HUMAN FLOURISHING

HUMAN FLOURISHING

Edited by
**Ellen Frankel Paul, Fred D. Miller, Jr.,
and Jeffrey Paul**

CAMBRIDGE
UNIVERSITY PRESS

Published by the Press Syndicate of the University of Cambridge
The Pitt Building, Trumpington Street, Cambridge CB2 1RP, England
40 West 20th Street, New York, NY 10011, USA
10 Stamford Road, Oakleigh, Melbourne, Victoria 3166, Australia

First published 1999

Printed in the United States of America

Library of Congress Cataloging-in-Publication Data

Human Flourishing / edited by Ellen Frankel Paul,
Fred D. Miller, Jr., and Jeffrey Paul.   p.   cm.
Includes bibliographical references and index.
ISBN 0-521-64471-2
1. Happiness.
I. Paul, Ellen Frankel.   II. Miller,
Fred Dycus, 1944–   III. Paul, Jeffrey.
B187.H3 H85   1999
170–dc21   98-50573
                                        CIP

ISBN 0-521-64471-2 paperback

CONTENTS

	Introduction	vii
	Acknowledgments	xvi
	Contributors	xvii
DOUGLAS B. RASMUSSEN	Human Flourishing and the Appeal to Human Nature	1
THOMAS HURKA	The Three Faces of Flourishing	44
LESTER H. HUNT	Flourishing Egoism	72
CHARLES LARMORE	The Idea of a Life Plan	96
RICHARD J. ARNESON	Human Flourishing versus Desire Satisfaction	113
THOMAS E. HILL, JR.	Happiness and Human Flourishing in Kant's Ethics	143
STEPHEN DARWALL	Valuing Activity	176
GEORGIOS ANAGNOSTOPOULOS	Ancient Perfectionism and Its Modern Critics	197
SARAH BROADIE	Aristotle's Elusive *Summum Bonum*	233
DAVID O. BRINK	Eudaimonism, Love and Friendship, and Political Community	252
JENNIFER ROBACK MORSE	No Families, No Freedom: Human Flourishing in a Free Society	290
RICHARD KRAUT	Politics, Neutrality, and the Good	315
THOMAS W. POGGE	Human Flourishing and Universal Justice	333
	Index	363

INTRODUCTION

The ancient idea that happiness or flourishing should be the end of human action, and that the nature of this end can be objectively derived from claims about human nature or function, stands opposed to some commonly held views in contemporary moral theory. Many contemporary theorists believe, for example, that happiness is a subjective matter, varying from individual to individual, that morality is chiefly other-regarding, and that the pursuit of one's own good, far from being the purpose of moral action, is often in conflict with morality. Yet in recent years a number of theorists have sought to revive or adapt classical notions of human flourishing in order to give a more satisfactory account of the ends of human action and the relationship between virtue and self-interest.

The essays in this volume examine the nature of human flourishing and its relationship to a variety of other key concepts in moral theory. Some of them trace the link between flourishing and human nature, asking whether a theory of human nature can allow us to develop an objective list of goods that are of value to all agents, regardless of their individual purposes or aims. Some essays look at the role of friendships or parent-child relationships in a good life, or seek to determine whether an ethical theory based on human flourishing can accommodate concern for others for their own sake. Other essays analyze the function of families or other social-political institutions in promoting the flourishing of individuals. Still others explore the implications of flourishing for political theory, asking whether considerations of human flourishing can help us to derive principles of social justice.

In the opening essay, "Human Flourishing and the Appeal to Human Nature," Douglas B. Rasmussen presents a neo-Aristotelian conception of the human good in which human flourishing is conceived as both objective and individualized with respect to particular agents. The key issue Rasmussen addresses is the extent to which this view of flourishing appeals to human nature. He argues that considerations of human nature can lead us to the discovery of generic goods and virtues, but that these can serve as no more than general guidelines and cannot alone determine what form of flourishing is proper for the individual. Rather, moral consideration has to be given to what is unique to the individual in determining what is best for him or her. Rasmussen offers a lengthy discussion of the role of practical reason in bridging the gap between generic goods and virtues and the particular circumstances of individual lives. On his view, practical reasoning is not best understood as a means of comparing possible acts or rules to determine which will produce the "the most" flourishing; it is, instead, a means of managing one's activities so that the necessary goods and virtues are achieved and sustained in an appropriate way over the course of one's life. Rasmussen concludes by responding to a number of potential objections to his neo-Aristotelian conception of flourishing and by defending the plausibility of the version of natural teleology on which it is based.

Like Rasmussen, Thomas Hurka is concerned with the relationship between human nature and human flourishing. In "The Three Faces of Flourishing," Hurka explores the idea that flourishing or the human good consists in developing properties that are fundamental to human nature. He also explores two related ideas: that virtues are those traits necessary for flourishing, and that all of a person's normative reasons for action derive from his own flourishing. Although these ideas are logically independent, Hurka notes, they are often found together. Yet Hurka argues that the first view—the view about human nature—is in conflict with the other two. If the good consists in the development of one's human nature, then we must specify what properties of human beings are central to their nature. One plausible candidate is rationality, but Hurka contends that the development of one's rationality need not be linked with the development of other-regarding virtues. If such virtues cannot be derived from arguments based on human nature, and if we believe that such virtues are part of a flourishing life, then we cannot ground our account of flourishing in terms of human nature. Hurka goes on to sketch a less ambitious account of flourishing, one which leaves aside human nature and attempts to justify other-regarding virtues in egoistic terms, but he maintains, ultimately, that such account does not succeed. A more promising approach, he suggests, might be to retain elements of the human-nature view, but to develop them within a nonegoistic framework.

Lester H. Hunt takes a different view of the relationship between egoism and human flourishing in his contribution to this collection, "Flourishing Egoism." Hunt notes that virtue and self-interest—notions which were closely linked in Greek philosophy—have tended to fall out of favor in modern moral theory, and he argues that the concept of flourishing allows us to forge a closer connection between virtue and self-interest than modern theorists would generally allow. Beginning with the idea that one's self-interest lies in living the sort of life that is most worth living—that is, in flourishing—Hunt shows how this flourishing-based notion of self-interest allows us to avoid a pair of troubling objections commonly raised against egoistic theories. Such theories are typically criticized for being unable to give a satisfactory account of other-regarding reasons for action, and for fostering a calculating, manipulative attitude toward other people that is ultimately self-defeating. Hunt argues that a flourishing-based egoism can avoid the first objection by rejecting the idea that regard for others only provides reasons for action if caring for others benefits the agent himself. Instead, on the flourishing-based account, caring for others is seen to be part of the best sort of life, regardless of its further effects on the agent. A similar reply can be made to the second objection: an egoistic theory need not promote a calculating attitude toward other people if the good of others is seen as partly constitutive of flourishing rather than as a means to achieving one's interests. A conception of self-interest based in flourishing, Hunt concludes, may provide the foundation for an egoistic ethical theory that is not vulnerable to the usual objections; what's more, it may provide a more fertile and interesting idea for use in nonegoistic theories as well.

In "The Idea of a Life Plan," Charles Larmore challenges a central claim that has united many moral theories from antiquity to the present day: the claim that each of us as a rational being should frame and follow a plan of life. The concept of a life plan, Larmore notes, expresses a certain attitude toward life, one according to which we flourish as human beings only if we take charge of our lives, shaping them ourselves, instead of leaving them at the mercy of circumstance and whim. He argues, however, that this view is false to the human condition, in that it draws too sharp a contrast between leading a life and responding to the unforeseen events that befall us. The view that life plans are central to flourishing misses the important truth that the happiness life affords is less often the good we have reason to pursue than the good that comes to us unexpectedly. Larmore develops this argument with special attention to the systematic treatment that John Rawls has given to the notion of a life plan. In the course of his discussion, Larmore touches upon a range of subjects, including the nature of prudence, Rawls's notion of deliberative rationality, and the stability of our purposes over time. He concludes that the best account of flourishing is one that acknowledges both the importance of planning and the need to leave ourselves open to the unexpected goods that we encounter in life.

The nature of a flourishing life is also the subject of Richard J. Arneson's contribution to this volume, "Human Flourishing versus Desire Satisfaction." Arneson defends an objective theory of the human good, according to which the things that make one's life go well have intrinsic value independent of one's attitudes or desires. He contrasts this theory with a pair of alternative accounts of the good: hedonism and desire fulfillment. Hedonism fails as a theory of the good because it identifies an individual's good with some aspects of his experience, but we care about more than the quality of our experiences. The desire-fulfillment theory seems inadequate for at least two reasons: because many of our desires do not bear on our well-being, and because some of our desires may be based on confusion, ignorance, or errors in reasoning. Arneson considers various refinements of the desire-fulfillment theory designed to overcome these problems, but he maintains that the only truly plausible version of this theory is one which holds that the good is that which is truly desirable. Yet this view is no longer really a desire-fulfillment theory at all; it has been transformed into an objective theory of the good. Arneson concludes by considering a constraint on objective theories of the good which holds that nothing can be good for an individual unless he endorses it. He contends that such a constraint, while appealing, is nevertheless unwarranted, since one's reasons for failing to endorse a particular good may be weak or misguided.

Modern moral theory has tended to shift away from viewing happiness as an objective state, and an influential figure in this shift has been Immanuel Kant. In "Happiness and Human Flourishing in Kant's Ethics," Thomas E. Hill, Jr. examines Kant's view of happiness and contrasts it with ancient notions of human flourishing. While ancient theorists believed that one of the primary aims of ethics was the achievement of one's own happiness or flourishing, Kant viewed happiness in terms of a subjective feeling of contentment and the achievement of desired ends. On Kant's view, happiness is not the aim of morality; indeed, morality is seen as a constraint on the pursuit of one's happiness. Hill proceeds by describing Kant's view in detail, showing why Kant believed that happiness is not an unconditional good, is not the ultimate criterion for judging right and wrong actions, and is not the unqualified goal of moral rules. Moreover, Hill explores Kant's reasons for defending strict moral rules that do not admit of exceptions, even when exceptions might prevent unhappiness; and he shows why Kant believed that the purpose of government is not to promote happiness but to secure justice. Although Kant is often thought to have denigrated happiness—arguing, for example, that we have only an imperfect duty to promote the happiness of others, and no duty at all to promote our own—Hill seeks to explain why Kant's distinctive view of happiness, and his concern for individual freedom, led him to this position.

The next four essays deal in various ways with ancient Greek accounts of flourishing. In "Valuing Activity," Stephen Darwall defends a version of what he calls the "Aristotelian Thesis," the idea that to live a good life is to engage in excellent, distinctively human activity. In Darwall's version of this thesis, one crucial kind of activity is "valuing activity"—appreciating or taking pleasure in values that have genuine worth. "Worth," on this view, is a kind of value that something has in virtue of being important or significant in itself; and "merit" is a kind of value belonging to persons and their actions in virtue of their being worthy of admiration or emulation. Darwall argues that people or their actions have merit to the extent that they respond appropriately to things or activities that have worth. On this view, valuing activity has both subjective and objective elements: if either element is lacking, the activity's contribution to one's flourishing is lessened. If an agent is engaged in a pursuit which he mistakenly believes has great worth, he is less well-off than he might be; similarly, if he is engaged in a genuinely valuable activity but does not appreciate its worth, he cannot be said to be fully flourishing. In the course of his discussion, Darwall distinguishes four versions of the Aristotelian Thesis which differ according to whether they give an account of the human good in terms of perfectionism, biology, welfare, or the pursuit of rational ends. He also discusses the connection between flourishing and personal relationships, such as the relationship between parents and children. He concludes with the suggestion that the Aristotelian Thesis may provide support for a certain theory of well-being: the notion that a person's good is what it would make sense for someone who cared about that person to want for him for his own sake.

Georgios Anagnostopoulos explores perfectionist theories of human flourishing in his contribution to this volume, "Ancient Perfectionism and Its Modern Critics." Anagnostopoulos begins by noting that traditional theories of human flourishing and perfectionism are founded on a metaphysical conception of human nature, teleology, or function, and that they imply that the good is objective and the same for all persons. He examines three accounts of the good that can be found in ancient Greek thought—the pre-philosophical perfectionism of Homer, and the views of Plato and Aristotle—and analyzes objections directed against their metaphysical presuppositions. Neither pre-philosophical nor Platonic perfectionism can succeed, Anagnostopoulos contends, if they are understood without any reference to a conception of human nature or teleology. Aristotle's account is more problematic, and Anagnostopoulos offers a critical examination of this account, comparing it with some of the views of modern liberal theorists and desire-satisfaction theorists. He argues that, while Aristotle cannot derive the conclusion that the good is one and the same for everyone from his conception of the good and considerations of rationality, he has plausible reasons for his conclusion that the best life for an agent is a life with a single end. This conclusion is strongly opposed by desire-satisfaction theorists and liberal theorists, and Anagnostopoulos maintains that the disagreement between Aristotle and contemporary theorists rests on different conceptions of the self.

Aristotle's view of the human good is also the subject of Sarah Broadie's essay "Aristotle's Elusive *Summum Bonum*." While Aristotle and other ancient philosophers focused on the material question, What is the *summum bonum* or highest good?, Broadie addresses the formal question, What, in the Aristotelian context, is it for something to count as the *summum bonum*? Broadie considers and rejects a utilitarian answer to this formal question: the idea that the highest good is that which we should strive above all to realize. Instead, she maintains that the *summum bonum* is that which renders other goods worthwhile. This formal description of the nature of the good, she argues, is in keeping with Aristotle's belief that the highest good is activity of excellence in a complete life—where "activity of excellence" is understood to consist in intellectual or imaginative activity, and where a "complete life" is understood to include such goods as friendship and pleasure. In the course of her essay, Broadie distinguishes two levels of practical thinking that are present in Aristotle's theory: that of the statesman, whose task is to establish and preserve principles of conduct, and that of the individual, who is to follow those principles in his own life. She frames her discussion with a consideration of Aristotle's concern to place practical rationality within a wider context of human weakness and human aspiration—a concern which, she suggests, is absent from much contemporary work in moral philosophy.

The part played by friendship in a good life—a topic that Broadie touches upon—is the central theme of David O. Brink's contribution to this volume. In "Eudaimonism, Love and Friendship, and Political Community," Brink examines the role of love and friendship in fostering happiness or flourishing by assessing certain ancient Greek views of love and friendship in light of doubts about whether they can accommodate concern for the loved one for his own sake. The central question is whether the eudaimonistic view held by many of the ancients—the idea that the proper end of rational action is the promotion of one's own *eudaimonia* or happiness—is compatible with a noninstrumental concern for others. Brink acknowledges that Socrates' eudaimonism may not be able to accommodate noninstrumental concern for one's friends, but he argues that Platonic and Aristotelian concern for the virtue of one's friends is not only consistent with, but essential to, a concern for one's friends for their own sake, and not simply for the sake of the contribution they make to one's own happiness. Moreover, Platonic and Aristotelian accounts of concern for the virtue of others have strong implications for political theory, since, on these accounts, one of the responsibilities of political leaders is to shape the virtue of their subjects. Brink observes that the theories of love and friendship embraced by Plato and Aristotle lead to certain antidemocratic tendencies in their views of the appropriate form and scope of political association—tendencies which are particularly troubling for contemporary political theorists. Brink argues, however, that the more general claims about love and friendship to which Plato and Aristotle are committed provide the resources for correcting this difficulty.

The remaining three essays, like Brink's, deal with the connection between individual flourishing and larger social-political institutions. Jennifer Roback Morse explores the function that families perform within the social order in her essay "No Families, No Freedom: Human Flourishing in a Free Society." Morse maintains that the family plays an indispensable role in transforming helpless infants from self-centered bundles of impulses, desires, and emotions, into adult people capable of social behavior of all kinds. The family teaches the ability to trust, cooperate, and exercise self-restraint, she observes; neither the free market nor self-governing political institutions can survive unless the vast majority of the population possesses these skills. Morse shows how people instill these qualities in their children as a side effect of loving interactions with them, and she examines the problems children have in forming attachments when such interactions are absent. The trust developed within families, she contends, is a crucial prerequisite for responsibility and reciprocity in later economic and political interactions. A society based on free political institutions and freedom of contract would be unworkable if families did not inculcate self-restraint and the disposition to cooperate in their children. Morse concludes by arguing that neither government institutions (such as state-run orphanages) nor private markets for child care can be legitimate substitutes for the family.

The role of the state in promoting human flourishing is the focus of Richard Kraut's essay "Politics, Neutrality, and the Good." Kraut challenges the view, commonly held among liberal political philosophers, that the state should adopt a stance of neutrality toward questions about the nature of the human good. He argues that the neutrality view does not provide us with an illuminating way to organize our intuitions about the manner in which a free and diverse society should be governed. On the contrary, he proposes that many modern liberal practices might better be seen as expressions of plausible and widely held ideas about human flourishing. Kraut defends this proposal by examining common attitudes toward assisted suicide, liberal education, autonomy, religion, democracy, and human dignity. A consideration of these attitudes reveals that in countries like the United States, civic support of certain intrinsic goods is widely accepted. In the course of his essay, Kraut discusses a variety of topics, including the distinction between principled and strategic neutrality, the difficulty of devising a rationally defensible account of human well-being, and the idea that allowing the state to take a nonneutral position opens the door to oppression. He concludes that strict adherence to a policy of state neutrality regarding the elements of a flourishing life would weaken or undermine some of our most familiar social institutions.

Government's role in promoting flourishing is also the subject of the final essay in this volume, Thomas W. Pogge's "Human Flourishing and Universal Justice." Pogge begins by noting that if we are to make sense of the great diversity of views about human flourishing, we must distinguish the perspectives from which questions about flourishing can be raised. One important perspective, Pogge believes, is that of social justice, defined as the moral assessment of social institutions in terms of how they treat the persons affected by them. Since the lives of individuals—and their potential for achieving happiness or flourishing—are increasingly affected by foreign and supranational institutions, we need a shared criterion of justice through which all institutions can be assessed. To be shareable, Pogge argues, such a criterion should be modest and abstract. It should not seek to provide a conception of what flourishing consists in; rather, it should aim to secure the essential contributors to human flourishing. The objective of social justice, then, should be to ensure that people have access to minimally adequate shares of the goods that are essential to leading worthwhile lives: food, clothing, shelter, education, and health care, as well as basic personal and political liberties. Pogge proposes a criterion of social justice which—unlike widely held consequentialist or contractarian views—differentiates among the various ways in which social institutions may affect the lives of individuals (for example, by mandating, authorizing, or insufficiently deterring certain harms). He concludes that such a criterion, based on a somewhat unconventional understanding of human rights, offers the most promising way of assessing institutions in terms of their ability to foster human flourishing.

The recent revival of interest in human flourishing among moral philosophers promises to shed new light on the ends of human action and the relationship between virtue and happiness. These thirteen essays offer important insights into the nature of flourishing, its place in moral theory, and the influence of ancient theorists on the views of contemporary philosophers.

ACKNOWLEDGMENTS

The editors wish to acknowledge several individuals at the Social Philosophy and Policy Center, Bowling Green State University, who provided invaluable assistance in the preparation of this volume. They include Mary Dilsaver, Terrie Weaver, and Carrie-Ann Biondi.

The editors would like to extend special thanks to Executive Manager Kory Swanson, for offering invaluable administrative support; to Publication Specialist Tamara Sharp, for attending to innumerable day-to-day details of the book's preparation; and to Managing Editor Harry Dolan, for providing dedicated assistance throughout the editorial and production process.

CONTRIBUTORS

Douglas B. Rasmussen is Professor of Philosophy at St. John's University in New York City. He is coauthor of *The Catholic Bishops and the Economy: A Debate* (1987), *Liberty and Nature: An Aristotelian Defense of Liberal Order* (1991), and *Liberalism Defended: The Challenge of Post-Modernity* (1997), and coeditor of *Liberty for the Twenty-First Century* (1995). He has published numerous articles on issues in epistemology, ethics, and political philosophy in various professional journals and books. He guest-edited the January 1992 issue of *The Monist* on the topic "Teleology and the Foundation of Value."

Thomas Hurka is Professor of Philosophy at the University of Calgary in Canada. He works in ethical theory, with a special interest in perfectionist theories of value and their implications for moral and political philosophy. He is the author of *Perfectionism* (1993) and of recent articles in *The Journal of Philosophy*, *Social Philosophy and Policy*, *Ethics*, and *The Journal of Political Philosophy*. He is currently completing a book entitled *Virtue and Vice: A Perfectionist Account*, which develops an account of the intrinsic goodness of virtue different from those promoted under the heading "virtue ethics."

Lester H. Hunt is Professor of Philosophy at the University of Wisconsin–Madison. He has taught at Carnegie-Mellon University, the University of Pittsburgh, and Johns Hopkins University. He is the author of *Nietzsche and the Origin of Virtue* (1991) and *Character and Culture* (1997). He is currently working on a book on ethical, legal, and political ideas in American literature.

Charles Larmore is Professor of Political Science and Philosophy at the University of Chicago. His publications include *Patterns of Moral Complexity* (1987), *Modernité et morale* (1993), *The Romantic Legacy* (1996), and *The Morals of Modernity* (1996). He is currently at work on a new book on the nature of the self, entitled *Les pratiques du moi*.

Richard J. Arneson is Professor of Philosophy at the University of California at San Diego, where he was department chair from 1992 to 1996. He has held visiting appointments at California Institute of Technology, University of California at Davis, and Yale University. He is an associate editor of the journal *Ethics*. He writes mainly on social and political philosophy, with an emphasis on contemporary theories of justice.

Thomas E. Hill, Jr. is Kenan Professor of Philosophy at the University of North Carolina at Chapel Hill, where he has taught since 1984. He previously taught for sixteen years at the University of California, Los Angeles, and more briefly at Pomona College, at Johns Hopkins University, and (on visiting appointments) at Stanford University and the University of Minnesota. He is the author of *Dignity and Practical Reason in Kant's Moral Theory* (1992) and *Autonomy and Self-Respect* (1991). He is currently editing a collection of his more recent essays on Kantian ethics for Oxford University Press.

Stephen Darwall is Professor of Philosophy at the University of Michigan, where he has taught since 1984. His work has concentrated on contemporary theorizing about the foundations of ethics and practical reason, on the history of fundamental moral philosophy, especially in the seventeenth and eighteenth centuries, and on the connections between these. He is the author of *Impartial Reason* (1983), *The British Moralists and the Internal 'Ought': 1640–1740* (1995), and numerous articles in moral philosophy, moral psychology, and the history of ethics.

Georgios Anagnostopoulos is Professor of Philosophy at the University of California, San Diego. His major research interests are in ancient philosophy and ethics. He is the author of *Aristotle on the Goals and Exactness of Ethics* (1994) and of a number of articles in ancient philosophy.

Sarah Broadie is Professor of Philosophy at Princeton University. She was trained in Classics and Philosophy at Oxford, and has taught at Edinburgh University, the University of Texas at Austin, Yale University, and Rutgers University. She is the author of *Ethics with Aristotle* (1991) and (as Sarah Waterlow) of *Nature, Change, and Agency* (1982) and *Passage and Possibility* (1982).

David O. Brink is Professor of Philosophy at the University of California, San Diego. His research interests are in ethical theory, history of ethics, political philosophy, and constitutional jurisprudence. He is the author of *Moral Realism and the Foundations of Ethics* (1989) and is bringing out a new edition of T. H. Green's *Prolegomena to Ethics* with Clarendon Press. He is currently working on issues in ethical theory and the history of ethics about practical reason and moral demands, and on issues in constitutional jurisprudence involving judicial review and individual rights in a constitutional democracy.

Jennifer Roback Morse is a Research Fellow at the Hoover Institution at Stanford University. She taught previously at Yale University and at George Mason University, where she was director of the Public Choice Outreach Program and the Diversity Studies Program. She was John M. Olin Visiting Scholar at the Cornell Law School in 1993, and lectured in Rome at the 1997 Acton Institute conference celebrating the anniversary of Centissimus Annus. She is the author of *A Matter of Choice: A Critique of Comparable Worth by a Skeptical Feminist* (1986) and of a forthcoming book entitled *The Family in a Free Society: An Economist Looks Beyond Economic Man.*

Richard Kraut is Professor of Philosophy at Northwestern University. He is the author of *Socrates and the State* (1984), *Aristotle on the Human Good* (1989), and *Aristotle's Politics, Books VII and VIII* (translation and commentary, 1997). He is also the editor of *The Cambridge Companion to Plato* (1992).

Thomas W. Pogge is Associate Professor of Philosophy at Columbia University. His research interests center on moral and political philosophy and Kant, with a special emphasis on issues in global justice, human rights, and contractualism. His recent publications include *Realizing Rawls* (1989) and numerous articles in journals such as *Ethics, The Journal of Philosophy, Philosophy and Public Affairs, Canadian Journal of Philosophy,* and *The Journal of Political Philosophy.*

HUMAN FLOURISHING AND THE APPEAL
TO HUMAN NATURE*

By Douglas B. Rasmussen

[Aristotle] certainly does think that the nature of man—the powers
and needs all men have—determines the character that any satisfying human life must have. But since his account of the nature of man
is in general terms the corresponding specification of the best life for
man is also general. So while his assumption puts some limits on the
possible answers to the question "how shall I live?" it leaves considerable scope for a discussion which takes account of my individual
tastes, capacities, and circumstances.

—J. L. Ackrill, *Aristotle's Ethics*

I. Introduction

If "perfectionism" in ethics refers to those normative theories that treat
the fulfillment or realization of human nature as central to an account
of both goodness and moral obligation,[1] in what sense is "human flourishing" a perfectionist notion? How much of what we take "human
flourishing" to signify is the result of our understanding of human
nature? Is the content of this concept simply read off an examination of
our nature? Is there no place for diversity and individuality? Is the belief
that the content of such a normative concept can be determined by an
appeal to human nature merely the result of epistemological naiveté?
What is the exact character of the connection between human flourishing
and human nature?

These questions are the ultimate concern of this essay, but to appreciate
the answers that will be offered it is necessary to understand what is
meant by "human flourishing." "Human flourishing" is a relatively
recent term in ethics. It seems to have developed in the last two decades

* Thanks are due to Roger Bissell, Robert Campbell, Douglas Den Uyl, Paul Gaffney,
Jonathan Jacobs, Irfan Khawaja, Tibor R. Machan, Eric Mack, Aeon Skoble, and Henry
Veatch for their comments on earlier drafts. Also, the helpful assistance of the editors of this
volume deserves mention. Finally, the generous support of the Earhart Foundation helped
to make this essay possible.
[1] Contrary to everyday usage, "perfectionism" in ethics does not typically refer to attempts to become God-like, immune to degeneration, incapable of harm, or anything nonhuman. Rather, it refers to becoming human, specifically, to fulfilling those potentialities
that make one human.

because the traditional translation of the Greek term *eudaimonia* as "happiness" failed to communicate clearly that *eudaimonia* was an objective good, not merely a subjective good.

The employment of "human flourishing" in the discussion of "happiness" has been successful for the most part in getting people to understand that *eudaimonia* is not merely subjectively determined. "Human flourishing," however, remains a technical notion, and its exact meaning varies with different theories of the human good. Further, "human flourishing" has developed a life of its own. It is now employed by neo-Aristotelian ethicists, myself included, as the central concept with which to develop an alternative to consequentialistic[2] and deontological[3] conceptions of ethics. It is a complex notion whose many interrelated features generate an elaborate conception of the human good and obligation.

This essay is only part of a larger argument for this view of the human good. However, it is my aim to move this viewpoint forward by showing that this neo-Aristotelian conception of human flourishing is more plausible than is generally thought. Accordingly, Section II of this essay will outline the central features of a neo-Aristotelian conception of human flourishing. Section III will discuss the role of practical wisdom in this conception of human flourishing. Section IV will deal with questions and difficulties faced by this conception, and Section V will take up a discussion of some of the questions noted in this essay's first paragraph. Overall, the concern will be with determining what type of connection there is between this conception of human flourishing and human nature. By clarifying the character of this connection, I hope to advance the plausibility of this neo-Aristotelian conception of human flourishing.

One cautionary note should be sounded, however. What follows does not purport to be textual exegesis of Aristotle. "Neo-Aristotelian" is used here to stand for "modern theorizing which incorporates some central doctrines of Aristotle. . . . Such theorizing should critically assess his claims in light of modern philosophical theory, scientific research, and practical experience, revise or reject them where necessary, and consider their application to . . . contexts not envisioned by him."[4] Though often found together, there is a difference between neo-Aristotelian theorizing and an exegesis of Aristotle's texts. It is in the foregoing sense that the following account of human flourishing is neo-Aristotelian.

---

[2] A consequentialistic theory is any theory in normative ethics that attempts to determine obligations *merely* by whether an action or rule produces the greatest, net expected "good" (or least "bad") consequences.

[3] A deontological theory is any theory in normative ethics that holds "duty" and "right" to be basic and defines the morally good in terms of them. Such theories attempt to determine obligations apart from a consideration of what promotes or expresses the good. For Kantians, this is accomplished primarily by a universalizability test.

[4] Fred D. Miller, Jr., *Nature, Justice, and Rights in Aristotle's "Politics"* (Oxford: Clarendon Press, 1995), p. 336, n. 1.

II. A Neo-Aristotelian Conception of Human Flourishing

This neo-Aristotelian conception of human flourishing offers a view of the human good that is (1) objective, (2) inclusive, (3) individualized, (4) agent-relative, (5) self-directed, and (6) social. I shall briefly and directly explain each of these interrelated features.

1. Human flourishing is an objective good. In terms similar to those used by Socrates in his question to Euthyphro,[5] human flourishing is an object of desire and choice because it is desirable and choiceworthy, not simply because it is desired or chosen. In other words, it is desired because of what it *is*. Its constitution is what makes it good. Thus, human goodness is something ontological. It is a state of being, not a mere feeling or experience.[6]

Ontologically considered, human flourishing is an activity, an actuality, and an end (or function). Human flourishing is a way of living that consists in certain activities. *Omne ens perficitur in actu*: flourishing is to be found in action. It is not something static. These activities are those that both express and produce in a human being an actualization of potentialities that are specific to its natural kind.[7] Finally, these activities also constitute the achievement of a human being's natural end or *telos*. Human flourishing is that-for-the-sake-of-which human conduct is done, and though flourishing is dependent on human agency for its achievement, it does not depend on such agency for its status as the ultimate end.

Obviously, the foregoing ontological considerations are complex and require further explanation. We will return to their discussion later when we explore the relationship between human flourishing and human nature. Before doing so, however, we need to grasp some of the other central features of this account of human flourishing, because they affect the character of that relationship.

2. Human flourishing is the ultimate end of human conduct, but it is not the only activity of inherent worth. It is not a "dominant" end that reduces the value of everything else to that of a mere means. Neither is it monistic and simple. Rather, it is "the *most* final end and is never sought for the sake of anything else, because it includes all final ends."[8]

---

[5] The question that Socrates asks Euthyphro is, of course, whether something is pious because it is loved by the gods, or whether it is loved by the gods because it is pious. Plato, *Euthyphro*, 10.

[6] This is not, however, to claim that having the proper feelings and experiences could not make up the good human life. Indeed, the good human life is traditionally understood as the satisfaction of *right* desire.

[7] As will be discussed later, however, human flourishing is not some abstract universal; potentialities unique to the individual are also involved.

[8] J. L. Ackrill, "Aristotle on Eudaimonia," in *Essays on Aristotle's Ethics*, ed. Amélie O. Rorty (Berkeley: University of California Press, 1980), p. 23.

Human flourishing is an "inclusive" end.[9] It comprises basic[10] or "generic"[11] goods and virtues—for example, such goods as knowledge, health, friendship, creative achievement, beauty, and pleasure; and such virtues as integrity, temperance, courage, and justice. These are valuable not as mere means to human flourishing but as partial realizations or expressions of it. As such, these goods and virtues are final[12] ends and valuable in their own right.

To understand this idea better, we should consider the difference between two relations of subordination to some end: the difference between (A) activities that are purely means or instruments to that end, and (B) activities that are ingredients in or constituents of that end. For example, consider the difference between the relationship of obtaining golf clubs to playing golf, and the relationship of putting to playing golf. While both activities are "for the sake of" playing golf, the former is only a necessary preliminary, while putting is one of the activities that makes golfing what it is. Furthermore, the actions taken to obtain golf clubs produce an outcome separate from that activity—namely, the possession of golf clubs that can be used—but putting has no end or result apart from itself. Its value is not that of a mere means. Its value lies in its being an expression or realization of the activity of which it is a constituent. As Ackrill states, "One does not putt *in order to* play golf. . . . Putting *is* playing golf (though not all that playing golf is)."[13]

---

[9] Irfan Khawaja has pointed out to me that the inclusive-dominant distinction is not logically exhaustive and that these terms contrast different issues. He suggests that the issues should be redefined as follows: the inclusive-exclusive distinction pertains to "What is included in human flourishing and what is not?" and the dominant-subordinate distinction pertains to "What is ordered to what and why?" This seems like a good way to discuss these matters. Nonetheless, the inclusive-versus-dominant terminology of W. F. R. Hardie and J. L. Ackrill is well-established and is sufficient for our limited purposes. For more on this issue, see Scott MacDonald, "Ultimate Ends in Practical Reasoning: Aquinas's Aristotelian Moral Psychology and Anscombe's Fallacy," *Philosophical Review*, vol. 100 (January 1991), pp. 31–66.

[10] These could be regarded as somewhat similar to what John Rawls calls "primary goods," that is, "things that every rational man is presumed to want." See Rawls, *A Theory of Justice* (Cambridge, MA: Harvard University Press, 1971), p. 62.

[11] For convenience this term is used to stand for considerations that involve both the genus and the species to which a human being belongs.

[12] "A is more final than B if though B is sought for its own sake (and hence is indeed a final and not merely intermediate goal) it is also sought for the sake of A." Ackrill, "Aristotle on Eudaimonia," p. 21.

[13] *Ibid.*, p. 19. As Ackrill implies, the relations of subordination are even more complicated than described here. See MacDonald, "Ultimate Ends in Practical Reasoning," for a discussion of these complications and a thorough defense of the idea that the human good is an inclusive end. MacDonald argues, however, that Ackrill's example of putting's relationship to golfing is not a good one for illustrating inclusivity, because it is logically possible to play a round of golf without putting. To illustrate inclusivity, MacDonald instead uses the example of running a ten-kilometer race as a constituent part of a triathlon. Yet it still seems that Ackrill's example of putting's relationship to golfing could be defended as a constitutive part if one noted that the end was doing well at golf or having the lowest score, not merely playing a round of golf.

Another point that is crucial to appreciating what it means for human flourishing to be an "inclusive" end is the idea that (C) some things can be done for their own sake and yet also done for the sake of something else. (C) is possible, since flourishing is not the result of the efforts of a lifetime; it is not something that one looks forward to enjoying in the future. Rather, it is a life that is worthwhile throughout. Thus, the constituents of such a life are more than merely means for bringing about what is to follow; they are also worthwhile in themselves. It is perfectly possible for something to be pursued for its own sake and still be a constituent of human flourishing.[14] Indeed, as Aristotle states:

> What is always chosen as an end in itself and never as a means to something else is called final in an unqualified sense. This description seems to apply to *eudaimonia* above all else; for we always choose *eudaimonia* as an end in itself and never for the sake of something else. Honor, pleasure, intelligence, and all virtue we choose partly for themselves—for we would choose each of them even if no further advantage would accrue from them—but we also choose them partly for the sake of *eudaimonia*. (*Nicomachean Ethics*, 1097bff.)

This view of human flourishing is open to the possibility that there may *not* be a preset weighting or evaluative pattern for the basic or generic goods and virtues that constitute it. Even if all the aforementioned goods and virtues are necessary to flourishing, an abstract analysis of human nature may not show us what their evaluative ranking should be. Such an analysis may not tell us how much time and effort should be spent in the pursuit of one necessary good or virtue as opposed to another. As we shall see, this possibility creates a basis for a conception of human flourishing that is different in many respects from that usually associated with perfectionist theories.

3. Human flourishing is individualized and diverse. It is dependent on *who* as well as *what* one is. Abstractly considered, we can speak of human flourishing and of basic or generic goods and virtues that help to define

[14] Thus, the theory of obligation generated by this inclusivist view of human flourishing is one in which it is not necessary to calculate what the expected consequences of every proposed course of conduct might be in order to determine what is good and ought to be done. Nor is it necessary always to be open to the possibility of such calculation. Though calculation would be appropriate for dealing with matters that are entirely instrumental to human flourishing, this is not so when it comes to the components of human flourishing itself. The first principle of practical reason is, as Aquinas noted: Pursue good and avoid evil. Thus, the major concern is determining what in the particular and contingent is really good or virtuous. Once one discerns what is good or virtuous, one knows what ought to be done. It is in this respect that an ethics of human flourishing is not consequentialistic (as defined in note 2), because some virtues and goods are seen as activities that characterize our human flourishing itself, not merely as external means. This is not to say, however, that there might not be other senses (for example, a nonmaximizing sense) in which this view can be termed "consequentialistic."

it. Yet this does not make human flourishing in reality either abstract or universal. Concretely speaking, no two cases of human flourishing are the same, and they are not interchangeable. Just as Mary's actualization of her potentialities is not the same as Bill's actualization of his, Mary's fulfillment is not the same as Bill's. There are individuative as well as generic potentialities, and this makes human fulfillment always something unique.

The generic goods and virtues of human flourishing are not like Recommended Daily Allowances for vitamins and minerals. Their weighting, balance, or proportion cannot be read off human nature like the back of a cereal box and applied equally across all individuals as if individuals were merely repositories for the generic goods and virtues.[15] Rather, it is only when the individual's particular talents, potentialities, and circumstances are jointly engaged that these goods and virtues become real or achieve determinacy. Individuals thus do more than locate human flourishing in space. Human flourishing exists neither apart from the choices and actions of individual human beings nor independently of the particular mix of goods that individual human beings need to determine as being appropriate for their circumstances.

Just as our humanity is not some amorphous, undifferentiated universal, so human flourishing is not something abstract and universal. Rather, it is determinate and particular. Flourishing is not merely something achieved and enjoyed by individuals; it is itself individualized. Thus, this account of human flourishing is a version of moral pluralism. There are many *summa bona*. Yet this does not require that human flourishing be subjective either in the sense that it consists in merely having favorable feelings or in the sense that its value is conferred upon it simply by someone's preference or endorsement. Thus, this account of human flourishing offers diversity without subjectivism.[16]

4. Human flourishing is agent-relative. Abstractly stated, human flourishing, G, for a person, P, is agent-relative if and only if its distinctive presence in world W_1 is a basis for P ranking W_1 over W_2, even though G may not be the basis for *any other* person's ranking W_1 over W_2. There is no human flourishing *period*. Human flourishing is always and necessarily the good *for* some person or other.

It is not that flourishing merely happens or occurs within some person's life, as if a person were simply a placeholder for this ultimate value. Rather, the relationship between flourishing and a person's life is much more intimate. The status of human flourishing *as the ultimate value* arises within and obtains only *in relationship to* some person's life. That is to say, its value is found in and exhausted by those activities of a person that

---

[15] Douglas J. Den Uyl, *The Virtue of Prudence* (New York: Peter Lang, 1991), pp. 37–38.

[16] There is nothing incompatible about human flourishing's being objective and its being diverse or individualized. This is discussed in Section IV below.

constitute that person's flourishing. Further, human flourishing involves an essential reference to the person for whom it is good as part of its description. Human flourishing is thus neither a *tertium quid* nor a value-at-large.

Perhaps the best way to understand what agent-relativity means is to contrast it with its opposing view, the view that basic values and reasons are agent-neutral and that ethics is impersonal. The following two statements, the first by Henry Sidgwick and the second by John Stuart Mill, express this viewpoint well:

> I obtain the self-evident principle that the good of any one individual is of no more importance, from the point of view (if I may say so) of the Universe, than the good of any other; unless, that is, there are special grounds for believing that more good is likely to be realized in the one case than in the other. And it is evident that as a rational being I am bound to aim at the good generally,—so far as it is attainable by my efforts—not merely at a particular part of it.[17]

> The happiness which forms the utilitarian standard of what is right in conduct, is not the agent's own happiness, but that of all concerned. As between his own happiness and that of others, utilitarianism requires him to be as strictly impartial as a disinterested benevolent spectator.[18]

Accordingly, we are to take on the viewpoint of the universe and become impartial when determining our conduct. In effect, we are to adopt the perspective of a rational agent, considered apart from all individuating conditions—be they natural, social, or cultural—and eschew all values, rankings, and reasons that could not be held by such a rational agent.

In an impersonalist ethical theory, the fact that course of action C results in assistance to one's own personal projects, family, friends, or country, where non-C does not, provides no ethical reason for preferring C over non-C. These factors might explain how a person would feel about the situation, but when a person is acting from an impersonalist perspective, considerations of a personal nature are irrelevant and should not weigh more heavily. By adopting the perspective of such a rational agent, a person could never legitimately use some value crucial to *who* he or she is as a reason to give extra weight or importance to that value when determining the proper course of action. The individual *qua individual* is not important in an impersonal moral theory. The individual only represents a locus at which good is achieved or right conduct performed.

[17] Henry Sidgwick, *The Methods of Ethics*, 7th ed. (Indianapolis, IN: Hackett Publishing Co., 1981), p. 382.
[18] John Stuart Mill, *Utilitarianism*, ch. 2.

Thus, we may say that an ethical theory is impersonal when all ultimately morally salient values, reasons, and rankings are "agent-neutral"; and they are agent-neutral when they do *not* involve as part of their description an essential reference to the person for whom the value or reason exists or the ranking is correct. One person can be substituted for any other. The individual is merely a placeholder around which rules and abstract principles revolve. "For any value, reason or ranking V, if a person P1 is justified in holding V, then so are P2–Pn under appropriately similar conditions. . . . On an agent-neutral conception it is impossible to weight more heavily or at all, V, simply because it is one's own value."[19] Accordingly, when it comes to describing a value, reason, or ranking, it does not ethically matter whose value, reason, or ranking it is.

According to the neo-Aristotelian view of human flourishing advanced here, an impersonal ethics and an agent-neutral conception of basic values and reasons are unsound. There is no great divide in the nature of things between the facts that can and cannot be ethically relevant. Particular and contingent facts can be ethically important. Of course, some may be more important than others in achieving human flourishing, but this cannot be determined from one's armchair alone. Certainly, there is, for this neo-Aristotelian view, no basis for holding that individual, social, and cultural differences among people are ethically irrelevant. They are, to the contrary, highly significant. Further, moral impersonalism's claim that values central to one's very conception of oneself may not be weighted more than less-central values is without foundation. The fact that a value is crucial to some person's deeply held personal project, but to no one else's, does not make it morally irrelevant. Indeed, the opposite is the case. Such value deserves consideration that is even more careful, precisely because of its relation to oneself. I will discuss these points further when I consider the role of practical wisdom in this conception of human flourishing.

There remain, however, three possible confusions about agent-relativity that must be considered at this time. The first has to do with the relationship between the objectivity of human flourishing and its agent-relativity. While aspects of this issue will be discussed in Section V of this essay, it should be noted that just because something is only valuable relative to some person does not necessarily make its value merely a matter of that person's attitude toward it or, indeed, merely something desired, wanted, or chosen. Nor is it merely a matter of a person's point of view. The old question "Relative to what?" is important here. Human flourishing is agent-relative in the sense that it is essentially related to some person or other, but this does not mean that it is essentially related to what a person merely desires, wants, or chooses. This neo-Aristotelian theory assumes that a human being is more than a bundle of passions and desires and that there are real potentialities, needs, and circumstances that characterize both what and who a person is. Thus, simply because one is interested in or has a desire for something does not necessarily mean that it is good *for* one. The agent-relative, as well as the individualized, character of human flourishing is not incompatible with its being something objective.

The second confusion is more subtle. It has to do with the issue of whether something can be valuable in its own right (that is, a final end, an end in itself) and nonetheless agent-relative. The problem seems to be that if something is an agent-relative value, then its value lies not in itself, but in something else. Thus, something cannot be valuable in its own right and agent-relative as well. This argument, however, confuses instrumental value with agent-relative value. Though all values may be related to some person or other, this does not mean or show that their value lies in their being mere means or instruments. As I noted in my earlier discussion of inclusivity, the constituent goods and virtues of human flourishing are, for example, valuable in their own right but nonetheless essentially related to the lives of individual human beings. Their value is not a matter of their being mere means to human flourishing; rather, it is a matter of their being expressions or realizations of it. There is no incompatibility, then, in something's being valuable in its own right and agent-relative.

What is even more to the point, however, is that there is no incompatibility in human flourishing's being the ultimate objective value[20] and agent-relative as well. As I have noted, there is no flourishing-at-large. There is no flourishing that is not essentially the flourishing-for-some-person. The human *telos* just is, then, the flourishing of each individual. Its value lies in the immanent activities that comprise the fulfillment of individual human beings. These activities are essentially a part of and thus are related to the lives of individual human beings. As such, human flourishing is not something that competes with the good of individual human beings, but is the very flourishing of their lives. Thus, it is perfectly consistent for the flourishing of individual human beings to be valuable in its own right *and* essentially related to individual persons. A commitment to the inherent value of human flourishing does not imply, then, that it is agent-neutral. Human flourishing is not something that can be exchanged or promoted regardless of whose flourishing it is. Agent-neutrality is not necessary for upholding either value-objectivity or choiceworthiness.[21]

---

[20] As Ackrill puts it, "the *most* final end . . . because it includes all final ends" ("Aristotle on Eudaimonia," p. 23).

[21] The foregoing discussion of features (3) and (4) of human flourishing revises, develops, and expands upon material from chapter three of Douglas B. Rasmussen and Douglas J. Den Uyl, *Liberalism Defended: The Challenge of Post-Modernity* (Cheltenham, UK, and Northampton, MA: Edward Elgar, 1997).

Finally, agent-relativity should not be confused with egoism. To say that human flourishing is agent-relative does not mean or imply that human flourishing cannot involve concern for others or that acting for the welfare of another could not be a value or reason for one's conduct. Acting for the sake of another could be only good-for-you and not necessarily anyone else. Parents sacrificing for *their* children, or friends helping and nurturing one another, are among the many examples of how flourishing can be agent-relative and nonetheless involve authentic concern for others. Further, even in situations that are not regarded as instances of flourishing, we find agent-relativity compatible with concern for others, as in the case of soldiers risking their lives for *their* comrades during battle. Therefore, agent-relativity and egoism should be distinguished.

5. Human flourishing is a self-directed activity. This view seems to be endorsed by Aristotle, who makes the following observation about the difference between good fortune and *eudaimonia* when speaking about god:

> [He] is *eudaimôn* and blessed, but not on account of any external goods but on account of himself and because he is by nature of a certain sort—which shows that being fortunate must be different from flourishing. For the goods external to the soul come of themselves by chance, but no one is just or temperate by or through chance. (*Politics*, 1323b24–29)

Human flourishing must be attained through a person's own efforts and cannot be the result of factors that are beyond one's control. Flourishing does not consist in the mere possession and use of needed goods.[22] Rather, human flourishing consists in a person's taking charge of his own life so as to develop and maintain those virtues for which he alone is responsible and which in most cases will allow him to attain the goods his life requires.

Aristotle also notes that if our knowledge and actions are to enable us to *be* good, as opposed to us merely knowing and doing good, three conditions must be met. "(1) The agent must act in full consciousness of what he is doing. (2) He must 'will' the action, and will it for its own sake. (3) The act must proceed from a fixed and unchangeable disposition" (*Nicomachean Ethics*, 1105a31–32). Only by initiating and maintaining the effort to gain the requisite knowledge, to cultivate the proper habits of character, to exercise correct choices, and to perform the right actions

---

[22] John Cooper notes that "for Aristotle, *eudaimonia* is necessarily the result of a person's own efforts; success, of whatever kind, could only count as *eudaimonia* if due to one's own efforts." John Cooper, *Reason and Human Good in Aristotle* (Cambridge, MA: Harvard University Press, 1975), p. 124.

can someone achieve moral excellence. Virtuous living is anything but passive.[23]

These statements, together with others,[24] suggest that Aristotle sees human flourishing as fundamentally a self-directed activity. Whatever his ultimate position may be, however, human flourishing is, according to this neo-Aristotelian conception, essentially self-directed. The point here is not that self-direction is merely necessary for the existence of human flourishing, for surely there are numerous necessary conditions for human flourishing's existence. Self-direction is not simply one of those many conditions. The point is rather that self-direction is necessary to the very character of human flourishing.[25] Human flourishing would not be human flourishing if there were no self-direction involved. Moreover, self-direction is the central necessary constituent or ingredient of human flourishing—that feature of human flourishing without which no other feature could be a constituent. In other words, self-direction is both a necessary condition for, and an operating condition of, the pursuit and achievement of human flourishing. Regardless of the level of achievement or specificity, self-direction is a feature of all acts of human fulfillment.

To appreciate this insight fully we need to discuss the role of practical wisdom as the central integrating virtue of human flourishing. This will be done later, as already noted. For now, it will suffice to see that the functioning of one's reason or intelligence, regardless of one's level of learning or degree of ability, does not occur automatically. It is something the individual initiates and maintains. It requires effort or exertion. Effort is needed to discover the goods and virtues of human flourishing as well as to achieve and implement them. The act of using one's intellectual capacity is an exercise of self-direction, and the act of self-direction is an

[23] See Jennifer Whiting, "Aristotle's Function Argument: A Defense," *Ancient Philosophy*, vol. 8 (1988), p. 43:

> A heart which, owing to some deficiency in its natural capacities, cannot beat on its own but is made to beat by means of a pacemaker is not a healthy heart. For *it*, the heart, is not strictly performing its function. Similarly, a man who, owing to some deficiency in his natural capacities, cannot manage his own life but is managed by means of another's deliberating and ordering him is not *eudaimôn*—not even if he possesses the same goods and engages in the same first order activities as does a *eudaimôn* man. For *he*, the man, is not strictly performing his function.... Aristotle's claim that *eudaimonia* is an activity of the soul in accordance with virtue shows that he thinks that *eudaimonia consists in* exercising rational agency.

[24] See Aristotle, *Nicomachean Ethics*, 1099b18–25 and 1168b34–1169a3. In *De Anima*, 417b18–26, Aristotle states that the exercise of reason, as contrasted to sense perception, is up to the agent, that is, dependent on the agent's effort, for its functioning. Fred D. Miller, Jr. first directed me to this passage.

[25] If human beings were attached to machines that satisfied their every need and thus made it unnecessary for them to do anything, that is, if everything were done for them so that they were essentially passive, their lives would not be worthwhile. There would be no self-direction, no reason, and no individualization. Fundamentally, their lives would not really be their own. There would be no such thing as human flourishing.

exercise of reason.[26] They are not separate acts of two isolated capacities, but distinct aspects of the same conscious act.[27]

Though the conclusions of practical reasoning can be shared, the act of reasoning that is an exercise of self-direction cannot. It is something each person must do for him- or herself.[28] Thus, if we were to speak of "human flourishing" as the "perfection" of the human being, then it would be fundamentally a process of *self*-perfection—where the individual human being is both the agent and the object of the process.[29]

6. Human beings are naturally social animals. We are social in the sense that our maturation requires a life with others. We do not achieve our maturity like mushrooms, suddenly, all at once, with no engagement with one another. We have potentialities that are other-oriented, and we cannot find fulfillment without their actualization. Human flourishing is thus not atomistic. It does *not* require gaining the goods of life exclusively for oneself and never acting for the sake of others.[30] Indeed, having other-concern is crucial to our maturation. As Aristotle makes clear, *philia* (friendship) is one of the constituents of human flourishing.[31] Further, in terms

---

[26] See Den Uyl, *The Virtue of Prudence*, pp. 183–86.

[27] Aquinas states that "man is master of his actions through his reason and will; whence, too, 'the free-will is defined as 'the faculty and will of reason'" (*Summa Theologiae*, IaIIae 1.1). See Scott MacDonald, "Egoistic Rationalism: Aquinas's Basis for Christian Morality," in *Christian Theism and the Problem of Philosophy*, ed. Michael D. Beaty (Notre Dame and London: University of Notre Dame Press, 1990), pp. 327–54.

[28] Henry B. Veatch puts this point well in his *Human Rights: Fact or Fancy?* (Baton Rouge and London: Louisiana State University Press, 1985), p. 84:

> For is it not evident that not only does a human being not attain his natural end by an automatic process of development and maturity after the manner of an animal? In addition, no human being ever attains his natural end or perfection save by his own personal effort and exertion. No one other than the human individual—no agency of society, of family, of friends, or of whatever can make or determine or program an individual to be a good man, or live the life that a human being ought to live. Instead attaining one's natural end as a human person is nothing if not a "do-it-yourself" job.

[29] See Douglas B. Rasmussen and Douglas J. Den Uyl, *Liberty and Nature* (La Salle, IL: Open Court, 1991), p. 40:

> In an ontological sense, the person is a unity seeking further actualization of the self. But since further actualization depends on choice reflected through action, the degree to which action and choice are consistent affects the degree of success the individual will have.... The Aristotelian eudaimonic person is not characterized by an aggregation of intentions, desires, or actions. It is rather that one's intentions, desires, and actions come to be a manifestation of a single core self developing towards its further realization.

[30] See Kelly Rogers, "Aristotle on Loving Another for His Own Sake," *Phronesis*, vol. 39, no. 3 (1994), pp. 291–302. Scott MacDonald notes that "the claim that one seeks the good of others as a part of one's own good does not mean that one does not seek the good of others for its own sake but only for the sake of one's own good. One can seek the constituents of one's own good for their own sakes, and also for the sake of the good of which they are constituents" ("Egoistic Rationalism," p. 352, n. 35).

[31] See John Cooper, "Aristotle on Friendship," in Rorty, ed., *Essays on Aristotle's Ethics*, pp. 301–40.

of origins, we are almost always born into a society or community, and it is in some social context or other that we grow and develop. Much of what is crucial to our self-conception and fundamental values is dependent on our upbringing and environment. Our lives are intertwined with others; we are not abstract individuals. It is thus a fundamental mistake to conceive of human beings achieving maturity apart from others and only later taking it upon themselves to join society or to have social concern. Human flourishing is achieved with and among others.

Contrary to what seems to have been the traditional Aristotelian view,[32] however, human sociality need not be confined to a select group or pool of human beings. Though relationships with others are founded on common values that form the basis for a continuum of relations—from those with close friends and acquaintances, to those with fellow members of communities and cultures—human sociality is open-ended. It imposes no *a priori* limitation regarding with whom one may have a relationship. Our sociality, in principle, allows one to be open to relationships with *any* human. Thus, one need not accept the social status quo. It is an unjustified limitation of human sociality to hold that persons cannot form relationships with persons with whom they do not yet share any common values.

The open-ended character of human sociality is important. It reveals the need for a perspective that is broad enough to explain how the possible relationships among persons who as yet share no common values and are strangers to each other can, nonetheless, be ethically compossible. In other words, it requires that attention be given to how it might be possible for different individuals to flourish and to do so in different ways (in different communities and cultures) without creating moral conflict. Thus, the open-ended character of human sociality requires a neo-Aristotelian ethics, which sees human flourishing as always lived in some community and culture, to consider questions of frameworks and modern political issues. Specifically, it requires a neo-Aristotelian ethics to consider the question of finding a political framework that is both compatible with the moral propriety of pluralism and yet based on something that can be mutually worthwhile for everyone involved. Moreover, since our sociality is essential to our self-understanding and well-being, this concern for political frameworks is not ethically optional for the individual. As Aristotle notes, "Only a beast or a god would live outside the polis" (*Politics*, 1253a27–29).

According to this neo-Aristotelian conception of human flourishing, then, one person's moral well-being cannot be exchanged with another's. The good-for-me is not, and cannot be, the good-for-you, but this is not to

---

[32] See Julia Annas, *The Morality of Happiness* (New York: Oxford University Press, 1993), pp. 250–52, for a discussion of this point.

say that any choice one makes is as good as the next. Rather, it is to say that the choice must be one's own and must involve considerations that are unique to oneself. The human good, then, is something objective, self-directed, socially achieved, and yet highly personal. It is not abstract, collectively determined, atomistic, or impersonal.

III. THE ROLE OF PRACTICAL WISDOM

Regardless of whether the foregoing outline of human flourishing turns out to be Aristotle's, it is clear that human flourishing is, for this contemporary view, something plural and complex, not monistic and simple. As already noted, this view of human flourishing amounts to a version of moral pluralism, because there are many goods that help to define human flourishing. Further, there is no single good or virtue that dominates all others and reduces them to mere instrumental values. Such goods as, for example, health, creative achievement, friendship, beauty, pleasure, and knowledge, and such virtues as, for example, integrity, courage, temperance, and justice, seem to be candidates for necessary ingredients or constituents of human flourishing. They are, as such, valuable in themselves, not as mere means.

Each is only one of the components, however. Each, like all the other necessary components of human flourishing, must be achieved, maintained, and enjoyed in a manner that allows it to be coherently integrated with everything else that makes up human flourishing. Further, since human flourishing is individualized, these goods and virtues must be achieved in light of a consideration of the set of circumstances, talents, endowments, interests, beliefs, and histories that descriptively characterize the individual—what I shall call his or her "nexus"—as well as the individual's community and culture. Thus, an examination of human nature may reveal basic or generic goods and virtues, but it does not reveal what the weighting or balancing of these goods and virtues should be for the individual.[33]

In other words, what human flourishing amounts to in terms of concrete activities for any particular individual is not something that can be simply read off human nature in some recipe-like manner. It is fundamentally erroneous to assume that abstract ethical principles *alone* can determine the proper course of conduct for any particular individual. Such ethical rationalism fails to grasp that ethics is practical and concerned with particular and contingent facts—facts that abstract ethical principles cannot explicitly capture. Such facts are crucial to determining

---

[33] This paragraph is taken, with slight alterations, from my entry "Perfectionism," in *Encyclopedia of Applied Ethics*, vol. 3 (San Diego: Academic Press, 1997), pp. 473–80. Further, the discussion of practical wisdom in this essay develops and expands upon ideas and themes presented there.

what ought to be done. Thus, contrary to much of modern and contemporary ethics, not all morally proper conduct need be something everybody should do.[34]

It might seem, however, that this rejection of ethical rationalism[35] goes too far. If knowing in what human flourishing generically consists does not solve the question of how individuals should conduct their lives, this inclusivist view of human flourishing can be charged with underdetermination. On such a view, ethical theory seems not very useful.

In other words, critics claim that this view of human flourishing places limits on practical reason's ability to determine what ought to be done regarding substantial matters.[36] Further, they claim that a view of human flourishing that allows for a plurality of inherent goods creates irresolvable conflicts when one tries to achieve them.[37] As an attempt to avoid the difficulties of a dominant-end account of human flourishing and the dogmatism of ethical rationalism, their overall complaint is that this neo-Aristotelian view has abdicated on its responsibility to provide ethical guidance.

My reply to these charges can be summarized as follows: (1) Underdetermination is a flaw only if one assumes that the aim of moral theory is to dictate a set of specific rules of conduct equally suited to all persons regardless of their nexus. But this is not necessary given that the human good is neither abstract nor agent-neutral. Practical wisdom deals with the contingent and the particular and can provide guidance regarding substantial matters, if we do not confuse it with theoretical reason or its features. (2) The existence of a plurality of inherent goods does not necessarily make them incompatible, if we do not confuse concrete with abstract considerations and if we recognize that it is by using practical wisdom, not rules, that potential conflicts are reconciled.

I will develop each of these responses. I will also, in the process, explain the central role of practical wisdom for this conception of human flourishing.

1. If it is indeed the case that human flourishing is a highly individualized, agent-relative activity, then a large measure of individualism

---

[34] The principle of universalizability will be discussed in Section IV.

[35] Ethical rationalism is understood here to be the position which holds (1) that abstract ethical principles *alone* can determine the proper course of conduct for any particular individual, and (2) that particular and contingent facts are not *morally* relevant when it comes to determining the proper course of conduct for an individual.

[36] "To admit an irreducible plurality of ends is to admit a limit to practical reasoning, and to admit that some substantial decisions are not to be explained, and not to be justified by any rational calculation. This is a possibility that cannot be conceptually excluded, even if it makes satisfying theoretical reconstruction of different uses of 'good,' as a target-setting term, impossible." Stuart Hampshire, *Freedom of Mind* (Princeton: Princeton University Press, 1971), p. 79.

[37] Loren Lomasky, *Persons, Rights, and the Moral Community* (New York: Oxford University Press, 1987), p. 51.

must be factored into the process of determining what a person should do. Yet, if this is so, then there might be a way to turn the tables on those who charge this neo-Aristotelian account with underdetermination. What appears to be a flaw might not really be one. In fact, it might be one of the principal advantages of this account, because it represents a theoretical openness to diversity. This account does not assume that abstract ethical reasoning can alone provide moral guidance or that the contingent and particular must somehow be eliminated from moral deliberations. Further, it does not suppose, as the Kantian (and utilitarian)[38] viewpoints appear to do, that the *sine qua non* of ethical reasoning is providing impersonal prescriptions.

Fundamentally, such a supposition is wrongheaded. The attempt to provide a set of specific rules of conduct equally suited to all persons regardless of their nexus, which has characterized so much of twentieth-century ethics, confuses agent-neutrality with objectivity, confuses law with ethics, and forgets the open-endedness of ethics.[39] Furthermore, it tends to confuse armchair pronouncements with the difficult task of determining what is the proper course of conduct for an individual in a given situation. Most importantly, however, the search for impersonal prescriptions overlooks the moral significance of what the individual *qua* individual brings to moral considerations.

The search for impersonal prescriptions also ignores the central role of the virtue of *phronesis* or practical wisdom for an ethics of human flourishing. Practical wisdom is the excellent or virtuous use of practical reason, and practical reason is the intellectual faculty employed in guiding conduct. This faculty can be properly or improperly used; when it is properly or excellently used, we have the virtue of practical wisdom. Practical wisdom is *the* intellectual virtue for this neo-Aristotelian conception of ethics, for it is central to the exercise of moral virtue. As Aristotle states, "virtue or excellence is a state of character involving choice and consists in observing the mean relative to us, a mean defined by a rational principle, *such as a man of practical wisdom would use to determine it*" (*Nicomachean Ethics*, 1107a1–3, emphasis added). It is extremely difficult to overstate the importance of practical wisdom for this view.

Practical wisdom is not merely cleverness or means-end reasoning.[40] Instead, it is the ability of the individual at the time of action to discern

---

[38] Utilitarianism is a consequentialistic theory of obligation whose aim is neither altruistic nor egoistic, but universalistic. One's own good should be considered, but not more than any other's; hence, it is an agent-neutral theory.

[39] Law must be concerned with rules that are universal and necessary, because it is concerned with the question of establishing social conditions that must apply to everyone equally. Ethics, on the other hand, need not be so construed. Ethical principles need to be open to the particular and contingent circumstances of the lives of different individuals.

[40] See Norman O. Dahl, *Practical Reason, Aristotle, and Weakness of the Will* (Minneapolis: University of Minnesota Press, 1984), p. 111.

in particular and contingent circumstances what is morally required.[41] Since there are for this view no *a priori* universal rules that dictate the proper weighting of the goods and virtues of human flourishing, a proper weighting is only achieved by individuals using practical wisdom at the time of action to discover the proper balance *for themselves*. The desirable and choiceworthy elements of flourishing need to be achieved, maintained, and enjoyed in a coherent manner, and this involves a consideration of generic, individuative, and circumstantial factors. This is no small task, and the ability to do it well characterizes the person who lives excellently. Such a person is practically wise. "Now it is thought to be the mark of a man of practical wisdom to be able to deliberate about what is good and expedient for himself, not in some particular respect, . . . but about what sorts of things conduce to the good life in general" (*Nicomachean Ethics*, 1140a25–28).

Moreover, the proper use of practical reasoning is not solely a process of maximization. The principal appeal of maximization is that given that something is desirable, it seems irrational not to choose a course of conduct that gives one more of it. However, if desirable goals are never pursued apart from other such goals, then practical reasoning has to encompass more than merely maximizing a good. It has to determine how to weight the pursuit of one necessary good or virtue relative to another so that the achievement of one does not eliminate the achievement of another. *Indeed, practical reason properly used, which is the virtue of practical wisdom, is the intelligent management of one's life so that all the necessary goods and virtues are coherently achieved, maintained, and enjoyed in a manner that is appropriate for the individual human being.*

Figure 1 illustrates the role of practical wisdom for this inclusivist, individualized, agent-relative conception of human flourishing.[42] The lines that divide the pie diagrams represent acts of practical wisdom. HF1, HF2, and HF3 are three different forms of flourishing, but there can be as many different forms of flourishing as there are individuals. The proportion of the pie diagram allotted each good[43] reflects the valuation or weighting (which is ultimately expressed by an individual's time and effort) that is proper for that person. There is no single, agent-neutral model to which each person's pattern or weighting of these goods must conform. None of these forms of flourishing is inherently superior to the other. Each has the necessary generic goods, but their proportions or weightings vary. The proper proportion must be worked out by

---

[41] Fred D. Miller, Jr., "Aristotle on Rationality and Action," *Review of Metaphysics*, vol. 38 (1984), pp. 499–520.

[42] The diagrams in Figure 1 come from Den Uyl, *The Virtue of Prudence*, pp. 192–93.

[43] The list of goods that comprise each pie comes from Aristotle's *Rhetoric*, 1362b10–28. It should be noted that health includes here action and life, and that intellectual ability involves speech.

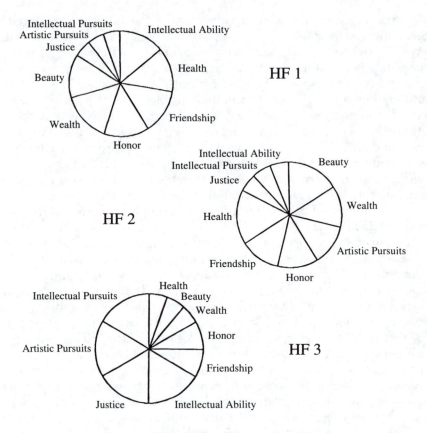

FIGURE 1. Three forms of human flourishing.

practical wisdom in light of each individual's nexus, community, and culture.[44]

Practical wisdom is crucial to the process of determining the proper course of conduct, but it does not replace or render unnecessary speculative or theoretical insight into the character of human flourishing. In fact, it depends on there being such abstract knowledge. Yet practical wisdom guides conduct by dealing with the contingent and the particular

[44] If we identify HF1 as the life of a businessperson, HF2 as the life of an athlete, and HF3 as the life of a philosopher, we see that a philosophic life is but one of the possible legitimate forms of flourishing. HF3 is not an inherently superior form of flourishing. There are no inherently superior forms of flourishing. The pie diagrams illustrate well the inclusivist, agent-relative view of human flourishing and the central role of practical wisdom. They also reveal clearly how much this neo-Aristotelian view, which I have been elucidating, varies from the dominant-end, contemplative model of human flourishing.

and thus does not have the features of theoretical reasoning. It is not impersonal, atemporal, or universal.[45] It is different, and if what has been said about the character of human flourishing is true, this difference does not make ethical theory any less useful for guiding conduct. We need both abstract knowledge of generic goods and virtues and practical wisdom's insight into the contingent and particular.

In other words, ethical living cannot be a matter of having theoretical knowledge alone or practical knowledge alone. Both are required. We need to have theoretical insight into the general character of human flourishing. For example, we need such knowledge as I attempted to provide when delineating the six features of human flourishing in Section II; or we need such knowledge as ethicists provide when they develop an account of the generic goods and virtues of human flourishing. This is knowledge about human flourishing that applies to all human beings regardless of their time or place or who they are. However, we also need to have practical insight at the time of action. We need to see what these generic goods and virtues amount to in concrete situations. We need to see what is their proper proportion or balance for us. Ethical living requires both theoretical and practical wisdom, but we should not forget their differences.

The reason there is a difference between theoretical and practical wisdom is that morality is not self-justifying. It serves a function or end, which is human flourishing.[46] Of course, flourishing always involves considerations of the contingent and particular. They are ineliminable. Thus, instead of trying to launder ethical reasoning through such devices as "veils of ignorance," "impartial ideal observers," or agent-neutral conceptions of practical reason, practical wisdom remains concerned with the temporal and individual. It is the central intellectual virtue for ethics because human flourishing is both individualized and agent-relative.

2. The existence of a plurality of ends that compose human flourishing does not, abstractly considered, logically entail that these ends are incompatible. Concretely considered, keeping them from becoming incompatible by discovering the proper weighting or balancing of these ends is an individual's central task. Yet this is only an insuperable difficulty if we assume that the goods and virtues that compose human flourishing are equal among themselves and identical across individuals. The view of human flourishing presented here accepts unequal weighting of its goods

---

[45] This point is developed further in the third subsection of Section IV.

[46] Morality requires both explanation and justification. It is not *sui generis*. For an ethics of human flourishing, morality exists for the purpose of helping human beings obtain a better life. The ultimate answer it offers to the question "Why be moral?" is "Because it is good for you." This may seem an implausible answer to some, but the deontological answer "Because it is your duty" is a nonstarter. It simply begs the question and does not take up the explanatory challenge.

and virtues[47] as central to the very character of human flourishing. Thus, conflicts are not as likely because some goods and virtues need not, given a person's nexus and circumstances, be emphasized or weighted as highly as other goods and virtues.

To appreciate better this viewpoint, it is worthwhile to quote at length what Douglas Den Uyl has observed regarding the role of the generic characteristics of our nature. These characteristics are seen

> as a package of capacities whose realization is required for self-perfection, but whose form is individuated by each person's own attributes, circumstances, and interests. These generic capacities, then, constitute the skeletal structure of one's life, but do not provide that life with specific content or direction. It is precisely the genericism of these capacities that often renders them impotent as specific guides of conduct or character development; for, although grounded in reality, they are nevertheless generalized abstractions of common needs and capacities and not independent realities in their own right. As such, unless the matter at hand concerns people in general, there is no reason to suppose identity of expression among individuals. Consequently, as components of a skeletal framework, these generic capacities serve to channel or corral individual expressions of self-actualization, but are not of themselves sufficient to identify the particular forms of that expression. And because of their generic quality, they are not in conflict, since they are not yet sufficiently substantive to identify a basis for conflict. Individuals or society may breathe content into these capacities in such a way that conflicts do develop.[48]

It remains the task for the individual to use his or her practical wisdom to avoid conflict when generic goods and virtues take concrete form. Simply following rules, or even abstract principles, will not suffice. Practical wisdom is required, but practical wisdom is not automatic. It must be initiated and maintained—it must be self-directed.

This task is, however, more than merely conflict avoidance; for if these generic goods and virtues are to be determinate, they must be appropriately individualized. As noted earlier, the individual does more than merely instantiate "abstract" goods and virtues. One must incorporate them into one's nexus by an act of reason or insight, not by mere mechanical application of universal principles to concrete cases.

In fact, abstractly conceived constitutive goods and virtues of human flourishing are valueless apart from the virtue of practical wisdom. They

---

[47] See Den Uyl, *The Virtue of Prudence*, p. 213.
[48] *Ibid.*, pp. 167–68. For a similar view, see Kathleen V. Wilkes, "The Good Man and the Good for Man in Aristotle's Ethics," *Mind*, vol. 87 (October 1978), p. 570.

are not like manna from heaven that somehow fit with each individual's needs and circumstances. Rather, they become valuable—that is, their proper combination, pattern, or weighting is achieved—only in relation to and because of the efforts of individual human beings. They are not goods apart from individuals and their efforts.

Though there is no abstract incompatibility among the goods and virtues of flourishing, making them compatible is not necessarily guaranteed. There may indeed be times when, though the principles are clear, the situation precludes achieving all the necessary goods. Tragedies are possible. Yet human flourishing remains a realistic ideal. We should be careful not to make of it something utopian. Human beings are neither omniscient nor omnipotent. Thus, ethics must be understood as being concerned only with what is, in principle, within the realm of human agency. Moreover, ethical principles only deal with what is for the most part, not with the contingent and the particular. Human lives are not numbers that can be neatly fitted into a mathematical equation. There is no single path or set formula. Despite what theologians, politicians, philosophers, and even friends may offer—and sometimes this can be valuable—only individuals exercising their own practical wisdom can make themselves whole.

The observations in this section do not mean or imply that one can ignore with moral impunity any of the necessary goods or virtues of human flourishing. Nor do they show that one course of action in a concrete situation is as good as the next. Neither conventionalism nor subjectivism[49] is implied. There are moral truths. These observations simply show that if this neo-Aristotelian account of human flourishing is true, then ethical rationalism is false and there is at least a form of pluralism that is morally appropriate.

IV. QUESTIONS AND DIFFICULTIES

There are many questions and difficulties that confront this neo-Aristotelian conception of human flourishing.[50] I will consider five of the more significant ones.

1. Can we speak of human flourishing or the human good "as such" and still describe this good as agent-relative? Does not the ability to know what human flourishing universally is—that is, our ability to abstractly consider generic ingredients or constituents of human flourishing—

[49] If we let P refer to the statement "X-ing is right and ought to be done" (or "X-ing is wrong and ought not to be done"), then conventionalism can be defined as the position which holds that "P is true" is semantically equivalent to "We think or believe P is true"; and subjectivism can be defined as the position which holds that "P is true" is semantically equivalent to "I believe or think P is true." In either case, the truth of a moral claim does not exist apart from its being thought or believed to be so.

[50] See Thomas Hurka, *Perfectionism* (New York: Oxford University Press, 1993), pp. 55–68.

conflict with the claim that it is agent-relative? Are we not, after all, required to adopt an agent-neutral conception of human flourishing?

This depends on what abstraction is. To think of the human good without regard to whose good it is is plainly possible, but does this entail thinking that the human good *is not* essentially the good for some person or other? Or does this only mean that one can think of the human good without thinking of whose good it is? If it is the latter, then it can still be the case that the good is always and necessarily the good for some person. There need not be conflict. The questions in the previous paragraph assume that the mode or manner of thinking something thus-and-so must determine the mode or manner of that something's being thus-and-so.[51] Yet there is no reason to accept such a view of abstraction. As Anthony Kenny has noted:

> To think a thing to *be* otherwise than it is is certainly to think falsely. But if all that is meant by "thinking a thing other than it is" is that the way it is with our thinking is different from the way it is with the thing we are thinking about, in its own existence, then there need be no falsehood involved. To think that Henry the VIII had no weight is to think a false thought; but there is no falsehood in thinking of Henry the VIII without thinking of his weight. Henry the VIII could never exist without having some weight or other, but a thought of Henry the VIII can certainly exist without any thought at all about his weight.[52]

To think of human flourishing without specifying the person whose flourishing it is, or without considering the myriad features of a person's nexus that give it determination, is not to deny either its relationship to the person or the existence of individuating features.[53] Nor does such abstract consideration require human flourishing to be agent-neutral, universal, or abstract.

It might still seem, however, that if we speak of human flourishing as the ultimate end of human conduct, then we are committed to something that is universalizable and, hence, not agent-relative, but agent-neutral. Yet it is not true that universalizability requires an agent-neutral view, for it is possible to hold a moral theory which claims that a person's good is agent-relative and still universalize the maxims of actions based on it. Let us say that human flourishing, G_1, for a person, P_1, is agent-relative if and

---

[51] As Aquinas observes: "Although it is necessary for the truth of cognition that the cognition answer to the thing known, still it is not necessary that the mode of the thing known be the same as the mode of its cognition" (*Summa Contra Gentiles*, II, 75).

[52] Anthony Kenny, *The Metaphysics of Mind* (Oxford: Clarendon Press, 1989), p. 134.

[53] The principle behind an abstract formulation of human flourishing can be stated as follows: Human flourishing must be human flourishing *for* some person, but it can be flourishing *for* any.

only if its distinctive presence in world W_1 is a basis for P_1's ranking W_1 over W_2, even though G_1 may not be the basis for *any other* person's ranking W_1 over W_2. Further, let us say the same holds true of goods G_2 through G_n for persons P_2 through P_n, respectively. Conduct based on such agent-relative goods can be universalized as follows: just as the production of P_1's good is a reason for P_1 to act, so is the production of P_2's good a reason for P_2 to act. P_1 cannot claim that G_1 provides him with a legitimate reason to act without acknowledging that G_2 provides P_2 with a legitimate reason to act. In other words, if one knows that attaining one's good provides one with a legitimate reason to act, because it is one's good, then one also knows that another person's attaining his or her good provides that person with a legitimate reason to act. The middle term is the knowledge that a person's attaining his or her good provides a person with a legitimate reason to act. This is what is universalized. But to know this does not show that human flourishing is not always essentially re-lated to some person. Thus, agent-relative values can be universalized. Being agent-neutral is not necessary for universalization.[54]

2. Maybe the real point of the previous questions has to do with uni-versalizability and what it involves. Perhaps universalizability creates difficulties for this conception of human flourishing, regardless of whether it implies agent-neutrality. There are two arguments for this claim: (A) If the human good is universalizable, then the human good *is* something universal, not individualized. (B) If the human good is objective, then it must be universalizable and hence universal and thus not individualized. In other words, it is argued that there is conflict between the human good's being universalizable and its being individualized and between its being individualized and its being objective. Thus, there is lack of coher-ence in the conception of human flourishing that has been presented.

Both of these arguments suppose, however, that if a good is the basis for universalizable conduct, then that good *is* universal and not individ-ualized. This assumes that what is necessary for the recognition of some-thing as a good and an object of conduct is also necessary for its existence as a good and an object of conduct. This assumption is not true. To say, for example, that knowledge is good for and ought to be pursued by every human being does not show that knowledge actually exists as some uni-versal, nonindividualized good. To think that knowledge is a good for everyone without thinking of the various individual ways it is a good does not show that knowledge does not exist as an individualized good for some human being. To claim that it does is but another instance of

---

[54] It should also be noted here that the ability of a value to be the basis for universalizable conduct is not sufficient to establish common values or a reason for other-regarding conduct among persons. This is so, because the universalization of agent-relative goods does not show P_1's good to be P_2's good, nor does it show that the production of P_2's good provides P_1 with a reason for action, or vice versa. Thus, if P_1's good should conflict with P_2's, universalizability would not provide a way out of this conflict.

assuming that the mode of our cognition of something must determine its mode of existence.

Similar considerations also apply to argument (B). As Henry Veatch has written:

> If the good of X is indeed but the actuality of X's potentialities, then this is a fact that not just X needs to recognize, but anyone and everyone else as well. And yet given the mere fact that a certain good needs to be recognized, and recognized universally, to be the good of X, it by no means follows that X's good must be taken to be Y's good as well, any more than the actuality or perfection or fulfillment of X needs to be recognized as being the actuality or perfection of Y as well.[55]

It can be true for everyone that some thing or activity is good for someone, even if it is not good for everyone. More generally, a truth about certain goods can be universalizable, even if those goods themselves are not. Further, it is false that some thing or activity cannot be actually good for anyone unless it is so for everyone.[56] More generally, the universality of the good is not a necessary condition for the objectivity of the good.

Another way of making these points is simply to note that universalizability is not the same as universality. If something is knowable, then it can be universalized, but this does not mean that it is universal. Human flourishing is objective and knowable and thus universalizable, but this does not make it something universal, something nonindividualized.

3. According to the account of human flourishing that has been presented, it is a mistake to treat practical reasoning as a process of comparing proposed acts or rules in terms of which produces "the most" human flourishing for someone. A mere maximizing view of practical reasoning mistakes abstractions for realities and treats one person's version of human flourishing as comparable to another's. Such comparisons are not possible, however. There is in reality no flourishing-at-large, no agent-neutral best end, by which to make a comparison. We cannot think of human flourishing as providing the basis for a unified race, with a single standard of swiftness, where everyone competes for the same prize. Versions of human flourishing are only valuable relative to some individual. Thus, the attempt to aggregate "total outputs" of actions or rules in terms

---

[55] Henry B. Veatch, "Ethical Egoism New Style: Should Its Trademark Be Aristotelian or Libertarian?" in his *Swimming against the Current in Contemporary Philosophy* (Washington, DC: The Catholic University of America Press, 1990), p. 194.

[56] For a recent discussion of this assumption, see Joseph L. Lombardi, "James Rachels on Kant's Basic Idea," *American Catholic Philosophical Quarterly*, vol. 71 (Winter 1997), pp. 53–58. See also Henry B. Veatch, "Modern Ethics, Teleology, and Love of Self," *The Monist*, vol. 75 (January 1992), pp. 52–70.

of some agent-neutral conception of human flourishing is not something in which practical reason can engage.

However, can this position be consistently maintained without lapsing into subjectivism or conventionalism? Surely, we must make comparisons with others and postulate an ideal standard in order to flourish. How else do we know if we are living up to our potentials? Further, if one is to have worthwhile relationships of any kind, let alone relationships such as character-friendships, one needs to be able to look at the world from the perspectives of others. Despite everything that has been said, it remains the case that in order to flourish people must be capable of transcending their own perspectives or points of view. Thus, flourishing seems to require that one treat value and practical reason in an agent-neutral manner. Agent-relativity will not suffice.

It is certainly true that the achievement of human flourishing requires individuals at times to adopt perspectives different from their own. Taking a perspective other than one's own—whether it is ideal, that of a friend, or that of *any* human being—is a valuable instrument for practical wisdom on an agent-relative view of human flourishing. An individual's moral growth, in both its personal and interpersonal dimensions, requires that this procedure be used, because flourishing requires learning about one's potentialities and understanding others.

Nonetheless, when we momentarily distance ourselves from or put ourselves outside our current situation in order to consider abstractly what is the best that is possible for human beings or in order to relate to others, we do not necessarily adopt an agent-neutral conception of human flourishing. It is a mistake to equate the value of taking such perspectives with the idea that values and reasons for conduct should or must be agent-neutral. Indeed, abstraction, imagination, empathy, interpersonal perspectives—speculative reason in general—are tools for practical reason, but they need to be used properly. We need to know when our concern is with knowing what is true and good and when it is with achieving what is good. We must be careful not to confuse speculative and practical reason. We need to distinguish the speculative activity of determining what the generic goods and virtues of human flourishing are and how they are ordered apart from their relation to any particular person, from the practical activity of determining their proper weighting and balance, that is, their value, relative to some individual. In other words, we need to distinguish intellectually discovering what in human flourishing "as such" is dependent on what, from the activity of achieving this good in its proper concrete form for some individual.[57] The former, abstract analysis is necessary for a general understanding of human flour-

---

[57] "To recognize that one must build the foundation of a house before one can build the second story does not require that one value the view from the basement more than the view from the balcony." Den Uyl, *The Virtue of Prudence*, pp. 196–97. See also his discussion of Thomas Nagel's view of practical reason (*ibid.*, pp. 29–34).

ishing, but, after engaging in such abstract considerations, we need to return to our own cases to practically determine what ought to be done. We still need to determine how to achieve a level of excellence with respect to our various potentialities that is compatible with the most complete enjoyment of the other necessary goods and virtues. Human flourishing remains an individualized and agent-relative affair.

4. Closely related to the previous concern is the issue of whether all the goods and virtues that comprise human flourishing can be weighted differently for each individual. Might it not be that there are some whose importance is not relative to the other goods and virtues and which should not be treated in an individualized and agent-relative manner? We need only consider, for example, justice to see this difficulty. Justice is too fundamental to be given different weightings by different people. Indeed, justice might seem to illustrate perfectly what is wrong with this neo-Aristotelian conception of human flourishing. One is either just or not just. It is not a matter of weighting, balance, or emphasis. It is "all or nothing."

This objection is very important; and not all the dimensions of a full response, especially the political dimension, can be developed here.[58] I can, however, begin a response by noting that there are at least two different senses of "justice." First, we can speak of justice as the overall condition or state of the person. This is the idea of the rightly ordered soul and is but another way of speaking of human flourishing. It certainly does not seem that justice in this sense is the concern of this objection. Second, we can speak of justice as concerned with the interpersonal or social. This is the sense of "justice" that is the concern of the foregoing objection, but we still need further to note two senses in which justice is interpersonal or social.

As stated earlier, human flourishing is achieved with and among others. The specific form in which human sociality is expressed can be termed an "exclusive relationship." Exclusive relationships cover a continuum of relations, and they involve a principle of selectivity on the part of the participants in the relationship. Some people are included and others excluded from the relationship because of some value(s) the participants share. These relationships include everything from close friends and confidants, to business and work relations, to mere acquaintances. It is through exclusive relationships that various types of groups, communities, and even cultures are formed.

Human sociality can also involve the exploration of relationships with new and different people and varied ways of living, working, and thinking. This is the open-ended character of human sociality that I also noted

---

[58] See Douglas J. Den Uyl and Douglas B. Rasmussen, "'Rights' as MetaNormative Principles," *Liberty for the 21st Century*, ed. Tibor R. Machan and Douglas B. Rasmussen (Lanham, MD: Rowman and Littlefield, 1995), pp. 59–75; Rasmussen and Den Uyl, *Liberalism Defended*; and Rasmussen and Den Uyl, *Liberty and Nature*.

earlier. It leads me to describe the relationships that might develop as being "nonexclusive." No principle of selectivity is involved, for I am noting that human sociality, prior to a person's choice and selection, imposes no limitation regarding with whom and under what circumstances one may have a relationship. Further, nonexclusive relationships often provide the wider context in which exclusive relationships are formed. Many, if not most, exclusive relationships come about only because there was first a nonexclusive relationship.[59]

To identify a need for sociality, regardless of the social or cultural form it takes, is to speak of relationships in a nonexclusive sense, because no principle of selectivity is involved. Yet the recognition of the nonexclusive side of human sociality reveals that two senses of interpersonal or social justice need to be distinguished. I shall call one (a) "metanormative" justice and the other (b) "normative" justice.

(a) When interpersonal or social life is understood in a nonexclusive sense—that is, when we are concerned with relationships with *any* human being—justice can be understood as concerned *not* with the guidance of individual conduct in moral activity, but rather with the regulation of conduct so that conditions might be obtained where morally significant action can take place. Justice, understood as a norm that regulates conditions under which moral conduct can take place, is a "metanorm."

As a metanorm, justice deals with social life in the nonexclusive sense and does not assume a shared set of values or commitments. Hence, the context is as universal as possible. Justice is only concerned with making possible relationships among humans, each of whom has a unique form of human flourishing, ethically compossible.[60] The type of moral requirement that is imposed for establishing this context must be both something that everyone's form of flourishing requires and something that everyone can in principle fulfill. Justice understood in this sense is not a matter of personal flourishing, but a matter of creating, maintaining, and evaluating the political/legal conditions for civil order.[61] It is *not* one of the constituents of human flourishing and thus cannot be weighted.[62] Rather, justice is the political/legal prerequisite for their achievement. Its fundamental importance is grounded in the social as well as individual character of human flourishing.

[59] Cf. Rasmussen and Den Uyl, *Liberty and Nature*, pp. 173–219.

[60] As noted in the sixth subsection of Section II, the open-ended character of our natural sociality creates the need for finding principles that will allow for the possibility that individuals might flourish in different ways (in different communities and cultures) without creating moral conflict.

[61] See note 58.

[62] The aim of "metanormative" justice is not the human flourishing of the individual. Rather, the aim is establishing a political/legal context so that social life in its widest sense might be possible without requiring the sacrifice of one person's form of flourishing to another's. Though the need for "metanormative" justice is based on the character of human flourishing—e.g., its individuality and sociality—the direct object of its concern is not the personal flourishing of the individual.

(b) When interpersonal or social life is understood in an "exclusive" sense, justice is concerned with directing personal conduct for the achievement of human flourishing. So understood, justice is the normative principle of "rendering each his proportionate due,"[63] and it is one of the central virtues of human flourishing. However, the proper application of the virtue of justice—that is, understanding what constitutes the correct proportion—is not conveyed by the virtue of justice itself, but, like the application of every other normative virtue, requires practical wisdom. Furthermore, not only does one have to determine what action in the contingent and particular situation is just, one also has to integrate the actions required by this virtue with those required by the other virtues and goods that constitute one's flourishing.

As I have said, the proper course of conduct does not come in some ethical recipe. Knowledge of circumstances, the character of the person one is dealing with, and how a possible course of action integrates with the other actions that one's flourishing requires is needed. Determining what conduct the virtue of justice requires thus involves knowing more than that one is in the presence of a fellow human being. The virtue of justice is neither blind nor applied in an impersonal way. It requires discernment of differences of both persons and circumstances. Therefore, what the virtue of justice concretely requires will vary according to circumstances and situation. Different courses of action will be required.

Accordingly, one can properly decide not to take up a just course of conduct because, although worthy in itself, that conduct does not fit well with all the other aspects of one's flourishing that have been given greater emphasis. This is not, however, merely a practical matter; that is, one does not decide to forgo just conduct because one does not have sufficient time or money. Rather, it is a matter of practical wisdom. Regardless of how worthy the course of conduct may be in itself, it is not one's own proper course of conduct, because it is not consistent with other aspects of one's flourishing. As Den Uyl has noted regarding this very issue, "it is not only acceptable that one not participate, but *right* that one not do so."[64] Justice as it applies to exclusive relations is, then, *not* an "all or nothing" affair.

5. I have claimed that self-direction is crucial to the character of human flourishing and that an act of self-direction is an exercise of reason. Yet what is it to be self-directed, or when is someone not self-directed? Surely, persons are not self-directed when they do not use their rational faculty. This occurs, of course, when one literally does nothing; but it also happens when one's desires and passions are in control. The core of self-direction is the exercise of reason; and when one's passions are responsible for one's conduct, then one is not self-directed.

[63] Aristotle did not clearly distinguish between the exclusive and nonexclusive senses of sociality. Nor, with his use of the term "polis," did he distinguish clearly between society and state. Thus, it should be noted that this account of the virtue of justice differs from his.

[64] Den Uyl, *The Virtue of Prudence,* 194–95.

If the foregoing is true, however, this seems to create a problem for the claim that human flourishing is an object of desire. If the human good is an object of desire, then how can one be self-directed? If it is our appetites that move us toward human flourishing, then we have lost control of the situation. Our self-direction is but a sham. It would seem that the only way to stay in control and maintain self-direction would be to confine practical reason to procedures that do not let personal desires play a role in the determination of conduct.[65] In other words, it seems that practical reason must, despite everything that has been said, only consider agent-neutral reasons and universal goods. Once again, then, we have a question about the internal consistency of the conception of human flourishing that has been presented. Can the self-directed character of human flourishing be reconciled with its individualized and agent-relative character?

The answer to this question will provide a useful transition to our discussion of the importance of human nature for this conception of human flourishing, because this answer depends on our understanding of what it is to be human. If human beings are rational *animals*, not merely rational *beings*, then human flourishing is not the flourishing of a pure mind. Flourishing is, of course, a *way* of living and is thus more than self-preservation or survival. Yet it is nonetheless a way of *living* and is thus not intelligible apart from a biocentric context. Desire and appetite are necessarily a part of the process. However, the relation of desire and appetite to human flourishing is even more fundamental than this. They are not merely necessary to achieving flourishing. They are, rather, necessary to the very character of human flourishing. Human flourishing is the enactment of right desire. Correctly valuing something is not distinct from desire. Rather, it just *is* right desire. Thus, only an excessively rationalist conception of human beings would attempt to conceive of flourishing without desire.

Desires and appetites are not fundamental, however. They are for the sake of flourishing. That is to say, they are judged by whether they are conducive to one's fulfillment. Thus, it is not a question of eliminating them or discounting their influence. Rather, it is a question of using and controlling desire and appetite for the sake of human flourishing. There is no necessary incompatibility between them and reason. As Kathleen V. Wilkes has noted:

> Aristotle's man is *active*, an agent. His highest good (*eudaimonia*, roughly translated as "flourishing") is glossed in terms of activity: living well, doing well. "A man seems to be a source of actions" (*Nicomachean Ethics*, iii. 3. 1112b31–2); and consider this; "choice is either de-

---

[65] Loren Lomasky summarizes this viewpoint well when he observes that Rawlsian contractors are "perfectly pure specimens of autonomy. None can be deflected from rational reflection by the force of any untoward inclination, because behind the veil one does not know what one's inclinations are" (*Persons, Rights, and the Moral Community*, p. 43).

siderative reason or ratiocinative desire, *and such a source of action is man,"* (*Nicomachean Ethics*, vi. 2. 1139b4–5). We become the people that we are by choosing, deciding, acting; we have the responsibility for shaping ourselves, our characters, and our lives. This stress on agency and activity, man *in* the world and not just an observer of it, is one of the most attractive features of his general theory.[66]

Rational desires or dispositions are possible, and it is when one's character is so disposed that we may say one is flourishing.

If it is possible that desires can embody an act of self-direction or an exercise of reason, then there is no basis to suppose that human flourishing cannot be an object of both reason *and* desire.[67] It is not necessary to adopt procedures that prevent personal desires or interests from playing a role in the determination of conduct. Practical reason need not confine itself to agent-neutral considerations. There need be no inconsistency between self-direction and the individualized and agent-relative character of human flourishing.

If we are to see the possibility of desire embodying self-direction, we must awaken from our Cartesian slumbers. We need to see, of course, that one's exercise of reason cannot be merely the result of factors beyond one's control. Self-direction cannot be reducible to some causal string. It cannot be, for example, the mere result of antecedent genetic or socio-cultural factors. This will not suffice.

Nor can self-direction be some sort of primitive, acontextual, inexplicable, unconditional act, however. It is not radically free. It does not create its context. Instead, it can be evaluated in terms of something other than itself. Self-direction is crucial to the discovery, implementation, integration, and enjoyment of the goods that constitute its end—that is, the actualization of human flourishing—but self-direction does not create its potentiality for that end. The end-oriented character of self-direction is not itself a matter of self-direction.

This neo-Aristotelian view of human nature sees self-direction as neither compelled by external, antecedent forces nor metaphysically unconditioned. This view clearly supposes that human beings are teleological in nature and that teleology provides a middle ground between compulsion and radical freedom. I will examine this view in the next section.

V. APPEALING TO HUMAN NATURE

The character of human flourishing is not discovered solely by a scientific study of human nature. Considerations of the requirements and conditions for human volition and action, cultural and social practices,

---

[66] Kathleen V. Wilkes, *Real People* (Oxford: Clarendon Press, 1988), p. 213.
[67] See Dahl, *Practical Reason, Aristotle, and Weakness of the Will*, pp. 93–99.

and common-sense observations are part of the process. Further, we need not assume that our beliefs and practices must be barriers to knowing what is real. It is not necessary to proceed in a Cartesian manner and raze all opinions in order to find some firm foundation. We must start somewhere, and the starting point of an inquiry into the character of human flourishing is with the opinions, *endoxa*, of our society and culture. Indeed, we seldom, if ever, appeal to human nature to understand human flourishing without already having a set of evaluative views. The point of entry for such reflection most often occurs when we examine our lives as a whole and wonder what they are for.[68] Our general aim is to make our lives as good as possible and to find unity for them.

Yet the fact that we do not begin our investigation of human flourishing *de novo* does not imply that we are confined to the status quo. The claim that rationality is always embodied in a tradition that provides the context that determines whether an argument is a good one[69] is subject to two interpretations. It can mean either that a tradition determines whether an argument *is* good or merely that it determines whether people *think* an argument is good. The truth of the latter, weaker claim certainly does not imply the truth of the former, stronger claim. Further, there seems little reason to give up the basic and well-established idea that it is an argument's adequacy to its subject-matter that constitutes its goodness and not its counting as so within some tradition.[70]

Of course, we are neither disembodied minds nor asocial beings, and thus it should be admitted that our rationality is always embodied in a tradition—at least in some loose sense of that term. Yet this does not mean or imply that we are thereby trapped and cannot, as a matter of principle, consider things from the viewpoint of other traditions or adopt radically different perspectives. We can appeal to other accounts of human flourishing and in fact attempt to see if there is anything about being human that will give us insight into how to live our lives. There are, of course, practical limitations, for we are limited and fallible. Such admissions do not, however, show that our understanding of reality in general or of human flourishing in particular must be confined to our tradition or point of view. At least, they do not show that we are bound in such a way that we can no longer distinguish between our thinking something thus-and-so and its being thus-and-so.

---

[68] John M. Cooper, "Eudaimonism, the Appeal to Nature, and 'Moral Duty' in Stoicism," in *Aristotle, Kant, and the Stoics*, ed. Stephen Engstrom and Jennifer Whiting (Cambridge: Cambridge University Press, 1996), pp. 264–65.

[69] See Alasdair MacIntyre, *Whose Justice? Which Rationality?* (Notre Dame: University of Notre Dame Press, 1988). For an important and powerful critique of this book, see T. H. Irwin, "Tradition and Reason in the History of Ethics," *Social Philosophy and Policy*, vol. 7, no. 1 (Autumn 1989), pp. 45–68.

[70] Also, it seems unfair to suppose that those who claim that reason is always embodied in a tradition mean to endorse the view that the truth of a proposition consists just in members of a tradition thinking or believing that it is so.

Human nature sets the general limit on what is ultimately included in or excluded from any account of human flourishing. This being said, it should be noted that the following discussion is essentialistic in a minimal sense: what and who human beings are is not entirely a function of social or cultural forces; and linguistic and conceptual schemes, or systems of interpretation, do not ultimately determine human nature. In other words, there are individual realities of a certain kind to which the term "human being" refers. Further, this discussion assumes that cognitive realism is possible; that is to say, it assumes that we can know what things really are. The manner or mode of our cognition does not determine the very character of the content of our cognition. In this case, this means that what human beings are can be known. These are important assumptions that require defense, which cannot be provided here, but has been provided elsewhere.[71]

The neo-Aristotelian view of human flourishing that has been presented appeals to human nature in two basic ways: (1) it assumes that human nature is teleological, that is, that human beings have a *telos* or natural function;[72] and (2) it assumes that this natural function has moral import. In other words, it assumes that knowing what our natural function is tells us something about the character of human flourishing. Both of these assumptions shall be explained. They cannot be defended, however, in any detail; that task is for a much larger project. My hope, however, is that these remarks will show at least that these assumptions are not as implausible as is sometimes thought.

1. That human nature is teleological is at once the most important and the most controversial assumption of this view of human flourishing. It is the most important, because it is the idea that human flourishing is the end (*telos*) or function (*ergon*) of human life that allows this theory to avoid the "naturalistic fallacy."[73] If human flourishing is the natural end

---

[71] See Douglas B. Rasmussen, "Quine and Aristotelian Essentialism," *The New Scholasticism*, vol. 58 (Summer 1984), pp. 316–35; Rasmussen, "The Significance for Cognitive Realism of the Thought of John Poinsot," *American Catholic Philosophical Quarterly*, vol. 68 (Summer 1994), pp. 409–24; Baruch Brody, *Identity and Essence* (Princeton: Princeton University Press, 1980); Tibor R. Machan, "Epistemology and Moral Knowledge," *Review of Metaphysics*, vol. 36 (September 1982), pp. 23–49; Edward Pols, *Radical Realism* (Ithaca, NY: Cornell University Press, 1992); and Anthony J. Lisska, *Aquinas's Theory of Natural Law* (Oxford: Clarendon Press, 1996).

[72] We commonly think of artifacts as having a proper function (*ergon*), e.g., the function of a knife is to cut. To claim that an entity has a natural function is to claim that an entity has a proper function in virtue of what it is, not as the result of someone designing it for a certain activity. "Proper" means essential to the entity. The claim that an entity has a proper activity that is its natural function is confined here to the biological realm. Thus, natural functions primarily occur in living organisms. The claim that living entities have natural functions rests, however, on the further claim that *living* entities have an end (*telos*) in virtue of their nature. Thus, the natural function of a living thing is understood in terms of its natural end. "End" means in this context that-for-the-sake-of-which, but it does not necessarily mean "conscious purpose." This claim is explained and defended below.

[73] This is the alleged fallacy of deducing a statement of what *ought* to be from a statement of what *is* the case, or deducing a statement about a *value* from a statement about a *fact*.

for human life, and if we understand the human good in terms of that end, then it is simply not the case that all facts are valueless. This means that for human beings their good is based on and understood in terms of facts pertaining to their nature. Indeed, for the class of beings that have natural ends or functions, goodness is ontological in the sense that it is a potentiality that is actualized.[74] Hence, it is not always a fallacy to go from a fact to a value, because some facts are inherently value-laden. Further, if self-direction is for the sake of the human good, then self-direction is not radically free in the sense described in the previous section. It has an innate potentiality for the good. Thus, reason and motivation need not always be separate, and the problem of finding motivation for being moral need not be insuperable.

That human nature is teleological is certainly a most controversial claim. For some, to link this claim to the neo-Aristotelian view of human flourishing is to render this view beyond the pale. Indeed, it must be admitted that teleology is often associated with dubious metaphysical views— for example, that the cosmos has some end, that species are fixed and do not evolve, and that there is a *scala naturae* ascending from simple elements to an unmoved mover. Alasdair MacIntyre termed such views "metaphysical biology."[75] Moreover, teleology is associated with such positions as theism, vitalism,[76] ineluctabilism,[77] and genericism,[78] as well as the fallacy of anthropomorphism. Not surprisingly, there are some advocates of an ethics of human flourishing[79] who seek to avoid making ontological commitments about the nature of human flourishing.

The situation is not so grim, however. Present-day advocates of natural teleology argue that their position does not require them to uphold any of the foregoing views or to commit any fallacies. It is not necessary to hold that the cosmos, history, society, or the human race is directed toward

[74] See Rasmussen and Den Uyl, *Liberty and Nature*, pp. 56–57, as well as Henry B. Veatch, *For an Ontology of Morals* (Evanston: Northwestern University Press, 1971).

[75] Alasdair MacIntyre, *After Virtue* (Notre Dame: Notre Dame University Press, 1981), p. 152.

[76] Vitalism holds that present in any living thing is an immaterial substance, an *élan vital*, that imparts to that thing powers that are neither possessed by nor result from the inanimate parts that compose it. Vitalism should, then, be distinguished from the view that present in any living thing are emergent properties, which are contingent on the organization of its inanimate parts, but not reducible to them.

[77] If one's *telos* is ineluctable, then the issue of being responsible for achieving it is irrelevant.

[78] Genericism is the view "that all developmental processes are generically equivalent across individuals such that individuals come to be little more than repositories of generic endowments" (Den Uyl, *The Virtue of Prudence*, p. 36).

[79] See Hurka, *Perfectionism*, for an account of human flourishing which does not assume a theory of human nature. See also Robert P. George, "Natural Law and Human Nature," in *Natural Law Theory*, ed. Robert P. George (Oxford: Clarendon Press, 1992), pp. 31–41, where George argues that basic goods such as knowledge and friendship are self-evidently good and do not require an anthropological basis. See Lisska, *Aquinas's Theory of Natural Law*, for a critique of George's view.

some grand *telos*. Instead, it is only necessary that individuals have ends. Moreover, there are individuative potentialities that are actualized. It is not the case that individuals are little more than repositories for generic endowments and add nothing to the developmental processes. It is not necessary to accept genericism. Thus, the existence of a human *telos* need not be in conflict with the individualized character of human flourishing, as it seems to be for traditional versions of Aristotelian ethics. Nor is it necessary to hold that God has created the universe or individual things to serve some end to which they are drawn. There need only be a *naturalistic*[80] teleology.

James G. Lennox has argued that there are basically two different models of teleology, or final causation.[81] According to the Platonic model,[82] which has its origin in the divine craftsman of the *Timaeus*,[83] the operation of ends as causes requires the actions of a rational agent or mind whose intentions apply to the entire cosmos. It is in terms of this agent's intentions that processes in the natural world are judged good. Both the cause and the goodness are, for this model, "external" to what is being explained. It is in principle the same view of teleology that is used when speaking of artifacts. Just as we say that a good knife is one that fulfills the purpose for which it is created—that is, cutting—so we say the same regarding entities in the natural world.

According to the Aristotelian[84] model, final causation is only one of the answers to the question "Why?" and it does not require a rational agent whose universal intentions determine goodness. Instead, teleology is restricted to the biological domain and is "internal" or "immanent" to the organism that is being explained. It is the goal or function of the individual organism, not the "external" designer, that is under consideration. Further, it is not necessary to posit an immaterial, separable force, an *élan vital*, within an organism that provides direction and motivation. Rather, teleology can result from an internal directive principle

---

[80] "Naturalistic" is used here to rule out the necessity of any supernatural commitment. It does not mean the same thing as materialism or, at least, not eliminative or reductive materialism. See Elliott Sober's discussion of "Teleology Naturalized" in his *Philosophy of Biology* (Boulder and San Francisco: Westview Press, 1993), pp. 82–87.

[81] James G. Lennox, "Teleology," in *Keywords in Evolutionary Biology*, ed. Evelyn Fox Keller and Elisabeth A. Lloyd (Cambridge, MA, and London: Harvard University Press, 1992), pp. 324–33.

[82] James G. Lennox, "Plato's Unnatural Teleology," *Platonic Investigations*, ed. Dominic J. O'Meara (Washington, DC: Catholic University Press, 1985), pp. 195–218.

[83] The *Timaeus* is Plato's creation myth in which the divine craftsman, the "demiurge," gives purpose to nature.

[84] See Allan Gotthelf, "Aristotle's Conception of Final Causality," in *Philosophical Issues in Aristotle's Biology*, ed. Allan Gotthelf and James Lennox (Cambridge: Cambridge University Press, 1987), pp. 204–42; Gotthelf, "Understanding Aristotle's Teleology," in *Final Causality in Nature and Human Affairs*, ed. R. F. Hassing (Washington, DC: Catholic University of America Press, 1997), pp. 71–82; and Miller, *Nature, Justice, and Rights in Aristotle's "Politics"* (*supra* note 4), section 10.2, "Natural Teleology," pp. 336–46.

that is an irreducible feature of the developmental processes of the living organism itself. The process is irreducible in the sense that the movement from potentiality to actuality is inherent in the structure of the organism in such a way that other forms of explanation (e.g., mechanical or chemical) are insufficient to account for the phenomenon.

In other words, it is precisely the capacity for the development to maturity that cannot be accounted for by merely appealing to the potentialities of the basic material elements that compose a living thing. For Aristotle, these material elements were earth, air, fire, and water. For us, they are much more complex, but the principle is the same. Development to maturity does occur and requires explanation. Yet appealing to the potentialities of these basic material elements alone does not suffice. Only an inherent potential for the development to maturity will suffice.

Accordingly, contemporary advocates of natural teleology hold that what living things are and how they develop cannot be adequately understood except insofar as they are understood as functioning for the sake of the mature state of the organism. The process of pursuing and maintaining ends is the result of the very nature of living things. Teleology has a place in nature, then, not because the universe has a purpose or because God has created and endowed each creature with a purpose. Teleology exists because the nature of living things involves the potential that is irreducibly for development to maturity.

It is further argued that the theoretical core of Aristotle's teleology—namely, that life-forms are self-directing in virtue of inherent forms or structure—is vindicated by modern biology. Aristotle's accounts of the physical mechanisms (for example, vital heat) that are supposed to be the source of transmission of the formal principle, are, of course, not defensible, but he seems to have gotten the essentials right. As Max Delbrück, founder of molecular genetics, remarked about Aristotle's explanation of the generation of animals:

> What strikes the modern reader most forcibly is his insistence that in the generation of animals the male contributes, in the semen, a *form principle*, not a mini-man. . . . The form principle is likened to a carpenter. The carpenter is a moving force which changes the substrate, but the moving force is not contained in the finished product. . . . Put into modern language [what Aristotle says] is this: The form principle is the information which is stored in the semen. After fertilization it is read out in a preprogrammed way; the readout alters the matter upon which it acts, but it does not alter the stored information, which is not, properly speaking, part of the finished product. In other words, if that committee in Stockholm, which has the unenviable task each year of pointing out the most creative scientists, had the liberty of

giving awards posthumously, I think they should consider Aristotle for the discovery of the principle implied in DNA.[85]

This naturalistic approach to teleology is also like "adaptational explanations"[86] in evolutionary biology, and it has value implications. As Lennox explains:

> [I]f a part comes to be because of its contribution to the organism's life, that sanctions its identification as *there for the sake of* that contribution. Taking its continued existence as good for it, those of the animal's parts and behavior that develop to contribute to its life in various ways can be described as for the sake of *the good* or *the valuable*. Thus, the use of evaluative language in the Aristotelian teleological tradition doesn't depend, as it does in the Platonic tradition, on the end being *seen as* valuable by a rational agent.[87]

Broadly speaking, then, we may "define"[88] goodness as the actualization by a living thing of its potentialities, since the needs and requirements of a living thing are what give rise to that actualization being an end. Values are not separate from facts when it comes to living things. Further, it is in this sense that goodness might be understood as "ontological" but still ultimately relational. In other words, certain actions of a living thing at a given time benefit its life; that is, they promote its development to maturity. Now these actions, in turn, make possible the repetition by the living thing of those actions in the future, and so on. These actions thus both produce and express the life of the entity. They constitute its life although they are also *for* it. Goodness is therefore neither an intrinsic

[85] Max Delbrück, "Aristotle-totle-totle," in *Of Microbes and Life*, ed. Jacques Monod and Ernest Borek (New York: Columbia University Press, 1971), pp. 54–55. Fred D. Miller's work (see note 84) first drew my attention to this statement by Delbrück. See also Francisco J. Ayala, "The Autonomy of Biology as a Natural Science," in *Biology, History, and Natural Philosophy*, ed. A. D. Breck and W. Yourgrau (New York: Plenum Press, 1972), pp. 1–16; Ayala, "Teleological Explanations in Evolutionary Biology," *Philosophy of Science*, vol. 37 (1970), pp. 1–15; Robert N. Brandon, "Biological Teleology: Questions and Explanation," *Studies in the History and Philosophy of Science*, vol. 12 (1981), pp. 91–105; Jonathan Jacobs, "Teleological Form and Explanation," in *Current Issues in Teleology*, ed. Nicholas Rescher (Lanham, MD: University Press of America, 1986), pp. 49–55; Charles Taylor, *The Explanation of Behavior* (London: Routledge and Kegan Paul, 1964); W. C. Wimsatt, "Teleology and the Logical Structure of Function Statements," *Studies in the History and Philosophy of Science*, vol. 3 (1972), pp. 1–80; Andrew Woodfield, *Teleology* (Cambridge: Cambridge University Press, 1976); Larry Wright, *Teleological Explanations* (Berkeley: University of California Press, 1976).

[86] "Characteristic c is an adaptation for task t in a population if and only if members of the population now have c because, ancestrally, there was a selection for having c and c conferred a fitness advantage because it performed task t" (Sober, *Philosophy of Biology*, p. 84).

[87] Lennox, "Teleology," in *Keywords in Evolutionary Biology*, p. 327.

[88] See Rasmussen and Den Uyl, *Liberty and Nature*, pp. 51–57, for a critique of G. E. Moore's "open-question argument" and his claim that goodness cannot be defined.

(nonrelational) feature of things or actions, nor is it merely a subjective phenomenon of consciousness. Instead, it is an aspect of reality *in relation* to the needs of a living thing. Indeed, we might say that apart from living things there are no intrinsically good, right, or beautiful things. Things are only good, right, or beautiful in relation to living entities.[89]

For human beings, becoming good, flourishing, is not something to which they are driven. Teleology does not require ineluctability. Human beings, insofar as they are moral agents, actualize their ends through their own self-direction. This occurs through a person's dispositions for the proper desires and actions—dispositions which are ultimately a matter of moral responsibility. It is human reason that forms the conception of what is good for a person that is expressed in one's character or dispositions.[90] It is the ability to have a conception of what is good for oneself (that children and nonhuman animals do not possess) that creates the causal power necessary for the nonaccidental production of good outcomes. This is crucial for a given activity's being morally right or wrong and thus for someone's being morally responsible.[91] As Aristotle states:

> [R]eason is for distinguishing the beneficial and the harmful, and so too the just and the unjust. For this distinguishes a human being from the other animals—that he alone has perception of the good and bad and just and unjust and the rest. (*Politics*, 1253a14–18)

Human beings are part of the natural order and are not immune from its influences. Self-direction is part of the process, but it is, nonetheless, an activity for which beings of our kind are responsible.

2. The claim that human flourishing is a *telos* is intimately connected with the idea that there is a distinct human nature. It is in terms of one's nature that the activity of flourishing or the process of "perfection" is measured. To "perfect," to "realize," or to "actualize" oneself is not to become God-like, immune to degeneration, or incapable of harm, but it is to fulfill those potentialities and capacities that make one human. This is to achieve one's natural end or perform one's natural function.

There are, however, some important objections to this line of thought. They are as follows:

(A) Even if we know what the function of a human being is, this does not entitle us to speak legitimately of what a good human being is, because this inference requires that human beings have instrumental functions and purposes in terms of which they are judged good or useful.

---

[89] Tibor R. Machan, *Human Rights and Human Liberties* (Chicago: Nelson-Hall, 1974), p. 66.
[90] Aquinas, *Summa Theologiae*, Ia.5.1.
[91] Susan Sauvé Meyer, *Aristotle on Moral Responsibility* (Oxford, UK, and Cambridge, MA: Basil Blackwell, 1993), p. 166.

Yet human beings are not tools that have instrumental functions or purposes.[92]

(B) From the fact that some capacity is peculiar or unique to human beings, it does not follow that a good human being is one who exercises this capacity. Neither does it follow that it is good for human beings to exercise this capacity.[93]

(C) Even if performing one's natural function determines what makes someone a good human being, it does not follow that it is good for any individual human being to exercise the capacities that comprise this function. There is a difference between what is a good human being and what is good for a human being.[94]

I shall respond to each objection. Regarding (A), it is not necessary to assume that human beings have instrumental functions like tools in terms of which their conduct can be judged as functioning well or poorly. In fact, not only is it not necessary that people be viewed instrumentally, it is necessary that they *not* be viewed instrumentally. Human beings have a function because of what they are. Their function is "internally," not "externally," determined. They are living organisms, and the performance of their function by them is for their sake or benefit, not for some further end. The inference from what the function of a human being is to what it is to be a good human being is confined to individual living things that are members of a natural kind and whose benefit is at least in part determined by the characteristics in virtue of which each is a member of that kind. The activities that compose the function, which I will discuss shortly, serve no further ends or purpose but are inherent to those characteristics that are responsible for membership in that kind. Yet it should be emphasized that for this neo-Aristotelian view one cannot identify the function of a certain kind of living organism without introducing the notion of benefit for members of that kind. Thus, formal and final causes coincide.[95] As noted earlier, when it comes to the nature of living things, giving an account of an organism's function is not merely a matter of moving from a purely descriptive account to an evaluative account. There are values "all the way down."[96]

Regarding (B), a human being's function is not determined by what is peculiar or unique.[97] Instead, a human being's function is determined by

---

[92] W. F. R. Hardie, *Aristotle's Ethical Theory* (Oxford: Clarendon Press, 1980), pp. 23–24.

[93] Robert Nozick, "On the Randian Argument," *The Personalist*, vol. 52 (1971), pp. 282–304. See also Thomas Nagel, "Aristotle on Eudaimonia," in Rorty, ed., *Essays on Aristotle's Ethics* (*supra* note 8), pp. 7–14.

[94] P. Glassen, "A Fallacy in Aristotle's Function Argument about the Good," *Philosophical Quarterly*, vol. 7 (1957), pp. 319–22.

[95] That is to say, what a human being is (its formal cause) and what a human being is for (its final cause) synchronize in the idea of benefit for members of a kind.

[96] Whiting, "Aristotle's Function Argument: A Defense," p. 39.

[97] T. H. Irwin, "The Metaphysical and Psychological Basis of Aristotle's Ethics," in Rorty, ed., *Essays on Aristotle's Ethics*, p. 49.

what is "proper" or "essential" to a human being. It is human nature as a whole, not some part of it, that is being considered.[98] In other words, if human beings are defined as rational animals, then any account of a human being's function must consider not only the referent of the differentia, but the referent of the genus as well. For human beings, this involves animality and all that goes with it, particularly the fact that a human being is a living creature. Moreover, it needs to be realized that any definitional statement of an entity's nature is a condensation of a vast number of facts and is meant to provide the means by which it is sorted conceptually from other things. It thus implies the presence of many qualities and features other than those explicitly noted by the definition.[99] The character of the human *ergon* is not settled in terms of what is distinctive alone.

For the neo-Aristotelian theory I have been describing, then, fulfilling our human function—not disembodied reasoning—is "the practical life of man possessing reason." Fulfilling our function includes exercising capacities shared by other animals, such as those for pleasure and health, and, as will be noted, many other things as well. What the distinguishing characteristic does is to characterize the *modality* through which the development of these other faculties will be successful:

> The *ergon* of man is indeed "activity of the *psuche* in accordance with a rational principle," the "rational principle" in question is, broadly, intelligence in general: intelligence that may be applied to art, craft, science, philosophy, politics, or any other domain.[100]

Regarding (C), the distinction between what is a good man and what is good for a man is a distinction without a difference, *if* the beneficial sense of "function" is recognized. One cannot determine a human being's function or excellence apart from a consideration of the specific needs and requirements a human being has in virtue of the kind of living thing he or she is. Such a determination cannot be divorced from the biocentric context. Further, if the human function is taken to be the life of practical reason,[101] not contemplation, and if the inclusive, individualized, and agent-relative character of human flourishing is recognized, then the alleged conceptual gap between what perfection requires (what is a good human being) and what is beneficial (what is good for a human being) is

---

[98] See Aquinas's discussion of abstracting the "whole" nature of a being in *Being and Essence*, 2nd ed. rev., trans. Armand Mauer (Toronto: The Pontifical Institute for Mediaeval Studies, 1968), pp. 37–44.

[99] See Rasmussen, "Quine and Aristotelian Essentialism" (*supra* note 71), pp. 328–29.

[100] Wilkes, "The Good Man and the Good for Man" (*supra* note 48), p. 568.

[101] Henry B. Veatch, in his classic *Rational Man* (Bloomington and London: Indiana University Press, 1962), calls the human function "rational or intelligent living."

closed.[102] Whatever remaining basis there is for it will not be a matter of principle but of situation and circumstance.

Isaiah Berlin has argued against the usefulness of any appeal to human nature when it comes to providing ethical knowledge. For Berlin, the dominant ethical fact is the diversity of moral values—what he calls "value pluralism." By this, however, he does not intend to claim that ethical relativism, in either subjectivist or conventionalist form, is true. Instead, he means that there are many objective values of inherent worth and that these are not compatible. Thus, it is futile to attempt to find some ethical standard that will provide universal guidance. Whether Berlin consistently avoids ethical relativism and whether he ever shows these objective values to be *inherently* incompatible are not issues that concern me here.[103] What concerns me are two brief remarks that he makes in passing. He notes that

> forms of life differ. Ends, moral principles, are many. But not infinitely many; they must be within the human horizon.[104]

Also, he states that ultimate objective ends, though incompatible,

> cannot be unlimited, for the nature of men, however various and subject to change, must possess some generic character if it is to be called human at all.[105]

It is to what Berlin calls the "generic character" of human beings that the conception of human flourishing described in this essay appeals.

The general parameters of human flourishing are provided by human nature. Their concrete form is not. As I have noted many times, this conception of human flourishing does not suppose that the pattern or weighting of the goods and virtues that comprise human flourishing can be determined by simply appealing to human nature. Thus, without endorsing Berlin's characterization of value pluralism, this conception of human flourishing accepts the idea that there are many objective goods that are valuable in their own right. Yet this form of value pluralism does not suppose that these goods must be incompatible. As noted earlier,[106] the existence of a plurality of goods does not in itself entail any incom-

---

[102] This gap is discussed in L. W. Sumner, *Welfare, Happiness, and Ethics* (Oxford: Clarendon Press, 1996), pp. 78–79. However, Sumner does not consider a view of human flourishing that is inclusive, individualized, and agent-relative.

[103] See Rasmussen and Den Uyl, *Liberalism Defended*.

[104] Isaiah Berlin, "The Pursuit of the Ideal," in Berlin, *The Crooked Timber of Humanity* (New York: Alfred A. Knopf, 1991), p. 11.

[105] Isaiah Berlin, "Alleged Relativism in Eighteenth-Century European Thought," in *ibid.*, p. 80.

[106] See reply (2) in Section III above.

patibility. Rather, the question of their compatibility must be worked out in light of each individual's nexus and thus cannot be decided *a priori*. Further, since an agent-neutral conception of human flourishing has been rejected, there is no single model to which each person's pattern or weighting of these goods must conform. Such ethical rationalism has been rejected.

A consideration of human nature does allow one to make a list of generic goods. These goods form a cluster concept that is open-ended and subject to revision. Such a list is not intended to be exhaustive; nor is the list particularly novel. Indeed, it is not meant to be. It involves knowledge, friendship, justice, creative work, leisure, pleasure, health, aesthetic appreciation, honor, self-esteem, and moral virtue. These seem to be goods that no one, as Aristotle states, would choose to be without. They are, however, wide abstractions that help to outline the general character of human flourishing; they take on actuality and value only in relation to and because of the efforts of individual human beings. It is thus an error to suppose that they can be fulfilled in any manner apart from individuative and agent-relative considerations. These goods are manifested in various activities in individual lives and take diverse forms in different cultures.[107]

Since human beings are not purely minds, the pivotal role of moral virtue in assisting practical wisdom should not go unmentioned. We have feelings and emotions that move us toward objects of apparent benefit and away from objects of apparent harm. We are eager for the former and fearful in the case of the latter. However, what we desire as worthwhile and fear as harmful might not really be so. The problem is not with our emotions and feelings themselves. Being eager or afraid, pleased or sad, excited or bored, satisfied or discouraged—indeed, the whole range of emotional responses—are forces of our very being. We cannot flourish without them. Rather, the question is whether the objects of such emotions and feelings merit the responses and reactions that we give them. Is the implicit value judgment behind our emotional responses accurate? It is thus important to have the ability to use and control our emotions and feelings so that they will more accurately respond to what the situation merits.

Not surprisingly, if we do not properly use and control our emotions, they can be sources of conflict. We can come to have rational desires for some things and mere appetites for others. We can be emotionally pushed and pulled, torn apart, rendered dysdaimonic. Hence, our creation of moral virtues, that is, rational dispositions, that form our moral character is extremely important. Our appetites and desires can be revamped or reshaped into rational dispositions by our intelligence so that what we

---

[107] However, these goods may not all be on the same level; some may be more fundamental than others. But this is a matter for further investigation.

ought to desire and what we in fact do desire can be in harmony. This is where such rational dispositions as integrity, courage, temperance, and honesty play a crucial role in assisting practical wisdom in its task. When considered as a whole, moral virtue is necessary for the coherent achievement and use of multiple basic human goods, and, along with practical wisdom, pervades the entire activity of flourishing. Moral virtue aids practical wisdom in finding the mean. In fact, moral virtue and practical wisdom are mutually interdependent, because the compossibility they seek is one of thought and feeling, not mere abstract goods.[108]

Yet, when considered not as a whole but as one good among many, moral virtue can be given more or less emphasis—for example, a person with a career in the military might require greater emphasis on the virtue of courage than would otherwise be the case. Thus, an individual needs to achieve a proper weighting or balance of the moral virtues or rational dispositions that define his or her character as well.

Obviously, any complete account of this neo-Aristotelian conception of human flourishing will have to consider the relationship of the moral virtues to practical wisdom in detail.[109] Moreover, a thorough investigation of all these proposed goods and virtues is required—particularly, such goods as nobility, honor, and self-esteem. Nonetheless, the crucial feature of this conception of human flourishing remains: an individual must use his practical wisdom if he is to fashion a worthwhile life. It is the task that our nature gives us, but does not do for us.

VI. CONCLUSION

The final question for this account of human flourishing remains: Is this a perfectionist theory? If we judge "perfectionism" as it has been traditionally understood, then the answer to this question must be "no." Though the conception of human flourishing that has been presented does appeal to human nature to discover generic goods and virtues, these goods and virtues are no more than general parameters. They cannot alone determine what form of flourishing is proper for the individual. Rather, in determining what form of flourishing is best for the individual, moral consideration has to be given to what is unique to the individual. Seldom has the role and importance of the individual for an understanding of the human good been given such emphasis.

By offering an account of the human good that is not agent-neutral, while still being objective, and a view of practical wisdom that avoids the hubris of ethical rationalism, while still allowing a place for rational desire, this essay presents a view of human flourishing that is a form of moral pluralism. Human flourishing can be both objective and agent-

---

[108] Veatch, *Rational Man*, pp. 86ff.
[109] See Den Uyl, *The Virtue of Prudence*, pp. 200–213.

relative as well as universalizable and individualized. Further, it can be socially achieved and still personal. This is certainly not a view of the human good that is usually associated with a theory that appeals to natural teleology, even a natural teleology understood in a contemporary manner. Indeed, it might even be the case that the view of human flourishing that has been presented is more quasi- than neo-Aristotelian.[110]

Be this as it may, the view of human flourishing that has been presented combines plausibly an appeal to human nature with a recognition of human individuality. The fundamental intuition behind this project has been not only that it is the flourishing of individual human beings that ultimately matters but the individuality of flourishing as well. David L. Norton expressed this point well by noting that

> to emulate a worthy man is not to re-live his individual life, but to utilize the principle of worthy living, exemplified by him, toward the qualitative improvement of our individual life.[111]

Thus, one's aim in using practical wisdom is not to imitate "the worthy man," but to emulate him. It certainly seems fair to call such an activity as this *self-perfection*.

Philosophy, St. John's University

---

[110] See Richard Kraut, *Aristotle on the Human Good* (Princeton: Princeton University Press, 1989), for an important criticism of the inclusivist interpretation of Aristotle's ethics.
[111] David L. Norton, *Personal Destinies* (Princeton: Princeton University Press, 1976), p. 13.

THE THREE FACES OF FLOURISHING*

By Thomas Hurka

I. Introduction

To my knowledge, the term "flourishing" was introduced into contemporary philosophy in Elizabeth Anscombe's 1958 article "Modern Moral Philosophy."[1] In this article and in much of the writing subsequent to it, the concept of flourishing seems to have three principal facets, or to be associated with three philosophical views.

First, it indicates an objective theory of the human good based on some theory of human nature. The flourishing of a human being is a desirable state, one that constitutes part or even all of his good.[2] As the term's etymological connection to "flowering" suggests, however, we are to understand human flourishing by analogy with similar states of other organisms such as animals and even plants. A plant or animal flourishes when the properties that constitute its nature are developed to a high degree. By analogy, it is said, there are properties central to human nature, and their development is what makes for human flourishing and a good human life. According to this first view about flourishing, the human good is not characterized subjectively, as depending on what someone takes pleasure in or desires, but objectively, in terms of a development of human nature that is good whatever anyone's attitude toward it.

Second, the concept of flourishing is used to identify the moral virtues, including other-regarding virtues such as justice and benevolence. In "Modern Moral Philosophy," Anscombe proposes an ethical view in which the primary evaluation of actions is as virtuous or vicious, that is, as reflecting a virtue such as justice or a vice such as injustice. And she proposes that the virtues themselves be identified as those traits a human needs to live a flourishing life, or to flourish *qua* human. According to this second view about flourishing, we start our ethical thinking with the concept of human flourishing, identify the virtues as those traits necessary for flourishing, and, finally, evaluate actions as virtuous or vicious.

* For helpful comments and discussion I am grateful to Dennis McKerlie, Ellen Frankel Paul, Michael Slote, Christine Swanton, and the other contributors to this volume.

[1] G. E. M. Anscombe, "Modern Moral Philosophy," *Philosophy*, vol. 33 (1958), pp. 1–19.

[2] Many contemporary philosophers distinguish between claims about what is simply a "good in" someone, that is, a state that is simply good and is also a state of him, and what is "good for" him, or constitutes his "well-being." In this essay I will ignore this distinction and speak indiscriminately of a person's "good" and of theories of it.

But the crucial list of virtues is constructed by reference to their contribution to flourishing.

Third, the concept of flourishing is used as the central concept in a normative theory that is formally egoistic, deriving all of a person's normative reasons for action from a fundamental reason he has to pursue his own flourishing, or his own good. This theory may acknowledge derivative reasons to act that are other-regarding, such as reasons to benefit others or to refrain from harming them. But it insists that if these are reasons, it is only because they can be connected to each person's fundamental interest in his own achievement of flourishing.

These three views are logically independent. It is possible to hold any one of them apart from the other two, and some philosophers do. Nevertheless, the views are often taken to go together, and their combination is a central subject in the recent literature on flourishing. Much of this literature assumes the following three-part understanding of flourishing: (1) each person's good consists in developing his nature, which (2) involves as an important element his acting virtuously toward others, and (3) is all he ultimately has normative reason to do.[3] Nor is this surprising, since despite their logical independence the views complement each other in important ways. On the one side, an egoistic theory of reasons will be intuitively acceptable only if it somehow captures other-regarding moral duties such as the duty not to harm other people. But it can do that only if its theory of the good includes something like the exercise of the other-regarding virtues as a constituent, and it can justify that inclusion only given some objective theory of the good, such as one based on human nature. On the other side, the identification of the virtues in terms of flourishing seems to presuppose formal egoism. Why insist on connecting the virtues to the agent's own good unless that good has special rational importance, or is uniquely the source of reasons for action?

In this essay I will examine this three-part understanding of flourishing and, especially, the mutual relations of its three components. My examination will be largely critical and skeptical. In Section II, I will argue that the first view grounding flourishing in human nature is in conflict with the second and third views about the virtues and egoism. If we take seriously a theory of the good based on human nature, we cannot hold that the good as this theory characterizes it includes the other-regarding virtues as constituents, and we cannot plausibly embed the theory in an egoistic structure. This is not to say that a theory of the good of this kind should be rejected. If we retain it, however, it must be in a framework

---

[3] For recent discussions of this three-part understanding of flourishing, see Sarah Conly, "Flourishing and the Failure of the Ethics of Virtue," in *Midwest Studies in Philosophy, Volume XIII, Ethical Theory: Character and Virtue*, ed. Peter A. French, Theodore E. Uehling, Jr., and Howard K. Wettstein (Notre Dame, IN: University of Notre Dame Press, 1988), pp. 83–96; Richard Taylor, *Virtue Ethics: An Introduction* (Interlaken, NY: Linden Books, 1991); and Justin Oakley, "Varieties of Virtue Ethics," *Ratio*, vol. 9, no. 2 (September 1996), pp. 133–34.

where each person has as fundamental a reason to pursue the good of others as he has to pursue his own. Section III will consider a less ambitious understanding of flourishing containing only the second and third views, one that is still egoistic and still defines the virtues by reference to flourishing but does not ground flourishing in human nature. I will argue that despite avoiding objections arising from inclusion of the first view, this two-part understanding cannot explain why the exercise of virtue is good (rather than simply asserting that it is so), and cannot give other-regarding duties their proper weight and scope without making claims about each person's good that are not plausible. Section IV will propose some further in-principle objections to any egoistic justification of other-regarding duties of the kind proposed in much of the recent literature on flourishing. Again, it is not that every element of the two-part understanding should be rejected. In particular, the idea that virtue is a constituent of each person's good is attractive and should be retained, but this is best done in a nonegoistic framework where virtue does not have priority over other goods and does not have the centrality for the evaluation of actions that Anscombe and others propose.

In developing these arguments I will abstract from another important aspect of the concept of flourishing: its connection to Aristotle's concept of *eudaimonia*. Anscombe proposes an ethical view based on flourishing and virtue as a specifically Aristotelian view, and there are strong affinities between the three-part understanding of flourishing and a common interpretation of Aristotle. Aristotle is widely thought to have a formally egoistic theory of normative reasons, in which all of a person's reasons for acting derive from his interest in his own *eudaimonia*. Aristotle is also widely thought to ground *eudaimonia* in human nature, in the famous *ergon* argument of *Nicomachean Ethics*, Book I, chapter 7, and he clearly thinks the virtues are constituents of *eudaimonia*. Because of this, the term "flourishing" is often proposed as a translation of Aristotle's term "*eudaimonia*," and much of the best writing about flourishing has appeared in commentaries on Aristotle. But I do not want to become embroiled in the intricacies of Aristotelian exegesis. My interest is in whether certain combinations of philosophical views are tenable in themselves, and I will pursue that question independently of whether they happen to have been held by any particular ancient philosopher.

II. FLOURISHING AND HUMAN NATURE

The first view about flourishing, that the human good consists in developing human nature, has several attractive features.[4] It is intuitively appealing in itself, or at least has been found so by a long list of adherents

---

[4] For a fuller discussion of this view, and of many of the ideas in this section, see my *Perfectionism* (New York: Oxford University Press, 1993).

from Plato and Aristotle through Marx and Nietzsche. It also offers to unify a variety of objective goods. If we ask which states of humans are objectively good, we will probably produce a mixed list: knowledge, achievement, athletic excellence, and more. The first, or *human-nature*, view about flourishing, if successfully developed, can unify these goods in a single foundational ideal.

In my view, a contemporary presentation of this view should dispense with three further claims often associated with it. First, it should not claim that developing human nature is each human's function or metaphysical purpose as a human. The view is less metaphysically contentious if it holds simply that the development of human nature constitutes the human good whatever its connection to functions or purposes. Second, the view should not claim that premises about human nature directly entail conclusions about the good, as in a version of metaethical naturalism.[5] It does better to present its general ideal as one that is not logically true but needs to be defended on substantive moral grounds. Then conclusions about the good follow from premises about human nature only given the further evaluative premise that developing whatever constitutes human nature is good. Finally, the view should not claim that developing human nature is what each human above all desires, perhaps desiring all other ends as means to this single all-organizing one. If this claim about desire were true, it would diminish the difference between objective and subjective theories of value, since then the life that most developed a human's nature would also most satisfy his desires. But any such claim about desire is surely false. As Joseph Butler in particular urged, humans have many desires, some more or less organizing but many just for particular ends regardless of their place in larger patterns.[6] (Consider the desire for strawberry ice cream now.) There is likewise great variety in the ends desired by different humans. Some philosophers claim that humans desire to develop their nature only indirectly, by desiring some x that is identical to the development of their nature whether they know this or not. For example, some claim that all humans desire above all what is good, so if the good is the development of their nature, their strongest desire will not be fulfilled unless they develop their nature.[7] But even this indirect claim about desire is false. The desire for something as good involves a sophisticated evaluative thought about an object that is not present in many desires, and certainly does not organize all desires. (The desire for strawberry ice cream now is not normally a desire for whatever

[5] Metaethical naturalism is the view that evaluative (and *a fortiori* moral) claims are either equivalent to or follow from nonevaluative ones. In the present context this means that claims about the human good are equivalent to or follow from ones about human nature.

[6] Joseph Butler, *Five Sermons*, ed. Stephen L. Darwall (Indianapolis: Hackett, 1983).

[7] For an especially explicit version of this claim, see Jennifer Whiting, "Aristotle's Function Argument: A Defense," *Ancient Philosophy*, vol. 8 (1988), p. 44. That desire is always for the good is also a claim of Anscombe's; see her *Intention*, 2d ed. (Oxford: Basil Blackwell, 1976), pp. 70–72, 76–78.

will now contribute to an overall best life.) This point may be obscured if the good is defined subjectively, as whatever a person desires, but that definition reduces the indirect claim about desire to the tautology that humans desire what they desire. When the claim is read non-tautologically, so that people can be wrong about their good, it is not true that they always desire the good.

Having dispensed with these claims, the human-nature view needs to explain what type of properties it takes human nature to consist in. There are several possibilities: the properties distinctive of humans, those essential to humans, those distinctive of and essential to humans, and more. But I will take it that any plausible version of the view values the development of at least some subset of the properties essential to humans. These are the properties any being must have to count as human. In that sense, these properties make humans human and are in the appropriate sense fundamental to their nature. But valuing essential properties has important implications for the attempt to combine the human-nature view with the two other views connecting flourishing to virtue and to formal egoism.

On a contemporary understanding, such as that of Saul Kripke or Hilary Putnam, a kind's essential properties are, in part, those that play a central role in explaining its other properties.[8] Thus, a common view holds that essential properties are identified precisely by their explanatory priority over other properties. It does not follow that every essential property must explain all of a kind's behavior. If the kind has several essential properties, each may explain a different aspect of its behavior. But every essential property of a kind must explain at least a large portion of the kind's behavior rather than just some arbitrarily restricted part. It cannot be just a narrower version of some more generally explanatory property.

Consider human behavior. Some of it, such as the operation of our digestive system, is purely physiological and will be explained by physiological properties. But another part involves or issues from psychological states such as beliefs and desires, and the essential properties of interest to the human-nature view will come primarily from the explanation of this behavior. But note how heterogeneous the behavior is. Some is morally virtuous, as when a person benefits another from a desire to do him good. But a great deal is morally neutral, such as eating ice cream, and some is morally vicious, as when a person hurts another from malice or spite. Given this heterogeneity, a plausible human-nature view cannot claim that humans are essentially virtuous, so the exercise of virtue directly realizes an essential property. That would make essential a

---

[8] Saul Kripke, *Naming and Necessity* (Cambridge, MA: Harvard University Press, 1980); and Hilary Putnam, "Is Semantics Possible?" and "The Meaning of 'Meaning'," in Putnam, *Mind, Language, and Reality: Philosophical Papers*, vol. 2 (Cambridge: Cambridge University Press, 1975).

property that at best explains a subset of psychological behavior, and does so only in conjunction with whatever more fundamental properties explain all such behavior. Nor, in my view, can a plausible human-nature view claim that humans essentially have some property that is developed more fully in virtuous behavior than in vicious behavior. The relevant explanatory property functions uniformly in the explanation of virtuous, vicious, and neutral behavior; it is equally present in them all. It is therefore false to its explanatory role to claim that it is somehow specially realized in virtue.

Consider rationality, a property central to many versions of the human-nature view. With a theoretical aspect expressed in beliefs and a practical aspect expressed in desires and actions, rationality has just the centrality to psychological explanation needed for an essential property. Whenever we explain a person's belief by saying he had evidence pointing to its truth, or explain his action by saying he desired an end and believed the action would achieve that end, we assume in several ways that he was exercising theoretical or practical rationality. Rationality is also a property whose development is an attractive intrinsic good. However, a fuller characterization of this good must respect rationality's role in explaining the whole range of psychological behavior.

This characterization can take rationality to be expressed in particular psychological states, so that the more such states a person has, the more he develops his rational powers. On one view the relevant states for theoretical rationality are items of knowledge, that is, beliefs about the world that are both true and (something like) justified. The parallel states for practical rationality are successful achievements of an end, given a justified antecedent belief that this would happen. The requirement of successful achievement parallels that of truth in beliefs, involving a similar correspondence between a mind and the world, while the requirement of justified belief rules out ends achieved by luck. And just as more items of knowledge make for a better life, so do more non-lucky achievements.

But a person's rational development cannot depend just on the number of such states he has. Clearly some psychological states have more value and represent more of a rational achievement than others. The characterization therefore needs measures of the quality of items of knowledge and non-lucky achievements. To respect rationality's explanatory role, these measures cannot say that the best knowledge is of a certain subject-matter or that the best achievements are of certain substantive ends. Instead, these measures must value certain formal properties that can be present to some degree in all beliefs and ends. There are at least two such formal properties.

The first is the extent of a belief's or an end's content across times, objects, and persons. When this content is more extended, knowing it or achieving it involves a greater exercise of rationality and therefore greater value. For theoretical rationality, this means that it is better to know

scientific laws, which govern many objects, than to know isolated particular facts. For practical rationality, it means that it is better to achieve ends
that extend through one's whole life or involve many people, as a political
leader's do, than to achieve just a state of oneself now.

The second formal property arises from our human ability to arrange
beliefs and ends hierarchically. On the theoretical side, we use some beliefs to explain others—say, more general laws to explain less general
laws, which in turn explain particular facts. On the practical side, we
pursue some ends as means to other ends, which in turn serve an overarching end that unifies them all. The second measure of quality says that
a person's psychological states involve a greater exercise of rationality the
more they are arranged in this hierarchical way. A person's knowledge is
better the more it is explanatorily unified, and an achievement is better
the more it involves a large number of subordinate achievements. This
last, practical structuring can be found either in a whole life, where many
activities serve a single life-goal, or in particular activities that are complex and difficult.

This purely formal account of rational development has many attractive features. It finds value in unified explanatory knowledge, in a life
organized around one or a few goals, in activities that are intricate and
challenging, and more. It also unites these various values in a single
foundational idea that applies in parallel to theoretical and practical rationality. However, it does not imply, as many versions of the three-part
understanding do, that the development of rationality requires other-
regarding virtuous action.

It is not that the account denies value to such action. Imagine that
someone devotes his life to working benevolently for the benefit of large
numbers of people and successfully achieves his goal. His activity may
score highly on the two measures of quality and therefore may involve a
high rational achievement. But it is not a rational achievement because it
is benevolent. The qualities that make it rational differ from those that
make it virtuous, and thus there is no necessary coincidence between
rationality and other-regarding virtue.

First, even when virtuous activity is highly rational, it need not be the
most rational activity available to a person. Perhaps he can devote his life
to working benevolently for others, but he can also devote his life to
acquiring scientific knowledge or exercising practical skill in mountain
climbing or chess. And his development, on balance, of his rational powers may be greater in the latter activities than in the former.

Second, even positively vicious activity can have high rational value.
Imagine that someone devotes his life to trying maliciously to cause many
people pain and, through complex steps, achieves his goal. His activity
too may score highly on the two measures of quality and may involve a
high rational achievement. It may even be the greatest rational achieve-

ment available to him, in which case a formally egoist theory not only does not forbid this large-scale harming but positively requires it.[9]

It may be objected that my argument misunderstands practical rationality, because it misconstrues the parallel between theoretical and practical goods. The practical analogue of truth in belief is not the successful achievement of an end but the goodness of that end. Whereas beliefs aim at the true, desires aim at the good,[10] and this crucial fact about desire must be reflected in an account of practical rationality. Practical rationality must be characterized not in the formal way I have proposed but as involving reasoning about, identifying, and effectively pursuing what is good.[11] When it is characterized in this way, practical rationality can involve the virtues as constituents or necessary parts.

This proposal faces three difficulties. First, practical rationality as characterized here could only be essential to humans if all human action aimed at what is good. As I have said, however, the desire for something as good is an unusually sophisticated desire, one not present in all or even a majority of human actions.

Second, the proposal abandons many of the unifying ambitions of the human-nature view. If practical rationality consists in reasoning about what is good, there must be goods independent of practical rationality for it to reason about. (It would obviously be circular to say that practical rationality consists in the identification of a good that itself consists entirely in practical rationality.) Some of these goods, such as knowledge, may be realizations of theoretical rationality, but if there are any nontheoretical goods, as there surely are, they must be entirely independent of rationality. Their goodness cannot be explained by their realizing through rationality an aspect of human nature; it must simply be taken as given by the human-nature view, which therefore gives no account of these goods at all. In fact, the proposal treats practical rationality as a second-order good, one consisting in a correct or appropriate response to other goods. And as I will argue below, second-order goods are in general less impor-

---

[9] In *Aristotle's First Principles* (Oxford: Clarendon Press, 1988), Terence Irwin both ascribes to Aristotle and defends a version of the human-nature view focused on practical rationality as an essential property of humans. (He somehow ignores theoretical rationality.) Irwin connects practical rationality to other-regarding virtues such as friendship and justice by saying that these virtues "extend" a person's exercise of practical rationality, and in particular extend "his practical reason and deliberation beyond his own life and activities" (p. 401; see also pp. 394–95, 405–6, 409–10, 415, 431, 433). But if "extent" here means what it seems to, our two questions arise. If extent is not the only measure of rational development, why cannot purely self-regarding activities such as research and chess develop the agent's own rationality more, on balance, than other-regarding virtue? Even considering only extent, why is rationality not increased just as much in a malicious attempt to cause others pain?

[10] See Anscombe, *Intention*, p. 76; and Ronald de Sousa, "The Good and the True," *Mind*, vol. 83 (1974), pp. 534–51.

[11] Irwin might press this alternative understanding of practical rationality; see *Aristotle's First Principles*, ch. 15.

tant goods. As between a first-order good such as knowledge and a second-order good that consists in correctly responding to it, the first-order good has greater moral weight.

Finally, it is not clear how the proposal does justify other-regarding virtues. If practical rationality involves reasoning about the good, whose good is this: just the agent's, or all people's? In a formally egoistic theory the answer must be: just the agent's. But then why should correct reasoning about his own good lead him to other-regarding action? This conclusion might follow if among the goods that reason was to identify were the exercise of other-regarding virtue itself. But then the human-nature view would not explain the goodness of such virtue; it would take it as given. It would not justify other-regarding duties, but would presuppose them at the start.[12]

Where does the argument of this section leave us? I have claimed that the first view about flourishing—that the human good consists in developing human nature—is in conflict with the second and third views about virtue and formal egoism. One response to this argument is to abandon the first view about flourishing and retain the other two; I will examine this response in the next two sections. Another response is to retain the first view in a more favorable formal setting. This is within a normative theory that is nonegoistic, giving each person a nonderivative reason to care about the flourishing of others in the same way that he cares about his own. This theory may be strictly agent-neutral, telling him to care equally about all people's good, or partly agent-relative, telling him to care more about his family's and friends' good than about the good of strangers. Either way, the theory derives other-regarding duties from its nonegoistic form, forbidding any person to pursue his own rational development in ways that do more to impede the similar development of others, and also requiring him to promote their development, say, by teaching them or sharing resources. It is open to question whether a nonegoistic theory valuing only the flourishing of human nature can capture all the other-regarding duties it should. For example, how can it capture a duty to give others pleasure and spare them pain if pleasure and the absence of pain are not realizations of rationality? But this difficulty, if it is one, can be met by expanding the account of each person's

---

[12] It is sometimes argued that those who hold the human-nature view should not understand the concept of human nature descriptively, as involving properties identified by descriptive criteria such as those drawn from scientific explanations. They should instead understand the concept as partly evaluative, so that its content is partly determined by claims about the human good (see, e.g., Whiting, "Aristotle's Function Argument: A Defense," pp. 35, 38–39; and Martha C. Nussbaum, "Aristotle on Human Nature and the Foundations of Ethics," in *World, Mind, and Ethics: Essays on the Ethical Philosophy of Bernard Williams,* ed. J. E. J. Altham and Ross Harrison [Cambridge: Cambridge University Press, 1995], pp. 93–95, 100–102). As several critics have pointed out, however, this proposal robs the human-nature view of its explanatory point. If we include certain properties in human nature only because we think their development is good, how can we explain that goodness by saying they make up human nature?

good to include more than just his flourishing, so that, for example, pleasure is a coordinate aspect of that good. This expansion would be problematic if flourishing were the sole source of a person's reasons for acting, as in the three-part understanding sketched in Section I. But it is less so when flourishing does not carry that heavy theoretical load. Then flourishing can be one element in an account of the good that does not itself generate other-regarding duties but takes those to follow from non-egoistic formal principles. The idea that the human good consists in developing human nature has many attractive features. It yields an impressive list of particular goods and unifies those goods in a single ideal of developing essential rationality. Though this idea cannot itself ground an entire moral theory, it can be an important element in a theory with other elements to capture other moral claims.

III. FLOURISHING AND VIRTUE

Some philosophers may deny that the human-nature view ever was part of the most common understanding of flourishing or can figure in a plausible understanding. And the second and third views certainly can be detached from it. A less ambitious two-part understanding of flourishing still identifies the virtues as necessary for flourishing (hereafter "the virtue view") and still holds that all of a person's normative reasons for acting derive from his own flourishing; but it does not characterize flourishing in terms of human nature and is not open to objections based on its doing so. The components of this understanding still seem to fit together. An egoistic theory which derives reasons for acting from the agent's own flourishing needs something like the virtue view to generate other-regarding reasons, and the virtue view seems to presuppose formal egoism. By insisting that the virtues contribute to the agent's own good, it implicitly treats that good as having special rational importance. Let us therefore examine this two-part understanding, and especially its virtue view requiring the virtues for flourishing. To do so, we must first clarify this view's central claims.[13]

First, when the virtues are said to be "necessary" for flourishing, what kind of relation is intended? In the three-part understanding, the virtues

---

[13] For recent discussions of virtue and flourishing that do not seem to connect the latter to human nature, see Charles E. Larmore, *Patterns of Moral Complexity* (Cambridge: Cambridge University Press, 1987), pp. 30–34; John Casey, *Pagan Virtue: An Essay in Ethics* (Oxford: Clarendon Press, 1990), p. v; Rosalind Hursthouse, "Virtue Theory and Abortion," *Philosophy and Public Affairs*, vol. 20, no. 3 (Summer 1991), pp. 223–46; Justin Oakley, *Morality and the Emotions* (London: Routledge, 1992), pp. 39, 78, 87, 163, 177; Julia Annas, "The Good Life and the Good Lives of Others," *Social Philosophy and Policy*, vol. 9, no. 2 (Summer 1992), pp. 133–48; and Annas, *The Morality of Happiness* (New York: Oxford University Press, 1993). (Annas uses "happiness" to translate the Greek "*eudaimonia*" that others translate as "flourishing.") Formal egoism is more explicit in some of these discussions, e.g., Oakley and Annas, than in others, but as I have said, the insistence on connecting the virtues to the agent's good seems to presuppose egoism.

are constituents of flourishing or instantiate it, by instantiating the development of some essential property. And a natural reading of the two-
part view has it assume the same relation, so the virtues are still constituents
of flourishing. But some versions of the virtue view seem to assume a
causal relation between virtue and flourishing. This is especially so when
the virtues are said to contribute not just to the good of the agent but
either to the good of the agent or to the good of other people.[14] Since one
person's virtue cannot instantiate another's good, the relation here must
be the causal one of promoting that good. And we can imagine an egoistic
view on which the virtues are necessary for the agent's flourishing, but
only causally, as means to a separately existing end-state of flourishing.

This causal interpretation, however, is not suitable even in the two-part
understanding of flourishing. Any merely causal relation between virtue
and flourishing will be contingent, requiring the presence of other causal
conditions. And a merely contingent relation cannot ground sufficiently
universal or stable other-regarding reasons for action; people will have
reason to care for others only in some circumstances. The causal interpretation is also hard to reconcile with another feature of the virtue view.
After proposing that the virtues be identified by reference to flourishing,
Anscombe suggests they be used to evaluate actions, so that actions are
primarily judged as just, unjust, and so on. She here states the core idea
of what has since become known as virtue ethics: that the primary evaluation of actions does not derive from their consequences or from deontic
considerations such as duties and rights, but from their status as virtuous
or vicious. But an instrumental definition of the virtues is in tension with
this virtue-ethical idea. If the virtues are identified as causing some separately existing good, then that good seems primary and the virtues only
secondary. So should actions not be evaluated directly in terms of the
good they produce rather than by the derivative concept of virtue? Neither of these difficulties arises so directly if the relation defining the
virtues is noncausal. If the virtues are necessary constituents of flourishing, then the reason a person has to act virtuously is always present. And
if the virtues have the right kind of priority over other constituents of
flourishing, it may be reasonable to evaluate actions primarily as virtuous
and vicious.

Second, what degree of virtue does the view take to be necessary for
what degree of flourishing? As Anscombe recognizes,[15] a person can
flourish more or less, and he can also be more or less virtuous. Thus,
different versions of the virtue view are possible. A very weak version
says that to flourish to the highest degree possible a person need only be
virtuous to some minimal degree, say, any degree above zero. A very

---

[14] See, e.g., Philippa Foot, "Virtues and Vices," in her *Virtues and Vices and Other Essays in
Moral Philosophy* (Berkeley, CA: University of California Press, 1978), pp. 1–18; and James D.
Wallace, *Virtues and Vices* (Ithaca, NY: Cornell University Press, 1978).

[15] Anscombe, "Modern Moral Philosophy," p. 18.

strong version says that to flourish to any degree above zero a person must be virtuous to the maximal degree; if he is not completely virtuous, he does not flourish at all. But I take it that what is most often intended by the virtue view is something intermediate between these claims. The view says that to flourish to a reasonable degree, which is not the highest possible but is sufficient for a person to count as simply flourishing, that person must be virtuous to a reasonable degree.

Third, is each of the virtues individually necessary for reasonable flourishing, or only the virtues in some weaker collective sense? This question would not arise given the classical doctrine of the unity of the virtues, according to which a person cannot have any one of the virtues unless he has them all. If the virtues are independent of each other, however, we can consider a stronger view requiring that each of the virtues be present for reasonable flourishing, and a weaker view requiring only that some reasonable proportion of them be present, so that someone who lacks one or two virtues can still flourish if he has the rest. The weaker of these views seems to fit well with the interpretation of degrees of virtue and flourishing just given, but many discussions of the virtue view seem to assume the stronger view. There is a good reason why. If what people have strong reason to pursue is only their reasonable flourishing,[16] which requires only a reasonable proportion of the virtues, then anyone who has enough other virtues has no strong reason ever to act, say, justly or temperately. This is surely counterintuitive. The parallel implication about a single virtue is not similarly problematic. If reasonable flourishing requires only the reasonable exercise of a virtue such as justice, then someone who is already acting reasonably justly does not have the same strong reason to act more justly. There is a kind of supererogation with respect to justice, which is demanded strongly up to a certain level but not so strongly beyond it. This is not an unattractive implication, and some may welcome it.[17] But to give people strong reason to exercise each virtue to a reasonable degree, the virtue view must require each virtue for reasonable flourishing.

The most important question about the virtue view is whether its conception of flourishing is substantive or merely formal. A substantive conception equates human flourishing with some state of humans F that is independently good and whose goodness can explain the goodness of virtuous action. The human-nature view understands flourishing substantively, equating it with a development of human nature whose goodness is prior to and explains that of its instances. The two-part understanding also understands flourishing substantively if it says that some other human state F is ultimately good and is instantiated

---

[16] I again assume that if the virtues are defined by reference to some state x, it must be because x has some special rational importance.

[17] See Christine Swanton, "Satisficing and Virtue," *Journal of Philosophy*, vol. 90 (1993), pp. 33–48; and Oakley, "Varieties of Virtue Ethics," pp. 143–44.

by the virtues, whose goodness is explained by that instantiation. By contrast, a merely formal conception does not equate flourishing with any substantive state F but only with the general idea of the human good, whatever its content. In identifying the virtues as necessary for flourishing, therefore, a merely formal virtue view does not say that the virtues instantiate some more fundamental good, but only that they are constituents of a good life, that is, in themselves and underivatively good. A merely formal virtue view therefore abandons a central aim of the substantive approach: to justify and explain the claim that virtue is good. Instead, it simply asserts that claim or takes it as given. To remain consistent with egoism, the formal view must still understand flourishing as constituting the agent's own good, that is, as making *his* life go best regardless of its effects on others. It cannot so empty the concept of flourishing of content that flourishing consists just in the state where a person acts on all the normative reasons that apply to him, among which are underivative other-regarding reasons.[18] A person's flourishing must still be a desirable state of him. Subject to that constraint, however, a merely formal conception adds no substantive content to its concept of flourishing.

Of these two conceptions, the substantive one makes for a more interesting, because more philosophically ambitious, virtue view. The difficulty facing this view is to find an appropriate state F that is both good independently of its connection to virtue and instantiated by virtue. This difficulty is evident in a recent defense of the virtue view by Rosalind Hursthouse.

Hursthouse identifies a virtue in the familiar way, as "a character trait a person needs to flourish or live well."[19] It is not clear whether her conception of flourishing is substantive or formal, but let us assume it is substantive. Hursthouse recognizes that her identification of the virtues must connect them to flourishing *as* virtues, or for the properties that make them virtuous rather than for some other properties. This is evident in her treatment of benevolence, which she defines as "the virtue whose concern is the *good* of others" or is what is "*worthwhile*" for others.[20] This raises very sharply the difficulty for the substantive virtue view. This view must find some human state F that is both independently good and instantiated by concern for others *as* concern for others. What can this

---

[18] On this, see Dennis McKerlie, "Aristotle and Egoism," *Southern Journal of Philosophy*, vol. 36, no. 4 (Winter 1998).

[19] Hursthouse, "Virtue Theory and Abortion," p. 226.

[20] *Ibid.*, p. 227. One question about Hursthouse's view is how it relates the concepts of flourishing (on the one hand) and a person's good or what is worthwhile (on the other). Are these the same concepts, so that in caring benevolently about another's good I am caring about his flourishing? If so, Hursthouse's view is close to the nonegoistic recursive view I sketch below. If not, can I also care about another's flourishing, and is it virtuous of me to do so? Does caring about another affect my good as well as my flourishing?

state be? It cannot be the exercise of rationality as formally characterized, for the reasons given in Section II. Nor can it be the exercise of rationality defined as identifying the good. This definition is no longer objectionable for flouting rationality's status as an essential property, but it still treats rationality as a merely second-order good and still cannot justify other-regarding duties. In an egoistic framework the good that rationality identifies can only be the agent's own, and why should a correct identification of that good lead him to other-regarding action? So what can the crucial state F be?

The substantive view's difficulty can be underscored by contrasting it with a rival view that does explain virtue's goodness, but in a different theoretical context. This view starts with the nonegoistic claim that, from each person's point of view, states of others can be good and evil in the same way as his own. Thus, others' pleasure and knowledge are good in the same way as his own pleasure and knowledge are good, giving him the same kind of reason to pursue them, and their pain is evil in the same way as his pain is evil. The view then adds the perfectly general recursive claim that whenever a state is good or evil, certain attitudes toward it are also good or evil. The good attitude toward a good is the positive one of loving it for itself, that is, desiring, pursuing, or taking pleasure in it for itself; and the good attitude toward an evil is the contrary one of hating it, for example, being pained by it, for itself.[21] This recursive view implies that desiring another's pleasure for itself is a good in the desirer's life, as is feeling compassion for another's pain. And if the view goes on to identify the virtues as those goods that consist in attitudes toward other goods and evils, it implies that the virtues are good in their possessor's life and the vices evil. What is more, it does so in a way that satisfies Hursthouse's condition. What makes benevolence a good in the benevolent person's life is the very property—its being concerned with another's good—that makes it benevolence. Other virtues receive a similar treatment. There are self-regarding virtues that involve attitudes toward the agent's own good and evil, and in fact there are as many different virtues as there are different kinds of good and evil. So the view's treatment of benevolence is not ad hoc but part of a larger explanatory scheme. However, that treatment relies crucially on the nonegoistic claim that, from each person's point of view, states of others are good. Only given that claim can attitudes toward those states also count, in the recursive framework, as good. But nonegoism is excluded by the formal assumptions of the two-part understanding of flourishing. So how can that understanding find a substantive state F of which other-regarding virtue is an instance?

[21] See my "Virtue as Loving the Good," *Social Philosophy and Policy*, vol. 9, no. 2 (Summer 1992), pp. 149–68.

In fact, the difficulty facing the substantive view is even greater. As Hursthouse recognizes, there can be conflicts among virtues.[22] Imagine, therefore, a conflict between an other-regarding virtue and a self-regarding one, say, between benevolence and temperance, in which the other-regarding virtue has greater weight. To take a fanciful example, imagine that a tyrant will kill a hundred innocent people if a certain person does not overeat for one week. Here benevolence clearly has priority over temperance and the person should overeat. But the substantive view can yield this conclusion only if it shows that acting benevolently in this situation instantiates state F more fully than acting temperately. More generally, it must somehow match the degree to which various actions instantiate F to the degree to which they are intuitively morally required, and how can it do that? The rival recursive view does not have this difficulty. Having said that certain attitudes toward goods and evils are intrinsically good, it can plausibly add that, other things equal, the appropriate attitudes toward greater goods and evils are better and more virtuous than attitudes toward lesser ones. This implies that a person who acts from concern for the hundred people's lives in the above example acts more virtuously than if he cared only about his own health. This is the intuitively plausible conclusion, and it is here given a satisfying rationale. But how can it follow from a view deriving the virtues from the agent's own flourishing as substantively conceived?

These difficulties suggest that the defensible version of the virtue view is the merely formal one, which conceives a flourishing life just as a good life, with no substantive claims about its content.[23] This formal view is considerably less interesting than the substantive one, since instead of explaining why the exercise of virtue is good it simply asserts or assumes that this is so. It likewise simply asserts that some exercises of virtue are better or involve more virtue than others. This yields the right conclusion about conflict cases like the tyrant case above, but, again, yields it by assertion rather than with any justification for that conclusion. Still, the formal view is not entirely without point, since it attempts a task that, as I will now explain, is necessary for any virtue view, formal or substantive.

Proponents of the virtue view hold that the virtues are constituents of a flourishing life, but they do not usually hold that the virtues are the only constituents. This last view would imply that a person who was virtuous but suffered excruciating agony and had massively false beliefs would have an ideal life, one that could not be made better with respect to flourishing. Finding this implication unacceptable, most proponents hold

---

[22] Hursthouse, "Virtue Theory and Abortion," p. 229.

[23] The most explicitly formal account is that of Annas; see "The Good Life and the Good Lives of Others," and *The Morality of Happiness*. Annas does not use the virtue view to identify the virtues; rather, she assumes we know independently what they are. But she does use claims about the place of virtue in an agent's good to derive, within an egoistic framework, normative reasons to act virtuously.

that there are other constituents of flourishing, such as pleasure and knowledge. But then it is not a sufficient identification of the virtues to say they are constituents of flourishing; that does not distinguish them from pleasure and knowledge. And most versions of the view do not say only this; they add that the virtues have a certain priority over other constituents of flourishing. Anscombe suggests this priority when she says that even if a person "flourishes less, or not at all, in inessentials by avoiding injustice, his life is spoiled in essentials by not avoiding injustice."[24] And the same priority seems implicit in the standard formulation of the virtue view: that the virtues are *necessary* for flourishing. This formulation seems to separate the virtues from other desirable states that, though contributing to a good life, are not in the same way vital to it. If a merely formal virtue view affirms this priority, it does have philosophical interest. Though it assumes without argument that the virtues are good, it claims in addition that they are specially or necessarily good and distinguishes them from other goods on that basis.

This priority claim is needed for another reason. The virtue view is standardly coupled with the virtue-ethical idea that actions are to be evaluated primarily as virtuous and vicious. This idea might seem natural if the virtues were the only constituents of flourishing, but it becomes problematic if they are not. If pleasure and knowledge are also goods, why should we not also evaluate actions in terms of them, say, as expressing or conducing to pleasure or knowledge? And why should we think people have more reason to act on virtue-ethical evaluations than on these other good-based ones? These questions may be answered if virtue has the right priority over other goods. Then evaluations of acts as virtuous will have an importance for a person's flourishing that other evaluations do not, and may be a uniquely important source of reasons for action.

The priority claim should not be read too strongly, and in particular should not be taken to require a person always to sacrifice his own pleasure and knowledge. An important part of virtue involves weighing one's own good properly against other people's, which may mean weighing it equally against other people's. Given this latter view, a person who faces a choice between a greater pleasure for himself and a lesser pleasure for another acts most virtuously if he prefers the greater pleasure for himself. (If he does the opposite, he may manifest a vice of self-abnegation or lack of self-respect.) But if he has a choice between a lesser pleasure for himself and a greater pleasure for another, he acts most virtuously if he prefers the greater. The question then is whether the greater virtue involved in acting this way outweighs in his own life the loss of the lesser pleasure. Only if an egoistic virtue view can say yes can it say that he has most reason to act most virtuously.

[24] Anscombe, "Modern Moral Philosophy," p. 18.

The question, however, is what specific priority claim the virtue view makes and whether this claim is plausible as a claim about each person's good. Is it true that the desirability of a life depends more on its virtue than on its share of other goods?

The simplest priority claim is that virtue has infinite value compared to other goods and vice infinite disvalue. W. D. Ross defended this infinite priority claim, which is also affirmed in some recent writing about virtue.[25] And the claim is of just the right kind to justify the virtue-ethical evaluation of actions. If virtue has infinite value compared to other constituents of flourishing, it can never be outweighed by them, and the best thing anyone can ever do to promote his flourishing is to act in the most virtuous way possible.

But the infinite priority claim is simply not plausible as a claim about each person's good. It implies that the virtuous person who suffers agony has an overwhelmingly good life, one with only an infinitesimally small element of evil. It also implies that if one person is slightly more virtuous than another, feeling a tiny bit more compassion, but also suffers agony, his life is on balance better even if the second person experiences ecstasy. These implications are barely less unacceptable than those following from the view that the virtues are the sole constituents of flourishing. It may be said that the virtue view need not hold that all virtue has infinite priority over other goods, but only that reasonable degree of virtue that makes for reasonable flourishing. But this restriction of the priority claim does not remove the first implication noted above or all cases of the second. Imagine that one person is slightly above the level of reasonable virtue, while another is slightly below it. The restricted priority claim still says the first person's life is better even if it involves excruciating agony. And what do we say about two people who are both below the level of reasonable virtue? If they are to have a sufficiently strong reason to act virtuously rather than to pursue other goods such as their own pleasure, every increment of virtue in them must have infinite priority over pleasure; but then the one who is slightly more virtuous has a better life whatever his level of pleasure or pain.

In my view, far from having priority over other goods, virtue is in fact a lesser good in the following sense: the value of a virtuous attitude toward an object is always less than the value, either positive or negative,

---

[25] W. D. Ross, *The Right and the Good* (Oxford: Clarendon Press, 1930), pp. 150, 152; and Ross, *The Foundations of Ethics* (Oxford: Clarendon Press, 1939), p. 275. See also Cardinal Newman's frequently quoted remark that it would be less evil for all humankind to die "in extremest agony" than that "one soul ... should commit one venial sin" (John Henry Cardinal Newman, *Certain Difficulties Felt by Anglicans in Catholic Teaching*, vol. 1 [London: Longmans, 1901], p. 240); see also J. L. A. Garcia, "The Primacy of the Virtuous," *Philosophia*, vol. 20 (1990), pp. 78–79. Annas discusses a priority claim that, though not strictly infinite, is so strong as to be effectively equivalent to infinite priority; see *The Morality of Happiness*, pp. 122–23, 393–94.

of that object. This is most clearly shown within the recursive account of virtue sketched above.[26]

Consider one person's evil and another's virtuous attitude toward that evil, say, one person's pain and another's compassion for that pain. If virtue had even finite priority over pleasure and pain, this combination of states would be on balance good, and better than if there were no pain and no compassion; but this is unacceptable.[27] The compassion may be good, and may make the overall situation better than if there were pain and no compassion, but it cannot outweigh or justify the pain. Its positive value must be less than the negative value of the pain that is its object.

Or consider one person's good and another's virtuous love of that good. Imagine that a teacher works to instill knowledge in a student from a benevolent desire for the student's betterment, and that as a result the student acquires knowledge. If you learn of these facts, what should you be more pleased by, the student's knowledge or the teacher's virtuous attempt to instill knowledge? Surely you should be more pleased by the former; it is the point of the exercise. But then assuming that it is in general best to care more about greater goods, the knowledge must be the greater good. Or imagine that you can produce only one of these goods but not both. Suppose that right now an uncaring teacher is teaching using methods that do not work, so his student is not acquiring knowledge. You can either change the teacher's attitude while leaving his methods unchanged or change his methods but not his attitude. Surely in this case it is better to change the teacher's methods, so that the student acquires knowledge. But then, again, the knowledge must be better.

This comparative claim about virtue and other goods can be extended within the virtuous person's life. In a nonegoistic theory there is some pleasure or knowledge of this person's own that is equivalent in value to the pleasure or knowledge of others that he cares about. But then the virtuous attitude that has less value than those states of others also has less value than the equivalent states of himself. It does not have priority over all other constituents of his good, but is sometimes outweighed by them. The claim also seems plausible if we consider only the person's own goods, as we must do in a formally egoistic theory. Imagine that someone pursues knowledge for its own sake and successfully achieves knowledge. Here again the knowledge seems to be the central value and the virtuous attitude toward it seems secondary. The attitude is certainly

[26] For a fuller discussion of this issue, see my "How Great a Good Is Virtue?" *Journal of Philosophy*, vol. 95, no. 4 (March 1998), pp. 181–203.

[27] See G. E. Moore, *Principia Ethica* (Cambridge: Cambridge University Press, 1903), p. 219. Some philosophers distinguish between the "moral" goodness of compassion and other virtues and the "nonmoral" goodness of pleasure and evil of pain. In my view this is not a substantive distinction: moral goodness is just goodness—the very same property—when had by certain objects, namely, attitudes when evaluated in terms of their objects.

good, and makes the person's overall state better than it would be with only the knowledge, but it does so by adding a derivative and secondary good.

Let us apply this comparative claim to the virtuous person who suffers agony. If virtue is a lesser good, this person's life can be on balance undesirable. Though its virtue makes it better than if it contained the same agony and no virtue, this life can still be on balance evil and can be a life it would be better not to live. This conclusion is surely more plausible than the infinite-priority claim that such a life is overwhelmingly good. Or consider a vicious person whose life contains great pleasure, knowledge, and other non-virtue goods. If his vice is directed at sufficiently evil objects, such as the intense agony of many people, his life can be on balance evil. But if his vice is less extreme it can be outweighed by those other goods, so that his life is on balance good. This again seems preferable to saying that his life, once it contains any vice, is overwhelmingly evil. It may be morally objectionable that a vicious person has an on-balance good life, especially if a virtuous person does not; this can seem a kind of unfairness. As several writers have pointed out, however, its being objectionably unfair presupposes that what the vicious person has is a good life, one that constitutes a benefit to him.[28]

The virtue view, then, cannot plausibly hold that virtue has infinite or even any general priority over other constituents of flourishing. But there is another priority claim to consider. This claim can allow that when a person has both virtue and, say, pleasure or knowledge, the pleasure or knowledge makes a greater contribution to his good than does the virtue. But it still holds that virtue has priority over other goods, because it holds that virtue is a condition of those goods' having worth. Only when a person is reasonably virtuous, this conditionality claim says, do these other states contribute to his flourishing; otherwise they do not. Virtue is therefore necessary for flourishing in two ways: it is both a constituent of flourishing and a condition of other states' contributing to flourishing. This implies, as desired, that a person can never have reason to pursue other states at the expense of reasonable virtue. If he does prefer those states, they will not be goods in him.[29]

This conditionality claim is most appealing when applied to positively vicious states such as sadistic pleasure, where one person takes pleasure in another's intense pain. Here, many will say, the sadist's pleasure has no

[28] Noah M. Lemos, *Intrinsic Value: Concept and Warrant* (Cambridge: Cambridge University Press, 1994), pp. 43–44; Michael Slote, "The Virtue in Self-Interest," *Social Philosophy and Policy*, vol. 14, no. 1 (Winter 1997), pp. 273–74; and Robert Audi, "Intrinsic Value and Moral Obligation," *Southern Journal of Philosophy*, vol. 35, no. 2 (Summer 1997), p. 140.

[29] This claim is attributed to Aristotle by Sarah Broadie in *Ethics with Aristotle* (New York: Oxford University Press, 1991), p. 376; and Broadie, "Aristotle's Elusive *Summum Bonum*," elsewhere in this volume; the claim is attributed to Kant by Christine M. Korsgaard in "Two Distinctions in Goodness," *Philosophical Review*, vol. 92 (1983), p. 179; and to Ross and Kant by Lemos in *Intrinsic Value*, pp. 41–42.

value as pleasure because it derives from a vicious attitude. Even this claim is open to question, however. I think the preferable view is that even pleasure in another's pain has some value as pleasure: it is good as a pleasure and evil as a pleasure in evil, with its value on balance depending on how these two features weigh against each other. In some cases this value on balance may be positive. Imagine that a person takes pleasure in another's minor evil, such as his slipping on a banana peel, or laughs at a slightly malicious joke at his expense. Though the first person's pleasure is vicious and therefore evil in one respect, it is probably on balance better if he enjoys this pleasure than if he has no pleasure at all. Pleasures in great evils, such as pleasure in another's intense pain, seem a different case; here we do want the pleasure always to be on balance evil. And given the right valuing of pleasure and pain this conclusion does follow.[30] But even these much more vicious pleasures have some goodness as pleasures; though outweighed, this goodness is still present.

Let us grant, however, for argument's sake, that pleasures involving vicious attitudes have no value as pleasures. This initial conditionality claim is far from sufficient for the virtue view's needs. That view must claim that even pleasures that are not themselves vicious, that involve no evil attitude, lack value if they are not part of a reasonably virtuous life. Consider a morally neutral pleasure such as that of eating ice cream. The required conditionality claim must say that this nonvicious pleasure has no value if it is not enjoyed by someone of reasonable virtue. This implies, first, that the pleasure of eating ice cream has no value in the life of a vicious person. Some may be willing to accept this, though it again leaves them unable to explain what is objectionable about a vicious person's getting more of such pleasure than a virtuous person gets. But it also implies, more dubiously, that the pleasure of eating ice cream has no value in the life of a person who is somewhat virtuous but not quite virtuous to the reasonable degree. This person is not vicious; he has good traits, if only to a limited degree. But the conditionality claim must say that even his morally neutral pleasure has no worth, and that is highly counterintuitive. Or consider a positively virtuous pleasure of this somewhat virtuous person, say, a mild pleasure he takes in someone else's pleasure. The conditionality claim must say that this pleasure too lacks

---

[30] The difficulty about pleasures in great evils derives from the comparative claim that virtue and vice are lesser values, with less positive or negative value than their objects. This claim implies that a sadist's pleasure in another person's pain is less evil than that pain is evil, which in itself seems right. But if equal units of pleasure and pain have equal value, it also implies that if the sadist's pleasure is sufficiently intense, its goodness as pleasure can outweigh its evil as vice, so that it is on balance good. We can avoid this implication if we deny that equal units of pleasure and pain always have equal value. More specifically, if we hold that there is an upper limit on the goodness of any pleasure whatever its intensity, but no upper limit on the evil of any pain, there will be some pains such that pleasure in them can never be on balance good. (For a fuller discussion, see my "How Great a Good Is Virtue?")

value as a pleasure; though it derives from a good attitude, it is not good itself. This is surely impossible to accept. These last implications might be less objectionable if the level of reasonable virtue were set sufficiently low, so that even the somewhat virtuous person exceeds it. But here the virtue view faces a dilemma. It needs a priority claim such as the conditionality claim to explain why, assuming formal egoism, people have more reason to act virtuously than to pursue other goods such as their own pleasure. It can plausibly allow that when people are sufficiently virtuous this priority lapses, so that action that is even more virtuous then is super-erogatory. But the lapse must occur at a fairly high level of virtue, so that the view still affirms fairly strong other-regarding duties. But then the level of reasonable virtue is set too high for the conditionality claim to be plausible as a claim about each person's good, since it implies that the neutral and even virtuous pleasures of someone who is only somewhat virtuous have no value as pleasures.[31]

Nor is it only pleasure and knowledge that the conditionality claim must say have only conditional value. As many writers on virtue ac-knowledge, there can be cases where a person is morally required to sacrifice his life, say, in battle in a just war. Within the two-part under-standing of flourishing this can only be so if virtuously dying in battle does more to promote the person's own virtue and flourishing than any alternative. How can this be? After avoiding battle, the person could, perhaps after repenting of his cowardice, perform countless virtuous ac-tions in the many remaining years of his life. Would the resulting life not contain more virtuous action and flourishing than if he died in battle now? To avoid this conclusion, the virtue view must claim not only that virtue has priority over other goods but that present virtue has priority over future virtue. Within the infinite-priority claim, this means that present virtuous action has infinite value compared to future virtuous action. Within the conditionality claim, it means that present virtuous action is a condition of the value of future virtuous action. But is this last claim plausible? If a person who avoids battle later repents and devotes the rest of his life to virtuous action, does that later action have no value? To give intuitively sufficient weight to other-regarding duties, the virtue view again seems to be required to ground them in implausible claims about each person's good.

---

[31] In "The Virtue in Self-Interest," Slote defends a weaker conditionality claim, saying that states other than virtue are good only when accompanied by a particular virtue appropriate to them. Thus, pleasure is good only when accompanied by moderation, knowledge only when accompanied by courage, and so on (pp. 274–83). This weaker claim of Slote's still seems exaggerated. Pleasure without moderation may be less good than pleasure with moderation, but it still strikes me as good to some degree. More importantly, however, Slote's claim is too weak to serve the virtue view's needs. As Slote recognizes (p. 275), his claim allows that a pleasure in an overwhelmingly vicious person's life can be good so long as it is accompanied by the one virtue of moderation. The claim therefore by no means guarantees that a person always has more reason to act virtuously than to pursue his own pleasure.

There may be other priority claims I have not considered, but I do not see how they can avoid this general difficulty. To give people sufficiently strong reason to act from other-regarding virtue, they must give the exercise of such virtue a centrality in each person's good that it cannot plausibly have. And there is a further difficulty for the virtue view, concerning its account of other-regarding duties for those who cannot fulfill these duties virtuously.

Proponents of the virtue view do not hold that it is sufficient for virtuous action that a person merely act as a virtue requires, for example, by benefiting other people. He must also act in a virtuous way, which involves his satisfying two further conditions. First, he must act from a virtuous motive, either from a desire to act virtuously for its own sake or, more plausibly, from a desire for the other's good· for its own sake. Second, his virtuous motive must issue from a stable disposition, so that it reflects a permanent part of his character. Only when these two conditions are satisfied is action in accordance with virtue also virtuous and a contributor to his flourishing.[32]

But then there can be people who are able to act in accordance with a virtue and thereby fulfill an other-regarding duty but who are not able to do so virtuously. Imagine that a person does not now have the virtuous motive for other-regarding action and also does not have a disposition to have that motive. He cannot produce the required motive in himself from one moment to the next, as people generally cannot produce motives from one moment to the next, and he likewise cannot produce the disposition. So what reason does the two-part understanding give him to fulfill the other-regarding duty? A common answer is that although his doing so will not contribute to his flourishing now, it is the best way to promote his flourishing in the future. Because the virtues are acquired by habituation, the best way for him to develop a virtuous concern for others in the future is to start acting now in ways that benefit them, and to let the requisite concern grow out of that pattern of action.[33]

This argument requires the contingent assumption that virtuous motives will in fact result from other-regarding action, and has no force when that assumption is false. But surely it often is false. A person's character may be so set in vicious lines that no virtuous reform of it is possible. What normative reason does the two-part understanding then give him for benefiting others? Or even if reform of one's character is always in principle possible, a person may lack the necessary time. Imag-

---

[32] For the original of these conditions, see Aristotle, *Nicomachean Ethics*, 1105a31–34. My own view is that the second condition, about a stable disposition, should be rejected. If it is to make more than a verbal point about the word "virtue," this condition must imply that actions done from a stable disposition are better, or contribute more to flourishing, than actions done from a similar motive but in a manner that is out of character. Since I see no reason to accept this, that is, no reason to hold that a genuinely benevolent act is less good if not connected to a benevolent disposition, I would dispense with Aristotle's second condition. His first condition, however, is vital to any account of virtue.

[33] See, e.g., Annas, *The Morality of Happiness*, pp. 56–57.

ine that it takes one year of habituation in other-regarding action for virtuous other-regarding desires to appear, and another year for those desires to settle into a stable disposition. A person may have a disease that will kill him in eighteen or even six months. In this case no other-regarding action now can lead to any virtue or flourishing in the future, so what egoistic reason does he have to perform such actions now? It is not that the virtue view gives him a positive reason to perform some other action. If this view accepts the conditionality claim, for example, it denies that any other states of the person are worth pursuing in the absence of virtue. But the view is surely objectionable in denying that he has any positive reason to act in accordance with virtue. This difficulty would not arise if the view held that any other-regarding action, whatever its motive, contributes to flourishing. But this claim is again not plausible. While it is indeed attractive to hold that actions motivated in a certain way contribute to the agent's good, it is not plausible to say that about actions apart from their motivation. In fact, this is but another instance of a central problem with the two-part understanding of flourishing. To derive other-regarding reasons for action from an egoistic concern with the agent's own good, this understanding requires claims about that good that, considered as such, are not plausible. The claim that a person has reason to perform a given action is one thing, the claim that the action will make his own life best wholly another. Unfortunately for the two-part understanding, often the first claim is true when the second is not.[34]

IV. VIRTUE AND EGOISM

In the previous section, I argued that the two-part understanding of flourishing cannot successfully derive other-regarding duties within a formally egoistic framework. I will now argue that even if this derivation could be completed it would not be philosophically acceptable, because there are in-principle objections to any egoistic derivation of other-regarding duties. One of these concerns the motivation of the virtuous agent; another concerns the explanation of his other-regarding reasons.

It is a commonplace in writing about virtue that a truly virtuous person cannot be motivated primarily by thoughts of his own virtue or of how

---

[34] This problem is even greater for those versions of the two-part understanding that take a person's flourishing to be not just good but "good for" him, or to constitute his "well-being" (see note 2 above). For however dubious it is that virtue is simply better than other elements of well-being, it is even more dubious that it is better for its possessor. Not surprisingly, even those philosophers who associate flourishing with well-being rarely argue, as their assumptions require them to, that virtue is better for its possessor than anything else. Instead, they retreat to the easier claim that virtue is simply better; see George Sher, "Knowing about Virtue," *NOMOS XXXIV: Virtue*, ed. John W. Chapman and William A. Galston (New York: New York University Press, 1992), p. 113, n. 7. But even that easier claim, I have argued, is false.

his action will contribute to his own good. On the contrary, there is a moral failing and even vice—called variously moral self-indulgence, priggishness, and narcissism—that consists in caring more about one's own virtue than about its object, which in the case of other-regarding virtue is the good of others.[35] It would be going too far to say that a virtuous person cannot be motivated at all by thoughts of his own virtue. He can have as one motive in acting for others' benefit that he will thereby act virtuously, so long as this is a secondary motive. His primary motive, if he is truly virtuous, must be a desire for the others' good for its own sake.

This commonplace may seem inconsistent with the egoistic virtue view. If that view says the ultimate reason for other-regarding action is to increase the agent's flourishing, does it not encourage him to act from a desire for that flourishing? As Julia Annas in particular has argued, there is no strict inconsistency here.[36] An egoistic view can say that what is needed for flourishing is *virtuous* action, which it can insist is action directed primarily at the good of others. If an agent acts primarily from concern for his own flourishing, he does not act virtuously and therefore does not achieve the flourishing that is his goal.

Though there is no inconsistency here, there is nonetheless a difficulty. If an agent reflects at the time of acting on the egoistic virtue view, he will believe that his ultimate reason for benefiting others is to increase his own flourishing. And if he reflects on that belief he will naturally be motivated by it and therefore act self-indulgently. So the virtue view must tell agents not to reflect on or even be aware of its own claims when they act. It must be what Derek Parfit calls "self-effacing," saying that agents will achieve the goals it sets them only if they are not motivated by those goals.[37] This property of being self-effacing is most commonly associated with utilitarianism, whose indirect or two-level versions say that agents will produce better consequences if they do not try to choose actions by evaluating their consequences. But it is also a feature of the egoistic virtue view, which says that people will achieve their ultimate goal of flourishing only if they are not motivated by thoughts of flourishing's role as the source of their reasons. Perhaps they can think about that role in a "cool hour," when they are not acting; but when they act they must ignore the view's central claim.

---

[35] See, e.g., Bernard Williams, "Utilitarianism and Moral Self-Indulgence," in his *Moral Luck* (Cambridge: Cambridge University Press, 1981), pp. 40–53; Williams, *Ethics and the Limits of Philosophy* (Cambridge, MA: Harvard University Press, 1985), pp. 10–11; and Noah M. Lemos, "High-Minded Egoism and the Problem of Priggishness," *Mind*, vol. 93 (1984), pp. 542–58.

[36] Annas, *The Morality of Happiness*, pp. 118, 127–28; see also Swanton, "Satisficing and Virtue," pp. 42–43.

[37] Derek Parfit, *Reasons and Persons* (Oxford: Clarendon Press, 1984), p. 24. This feature of Annas's view is pointed out in Christine Swanton, "Virtue Ethics and the Problem of Indirection: A Pluralistic Value-Centred Approach," *Utilitas*, vol. 9, no. 2 (July 1997), pp. 168–70; and McKerlie, "Aristotle and Egoism."

The literature on utilitarianism has included debate over whether its being self-effacing is an objectionable feature of a normative theory, with opponents of utilitarianism tending to say that it is and defenders saying that it is not.[38] But whatever the outcome of this debate, the situation facing the virtue view seems worse. In utilitarianism the reasons why it is best for agents not to apply the utilitarian standard of action-evaluation directly are contingent, turning on contingent facts about humans' reasoning ability and psychology. In the virtue view, however, the parallel reason must be noncontingent. To avoid encouraging moral self-indulgence, the view must say that being motivated primarily by concern for one's own flourishing is in itself and directly objectionable. Is it not odd for a normative view to in that direct way remove itself from the scene?

Even apart from this difficulty, an egoistic view cannot *explain* why self-indulgent motivation is contrary to virtue. It simply asserts that it is, with no further grounding for its claim. This is characteristic of the view, which in its merely formal rather than substantive versions simply asserts that virtue is good. But it is problematic when there is a satisfying explanation in the wings, one given by the recursive account of virtue sketched in Section III.

This account, recall, holds that from each person's point of view the pleasure and knowledge of others are good in the same way as his own. It then adds that whenever a state is good, certain attitudes of loving it for itself are also good and constitute virtue. Finally, it holds that virtue is a lesser good in the sense that the value of a virtuous love of an object is always less than that of the object. Taken together, these three claims explain why moral self-indulgence is objectionable. Consider the teacher teaching from a benevolent desire for his student's betterment. The teacher's virtuous pursuit of the student's knowledge is indeed a good, but a lesser good than that knowledge. Assuming that it is part of virtue to care more about greater than about lesser goods, the teacher should have as her primary motive in acting a desire for the student's knowledge, with a desire to act virtuously only secondary. In other cases, caring more about a lesser good than about a greater one—say, caring more about one's own minor pleasure than about another's great pleasure—is a moral failing and even a vice.[39] And it is similarly a failing or vice to care more about one's virtue than about the states, often of others, that are its object. Here the recursive account of virtue explains, and in a philosophically

---

[38] Annas thinks two-level versions of utilitarianism are highly objectionable (see *The Morality of Happiness*, pp. 234–35, 240–42, 299–301, 342). But she claims that the same feature in her own view is not objectionable because in this case the agent's two motivating thoughts do not conflict (p. 260, n. 49). This claim, however, is unpersuasive. To benefit others only because one cares about their good is one thing; to benefit them because one believes that caring about their good will contribute to one's own flourishing is entirely another. Since only one of these can be a person's dominant motive, they do conflict.

[39] See my "Self-Interest, Altruism, and Virtue," *Social Philosophy and Policy*, vol. 14, no. 1 (Winter 1997), pp. 296–97.

satisfying way, what the egoistic virtue view, characteristically, can only assert.

There is another aspect to this difficulty. The main assumption of the explanation just given is that it is best and most virtuous to care more about greater goods than about lesser ones. But if the virtue view accepts this assumption it must positively applaud moral self-indulgence. Within an egoistic framework, states of others such as their pleasure and knowledge are not, from the agent's point of view, good; what is good is only his virtuous love of those states. But then, given the aforementioned assumption, the virtue view will tell the agent to care as much as possible about his virtuous love and as little as possible about the states of others. Of course, the virtuous love cannot be present unless the agent has some concern for these states of others, but to say this is not to say how intense that concern should be, especially in comparison with his second-order concern for his own virtue. And given the relevant assumption, the latter concern should be as intense as possible. To avoid applauding self-indulgence, then, the virtue view must deny that it is best and most virtuous to care more about greater goods. But is that not a highly counterintuitive denial? Is it not overwhelmingly plausible that one should care more about what has more value? Not only does the virtue view merely assert that self-indulgence is objectionable, but the assertion contradicts a seemingly undeniable claim about the best division of virtuous concern.

A different objection to the egoistic virtue view concerns the explanation or philosophical ground it gives for other-regarding reasons. If one person has normative reason to benefit another, what is the ultimate explanation for this reason? The egoistic view says that the explanation is self-regarding: to make his own life better or more flourishing. But this is not, intuitively, the right explanation. The right explanation is other-regarding: to make the other person's life better. Effects on the agent's good may provide a secondary reason for other-regarding action, but the primary reason concerns the action's effect on the other. That is, after all, the point of the action. So in deriving other-regarding reasons from egoistic ones, the virtue view gives the wrong explanation of their force. Annas seems to be addressing this objection when she says that the virtue view "does not imply that its forming part of my good is the *reason why* I should care about the good of others. I care about others for their own sake. Their good is part of my own final good. The second thought does not undermine the first."[40] But her answer concerns only a person's motivating reasons and not the explanatory normative reasons that are currently at issue. We are now granting, despite the first objection above, that the two-part understanding can require a virtuous person not to be motivated by thoughts of his own flourishing. The current objection asks,

[40] Annas, "The Good Life and the Good Lives of Others," p. 137.

granting this, about the explanation the view gives of his having a normative reason to benefit another. The explanation is, in the end, that this action will make his own life better, and that is, intuitively, the wrong explanation. The right explanation is that the action will make the other's life better.

These objections would have no force if there were some necessity for all of a person's normative reasons to derive from his own good, as defenders of egoism assume. Though I cannot discuss the issue fully, I see no basis for this assumption. A person's normative reasons must be reasons for him or concerning his actions; that is, they must have him as their subject. But that does not make them egoistic in their content, and the virtue view denies that they must be egoistic in content. They can be reasons to benefit others, and even to benefit others from a desire for their good for its own sake. But if reasons need not be egoistic in their content, why must they be egoistic in their ground? Why do we not have a satisfactory explanation of a reason to benefit others unless we have connected it to the agent's own good? At least one argument for this conclusion is not available in the present context. It is sometimes held that all of a person's reasons must be internal to his own motivations, arising from within his desires as they now are or would be in more favorable circumstances.[41] But this argument cannot be made given an objective theory of the good of the kind assumed by the virtue view. That view says a person has reason to do what will give him the objectively best life whether he wants that life or not, for example, to develop the virtues whether he wants the virtues or not. Why can it not then also say that he has reason, and nonderivative reason, to benefit others whether he wants to or not? Formal egoism is often assumed in discussions of flourishing but not, I believe, on any sound basis. And if it need not be assumed, there are in-principle reasons why it should not be.

V. CONCLUSION

I have considered three views associated with the concept of flourishing: that the human good consists in the development of properties fundamental to human nature, that the virtues can be identified as those traits necessary for flourishing, and that all a person's normative reasons for acting derive, egoistically, from his interest in his own flourishing.

I have argued that the first of these views is in conflict with the second and third. If we take seriously the idea that the good rests on human nature, we cannot hold that that good involves the virtues as constituents and we cannot plausibly treat all reasons as egoistic. I have also raised objections to the second and third views considered apart from the first.

[41] See, e.g., Bernard Williams, "Internal and External Reasons," in his *Moral Luck*, pp. 101–13.

These views cannot explain why the exercise of the virtues is good rather than simply asserting that it is so, and cannot explain either the force of other-regarding reasons or their application to people who are not virtuous without making claims about that good that are not plausible. In addition, there are in-principle objections to the views' derivation of other-regarding duties from the agent's own good.

Though these arguments have been largely critical, their purpose has not been wholly negative. I believe there are elements of the standard understanding of flourishing that are worth retaining, even if in a different theoretical context. One such element may be the view that the good consists in developing human nature. This both yields and unifies an impressive list of human goods and may figure in an attractive nonegoistic theory where agents are to pursue, perhaps as one goal among others, all people's development of their human nature. Also worth retaining is the view that the exercise of the virtues, including the other-regarding virtues, is a constituent of each person's good. But this view too is best retained in a nonegoistic framework, where agents have nonderivative reasons to pursue the good of others. In this context the view can explain why a given virtue is good, by saying it involves an attitude toward a good or evil that, as that attitude, is virtuous and good. The view can also dispense with the dubious further claims about virtue required in the more common understandings of flourishing. It need not hold that virtue has priority over other goods, but can instead treat virtue as a lesser good, one whose value is always less than that of its object. It also need not and should not use the concept of virtue to evaluate actions, as in virtue ethics. Having identified the virtues in terms of other goods and evils, it should say that what people have reason to do is what will promote good and prevent evil, both in themselves and in other people. Of course, if virtue is a good, then any evaluation of an action's outcome must consider any virtue the action will lead to or express. But if virtue is a lesser good, its contribution to that outcome will usually not be decisive, and in fact in most cases will not make a difference. If what is most virtuous is aiming in the right way at the greatest available goods, then what is most virtuous in a person now is in most cases what he already and independently has most reason to do. In a nonegoistic framework, the concept of virtue does not carry the heavy theoretical load it does in the more common understandings of flourishing. For precisely that reason, however, this framework allows us to affirm the view that virtue is good in a less exaggerated and far more credible way.

Philosophy, University of Calgary

FLOURISHING EGOISM*

By Lester H. Hunt

I. Virtue and Self-Interest

Early in Peter Abelard's *Dialogue between a Philosopher, a Jew, and a Christian*, the philosopher (that is, the ancient Greek) and the Christian easily come to agreement about what the point of ethics is: "[T]he culmination of true ethics . . . is gathered together in this: that it reveal where the ultimate good is and by what road we are to arrive there." They also agree that, since the enjoyment of this ultimate good "comprises true blessedness," ethics "far surpasses other teachings in both usefulness and worthiness."[1] As Abelard understood them, both fundamental elements of his twelfth-century ethical culture—Greek philosophy and Christian religion—held a common view of the nature of ethical inquiry, one that was so obvious to them that his characters do not even state it in a fully explicit way. They take for granted, as we take the ground we stand on, the premise that the most important function of ethical theory is to tell you what sort of life is most desirable, or most worth living. That is, the point of ethics is that it is good for you, that it serves your self-interest.

This idea sounds very strange to modern ears, and is scarcely made less so when it is stated, as it is by Abelard, in terms of the concept of happiness or, to use the somewhat broader term that is now widely used, of "flourishing." It still sounds as if things are being combined that cannot be put together. Nonetheless, Abelard's depiction of his intellectual heritage suggests—at least to me—a historical generalization which I think is at least close to being right: the idea of self-interest, as expressed through the notions of happiness or flourishing, dominates the ethical thinking of both ancient Greek and medieval Christian philosophy in more or less the way I have just described. It is also fair to say that there is at least one other idea that very characteristically dominates thought during the same periods: namely, the idea of virtue. It was generally assumed at that time

* I have benefited from comments by many people on various drafts of this essay. Tara Smith served very ably as the commentator when it was presented at the 1996 annual meetings of the Ayn Rand Society. Ellen Frankel Paul was good enough to send me comments in writing, as did Irfan Khawaja, Eyal Mozes, Chris Sciabarra, and Douglas Rasmussen. Remarks made in oral discussion by Richard Kraut and Richard Arneson also proved to be helpful.
[1] Peter Abelard, "Dialogue 2: Between the Philosopher and the Christian," in Abelard, *Ethical Writings*, trans. Paul Vincent Spade (Indianapolis: Hackett, 1995), pp. 93-94.

that ethics tells you what sort of person you should be: it discovers which traits, if you should have them, would make you a good person.

This close historical association between virtue and self-interest suggests (again, to me at any rate) a further hypothesis: that there is some close connection between the concept of virtue and that of self-interest. This impression is reinforced by the fact that, as the concept of self-interest and related notions receded from the focal point of Western ethics, the idea of virtue did so as well. Both ideas were already sharply demoted in the work of Hobbes, beginning a trend that resulted (sometime in the middle of the twentieth century) in an ethical orthodoxy within which virtue was never mentioned and the agent's own well-being was regarded as at best irrelevant to his or her ethical merit, and at worst in conflict with it.

In what follows, I would like to present one piece of evidence that these two ideas do indeed belong together, related in something like the way they are in the classical, pre-Hobbesian tradition. More precisely, I will argue that the notion of happiness or (the term I will use hereafter) "flourishing" enables us to entertain a much closer connection between virtue and self-interest than modern prejudices will generally allow.

To make this point, I will focus on an ethical doctrine in which this connection is alleged in its most extreme form, namely, ethical egoism. It is perhaps obvious that the notion of flourishing can be relevant to the development of egoistic theories. Though there are various forms of egoism, it must by definition hold, in one way or another, that a distinguishing mark of the right or the good in human conduct is the fact that it conduces to the self-interest of the agent. The concept of flourishing can readily serve as a first approach toward understanding what self-interest is, as an outline sketch that can be filled in later in various ways. One way to explain what self-interest is—among other ways, some crucially different—would be to specify that what is in a person's self-interest is to live the sort of life that is most desirable, most worth living. In a word, self-interest is flourishing. One can then inquire about what sort of life this is, and what it is that makes it the best life.

If flourishing can be used to explain, or begin to explain, what self-interest is, then it can also be used to specify the content of a doctrine of ethical egoism. I will argue in what follows that it makes a great deal of difference whether an egoistic theory begins in this way or in a certain alternative way. It makes a difference to the plausibility of ethical theories and, more fundamentally, to the relevance of self-interest to ethics and to central ethical concepts, most particularly including virtue.

I will begin by setting out some familiar difficulties confronting egoistic theories, together with solutions to these difficulties which can be drawn from the work of one proponent of flourishing-based egoism, one who is often mentioned in discussions of egoism but seldom read closely or discussed with care by professional philosophers. I am referring, as some readers may already have surmised, to Ayn Rand.

II. DIFFICULTIES FOR EGOISM

The first difficulty I want to focus on is a very simple but also, I think, very influential objection to ethical egoism. It is based on the fundamental fact that ethical egoism is, as one might put it, a theory of reasons: it does not, as such, pass judgment on people, their traits, their ways of life, or the acts that they do, but, rather, tells us what constitutes a good reason for such judgments. Egoism says that in some ultimate way, actions, traits, and ways of life have value because they are beneficial to the agent who has or does them. This is what gives us a reason to do actions, to have traits, to live a given way of life, or to admire them in others. The objection I have in mind alleges that egoism, regarded as a theory of reasons, and in particular as a theory of reasons for action, clearly clashes with common sense.[2] Most of us think that the good of others is, to take a phrase used by Michael Slote in a similar context, a "ground floor" reason for action—that the fact that an action produces some good for some other person is sometimes, simply in itself, a reason for doing it.[3] Yet this seems to be just the sort of thing that egoism denies.

To the extent that a theory does clash with common sense, it must present people with arguments to change their minds, at least if its proponents mean to convince people who do not already agree with them. Here the clash with common sense seems very deep, and the burden of proof correspondingly large. In the absence of compelling arguments to the contrary, Slote says, "a properly conservative approach seems to dictate . . . that we prefer a common-sense account . . . to the egoistic view."[4]

The second objection I want to consider is one to which Derek Parfit drew attention a few years ago. Like the first one, it arises, more or less naturally, when we regard egoism as a theory of reasons for action. It goes like this: Egoism, interpreted as a theory of reasons for action, distin-

---

[2] "Common sense," in this context, means: the views that people in a given culture hold before theoretical considerations convince them to change those views.

[3] Michael Slote, *From Morality to Virtue* (New York: Oxford University Press, 1992), p. 91.

[4] *Ibid.*, p. 92. The objection to egoism that Slote raises in this passage is actually about egoism regarded as a theory of what makes actions admirable, and not (at least not explicitly) about egoism as a theory of reasons for performing actions. His claim is that egoism clashes with "the ground floor admiration for acts and traits that help others" which "most of us are disposed—and happy to be disposed—to feel." The objection I have just presented is stated as an objection to egoism as a theory of reasons for acting and thus constitutes a different, though related, problem. It seems likely that a satisfactory response to the objection I am considering would contain clues pointing to a response to the problem Slote raises, but an adequate discussion of the latter problem would require more attention than I will be able to devote to it in this essay.

guishes between good reasons and bad ones by using a certain aim, or outcome, as the standard: namely, the agent's own good. The problem, according to this objection, is that this outcome will probably not be achieved most effectively by people who are trying to achieve it, and who have no other ultimate aim. We can readily imagine reasons why this might well be the case. If people were to realize that I act as if I value their well-being simply in order to get something out of them, all sorts of results that are bad for me will tend follow: to one extent or another, other people will object to being "used" in this way and will refuse to cooperate with me. They will also dislike me, and they will think I am a bad person. However, it is good for me that others cooperate with me, like me, and think I am a good person; thus, to the extent that these results can be expected to follow from it, egoistic behavior undermines the aim of egoism.

As Parfit has pointed out in his own response to this sort of objection, the problem it raises is not a logical contradiction: it does not mean that egoism logically entails its own falsity.[5] We could take it to mean, rather, that egoism advises us to conceal our ultimate aim from others and perhaps from ourselves. It may actually be easier to get others to respond in a favorable way to us if we actually come to value their well-being as an end in itself. This, in turn, may mean that egoism would require us to believe theories that are inconsistent with itself, that it would require us to think (for instance) that things are actually good that, according to egoism, are really worthless. It would not follow from this, however, that according to egoism, egoism is false. Strictly speaking, it would only entail that, according to egoism, we really should have these attitudes and believe these theories. Egoism would (according to itself) give the true account of why we ought to do and believe these things.

Parfit has apparently taken the position that, if this objection does not convict egoism of self-contradiction, it is no objection at all.[6] It seems to me, though, that it *is* an objection, and one that should be taken seriously. Ethical egoism, like any other ethical doctrine, is meant to guide the conduct of life. If it should turn out to be true that it can only be followed by using secrecy, lying, self-deception, and holding contradictory beliefs, this would raise several problems for anyone who wants to believe the doctrine. To mention only the most obvious one, it would seem to mean that this guide to life is an extremely difficult one to follow. To the extent that one guide is difficult to follow and another is not, that other is, all other things being equal (for instance, if the reasons for thinking they *are* true are about evenly balanced), clearly preferable as a guide. Later, I will say more to reinforce the idea that this constitutes a problem. For the time

---

[5] This theme runs throughout much of Derek Parfit's *Reasons and Persons* (New York: Oxford University Press, 1984), ch. 1, esp. sections 1–8.

[6] See the preceding footnote.

being, I hope it has enough intuitive appeal to at least motivate the reader to continue to follow what I am saying.

III. One Version of Egoism

Neither of these two objections, as I have described them, is a knock-down refutation of ethical egoism. Both have the character, rather, of considerations that weigh against it and must somehow be balanced by considerations that weigh on the other side, creating a burden of proof that apparently must be shouldered by anyone who wishes to defend ethical egoism to people not already convinced of its truth. Despite this appearance, I will argue in what follows that there is at least one sort of egoism that can afford to lay down this burden. I am referring to egoistic doctrines that make suitable use of the idea of flourishing. Such theories can be formulated in such a way that the above objections simply do not apply to them. This, in fact, is one of the principal advantages these theories enjoy over other varieties of ethical egoism, for there are varieties to which these objections do apply. To make a case for these claims, I will, as already indicated, focus on one particular example of flourishing-based egoism: the one formulated and defended by Ayn Rand. In the present section of this essay, I will describe this version in what I hope is enough detail to provide a basis for discussion. In the next section, I will briefly show how the possibilities opened by the flourishing-based approach enable it to side-step these two otherwise persuasive objections.

One of the most direct and revealing statements of Rand's ethical egoism is a statement in her philosophical novel *Atlas Shrugged*, one that she deemed important enough to quote some years later in her essay "The Objectivist Ethics":

> Man has to be man—by choice; he has to hold his life as a value—by choice; he has to learn to sustain it—by choice; he has to discover the values it requires and practice his virtues—by choice. A code of values accepted by choice is a code of morality.[7]

There is much in this statement that invites comment of one sort or another, but for the present I will only call attention to one aspect of it, one that I will later argue is important. She does not describe the moral task as, fundamentally, one of selecting acts nor, by the same token, as one of selecting acts that optimally achieve some goal. In place of a goal, she presents something that cannot in any straightforward sense be maximized, something we would not ordinarily think of as a goal at all:

---

[7] Ayn Rand, "The Objectivist Ethics," in Rand, *The Virtue of Selfishness* (New York: Signet, 1964), p. 23.

namely, one's own life. It is the value that must be achieved—or, as she says, "sustained." Further, she presents this task as one that apparently can *only* be carried out by one means or method: by identifying the requisite values and—what is evidently a closely related matter—practicing the appropriate virtues.

When she gives an even more explicit statement of her ethical egoism, a few pages after quoting the passage from *Atlas Shrugged*, she says:

> The Objectivist ethics proudly advocates and upholds *rational selfishness*—which means: the values required for man's survival *qua* man.[8]

Here, again, though the reference to virtue is dropped, there is still no direct reference to action at all. This pattern, as far as I know, is sustained throughout her work: in her direct statements of her doctrine, she does not present it as a thesis that is *directly* about what we should do.

Naturally, as with any ethical theory, action must come into it at some point. In a rough sort of way, it is relatively easy to say how action enters into this one. Among the many values that can become helpful in sustaining the ultimate value, three are of such importance that they can be singled out as *the* means to its achievement:

> The three cardinal values of the Objectivist ethics—the three values which, taken together, are the means to and the realization of one's ultimate value, one's own life—are Reason, Purpose, Self-Esteem.[9]

In turn, "these three values," as she has her character John Galt say, "imply and require all of man's virtues."[10] In "The Objectivist Ethics" she selects three virtues for special consideration as "corresponding" to the three cardinal values: rationality, productiveness, and pride.

Finally, though Rand does not directly connect self-interest with action, she does establish such a connection between action and virtue: "*Value*," she says, "is that which one acts to gain and/or keep—*virtue* is the act by which one gains and/or keeps it."[11] Self-interest as an ethical standard is connected with action, but the connection is made indirectly, through the intermediary concepts of value and virtue. One's interests are sustained only by achieving that which is of value, while that which is of value is achieved by means of virtue. The acts of which such virtue consists,

---

[8] *Ibid.*, p. 31.
[9] *Ibid.*, p. 27.
[10] Ayn Rand, *Atlas Shrugged* (New York: Random House, 1957), p. 1018.
[11] Rand, "The Objectivist Ethics," p. 25.

whatever they might be, are the ones that her ethical standard singles out for praise and commendation.

To see just what these connections between standard and action amount to, it is probably most helpful to understand what self-interest means for Rand. To that end, consider the following story, which I draw from the life of the great architect Louis Sullivan. In 1917, Sullivan's career was in desperate condition. His innovative aesthetic was out of fashion, and he had completed no projects of any importance for three years. If he did not receive a commission soon, he was facing the degrading possibility of real poverty. Then the directors of a small banking firm in Sidney, Ohio approached him about designing a building for them. He traveled to Sidney and, after inspecting the site and reflecting on their specifications, had a meeting with the directors which an early biographer describes in this way:

> He announced to the directors that the design was made—in his head—proceeded to draw a rapid sketch before them, and announced an estimate of the cost. One of the directors was somewhat disturbed by the unfamiliarity of the style, and suggested that he had rather fancied some classic columns and pilasters for the façade. Sullivan very brusquely rolled up his sketch and started to depart, saying that the directors could get a thousand architects to design a classic bank but only one to design them this kind of bank, and that as far as he was concerned, it was either the one thing or the other. After some conference, the directors accepted the sketch design and the bank was forthwith built with not a single essential change in the design.[12]

This incident presents us with a definite narrative sequence, concluding with a happy ending: Sullivan is in serious danger, yet faces it with unflinching courage and, perhaps because of this, things turn out very well for him. He is able to pay his rent a while longer, and he avoids violating his architectural ideals. But wherein does this "turning out well" consist?

Rand created a memorable fictional incident, probably inspired by this historical one, which poses a striking answer to this question. There is an episode in her novel *The Fountainhead* in which the architect-hero, Howard Roark, confronts a professional crisis virtually identical to the one we have just seen Sullivan facing: if he does not get an architectural commission almost immediately, he will have to go to work as a laborer, possibly giving up his career forever. He is asked to design a commercial building, and there is a request for classical ornaments that are inconsis-

---

[12] Hugh Morrison, *Louis Sullivan: Prophet of Modern Architecture* (New York: Norton, 1935), pp. 180–81.

tent with the rest of the design. But Roark is not as lucky as Sullivan was. The board makes it clear that this represents their final offer. As he prepares to leave, a representative of the company begs him to reconsider, if only for the sake of his own well-being:

> "We want your building. You need the commission. Do you have to be quite so fanatical and selfless about it?"
>
> "What?" Roark asked, incredulously.
>
> "Fanatical and selfless."
>
> Roark smiled. He looked down at his drawings. His elbow moved a little, pressing them to his body. He said:
>
> "That was the most selfish thing you've ever seen a man do." [13]

By making things turn out worse for Roark than they did for Sullivan, Rand compels us to consider what self-interest really is. Sullivan manages to secure for himself two sorts of goods: those involved in designing the sort of building he believes in, and those involved in being able to pay his rent. Because he achieves both, we have no need to think about the relative roles of these two sorts of values—which we might roughly capture by calling them "ideals" and "money"—in constituting the interests of the individual involved. In Roark's case these two sorts of goods conflict, and he must choose between them. In evaluating the effect of this episode on the hero's fortunes, we must consider which choice better supports his well-being.

Rand and her character make it very clear that their solution to this problem is not the one that many people would give, including many philosophers who have discussed ethical egoism. Typically, one's ideals are thought to be for the most part antithetical to one's interests, while money is treated as if it were infallibly conducive to them, and this is clearly not what Rand and Roark think. Obviously, there is a heterodox theory about the nature of self-interest involved here.

Whatever this theory might be, it certainly cannot simply amount to the claim that acting on one's ideals is necessarily in one's interest. It is too evident that some people's ideals really are bad for them. What, then, *is* self-interest? Rand never says, quite directly and explicitly, what "interest" or "self-interest" mean when she uses them, but she does make some relevant and highly illuminating comments on the thing that she takes as representing the opposite of these things: namely, sacrifice. "'Sacrifice'," she tells us, "is the surrender of a greater value for the sake of a lesser one or of a nonvalue." [14] She goes on to give an example:

---

[13] Ayn Rand, *The Fountainhead* (New York: Bobbs-Merrill, 1943), p. 206.

[14] Rand, "The Ethics of Emergencies," in *The Virtue of Selfishness* (*supra* note 7), p. 44.

If a man who is passionately in love with his wife spends a fortune
to cure her of a dangerous illness, it would be absurd to claim that he
does it as a "sacrifice" for *her* sake, not his own, and that it makes no
difference to *him*, personally and selfishly, whether she lives or dies. . . .
But suppose he let her die in order to spend his money on saving the
lives of ten other women, none of whom meant anything to him. . . .
That would be a sacrifice.[15]

Now I am in a position to say more about how it is, in Rand's theory,
that value and virtue connect action with self-interest. An account of the
connection that is both suggested by and consistent with the passages I
have quoted in the last several paragraphs would go like this. One's
interests consist in achieving what is of value. Since things that are of
value are unequally valuable and conflict with one another, this would
have to mean achieving what is of *greatest* value. But this cannot be
accomplished without knowing what is, in a given situation, of greater
value and what is of less. Since acting on the basis of this understanding
is what virtue is, this also means that achieving one's own interest would
be impossible without virtue.

IV. Difficulties Avoided

How does this version of ethical egoism fare in the face of the objections
against egoism that I raised earlier? In the case of the first one, I think the
answer is fairly straightforward. This objection rested on the claim that
egoism clashes with the idea that the good of others is a "ground floor"
reason for action, and that, consequently, egoism is incompatible with
common sense. As I have presented it, this claim could mean two different things.

First, it could mean that common sense holds that the fact that a given
act advances the good of others is a reason for doing that act and, further,
that there is no reason why *this* is so. There is no reason why it is a reason.
This, of course, does not seem to be a tenet of common sense at all.
Indeed, it seems consistent with common sense to say that the good of
people you know is a reason for action because other people are of great
value to you, that promoting the good of others, at least of certain others,
is an indispensable part of the sort of life that it is best to live, the sort of
life that is the most desirable. In fact, parents—most of whom can be

---

[15] *Ibid.*, pp. 44–45. Rand has John Galt put the same idea this way: "If you exchange a
penny for a dollar, it is *not* a sacrifice; if you exchange a dollar for a penny, it *is*. If you
achieve the career you wanted, after years of struggle, it is *not* a sacrifice; if you then
renounce it for the sake of a rival, it *is*. If you own a bottle of milk and give it to your starving
child, it is *not* a sacrifice; if you give it to your neighbor's child and let your own die, it *is*"
(Rand, *Atlas Shrugged*, p. 1028).

taken to represent common sense to some extent—often try to convince their children that this is true. Of course, it is debatable whether such common-sense ways of explaining the value of the good of others are egoistic; but it is worth noting that, if they are, they are instances of flourishing-based egoism. We show that something is in one's self-interest by showing that it is part of a certain sort of life. This sort of life, it is assumed, is what self-interest is.

However, it seems likely that few people would be influenced by this objection to ethical egoism if this is what it meant. An alternative and more persuasive way of understanding the objection would be to view it as the claim that common sense denies a *certain* conception of the reason why the good of others is a reason for action. According to this conception, the *only* reason for which we should seek to bring about the good of others is that their well-being in turn brings about a certain further result—namely, of course, our own self-interest.

It is certainly very plausible to say that this conception clashes with common sense. However, it is not so obvious that it is implied by ethical egoism. In particular, Rand's theory seems to have no such implication. It does not recommend that we seek the well-being of others on the grounds that their well-being causes one's own interests to be realized. Rather, one's own interest is (consists in) the attainment of value, and one of the most valuable things is the good of other—that is, certain other—people. One's own self-interest is not some further result, in addition to the attainment of one's values; and one's values include, as a part of them, the good of certain other people.

What this means is that, as I have already hinted, Rand's egoism is of the flourishing-based sort. The notion of attaining value functions here as part of her account of which sort of life is best. We show that things are in one's interest by showing that they are part of this sort of life. The reason why something does fit into such a life—why it is a value—may be a matter of what further effects it has on the agent, but that is another matter. Saying that the good of others fits into such a life is not the same thing as saying that it has such effects. This is why Rand can claim that she is an ethical egoist and yet embrace the common-sense view that the good of others *is* a ground-floor reason for action in that it is worth pursuing in itself.

So much for the first objection to ethical egoism. As for the second one, which alleges that egoism requires one to adopt a certain self-defeating attitude toward other people, a closely related reply is also available. The reply I just gave to the second, and more likely, interpretation of the first objection rested on the idea that it assumed an arbitrarily narrow notion of egoism as a theory of reasons. The existence of flourishing-based explanations of self-interest opens up the possibility of an egoism that is more inclusive in the reasons for action that it treats as legitimate. The same sort of thing can be said in connection with the second objection. In both cases, it is assumed that, according to egoism, a consideration becomes a good reason for action simply and solely because, if one acts on it, it brings about a certain result: the agent's own self-interest. In the second objection this assumption implies that, if we act as egoism recommends, we are viewing the interests of others in a certain way: as mere instruments to be manipulated to produce a certain result. As we have already seen, this assumption is not necessarily true, and, in particular, it is not true of Rand's egoism. In her view, the achievement of one's values is related to self-interest, not by causality, but by identity. That is what self-interest is. Given that the good of (at least certain) others properly is among one's values, it is in one's self-interest to pursue it, even apart from further, future results it might bring. To put the same idea in more abstract and theory-neutral language: it is in one's self-interest, not because it causes flourishing, but because it is partly constitutive of it.

Of course, whether an ethical egoism that is formulated in this way is true, or even fully coherent, is another matter; but at least we can say that this form of egoism is not logically committed to a repulsively manipulative attitude toward other people, an attitude which, according to the second objection, must be concealed from them and, possibly, from oneself.

V. CONSEQUENTIALIST EGOISM

My responses to the two objections, as I have presented them so far, are very brief. Obviously, much more remains to be said about them; in particular, I must deal with the inevitable replies, and that is what I will do for most of the remainder of this essay. I have claimed that these objections do not necessarily apply to a certain sort of egoism: namely, the sort that, at least implicitly, uses the flourishing-based approach to explaining what self-interest is. In addition, some of my comments have suggested rather strongly that such objections *do* apply to a certain other sort of egoism, and may even cause it some serious damage. Accordingly, I have exposed myself to two sorts of attack: one from people who find fault with the type of egoism I have defended, and the other from people who find fault with the way I have implicitly rejected the other type. Some people would likely wish to claim that the notion of flourishing cannot help egoism in the way I have suggested it can, while others will say that non-flourishing-based egoism has no need of such help.

I will take the latter sort of attack first, using as my principal focus a version of the attack presented by Peter Railton.[16] Following some suggestions by Parfit to which I have already referred, Railton contends that,

---

[16] My main source is Peter Railton, "Alienation, Consequentialism, and the Demands of Morality," *Philosophy and Public Affairs*, vol. 13, no. 2 (Spring 1984), pp. 134–71. See also his "How Thinking about Character and Utilitarianism Might Lead to Rethinking the Character of Utilitarianism," *Midwest Studies in Philosophy*, vol. 13 (1988), pp. 398–416.

contrary to what I have supposed, the second objection, properly understood, really presents no problem at all for the theories at which it is aimed: the self-defeatingness with which it charges them is actually not a bad thing. What prevents it from being a bad thing, in part, is the concept of virtue. Railton states his argument in terms of egoistic hedonism, but it is easy to see how it can be generalized to apply to egoism in general.

Egoistic hedonism ("hedonism" for short) is the theory that says that all actions that an agent might do are good only if they cause a certain state of consciousness in the agent: namely, happiness or pleasure (which, for brevity, I will call "pleasure" from now on). Stated as a problem about hedonism, the second objection rests on the familiar truism that people who make pleasure their sole ultimate aim often achieve this end less well than people who have ultimate ends—goods sought as good in themselves—other than (perhaps in addition to) pleasure. Doing something because it results in a certain state of consciousness in oneself is quite a different thing from doing it for love of the activity itself. They are different, in spite of the fact that the latter way of acting will also produce pleasure. In fact, for a number of reasons, a life filled with these sorts of activities will probably contain more pleasure than a life in which everything is calculated to achieve this result.

As Railton treats it, this problem is simply an instance of a more general psychological one, which is created by the fact that the temptation to indulge in excessive reflection about one's ends tends to interfere with the achievement of those ends. A problem that seems to function as a paradigm for him is one that he calls "a famous old conundrum for consequentialism": If all actions are to be judged by their outcomes, then it would seem that we must deliberate not only about actions but about how much time to spend on any deliberation, including these deliberations about our deliberations, and so on to infinity.

One can avoid this problem, he says, simply by refraining from deliberating about time allocation. The "sophisticated consequentialist" can "develop standing dispositions to give more or less time to decisions depending upon their perceived importance, the amount of information available, the predictability of his choice, and so on."[17] Similar things, he points out, can be said of a wide range of problems involving self-defeatingly goal-based thinking. There is the tennis enthusiast who is so obsessed with winning that he would actually win more if he forgot the score and became absorbed in the details of the game,[18] the timid employee who will never have the nerve to ask for a needed raise if he deliberates about whether to do it, the self-conscious man who, if he thinks about how he should act at a party he is attending, will fail to achieve the goal of such thinking, which is to act naturally and, ulti-

---

[17] Railton, "Alienation, Consequentialism, and the Demands of Morality," pp. 153–54.
[18] *Ibid.*, p. 144.

mately, to enjoy the party. Finally, there is the tightrope walker who will not be able to concentrate if he consciously focuses on the fact that his life depends on his keeping his concentration. In each of these cases, Railton tells us, the individuals involved can improve the consequences of their action by avoiding "consequentialist deliberation." This can be done by developing personal traits, "habits of thought," which tend to forestall such deliberation.[19] Because of their manifest importance in enabling us to live as we should, such traits would naturally be regarded as virtues.

This argument brings to the surface two important threads in the tangle of issues I am treating here, threads I want to comment on very briefly before going on to the question of the cogency of Railton's argument. First, one moral that can be drawn from examples like the case of the tightrope walker and the others just cited is that deliberation and conscious reflection are not the same thing as rationality, even when they contain only factually accurate thoughts and are carried out without violating the formal constraints of logic. There are times when conscious reflection, just because it is conscious reflection, would be profoundly irrational.[20]

The other thread that deserves some immediate comment has to do with the nature of Railton's ultimate concerns. He is not defending egoistic hedonism against attack because he believes it is true. His interest is based on the fact that his own doctrine, what is usually called consequentialism, has been subjected to the same attack, and he believes both can be given the same defense. Fundamentally, the defense he offers for egoistic hedonism is the one he also offers for consequentialism. The fact that an intelligent person could find such a strategy plausible rather obviously suggests a further fact, which I believe is both true and important: namely, that consequentialism is indeed closely related to egoism. This, however, is only true of a certain sort of egoism.

Consequentialism decides the rightness or wrongness of actions based on their total causal outcome, their effects on *everyone* who is affected by them. The relevant sort of egoism decides the rightness or wrongness of acts based on their effects on the agent alone. Obviously, these two ideas have something in common: both are ethical theories which decide the rightness of acts, and both do so based entirely on the results that these acts produce. Since both of these views appeal only to consequences, they probably should both be treated as varieties of "consequentialism": one might be called "collective consequentialism," and the other could be called "individual consequentialism." It is worth bearing in mind the

---

[19] *Ibid.*, p. 154.

[20] For discussions of the ways in which human reason is able to avoid pointless or counterproductive thinking, see Michael Polanyi, *The Tacit Dimension* (New York: Doubleday, 1966), ch. 1; and Polanyi, *Knowing and Being* (Chicago: University of Chicago Press, 1969), Part III.

possibility that the problem Railton poses and tries to solve for egoistic hedonism is indeed a problem for consequentialism in general, including all consequentialist varieties of egoism, as well as his favored collective variety of the doctrine. If his solution is not a satisfactory one, then this doctrine may be flawed in all its varieties.

I say this is worth bearing in mind because I think that, in fact, the proposed solution is not a satisfactory one. The reason for this has to do with the nature of the traits that are to solve the problem faced by the tennis player, the tightrope walker, and the others who experience the temptation to become irrationally reflective and deliberative.

Those traits are, as Railton says, "habits of thought." It is important to ask exactly what this means. Habits are traits on the basis of which individuals act. The fact that an act is done from habit has no necessary connection with the thoughts, beliefs, or values of the person who does it. It is in this sense that habits might be said to be mindless. Suppose that I develop a habit of abstaining from fatty foods because I value health. Later, I change my way of thinking and no longer value health, but from habit I still refrain (for a while) from eating those foods. In both cases the actions involved (which happen to be abstentions) are habitual and are done from the *same* habit. The relation between habit and thought is loose. This does not mean that there is tension or incompatibility between habit and thought, any more than there is any tension between an inert hammer and the skillful deliberation of the carpenter. It means that, to the extent that it is habitual, the act does not necessarily proceed from any thought or any valuation.

It is partly for this reason that such habits are not traits of character. If I develop a habit of not thinking about my score while playing a game, this might be a result of wisdom. It might also be a cowardly evasion, in which I conceal from myself the fact that my real goals and interests are of a sort that I despise. Wisdom and cowardice are traits of character, while the habit of thinking or not thinking of something is not. This is, in part, because conduct that is wise or cowardly necessarily arises from what one thinks or values, while habitual behaviors, including habitual thoughts, do not.[21]

In spite of their mindlessness, or perhaps because if it, these habits of thought serve to advance the purposes set by our thoughts and evaluations. This can be so, for instance, when conscious thinking would take more time than we should spend on it, or when its results would be so inaccurate that a very rough but readily available approximation to the right answer would actually serve better. Things that do not have the nature of thought can serve as a substitute for thought. These particular

---

[21] For further discussion of the difference between habits and traits of character, see my *Character and Culture* (Lanham, MD: Rowman and Littlefield, 1997), ch. 1.

substitutes can mimic, approximately, the results that conscious thought could be expected to produce if it could only work in some ideally rapid, logical, and well-informed manner.

There are times when such thought-substitutes are desirable, and the particular way in which they are desirable can help to explain why they are feasible as well. To see why such an explanation is necessary, consider the state of mind of the tightrope walker who finds that he must develop a habit of avoiding certain states of consciousness: he must not look down; he must not think about what it would feel like to lose his balance; he must not visualize the ugly results of landing on the ground beneath him. Usually, avoiding thought in a situation where there are important problems to solve is not only undesirable but, for the sort of person who is good at solving problems, difficult to do. Why, then, is the performer able to do so in this case?

Part of the answer, no doubt, lies in the fact that here one is not avoiding thought in general, but only certain particular thoughts. These particular thoughts, moreover, are, from the agent's point of view, eminently worthy of being avoided. Admittedly, the information that the tightrope walker can represent to himself by imagining his mangled body lying far beneath him might be accurate, but this is not a situation in which the collection of accurate data is per se valuable. His only concern at the moment is what he should do, and only the data that can inform him on that point have any legitimate interest. The data that he fails to collect by not looking down have no implications that go beyond what he already knows—indeed, beyond what he is already doing. The fact that he would become a bloody mess if he were to fall is all the more reason why he should focus his consciousness on the rope and on his destination at the other end. If he refrains from thinking about this fact, the only thing he misses that is connected with his present concerns is the emotional power the fact has to confuse and disorient him.

It would be easy, though tedious, to show that similar things can be said about the tennis enthusiast, the self-conscious man, and the timid employee. The general idea that applies to all of them is this: When we deliberate, we think about which particular act is the right one to do. There are various thoughts which, if we experience them, can interfere with identifying and doing the right thing. Under such circumstances, developing a certain habit of thought, in which such thoughts are avoided, can help to achieve the end of deliberation. Developing such a habit is possible, in part, because the individual literally *has no reason* to think these thoughts. In such situations, though habit does not have the nature of a mental process, it serves, so to speak, as a mind-mimic.

Railton's argument fails because the problem faced by the hedonist, and by consequentialists in general, whether individual or collective, is fundamentally different from situations of this kind. In particular, the problem lacks the characteristic that, as we have just seen, allows habits of thought to be a feasible solution. To see why, we must look a little closer at what this problem actually amounts to.

First, it has to be admitted that the problem involved in this sort of case is in one way the same as that faced by the tightrope walker and the others: in both cases, the problem is how to avoid having certain thoughts. Consider, however, concrete instances of the thought to be avoided in the case of the hedonist. A plausible example of the sort of thought that would give me trouble if I were an egoistic hedonist would be the realization that, by stealing the contents of my friend's wallet, I can expect to be better off on balance than I am now. Insofar as the consequences of individual acts can be calculated, this seems to be the sort of thought that can be supported by the preponderance of evidence. Further, it seems to be a plausible thought, not only from the point of view of an egoistic hedonist, but from that of any sort of consequentialist egoism.

It is easy to find examples of thoughts that would have the same sort of plausibility for the collective consequentialist and would create the same sort of trouble. Consider, for instance, the following facts. I spend some of my income on making my son's diet nutritious, varied, and interesting to him. This is not needed to keep him alive; it only serves to improve the quality of his life. If I were to give this money to the right charities, I could probably save the life of some child in the Third World. Resources at my disposal that merely bring goods like improved health to my son might very likely mean the difference between life and death to a stranger on the other side of the earth.

There is one good reason for avoiding the thoughts involved in these two cases that applies equally to both of them. At the moment when I see increasing my property as a good enough reason to take my friend's wallet, I view my friend as having a definite and very limited sort of value. Similarly, at the moment when I decide to divert resources away from my son simply because it would benefit the larger group of which he is a mere part, I am viewing his value as limited in exactly the same way. In both cases, the other person is seen as an entity whose interests can conflict with that of some other entity, and that conflict is seen as, in itself, a good enough reason to sacrifice the interests of the person.

Obviously, it would be very bad if one's attitude toward other people amounted simply to this. In particular, it would be regarded as bad within the points of view of both individual and collective consequentialism. As far as the individual standard is concerned, this willingness instantly to sacrifice everyone for the sake of some advantage to oneself is the source of the problems I cited earlier, involving loss of trust and respect from others and resulting in damage to one's own well-being. It also harms one's interest in a more immediate and possibly more devastating way. Anyone who, supposing it is possible, has this attitude toward others is obviously incapable of forming close personal attachments to other people, the sorts of attachments that are involved in love and friendship.

Such attachments seem to be absolutely essential components of human well-being.

From the point of view of individual consequentialism, this fact is very important. It is also important, and equally so, from the point of view of collective consequentialism. If everyone used consequentialist ideas in the daily course of deliberation, everyone would be incapable of close personal attachments to others. But this would mean that no one would be living a good life, which runs directly against the standard that defines this point of view.

From the point of view of consequentialism, whether individual or collective, it is crucial that this same point of view be kept out of the perspective of deliberation, in which human beings actually choose their conduct. One problem faced by the consequentialist, the one we are now considering, is how to do this. We can now see why habits of thought are not a feasible solution to it: we have reason to think that a genuine consequentialist—someone who consistently believes consequentialism— will likely not be able to develop effective habits of suppressing the relevant thoughts.

The problem of the consequentialist differs from the sort of problem for which habits of thought are clearly a workable solution in at least two relevant ways. First, the troublesome thoughts in the case of the tightrope walker (and related cases) are simply a miscellaneous collection of facts united only by an emotional connection with the issue faced by the de- liberator. In the consequentialist cases, the thoughts really are about the issue at hand: the problem of which course of action is the right one to follow. This, of course, is exactly what deliberation is about. This imme- diately creates a problem, for people whose habits of mind are those of a rational human being, of how to motivate oneself to screen these thoughts out of one's consciousness. Such people would view the possibility of developing such a habit with deep suspicion, partly because they would need assurance that such habits would not also suppress thoughts that they really should be having.

Naturally, if we know that these habits only suppress certain thoughts, and if we know that if they have any bearing on the issue at all, they have the same implications that the preponderance of one's unsuppressed thoughts have, then we have the assurance we need. As I have pointed out, in cases like that of the tightrope walker, this is just what we do have. In the consequentialist cases, however, this assurance is starkly absent, and this is the second way in which such cases differ from the others. In fact, the thoughts to be avoided would imply that the action supported by one's unsuppressed thoughts would be *wrong*. According to individual consequentialism, failure to steal my friend's wallet, under the circum- stances we have imagined, would be the wrong thing to do. The same thing is true, according to collective consequentialism, of failure to de- prive one's child of resources that could bring greater benefits to the children of strangers in other countries.

It is crucial, from the point of view of consequentialism, to keep such thoughts out of one's deliberative thinking. One thing that makes this particularly difficult to do is the fact that, to put it bluntly, such thoughts *should not* be systematically suppressed. After all, according to any conceivable ethical standard, there really are times when we ought to prefer our interests to those of our friends, and there really are times when we ought to prefer the interests of stricken and desperate strangers over the desires of our children. However, for consequentialists, thinking about the consequences of one's conduct in such contexts is not a safe enterprise. For nonconsequentialists, such considerations are a normal and inevitable part of deliberation. For consequentialists, ironically, they are not: such thoughts threaten to engulf their deliberative thoughts and poison their relations with others and with themselves.

The problem is a particularly nasty one because of the nature of the obstacles that consequentialists, whether individual or collective, must try to overcome. Among the things they would have working against them are their desire to consider everything that is relevant to issues about which they are thinking, and their eagerness to identify the things that, by their standards, are the right things to do. I think this means that their adversaries would include both their rationality and their moral integrity. These are not the sort of obstacles we ought to be contending with.

VI. The Possibility of Flourishing-Based Egoism

I think it is clear from what I have already said that flourishing-based egoism is not doomed to face these problems. The flourishing-based explanation of self-interest makes it possible for me to say that my friend's good is partly constitutive of my own good. If I do take this position, there is no prima facie reason to think that I will advance my interests by stealing his wallet, even if he never suspects me and, in purely consequentialist terms, I "get away with it." If my relationship with my friend is, to use Rand's terminology, "one of my highest values," then by betraying his trust and victimizing him I would be damaging my own life just as I am damaging his.

This said, however, I must deal with the remaining one of the potential attacks on my line of reasoning as set out at the beginning of Section V: the one that I can expect to be launched by people who find the notion of flourishing-based egoism, in one way or another, implausible. Here I face a somewhat awkward problem. The particular aspect of this sort of egoism that I have chosen to focus on and defend, the aspect that is relevant to the point I wish to make, is its potential for being developed in nonconsequentialist ways. The problem is that, as far as I know, this aspect of this sort of theory has never been clearly and unambiguously identified and attacked. I will have to guess what sorts of criticisms might be made against it.

The apparent fact that this sort of view has not been criticized suggests that the most likely doubts that people might have about it would concern whether there really is such a thing as nonconsequentialist egoism. That is, one might doubt that the doctrine can be fully formulated without collapsing either into consequentialist egoism or into some nonegoist doctrine. The following would be one way of setting out these doubts: One's interests, one might say, consist in achieving what is of value or, in more antique language, possessing the good. But not just any value or good will do. It is not in my interest to have what is good for, or of value to, someone else but is not good for or of value to me. It must be good for me, of value to me. If something is good for me, it must have some effect that falls on me rather than someone else, an effect that is in some way favorable to me. Now, if self-interest is the standard of ethical merit, that would have to mean, in one way or another, that actions are evaluated on the basis of how much good they produce for the agent, and this would mean that actions are evaluated on the basis of the effects that they have on the agent. But this, of course, is consequentialist egoism. The only way egoism can avoid being consequentialist is by avoiding egoism, probably by opting for an impersonal, non-agent-relative notion of the good.

What should immediately arouse suspicion against this argument is the fact that the conception of self-interest that it uses carries the implication—in fact, this is virtually the point of it as employed here—that actions can never have value in themselves for the agent who performs them. Presumably, insofar as an act has value in itself, it is not good for any one person as distinguished from everyone else. This is not plausible on the face of it. People treat many of the things that they do with friends and lovers as good in themselves and, precisely as such, as good for them. There is no obvious reason why they should not do so. Further, most people live their lives as ends in themselves, and not as processes that only have value because they serve some end other than themselves. Since a life is made up of actions—one's life is simply everything one does—this would seem to mean that many actions, and probably many kinds of actions, are being treated as good for the individuals who do them, *and* as good in themselves. The people who would raise the objection I am considering here would have to say what is wrong with this— and it is not obvious what their explanation could be.

No doubt such people would also claim that nonconsequentialist egoists also have something *they* need to explain. One might well ask precisely how the good of others can become good for oneself in a nonconsequentialist way. This seems a very reasonable question. Consider the image that is most naturally formed when we try to imagine how it is that human beings are actually related to each other. I am here and my friend is over there. Between us, there is empty space through which a slight draft is blowing. Nonetheless, there are many sorts of relations that hold between us. Inclusion is obviously not one of them, however; I am not included in him, and he is not part of me. How then can his good be included in mine, as a part of it?

There is no way I can present a full answer to this interesting question here, but I think it will suffice if I suggest a way in which it *can* be answered.[22] What I would like to suggest is this. My friend's good is not a characteristic of my friend as an inert object, but as a living being. More precisely, it is characteristic of his life, of the way he lives and functions. This, of course, is simply a way of putting the matter in flourishing-based terms. But events in my friend's life can also be, and often are, events in my life as well. This is partly because many of our actions are actually shared projects, or things that we both do. The dinner we shared the other day in a Vietnamese restaurant, the book we are writing together, the long conversation we had with his former classmates from Germany—these are all things we *both* did. Thus, although my friend's body does not overlap my body, his life does overlap my life. Beyond that, many of the other events in my friend's life, the ones in which I do not share as fellow-agent, are things of which I am conscious, and my well-being is raised or lowered by this consciousness. For these reasons, good things in my friend's life will be goods in my life as well.[23]

There is at least one more thing, however, that critics of nonconsequentialist egoism would probably say its proponents would need to explain. Whatever the faults of consequentialism might be, these critics might point out, at least it has an explanation of how a course of action can be

---

[22] I can also refer the reader to Aristotle's account of the value of character friendship, which is both egoistic and nonconsequentialist; see Aristotle, *Nicomachean Ethics*, Book IX, chs. 4 and 9. Another example would be Rand's account of love relationships, which is actually rather similar to Aristotle's account of character friendship, and which can be found dramatized and discussed in various passages in *Atlas Shrugged*, but especially in the character Francisco d'Anconia's speech about the meaning of sex (Rand, *Atlas Shrugged*, pp. 489–95).

[23] The fundamental idea that underlies what I have just said is a point made in a number of ways by Aristotle: my friend and the good of my friend can be valuable in themselves and for me, if only because my being conscious of them is valuable in the same ways. An episode from Ayn Rand's life illustrates this idea vividly. In a letter to John Hospers, she explained why a favorable letter from him about a book she had just published was more important to her than a blisteringly unfavorable review in *Newsweek*: "It is not an issue of how many people will see your letter vs. how many people will see the review. Your letter proves the existence of a man of intelligence and integrity; the review proves the existence of a fool and a knave. The first is important, the second is not. (Or, to use *your* terms: the existence of the former is an 'intrinsic' good—while the existence of the latter is not even an instrumental evil.)" Michael S. Berliner, ed., *The Letters of Ayn Rand* (New York: Dutton, 1995), p. 562. It would not be so plausible to say that, if Hospers had written the same letter to someone else and Rand had never learned of it, the letter and its author would still be "intrinsic" goods (i.e., good in themselves) for her. But she does know about them, and that in itself seems to suffice to give them that status. This suggests a solution to a problem that I have so far not touched on directly: What about the good of strangers? To avoid wildly counterintuitive results, it seems that the nonconsequentialist egoist would need to show how the good of strangers, and not just the good of my friends, can to some degree be included in my own good as a part. The solution I have in mind would be based on the notion that strangers I do not know about pose no ethical problems, but once I become aware of them, to some extent my consciousness of their weal or woe adds to mine.

good for or of value to me and not to someone else. Supposing that this explanation is not adequate, what is it that *does* make the things we do good for, of value to, or in the interests of one person rather than another?

This, of course, is a reasonable question and must be answered by any theory that claims to be egoistic. All I am prepared to do here is to make a few comments about how one sort of answer can begin. We can find an interesting clue to an answer in a comment that Rand makes immediately after she presents the definition of sacrifice I quoted in Section III above:

> The rational principle of conduct is the exact opposite [of sacrifice]: always act in accordance with the hierarchy of your values, and never sacrifice a greater value to a lesser one. This . . . requires that one possess a defined hierarchy of *rational* values (values chosen and validated by a rational standard). Without such a hierarchy, neither rational conduct nor considered value judgments nor moral choices are possible.[24]

Presumably, the exact opposite of sacrifice would be doing what is in one's own interest. The argument involved here seems to be this. The reason it would be a sacrifice on my part to save the lives of ten women I do not know while letting my own wife die is that it would involve preferring a lesser value to a greater one. In that case, the reason a particular act is an instance of acting in my own interest must be that it would involve preferring a greater value to a lesser one. Of course, it is possible for people to have perverse or foolish values or to rank their values in perverse or foolish ways, so not just any values will count. There must be a way to limit which ones count. The way that Rand uses is the same as the one employed by the Stoics: the values and their ranking must be rational.[25] Given that assumption, a course of action will be in your interest—and thus of value to you or good for you—if it meets two conditions: first, that it is in accordance with your values, and, second, that your values and their hierarchical order are rational.

Of course, this way of answering our question is no doubt apt to be controversial, in no small part because some people would disagree with the conception of reason it employs. Given my rather limited objectives, I will confine my comments to two other aspects of this answer, ones that should be considerably less controversial.

First, the explanation of self-interest Rand has given is plainly a flourishing-based one. Describing a settled hierarchy of values is equivalent to describing a way of life: the sort of life that is lived on the basis of that hierarchy. She has explained what self-interest is, not by tracing the consequences of the actions involved, but by asserting that self-

---

[24] Rand, "The Ethics of Emergencies," p. 44.
[25] See Epictetus, *The Discourses*, I.2 and I.4.

interest must fit into a way of life, one that is good or the best, and by offering an account of what it is that makes this life good or the best.[26]

Second, this way of explaining self-interest leads very naturally to an explanation of virtue or, more precisely, of why certain traits have the status of virtues. Many traits that are traditionally viewed as vices could be seen as errors which involve valuing something too much or too little. Cowardice is valuing safety too highly, for instance, and gluttony is valuing certain pleasures too highly. The contrary virtues, then, would seem to consist in placing the right value on the same goods, neither valuing them too much nor too little. This is precisely what having a rational hierarchy of values would mean. This, on the flourishing-based notion of self-interest we are now considering, can explain why they *are* virtues. They are essential to human well-being, not because they lead to it, in a consequentialist sense, but because they are constitutive of it. The order that these traits bring to our values is what well-being is, or an essential part of it.[27]

VII. VIRTUE AND SELF-INTEREST, AGAIN

If we adopt the flourishing-based explanation of self-interest, ethical egoism loses some of the wildly counterintuitive appearance it is apt to present on first hearing. It is, in that case, not liable to the two rather obvious objections I have discussed, which might otherwise provoke rea-

[26] This may be the place to briefly raise an exegetical issue. Tara Smith and Irfan Khawaja have pointed out to me that Rand, in one of her later writings, uses strongly consequentialist language which appears to conflict with the nonconsequentialist interpretation of her position that I am presenting here. See Rand, "Causality versus Duty," in her *Philosophy: Who Needs It?* (New York: Signet, 1982). In the main, this essay is a critique of Kantian deontology on the grounds that thinking in terms of consequences and, more generally, causal thinking, is absolutely essential to rationality. I think the first thing to say about this is that this argument is, so far, perfectly consistent with the view I am attributing to Rand. Nonconsequentialist egoism does not claim (as deontology does) that thinking in terms of consequences does not belong in the ethical realm; it only denies the consequentialist claim that nothing else *does* belong there. It can also claim (what seems clearly true) that thinking in terms of consequences (e.g., Will this food nourish me or poison me?) is an absolutely indispensable part of discerning what one's interests are. It only denies that the relationship between them is identity. There is, however, one passage in which Rand seems to go beyond this and claim that thinking in terms of consequences *is* identical to rationality in ethics ("Causality versus Duty," p. 99, third full paragraph). I would argue that here she is falling into the understandable temptation of overstating the difference between herself and Kant, and that the argument she is giving in that passage can be stated in overtly nonconsequentialist terms.

[27] If we introduce the assumption that the function of virtue is precisely to maintain this rational hierarchy of values, then virtue and self-interest would appear to be very nearly the same thing. The idea that something like this is indeed the case is typical of philosophers in the tradition of flourishing-based egoism, including Plato, Aristotle, and the Stoics. For an insightful discussion of the views of the Stoics on this issue, see Michael Slote's comments on Stoicism and Epicureanism as opposed forms of ethical egoism in *From Morality to Virtue*, pp. 201–10. The Epicureans, of course, were proponents of consequentialist egoism.

sonable people to reject it. Of course, one might still reject it on other grounds, and nothing I have said here is meant to affect that possibility.

Nonetheless, I hope that what we have seen here might prove to be useful even to people who have no interest in this particular ethical doctrine. After all, the features of the consequentialist notion of self-interest that give the egoistic doctrines that make use of it their strange and repugnant appearance are problematic for nonegoists as well. The consequences that we have seen following from the idea that self-interest is simply a matter of the causal outcome of one's acts make the notion unattractive for any sort of ethical use at all. If this is what self-interest is, then pursuing it would seem to require a state of mind dominated by a calculating sort of attitude toward the future, and toward other people. In particular, the attitude toward other people that would seem to be required is manipulative and possibly dishonest. To try to explain the value of a virtue by connecting it with self-interest in this sense is to degrade it somewhat, to make it seem less lofty than other virtues. It is very natural to try to segregate an idea like self-interest from all issues having to do with ethical merit. That, of course, is just what the post-Hobbesian tradition did.

On the other hand, if we accept an appropriate flourishing-based explanation of self-interest, it becomes equally natural to see self-interest and considerations of merit as far more closely related.[28] This is true even if one balks at making the relation as close as the ethical egoist does. In particular, the ancient, flourishing-based conceptions of self-interest have an especially close connection with the ancient and long-ignored notion of virtue. At the very least, such notions of self-interest can explain why certain traits are virtues: they are traits that maintain a properly hierarchical relationship among the values that the agent holds. This is surely an important fact even if one holds that self-interest is not the *full* explanation of why these traits are virtues, and even if one thinks that there are other virtues to which this explanation does not apply.[29]

Egoists are distinguished by the fact that they hold that self-interest in some sense is *the* explanation for one feature or another of the ethical

---

[28] I cannot resist making the following comment, which will have to wait for fuller development. One could say that what flourishing traditionally did for the concept of self-interest is precisely analogous to what virtue traditionally did for the concept of ethical merit. In both cases, there is a certain shift from the act to the agent and from the episodic to the settled and the structural. When we evaluate what a person does from a virtue-based point of view, we do so on the basis of what an act indicates about the person who performed it, and the things that it indicates are relatively enduring aspects of the person. In that case, the value of the act is explained by the sort of life of which it is a part. This is exactly what happens when we understand self-interest by way of the notion of flourishing.

[29] I should mention that, according to my own view of these matters, there are a number of radically different sorts of virtues, and only one of them has the hierarchy-preserving function that is essential to the argument I have just given. See my *Character and Culture*, chs. 1–4. The virtues that do have this function are the subject of ch. 2. It would take us too far afield to discuss how self-interest and egoism are related to the other sorts of virtues and, to tell the truth, my views on this subject are presently amorphous and changing.

realm, and perhaps of the entire realm itself. In a way, they are monists. Those who resist monistic views can at least be open to the possibility that self-interest is *an* explanation. To the extent that one accepts the flourishing-based explanation of self-interest, this possibility ought to be an attractive one. Then another possibility will arise, as eminently worthy of exploration: that at least *part* of the point of ethics is that, as Abelard was trying to tell us, it is good for us.

Philosophy, University of Wisconsin–Madison

THE IDEA OF A LIFE PLAN

By Charles Larmore

En échange de ce que l'imagination laisse attendre et que nous nous donnons inutilement tant de peine pour essayer de découvrir, la vie nous donne quelque chose que nous étions bien loin d'imaginer.

—Marcel Proust[1]

I. Introduction

When philosophers undertake to say what it is that makes life worth living, they generally display a procrustean habit of thought which the practice of philosophy itself does much to encourage. As a result, they arrive at an image of the human good that is far more controversial than they suspect. The canonical view among philosophers ancient and modern has been, in essence, that the life lived well is the life lived in accord with a rational plan. To me this conception of the human good seems manifestly wrong. The idea that life should be the object of a plan is false to the human condition. It misses the important truth which Proust, by contrast, discerned and made into one of the organizing themes of his great meditation on disappointment and revelation, *A la recherche du temps perdu*: The happiness that life affords is less often the good we have reason to pursue than the good that befalls us unexpectedly.

The mistake to which I refer has molded the way that philosophy on the whole has dealt with the most fundamental question we ask ourselves, the question of how we are to live our lives. I do not believe that there has been anything inevitable about this development, anything inherent in the philosophical enterprise that has led to the mistaken ideal of a life plan. It is not the very nature of philosophy which is to blame, for philosophy really has no essence beyond the goal of comprehensive understanding, and that may mean a great many things. But I am convinced that philosophers have by and large proceeded on the wrong track in dealing with this question, and that their error is more than accidental, stemming as it does from what has been one of their abiding preoccupations.

Before explaining this point further, I should indicate what precisely I believe is wrong in the idea of a life plan. The mistake lies at its very core, in the basic attitude toward life to which it gives expression. That attitude

---

[1] Marcel Proust, *Albertine Disparue* (Paris: Gallimard/Folio, 1992), p. 83. "In exchange for what our imagination leads us to expect and which we vainly give ourselves so much trouble to try to discover, life gives us something which we were very far from imagining."

is the view that a life is something we are to lead and not something we should allow to happen to us. We flourish as human beings, it supposes, only if we shape our lives ourselves, instead of leaving them to be the hostages of circumstance and whim. If this is our outlook, then we should obviously seek to live in accord with some unified conception of our overall purposes and of the ways to achieve them. In other words, we should devise for ourselves some "plan of life" at least in its broad strokes, if not fine-tuned in its smallest details. To the extent that we work out our plan in a rational way, giving due weight to our beliefs about what is valuable, our knowledge of our own abilities, and our grasp of the possibilities the world provides, we will have determined the character of our good and the way to achieve it. Success is not guaranteed, of course; but we will have done the best we could.

This conception of life seems perhaps so sensible that we may wonder what could be amiss. The rub, I am inclined to say, is that it is too sensible. But no doubt the better and more straightforward way to put the objection is by observing that this frame of mind embodies too great a timidity in the face of the power that experience has to change our sense of what makes life worth living. Its guiding assumption is that we should take charge of our lives, bringing them under our rule as best we can. And yet we go wrong in making so much of a contrast between leading a life and letting life happen to us. The good lies between these two extremes. It belongs to a life that is not just led but met with as well, a life that is both self-directed and shaped from without. We miss an important aspect of what gives our lives meaning, when we suppose that we live well by living in accord with an all-embracing plan of our own devising. The happy life spans, not just the good we plan for, but also the unlooked-for good which befalls us.

The basis of my opposition to the idea of a life plan is not, I should observe, the age-old perception that the best-laid schemes of mice and men go oft awry. Our plans, when we put them into practice, certainly risk defeat at the hands of reality. And disappointment may seem inescapable when so complicated a matter as life itself is made the object of a plan. Many people have raised this sort of difficulty, none perhaps so movingly as Samuel Johnson in *Rasselas* (published in 1759). In this novel, the young prince Rasselas, cloyed by his pampered existence in the Happy Valley, escapes to make his own way in the world. His faith is that with experience will come the ability to make, as he says, the proper "choice of life." But Imlac, his tutor, tries to disabuse him of this hope. Our grasp of how the world is put together is too unreliable for any such choice to stand a real chance of success. "The causes of good and evil," Imlac insists,

> are so various and uncertain, so often entangled with each other, so diversified by various relations, and so much subject to accidents

which cannot be foreseen that he who would fix his condition upon
incontestable reasons of preference, must live and die inquiring and
deliberating. . . . Very few live by choice. Every man is placed in his
present condition by causes which acted without his foresight, and
with which he did not always willingly cooperate.[2]

There is considerable wisdom in these observations, but they do not
really suffice to undermine the idea of a life plan. Snarled and unpredict-
able though the ways of the world may be, we can set our sights on ends
whose achievement seems minimally imperiled by chance or misfortune.
To choose our purposes with an eye to lessening the likelihood of frustration has been, after all, the almost universal advice of the philosophical
tradition, the grounds on which it has often elevated, for example, the life
of virtue above the pursuit of more fickle goods such as honor or wealth.
Probably no way of life can escape altogether the play of luck.[3] But the
fragility of whatever good we may achieve is not the point I am concerned to make.

My protest against the idea of a life plan is of a different and more
fundamental kind. It arises not from the precariousness of our plans, but
rather from the drawbacks of planning. A significant dimension of the
human good escapes us if we believe that our attitude toward life must
be at bottom one of foresight and control, as the idea of a life plan entails.
On the contrary, we live well when we are not simply active, but passive
too. There is an openness to life's surprises which we do well to maintain.
For the unexpected can turn out to be, not just the mishap that defeats our
plans, but also the revelation that discloses new vistas of meaning, new
forms of happiness and understanding which we least suspected or never
imagined and which may change our lives and who we are in the deepest
ways.[4] Sometimes we then learn that we have been mistaken in the things
we have hitherto had reason to value. Other times we find simply that we
must add a new element to our notion of our good (though the addition
often ends up affecting the complexion of our other commitments as
well).

The unexpected good, I thus assume, possesses a certain "objectivity."
It is something we discover, something whose value we could not appreciate in the light of all that we thought and felt before, but come to grasp
only in and through new experience. That the good in general need not
be a projection of desire, but rather can offer a standard by which to judge
our existing preferences, is not an assumption I will argue for here. I

---

[2] Samuel Johnson, *The History of Rasselas, Prince of Abissinia* (1759; London: Penguin, 1976),
ch. 16.

[3] This is the theme of Martha Nussbaum's magnificent book *The Fragility of Goodness*
(Cambridge: Cambridge University Press, 1986).

[4] In this essay I elaborate a thesis which I first sketched in *The Romantic Legacy* (New York:
Columbia University Press, 1996), p. 95.

simply observe that it is a way we ordinarily think of some goods, if we are not under the sway of particular philosophical theories.[5]

There are two important roles the unforeseen good can play in our lives, and, though connected, they need to be distinguished. The first is that our conception of our good, drawing as it does on previous experience, is bound to fall short of the forms of value which life has yet to show us. Though this fact acquires a greater significance in societies such as our own where circumstances tend to change dramatically and unpredictably, and usually not for the worse (as was the rule in premodern times), it has always been part of the human condition, and not least because the unexpected good may also come through memory, when new experience amounts to a novel reappropriation of old. The second role involves an element of reflection. It is that being surprised by a good of which we had no inkling is itself an invaluable element of what makes life worth living. Our lives would be the poorer, if our happiness unfolded perfectly according to plan.

I do not deny, of course, that planning has an important place in life. But the vital thing is to see that life itself is not properly the object of a plan. Many factors may impel us to miss this truth. The error is not limited to philosophy. It represents a temptation to which anyone, once bruised by life's vicissitudes, can succumb. All the same, this conception seems to me to have the stamp of a philosophical prejudice as well. The near unanimity with which philosophers have embraced it is not accidental. The idea of a life plan grows out of what has been one of philosophy's characteristic aspirations, fueled by a notion of reason which has always enjoyed a certain plausibility.

Let me explain. That the human mind should be able, in principle, to make sense of how everything ultimately hangs together is a thesis on which philosophers have always disagreed. But the rational transparency of the world, though scarcely an uncontested article of faith, has proven to be a widely influential notion nonetheless. It has been taken to be the goal which our picture of the world should approximate as much as possible. And, most importantly, philosophers have almost without exception believed it to be a demand of reason that we create in our own lives the sort of rational order which we seek, with perhaps only variable success, in the world around us. A life of reason would be one whose various activities were governed by overarching principles, which assign these activities their appropriate and mutually harmonious places—in other words, a life we regulate ourselves in accord with a plan. Such a life has seemed indeed to offer the best security against the failures we are likely to encounter in trying to achieve a comprehensive understanding of the world. I do not say that the notion of rational conduct has to

---

[5] Cf. Charles Taylor's idea of "strong evaluation" in "What Is Human Agency?" in Taylor, *Philosophical Papers*, vol. I (Cambridge: Cambridge University Press, 1985), pp. 15–44.

assume this form. But this is the direction in which the philosophical imagination naturally moves.

II. Ancient Roots

Today the idea of a life plan is rightly associated with John Rawls and the systematic exposition he gave it in his *A Theory of Justice*.[6] (My discussion so far bears the mark of his account.) But the idea goes back to the beginnings of moral philosophy. I suspect that it plays an important role in Socrates' famous declaration that "the unexamined life is not worth living."[7] It will be helpful in any case if I bring out the other significant assumptions at work in that Socratic proposition, for then we may get a firmer grasp of what is special about the belief that flourishing requires a rational plan of life.

The idea that only the examined life can be worth living may seem little better than a truism. Yet in reality this impression shows how accustomed we have grown to conceiving of the good life along the line of thought that Socrates (or Plato at least) did much to introduce. The Socratic claim is not so innocent as it may appear. The most obvious among its key elements is the conviction that a life as a whole, and not simply this course of action or that trait of character, can become the object of ethical evaluation. This assumption is certainly not beyond question. Convinced as I am that philosophical thinking has gone wrong in its devotion to the idea of a life plan, I have sometimes wondered whether the fault does not lie with the very notion that a life in its entirety might count as good or bad. Yet I continue to share that assumption here—if only to present an image of the good life which gives a subordinate role to planning and which appears more faithful to the dynamics of human experience.

There is another presupposition no doubt underlying Socrates' statement that is more problematic. It is that in reflecting upon our life as a whole we are to look at it from the outside—timelessly, as it were. Though we begin our thinking in the present, we are to regard our life as spread out in time, not only giving each point equal consideration, but also looking beyond our commitments of the moment as we determine how our life would go best. Bernard Williams, who has done much to illuminate the presuppositions of the Socratic standpoint, has given considerable attention to this assumption and has attacked it directly.[8]

I shall have occasion later to look more closely at Williams's argument and at its relation to the error I find in the idea of a life plan. But for now

---

[6] See in particular John Rawls, *A Theory of Justice* (Cambridge, MA: Harvard University Press, 1971), section 63.

[7] Plato, *Apology*, 38a.

[8] Bernard Williams, *Ethics and the Limits of Philosophy* (Cambridge, MA: Harvard University Press, 1985), pp. 4, 19.

we may note that the object of Williams's discontent seems to be a different assumption about what it is to reflect upon the nature of the good
life than the one which interests me. His focus is the standpoint from
which such deliberation should supposedly proceed, whereas my concern lies with the sort of result—the construction of a life plan—to which
it has been supposed to lead. The one topic has to do with where we
reason from, the other with what we reason to.

We would not go wrong, I believe, if we saw in Socrates' commitment
to the examined life this further assumption as well, that is, the idea that
the good life is one lived in accord with a plan. For example, the Myth of
Er at the end of Plato's *Republic* seems intended to illustrate the belief that
ultimately each of us chooses, more or less thoughtfully and so for better
or worse, the sort of life we lead. Socrates (or rather Plato speaking
through him) explains the moral thus:

> That is why our chief concern should be to put aside all other forms
> of knowledge, and seek to discern that which will show us how to
> perceive and find someone who will give us knowledge and ability
> to tell a good life from a bad one and always choose the better one so
> far as possible.[9]

To some it may seem that my remarks read too much into Socrates'
statement that only the examined life is worth living. Obviously, any
account of the opinions supposedly advocated by the historical Socrates
will be conjectural. And besides, there are good reasons not to assume
without question that the words Plato puts into Socrates' mouth represent
the latter's own convictions—an element of uncertainty only compounded
by the notorious difficulties bound up in deciding how to interpret Plato's
myths. But whatever hesitation we may feel about saying what Socrates
or Plato thought about this matter, there can be no dispute about the
allegiance that other ancient philosophers showed to the ideal of a life
plan. Consider, for example, the words with which Aristotle begins his
discussion of the good life in the *Eudemian Ethics*:

> Everyone who can live according to his own choice should adopt
> some goal for the good life (*tina skopon tou kalos zen thesthai*), be it
> honor or reputation or wealth or culture—a goal that he will keep in
> view in all his actions. (For not to have ordered one's life in relation
> to some end is a sign of extreme folly.) Therefore, before all else, he
> should settle in his own mind, neither hastily nor carelessly, in which

---

[9] Plato, *Republic*, 618c. The Myth of Er describes an afterworld where souls, who are about
to be reborn, choose the sort of life which they will lead.

of our concerns living well consists, and what are the things which make it possible for human beings.[10]

One could not hope for a clearer statement of the view that the good life depends on organizing our existence around a plan, choosing all our actions with a view to making possible the overall goal we have set for ourselves. For Aristotle, as John Cooper has rightly observed, "it is re-pugnant ... to our idea of what it is for a human being to flourish, to allow that anyone is flourishing except insofar as he has taken charge of his own life."[11] Either planning or folly—that is the alternative Aristotle presents us with. Since the choice is clear, or so it seems to him, our business must be to determine what is the plan of life which reason recommends—a question which in this ethical treatise, as in others, Ar-istotle goes on to answer.

I will not run through all the different thinkers, from ancient to modern times, who have endorsed the assumption that the good life is one which relies upon a plan.[12] In some regards, such a survey would be very useful. It would make plain how extensive the commitment to this assumption has been; it might also serve to bring out some significant differences of emphasis within this enduring tradition. However, my interest lies prin-cipally in the cogency of the notion of a life plan. To pursue this question systematically, I can do no better than to look in detail at Rawls's expo-sition of the idea. It is philosophically the most elaborate account there is and the one which has become authoritative for our time.[13]

III. THE RAWLSIAN CONCEPTION

Rawls models his account of a life plan on some striking formulations in the lectures on ethics which Josiah Royce published in 1908 under the title *The Philosophy of Loyalty*. "A person, an individual self," Royce de-

[10] Aristotle, *Eudemian Ethics*, trans. Michael Woods (Oxford: Clarendon Press, 1982), Book 1, ch. 2, 1214b7–13.

[11] John M. Cooper, *Reason and Human Good in Aristotle* (Cambridge, MA: Harvard University Press, 1975), p. 125.

[12] For elements of a bibliography, see John Finnis, *Natural Law and Natural Rights* (Oxford: Oxford University Press, 1980), pp. 129–30.

[13] I shall be examining Rawls's notion of a rational life plan as an overall moral ideal, abstracting from the political role he gives it in *A Theory of Justice*. In later writings, Rawls has said that he wishes that notion, along with the associated account of goodness as rationality, to be understood simply as part of a political conception, and not as an element of a comprehensive moral doctrine (Rawls, *Political Liberalism* [New York: Columbia University Press, 1993], pp. 176–77n.). I am unsure whether my criticisms touch the more circumscribed status he now assigns to the idea of a life plan, or whether, more generally, they have an important bearing on the foundations of a liberal theory of justice. Here I am pursuing a topic in ethics, and my reason for taking Rawls's views out of their political context is that they constitute by far the most powerful statement of the outlook I mean to question.

clared, "may be defined as a human life lived according to a plan." The point is that our identity, whatever unity of self we possess, consists in our goals and the degree of consilience among them. "The answer to the question, 'Who are you?' really begins in earnest," Royce wrote, "when a man mentions his calling, and so actually sets out upon the definition of his purposes and of the way in which these purposes get expressed in his life."[14]

There is certainly something right about the view Royce expounds. The question is whether it goes deep enough. Our self-understanding may indeed find expression in our aims. But rooted as it is in our past experience, does it not also involve the memory of things which have fortunately happened to us despite our goals at the time? If this is so, then though our self-conception revolves around our purposes, it does not follow that our good is determined by the purposes we pursue. Our good may instead involve the sort of bafflement of our aims which provokes us to change our idea of who we are. Rawls, however, seems to believe that if our self-conception is defined by our purposes, our individual good is so defined as well. For from Royce's notion of the person Rawls moves directly to the proposition which forms the center of his theory of the good life: "The rational plan for a person," he holds, "determines his good."[15]

This statement is the epitome of the outlook that I reject. It allows Rawls to conclude that happiness consists in the successful execution of a rational plan of life.[16] Yet the happy life, as I conceive it, cannot be in this way so much a matter of our own making—and not just because of the fact that, as Rawls himself notes, the conditions under which we draw up a life plan are never under our complete control and may prove too unpropitious for the design of any life worth calling happy. Instead, the objection is that we are never in a position to grasp in advance the full character of our good, even in its broad outline. As a result, our happiness includes not just the anticipated good we achieve, but also the unexpected good which happens to us. It even involves this very experience of surprise.

What is the line of thought by which Rawls arrives at his thesis that a person's rational plan of life determines his good? It is important to retrace his steps carefully, so that we may locate precisely where the error lies.

Rawls's idea of a life plan grows out of a general theory of the good, a theory which seeks to explicate goodness in terms of rationality. In general, he writes, "A is a good X, if and only if A has the properties (to a higher degree than the average or standard X) which it is rational to want

---

[14] Josiah Royce, *The Philosophy of Loyalty* (New York: Macmillan, 1908), p. 168.
[15] Rawls, *A Theory of Justice*, p. 408; see also pp. 421, 424.
[16] *Ibid.*, pp. 93, 409, 548–60.

in an X." In the same spirit, something will be good for a person if and only if the thing has the properties which it is rational for that person to want in it, given his "circumstances, abilities, and plan of life (system of aims)."[17] Even with this definition, however, we still have an inadequate, incompletely objective notion of the good. For if goodness is understood along these lines, a thing will not count as truly good unless the grounds on which the person determines what he should want can themselves be certified as rational. That is why Rawls directs himself to the question of what it is that makes a life plan rational. Such a plan is rational, he holds, when it accords with the principles of rational choice and is such as would be chosen by the person with "full deliberative rationality, that is, with full awareness of the relevant facts and after a careful consideration of the consequences."[18]

In one sense, Rawls observes, the life plan which determines a person's good depends on purposes he can formulate at the time of the plan's conception. Thus, there is an essential reference to the present in the reasoning by which life plans are to be constructed. "A person's future good on the whole," Rawls writes, is "what he would now desire and seek if the consequences of all the various courses of conduct open to him were, at the present point of time, accurately foreseen by him and adequately realized in imagination."[19] Yet the role this proposition gives to the present supposedly entails no more than the trivial fact that it is always in the present that we deliberate. What we are reflecting about clearly extends beyond the present, and the way we are to carry out our deliberation aims at neutralizing any substantial kind of dependence on the given moment. According to Rawls, we are to give full consideration to all of our possibilities and to look to our future good as a whole. That means that we are not to determine the nature of our good by appealing simply to our commitments at the time, for they too must be pondered and weighed. Reflecting upon our life as a whole, we are to stand free from the perspective of any particular moment within it. We are no less our later selves than the person we are now, and thus our choice of a life plan should find its footing in our identity across time.

Deliberative rationality, so Rawls gives us to understand,[20] is impartial, not just in its basis, but in its object too. That is, it also requires that we show an equal regard for all moments of our life. No life plan is rational if it resorts to "pure time-preference." It may not accord greater weight to interests we have at one time—and, in particular, to the interests we have

----

[17] *Ibid.*, p. 399.
[18] *Ibid.*, p. 408. More exactly, a person's plan is "subjectively rational" if it is based on an accurate conception of his existing wants and the available knowledge concerning the consequences of his actions; it is also "objectively rational" if the future actually goes as he supposes (pp. 417, 422).
[19] *Ibid.*, pp. 416–17.
[20] See *ibid.*, p. 420.

at present—than to those we would have at another, simply because of their difference in time. On the contrary, the preference given to some interests over others must reflect the belief that they contribute more to our good as a whole.

In general, we could say that Rawls's notion of deliberative rationality is really prudence under another name, that is, the careful management of life's affairs. Prudence, of course, is no guarantee of happiness. Our plan of life, though rational, may be defeated by events we could not have foreseen. But in Rawls's view prudence does ensure that, should we be disappointed by unexpected developments, we still will have nothing to blame ourselves for.[21] We will have done the best we could. No doubt this sort of satisfaction forms, for Rawls as for others, one of the preeminent values in the idea of a life plan.

IV. Some Other Objections

Such, at least at first approximation (more details will prove necessary later), is the line of argument by which Rawls works out his conception of a life plan and gives it the pivotal role in his theory of the good life. A number of steps might be reasonably contested—not just the neglect of unexpected goods which I have been concerned to emphasize, though that, I believe, is the fundamental issue. Before showing at what stage this error makes its appearance, I want to consider two other objections which Rawls's argument has aroused. These criticisms are important, even if they do not latch onto what is crucially amiss. They provide, in fact, a helpful contrast to the point I wish to make.

The first of these objections is that Rawls has lost touch with the natural rhythm of human finitude. By defining an individual's good in terms of a life plan, he contradicts the shape our lives inevitably take by virtue of the fact that we are born and die.[22] We begin life as children. And though children should certainly imagine and act out various ways of life, those who trade this play for planning, weighing their interests and capacities, making up their mind about their goal in life and devoting themselves to achieving it are a dreary lot, who have missed the blessings of childhood. Prudence about life is a "relative virtue," as Michael Slote has said: it does not fit every period of life. It is desirable when we are grown up, but not when we are young. To say that our rational plan of life determines our good cannot therefore be right as a general claim. It forgets that we are not always adults.

---

[21] *Ibid.*, p. 422. A rational person, Rawls there observes, "does what seems best at the time, and if his beliefs later prove to be mistaken with untoward results, it is through no fault of his own. There is no cause for self-reproach."

[22] A fine development of this objection is to be found in Michael Slote, *Goods and Virtues* (Oxford: Oxford University Press, 1983), chs. 1 and 2.

It also forgets—so the objection continues—the other end of our finite condition, the fact that we die and die at a roughly foreseeable age, at least in the natural course of events. On Rawls's telling, a rational plan of life gives equal weight to all the moments of one's life; it refuses pure time-preference. But in reality, it is argued, a proper sense of mortality makes us anything but impartial with respect to time. Not only do we accord greater importance to that part of our life when we are at the height of our powers than to childhood or senescence, but we also give priority within that period to later over earlier moments. That is, we prefer the life in which failure gives way to success, to one marked by success and failure of a similar magnitude occurring in the opposite order. We do so because we are mortal and, knowing that our lives will end, want them to end well. We want them to achieve a form of completion.[23] If our life extended indefinitely before us, we would not regard the order of success and failure (if they were of finite duration) as inherently significant; for after every failure there would always be more than enough time to make up for it.

This objection has a mixed validity. Though earlier and later moments may well enjoy within the prime of life a differential significance, the pure time-preference which Rawls excludes is not thereby legitimated. If later success counts for more than the same success at an earlier time, that is not because of temporal position alone, but because the biological givens of birth and death invest the human good with a certain inevitable shape. This fact does not conflict with the idea of rationality that Rawls assigns to the construction of a life plan. It simply makes more specific the form such deliberation must take for beings who are mortal as we are. Indeed, this first objection as a whole does not really question the primacy of prudence in the composition of the good life. It rightly observes that a life plan has no proper role to play in the goods of childhood. But it says nothing to challenge the assumption that mature persons should bring their lives under the rule of a rational plan.[24]

A second prominent objection to Rawls's argument also takes issue with the idea that deliberative rationality looks beyond the present. Here, however, the focus is not the axiom forbidding "time-preference" in the content of a life plan, but rather the ambition of transcending the local perspective defined by our present concerns as we think about our life as a whole. If the first objection urges us to retain a sense of the finitude of the life we deliberate about, the second seeks to remind us that in this

[23] Cf. Robert Nozick's reflections on the "narrative direction" of the happy life, in *The Examined Life* (New York: Simon and Schuster, 1989), pp. 100–102.

[24] In his presentation of the objection just described, Slote introduces some interesting criticisms of this assumption as well (*Goods and Virtues*, pp. 43–45). There is also a very suggestive critique of this assumption in Martin Seel, *Versuch über die Form des Glücks* (Frankfurt: Suhrkamp, 1996), pp. 102–13.

matter as in others deliberation is always situated, dependent upon the beliefs and interests which are ours at the time.

This objection we have met before. It is Bernard Williams's complaint about the timeless form into which Socrates cast the question "How should one live?" And Williams has brought the same charge against Rawls's conception of what it is to devise a life plan. "The perspective of deliberative choice on one's life," Williams argues, "is constitutively *from here*."[25] In other words, the fact that our deliberation takes place in the present is not so trivial as it may seem. The results of practical deliberation—as I understand the gist of Williams's argument—cannot be more substantive than the premises from which it sets out. Present commitments can certainly be weighed and may be revised, but not in a wholesale fashion, for our examination of them must rely on the materials at hand. As a result, our thinking, even when directed toward our life as a whole, must draw its bearings from our present perspective. It always carries the mark of where we are at the time.

With the validity of this thesis I am in complete accord. There is no escape from time, no means by which reason may transcend history and still prove to be any sort of guide to thought or action. The point has often been made before, though apparently it cannot be repeated enough.[26] No doubt the trouble involves yet another deep-seated philosophical illusion.

Williams himself, I should add, finds something more than I do in this substantial rootedness of deliberation in the here and now. For he believes that it serves to distinguish practical from theoretical reason. Our scientific beliefs aim to view the world as independently as possible from our historical or local context, in contrast to deliberation about action, which in his view concerns essentially what we should do as the situated beings we are:

> My life, my action is quite irreducibly mine, and to require that it is at best a *derivative* conclusion that it should be lived from the perspective that happens to be mine is an extraordinary misunderstanding. Yet it is the idea that is implicitly contained in the model of the point of view of the universe.[27]

I cannot see the sense of this distinction between theory and practice. Williams's dichotomy is unfounded. On the one hand, objectivity does not cease to be the aim of science once we admit, as certainly we should,

---

[25] Bernard Williams, *Moral Luck* (Cambridge: Cambridge University Press, 1981), p. 35.

[26] I develop the point somewhat in *The Morals of Modernity* (Cambridge: Cambridge University Press, 1996), particularly in ch. 2.

[27] Bernard Williams, *Making Sense of Humanity* (Cambridge: Cambridge University Press, 1995), p. 170; see also Williams, *Ethics and the Limits of Philosophy*, pp. 67–69.

that our conception of nature as it is in itself depends on what happens to be the existing state of scientific doctrine, on the beliefs we have reason to accept and the methods we have reason to deem reliable. On the other hand, we may derive what we should do, as practical beings, from impartial considerations about what anyone should do, as judged from the "point of view of the universe"—though again our reasoning, and even our conception of impartiality, will be shaped by the convictions that make up our historical context. The only difference I discern between theoretical and practical reason involves simply their subject matter: the one governs what we are to believe, the other what we are to do.[28]

But let us consider the situatedness of practical deliberation alone. In what way is this second objection supposed to cut against Rawls's conception of a life plan?

V. The Limits of Purpose

Williams argues that this objection undermines the ancient conviction, at work still in Rawls's thinking, that the prudent man lives so as to avoid self-reproach. Our decisions can never enjoy an immunity to the regret which we might feel in the future, for our later self will judge our earlier choices on the basis of the preferences which then will be ours and which will be the fruit of all that we have been and done in the meantime.[29]

About this objection I also have reservations, this time on the score of ambiguity. In one sense, it seems wrong. There is no point in reproaching ourselves for not having deliberated better than we could have in the given situation. Consider the parallel case of our attitude toward others: should we not judge the rationality (though not perhaps the worth) of another's decision in the light of his view of the world and not our own? However, on another construal the objection is valid, and then indeed it reflects the proposition I am concerned to establish. We may rightly reproach ourselves for having been prudent at all. In retrospect we may wish that, instead of weighing our options judiciously, we had acted impulsively, letting ourselves be carried away by the passions of the moment, since then a good would have been ours whose value we only now appreciate. Prudence, however important, is not the highest value, for as a matter of fact no single value is supreme. This sort of pluralism, I would say, is the very essence of my view. And it provides for one clear sense in which the prudent person cannot be certain to escape self-reproach.

Such is not, however, the direction in which Williams himself develops his remarks about regret. (Though they are compatible with this interpretation, much of what he says suggests the other interpretation I noted

---

[28] For further reflections along these lines, see my "Denken und Handeln," *Deutsche Zeitschrift für Philosophie*, vol. 45, no. 2 (1997), pp. 183–95.

[29] Williams, *Moral Luck*, pp. 34–36.

above.) Williams regards his objection to Rawls's idea of a life plan as presenting a more sensible account of deliberative rationality, one which keeps in mind the situatedness of reflection even when directed toward the course of one's life as a whole. Focusing on the way Rawls supposes a life plan is to be devised, Williams aims simply at presenting a more realistic view of prudence. As a result, his criticism does not challenge directly the notion that prudence should be the rule of life.

That is why the mistake I find in Rawls's argument lies deeper than the level at which Williams's discussion operates. Williams's objection, like the previous one, leaves intact the idea that the mature person is to understand his good in terms of a rational life plan, for the two objections urge only that this view take more seriously certain givens of the human condition, namely, our mortality and the time-boundedness of deliberation. My concern, by contrast, is to point out why that view itself is wrong. In fact, the mistake by which Rawls is led to it occurs early on in his argument—at a point, as I now shall show, prior to his exposition of the notion of a life plan.

Rawls stipulates that something is good for a person depending on his "circumstances, abilities, and plan of life." Note that this is a rather heterogeneous set of conditions. A person's circumstances and in some cases his abilities too may define, not only what he does, but also what he is or has become. Thus, something may appear good in their light yet belong among the things which happen to him, instead of among the things he pursues. It is just the opposite with a person's life plan, for it can allow something to appear good only in view of the purposes with which he acts. Now if these various conditions were understood as forming merely a list of factors any one of which might serve to determine whether something were good for a person, there would be no grounds for quarrel. But Rawls unmistakably chooses to regard them all as belonging to our purposive being. Without seeming to notice the narrowing of focus, he restates, for example, his definition of a thing's being good for a person as its having the properties which it is rational for him to want in it "in view of his interests and aims."[30] Once it is thus assumed that a person's good is to be judged by reference to his purposes, it is but a short way to Rawls's general but, in my view, erroneous conclusion that "the rational plan for a person determines his good." One need only suppose that a person's real good must be determined by his rational purposes and that their rationality depends on their being part of a life plan.

In my view, the fatal assumption is precisely the idea that what is good for a person must hinge on his purposes. Of course, a person's purposes may not match his good because he has framed them faultily, failing to recognize his abilities, past experience, or interests for what they are, or failing to reflect properly upon such information. But this is not the sort

---

[30] Rawls, *A Theory of Justice*, p. 407.

of situation I have in mind. My point is that something may form part of our good without conducing to the realization of our rational purposes and may even conflict with them. New experience may upset our existing plans, providing us reason to alter, even recast, our understanding of what our goals should be. For it can reveal forms of relationship, ways of being and acting, whose value we could never have suspected, given all that we could have known. Consider, for example, the happiness that comes with having children. No doubt we can frame some idea of it beforehand, but we cannot appreciate it truly, nor realize how it colors the value of other things we hold dear, except in and through the experience of being a parent.

The unexpected good our rational purposes do not anticipate is hardly apt to appear valuable, if judged by their light. But in this fact is expressed only the limitations of the point of view these purposes embody. It may be true that nothing unexpected could be good for a person if it did not make some sense in view of his past experience. The point in doubt, however, is whether his purposes must form the criterion for deciding that it is good. If we take to heart the fact that there are important goods which befall us contrary to all we have reason to expect, we cannot then accept the Rawlsian principle—which is the predominant view of our philosophical tradition—that "the rational plan for a person determines his good."

To distinguish my point from yet another objection one might be tempted to bring against Rawls's idea of a life plan, let me remark that I am not arguing that some goods by their very nature elude the art of planning. Spontaneity, for example, is a virtue which, as it is often said, cannot be the object of direct pursuit. True, but we may still devise methods of indirection by which we can bring ourselves into the desired state of acting unreflectively.[31] Nothing prevents spontaneity from figuring among the elements of a suitably sophisticated plan of life, as Rawls himself observes.[32] In my view, the real question is not whether certain goods cannot be sought by planning, but whether life itself can properly be the object of a plan.

Thus, I am willing to agree that for something unexpected to count as good the person must be able to integrate it into a new set of purposes. That is, he will regard it as something worthy of pursuit in the light of a revised conception of his ends which he has designed in its wake. The crux, however, is that this fact does nothing to rescue the definition of good in terms of an agent's purposes. For the unforeseen good he now pursues does not fit a purpose he had at the time, but instead is the source of the one he has subsequently devised. In this case, the good is not being judged by reference to his purposes; rather, his purposes are justified by appeal to something he understands to have been good for him.

---

[31] See Jon Elster, *Sour Grapes* (Cambridge: Cambridge University Press, 1983), ch. 2.
[32] Rawls, *A Theory of Justice*, p. 423.

We can see, therefore, what is wrong with defending the criterion of purpose by arguing that to regard something unexpected as good is tantamount to supposing we would have had reason to aim at it, had our purposes been sufficiently well-informed or rational. The objection is wrong on two counts. First, there is the point, far from negligible, that the element of surprise forms part of the value of what proves unexpectedly good and that we would live less well if our projects, however rational, were never tripped up by experiences that impel us to rethink the way we live. But the primary defect in this response is that it puts the cart before the horse. In the case at hand, it is a good—a good which befalls us—that acts as the criterion of rational purpose, and not the other way round. If our purposes at the time were rational, given what we knew, then the only way we can say that we would have aimed at the unexpected good, had we known better, is by imagining we had learned earlier than we did that, contrary to our purposes, it was good. There is no getting by the fact that rational purpose cannot suffice as a criterion of the good.

VI. Conclusion

Life is too unruly to be the object of a plan, and again not simply because our schemes may founder when applied. Obviously, we often fail to achieve the good we pursue. But more important and certainly more neglected by philosophy is the happy fact that the good we pursue, the good we have reason to pursue, is bound to fall short of the good that life has yet to reveal. From this insight we should not infer that the nature of the good life is a question not worth trying to answer since every answer will prove inadequate. It is natural to think about what elements go into making up our good, and my remarks have not been meant to deny that each of us lives, or ought to live, with an idea in mind of the good life. The target of my criticism has been the view that any such idea must be of a life we have taken charge of and brought under the rule of our own purposes. The good life is not, I have argued, the life lived in accord with a rational plan. It is the life lived with a sense of our dual nature as active and passive beings, bent on achieving the goals we espouse, but also liable to be surprised by forms of good we never anticipated. A life lived in the light of this more complex ideal can accommodate, it can even welcome, the way in which an unexpected good may challenge our existing projects. We will not thereby avoid being surprised (nor should we want to), but we will know enough not to be surprised at being surprised.

Nothing I have said should suggest, either, that planning is wrong or pointless. Prudence is an undeniable virtue, and not solely in the handling of the little things of life. We cannot hope to live well if we do not direct ourselves toward achieving goals which have a ramifying significance, which organize our various activities and give our lives meaning. But we err if we suppose that prudence is the supreme virtue and that the good life is one which unfolds in accord with a rational plan.

Some may be tempted to reply that in constructing a life plan we could always allot a certain role for the value of surprise. But this rejoinder misses the point. The sort of unexpected good whose importance I wish to underscore does not simply fill in a space left blank. It overthrows existing expectations. No doubt we could plan for a bit of surprise, if that is what we wanted to do. But this plan, like any, would have to involve some scheme of ends and means, and such schemes may always be tripped up by the good that life has yet in store.

The belief in the supremacy of prudence is mistaken for two reasons. The basic point is that, if we give life a chance, it always turns out to be richer in possibilities than the idea we have at the time of what it would be to flourish. To make our life the object of a plan, however well-informed and carefully arranged the plan might be, means closing our minds to the lessons future experience will impart. But, in addition, there is the fact that our lives would mean less if they did not contain moments of wonder and redirection, when we find that earlier choices have led to a happiness we never imagined, or when we see our existing purposes thrown into disarray by the realization that our fulfillment lies elsewhere. Not only do we then encounter a good we did not foresee, but these experiences are themselves of inestimable value, for they teach us an important truth about what it is to be human.

That truth is the essential contingency which lies at the heart of whatever, for each of us, happiness may signify. Precisely because the unexpected good can upset the most rational plans, it is best understood, not as a part of what our overall good has always been, but instead as a new turn in what our good has come to be. Had our experience gone otherwise, as it could well have done, the very meaning of our life (and not just our efforts to discern it) would have been different. We are creatures for whom the character of our good takes shape only in time and with the impress of chance. At no point does our good exist as a finished end, waiting to be discovered and made the object of pursuit. The goodness itself of what we meet with may exist independently of our recognition of it; but when a good comes to form part of our good, contrary to all we had reason to expect, our good itself has changed. Developing over the course of a lifetime, our good is in large part the fruit of experiences we stumble into, and thus is as much the unintended result of our actions as the goal they may set out to achieve. The good life outruns the reach of planning because its very nature is to be the child of time. To recognize this truth is the beginning of wisdom, for it is to understand why wisdom is something more than prudence.

Philosophy, University of Chicago

HUMAN FLOURISHING VERSUS DESIRE SATISFACTION

By Richard J. Arneson

I. Introduction

What is the good for human persons? If I am trying to lead the best possible life I could lead, not the morally best life, but the life that is best for me, what exactly am I seeking?

This phrasing of the question I will be pursuing may sound tendentious, so some explanation is needed. What is good for one person, we ordinarily suppose, can conflict with what is good for other persons and with what is required by morality. A prudent person seeks her own good efficiently; she selects the best available means to her good. If we call the value that a person seeks when she is being prudent "prudential value," then an alternative rendering of the question to be addressed in this essay is "What is prudential value?" We can also say that an individual flourishes or has a life high in well-being when her life is high in prudential value. Of course, these common-sense appearances that the good for an individual, the good for other persons, and the requirements of morality often are in conflict might be deceiving. For all that I have said here, the correct theory of individual good might yield the result that sacrificing oneself for the sake of other people or for the sake of a morally worthy cause can never occur, because helping others and being moral always maximize one's own good. But this would be the surprising result of a theory, not something we should presuppose at the start of inquiry. When a friend has a baby and I express a conventional wish that the child have a good life, I mean a life that is good for the child, not a life that merely helps others or merely respects the constraints of morality. After all, a life that is altruistic and perfectly moral, we suppose, could be a life that is pure hell for the person who lives it—a succession of horrible headaches marked by no achievements or attainments of anything worthwhile and ending in agonizing death at a young age. So the question remains, what constitutes a life that is good for the person who is living it?

Some components of a good life are good because they are efficient means to getting other goods. A college education is good (among other reasons) because it usually enables the recipient to have a higher income, and high income is good because money is a means to what-

113

ever is for sale. Our concern is with the characterization of what is intrinsically good, good for its own sake, rather than as a means to other goods.[1]

In this essay I discuss the distinction between subjective and objective theories of good (that is, well-being or prudential value). I defend a type of objective theory, the objective-list account. The defense proceeds by contrasting this account with two rivals, hedonism and desire fulfillment. These terms will be explained shortly. At several points I try to draw out the difficulties in these two rival accounts by considering internal tensions in the theory of the good developed by John Stuart Mill, which attempts to combine the advantages of hedonism and desire fulfillment by fusion. Hedonism, as I construe it, is unsatisfactory for a general reason: it implies that nothing can matter prudentially to an individual except the quality of her experience, but this seems counterintuitive. The desire-fulfillment account resolves this difficulty, but gives rise to others, and the accounting of the strengths and weaknesses of this account, especially in its refined form, is complex. The desire-fulfillment view has the resources to resist some criticisms, but succumbs to others. The devastating force of the objections against its main rivals is good news for the objective-list theory, but this theory is also subject to strong criticisms. One criticism consists in skeptical doubt that there is no uniquely rational way to determine what putative goods qualify as entries on the list. Skepticism here is a genuine worry, but not one this essay considers. But, setting aside skeptical doubt, I note another criticism that threatens to be devastating. The objective-list account allows that something I get can intrinsically enhance my well-being even though I hate it, and some will find this result puzzling or worse. A mixed or composite account deals with this latter difficulty by stipulating that nothing can intrinsically enhance an individual's well-being unless it is both truly worthwhile and also affirmed or endorsed by that very individual. Roughly speaking, this mixed view combines the desire-fulfillment theory and the objective-list theory. The essay concludes by finding grounds to resist the mixed account and to favor the pure objective-list theory.

II. SUBJECTIVE AND OBJECTIVE THEORIES

Philosophers have debated whether good is objective or subjective. Different questions have been asked under this description. Subjective theories of human good are sometimes taken to be those that "make

---

[1] In this essay I use "intrinsically" interchangeably with "for its own sake." What is good in these ways is distinguished from what is good as a means to some further goal. The distinction between what is intrinsically and extrinsically good, intended to mark a different contrast from the distinction between what is good for its own sake and what is good as a means, plays no role in this essay.

welfare depend *at least in part* on some mental state."[2] The intended contrast is with objective theories of well-being which make the well-being of an agent depend entirely on states of the world apart from the state of mind of the agent whose well-being is under review. This is a coherent usage, but a potentially confusing one. A Platonic theory which held that the good for humans was perception and understanding of the Forms would count as subjective on this usage, even though most philosophers would deem Plato's theory to be a paradigm case of an objective theory. I would prefer to let the contrast between objective and subjective mark the contrast between (1) views which hold that claims about what is good can be correct or incorrect and that the correctness of a claim about a person's good is determined independently of that person's volition, attitudes, and opinions, and (2) views which deny this. On the revised distinction, Plato's position counts as an objective theory of the good.

Derek Parfit has distinguished three types of theories about what makes someone's life go best: (1) hedonistic theories, according to which "what would be best for someone is what would make his life happiest"; (2) desire-fulfillment theories, according to which a person's good "is what, throughout his life, would best fulfill his desires"; and (3) objective-list theories, according to which, "certain things are good or bad for us, whether or not we want to have the good things, or to avoid the bad things."[3] The three theories do not exhaust the possibilities, but this is not a serious defect, because the known plausible candidates are included. The trouble with the definitions of these categories is that they do not establish the three theories as mutually exclusive and clearly counterposed. Suppose it should turn out that the objective-list contains one item, namely, happiness. In this case, (1) and (3) come to the same thing. Suppose that the objective-list contains one item, namely, desire fulfillment. In this case, (2) and (3) come to the same thing. With desire fulfillment as the sole entry on the list, the objective-list theory then holds that desire fulfillment is good for a person, and desire nonfulfillment bad, whether or not the person wants to have desire fulfillment or to avoid desire nonfulfillment.

We could secure the result that Parfit's three theories are mutually exclusive if we revise them as follows: the hedonistic theory holds that happiness, and happiness alone, is prudentially valuable for its own sake, whereas the desire-fulfillment theory holds that desire fulfillment, and only that, is prudentially valuable for its own sake, and the objective-list theory holds that more than one type of thing is prudentially valuable for its own sake. On the revised view, the essence of the objective-list theory is that there is more than one entry on the list.

[2] L. W. Sumner, *Welfare, Happiness, and Ethics* (Oxford: Oxford University Press, 1996), p. 82.
[3] Derek Parfit, *Reasons and Persons* (Oxford: Oxford University Press, 1984), p. 493.

But it would be unsatisfactory to transform the objective-list theory into the plural-entry-list theory. My main quarrel with Parfit's classification scheme is that a theory that intuitively is not an objective theory at all could qualify as a version of the objective-list theory. To see this, notice that a theory which holds that what is good for each person is definitively fixed by that very person's subjective opinions about what is good for her qualifies as an objective-list theory on Parfit's definition. We can do better by noting several claims about the nature of prudential value that play a role in classifying theories of prudential value as subjective or objective. One claim is that what is good for each person is entirely determined by that very person's evaluative perspective. Call this the claim of agent sovereignty. What I will call subjective theories affirm this claim, and objective theories deny it.

This denial, however, is not enough by itself to render a theory objective. Rejecting the name "objective-list theories" for the theories that Parfit characterizes under that name, Thomas Scanlon asserts that what "is essential is that these are theories according to which an assessment of a person's well-being involves a substantive judgement about what things make life better, a judgement which may conflict with that of the person whose well-being is in question."[4] Scanlon suggests the label "substantive good theories" for this class of views on the ground that they "are based on substantive claims about what goods, conditions, and opportunities make life better." But consider an "observer theory" of prudential value, according to which what is good for a person is fixed by the substantive judgments of some observer as to what would make the person's life go best, and what is good for a person must then be specified relative to some observer. If Smith observes that what would make Jones's life go best is eating corn, and Black observes that what would make Jones's life go best is eating peas, then, according to the observer theory, Jones's good is eating corn, relative to observer Smith, and eating peas, relative to observer Black. The observer theory fits Scanlon's characterization of a substantive good theory, but not his evident intent. Rejecting subjectivism rooted in the agent's evaluative perspective and plumping for subjectivism rooted in the observer's evaluative perspective does not yield an objective theory. The denial of the claim of agent sovereignty does not suffice to characterize an objective theory, for the same reason. So let us add to the denial of agent sovereignty the assertion that there is a fact of the matter as to what is prudentially valuable for a person, so that claims about what types of things are prudentially valuable are true or false, and thus can be mistaken, and no person's actual evaluative perspective necessarily fixes what is genuinely prudentially valuable. Call this the claim of realism about prudential value.

[4] Thomas Scanlon, "Value, Desire, and Quality of Life," in *The Quality of Life*, ed. Martha C. Nussbaum and Amartya Sen (Oxford: Clarendon Press, 1993), pp. 185–200; see p. 188. My views defended here have been strongly influenced by Scanlon's essay.

The objective-list theory of what makes someone's life go best, as I will construe it, is a complex animal. A theory of this type is one that denies the claim of agent sovereignty, asserts the claim of realism about prudential value (which includes the former denial), and asserts that there exists a plurality of types of good. Note that an objective-list theory so understood does not deny that an individual's attitudes may partly determine what is prudentially valuable for her. An individual's attitudes do not determine what items properly belong on her objective list, but among the items that appear, some may include requirements concerning her attitudes and opinions. For example, an objective-list view might well hold that one good thing for an individual is that her important life aims be satisfied, with importance determined by her own subjective ranking of her aims.

III. Subjectivity and Relativity

Subjective theories gain an unmerited halo of plausibility from the suspicion that standards of well-being cannot be the same across the class of human persons but are relative to the individual whose good is in question. But the good can be objective even if it is relative to each individual. A glance at J. S. Mill's writings on the good confirms this point.

One of the more puzzling features of Mill's analyses of human good in *Utilitarianism* and in *On Liberty* is that the two accounts are opposed on a significant point.[5] In *Utilitarianism*, Mill asserts that human good is to be equated to happiness, that happiness is pleasure and absence of pain, and that the quality of one pleasure as compared to another is determined by the preference of experienced and competent judges for one over the other. It is obvious that Mill aims to avoid the result that the welfare an individual gains from some putative good is determined by her own, perhaps idiosyncratic or confused, appraisal of her experience of the good. To achieve this end, Mill proposes an analysis with the feature, which some will find peculiar, that the value of the pleasure I get from eating a peach, compared to the value I get from a pear, is determined not by my own experience of the peach and the pear but by the preferences and judgments of a panel of fruit-tasting experts who sample each fruit.

In *On Liberty*, Mill follows a quite different line. Arguing against paternalistic restriction of individual liberty in self-regarding matters, Mill observes that what is good for each of us is set by our individual nature, which is nontransparent, and which may differ from person to person.

[5] J. S. Mill, *Utilitarianism*, in his *Collected Works*, vol. 10, ed. J. M. Robson (Toronto: University of Toronto Press, 1969), pp. 210–14; and Mill, *On Liberty*, in his *Collected Works*, vol. 18, ed. J. M. Robson (Toronto: University of Toronto Press, 1977), ch. 3, pp. 260–75.

The conventional judgments in a society about what ways of life are worthwhile may give untrustworthy guidance for a given individual for several reasons. The conventional judgments may be just mistaken. Even if they are correct as generalities, they may not apply to this individual, for her circumstances may be unusual. Moreover, even if the individual's circumstances are of the standard variety, the customs are designed to suit ordinary characters, and her character may be extraordinary. Mill is conceiving of ways of life as including both ultimate goals and plans of life to achieve the goals. Concentrating now just on the former component, we can say that for Mill in *On Liberty*, what is intrinsically good for me cannot in principle reliably be determined just by consulting the judgments of other persons even if they are reliable judges of their own good, because what is good depends on the type of person one is, and my type may differ from that of the judges. If we make the division of types of persons sufficiently fine-grained, it will turn out that each individual nature is unique, and thus what is intrinsically good may vary to some extent from person to person.

A hedonistic theory of the good of the type that Mill asserts in *Utilitarianism* can allow that what is good is relative to the individual without endorsing subjectivism about the good. According to Mill, the relative values of the pleasures available to an individual are fixed by that individual's nature. This is compatible with the further claim that the individual may be mistaken in his own assessments of quantity and quality of pleasure. But what he would be mistaken about is the quantity or quality of pleasure that he himself would derive from various sources. Where Mill seems to go wrong is in trying to fix by stipulation that the consensus of expert judgment (the judgment of other, experienced people about their own experiences) determines the quantity and quality of pleasure that I would get from one or another sort of experience. This move insists on objectivity by denying relativity to the individual, but this move is unnecessary.

IV. Is the Objective-List Theory a Theory?

There is a rudimentary theory associated with the objective-list account of the good. The theory holds that what is intrinsically good for an individual, good for its own sake rather than as a means to some further good, is to get or achieve the items that are specified on a correct and complete list of such goods. The more that one gets or achieves the listed goods over the course of one's life, the better for oneself is the life that one has lived. Different versions of the theory may stipulate that there is one list for all persons, or that there are different types of persons and a distinct list for each type, or that the objective list for each person is unique to that person. The idea of the objective list is simply that what is intrinsically good for a person is fixed independently of that person's attitudes or opinions; the items on the list for an individual are there independently of whether the individual has favorable attitudes toward them or himself judges that the items are valuable for him.

Wayne Sumner remarks that virtually all theories of the good, including subjective theories, will assert similar lists of the things that are sources of value. But a list of the things that are prudentially valuable is not the same as an account of what it is that makes something valuable for an individual. Just providing what purports to be an objective list, then, is not yet to advance an objective account of the good that can compete with subjective theories, according to Sumner. Thus, the objective list is not, according to Sumner, a candidate rival view which an advocate of subjectivism is obliged to rebut in order to provide a complete and successful defense of subjectivism.

But Sumner sweeps aside the objective-list idea too swiftly. Even if a subjective account and an objective-list account generate similar lists of things that are valuable, the status of the items on the lists is different in the two accounts. Suppose accomplishment and relations of love and friendship appear as items in both lists. For the subjectivist, the list is provisional and defeasible, at least in theory. What renders something intrinsically good for someone is that she (under the appropriate conditions specified by the particular subjective theory) has a favorable attitude toward it. If it turns out that our lore about what people will in fact regard favorably under appropriate conditions is mistaken, then the subjectivist is prepared to revise and rewrite the list of valuable things. Not so for the objective-list advocate. The items on the list do not belong there depending contingently upon the attitudes that people come to have toward them. We might be mistaken now about our assertion that any particular item belongs on the objective list, but what we would be mistaken about is not a conjecture about what people's attitudes under specified conditions would turn out to be, but rather about what there is most reason to regard as truly valuable. Contrary to Sumner, the objective-list theory is not merely the provision of a list of putative goods. It is also a claim that what it is to be intrinsically valuable for a person, to make that person's life go better for herself, is to be an item that belongs on such a list.

The objective-list theory may be a mistaken rival theory, but it is a rival theory, and cannot be dismissed without a hearing as Sumner attempts to do.

V. Perfectionism versus the Objective List

An objective theory about human good should also be distinguished from perfectionist theories of the good as these are usually understood. Perfectionism is the doctrine that the good or intrinsically desirable human life is one that develops to the maximal possible extent the properties that constitute human nature. Thomas Hurka identifies these properties as "those that are essential to humans and conditioned on their being living things."[6] The good life according to perfectionist theory is the life in which the individual develops the excellences of the species to a high degree. Perfectionism might be understood as a moral theory that sets a goal that determines how we ought to conduct our own lives and help others to live, or it might be understood as a specification of prudential value, of what makes someone's life go best. Hurka himself understands perfectionism in the former way and holds that the historical tradition of philosophers in this camp from Plato onward is, broadly speaking, better understood this way. Still, we might identify well-being (i.e., the idea of what makes someone's life go best, of what is noninstrumentally prudentially valuable) with the perfection of our nature. If perfecting someone's life does not make the life better for the one who lives it, the imperative to maximize perfection strikes me as very uncompelling, so I would suppose the best strategy for perfectionist theory is to claim that perfection equals welfare.

Perfectionism should not be identified with objective-list theories of what makes someone's life go best. Perfectionism is not the family, just one member (or branch) of this family of views. Moreover, perfectionism takes a narrow view of human good. The excellences it takes to be valuable do seem valuable, but it denies value to much that seems worthwhile.

Among the goods that intrinsically enhance the quality of someone's life, some may have nothing whatsoever to do with fashioning oneself as a more perfect specimen of the human species or as a more perfect specimen of the type of individual one is. Consider what are sometimes called "cheap thrills," activities that provide pleasure and excitement without any significant effort or sacrifice on the part of the agent and also without the exercise or development of any of the agent's significant talents. Cheap thrills are pleasures with no redeeming social value beyond their pleasantness. The world being as it is, and human nature being what it is, such pleasures seem to me to be important sources of enjoyment that significantly enhance many people's lives in ways for which there is no practical substitute. I take it that the pleasures of cheap thrills will not register at all on a perfectionist measure of the prudential value of people's lives, but I would think that if these pleasures were to disappear without replacement, the world would be immensely worse and most human lives would be significantly blighted. At least, the issue will surely be open for discussion on an objective view, whereas according to the more narrow doctrine of perfectionism, the insignificance of cheap thrills to the prudential value of lives is a simple closed issue.

---

[6] Thomas Hurka, *Perfectionism* (Oxford: Oxford University Press, 1993), p. 16.

VI. Experience and Well-Being

Mill's position on the nature of the good in *Utilitarianism* is contentious in another way that sheds light on the comparative assessment of hedonism, desire fulfillment, and the objective-list theory. Following Bentham, Mill equates the good for persons with happiness and happiness with pleasure and the absence of pain.[7] This set of equations raises issues about how we are to understand the notions of pleasure and pain as they are used in Mill's theory of the good. Quite aside from these issues, Mill's position looks to be unsatisfactory for a quite general reason. As Robert Nozick has noticed, a hedonistic view such as Mill's, which takes pleasure to be constitutive of good, is a member of a wider family of views, which take the good to be constituted by some quality of experience.[8] "Experience" here refers to an individual's conscious awareness of aspects of his life as it unfolds moment by moment. Experience is what an individual has when awake or dreaming and does not have in a condition of coma or dreamless sleep. A quality-of-experience view identifies the good with some aspects of experience. Nozick has a powerful objection against the class of quality-of-experience views. The objection is expressed in an example. We care, and it is reasonable for us to care, about things other than the quality of our experience. Realization of this point emerges if we contemplate our reaction to an imaginary "experience machine," which could give an individual a perfect simulacrum of any life so far as the experience of that life is concerned. Hooked up to the experience machine, you would have the experience of leading any life you might choose, while really being, as Nozick states, "an indeterminate blob" floating in a tank.[9] If we care only about quality of experience, it is irrational to refuse to plug into the experience machine, just as it would be irrational, if my only aim is to open a bottle of beer[10] swiftly, to reject the mechanical aid of a bottle opener and insist upon the slower method of opening the bottle with my teeth. If we nonetheless think that it need not be unreasonable to refuse to live our lives plugged into the experience machine, this signals that we have aims other than achieving any specified type of experience. We want to have faithful friends and be a good friend ourselves, not merely to have the experience of such friendship, and we wish actually to accomplish something significant in the world, not just to have the experience of doing that, and so on.

[7] Mill, *Utilitarianism*, ch. 2.

[8] Robert Nozick, *Anarchy, State, and Utopia* (New York: Basic Books, 1974), p. 42. The point is also well stated in Ronald Dworkin, "What Is Equality? Part 1: Equality of Welfare," *Philosophy and Public Affairs*, vol. 10, no. 3 (Summer 1981), pp. 185–246; see pp. 192–93.

[9] Nozick, *Anarchy, State, and Utopia*, p. 43.

[10] That is, a bottle of the old-fashioned variety that lacks a twist-off top.

VII. THE HYBRID VIEW

Despite the experience-machine example and its lessons, one might hold fast to the thought that what is inherently good for a person must entirely consist in the quality of her experience. If we accept that, however thrilling it might be to experience, life in the experience machine is just floating as a conscious blob in a tank, and thus is not a genuinely good life, we might embrace a hybrid view according to which the character of one's experience can vary in value not just in virtue of its subjectively felt quality but also in virtue of its relationship to the world.

The hybrid view would allow us to judge that false pleasures contribute less to the value of the life of the person who experiences them than they otherwise would. A "false" pleasure here is one that is accompanied by significant false beliefs about the nature of the experience in which the agent finds enjoyment. Perhaps a better position would be that the value of a pleasure may vary not just in virtue of its felt quality but also in virtue of the actual character of the activity which one takes pleasure in experiencing. This position would allow discounting the value of pleasure taken in the supposed awareness that one's spouse is sexually faithful when this is not actually the case. But the position would be sufficiently flexible to allow that a pleasure can be more valuable if the agent's beliefs about the experience are false than would be the case if the agent's beliefs about the experience were all true. Consider that the pleasurable experience might sometimes be more valuable or admirable than the agent believes is the case. For example, one might hold that the bittersweet pleasure of completing a long-term project of writing an epic poem, which one believes to be weak but which is actually brilliantly effective, has more value than it would have if one's belief about the weakness of the poem were correct.

Mill's position in *Utilitarianism* might be an instance of a hybrid view.[11] One might interpret Mill as holding that nothing is prudentially valuable except the experience of one's activity, and experience must be pleasurable to be valuable. The pleasure of pleasurable activities varies in intensity and duration, and the more pleasure an activity contains, the more valuable it is. But besides differing in quantity of pleasure, pleasurable activities differ in their quality, which is measured by the preferences for one pleasurable activity over another by knowledgeable and competent experts. These experts might judge one activity such as surfing to be of higher quality than another activity such as sunbathing, so that surfing yields more prudential value per unit of pleasure it delivers than sunbathing does. Confronted with the experience-machine example, Mill on this interpretation should reply that whether, for example, the pleasures

---

[11] Mill is so interpreted in J. J. C. Smart, "Outline of a System of Utilitarian Ethics," in J. J. C. Smart and Bernard Williams, *Utilitarianism—For and Against* (Cambridge: Cambridge University Press, 1974).

of actual friendship are superior to the pleasures of experience-machine simulations of friendship is determined by the preferences of judges who have tried both types of pleasure and are fully capable of appreciating each. Nothing in Mill's testing procedure ensures that the judges, in arriving at their preferences in such cases, should attend only to the felt quality of the experiences. They might prefer actual-friendship pleasure over experience-machine pleasure because they regard the former as more fitting for human beings, more worthy, more dignified, and the like.

Whatever other difficulties the hybrid view might face, it seems deficient for a simple reason. An individual may have a strong and reasonable desire that a certain state of affairs concerning himself should obtain. This state of affairs might involve no experience of any sort on the part of the desiring agent. One desires that the novel one has written should prove to be a good novel. Here the state of affairs that is desired does not essentially involve any experience of any sort on the part of the agent. Yet it is plausible to suppose that a desire of this sort, if satisfied, contributes directly to the well-being of the agent. If this claim is correct, the hybrid view is doomed.

VIII. DESIRE SATISFACTION

If we reject the hybrid view, and with it the claim that "nothing can make our lives go better or worse unless it somehow affects the quality of our experience,"[12] the rival view that immediately becomes salient is the desire-fulfillment theory. We can always put the content of a desire in the form of a proposition; my desire for strawberries at breakfast is the desire that the proposition "Arneson eats strawberries at breakfast" should become true. A desire is fulfilled when the associated proposition becomes true. The fulfillment of a desire need not involve any experience of fulfillment, and the satisfaction of some desires can occur without the occurrence of any conscious episodes of any sort in the desirer. My desire that the novel I have written is praiseworthy is fulfilled just in case it is praiseworthy, whatever reasonable or unreasonable opinions on this matter I might come to hold. So the desire-fulfillment theory is not embarrassed by the fact that one's desires range beyond one's actual or possible experience. Fulfillment of basic (i.e., noninstrumental) desires can enhance well-being whether or not the fulfillment is experienced or even capable of being experienced.

According to the desire-fulfillment theory, one's life goes better, the more it is the case that one's basic desires are satisfied, with desires that rank as more important in the agent's hierarchy of desires counting for more if fulfilled.

---

[12] Sumner, *Welfare, Happiness, and Ethics*, p. 112.

This simple desire-fulfillment view is vulnerable to two significant objections. First, not all of an agent's desires plausibly bear on her well-being. I might listen to a televised plea for famine relief, and form the desire to aid distant starving strangers, without myself thinking (and without its being plausible for anyone else to think) that the fulfillment of this desire would in any way make my life go better. So one needs to restrict somehow the class of basic desires whose fulfillment contributes to well-being. It will not do to stipulate that each agent determines for herself which of her basic desires bear on her well-being. Surely an agent could make a mistake in making this determination, and we need some way of deciding when a mistake occurs. And an account is needed of what an agent is doing in making the determination that fixes which of her desires shall contribute to her well-being. If we say that she divides her basic desires into two piles, those whose satisfaction would contribute to her well-being and the rest, our account is rendered viciously circular, and requires that we already have an idea of well-being independent of desire fulfillment.[13]

It is perhaps worth noting that switching allegiance from a desire-fulfillment theory to an objective-list theory of well-being does not solve this difficulty but only reduces its scope. At least this is so if desire fulfillment ends up being an entry on the objective list, as is surely plausible. Surely satisfying the basic desires one regards as important over the course of one's life is one component of a good life. Then for this component, the problem of finding a principled restriction on the class of desires whose fulfillment contributes to well-being still remains.

The second objection against simple desire fulfillment is that some desires that are felt to be of great importance by the individual, and are desired for their own sake, not as a means to further goals, are only desired because the individual is confused, ignorant, or making reasoning errors. These desires would not survive reflective critical scrutiny. Why suppose their satisfaction is good for the desirer at all? Suppose my wife's ultimate desire in life is to construct a huge monument to my virtue in our back yard. She wants this for its own sake, and by dint of great personal sacrifice and effort succeeds in fulfilling this aim, so that our house is overshadowed by this statue. Yet if it is also the case that my wife would not have had this desire if she had not erred in her estimation of my virtue by wildly overestimating it, we will be reluctant to accept that satisfaction of this desire really contributes to her well-being. This reluctance is tantamount to an unwillingness to accept the simple desire-fulfillment view as a satisfactory account of what makes someone's life go well.

---

[13] James Griffin acknowledges the circularity worry and suggests it might not constitute a decisive objection in his *Well-Being: Its Meaning, Measurement, and Moral Importance* (Oxford: Clarendon Press, 1986), p. 22.

IX. The Problem of Nonprudential Desire

Of the two objections against the desire-satisfaction account just raised, the first may be the more intractable. The second invites the response that only those basic desires that do not arise from cognitive error or ignorance intrinsically enhance a person's well-being if they are satisfied. This response is explored in the next three sections. Whether or not it ultimately succeeds, this strategy of refining the desire-satisfaction account surely has some initial plausibility. But this strategy does nothing to resolve the first difficulty. A person may well desire for its own sake something other than her own well-being, and may continue to do so even after ideal critical scrutiny with full information.

To save the desire-satisfaction account, one must find a principled way of restricting the portion of an individual's basic desires, satisfaction of which constitutes her well-being. Examples such as desiring that life be discovered somewhere in outer space, or desiring that distant strangers should not suffer in poverty, might suggest the proposal that only desires that concern the agent's own life qualify as welfare-determining for that agent. But the desire to sacrifice one's life for the sake of others evidently concerns one's own life but intuitively is not such that its satisfaction intrinsically increases one's well-being.

Another possible restriction is to exclude from the set of welfare-determining desires those that are adopted by the agent from moral considerations. If I desire to keep a promise because I believe that promise-keeping is morally obligatory, it does seem sensible to deny that my life goes better if this desire is fulfilled. But there are other examples. I might come to have a strong desire that endangered animal species survive or that distant strangers should not live in poverty even if I am moved to adopt the desire by sympathy for the plight of the species and the strangers quite independently of moral considerations.

Without pursuing this issue further, I will simply register my conviction that there is no viable solution to the problem of nonprudential desire. The next sections pursue the strengths and weaknesses of simple and refined desire-satisfaction accounts on the assumption that this problem can be solved despite the doubts registered here. It turns out that even if there were no nonprudential desire problem, the desire-satisfaction account would still be plagued with troubles.

Another road might be taken at this juncture. One might reinterpret the desire-satisfaction account as giving a necessary, not a sufficient, condition for prudential value. Nothing can intrinsically enhance an individual's well-being unless she desires that thing. The fact that one can seemingly have desires for what does not enhance one's well-being is no embarrassment for this less ambitious account.

Desire satisfaction construed as a necessary condition might play a role in many types of analysis of prudential value. Perhaps the most plausible mixed theories of this sort will combine desire satisfaction with either a quality-of-experience requirement or an objective-list requirement. The first view would maintain that if something intrinsically enhances an individual's well-being, it must be desired by that individual and must be pleasurable. The second view would maintain that if something intrinsically enhances an individual's well-being, it must be desired by that individual and objectively worthwhile. The second view is discussed, and rejected, later in this essay, when the endorsement constraint is examined and found wanting. The claim that nothing can intrinsically enhance an individual's welfare unless she desires it is one specific version of the endorsement constraint. The first view supposes that nothing can intrinsically enhance an individual's well-being unless the experience of that putative good is pleasurable (or, in the more general case, has a desirable quality). Section VII of this essay already has criticized this position, which cannot be upheld by anyone who acknowledges that some contributors to well-being are not experienced at all. For example, the desire that one's child-rearing activity should be successful in the sense that one's child comes to have a good life is not a desire to have any sort of experience. If the fulfillment of such a desire can contribute to one's well-being, then no mixed view that includes an experience requirement as a necessary condition for prudential value can be correct.

X. Informed-Desire Satisfaction

Consider again the claim that the satisfaction of any of an individual's basic desires intrinsically enhances her well-being, and assume that the nonprudential-desire problem can be solved. In response to the objection that some desires are based on mistakes and ignorance, turn now to refinements of desire-fulfillment theories that hold that the desires whose satisfaction increases well-being are those an agent would form under ideal conditions for desire formation. Among these conditions, avoidance of the influence of mistaken belief and of ignorance of material facts looms large, so the class of theories has been labeled "informed-desire theories of well-being."[14]

Immediately doubts arise as to whether this theoretical move is in the right direction. Suppose that in my actual benighted state I strongly desire to learn quantum physics, but if I were fully informed about the matters that bear on the reasonableness of this choice, I would already know quantum physics, and hence would have no desire to acquire further understanding of this field. This counterfactual does not intuitively

---

[14] Views of this type are developed in Richard B. Brandt, *A Theory of the Good and the Right* (Oxford: Clarendon Press, 1979), chs. 6–7; John Rawls, *A Theory of Justice* (Cambridge: Harvard University Press, 1971), pp. 417ff.; and Griffin, *Well-Being: Its Meaning, Measurement, and Moral Importance*. Griffin's account is thorough in its examination of difficulties and creative in its attempts to resolve them, but the position he ends up defending is complex, and not unambiguously a full-information account.

diminish the attractiveness of my present desire, but the informed-desire theory seems to grind out the result that satisfaction of my desire to learn physics would not increase my well-being because the desire would not be formed under ideal conditions. To avoid this result, Peter Railton has suggested a sophisticated formulation of the idea: "an individual's good consists in what he would want himself to want, or to pursue, were he to contemplate his present situation from a standpoint fully and vividly informed about himself and his circumstances, and entirely free of cognitive error or lapses of instrumental rationality."[15] We construct in thought a cognitively ideal version of myself, an ideal advisor, and what this guardian angel would want me to want fixes the set of basic desires whose satisfaction constitutes my well-being.

According to the ideal-advisor versions of informed-desire theories, what is intrinsically good for an individual is determined by what an ideally informed and reflective version of the individual would want the actual (perhaps not fully informed and reflective) individual to want for its own sake. If my ideal advisor would want me to want to eat fish, then eating fish is intrinsically good for me.

Informed-desire satisfaction theories of the good have received rough treatment recently at the hands of philosophical critics. Some of these criticisms strike me as unfair, or at least as nondecisive. The numbered list below contains five such nondecisive objections and my reasons for finding them so.

1. One objection raised against this type of account is that perhaps my ideal advisor would not be favorably disposed to me, so his advice about what I should want might be hostile.[16] Starting from my personality, and then becoming ideally informed, the advisor in the process of becoming informed might develop a revulsion against my personality type, and be indifferent to my welfare. Hence, I should not necessarily take the dictates of the ideal advisor as determinative of my welfare.

To block this objection, it suffices to stipulate that the ideal advisor will be sympathetic to the individual whose welfare his desires fix. The ideal advisor's sole aim is to advance the well-being of the advisee.

2. Another set of objections begins with the speculation that in the course of becoming fully informed, the ideal advisor, even though starting with my personality, may alter psychologically to such an extent that I should not necessarily regard the desires of this very different individual for my well-being as normative for me.[17] The fact that my ideal advisor would want me to want X might not induce me to want X. But, so the objection runs, it was supposed to be part of the attraction of ideal-advisor views· that they would satisfy an internalist constraint. And according to internalism, any valid claim as to what is good for me

---

[15] Peter Railton, "Facts and Values," *Philosophical Topics*, vol. 14 (1986), pp. 5–31; see p. 16.
[16] See Connie S. Rosati, "Persons, Perspectives, and Full Information Accounts of the Good," *Ethics*, vol. 105, no. 2 (January 1995), pp. 296–325; see pp. 307–13.
[17] This difficulty is explored in *ibid.*, pp. 299–314.

must motivate me to want that thing, at least under some ideal conditions. As Railton observes, "it would be an intolerably alienated conception of someone's good to imagine that it might fail in any way to engage him."[18]

My response to this objection is that internalism is too demanding a condition to impose on theories of the good, so the fact that informed-desire theories fail to meet the condition, if indeed it is a fact, casts no discredit on these theories. It may be that some psychological defect, some missing screw in the desiring department of my brain, prevents me from desiring some things that are in fact good for me. My ideal advisor will want me to want these things, and regret my psychological incapacity. Given the incapacity, if I were to discover that my ideal advisor would want me to want these things which seem undesirable to me, this knowledge would, *ex hypothesi*, not be sufficient to cause me to desire them. Without further argument to motivate an internalist constraint on acceptable theories of well-being, this possibility by itself does not reveal a defect in the ideal-advisor account.

3. Wayne Sumner has found troublesome what he takes to be the prospective nature of desire. Desires, according to Sumner, are always future-oriented. I can have a wish, but not a genuine desire, that the past be other than it turned out to be. But some goods fall into my lap without my having formed any antecedent desire for them. I never desired to witness the sunrise's orange glow on the cliffs below Mount Whitney, but there it is, and it's wonderful. But since I failed to entertain a prospective desire for this treat, and cannot logically form a desire about a past occurrence, this good slips between the slats of the ideal-advisor account, and does not register in that account as a contribution to my well-being.[19] One might wonder whether the counterexample could be deflected by finding a more abstract desire that the unique sunrise experience qualifies as satisfying. But I have a prior worry. It seems incorrect to assert that desires cannot be retrospective. I performed miserably in the last tournament of my dismal high-school wrestling career, and ever since then I have strongly desired that I had performed better. This is not a mere idle wish; I would give up resources to satisfy this aim if doing so would be useful. Or if one insists that "desires" regarding the past properly are characterized as wishes, then we can readily construct a new notion of *desire* that incorporates the prospective attitudes that Sumner counts as desires plus heartfelt wishes regarding the past, and reconstruct the ideal-advisor informed-desire view with this revisionary understanding of desire.

4. Another objection is that the idea of becoming fully informed is radically indeterminate.[20] Information can be presented to an individual

---

[18] Railton, "Facts and Values," p. 9.

[19] Sumner, *Welfare, Happiness, and Ethics*, pp. 130–33.

[20] See J. David Velleman, "Brandt's Definition of 'Good'," *Philosophical Review*, vol. 97, no. 3 (July 1988), pp. 353–71. Velleman develops criticisms of full-information accounts, with a focus on Brandt's proposal, beyond those this essay considers.

in different ways through different media. A television broadcast, a rousing speech, a novel, a poem, a painting, a popular song can all present the same propositions to an audience of would-be ideal advisors who are becoming fully and vividly informed. But there is no determinate answer to the question: Which mode of presentation conveys a more vivid impression? There are many dimensions of vividness corresponding to the various modes of presentation. Being more vividly informed along one dimension is being less vividly informed along other dimensions. Presenting information in all possible modes of presentation seriatim is no solution, even if the idea is coherent, because this would just be a mind-deadening, nearly interminable, and devastatingly boring presentation.

If the notion of becoming fully and vividly informed is indeterminate, this slack will be transmitted to yield indeterminacy in the idea of what is good for a person according to the ideal-advisor account. However, this is an objection against the account only if it can be shown that the ideal-advisor account yields indeterminacy where we have good reason to believe there should be none. But perhaps the correct inference to draw is that the notion of what is good for a person is inherently indeterminate, so that it is (for example) neither the case that eating fish nor eating fowl is a better culinary experience for me, because the judgment of my ideal advisor on these putative goods is unstable in response to various modes of presentation of the relevant information. It might turn out to be a strength of the ideal-advisor account that it allows for only limited commensurability of prudential value. One's ideal advisor will know the psychological laws and propensities that govern responsiveness of creatures such as us to varying types of presentation of information, and will take steps to prevent arbitrary contingencies such as order of presentation from affecting the desire-formation process unless this is unavoidable. But if it is a deep truth about my individual nature that a person of my type likes fowl better than fish if fowl is tasted first in life, and likes fish better if the taste of fish comes first, then neither fish nor fowl is inherently better, and if I have not yet tasted either, then which I get is a "don't care" in the judgment of my ideal advisor.

5. An objection along somewhat the same line denies that one could actually become fully and vividly informed as the application of the ideal-advisor account requires.[21] In one possible life I might lead, I am as innocent as a choirboy, and in another possible life, I become conversant with sin; in one life, I become a fierce warrior; in another, a gentle, sensitive soul. These traits cannot be combined in a single person. I cannot then hold in one consciousness all of these and the myriad other possible experiences I would have to have in order to qualify as fully informed so that my ideally informed self could give me authoritative guidance about well-being.

---

[21] For criticisms along this line, see David Sobel, "Full Information Accounts of Well-Being," *Ethics*, vol. 104, no. 4 (July 1994), pp. 784–810; and Rosati, "Persons, Perspectives, and Full Information Accounts of the Good," pp. 307–24.

The difficulties proposed in this objection arise from the assumption that to be fully informed, one must actually experience all of the putative goods which are to be ordered for choiceworthiness. The assumption seems misguided, however. The ideal advisor starts with an individual personality, including whatever fund of experience the particular individual has had. In the process of becoming ideally informed, the advisor gains all relevant propositional knowledge that is material to this ordering of goods. No experience is necessary, so the alleged psychological difficulties of combining opposed and mutually incompatible experiences are of no concern.

If I am wondering whether the joys of heroin render heroin usage an important constituent of my good, it is not (I am claiming) necessary for me to sample heroin; and to become fully and vividly informed, it would not be necessary for the ideal-advisor version of myself to live a complete life as a drug addict on the streets. It suffices to know all about heroin usage and drug addiction.

If one denies this last claim, the following problem emerges. Suppose that I know that a certain experience will be (as matters now seem from my present evaluative perspective) corrupting. The experience of lording it over others in Simon Legree fashion will, I know full well, give me a strong taste for the pleasures of domination, which I do not now admire. Suppose that if propositional knowledge suffices for becoming fully informed, I can become in the relevant sense fully informed about Simon Legree pleasures without actually experiencing them and becoming addicted to them. But if full and vivid experience is necessary for becoming a being whose desires are authoritative determiners of my well-being, then to become an ideal advisor I must let myself become corrupted against (what I now regard as) my better judgment. There is no cognitive defect in my present aversion to Simon Legree pleasures, and the aversion is based on no reasoning errors and, let us suppose, no factual ignorance or confusion of any kind. I wish the ideal-advisor account to allow that I can be relevantly fully informed without actually undergoing the experience that I judge would have a bad effect on my desire formation. That requires not interpreting "fully informed" as "fully experienced."

XI. Informed Desire and the Badness of Pain

An apparent attraction of a full-information ideal-desire theory is that it offers a solution to the following puzzle about the badness of pain and the goodness of pleasure. Pain is evidently undesirable, and pleasure desirable, for their own sakes and quite independently of their instrumental value and disvalue. Suppose we say that pain would not be undesirable if it were not disliked by the one who experiences it, and pleasure would not be desirable if it did not evoke liking. But if we opt for the position that our likings and dislikings determine what is valuable, we seem to be drifting back toward some version of a simple desire-satisfaction view. Moreover, if my desire to avoid pain determines that pain is bad, why does not the desire of an anorexic to forgo continued life if that conflicts with her ideal of a thin body determine that continued life, in these circumstances, is bad for her? On the one hand, if we want to say our likings and dislikings play a constitutive or determining role in the badness of pain and the goodness of pleasure, what distinguishes these cases from others in which we do not want to take this line? On the other hand, if we consistently reject the possibility that our likings and dislikings do play such a constitutive or determining role, we seem stuck with the unappealing consequences that the badness of pain and the goodness of pleasure are thrown into doubt.[22]

If we say that the desires whose satisfaction enhances our well-being are those that would survive ideal critical reflection with full information, we have a response to the puzzle. The desires for pleasure and against pain survive critical reflection for an odd reason. We cannot think of anything to say for or against either pleasure or pain, and our inability to find reasons bearing on these matters does not shake our initial aversion from pain and attraction to pleasure. Nor can we imagine that further information of any sort would alter our inchoate confidence. The conviction that pain is bad and pleasure good does fit smoothly into the set of our considered judgments in the widest reflective equilibrium we can attain. If one imagines a life that is wonderful in every detail, and then adds the further stipulation that the person is either miserable throughout her life or thoroughly enjoys almost every minute of it (without the pain being debilitating, or the pleasure stimulating, in ways that affect the degree to which any other goods are attained), one is strongly inclined to prefer, and to prefer for those one cares about, the life with pleasure to the life that is pain-filled, all else being equal.

In this picture, however, desire is an idle wheel. The work is done by the plausibility of the suggestion that the conviction that pain is bad and pleasure good would withstand ideal critical reflection. Ideal critical reflection puts us in an ideal position to appreciate the true worth of putative goods and bads. Pains and pleasures are kinds of sensations, or rather a distinctive kind of aspect that colors a wide range of kinds of experiences. Pleasure and pain feel a certain way that uniformly evokes liking in the case of the former and disliking in the case of the latter. Although it sounds stodgy to say it, the way pain feels is a good and sufficient reason to dislike it. The peculiarity of pleasure and pain is that

---

[22] Richard Kraut accepts the claim that this dilemma poses an exhaustive choice and opts for the latter horn in "Desire and the Human Good," *Proceedings and Addresses of the American Philosophical Association*, vol. 68, no. 2 (November 1994), pp. 39–54.

the quality of experience they provide yields inchoate reasons that might be supposed to resist articulation. There is nothing to say that warrants the claim that a headache is bad, beyond the bare observation that it is bad owing to the way it feels. If someone claims to like a sensation that is identical to the experience of a headache I find horrible, the possibilities are either that the phenomenology is really different (the person, on morphine, feels the pain but not its painful aspect) or that the person's mechanism that induces liking and disliking is faulty. If the person experiences a headache just like mine, the attitude of liking is an inappropriate reaction.[23] I conclude that accounting for the badness of pain does not require embracing a desire-fulfillment account.

XII. Informed-Desire Fulfillment versus the Objective List

We can try to test a sophisticated ideal-advisor version of a desire-fulfillment view against the rival objective-list doctrine by imagining a scenario in which an individual has a life that is rich in objective-list goods but poor in the amount of informed-desire fulfillment that is attained. Suppose an individual in very favorable circumstances forms extremely demanding ambitions. Her most important desires are grand in their nature—she wants to become an important public figure who changes the course of history, a consummate world-class artist whose achievements are extensive, strikingly original, brilliantly executed, and well recognized in her day, and a powerful matriarch who molds her family into a lasting dynasty devoted to her memory. In all of these cases the person desires not merely to make a good try at achieving these ambitions but to be successful in these diverse domains. These life goals are reasonable, let's say, and where the height of the ambition creates a high risk of failure, the risks are worth taking all things considered. Measured by the self-chosen standards of her own well-considered desires, the woman's life turns out to be a failure. What the person most cares about does not come about as she wishes. Yet in the course of piling up these failures, the person gets all of the goods on the objective list to an extraordinarily high degree. Even if satisfying one's major defining life goals is one item on the objective list, the woman's failure to achieve this item is outweighed by her striking success in other dimensions of the good life as rated by the objective-list measure. If in contemplating cases of this sort we come to think that one can lead an excellent life that is high in prudential value despite being a failure on the dimension of informed-desire

---

[23] For an opposed view on this issue, one which supposes that the badness of the sensation of pain resides in its being disliked, and that pain that does not evoke dislike is not intrinsically bad, see Parfit, *Reasons and Persons*, p. 493. C. D. Broad analyzed the notion of pleasure in a similar way in his *Five Types of Ethical Theory* (London: Routledge and Kegan Paul, 1930), pp. 237–38.

fulfillment, we are then inclining toward acceptance of the objective-list conception of what makes someone's life go best.

The flip side of this test is to imagine that someone in unfortunate circumstances forms quite limited and unambitious desires that are reasonable given the bleak conditions she faces. Being blind, I don't form ambitions that require eyesight; being impoverished, I don't form ambitions that require wealth to have a reasonable prospect of success; being unintelligent, I don't form ambitions that would strain my limited brain power; and lacking social connections, I don't form ambitions that can be achieved only with the help of powerful allies. Judged against the baseline of my original grim life circumstances, I am reasonably lucky, and most of my important desires are fulfilled over the course of my life. These desires are not ill-chosen; they would be endorsed and affirmed by the fully informed and rational ideal advisor whose advice determines what is prudentially valuable for me according to full-information accounts of the good. In these circumstances it seems that I succeed in leading a good, choiceworthy life according to the informed-desire fulfillment reckoning, but not according to a plausible application of an objective-list theory. The latter but not the former accounting will register at full value the important life goods I did not achieve and which did not enter (fully) into my set of basic life desires because I foresaw that insofar as I could affect by careful planning the desires I came to have, it would do me no good to develop desires that would stand virtually no chance of fulfillment.

In cases where informed-desire and objective-list accounts give different verdicts on the quality of a life, the objective-list verdicts are more compelling. But it should be noted that this position requires backing of a type this essay does not try to supply. I have not introduced any way to measure the success of a life according to informed-desire and objective-list standards. I have relied on hunches as to what the upshot of applying plausible measures derived from both theories would be. To go further would require an investigation of the prospects for an objective standard of interpersonal comparison of well-being. This would be to take up the skepticism issue that I stated at the outset I would not be exploring in this essay.

XIII. The Decisive Objection[24]

One line of objections against the informed-desire view might appear to have a gimmicky and ad hoc flavor, but in fact it raises a central issue. An example in this vein is offered by Allan Gibbard, who observes that if you became fully and vividly informed of the internal processes of di-

---

[24] The objection discussed in this section is borrowed from Donald C. Hubin, "Hypothetical Motivation," *Noûs*, vol. 30, no. 1 (March 1996), pp. 31–54.

gestion of a delicious meal, you might lose your desire for savoring delicious food, but even if this should be so, this odd fact should not undermine the claim that enjoyment of good food is a constituent of the good life.[25] The objection invites the reply that one's ideal advisor will know about this possible psychological link and will discount its influence, so that even if the advisor becomes nauseated by revulsion at the thought of digestion, he will still want his advisee to want to enjoy good food.

Put in more general terms, Gibbard's point, and the point of several other objections canvassed above, is that the essence of the informed-desire view is that what the process of becoming fully informed and critically reflecting causes one to desire for its own sake is good for one (for ideal-advisor views, the point is that what the process of learning and reflection causes the advisor to want one to want for its own sake is good for one). But nothing bars this causal process from generating outcomes in a way that does not intuitively confer any desirability on the resultant basic desires. It might simply be a brute psychological fact about me that if I were to become fully informed about grapes, this process would set off a chemical process in my brain that would lead me to crave counting blades of grass on courthouse lawns as my primary life aim. This would seem to be an oddity of my brain, not an indicator of my true well-being. If this were true of everyone, not just me, the same point would still hold. The informed-desire theories purport to establish that a certain causal process confers desirability; but the characterization of the causal process does not secure this result, and it does not seem that it could be altered to guarantee the right result. Griffin evidently is responding to this worry when he interprets the information requirement in an informed-desire account as, in effect, whatever it takes to produce an adequate response to the possible objects of desire. He writes: "So an 'informed' desire is one formed by appreciation of the nature of its object, and it includes anything necessary to achieve it."[26] The critic of the account will dig in her heels and insist that people's psychology, due to some quirk of evolution, might be such that fully appreciating the nature of some objects produces bizarre desires regarding them, but the fact that the objects do not appear as desirable in the light of this causal process does not detract from their desirability. One might further refine Griffin's proposal by demanding that an informed desire must be formed only by correct appreciation of its object and not by anything else, including any extraneous causal process that happens to accompany correct appreciation. At this point, however, it does seem that the account has been refined into nonexistence. We are no longer appealing to what people would desire under ideal circum-

[25] Allan Gibbard, *Wise Choices, Apt Feelings* (Cambridge: Harvard University Press, 1990), p. 20. It should be noted that Gibbard is discussing a specific full-information analysis by Richard Brandt, not an ideal-advisor theory.

[26] Griffin, *Well-Being: Its Meaning, Measurement, and Moral Importance*, p. 14.

stances of desire formation as theoretically determining what is prudentially valuable. Instead, the work is done by appeal to "correct appreciation," which can only mean finding desirable what truly is desirable.

XIV. The Endorsement Constraint

Suppose one holds that gaining well-being is to be identified with attaining what is objectively choiceworthy—the items on the objective list. It then turns out to be entirely a contingent matter whether or not an individual has any positive attitude of any sort toward the attainments that render her life good. My life might be rich in the goods that are prominent on the objective list even though I find these constituents of my life to be utterly repulsive.

Even if the position is taken that one of the entries on the objective list is being psychologically related in the right way to one's achievements of other goods on this list, this attitudinal good will be just one of several entries. The possibility is still open that one could score sufficiently high on the other dimensions of the good that register on the list that one could qualify as living a fine life even though one lacks any positive attitude toward any of the items that constitute one's well-being.

Discomfort with this result motivates the construction of mixed theories of prudential value that require that any occurrence that contributes intrinsically to an individual's well-being must be accompanied by some positive attitude on the part of the individual toward that occurrence. On such a view, nothing counts as an objectively valuable attainment unless it is subjectively affirmed by the one who has gained the attainment.

This endorsement constraint can take various forms. I shall consider two versions in this section and a general form of the constraint in the next. One idea, given eloquent expression by Ronald Dworkin, is that nothing can make a basic, noninstrumental contribution to the goodness of a person's life unless it is endorsed by that very person.[27] A second version has been proposed by James Griffin as a constraint on hypothetical-ideal-desire satisfaction accounts of the good.[28] The constraint is that any noninstrumental, basic desire whose satisfaction contributes to an individual's well-being must be actual when satisfied. That is to say, the hypothetical ideal desire must be endorsed by the person and so become her desire in order for its satisfaction to contribute to her well-being.

The attraction of the proposals is evident. It is disagreeable to think that one can improve the quality of a person's life by manipulating him or

---

[27] Ronald Dworkin, "Foundations of Liberal Equality," in *The Tanner Lectures on Human Values*, vol. 11, ed. Grethe B. Peterson (Salt Lake City: University of Utah Press, 1990), pp. 1–119; see pp. 80–83.
[28] Griffin, *Well-Being: Its Meaning, Measurement, and Moral Importance*, p. 11.

forcing him to gain putative goods that he does not regard as valuable and would not seek on his own absent the manipulation or forcing.

The endorsement constraint allows us to say that regardless of whether the good that we are contemplating gaining for an individual even though she does not endorse it is great or puny, the "good" gained for the person under this condition will be illusory, because no unendorsed good can contribute to the value of someone's life. In his discussion of the endorsement constraint, Dworkin skillfully exhibits how it enables one to combine an objective or perfectionist account of human good with a strong liberal moral presumption against just the type of paternalism that arouses our strong antipathy. *Paternalism* in general is restricting someone's liberty against her will for her own good. The type of paternalism that the endorsement constraint seems firmly to prohibit is restricting a competent individual's liberty against her will in order to secure for her a basic, noninstrumental good that she does not recognize as such.

Griffin's version of the endorsement constraint reveals a similar attraction. Some examples will incline us toward accepting it. For example, even if an ideally informed and reflective version of myself would love drinking champagne, if my actual uninformed and unreflective self is averse to the stuff, no gain in my utility can be secured by getting me to drink some when I lack all desire to do that.

Despite their glittering attractive qualities, both versions of the endorsement constraint should be resisted. The objection to the endorsement constraint is that people's reasons for declining to endorse some putative good that they are seeking or that is falling in their lap can be weak, confused, or even nonexistent. Suppose Samantha writes a brilliant poem but denies that this achievement has any value or in any way enhances her life. Her ground for this dismissal is a shallow and silly aesthetic theory which she has thoughtlessly embraced. In these circumstances, her failure to endorse her achievement does not negate its value for her. No doubt her utility would be higher, other things being equal, if she were to endorse it, because a subjective sense of accomplishment is itself a not inconsiderable good, especially when it is well grounded on genuine accomplishment. But this point is fully compatible with rejection of the endorsement constraint. Note also that often other things are not equal. Samantha might be so disposed that becoming the sort of person who would endorse her achievements according to a sensible scale of merit would also involve becoming the sort of person who is not likely to achieve much. In such a case, we might prefer for Samantha's own good that she not develop her capacity for self-endorsement but instead develop and exercise her capacity for significant achievement.

There are several possible lines of objection against this criticism of the endorsement constraint, but none proves successful. One might insist that the objection fails to distinguish the value of Samantha's achievement, impersonally regarded as an achievement, and its value regarded as a contribution to Samantha's life. Not everything Samantha does that is good is plausibly viewed as good for Samantha. How can an achievement that is utterly futile and worthless in Samantha's eyes nonetheless qualify as an enhancement of her well-being?

To blunt the force of this rhetorical question, it suffices to note that Samantha's disposition to nonendorsement might be an odd outlier among her psychological traits. She might enthusiastically work on her poem, organize a large stretch of her life around the project of its construction, and take pleasure in the process and the product. She just regards what she is doing as worthless on the strength of a bad aesthetic theory which she accepts. To explain how a nonendorsed achievement can increase someone's utility is to appeal to the strength of the objective-list account of well-being. Some things are important components of the good life. Having them, one's life is enriched. Lacking them, one's life is impoverished. Failing to endorse them just means one is making mistaken evaluations, and this nonendorsement does not automatically or necessarily alter their value. Lacking a desire for them merely means one's desires are defective because they do not arise from a proper appreciation of their possible objects. Suppose, improbably, that a person attains all of the significant items on the best formulation of the objective list (other than the single good of authentically endorsing and approving the shape of the life one is living) but fails to endorse any of them for miscellaneous reasons, none of which would withstand scrutiny. The person has it all, but fails to endorse her great riches. I find that it stretches credibility past the breaking point to maintain that this single quirk of her valuations reduces all of her riches to nothing.

Another line of objection begins with the suspicion that if an individual is correctly characterized as seeking or pursuing some good, she must see it as valuable or good in some way. We do not seek things in the belief that they are bad. This objection is mistaken, however; and in any case it would be powerless to support the endorsement constraint. This last point comes into view once we notice that some goods of human life do not come to us as a result of our striving. They simply happen. These manna-from-heaven goods would not have to be endorsed by us to count as genuine goods even if it were the case that in order to seek or pursue a good one must endorse it as good. But in any case it is not true that in order to seek or pursue a good one must endorse it as good. One might see the object of one's pursuit as bad in itself, but as a useful means to some further goal. In this spirit, Samantha might regard her poetry-writing as hackwork but useful nonetheless for producing her livelihood. Or one might pursue something, no doubt finding it attractive in some respect, even though one steadily believes the object of one's striving is bad all things considered, and pursues it just the same due to weakness of will. Or one might strive to gain something on a whim, without considering the true merits of what one is striving for, and when one contemplates this heavy issue of true merits, one is befuddled by it, and emits a confused dismissal.

When an individual fails to endorse a putative good that she either seeks and gets or just gets without seeking, there are two cases to consider. In the first type of case, the individual does not endorse the good but does not herself regard her endorsement as a necessary condition for the putative good's having some positive value. She has either not considered the issue or has considered it and does not take her endorsement to be a *sine qua non* for value. In the second type of case, the individual does believe that if she does not endorse the putative good, it cannot contribute noninstrumentally to the value of her life. Even in the second type of case, however, we may believe the individual is just wrong on this matter, and the grounds for overriding the individual's own judgment may be powerful. Evaluative judgments are not self-certifying, not in this or any other case.

The endorsement constraint gains unmerited plausibility if one fails to distinguish a general claim about human psychology from a conceptual claim. It is often the case that putative goods that are not regarded as goods by those who get them lack zest, intensity, and strength. If I do not regard professional wrestling to be a worthwhile activity and do not believe that enjoyment gained from watching it adds much value to anyone's life, I am very unlikely to get much value from time spent watching professional wrestling. I probably cannot reach the level of enjoyment to which an avid fan has ready access. But homely truths of this sort will not add up to a justification of the endorsement constraint.

The endorsement constraint only holds that a precondition of value for an agent is endorsement by the agent, and does not contain any commitment to the further idea that if something is endorsed by an agent, it has some value. Nor does the endorsement constraint per se make any claim to the effect that the stronger one's endorsement of a putative good, the greater the value of the good, provided one gets it. The former claim is obviously incorrect. With respect to the latter claim, I would hold it more plausible to think that, other things equal, the value of a putative good for an agent is enhanced if the agent has a proper and reasonable understanding of the value of the good. If I am listening to a great performance of a great symphony, my appreciation heightens the value of the experience, and if I am listening to (what I know to be) a schlocky performance of a mediocre symphony but enjoying it anyway, the value of the experience is enhanced since it is not tinged with false valuation.

The actual-desire version of the endorsement constraint goes astray for much the same reason that the Dworkin version of the endorsement constraint is defective. If I have a minor talent of a not especially significant sort, I may be led by snobbery or shame to have an aversion against exercising the talent. Suppose the talent is for singing moderately well in a choir, or for being a moderately efficient bookkeeper. But singing in a choir and keeping accurate accounts may be the best things I can do, and doing these activities may produce genuine but modest accomplishment, which does not cease to be accomplishment, and genuinely prudentially valuable, despite my lack of desire for it.

XV. The Weak Endorsement Constraint

Consider the further proposal that for something to qualify as intrinsically enhancing the quality of a person's life, either the thing must be desired by the individual who gets it or endorsed by her. Or consider the still weaker version of the endorsement constraint, which I call the "weak endorsement constraint." It simply holds that nothing can intrinsically enhance the quality of a person's life unless that person has some positive, affirmative attitude toward that element of her life. The root idea is that a purportedly happy occurrence in one's life that leaves one utterly cold cannot intrinsically enhance one's well-being. Some of my objections against the Dworkin and Griffin versions of the endorsement constraint have appealed to the possibility that an agent could be getting some great good and having some pro-attitude toward it but failing to have the precise attitude that Dworkin or Griffin insist is necessary. These objections might appear to concede the correctness of the weak endorsement constraint.[29]

One should also note another dimension along which the endorsement constraint might be relaxed. To this point I have been considering versions of the constraint that require simultaneous getting of the good and endorsing of it. One might weaken the constraint by requiring that nothing intrinsically enhances my well-being unless I have some positive attitude toward it, but allowing that I might have the requisite attitude at any time of my life, not necessarily at the time that the good is obtained. (This relaxed version of the constraint might strike some adherents of it as too weak. Imagine that at age ten I wanted very much to climb El Capitan on my sixtieth birthday and that doing this would rank high on the objective-list standard, but that at age sixty my actual desires are oriented toward sedentary activities and the prospect of satisfying this past desire now seems repulsive to me. The spirit of the endorsement

---

[29] Derek Parfit appears to affirm a version of the endorsement constraint in *Reasons and Persons*, p. 502: "Pleasure with many other kinds of object [those that lack objective value] has no value. And if they are entirely devoid of pleasure, there is no value in knowledge, rational activity, love, or the awareness of beauty. What is of value, or is good for someone, is to have both: to be engaged in these activities, and to be strongly wanting to be so engaged." Richard Kraut asserts a somewhat similar view in his "Desire and the Human Good"; see p. 45 and footnote 13. Kraut holds that to be living a good life one must love something and what one loves must be worth caring about, but "that cannot be the whole story," because in addition "one must be related in the right way to what one loves." Sumner's *Welfare, Happiness, and Ethics* is an extended sophisticated argument for the weak endorsement constraint.

constraint surely yields the verdict that if I do the climb but remain utterly alienated from it in my attitudes, it cannot intrinsically enhance my well-being.) Another possible relaxed version would insist that one must have some pro-attitude toward any putative good one obtains, no matter how objectively choiceworthy it is, and that one must have the affirmative attitude either simultaneously with the achievement or in retrospect. My further remarks concern the simultaneous version of the weak endorsement constraint. I believe that the difficulties I raise for it apply also to versions that relax the simultaneity requirement, but I shall not pursue this issue.

One might have the thought that the person who lives well according to the objective-list account but fails to satisfy the weak endorsement constraint goes through life unhappy, entirely frustrated in that none of her important desires and life ambitions are fulfilled, and completely lacking in subjective satisfaction. Such a life would doubtless be barren and low in prudential value. But the life that does well according to the objective-list account but fails to satisfy the weak endorsement constraint could not be entirely lacking in subjective satisfaction if (1) the objective list includes (some types of) subjective satisfaction among its entries, and (2) the objective list has a structure such that some threshold level of subjective satisfaction must be attained (no matter how high one's score on other dimensions of the good life) in order for the life to qualify as attaining a satisfactory level of overall well-being. Features (1) and (2) do seem plausible, so it may well be that the correct objective-list account would include them. But a life which qualifies as high in well-being according to the objective-list account that includes features (1) and (2) need not satisfy the weak endorsement constraint, because the sources of subjective satisfaction that satisfy features (1) and (2) need not include any subjective satisfaction taken in, or positive attitudes toward, any components of one's life that are entries on the objective list and that significantly intrinsically enhance one's well-being.

Suppose that Samantha experiences reciprocal love. She deeply loves another who loves her in return. Suppose that having such a loving relationship is deemed objectively choiceworthy, so that having it intrinsically enhances one's well-being according to the objective-list account. But Samantha entirely lacks positive attitudes toward this aspect of her life. She neither endorses this loving relationship nor actually desires it. She subscribes to a Stoic philosophy of life according to which such an attachment to a person lowers the quality of her life as she conceives it, and her desires follow her (false, we are assuming) theoretical beliefs. She experiences the choiceworthy thing, having a loving relationship, but her attainment of this good is due to weakness of will on her part. Of course, she has the desires that are part of having a loving relationship, but she has no positive attitude of any sort toward the having of this relationship. And so it goes for other elements of her life. She attains many important goods that qualify as choiceworthy according to the objective-list account, and she experiences a wealth of happiness, pleasure, and related subjective satisfactions. However, her satisfactions and desire fulfillment fail to connect to her objectively choiceworthy achievements in the right way so as to satisfy the weak endorsement constraint. (It may be hard to imagine the case of Samantha as psychologically plausible, but our concern is the logic of the concepts of human flourishing, not what is empirically likely.) Once the issue is squarely posed and irrelevant issues are put aside, I find the weak endorsement constraint deeply counterintuitive in the verdict it must yield on Samantha's life. The weak endorsement constraint requires us to hold that even if we concede that having a loving relationship is a great human good and that Samantha has one, this attainment counts for nothing so far as her well-being is concerned, given that she lacks positive attitudes toward her great achievement. And the same goes for the other objectively valuable achievements in her (as we are imagining it) rich life. She is happy and has gained many objectively valuable attainments, but her alienation from these attainments means not just that her life is less valuable than it ideally might have been, but that none of her attainments intrinsically enhances her well-being at all. My sense is that the weak endorsement constraint has us swallowing a camel of implausibility to avoid ingesting an epistemic gnat.

Rejection of the weak endorsement constraint is compatible with insistence on internal structure in the objective list. Features (1) and (2) noted above would have it that to be living a good life, one must have at least a threshold amount of subjective satisfaction (pleasure and desire satisfaction). No doubt one should also add a feature (3): that to be living a good life, one must have at least a threshold amount of objective goods other than subjective satisfaction. These requirements allow that any attainment of some of any good that is an entry on the objective list intrinsically enhances one's well-being. The entries on the objective list also exhibit positive and negative complementarities. The prudential value of pleasure is enhanced, I am inclined to hold, when what one takes pleasure in is itself objectively valuable, and the prudential value of pleasure is reduced to some extent when the pleasure is accompanied by ignorance or significantly mistaken belief about the character of the source of the pleasure.[30]

XVI. CONCLUSION

Some goods in an individual's life are objectively worthwhile. They are good for their own sakes quite independently of the individual's own

---

[30] Acknowledging complementarity, I need not disagree with Stephen Darwall's analysis of how a person's life is enriched by engagement in activities that are truly valuable, that she appreciates as truly valuable, and that she enjoys in virtue of her appreciation of their value. See Darwall, "Valuing Activity," elsewhere in this volume.

attitudes toward them and opinions as to their worth. These goods form the entries on a list, the objective list. An element in an individual's life intrinsically augments her well-being just in case that element corresponds to some entry on the objective list. An individual's life goes better, has more well-being, counts as flourishing to a greater extent, the more the individual gets goods that are entries on the objective list. The entries on the list are ranked in importance, and getting items that correspond to more important entries does more to augment one's well-being, other things being equal. No doubt many entries on the list have psychological prerequisites: for example, one cannot write a good novel without intending to write something and without doing some writing intentionally. But there is no attitude that an individual must have toward an element in her life if that element is to qualify as intrinsically augmenting her well-being according to the objective-list theory. To count as such, the goods in an individual's life need not be tinged with enjoyment nor colored by desire. In other words, for something to qualify as intrinsically enhancing an individual's well-being, it (1) is neither necessary nor sufficient that the individual actually desire that thing, and (2) is neither necessary nor sufficient that the individual actually enjoy (or have some other sort of positive experience of) that thing. These are the main claims I have tried to defend in this essay.

Philosophy, University of California, San Diego

HAPPINESS AND HUMAN FLOURISHING
IN KANT'S ETHICS

By Thomas E. Hill, Jr.

I. Introduction

Ancient moral philosophers, especially Aristotle and his followers, typically shared the assumption that ethics is primarily concerned with how to achieve the final end for human beings, a life of "happiness" or "human flourishing." This final end was not a subjective condition, such as contentment or the satisfaction of our preferences, but a life that could be objectively determined to be appropriate to our nature as human beings. Character traits were treated as moral virtues because they contributed well toward this ideal life, either as means to it or as constitutive aspects of it. Traits that tended to prevent a "happy" life were considered vices, even if they contributed to a life that was pleasant and what a person most wanted. The idea of "happiness" (or human flourishing) was central, then, in philosophical efforts to specify what we ought to do, what sort of persons we should try to become, and what sort of life a wise person would hope for.

In modern philosophy this ancient conception of happiness has been largely replaced by more subjective conceptions. Not surprisingly, then, happiness plays a different, and usually diminished, role in modern moral theories. Immanuel Kant is a striking, and influential, example of this trend. Viewing happiness as personal contentment and success in achieving the ends we want, he argues that morality is a constraint on the pursuit of a happy life rather than a means to it or an element of it. Even the moral duty to contribute to the happiness of others is more limited in Kant's moral theory than in most other modern theories that (like Kant) abandon the common ancient conceptions of "happiness."

These are apparently major disagreements about the importance of happiness and "human flourishing" in a moral life, and it is natural to wonder what are the reasons for the disagreements and how deep they run. As a step toward understanding the contrasts better, I shall try to sort out and describe briefly several different aspects of Kant's moral theory, as I understand it, especially concerning how happiness and human flourishing are (or are not) relevant to ethics. My project here is not to defend Kant's position, but to clarify it and at times to explore Kant's reasons for holding it. Some of Kant's points, as we shall see, are widely accepted, but others are highly controversial. Some are basic to his ethical theory, but others prove not to be. All of the points are open to dispute, but in some cases, I suggest, the dispute rests on a misunderstanding of Kant's position.

143

My discussion here is part of a larger project, which is to distinguish Kant's basic moral theory from unwarranted particular conclusions, to show its appeal so far as possible, to call attention to its shortcomings as I see them, and to suggest modifications to make Kantian ethics more plausible at least on some issues.

Since happiness (*eudaimonia*) in ancient ethics, understood as human flourishing, is generally distinct from what Kant calls happiness (*Glück-seligkeit*), I need at first to explain what I take these ideas to be, at least sufficiently for purposes of subsequent discussion. Then my questions are: How did Kant restrict the role of happiness in his moral theory? And why did he endorse happiness, rather than human flourishing, as the primary nonmoral good for individuals?[1]

II. THE IDEAS OF KANTIAN HAPPINESS AND HUMAN FLOURISHING

What is happiness, and what is it to flourish? Much of the history of Western ethics is devoted to these questions, and the answers have varied in complex and subtle ways that defy brief summary. For present purposes, however, what we need are some stipulations sufficient to fix ideas for subsequent discussion. Here, then, I will merely propose a working understanding of *human flourishing* that I hope will be sufficient to pose the issues on which I want to focus, and then I will contrast this with *happiness* as Kant conceived this.

Plants, animals, and human beings are said to flourish, or not, depending on how well they are doing by some presupposed conception of what is good for things of their kind. They flourish, or thrive, *as* plants, *as* animals, or *as* human beings. They may be said to flourish as a more specific kind of thing, natural or conventional. For example, a particular plant may be said to flourish as a bush (or as a decorative rose bush); a certain animal may be said to flourish as a bird (or as a wild bird of prey); and a particular person may be said to flourish as a hunter (or as a nomadic Buffalo hunter). The relevant criteria of flourishing (as an X) are sometimes part of the meaning of "flourishing" and the term for the kind in question, but they may be merely commonly accepted evaluative standards. As the ancients emphasized, they are typically associated with

---

[1] By calling happiness a "nonmoral" good in Kant's ethics, I have in mind several points. For example, in Kant's view, a happy person is not necessarily a morally good person and a vicious person is not necessarily unhappy. Happiness is a natural end that each person has, but the pursuit of (one's own) happiness is not a moral requirement—except indirectly, when its neglect would increase our temptations to neglect our duties. So far as it is compatible with morality, each person's happiness is a (conditional) good for that person, that is, something rational (but not a duty or virtue) for the person to pursue. We have a duty of beneficence to others, but this directs us to help them to achieve the (permissible) ends they choose, not to improve their characters or to fulfill a moral ideal. Having a good will (roughly, a will to do what is right) is, by contrast, a moral good, for maintaining a good will is necessary and sufficient for being a morally good person. It is an unconditional good, a fundamental requirement of morality.

natural tendencies: birds fly, fish swim, plants grow and draw nourishment through roots, etc. We think of things as not fully flourishing (as a certain kind) when they are impeded in these characteristic functions, when they are "damaged," "injured," "deformed," or "degenerate." In speaking of human beings, animals, and even (sometimes) plants, we invoke notions of striving and fulfillment: in general an X flourishes more fully as an X when the strivings it has as an X are fulfilled or at least partially successful. In human beings and higher-order animals, flourishing (as human or animal) is commonly thought to be marked by a sense of well-being and a significant degree of contentment about one's present condition or prospects. Being content, however, does not mean that one is flourishing, for contentment is merely a subjective sense of well-being that can persist despite serious disease, malfunctioning natural capacities, and imminent collapse. Notoriously, in human beings, narcotic drugs cause feelings of contentment in diseased, mentally damaged addicts who are far from flourishing as human beings.

These points seem obvious, I hope, because they reflect more or less how flourishing is usually understood today, even apart from philosophical theories. Together the points make the term "flourishing" in some respects less misleading than "happiness" for purposes of expressing ancient ideas of the final good for human beings. "Happiness," as often noted, now often stands for temporary euphoria, mindless contentment, a warm glow, or pleasure without worry. By common opinion now, one can be happy for a few moments, then unhappy, then happy again, and so on; but the same does not hold for *flourishing as a human being*. Admittedly, a person who is flourishing could be suddenly incapacitated or destroyed, but the description typically refers to a pattern of strivings and fulfillments, etc., over a significant period of time, not to something as variable as moods, sensations, and other passive states.

This current view of human flourishing reflects some of the basic ideas of "happiness" in ancient philosophy, and no doubt owes much to that source.[2] Ancient moral philosophy includes variations as well as similarities, of course, but for present purposes we may treat Aristotle's account

---

[2] My brief sketch of a contemporary view of human flourishing is just a summary of how I interpret common understandings of the idea, but few philosophers seem to discuss it independently of the texts of Aristotle and other ancient philosophers. John Cooper uses the term "human flourishing" to capture (roughly) Aristotle's idea of *eudaimonia* or "happiness," and he credits Elizabeth Anscombe for suggesting this translation. See John Cooper, *Reason and Human Good in Aristotle* (Cambridge: Harvard University Press, 1975), pp. 89–143, esp. p. 90n.; and G. E. M. Anscombe, "Modern Moral Philosophy," *Philosophy*, vol. 33, no. 124 (January 1958), pp. 1–19. Other scholars prefer "happiness" as the appropriate translation, while making clear that Aristotle's conception of "happiness" differs from familiar contemporary conceptions. See, for example, Julia Annas, *The Morality of Happiness* (Oxford and New York: Oxford University Press, 1993); Nancy Sherman, *The Fabric of Character* (Oxford: Oxford University Press, 1989); Anthony Kenny, *Aristotle on the Perfect Life* (Oxford: Oxford University Press, 1992); and Richard Kraut, *Aristotle and the Human Good* (Princeton: Princeton University Press, 1989).

of "happiness" (or human flourishing) as a paradigm.[3] The core of this idea, as I understand it, is as follows. "Happiness," properly conceived, describes an active, complete life that necessarily includes being virtuous and using practical reason in deliberation. Characteristic, natural, "essential" human capacities are developed and fulfilled together in a "happy" life. Community, moral exemplars, effort, and good fortune are supposed to be necessary, at least as causally enabling conditions. Whether acting in certain ways is conducive to a person's "happiness" or not is an objective matter that the person can discern if wise and virtuous; but ordinary, imperfect people often misjudge what is required. The particulars of a "happy" life vary from person to person, but not simply with their actual desires, considered preferences, or chosen ends. A "happy" life is pleasant and all that a wise person could (realistically) want, but a pleasant and content life is not necessarily a "happy" one. In a perfectly "happy" (and so virtuous) life, natural desires have been shaped into a harmonious system appropriate to the circumstances, and thus, in a sense, our main desires would be satisfied, not frustrated or repressed, in such a life. Without this special shaping, however, the goal of "satisfying all our desires" is far from the ideal of a "happy" life.

Kant seems to shift between several ideas of happiness. In all cases, though, happiness is conceived as something more subjective, indeterminate, and variable from person to person than human flourishing is typically thought to be. Kant agrees with Aristotle and others that *virtue* (at least as Kant understands this) requires much more than satisfying our desires and feeling content. We must use practical reason to determine objectively what is morally right and virtuous to choose. But by sharply distinguishing virtue and happiness, Kant splits elements that are apparently *combined* in Aristotle's idea of human flourishing.[4] The moral element (virtue) Kant then treats as objective, common to all human beings, distinct from desires, and discerned by reason. But the other element (happiness) he treats as subjective, relative to individuals, desire-based, and not very well served by reason.

---

[3] See Aristotle, *Nicomachean Ethics*, trans. Terence Irwin (Indianapolis: Hackett Publishing Co., 1985), esp. Book I. Many similarities and variations are described in detail in Annas, *The Morality of Happiness*. Since my aim is to emphasize the contrasts between Aristotle's idea of "happiness" (or human flourishing) and quite different Kantian ideas, in referring to Aristotle's *eudaimonia* I will either use the term "human flourishing" or else use quotation marks ("happiness").

[4] Strictly speaking, Kant splits virtue (as he conceives it) from happiness (as he conceives it), but not Aristotelian "virtue" from Aristotelian "happiness." "Virtue," according to Kant, is a "capacity and considered resolve" and "strength" to resist "what opposes the moral disposition *within us*." Immanuel Kant, *The Metaphysics of Morals*, trans. Mary Gregor (Cambridge: Cambridge University Press, 1991), pp. 186 [380], 194 [390], and 197 [394]. (The numbers in brackets here and later indicate pages in the standard Prussian Academy edition.) A virtuous person, then, must have not only a will to do what is right (a "good will") but also a resolve to resist temptations and strength of will to do so. Virtue, according to Aristotle, requires reshaping or getting rid of desires that might compete with our doing the right thing; and thus Aristotle's fully virtuous person, being temperate rather than merely continent, has no need for the *strength of will to resist temptations* that Kant refers to.

Sometimes Kant writes of happiness as something familiar and attainable (with luck): e.g., as "preservation," "welfare," and "well-being."[5] Most often, however, Kant characterizes happiness as an unattainable goal, something we can only approximate: e.g., as "an absolute whole, a maximum of well-being in my present, and in every future, state."[6] Sometimes the goal seems to be lasting *contentment*: e.g., "satisfaction with one's state, so long as this is lasting," and "a rational being's consciousness of the agreeableness of life which without interruption accompanies his whole existence."[7] At other times the central idea is *getting all that we desire*: e.g., "total satisfaction" of our "needs and inclinations" and "all inclinations combined in a sum total."[8] The differences here seem not to have concerned Kant. In fact, sometimes he brings the different ideas together: e.g., happiness is "that everything should always go the way you would like it to—[that is,] continuous well-being, enjoyment of life, complete satisfaction with one's condition."[9]

Kant realizes that all of our inclinations cannot be jointly satisfied and that we do not have any determinate idea of what this total satisfaction would be for us. Usually we have an even less determinate idea of the happiness of others. For practical purposes, then, the aim of promoting happiness, for oneself or another, must be understood more modestly: roughly, as trying to contribute to the satisfaction of some significant portion of the person's set of inclination-based ends.[10] Similarly, when happiness is interpreted as contentment, promoting happiness must be understood as increasing a person's contentment or subjective sense of well-being. The aim of promoting someone's happiness, understood as a practical aim, cannot be that the person will achieve total satisfaction of desire or uninterrupted contentment for a lifetime. That is obviously impossible to achieve, and, knowing this, we cannot seriously count it as a goal.

III. THE LIMITED ROLE OF HAPPINESS IN KANT'S ETHICS: OLD ISSUES

Kant reacted strongly against moral theories, ancient and modern, that, in his opinion, misunderstood and overrated the value of happiness or failed to acknowledge adequately the moral constraints on the pursuit of

---

[5] Immanuel Kant, *Groundwork of the Metaphysic of Morals*, trans. H. J. Paton (New York: Harper and Row Publishers, 1964), hereafter *Groundwork*, p. 93 [395]. See also Kant, *Metaphysics of Morals*, p. 193 [389].

[6] Kant, *Groundwork*, p. 67 [399].

[7] Kant, *Metaphysics of Morals*, p. 193 [389], and Immanuel Kant, *Critique of Practical Reason*, trans. Lewis White Beck (New York: Macmillan, 1993), p. 20 [22].

[8] Kant, *Groundwork*, pp. 73 [405] and 67 [399].

[9] Kant, *Metaphysics of Morals*, p. 269 [480].

[10] This characterization is quite vague, but inevitably so, for several reasons. Our ends tend to be indeterminate; our priorities for cases of conflict are often undecided; and it is unclear to what extent ignorance, irrationality, and misjudgment in a person's adoption of ends is supposed to modify or cancel the judgment that helping the person to realize those ends would be promoting the person's happiness.

happiness. Much of his work in ethics in fact seems devoted to putting happiness in its place. There are several distinguishable ways that he attempted to limit the role of happiness in moral theory, and each has been disputed. The controversies on most of these points have been debated for many years, and thus I shall comment only briefly on them. But a recent objection raised by Michael Slote has not been so thoroughly aired.[11] Since I think that it rests on an important misunderstanding that should be corrected, I examine it critically in Section IV.

A. Happiness is not an unconditional good

In Kant's moral theory, happiness is not valuable in some of the ways, and to the degree, that it is in other moral theories. According to Kant, only a good will is "good without qualification," and thus happiness is only conditionally good.[12] Qualified or conditional goods, in Kant's sense, are not worthy of pursuit by rational agents in all possible contexts, but only when certain conditions obtain. Conditional goods, like happiness, might seem good when we try to consider them apart from particular contexts, but an unqualified good must be worthy of choice in all contexts.[13]

Kant grants, however, that happiness is an end that all human beings have. It is human nature to seek happiness for oneself. Moreover, we tend to pursue it for its own sake, not merely as something good as a means to other things. Thus, even though Kant denies that happiness is an unqualified good, he grants that we tend to treat happiness, at least from our individual perspectives, as "good in itself" in a familiar, everyday sense.[14]

[11] Michael Slote, *From Morality to Virtue* (New York: Oxford University Press, 1992), pp. 39–57.

[12] Kant, *Groundwork*, pp. 61–62 [393–94]. I rely on a (possibly controversial) interpretation explained in my paper "Is a Good Will Overrated?" *Midwest Studies in Philosophy, Volume 20: Moral Concepts* (Notre Dame, IN: University of Notre Dame Press, 1996), pp. 199–217.

[13] G. E. Moore thought that the way to see what is "good in itself" is to consider the item in question "in isolation" from everything else, i.e., "apart from all effects and accompaniments." Here "in itself" is taken quite literally: just look into the thing itself and you will see its goodness. (See G. E. Moore, *Principia Ethica* [1903; Cambridge: Cambridge University Press, 1959], and Moore, *Ethics* [1912; Oxford: Oxford University Press, 1965].) This is not the ordinary use of the term, I think, nor is it Kant's. Crucially, it is not what Kant means by "unconditionally good." See Christine Korsgaard, "Two Distinctions in Goodness," *Philosophical Review*, vol. 92, no. 2 (April 1983), pp. 169–95; and my "Is a Good Will Overrated?"

[14] There is some disagreement among Kant scholars, I think, about whether Kant admits that there are individual-agent-relative values, things that are merely *good to or for a person* in a sense that does not necessarily give others reasons to act (e.g., to help or refrain from interference). (I say "individual-agent-relative" here to distinguish the values in question from those that might be described as "rational-agents-relative." In a sense, all value according to Kant stems from what persons rationally will and thus is not something that could exist independently of all [possible] valuing agents.) Of course, it is agreed that Kant's view is that insofar as attainment of happiness is consistent with morality, the happiness of every person is something that we have some moral reason to promote; and thus "morally permissible happiness," in Kant's view, is not *simply* valuable to the person who would attain it. The disagreement, I think, concerns whether Kant acknowledged the category of value judgments entirely relativized to individual agents.

We want happiness not for any further purpose it may serve, but just for what it is, and it is fully rational to act on this desire if doing so is compatible with duty and virtue.

Kant, however, does not treat happiness as something that has "intrinsic value" in the ways that this term has been understood by G. E. Moore, W. D. Ross, R. B. Perry, C. I. Lewis, and others.[15] In Kant's theory there are no *intrinsic values* as Moore understood the term; that is, there are no intuited nonnatural properties that "supervene" on natural properties (e.g., aspects of experiences of sentient beings). Kant's theory is also incompatible with the view that intrinsic values exist as natural properties, such as being "objects of interest" (Perry), satisfying "experiences" (Lewis), or being desired for themselves when we are fully informed (Brandt). Kant's view, as I understand it, is that things are good or valuable by virtue of being the objects of rational willing, and what it is rational to will is not a question that can be settled entirely by empirical means—or by intuition. In deliberating about right and wrong, then, we cannot assume that happiness has a natural or intuited "intrinsic value" always tending in favor of the acts that promote it. Unlike many philosophers, Kant does not think that each potential increase in someone's happiness has a quantity of value on a scale of commensurable values so that we have good reason for doing what will bring about that increase unless that bit of value is "outweighed" by more value that we can bring about by other options.[16]

Although Kant says that happiness is a natural end for human beings, he rejects the idea that happiness is a final, self-sufficient end for human beings in Aristotle's sense.[17] For Aristotle, as I understand him, a life of "happiness" (in his special sense) contains within it all the valuable sorts of things that any human being could reasonably want, mixed in the proportions appropriate to the context as judged by a practically wise person. Moral virtue, in Aristotle's view, is an essential constituent of such a "happy" life, and Aristotle apparently thought that no one would be wrong to live such a life, or to aim to do so, in any circumstances.[18]

---

[15] See, for example, Moore, *Principia Ethica*; Moore, *Ethics*; R. B. Perry, *General Theory of Value: Its Meaning and Basic Principles Construed in Terms of Interest* (New York: Longmans, Green, 1926); C. I. Lewis, *An Analysis of Knowledge and Valuation* (La Salle, IL: Open Court, 1947); and W. D. Ross, *The Right and the Good* (Oxford: Oxford University Press, 1930). These are classics of intrinsic value theory. In discussions of environmental ethics the term has reappeared in recent years, but without much attention to the controversies that earlier theories of intrinsic value raised. See, for example, *Environmental Philosophy*, ed. D. S. Mannison, M. A. McRobbie, and R. Routley (Canberra: Australian National University Research School of Social Sciences, 1980). For more contemporary use of the term, see Thomas Hurka, *Perfectionism* (New York: Oxford University Press, 1994).

[16] Kant, *Groundwork*, p. 102 [434–35].

[17] *Ibid.*, p. 83 [416]; Aristotle, *Nicomachean Ethics*, Book 1, ch. 1.

[18] I distinguish living a happy life from aiming to do so because it seems possible that fully virtuous persons could be living a happy life (in Aristotle's sense) while for the most part not holding the ideal of this sort of life as a deliberative goal; for example, they could

Kant conceives of "happiness" more narrowly (without virtue as a necessary ingredient) and insists that a happy life (so conceived) would not be a good life, or a worthy end, unless it could be pursued and achieved without violating moral requirements (which are not derived from a prior assumption that happiness is always good as an end).

Kant's position here on the value of happiness is controversial, of course, but it is perhaps more widely shared than we might at first think. Aristotelians should have no *substantial* disagreement with Kant on these points about the limited value of happiness as Kant, more narrowly, conceives it; for Aristotelians do not affirm the unqualified goodness of happiness in that sense.[19] Even intuitionists, such as Moore and Ross, are not committed to the idea that happiness is something unqualifiedly good—that is, good to pursue in all contexts—and their intuitionism of value allows that there may be better ends to pursue than happiness, better even than the greatest happiness of the greatest number.[20]

When Kant's position is properly understood, then, objections stem mostly from two sources: (1) classic utilitarians who treat "the greatest happiness" as an unconditionally good end to pursue, and (2) advocates of intuitionism and naturalism in value theory who rightly see Kant as denying their understanding of what constitutes value. These are old, much debated issues, and among contemporary philosophers Kant has much good company on his side.[21]

B. *Happiness is not the ultimate criterion of right action*

Kant holds that it is not always morally right to do what you expect will maximize happiness. This is not merely because consequences are

---

be concentrating instead on the particular choices at hand (in the manner of one with acquired virtues). The deliberate pursuit of a happy life might be more appropriately the ideal for novices who are not yet fully virtuous or for certain special decisions that require consciously reviewing one's life as a whole.

[19] Kant would not fully accept Aristotle's view about the value of happiness even in Aristotle's sense, but their views are closer regarding that.

[20] Ross, like Moore, was an intuitionist regarding "intrinsic value," but, unlike Moore, he was not a consequentialist who thought that the right thing to do is always to maximize intrinsic value. See Ross, *The Right and the Good*.

[21] Although interpretation is controversial, Bentham and Mill, as usually understood, represent classic utilitarianism; see Jeremy Bentham, *The Principles of Morals and Legislation* (1789; Buffalo, NY: Prometheus Books, 1988); and John Stuart Mill, *Utilitarianism*, ed. George Sher (1863; Indianapolis: Hackett Publishing Co., 1979). G. E. Moore and W. D. Ross are intuitionists with regard to intrinsic value; R. B. Perry and C. I. Lewis advocate the sort of naturalism that is intended here. Few, if any, contemporary philosophers defend the intuitionist position. Critics of classic utilitarianism are legion, but the most often cited is John Rawls, *A Theory of Justice* (Cambridge: Harvard University Press, 1971). Naturalistic definitions of value are also widely rejected. See, for example, R. M. Hare, *Freedom and Reason* (Oxford: Oxford University Press, 1963); Allan Gibbard, *Wise Choices, Apt Feelings* (Cambridge, MA: Harvard University Press, 1990); Simon Blackburn, *Spreading the Word* (Oxford: Oxford University Press, 1984); and Christine Korsgaard et al., *The Sources of Normativity* (New York: Cambridge University Press, 1996).

uncertain, for Kant is also committed to the stronger claim that there are many things that would be wrong to do even if we knew that they would actually maximize happiness. This goes beyond what I have already said, although perhaps not in an obvious way. Utilitarians often base their thesis that we always *ought* to do what promotes the greatest happiness on an assertion that happiness is *good* in itself, or intrinsically valuable; but they can affirm the former without the latter. That is, they can endorse a utilitarian theory of right without taking a stand in value theory. They can do this simply by asserting that the right thing to do is whatever maximizes happiness (or expected happiness) without arguing for this from the prior premise that happiness is intrinsically valuable. They may be challenged to produce new "grounds" for their utilitarian principle, but they would at least avoid dispute with Kantians (and others) about whether happiness is *unconditionally good*. Perhaps needless to say, their main dispute with Kantians (about what is right to do) would remain unsettled.

C. Happiness is not the unqualified goal of moral rules

Kant's theory not only affirms moral principles that constrain the pursuit of the general happiness, it is also incompatible with the rule-utilitarian idea that these principles themselves are justified because their general adoption as norms promotes the greatest happiness in the long run.[22] There is, I believe, a reasonable reconstruction of Kant's fundamental framework for moral deliberation that, like rule-utilitarianism, distinguishes deliberation about moral rules from deliberation guided by moral rules, but in Kant's theory, unlike in rule-utilitarianism, specific rules are not identified or "legislated" because their adoption would maximize

[22] For often-cited statements of rule-utilitarianism, see J. O. Urmson, "On the Interpretation of the Philosophy of J. S. Mill," *Philosophical Quarterly*, vol. 3 (1953); Richard Brandt, "Toward a Credible Form of Utilitarianism," in *Morality and the Language of Conduct*, ed. Hector-Neri Castaneda and George Nakhnikian (Detroit: Wayne State University Press, 1963); John Rawls, "Two Concepts of Rules," *Philosophical Review*, vol. 64 (1955), pp. 3–32; and David Lyons, *Forms and Limits of Utilitarianism* (Oxford: Clarendon Press, 1965). Rule-utilitarianism developed in response to objections to "act-utilitarianism," which holds that in every case we ought to act in the way that would maximize utility even if this would contravene important rules (actual and ideal) that are generally useful. The standard objection was that act-utilitarianism would endorse acts of injustice (e.g., false witness, even murder) in cases where these acts would promote (even slightly) more utility. Rule-utilitarianism tries to block this objection by maintaining that we should follow the generally useful rules of justice, even in these cases. But there are subtle differences in different versions of rule-utilitarianism.

David Cummiskey argues that, despite Kant's own beliefs contrary to utilitarianism of all sorts, features of Kant's basic moral theory, when followed out consistently, lead to a kind of consequentialism that is akin to rule-utilitarianism. See David Cummiskey, *Kantian Consequentialism* (New York: Oxford University Press, 1996). I disagree, but cannot argue the point here.

happiness.[23] Kantian deliberation about norms is constrained by the requirements implicit in the formulas of the Categorical Imperative, especially the idea of persons as ends in themselves.[24] Even at the highest level of deliberation about rules, then, we cannot endorse rules that express or encourage the idea that individuals are like exchangeable commodities, each having some value of a sort that is commensurable and permits calculated trade-offs.

D. Strict moral rules forbid exceptions that might prevent unhappiness

Kant does not merely reject the extreme utilitarian stand regarding the morality of promoting happiness. That alone would disturb only relatively few contemporary moral philosophers. Notoriously, Kant also severely limited the role of happiness in his moral theory by endorsing substantive rules of conduct that make very strict demands and admit few, if any, exceptions. The most often cited example is probably Kant's stand on lying (even for "benevolent purposes"), but his condemnation of "defiling oneself by lust," adultery, "unnatural crimes," "murdering oneself," revolutionary activity, and other matters is also unconditional.[25] Even when Kant explicitly mentions a permissible exception to principles in his theory of justice, this often merely highlights how unusually strict and inflexible his principles are. For example, at one point Kant grants that we may (and must) disobey an official state order if it requires us to

[23] I sketch such a reconstruction in "A Kantian Perspective on Moral Rules," *Philosophical Perspectives*, vol. 6 (1992), pp. 285–304. See also chapters 10 and 11 in my *Dignity and Practical Reason in Kant's Moral Theory* (Ithaca: Cornell University Press, 1992), pp. 196–250; and my essay "A Kantian Perspective on Political Violence," *The Journal of Ethics*, vol. 1 (1997), pp. 105–40.

[24] In Kant's moral theory, "the Categorical Imperative" represents the most fundamental moral requirements, expressed in an imperative form—as a "*command* of reason" (*Groundwork*, pp. 83, 84 [413, 416]). It is supposed to be an unconditional requirement of reason that grounds particular moral duties, which are morally and rationally binding even if they do not serve our self-interest or further our chosen ends. Kant presents the Categorical Imperative in several formulas, which he suggests amount to the same basic idea (*ibid.*, pp. 103–4 [436–37]). The interpretation of these formulas, whether they are equivalent, and even how many there are remain controversial. The first formula is: "Act only on that maxim through which you can at the same time will that it should become a universal law" (*ibid.*, p. 88 [421]). A variation, used in Kant's examples, is: "Act as if the maxim of your action were to become through your will a universal law of nature" (*ibid.*, p. 89 [421]). This is followed by the influential "humanity formula": "Act in such a way that you always treat humanity, whether in your own person or in the person of any other, never simply as a means, but always at the same time as an end" (*ibid.*, p. 96 [429]). Kant writes of both "humanity" and "persons" as "ends in themselves," which have an "unconditional and incomparable worth" as opposed to mere "price" (*ibid.*, p. 102 [434]).

[25] In a late essay, Kant takes the extreme stance that a person would not have a right to tell a lie to an assassin to save a friend from murder. See Immanuel Kant, *Grounding for the Metaphysics of Morals, with On a Supposed Right to Lie because of Philanthropic Concerns*, trans. James W. Ellington (Indianapolis: Hackett Publishing Co., 1981), pp. 63–67. Most contemporary admirers of Kant, I think, reject this position. See, for example, Alan Donagan, *The Theory of Morality* (Chicago: University of Chicago Press, 1977), pp. 88–89. For Kant's controversial position on other matters, see *Metaphysics of Morals*, pp. 220–21 [424–45], 96–97 [278–79], 168–69 [363–69], 218–19 [422–33], 127–33 [316–23].

do something "immoral in itself," but this (rarely mentioned) concession calls attention, by way of contrast, to Kant's remarkably strong claim that in all other cases we must obey the law, even when the law is maliciously imposed by a tyrant.[26] To take another example, Kant concedes that the strict duty of state officials to execute those who commit murder excludes the case in which for the sake of "honor" a mother kills her "illegitimate" infant. Kant says that because the child "is born outside of the law," it has "stolen into the commonwealth (like contraband)" and so "the commonwealth can ignore its existence" and also "its annihilation."[27] Few of us, I imagine, will want to insist on execution of the mother in this case, but Kant's discussion of it (as only one of three exceptions) does little to improve, and may even worsen, Kant's image as an inflexible, insensitive, perhaps even callous, "man of principle."

By endorsing his strict principles, Kant goes far beyond others who agree with him on the weaker thesis that the pursuit of personal and general happiness is subject to moral constraints. Ross, for example, holds that the duty to promote happiness can be, and often is, overridden by other prima facie duties (fidelity, justice, reparation, noninjury, gratitude, and self-improvement), and other nonconsequentialists allow "built in" exceptions to moral rules to accommodate certain special cases in which sticking to the rules without those exceptions would have a disastrous effect on the happiness of many people. Similarly, rights theorists now usually characterize particular rights as "defeasible," even if the potentially overriding considerations cannot be spelled out in advance. Quite unlike the disputes mentioned earlier, then, the dispute provoked by Kant's stand concerning inflexible principles pits Kant against most other moral theorists.

Once again, I do not want to pursue further the issue that I have identified, but my reason is not the same as in previous cases. Here the Kantian side of the dispute is so extreme and (in my view) implausible that discussions of it seem to me quite tiresome and "academic" in the pejorative sense. Although Kant's rigoristic principles concerning lying, obedience to law, etc., were no doubt an important part of his own personality and moral thinking, there is little in his basic moral theory, I believe, to support his extreme stand on these substantive issues.[28] For example, as is often noted, a full and honest articulation of the maxim

---

[26] Kant, *Metaphysics of Morals*, pp. 127–33 [316–23], 176 [371]; see also Hans Reiss, "Postscript," in *Kant: Political Writings*, ed. Hans Reiss (Cambridge: Cambridge University Press, 1991), pp. 267–68. See also Immanuel Kant, *Religion within the Limits of Reason Alone*, ed. T. M. Greene and H. H. Hudson (New York: Harper and Brothers, 1960), p. 142n. [154n.].

[27] Kant, *Metaphysics of Morals*, pp. 144–45 [336].

[28] My point is that Kant endorsed some particular principles as absolute that are indefensible even within his own basic theory, not that there are no defensible principles that hold without exception. Much depends on how the forbidden activity is described. When motives are included in the description, it becomes more plausible that we can describe acts that are always wrong, e.g., "torturing someone merely for your amusement." Some labels — e.g., "murder" and "rape"—seem implicitly to indicate an unacceptable motive.

behind many conscientious lies would be more subtle and context-sensitive than those mentioned in Kant's examples. So to consider them "as if universal laws of nature," we should not be thinking of possible worlds in which everyone lies whenever they please, or for selfish reasons, or for many other reasons that we could not sensibly choose for everyone to act on.[29] Kant's polemical argument, given late in life, against the right to lie to someone who threatens to murder a friend is question-begging.[30] Kant argues that if one lied and unexpectedly the lie led the murderer to his victim, then the death of the victim would be imputable to the person who lied (as well as the killer); but this claim *presupposes* Kant's conclusion that telling the lie is wrong regardless of the circumstances. If we suppose, to the contrary, that lying is the right thing to do in the specified circumstances, then there is no reason to insist that the liar would be to blame for the death if, unforeseeably, the conscientious lie resulted in the murderer's finding the victim.

Also, the idea that we should not treat persons "merely as means," which is often cited as the source of Kant's strictest principles, does not really support them, at least if that idea is interpreted in the way that makes most sense of Kant's arguments for it.[31] Those arguments, I think, support a relatively formal prescription, which I call the "thin interpretation" of the humanity formula. The main idea is that, whereas Kant's universal-law formula explicitly calls for us to consider what we ourselves could will as universal laws, the humanity formula requires us to consider what the practical reason of those who are affected by our acts could approve. We must take up the perspective of those adversely affected by (or otherwise rationally opposed to) our treatment of them. Usually these are other people, but we can, in the relevant sense, mistreat ourselves. Thinking of the humanity (or "rational nature") of potentially mistreated persons as an end in itself requires that our principles be justifiable to them, at least insofar as they too take up the moral perspective. It also prevents us from basing our decisions of principle on the idea that the value of persons is (in principle) quantifiable and relative to their social standing, usefulness, capacity for happiness, etc. But none of this implies that substantive moral rules (e.g., regarding lying, sex, revolution, and punishment) must be absolute or subject to only a few rare exceptions.

From the thin idea of "humanity as an end," together with some further assumptions, Kant moved to a more substantive working notion of what

---

[29] Kant, *Groundwork*, p. 89 [421].

[30] Kant, "On a Supposed Right to Lie because of Philanthropic Concerns" (*supra* note 25).

[31] Kant, *Groundwork*, pp. 95–96 [427–29]. Kant's humanity formula has been interpreted in many different ways. My view is developed in my essay collection *Dignity and Practical Reason in Kant's Moral Theory* (*supra* note 23), pp. 38–57, 197–225; in my essay "Donagan's Kant," *Ethics*, vol. 104 (1993), pp. 22–52; and in my essay "A Kantian Perspective on Political Violence" (*supra* note 23).

we must do to treat persons as ends, rather than merely as means. This thicker idea, with which Kant works in *The Metaphysics of Morals*, places high priority on acting in ways that protect, develop, and "honor" rational nature in human beings, who are presumed to be free and equal (in certain Kantian senses). Respect for these "rationally necessary" values would guide Kantian moral "legislators" away from familiar consequentialist thinking and (arguably) would give them reason to adopt quite stringent principles regarding murder, coercion, deception, manipulation, treating people with contempt, and so on. These value priorities should also lead us, more than Kant himself acknowledged, to give positive support for institutions and practices that increase everyone's opportunities to live as rational, free persons. But the main point for present purposes is that merely by making our "rational nature" a higher value priority than "happiness," even Kant's thicker conception of "humanity as an end" does not provide grounds for his absolute, and nearly absolute, practical principles.

A question more interesting, and potentially more rewarding, than whether Kant was right to hold such inflexible principles is how a moral theory that is Kantian in a broad sense (i.e., one that starts from specified basic points in Kant's theory) can determine what exceptions to various moral principles should be acknowledged. To say that exceptions should be allowed whenever "much," or "very much," or "very, very much" happiness would be lost otherwise seems un-Kantian in spirit and invites a familiar "slippery slope" argument. (If it is all right to torture someone to save a million lives, why not a million minus one, a million minus two—and so on?) A reasonable response requires more thorough explanation and defense of the basic Kantian moral constraints on deliberation. These constraints are supposed to be expressed in the various formulations of the Categorical Imperative, but those fundamental prescriptions need to be combined and further refined before they can be used convincingly to answer the consequentialists' doubts.

E. The purpose of government is to secure justice, not to promote happiness

Kant maintains that the proper aim of government is not to promote happiness but to secure justice. The fundamental principle of justice says, in effect, that it is not right to hinder the "external freedom" of another person that would be allowed under a system of "universal laws" that respects the equality and freedom of all.[32] John Rawls's first principle of

---

[32] Kant, *Metaphysics of Morals*, p. 56 [230–31]. See also Reiss, ed., *Kant: Political Writings*, pp. 73–74, 80. "External freedom" is the ability to act as one chooses without hindrance from others. Kant holds that the exercise of external freedom is unjust when it is incompatible with the equal freedom of all under universal laws. We exercise our external freedom through intentional acts, but external freedom is contrasted with two kinds of internal

justice is quite similar to this, and was perhaps inspired by it.[33] Kant offers little explicit interpretation of his own principle, but his main focus was apparently on "negative" freedoms such as freedom from murder, slavery, and theft. Kant does, however, allow for government assistance to the needy, and it is arguable that Kant's basic theory of justice supports even stronger policies of assistance.[34] There are also reasons to believe that Kant's general moral theory, if applied with a fuller understanding of social realities than Kant apparently had, would justify us in taking a broader view than Kant did of what constitutes the "freedom" that justice is meant to protect.[35] In any case, it seems clear that Kant is committed to the view that the primary function of government is the protection of the equal liberties of citizens as opposed to promoting their happiness.

Discussion of the issue between Kant and others here would echo many contemporary debates in political philosophy, but it would have some special features. Kant's arguments do not depend on the claims that ("external") freedom is intrinsically valuable, that only individuals know what best promotes their happiness, or that our freedom (or right) to act as we choose is morally unlimited until we make a contract to the contrary. Rather, Kant begins with the idea that practical reason permits "external freedom" to act only in ways such that the exercise of this freedom could coexist with the similar freedom of others (the universal principle of justice).[36] The corollary, in Kant's view, is that coercion is justified to "hinder hindrances to freedom."[37] That is, violations of the principle of justice may be opposed by force, and, given the conditions of human life, we have reason to authorize a sovereign power to try to prevent such violations and reason to obey its commands. Kant holds that the sovereign power in a state ought to conform to the moral requirements of practical reason, but (notoriously) he insists that citizens ought to obey the de facto laws even if the sovereign power violates those moral requirements—except in the limiting case in which the sovereign demands

---

freedom presupposed by moral agency: that is, the ability to act without being determined by natural causes (negative freedom) and "being a law to oneself" (rational autonomy or positive freedom). See Kant, Groundwork, p. 114 [446–47].

[33] Rawls's first principle says that "each person is to have an equal right to the most extensive basic liberty compatible with a similar liberty for others." John Rawls, A Theory of Justice (Cambridge, MA: Harvard University Press, 1971), p. 60. The interpretation of this principle is discussed in a later section (ibid., pp. 201–51).

[34] See James Rosen, Kant's Theory of Justice (Ithaca: Cornell University Press, 1991), pp. 173–208; and Paul Guyer, "Kantian Foundations for Liberalism," Jahrbuch für Strafrecht und Etik/Annual Review of Law and Ethics, vol. 5 (1997), pp. 121–40.

[35] For example, freedom might be understood to include the more positive idea of having certain basic opportunities and resources to live a full life as a rational, autonomous person, and, if so, unjust "hindrances to freedom" might include more than murder, slavery, theft, and the like. Sarah Holtman develops this idea in an excellent Ph.D. dissertation, "Kant, Justice, and the Augmentation of Ideal Theory," University of North Carolina, Chapel Hill, 1996.

[36] Kant, Metaphysics of Morals, p. 56 [230–31].

[37] Ibid., p. 57 [231].

that we do something "wrong in itself."[38] The upshot is that, whether his political theory is interpreted narrowly or broadly, Kant would have sided with contemporary political philosophers who deny that the aim of government is to make citizens happy and who say, instead, that its only legitimate aim is to respect rights and maintain the conditions for just relations among citizens.

Kant's grounds for his position go back to the basic idea that moral principles, even regarding political matters, are just those principles that reasonable and autonomous persons would acknowledge, given adequate understanding and acceptance of the fundamentals of the moral point of view. The justifying framework is analogous to that of Rawls in some respects, but it is a mistake (as Rawls has acknowledged) to treat these as identical or even very closely similar. Kant's claim that "freedom," not happiness, is the primary value in political matters seems to depend on an implicit assumption that rational autonomous human beings would place a higher priority on state protection of their equal opportunities to live as rational end-pursuing agents than on state efforts to promote the various ends that they seek under the name of "happiness." Kant may have thought that empirical evidence would confirm this assumption, but I suspect that Kant also took for granted that it is a necessary feature of our *rationality* that we have a strong preference for "external" freedom over the merely desire-based values that we include under our conception of happiness.[39] The idea, perhaps, is that although being enslaved or imprisoned does not necessarily destroy our rationality and autonomy of will, we cannot develop and use our full powers to live as rational autonomous agents without external liberty.[40]

Although Kant's concern to preserve freedom under a just social order is not reducible to a concern to promote the happiness of citizens, it should be obvious that the former encompasses much that utilitarians would recommend as means, or necessary conditions, for maximizing happiness. Thus, it is not surprising to find that Mill agrees with Kant to

---

[38] *Ibid.*, pp. 56–58 [230–33], 129–33 [318–23]. My interpretation of Kant's views on these matters differs somewhat from that presented in Rosen, *Kant's Theory of Justice*, pp. 115–72.

[39] Kant divides human nature into rational nature and sensuous nature. We learn about our sensuous nature empirically—for example, by observing how we feel and act in various circumstances. We cannot help but think of ourselves also as persons with practical reason, and philosophical examination of the idea is supposed to show that this requires attribution to ourselves of some rational dispositions distinct from the desires, impulses, and inclinations attributed on the basis of experience. Kant seems to suppose that human beings have a preference for freedom to live as rational autonomous persons over satisfaction of other desires both because this is a common desire, hard to repress, and also because it is a rational disposition and we are rational (or so we must assume).

[40] The suggestion assumes that Kant thought we have a rational disposition, not only to avoid making irrational choices, but also to develop and exercise our practical rationality over time by pursuing morally necessary ends and pursuing happiness within the limits of our duties. Insofar as we think of the relevant "external liberties" as those needed to fulfill this rational disposition (with due respect to others), then it makes sense to say that it is not just our desires but also our rational nature that places a high priority on these external liberties.

a considerable extent on what justice requires, at least in ordinary cases.[41] Mill and Kant make their recommendations on different grounds, and they disagree about the permissibility of making exceptions for special cases; but Kant's rhetoric against making "happiness" the goal of government should not blind us from the fact that his ideal of justice, if realized, would provide much of what we need to be happy, but lack in an unjust world.

IV. CONCERN FOR HAPPINESS IN CHARACTER, MOTIVES, AND DELIBERATION

A. Old issues about happiness as a moral ideal, motive, and reason for acting

In several related ways, Kant denies that the moral assessment of our character, motives, and deliberation depends on our efforts and success in pursuing our own happiness. Consider, for example, the idea that human happiness has *moral value*, not merely in the sense that it is morally right to promote the happiness of others (or happiness in general) but also in a sense implying that living a happy life is a *moral ideal*. The suggestion, in other words, is that living a happy life is a mark of a *morally good person*. In this respect being happy would be like being honest and being courageous, except that it is a more comprehensive characteristic. Those who seem to accept this idea probably have a conception of "happiness" that is radically different from Kant's; nevertheless, it is worth noting that Kant does not endorse this idea. Kant counts happiness (in his sense) as *morally valuable* only in the sense that it is something we have a limited duty (and right) to promote: more specifically, in Kant's view we have an imperfect duty to adopt a maxim to promote the happiness of others as one of our ends and a qualified permission (as well as an indirect duty) to pursue our own happiness.[42]

Furthermore, in Kant's view, acting to promote our own happiness, while often permissible, is normally not something "of moral worth." A maxim of the form "I shall do X in order to increase my happiness," according to Kant, "has no moral content."[43] We do not become worthy of moral esteem by trying to be happy. Sometimes, Kant allows, we might

---

[41] See Mill, *Utilitarianism* (*supra* note 21), pp. 41–63; and J. S. Mill, *On Liberty*, ed. Elizabeth Rapaport (Indianapolis: Hackett Publishing Co., 1978).

[42] Kant, *Metaphysics of Morals*, pp. 190–93 [385–88], 243–48 [448–54]. An imperfect duty, according to Kant, is somewhat indefinite regarding what actions are required to fulfill it. Imperfect duties contrast with perfect duties, which have the form "Always do X" or "Never do X." Typically, as with beneficence, an imperfect duty is a duty to make it a matter of principle (maxim) to pursue a broadly described end (such as "the happiness of others") for moral reasons. This leaves open, as a matter of judgment (but not unlimited discretion), when, how much, and in what ways to promote the end.

[43] Kant, *Groundwork*, p. 66 [398].

act to increase our happiness out of respect for our "indirect" duty to do so (to keep ourselves from temptations), but here the morally commendable motive is duty, not desire for happiness. Kant says that reason directs us to work toward the *summum bonum*, which is the union of virtue and the morally appropriate happiness that virtuous persons deserve.[44] Again, however, the point is not that concern for happiness itself is morally commendable. Even pursuit of the *summum bonum* is of moral worth only when it is "from duty."

Similarly, in Kant's view, when we deliberate about what to do, the fact that an act will enhance our happiness is not in general a reason for assessing that act as a moral duty. The consideration "this will make me happy" is not something that usually weighs in favor of the conclusion "this is what I morally ought to do."[45] Kant concedes a minor exception; for, as noted earlier, he thinks that we should not ignore our own happiness to a degree that would make us so needy or depressed that we would be tempted to neglect our duties to others. The idea, I suppose, need not be just that if we are needy and depressed we will be inclined to steal, and the like. More generally, miserable people tend to dampen the spirits of others, and thus out of concern for the happiness of others we need pay at least some attention to our own happiness. Kant's main points remain, however: for the most part, we are not morally good by virtue of our rational pursuit of happiness; and the ends that should guide our moral deliberations are our own perfection and the happiness of others, not our own happiness.

B. A new issue: Does Kant make us devalue our own happiness relative to that of others?

Kant's views summarized above (in Section IVA) about the moral assessment of character, motives, and deliberation are widely shared, I believe, at least among those who conceive of happiness (more or less) as Kant did. But Michael Slote, in his recent book *From Morality to Virtue*, raises the possibility of a different way that effort and success in the pursuit of happiness might be relevant to the assessment of persons. Slote recommends that we should move beyond *morality* to nonmoral assessments of character as virtuous or vicious, admirable or despicable, from an ordinary, common-sense perspective. From this point of view, Slote argues, whether we are virtuous or not depends significantly on our attitude and conduct with respect to our own happiness. For example, if we are virtuous, we will affirm the importance of our own happiness and will not sacrifice it too readily. In fact, Slote suggests at one point that if

[44] Kant, *Critique of Practical Reason*, pp. 116–26 [110–20].
[45] *Ibid.*, pp. 19–26 [21–26].

we are virtuous we will count our own happiness as (approximately) equal in importance to us as the happiness of all other persons combined.[46]

The issue now is not, as before, a controversy about how severely our pursuit of happiness is constrained by moral requirements. Slote's opposition to Kant, as I understand it, is not merely the usual complaint that Kant's inflexible principles leave us too little permission (or right) to do what we think will make us happy. Rather, the objection is that Kant requires us to "devalue" our own happiness, relative to the happiness of others. He supposedly urges us *as moral agents* to value others' happiness but not our own—or at least to subordinate our own happiness to the happiness of others. Thus, it seems, there is an objectionable "asymmetry" in Kant's ethics between a virtuous attitude toward our own happiness and a virtuous attitude toward the happiness of other people.

Slote's charge against Kant's ethics is similar in kind to a suspicion raised by Nietzsche and Ayn Rand, namely, that traditional moralists, such as Kant, advocate a self-effacing, debilitating, self-sacrificing "altruism" that no clear-thinking, rational person could accept.[47] These writers prompt us to ask, Why is it a virtue to be more concerned for the happiness of others than our own? and, Why shouldn't we get as much credit for "doing for ourselves" as we get for "doing for others"? Taking these questions seriously makes virtue ethics seem more appealing than Kant's ethics because virtue ethics seems to place greater importance on the intelligent pursuit of our own happiness than on any duty to be concerned for the happiness of others.[48]

Why suspect Kant of requiring us to devalue our own happiness? One might think that Kant's denial that we have a direct duty to promote our own happiness reflects his belief that we should value our own happiness less than we should value that of others. In fact, Kant repeatedly implies that most people *care* much more about their own happiness than the happiness of others. This, in his view, is a natural fact, not subject to moral appraisal. In a sense, *valuing* is not merely caring but also implies a stable attitude that we adopt or reaffirm on reflection, a disposition that we have

[46] Slote may intend a somewhat different point, namely, that character traits that are virtues are so because our having them tends to promote our own good and the good of all others combined more or less equally. This claim would not imply that a virtuous person actually has the policy or attitude of weighing others' good equally with his or her own. Slote does not explicitly identify a person's good with "happiness," I think, and therefore the position that I describe is only "suggested" by his remarks. See Slote, *From Morality to Virtue* (*supra* note 11), pp. 4–57, 98.

[47] See, for example, Ayn Rand, *The Virtue of Selfishness* (New York: New American Library, 1964); and Friedrich Nietzsche, *On the Genealogy of Morals*, trans. Walter Kaufmann and R. J. Hollingdale (New York: Vintage Press, 1968).

[48] "Virtue ethics" refers to a cluster of moral theories that hold that the primary concern of moral theory should be to explain good and bad moral character traits (virtues and vices) rather than right and wrong action. How to define "virtue ethics" more specifically is a matter of controversy. See, for example, Roger Crisp and Michael Slote, *Virtue Ethics* (Oxford: Oxford University Press, 1997). This includes a useful bibliography.

for reasons and that we intend to maintain.[49] But, even so, I think that Kant also believes that it is human nature for us to tend to *value* our own happiness more than the happiness of others and that there is nothing immoral or unreasonable about this.[50] At times, it seems, we may love another so much that the other person's happiness means more to us than our own, but this is not the attitude toward others that we normally have and maintain on reflection.[51]

In the ordinary sense intended here, *valuing* our own happiness more than others' happiness does not imply that we will choose to act to further our happiness whenever we can. Valuing is a positive attitude involving many dispositions to make certain choices in various circumstances, but it is not like a steady vector force that constantly pushes us in a certain direction no matter what the conditions. When our pursuit of happiness conflicts with that of others, we need to make a moral judgment about the case. Is it a matter of fair competition? Or is it a violation of others' rights for us to continue to pursue happiness in the way we initially wanted to? If we value our own happiness more than the happiness of the others, we may *prefer* to win the competition ourselves (in the first case), and we may *wish* that we could have permissibly done what we first wanted to do (in the second case)—we may even wish this more than we wish that the others could satisfy their initial desires. But none of this is incompatible with a Kantian good will. A good will, the unconditionally good moral disposition, does not require us to care about and value equally the happiness of all persons, for all purposes, in all contexts. What it requires is wholehearted commitment to constraining all our pursuits by the principles that can ultimately, at the highest level of moral deliberation, be justified to all persons who have equal moral standing and who are

---

[49] I draw (and oversimplify) here from an excellent philosophy Ph.D. dissertation by Valerie Tiberius, "Deliberation about the Good: Justifying What We Value," University of North Carolina, 1997.

[50] I distinguish here *valuing* something from *judging that, all things considered, it is good to pursue or have in the relevant context*. I suppose that a person who is resolute in never immorally pursuing happiness might still *value* being happy in general—for example, might desire it, intend to satisfy the desire when doing so is morally permissible, feel disappointment at losing happiness even when this is morally necessary, and affirm these desires and attitudes on reflection. A fully *virtuous* person, perhaps, values happiness only insofar as it is not immoral to gain it or have it, for (in Kant's view) the correct moral *judgment* is that happiness is only a conditional good, and a fully virtuous person may have learned to *value* such goods only when the condition for their value is satisfied. The tendency to value our happiness over that of others, I think, Kant would ascribe to human nature as something that we cannot entirely overcome. Having the tendency is not our fault, in Kant's view, nor is it entirely regrettable (because it feeds competition on which progress depends). Our primary moral responsibility with respect to this tendency is not to try to transform or transcend it by training our sensibility, but rather not to let the tendency lead us to act in ways that violate or neglect our duties to others and to ourselves.

[51] In *Civilization and Its Discontents*, Freud stresses the rarity of such love and argues that the ideal of equal love of all persons is both contrary to human nature and not an admirable ideal. (See Sigmund Freud, *Civilization and Its Discontents*, trans. Joan Riviere [London: Hogarth Press, 1930].) Needless to say, many Christians profess a different belief.

willing *for purposes of this deliberation* to abstract from the particular features of their special attachments and circumstances. Kant's moral theory, as I understand it, attributes an equal basic moral standing, dignity, or "unconditional and incomparable worth" to all persons, but this is for purposes of determining our moral responsibilities and rights, not for governing our everyday preferences where these are not at issue.

One might think that Kant's ethics makes us devalue our own happiness in an objectionable way just because it requires us to recognize all persons as having equal basic moral worth. The objection might be that Kantian "equal worth" inevitably leads to a utilitarian (or consequentialist) moral decision procedure, and therefore makes us devalue our happiness in just the ways that utilitarianism is often thought to do. The argument might run as follows: If each person has the same value, then the happiness of each should have the same value, other things equal; and, since more value is better than less, the happiness of two persons must be more valuable than the happiness of one, other things equal, and in general the more happiness, the more value; therefore, if we acknowledge the equal moral worth of all persons, we are committed to bringing about, directly or indirectly, the happiness of each random person as much as our own. The objection, as should now be clear, relies on the mistaken assumptions that all "worth" or "value" in Kant's theory, even dignity, is in principle commensurable and quantifiable and that right action consists in maximizing value. The basic equality that Kant attributes to all persons is a not a matter of "same size shares" of value understood in this way but, rather, a matter of having the same standing in a system of rights and duties and in the ideal deliberative processes that determine what these rights and duties are.

Slote's main reason for saying that Kant's ethics makes us devalue our own happiness, as compared to that of others, seems to be Kant's thesis that the "ends which are duties" are the happiness of others and our own perfection, not our own happiness. Kant's corollary is that we have a quite extensive *direct duty* to promote the happiness of others but only a quite limited and *indirect duty* to promote our own happiness. If we assume (mistakenly, I think) that what we judge to be our duties must be a simple reflection of what we "value," then we might think that the asymmetry in Kant's claims about our duties regarding ourselves and others shows that Kant thinks that right-minded people will value the happiness of others more than their own. At least, it might seem that Kant thinks that we should act as if we valued others' happiness more than our own.

Slote's main objection, as I noted, is apparently not that Kant's ethics requires us to *do* more for others than for ourselves or even that it grants us no *right* to pursue our own happiness to a reasonable degree. The special feature of Slote's complaint is that it presses the charge that Kantian ethics makes us "devalue" our own happiness even if it "permits" us to pursue it to a reasonable degree. This, it seems, is because Kant makes it a *direct duty* (within limits) to promote other people's happiness but only an *indirect duty* and *permission* (within limits) to pursue our own. Slote's assumption seems to be that we must value more what we judge we have a duty to promote than what we have a right to pursue. This is a dubious assumption, but the best way to deflate the objection is to reconstruct Kant's reasons for his asymmetry thesis and its corollary. The most plausible reconstruction, I will argue, does not presuppose or entail that we should count our own happiness as less valuable than any other person's happiness. The reasons why promoting our own happiness is merely an indirect duty and a permission, while promoting that of others is a direct duty, do not reflect a difference in the "value" of the two kinds of happiness, but rather a difference in the way respect for autonomy is displayed when we are dealing with the interests of others and when we are dealing only with our own interests.

Kant's explicit reason for denying that we have a direct moral duty to promote our own happiness is that we are already naturally inclined to promote our happiness. He did not mean, I take it, that we can never have a duty to do something that we have a natural inclination to do. The idea of duty includes the idea of being "necessitated" or constrained by reason, but we can be constrained to act in a way that we are already inclined to act if, despite that inclination, we may still fail to act as we should. Otherwise, Kant would have to conclude that we can have no duty to promote the happiness of others if we have a natural inclination to do so, which seems absurd. So what is the point? Why does the natural inclination to promote our own happiness block a duty to do so, whereas a natural inclination to promote the happiness of others does not?

One might suppose that the answer is that Kant thought our desire for our own happiness is much stronger and more pervasive than our benevolent impulses. I have no doubt that Kant thought this, but the belief does not explain why Kant should think that there is *no* direct duty to promote one's own happiness. Perhaps, one might think, Kant's idea is that our self-love is so strong that it is not, on balance, worth the psychological costs to make "a moral case" out of our occasional failures to take up harmless opportunities to further our own happiness. Most of the time we do not need a moral reminder, much less a call to "duty," to pay attention to our own happiness, and multiplying our duties needlessly may have a depressing effect. By contrast, one might think, our benevolent impulses are so weak that unless there is an acknowledged duty to promote the happiness of others, we will rarely do so, to the detriment of us all. These are reasonable rule-utilitarian thoughts, but there is, I think, a better Kantian reason for denying that we have a direct duty to promote our happiness.

To see this, let us first try to construct a Kantian argument *in favor of* a direct duty of beneficence. Consider the issue from the point of view of a Kantian moral legislator, a member of "the kingdom of ends" who respects humanity as an end in itself. Suppose that prior duties of justice, respect, mutual aid, and self-perfection have already been agreed upon. A good case can be made for endorsing a further imperfect duty of benef-icence, at least provided that the duty allows a reasonable "playroom for free action."[52] Such a duty, let us suppose, requires us to count the hap-piness of others as a good end to promote, but it is indeterminate regard-ing exactly when, how, and how much one must do to promote the happiness of others, and thus allows space for the reasonable pursuit of one's own projects. The general adoption of such a principle can be ex-pected to benefit everyone, so far as we can tell in advance of particular situations, and it seems to violate none of the basic Kantian value prior-ities and constraints. If this is the argument for beneficence to others, one might wonder, why shouldn't Kantian legislators prescribe a similar prin-ciple of *self-beneficence*, making it analogously an imperfect duty to pro-mote one's own happiness? After all, one might think, this is just what we would do unless we fail to *value* our own happiness as much as others' happiness, or unless we imagine that each person's own happiness *should* be less important to him or her than others' happiness. On this line of thinking, then, Kant might at first seem to be committed to the idea that we should devalue our own happiness, relative to that of others, because he did not include in his moral system any direct duty to promote our own happiness analogous to his principle of beneficence.[53]

But we need to rethink the analogy. Let us consider more specifically what sorts of acts the duty of beneficence requires. Kant, like most of us, did not suppose that this is a duty to promote the ends of others *whether they want us to or not*.[54] We are supposed to help others in their projects but, barring special circumstances, not without regard to whether or not they consent. They need not always give express consent, of course, but the basic point is that we should not try to make people happy against their will. Coercion is justified in many circumstances to prevent people from violating others' rights, and giving crucial lifesaving aid to people who profess not to want it seems relatively unproblematic if those in

[52] There is controversy among commentators about how to interpret the indeterminacy or "playroom" in Kant's principles. This room for discretion is construed narrowly by David Cummiskey in his *Kantian Consequentialism* and by Marcia Baron in her *Kantian Ethics (Almost) without Apology* (Ithaca: Cornell University Press, 1995). Mary Gregor accepts a broader interpretation that allows more moral discretion regarding the balance between charity and our own projects. The main features of my understanding of Kant's principle, which is also broad, are indicated in *Dignity and Practical Reason in Kant's Moral Theory*, pp. 147–75, but some revisions, I now see, are needed.

[53] As noted earlier, Kant says that we have an "indirect" duty to promote our own happiness, but this does little to help meet Slote's objection because this duty is only an application of our more general duties, e.g., to respect the rights of others and to promote their happiness (along with our own "perfection").

[54] "I cannot do good to anyone in accordance with my concepts of happiness (except to young children and the insane), thinking to benefit him by forcing a gift upon him; rather, I can benefit him only in accordance with his concepts of happiness" (Kant, *Metaphysics of Morals*, p. 248 [454]).

danger are obviously unable at the time to think clearly. But doing un-
wanted "favors," working on others' projects for them without their consent, and so on, is meddlesome and disrespectful of the autonomy of
those we mean to help, even if they would be "happier" if we were
successful. Thus, we must understand the duty of beneficence to others as
qualified: one should promote the permissible ends of others *only if this is
what they choose*.[55] Our would-be beneficiaries normally have the right to
block our altruistic efforts on their behalf. If they choose for us not to
promote their ends, then doing so is no longer a way of fulfilling our
imperfect duty of beneficence.

Now consider what sort of "beneficent" acts an analogous duty of
beneficence to oneself would require, if such a duty were possible. It would
be an imperfect duty, limited by justice, respect, etc., to promote our own
permissible ends (the ends belonging to our conception of a happy life for
us), and it would be indefinite with respect to exactly what, in what way,
and how much one must do toward this end. But now it must be qualified
in the same way that the principle of beneficence to others is qualified.
That is, it would have to be our "duty" to promote our own permissible
ends provided that we (at least implicitly) consent to do so, that is, provided that doing so is not against our will. In other words, the "duty"
would tell us that we "must" contribute somehow, and to some extent, to
our own happiness, by trying to fulfill the (permissible) ends that we
already have, but that we are "morally required" to do this only if we so
choose. It is doubtful whether it is even coherent to suppose that I might
adopt a general policy of not furthering my own happiness, that is, a
policy of not taking the means to achieve the various (permissible) ends
that I have. But, supposing for now that this is possible, the analogy with
beneficence to others implies that if I, as the would-be beneficiary, with-
hold consent to the "self-beneficent" acts (by choosing not to do them),
then I, as the would-be benefactor, cannot fulfill a duty (not even an
"imperfect" duty) by performing such acts.

Now it becomes clear, however, that such a "duty" of self-beneficence
is conceptually impossible. We could cancel such an alleged duty at will,
and a "duty" that we could cancel at will is no duty at all. We are not
bound by chains if they are so loose that we can throw them off whenever
we choose. What comparing the duty of beneficence to others with a
supposed duty of self-beneficence reveals is just that the latter is an
incoherent idea. Kant's denial of such a "duty," then, does not show that
he thinks that we should devalue our own happiness relative to others.

The duty of beneficence to others (with its consent requirement) limits
our moral freedom in dealing with others in several ways that seem quite

---

[55] There are, of course, many refinements that would need to be made if we were trying
to articulate the principle as subtly and completely as possible. For example, qualifications
are needed regarding cases where the person who refuses help is incompetent, obviously
"not herself," etc. But what I have said is enough, I hope, for present purposes.

reasonable: we must make it a principle to regard their happiness as an end, and our contributions toward this end (typically) require at least the implicit consent of the intended beneficiary. Kant's position on beneficence, however, can be seen as respectful of freedom in another way. That is, it reaffirms our moral freedom to accept or decline anticipated efforts by others to promote our happiness. The duty of beneficence to others respects our freedom insofar as it permits us (as a rule) to reject the efforts that we do not want others to make to further our personal projects. Similarly, Kant's denial that there is a parallel duty of beneficence *to oneself* respects our freedom by permitting us (morally) to decline to make our own efforts to promote those projects when we do not want to. *Prudence* often counsels us, even when we are reluctant, both to make our own efforts and to accept the aid of others toward achieving the ends encompassed in our conception of happiness.[56] *Moral duty*, however, does not demand it.

It should be noted that the argument against a duty of beneficence to oneself does not amount to a general argument against Kant's "duties to oneself," even though that argument is similar to the argument M. G. Singer offers against all "duties to oneself."[57] The key to the argument is that we cannot be "bound" by a "duty" if we can release ourselves from that (alleged) duty at will, but the "duties to oneself" that Kant affirms, unlike self-beneficence and keeping "promises to oneself," are not the sort of duties from which we have reason to suppose that we could release ourselves. If we had obligations to keep "promises to ourselves" that were perfectly analogous to our obligations to keep promises to others, then it seems natural to suppose that we could (normally) "release ourselves" at will because (normally) the recipient of a promise can release the promisor whenever he or she chooses. But a duty not to debase the humanity of other persons and treat them with utter contempt is not a duty from which they can release us, and so the analogous duty to avoid debasing our own humanity in a self-contemptuous way would not be a duty from which we could release ourselves.[58]

Let us return to Kant's explicit argument against a duty to promote our own happiness, which appeals to our natural inclination to pursue our own happiness. This is not the argument that I suggested above, but it is compatible with that argument. One way of understanding the relevance of Kant's reference to natural inclination is as follows. Recall that the duty to promote others' happiness is indefinite; in its basic form, it is a duty to

---

[56] Even prudence, however, normally allows options, for it is a conditional rational imperative to promote our own happiness, and our working conceptions of happiness are neither fixed nor completely determinate. Insofar as Kant conceives of happiness as satisfying freely chosen, desire-based ends, we can often avoid doing something that previously seemed necessary for happiness by modifying the ends we choose to pursue.

[57] M. G. Singer, *Generalization in Ethics* (New York: Alfred A. Knopf, 1961), pp. 311–18.

[58] I discuss these issues more fully in "Promises to Oneself," in my *Autonomy and Self-Respect* (Cambridge: Cambridge University Press, 1991), pp. 138–54.

make it one's maxim to include the happiness of others among one's own ends. Basically, then, the analogous "duty" of beneficence to oneself would have to be an indefinite "duty" to include one's own happiness among one's ends. This is something that everyone is inclined to do, according to Kant. Adopting a maxim to pursue an end is supposed to be more than just being inclined toward that end; it presupposes some degree of reflection and the power to choose otherwise if there is a sufficient reason to do so. But all rational persons with that natural inclination, Kant assumes, will adopt at least a general, indefinite policy of pursuing a set of personal ends (their conception of happiness for them) at least when there is no sufficient reason not to. That is, Kant supposes not merely that we are inclined by nature to pursue our own happiness but also that we all "freely" endorse our own happiness as an end—a higher-order end that encompasses many particular ends, though it is not necessarily our dominant end. Given Kant's idea of duties (categorical *imperatives*) as rational principles that we can but *might not* follow, we cannot say, strictly speaking, that it is a *duty* to make our own happiness an end, even though it is rational to do so.

Our own happiness is always an end we have, but we do not always attend to it as much as we need to in order to fulfill our duties to others. Thus, we might fail to promote our own happiness on particular occasions when we should. This makes it possible for Kant to speak of an "indirect duty" to promote our own happiness, for this is not a duty to adopt happiness as a general (and indefinite) end but, rather, a duty to do particular things required by reason that we *might not* otherwise do. The upshot of this line of thought is that the analogy with a duty of beneficence to others is blocked, not because of our *inability to avoid* endorsing our own happiness as a general higher-order end, but because there is no reason to expect that any rational person would want to try. In any case, Kant's grounds for denying a duty of beneficence to oneself do not imply that we do or should count our own happiness as less valuable than the happiness of persons whom we dutifully try to help.

V. Kant's Focus on Happiness Rather Than Human Flourishing

We have seen many ways in which the concept of happiness (as Kant understands it) is of limited importance in his ethics. Many philosophers, ancient and contemporary, regard what they call "happiness" as more important in ethics than Kant regards happiness in his sense. They may agree with Kant on many points about happiness in his sense; but when contemporary philosophers turn to Kant to see his position on "happiness" in the ancient (human flourishing) sense, they are likely to be disappointed. This is partly because Kant has very little to say about flourishing as a human being, as distinct from happiness in his sense. Kant mentions ancient philosophers from time to time, but he seemed to suppose for the most part that their conception of happiness is more or less the same as his. The disappointment of many contemporary philosophers with Kant's position is also likely to be due to the fact that, although Kant does not discuss human flourishing explicitly, his theory commits him to placing more severe limits on the role of human flourishing in moral thinking than they can accept. In this section, I will simply summarize some of these limits, as I see them, and speculate briefly about why Kant might have insisted on them. The reason is not, I suggest, merely Kant's misunderstanding of ancient philosophers, his personal eccentricities, a preoccupation with other matters, or an insensitivity to the human desire to flourish. It has more to do with his awareness of the distinctness of individuals and his respect for freedom.

A. The limited role of human flourishing in Kant's ethics

The first thing to consider is whether Kant's limits on happiness (in his sense) also carry over to human flourishing. Comparison is difficult if we suppose that having a "good will" and having virtue (in Kant's sense) are necessary constituents of human flourishing—a possibility to be considered later. For now, let us suppose otherwise. That is, let us assume that, although fulfilling certain essential and good dispositions of human nature is necessary to flourishing as a human being, satisfying Kantian moral constraints, even the basic ones, is not included in the idea of human flourishing as a necessary part. We assume, then, that it remains an open question whether our having a Kantian good will is conducive to our flourishing as human beings. This is a common assumption and a reasonable one if we understand "flourishing" in the usual ways (without presupposing Kant's theory).

Now it seems clear, given the assumption just mentioned, that Kant is committed to a limited role for human flourishing as well as for happiness in his sense. For example, human flourishing cannot be an unconditional good or an "intrinsic value" as intuitionists and naturalists understand this. This is because one could flourish without having a good will, which for Kant is the only "unconditional good," and Kant does not acknowledge intuited or natural intrinsic values. Obviously Kant must deny that whatever maximizes human flourishing is morally right, for the price of bringing about the most flourishing could be treating humanity in some persons as a mere means. Similarly, since Kant holds that the sole or primary aim of government is to secure justice, he must disallow government efforts to promote human flourishing if they employ unjust means or fail to enforce justice among citizens. Also, the same grounds that support Kant's denial that we have a direct duty to promote our own happiness (in his sense) would also tend to undermine any alleged direct duty to further our own flourishing as human beings. Assuming that it is normally up to others whether or not we can dutifully contribute to their flourishing, acknowledging an imperfect duty to promote others' flourishing does not imply that we should acknowledge a parallel *duty* to promote our own.

In addition to these ways in which Kant limits the role of both happiness and human flourishing in ethics, there are at least two further ways in which Kant relies on judgments about happiness but not on judgments about human flourishing. The first concerns the principle of beneficence. This, in Kant's theory, is an imperfect duty to promote others' happiness (in Kant's sense), not a duty to contribute to others' flourishing as human beings.

Now, of course, if everyone wants to flourish as a human being, then regard for the (Kantian) happiness of others would often promote their flourishing. This is because, wanting to flourish, they would tend to include flourishing in their conception of their happiness, and, insofar as they do, our contributing to their flourishing would tend to promote their happiness. If, as many think, it is *wise* to make flourishing as a human being our dominant personal end (at least when this is compatible with moral requirements), then our respect for others as rational (and thus potentially wise) might lead us to encourage them to seek happiness in ways that promote their flourishing, and might lead us to prefer helping them when they do. Even so, however, Kant's idea of the duty of beneficence remains distinct from the idea of a duty to promote others' flourishing as human beings. Even if we, and they too, do not know what will contribute to their flourishing, the Kantian duty urges us to promote the (permissible) ends that they set for themselves. It is up to others to determine what will make them happy, and all such judgments, Kant thought, are uncertain. Within the "room for choice" allowed by the principle of beneficence, we may select our beneficiaries as we choose; thus, we may to some extent choose to promote happiness where it will best contribute to flourishing, but the principle does not demand this.[59]

The second way that Kant relies on judgments about happiness rather than judgments about human flourishing has to do with prudence. Kant suggests that we are under a hypothetical imperative to take the necessary means to our happiness (in his sense). This is supposed to be a nonmoral requirement of reason, the application of which is limited by

---

[59] It is important to keep in mind that the principle of beneficence, a quite indeterminate ("imperfect") duty to adopt the happiness of others as an end, is not the only moral consideration regarding how to treat others that we must take into account when deliberating about what to do in particular situations. We must also respect others' rights, treat them with respect, show proper gratitude, and so on. The principle of beneficence by itself does not tell us when, how, or how much to do for others. For this, we need good judgment guided by the Categorical Imperative. For example, the basic idea of humanity as an end in itself does not leave it as "optional" whether to throw a life-preserver to someone about to drown or to wait to "help" someone else later.

moral principles. Because of the indeterminacy, even partial incoherence, of our conceptions of our happiness, applying this general requirement only gives us inexact rules of thumb or "counsels of prudence." Like all hypothetical imperatives, these counsels are only conditionally rational to follow. The advice that they seem to give on particular occasions is overridden when it conflicts with our moral responsibilities, and also we may often set it aside without irrationality simply by altering the ends that we choose to include in our conception of happiness. In these ways, Kant views the imperative "to do what we must to be happy" as quite restricted. It is striking, though, that he does not propose a general imperative of prudence concerning human flourishing. Even if it would be a good idea to adopt flourishing as a dominant end, Kant's theory of rational prudence seems to allow us, within moral limits, to choose our ends and set our priorities independently of any guiding aim to realize as well as we can the natural ("essential") human potentialities required for "flourishing as a human being."[60] We would be under a (nonmoral) hypothetical imperative to do what we must to flourish only if we chose to make that our end.

As before, if we assume that human flourishing is something objective, discernible, and naturally desired, then following Kant's prescriptions regarding happiness should tend to promote it—but not always. By being prudent, in Kant's sense, we would generally contribute to our flourishing so long as our adoption of particular ends is guided intelligently by our natural desire to flourish. But Kantian prudence will not lead to flourishing if we have strong conflicting desires and adopt our ends more randomly. So the main point remains: Kantian prudence explicitly calls for intelligent pursuit of our (permissible) ends, whatever these may be, not for wise choices contributing to our thriving as human beings.

B. Possible explanations

Why would Kant want to focus on happiness (in his sense) rather than on human flourishing? If we speculate about causal influences, there are many possibilities. For example, Kant was probably influenced by the modern rejection (by Hobbes and others) of the models of human nature that dominated the ancient and medieval worlds. Although Kant believed

---

[60] Note, however, that Kant treats certain aspects of "human flourishing" as matters that it is *morally impermissible* to ignore or neglect. For example, according to Kant, there is a "perfect duty to oneself" to avoid suicide and an imperfect duty to oneself to "develop and increase (one's) natural perfection" of body and mind (*Metaphysics of Morals*, pp. 218–20 [422–24], 239–40 [444–46]). Unlike Aristotle, Kant insists on a sharp distinction between rational prudence and morality. Then he does not place the ideal of human flourishing under rational prudence as a necessary end, but rather makes the pursuit of some aspects of it an imperfect *moral duty* to oneself. Thus, although he denies the right of prudential reason to demand that we pursue the ideal of human flourishing as an end, he makes room in his moral theory to affirm aspects of that ideal as requirements of reason.

that for some purposes we should look at the world through teleological lenses, his view of human desires is closer to Hobbes's than to Aristotle's — that is, desires are seen as diverse, fluctuating, conflicting, unmalleable impulses that are, in themselves, not good or bad, rational or irrational. Kant thought that we tend to see happiness as the impossible ideal of satisfying all of our desires, but that with intelligence we can select a subset of compatible desires to try to satisfy (others need to be resisted or repressed). Like Hobbes, Kant denied that desires can be shaped by reason into a harmonious system of mutually cooperative motives in the way the classic ideas of human flourishing seem to presuppose.

Also, a partial explanation may be found by paying attention to Kant's project. He was not asking, in a general way, how a wise person would live. His primary questions, instead, were about the idea of moral duties and the necessary presuppositions of believing that we have such duties. His concern was to determine what, if anything, it is rationally *necessary* to think and to do. His method was to try to separate the elements of something familiar and then to focus attention on one aspect apart from the rest. The main elements of human nature, he thought, are reason, desire, and our ability to choose; accordingly, the main elements of a good life, he thought, must be governing one's choices by pure practical reason (a good will) and the satisfaction of our desires (happiness).[61] The more complex idea of human flourishing does not readily fit into this picture. There is more to living well than doing our duty, but Kant's main questions were about the latter — and about the constraints it imposes on satisfying our desires. Many of the concerns that generate philosophical theories about human flourishing lie beyond the ethics of duty, as advocates of virtue ethics often remind us. To some extent, then, Kant's leaving aside questions about human flourishing is understandable in that these questions lie outside his central project. But this cannot be the whole story.

Another partial explanation might be Kant's recognition of our vast ignorance about what exactly it takes to enable different individuals to flourish as human beings.[62] Even if we can say formally, or in very general terms, what it is to flourish as a human being, determining what in

---

[61] Kant treats "practical reason" as reason concerned to determine what we *ought to do*. This contrasts with "theoretical reason," which is concerned with understanding the world as it actually is. Practical reason is called "pure" when its serves to determine what we ought to do independently of our natural desire for happiness and our individual inclinations. This contrasts with "empirically conditioned" practical reason, which tries to determine what we ought to do *in order to* satisfy our desire to be happy and to achieve our personal ends. Kant argues that pure practical reason is the source of the most fundamental moral principle, the Categorical Imperative. A person fully committed to following the fundamental moral principle has a "good will" and is "worthy to be happy." The most complete good is a good will combined with deserved happiness, but having a good will alone is not enough to make one happy and being happy does not entail that one has a good will. See Kant, *Critique of Practical Reason*, pp. 15–20 [15–22], 116–19 [110–13].

[62] See, for example, Kant, *Groundwork*, pp. 85–86 [418–19].

particular this or that individual needs in order to flourish in various contexts is extremely difficult. What will contribute to individuals' happiness (in Kant's sense) should be easier to discern because it is a matter of promoting whatever particular ends they set themselves, and typically those who want help will tell us what their ends are. Thus, although certainty here is impossible, we can often be effective in contributing to someone's happiness, as the duty of beneficence requires, even when neither they nor we know what it would take to make them flourish. For similar reasons, it seems that we can often enhance our own happiness (in Kant's sense), as prudence requires, even though we are ignorant of what would really contribute most to our flourishing. We may not know what is best for us, in that sense, but we know what our goals are. Again, however, our relative ignorance of the requirements of flourishing is hardly a sufficient reason for disregarding it in ethics.

Another possibility is that we are not merely ignorant of the facts about what makes individuals flourish; rather, it may be that there is not "a fact of the matter" to discern here. We can conjecture, then, that Kant, like many contemporary philosophers, was skeptical about the concept of human flourishing itself—that he doubted whether the concept was sufficiently determinate and psychologically defensible to serve a vital role in moral theory. If Kant had this skepticism, however, we would expect him to express it in criticism of classic theories that make human flourishing central; but, as far as I know, he did not. Perhaps he thought that this task of criticism had already been done; but more likely, I suspect, he just did not raise the issue.

Although no doubt many factors contributed, I suspect that a major reason why Kant made happiness, rather than human flourishing, the operative concept in the principle of beneficence and the imperative of prudence was his intense concern for individual freedom. At least this seems to be so if we focus on Kant's idea of happiness as fulfilling freely chosen ends rather than as feelings of contentment. Consider beneficence first. When would it matter whether our duty is to promote others' (permissible) happiness or to promote their flourishing as human beings? If we know more about the one than the other, that would make a difference; but let us suppose that we are equally knowledgeable (or ignorant) regarding both. Given this, how might concern for others' happiness and concern for their flourishing diverge?

A contribution to their flourishing will help them fulfill certain ends toward which human beings are *characteristically* prone to act, but these are not ends that all individuals want or endorse as their personal goals. To flourish means to develop and exercise common human potentials that are widely regarded to be natural, good, rewarding, and admirable to fulfill, but it is not necessarily compatible with doing what one loves to do, prefers on reflection to do, or sees as most expressive of "who one is" as an individual. To promote others' flourishing when it diverges from their happiness (in Kant's sense) would be to place higher priority on their fulfilling their characteristic human dispositions than on their loves, considered preferences, and self-expression as individuals. Philosophers have often argued that these will not in fact diverge significantly for those who are thoughtful and well-informed (and perhaps well-trained), but our question presupposes that they can diverge. When moral responsibility and virtue are "built in" to the concept of flourishing, then virtually all moral philosophers rank it as more important than individual loves, considered preferences, and self-expression *when these conflict with morality*. Again, however, our question concerns flourishing in a sense that is not so morally loaded. We assume, then, that happiness and human flourishing can diverge, and it is not yet obvious why beneficence should be more concerned with one rather than the other.[63]

My suggestion is just that, in addition to other factors, respect for individual freedom to choose one's own particular way of life, within moral limits, may have been a significant reason for Kant's giving priority to happiness over human flourishing in the ways that I have described. Even if there is a discernible fact that certain individual ends contribute better than others to fulfilling characteristic, natural human capacities, Kant says only that our responsibility in helping others is to respect *their* choices of the ends they want to pursue, provided the ends are not immoral. If they respect their basic duties to others and to themselves, then it is up to them to decide what to include in their pursuit of happiness, and we should respect that, rather than trying to make them flourish in another way. Admittedly, Kant says that we all have a duty to develop our mental and physical capacities, but he classifies this as a duty *to ourselves* that is not the business of others to enforce. Moreover, the requirement is an imperfect duty that leaves wide discretion as to how much, and in what ways, to develop these capacities. Undeniably Kant was moved by ideals of human perfection, for individuals and humanity in general, but his moral theory reflects a strong counterbalancing concern for allowing individuals to choose, and judge, for themselves, even if they choose less than what would best promote their flourishing.

Admittedly, if the duty of beneficence were a duty to promote others' flourishing rather than their happiness, then we would still be free (as potential beneficiaries) to refuse others' efforts to promote our flourishing

---

[63] It must be remembered that we are concerned here with beneficence that does not violate justice, due respect for persons, or other obligations. Also, I assume that our duties to give lifesaving aid, to meet essential human needs, etc., are justifiable as high-priority duties in Kant's ethics on grounds that are not simply applications of the very general and indeterminate duty to promote others' happiness. That duty, as I understand it, concerns contributions to others' happiness beyond those more elementary duties (even though Kant does not separate these issues in *The Metaphysics of Morals*).

when it promised to interfere with the preferred personal projects that we count as part of our happiness. The requirement of the consent of beneficiaries discussed earlier, we can assume, should apply here as well. Kantian beneficence, however, urges others to give us positive aid in our efforts to achieve the (permissible) ends we prefer, not merely to "back off" when we do not want a certain kind of aid. In this it positively affirms and facilitates our attempts, within moral limits, to pursue the ends we choose for ourselves as individuals even if these are, at times, in conflict with the generic, supposedly objective, end of flourishing in characteristically human ways. If the normative appeal of the latter is as strong and pervasive as many think, then we can expect that wise individuals will freely choose to make it the core of their conceptions of happiness, and then promoting their flourishing would be a way of promoting their happiness. But this would not be because the idea of human flourishing necessarily has an overriding claim on us, but rather because we place a moral value on the ability of all human beings to choose and effectively pursue their happiness as they conceive it.

It seems a plausible conjecture that the same concern could lie behind Kant's limiting prudential requirements to the rational pursuit of happiness, rather than human flourishing. Prudence requires that we respect the Hypothetical Imperative regarding the ends that we actually choose, not that we do everything possible to promote our flourishing as human beings.[64] That is, the requirement of prudence is to adopt a set of desire-based ends and then, when one can, to take the necessary steps to achieve them or else revise the ends. Prudential reason does condemn us as irrational if, instead of doing all we can to flourish in a characteristically human way, we choose instead a more eccentric individual course.[65] Thus, at least if we attend adequately to the imperfect duty to develop our minds and bodies, and if we fulfill our other duties, then, in Kant's view, the requirements of prudence as well as morality would leave us free to choose the ends that we prefer even when we anticipate that they will not maximally promote our flourishing as human beings.

My remarks in this section, as I mentioned, presuppose that flourishing as a human being is conceptually independent of being virtuous. But we might look at the whole matter differently. In Kant's view, our rational predisposition to morality, like our sensible nature as desiring beings, is

[64] By "the Hypothetical Imperative" I mean the most general principle behind our reasoning that we ought to do various particular things because they are necessary as a means to furthering our ends. The Hypothetical Imperative tells us to take the necessary means (when available) to the ends that we choose to pursue or else abandon these ends. A more complete explanation is given in my *Dignity and Practical Reason in Kant's Moral Theory*, chs. 1 and 7.

[65] Critics of the Kantian perspective might object that it must be irrational to choose personal projects that we know are not "the best" for us, but the objection presupposes the controversial claim that the course that does most to cause us to meet the descriptive criteria for "flourishing as a human being" is also "best" in a normative sense.

an indispensable part of our nature—even if it is not, in the same sense, a "natural" part.[66] So none of us, Kant thought, could live without inner conflict and self-disapproval if we pursued personal happiness by plainly immoral means. In a sense, then, he granted that we, human beings, cannot completely fulfill our most fundamental dispositions without virtue. Moreover, like many of his religious predecessors, he held that we should have faith that if we are truly virtuous we may, somehow (but not in this life), receive the happiness we deserve.[67] Thus, despite having separated virtue and happiness for practical purposes of choice, he acknowledged an ideal of human flourishing that unites them, after all, at least as something to hope for.

VI. Conclusion

My aim here has been to distinguish, summarize, and (at times) explain the place that the ideas of happiness and human flourishing have (or lack) in Kant's ethics. It is easy in reading Kant to get the impression that Kant is out to "put happiness in its place," which he sees as more restricted than many moral philosophers do. And readers of ancient philosophers will readily notice that Kant tends to ignore human flourishing, the favorite concept in virtue ethics. But it is also easy to confuse Kant's various claims on these matters and to exaggerate some of them. In any case, my hope has been that identifying and sorting out these different claims may facilitate discussion between Kantians and others, making further discussion more fruitful by focusing it on more specific issues. Some of Kant's claims about happiness, I have suggested, are rather uncontroversial; some of them, admittedly, are indefensible even within his basic framework; and some of them, though controversial, remain in dispute partly because of misunderstanding. The traditional and familiar ideas of human flourishing (as distinct from happiness in Kant's sense) do not have a prominent role in Kant's ethics, and I have speculated about several reasons why this might be so. This was due, I suggested, not merely to historical influences, misunderstanding of ancient philosophy, or preoccupation with other matters, but also to Kant's respect for individual freedom to choose, within moral limits, the way of life we prefer.

Philosophy, The University of North Carolina, Chapel Hill

---

[66] The predisposition to acknowledge moral principles as authoritative in our decision making, according to Kant, is something that we must attribute to ourselves as rational moral agents, but it is not an aspect of our nature that we discover and understand empirically as, for example, we come to know our desires and feelings.

[67] See Kant, *Critique of Practical Reason*, pp. 128–38 [122–32].

VALUING ACTIVITY*

By Stephen Darwall

I. Introduction

Call the proposition that the good life consists of excellent (or virtuous), distinctively human activity the *Aristotelian Thesis*.[1] I think of a photograph I clipped from the *New York Times* as vividly depicting this claim. It shows a pianist, David Golub, accompanying two vocalists, Victoria Livengood and Erie Mills, at a tribute for Marilyn Horne.[2] All three artists are in fine form, exercising themselves at the height of their powers. The reason I saved the photo, however, is Mr. Golub's face. He is positively grinning, as if saying to himself, "And they *pay* me to do this?"

Mr. Golub's delight is a sign of his activity's value, not what makes it good. His pleasure "completes the activity . . . as an end which supervenes as the bloom of youth does on those in the flower of their age" (1174b33–35).[3] The metaphor is apt, since "eudaimonia," Aristotle's term for the human good, is frequently translated as "flourishing."[4] "Flourish" comes from the same Old French root as "flower" (*"florir"*). When applied to plants and trees, "flourish" meant to grow vigorously to the point of putting out leaves or flowers. And a "flourish" was originally the blos-

* I am indebted to the other contributors to this volume for their helpful comments and discussion, especially to Richard Arneson, David Brink, and Thomas Hurka, and to Ellen Frankel Paul for her suggestions on the draft. I also benefited from discussion with participants in a conference to which a version of this paper was presented at the University of Bari in December 1997, especially Tito Magri and John Broome, and from discussion following its presentation at St. Louis University. Thanks also to Kate Jacobson for her helpful comments. Finally, my thinking in this paper owes much to the work of Elizabeth Anderson and David Velleman.

[1] Aristotle's translators prefer "virtuous." We should bear in mind, however, that the excellences of character that Aristotle includes within *"aretê"* range significantly more widely than moral virtue as that idea is usually understood these days.

[2] The photograph accompanied "Stretching Boundaries to Honor a Diva," by Anthony Tommasini, in the national edition of the *New York Times* for September 28, 1996. It evidently did not appear in the full edition of the paper that was archived and microfilmed.

[3] Aristotle, *Nicomachean Ethics*. This and further references are to W. D. Ross's translation (revised by J. O. Urmson) and to lines of Immanuel Bekker's standard edition of Aristotle's Greek text. The Ross/Urmson translation has been published separately (New York: Oxford University Press, 1987), and as part of *The Complete Works of Aristotle*, ed. Jonathan Barnes (Princeton, NJ: Princeton University Press, 1991), vol. 2.

[4] Although it is not translated this way by Ross or by Terence Irwin, both of whom use "happiness." For a defense of translating *eudaimonia* as "flourishing," see John Cooper, *Reason and Human Good in Aristotle* (Cambridge, MA: Harvard University Press, 1975), pp. 89–90, n. 1.

som itself.[5] More generally, something flourishes when it thrives or prospers as a healthy plant does coming to full flower. Making the relevant substitutions, Mr. Golub's manifest enjoyment is the sign of his flourishing, its flower or "flourish." What his flourishing consists in, however, is the excellent activity that produces his delight.

In what follows, I aim to develop and defend a version of the Aristotelian Thesis that is suggested by my essay's title. On any interpretation, the Aristotelian Thesis "values activity" in one sense, since it holds that human good consists in certain activities. In addition, I shall argue that these activities themselves involve valuing and the appreciation of value. They are "valuing activities," where the appreciated values differ in kind from the good of a person or value *for* someone. My claim will be that a person's life is enriched, made better *for her*, through active engagement with and appreciation of values whose worth transcends their capacity to benefit. The benefit comes through the *appreciation* of the value.

A version of this idea is already implicit in Aristotle. Aristotle says that the virtuous actions in which *eudaimonia* consists are undertaken on account of having a distinctive intrinsic value, fineness, or nobility (*to kalon*) (1102a5, 1104b30–1105a1, 1105a31, 1115b12–13, 22–24, 1117b8–10, 1119b16). This already gives us two kinds of value: the goodness of a life lived well (*eudaimonia*) and nobility or fineness of action (*kalon*).[6] Noble activity is what makes up the good life, but the concept of nobility of action differs from that of the value of a life for the person leading it. Otherwise, there could be no substantive disagreement between those who believe that flourishing consists of virtuous activity and those who think that it resides in something else, such as pleasure or honor. The latter would simply be confused about the concept.

Noble action is conceptually tied to an *ideal* of action, a conception of certain actions as intrinsically worthy of emulation, admiration, and praise. To claim as the Aristotelian Thesis does, therefore, that human good consists in activity chosen as realizing an ideal of action is to put forward a substantive normative doctrine.[7] Aristotle is already claiming, then, that human flourishing involves valuing activity, since he holds that it involves guidance by a kind of value (the noble) that is distinct from the value of human flourishing itself.

---

[5] *Oxford English Dictionary*, 2d ed.

[6] Here I follow, e.g., John M. Cooper, "Reason, Moral Virtue, and Moral Value," in Michael Frede and Gisela Striker, eds., *Rationality in Greek Thought* (Oxford: Clarendon Press, 1996), pp. 81–114. See also Kelly Rogers, "Aristotle's Conception of Tὸ Καλὸν," *Ancient Philosophy*, vol. 13 (1993), pp. 355–71. For the possibly conflicting view that "*to kalon*" refers to the common good, see T. H. Irwin, "Aristotle's Conception of Morality," *Proceedings of the Boston Area Colloquium in·Ancient Philosophy*, 1986, pp. 115–43.

[7] A reflection of the conceptual difference between flourishing and nobility of action is that the former is an agent- or person-relative notion. A flourishing life is one that is good *for the person leading it*. Fineness of action, however, is not an agent-relative notion in this sense. I shall return to this point in Section VI.

I believe that Aristotle's proposal has the ring of truth. Human life is shot through with ideal (or, as Charles Taylor calls it, "strong") evaluation in ways that make it inconceivable to me that we can flourish without seeing our lives as expressing ideals we accept.[8] But these are not the only, or even, I think, the most significant, values that are appreciated in a flourishing human life. When I look at the photograph of David Golub, I don't question that he appreciates the fineness of his playing, but I doubt that this is the main object of his delight. Rather, I imagine that what his smile primarily reveals is an appreciation of values that *make* music-making a noble pursuit—values like the beauty and power of the music he and his colleagues are creating, values that give music significance or *worth*. And I imagine that the benefit he derives from his playing comes, in large measure, through his appreciation of this worth and his relation to it.

The contrast I have in mind is between a kind of value (which I shall call *merit*) that persons and actions have in being worthy of admiration or emulation, on the one hand, and a kind of value or "mattering" (which I shall call *worth*) that a thing has by virtue of being appropriately deemed significant or important in itself, on the other. To see one example of this difference, consider the distinction within Kantian ethics between the kind of value Kant believes a person of good will and her actions have and the value he thinks that any person has regardless of whether that person's actions have moral worth or not.

Goodness of will and moral worth of actions are kinds of *merit*. They are qualities of persons and actions that we credit, praise, admire, encourage, and desire to emulate. The value someone has just by virtue of being a person, on the other hand, is a kind of *worth*, dignity, or "mattering," a value status that makes appropriate certain forms of valuing *conduct* toward the person and certain feelings that are *as of* someone who is to be treated and regarded in those ways.[9] We respond to merit when

---

[8] Charles Taylor, "What Is Human Agency?" in *Human Agency and Language: Philosophical Papers I* (Cambridge: Cambridge University Press, 1985), pp. 16–21. Taylor contrasts "strong evaluation" with "weak evaluation," saying of weak evaluation that for something to be (weakly) judged good, "it is sufficient that it be desired." However, this probably misses the contrast he has in mind, since critically-informed-desire accounts of evaluation, such as Peter Railton's account of a person's nonmoral good (in Railton, "Moral Realism," *Philosophical Review*, vol. 95 [1986], pp. 5–31), will count as strong evaluation by that criterion. Strong evaluation seems rather to concern what Taylor calls the "worth" of desires, where worth is characterized in terms of such categories as "noble" and "base." When I discuss these matters below, I will use "merit" where Taylor uses "worth," reserving "worth" for values to which desires that have merit themselves respond. For an excellent critical discussion of Taylor's distinction, see Owen J. Flanagan, "Identity and Strong and Weak Evaluation," in Amélie O. Rorty and Owen J. Flanagan, eds., *Identity, Character, and Morality: Essays in Moral Psychology* (Cambridge, MA: MIT Press, 1991).

[9] Within the Kantian view of morality, the difference between merit and worth manifests itself as a distinction between two kinds of respect. (For a discussion of this distinction see my "Two Kinds of Respect," *Ethics*, vol. 88 [1977], pp. 36–49.) Moral "appraisal respect" is an attitude of moral esteem or admiration for morally good character—the good will—and

we admire or are humbled by another's conduct or character. We respond to worth when we see someone as a person who cannot (rightly) be treated in certain ways.

However, nothing in the general ideas of merit and worth ties them specifically to morality, narrowly conceived. The notion of merit can be connected to an ideal of virtually any kind, and merit-notions like the noble and the base are prominent in ethical theories, like Aristotle's and Nietzsche's, that are not best viewed as theories of moral right and wrong at all. Nor is there anything in the idea of worth or intrinsic importance that connects it specifically to morality, much less to Kantian ethics. I take it, for example, that readers of this essay would likely agree that philosophy and philosophical activity have intrinsic worth even if they disagree about philosophy's *moral* relevance.

Although they are distinct, I believe that merit and worth are fundamentally related. The relation between them, I think, is that traits or actions are worthy of admiration, they have merit, because they appropriately respond to matters of importance or worth.[10] Thus, parenting is a noble pursuit, it has merit, because it appropriately responds to the importance of children, their worth; the creation and appreciation of fine music has merit, because music has worth; and so on. Consequently, my claim will be that we flourish through (meritorious) activities such as parenting and music-making, because these activities involve an appreciation of things that matter, things with worth.

Merit, moreover, is itself a kind of worth, although it cannot be the only kind, for reasons I have just suggested. Being appropriately related to what has worth matters also. It also has worth. Or, to put the point in more neutral value terms, being rightly oriented toward intrinsic value is also intrinsically valuable. In what follows, I shall continue to speak of merit and worth as different value concepts. But nothing hangs on this claimed conceptual difference. We might as easily think of two kinds of worth (or intrinsic value): a basic class (worth) and a second (merit) that consists in being properly oriented to or guided by the first.[11]

The specific version of the Aristotelian Thesis I shall defend, then, is that a good human life consists of activities that involve the appreciation

---

actions that express it. It is *as of* moral merit. (On my use of the construction "as of," see note 32 below.) Moral "recognition respect," on the other hand, is as of the dignity of persons — the intrinsic worth any person has simply by virtue of her capacity for moral agency. As a response to merit, moral appraisal respect expresses itself in admiration and emulation. As a response to worth, moral recognition respect shows itself in forms of conduct that express appropriate recognition for worth of that distinctive kind, for example, by regulating conduct toward others by principles that they would not reasonably reject.

[10] Cf. Thomas Hurka's view that virtue consists in loving the good, in Hurka, "Virtue as Loving the Good," *Social Philosophy and Policy*, vol. 9, no. 2 (Summer 1992), pp. 149–68.

[11] I am indebted to John Broome and Thomas Hurka for very helpful discussion of this point.

of worth and merit. I do not claim that appreciating these values is the only source of human good. I only claim, somewhat vaguely, that it is the major source.

II. HUMAN *GOOD*?

Before I can begin to develop and defend this claim, I need to make some preliminary distinctions concerning what it could mean to say that human flourishing or good consists in a life of a certain kind. We can distinguish four broadly different interpretations of the Aristotelian Thesis: the perfectionist, biological, rational-end, and welfare readings.

Perfectionist interpretation. According to a perfectionist reading, human nature is intrinsically perfectible.[12] A proper understanding of what we are includes an understanding of what we are *to become*. By approximating this standard, we better realize our nature, and hence, ourselves. We get closer to what we ought to be. Departures, on the other hand, are faults or deficiencies, failures to be or achieve what we should. Since development and maturation are also part of our nature, human nature includes not just an ideal blueprint, but also an ideal developmental process.

Perfectionism seems most at home in a metaphysical teleology. The idea of a human *telos* just *is* the idea of an inherently normative human nature. However, perfectionism can also simply be asserted as a fundamental normative doctrine, without teleology.[13]

Having mentioned this interpretation, I shall set it aside. My aim is to defend a different version of the Aristotelian Thesis, and I can do this without taking a stand on perfectionism's main claims.[14]

Biological interpretation. The biological interpretation takes its cue from the etymology of "flourishing" and our conception of what it is for a living being to be in a healthy, prospering condition. This is a familiar enough notion and one that has a sufficiently clear application to human beings, no less than to other life forms. No one denies that there is such a thing as human physical health, and talk of psychic or mental health can also be relatively unproblematic.

On the biological interpretation, the Aristotelian Thesis asserts that healthy human functioning consists in virtuous activity. This idea has definite appeal, but I shall set it aside as well, also without prejudice.

---

[12] See, e.g., Thomas Hurka, *Perfectionism* (New York: Oxford University Press, 1993), esp. pp. 3–23.

[13] This seems to be Hurka's view.

[14] For the record, however, I do believe that perfectionism fails to appreciate the role that appreciated values play in warranting the claims of self-perfection. What we are prepared to count as perfecting or cultivating ourselves itself depends on what we can see as developing our powers to appreciate values, which cannot in turn reduce to the value of developing those very powers.

Even if the biological interpretation is true, its normative bite will depend upon being subsumed under one of the remaining interpretations, the rational-end or the welfare interpretation.[15] Only if health is an essential component of human well-being or if, for some other reason, it is a rational human end will the biological interpretation have compelling interest. We may turn, therefore, to these two remaining interpretations.

Rational-end interpretation. On some readings, what Aristotle means by the "good for man" is nothing necessarily to do with human welfare, but simply whatever is most finally choiceworthy for human beings.[16] Read this way, the Aristotelian Thesis says that virtuous activity is the single most final and choiceworthy end. Since I will be arguing that merit is grounded in its relation to worth, the rational-end interpretation is not one I can accept. Virtuous activity cannot be the most final end if it is made meritorious by responding appropriately to things of worth, since it will then also be pursued for their sake.

Welfare interpretation. This leaves the welfare interpretation, according to which the Aristotelian Thesis asserts that a life of virtuous activity is best *for the person herself*, what benefits *her* most.

Although the idea expressed by "benefit," "welfare," "a person's good," "well-being," "prudential value," and so on, is a common one in ethical discussion, it turns out to be difficult to say exactly how it should be understood and what its normative status actually is.[17] Many attempts go wrong, I think, because they implicitly make the (Aristotelian) assumption that the agent's own good is a highest-level, or most final, rational end that structures all of his first-order rational pursuits. I believe that these accounts go wrong in two ways. They misunderstand the proper scope of well-being, and they mislocate its normative status.[18] As to scope, they mistake whatever a person rationally takes an interest *in*, the set of her rational *interests*, with what is *in her own interest*. To put it another way, they conflate what is good *from* her point of view with what is good *for* or benefits *her*.[19] As I see it (and as I have argued elsewhere), however, what

---

[15] Unless, of course, it can be fit within a defensible teleological metaphysics.

[16] For the idea of a "final" or "more complete" end, of more or less final ends, and of the most final end, see *Nicomachean Ethics*, 1097a24–34. An end is final if it is aimed at for its own sake. One final end is "more final" than another if the second is also appropriately pursued for the sake of the first.

[17] I take the term "prudential value" from James Griffin, *Well-Being: Its Meaning, Measurement, and Moral Importance* (Oxford: Clarendon Press, 1986).

[18] I argue for these claims in "Self-Interest and Self-Concern," *Social Philosophy and Policy*, vol. 14, no. 1 (Winter 1997), and in "Empathy, Sympathy, Care," *Philosophical Studies*, vol. 89 (1998), pp. 261–82. Thomas Scanlon's 1996 Tanner Lecture, "The Status of Well-Being," delivered at the University of Michigan, sounds some related themes.

[19] Think here of informed-desire accounts of rationality, such as Richard Brandt's, combined with similar accounts of a person's (nonmoral) good, such as Peter Railton's. See Brandt, *A Theory of the Good and the Right* (Oxford: Oxford University Press, 1979); and Railton, "Moral Realism."

benefits a person is not what she rationally wants. It is what someone, perhaps she herself, would rationally want insofar as he or she cared about *her*.[20]

Thinking about a person's good in this way has implications for its normative status. As I see it, a person's well-being does not exhaust or summarize his rational concerns. Indeed, even though I agree that everyone has reason to be concerned about his own good, I do not think that this proposition has anything like the fundamental standing in practical reasoning it is frequently assumed to have. Rather, I believe that a person has reason to care about his own good because he has reason to care about *himself*.[21] And he has reason to care about himself because he, like any person, has *worth*—he matters. If this is right, rational egoism actually gets things backwards. The reason my welfare should matter to me is no different from the reason my welfare should matter to anyone—I am someone who matters (like anyone).

Nothing in what follows will depend on this particular metaethical theory of prudential value. The Aristotelian Thesis is a proposition of normative ethics, and my claims will be intended to be neutral as between different metaethics. I will assume that the idea of welfare is more or less familiar and available to be employed in normative ethical claims. For purposes of this essay, the relevant test is whether the version of the Aristotelian Thesis I am defending seems plausible as a normative proposition.

III. IDEALS AND MERIT

Merit and demerit are distinctive forms of value and disvalue. Consider the difference, for example, between the intrinsic value of a pleasurable feeling to the person experiencing it (say, the feeling of a warm shower on a cold day), and the intrinsic value of some meritorious activity (say, a creative endeavor such as writing a play). Both are intrinsically desirable, good things to do in an obvious sense, but only the latter is intrinsically *estimable*. Only the latter can support self-esteem, pride, and other self-evaluations that respond to merit.

What distinguishes merit and demerit as distinctive value forms is their essential connection to distinctive evaluative attitudes—esteem and disesteem, respectively, as these are involved in such emotions and attitudes as admiration, looking up to, being inspired by, desiring to emulate, on the one hand, and contempt, looking down upon, being repelled or repulsed by, desiring to reject, on the other.[22] What has merit is what is

---

[20] I argue for this in "Self-Interest and Self-Concern" and in "Empathy, Sympathy, Care."

[21] Here I have been much influenced by Elizabeth Anderson's *Value in Ethics and Economics* (Cambridge, MA: Harvard University Press, 1993), pp. 19–30.

[22] For an elaboration and defense of the idea that distinctive values are normative for distinctive valuing attitudes, see Anderson, *Value in Ethics and Economics*.

appropriately an object of such esteem, what it "makes sense" to esteem;[23] and what has demerit is what warrants disesteem.

Consider also the difference between the way in which feelings relate to value in the case of simple pleasures and pains and the way these are related in the case of merit and demerit. Compare the painful feeling of a pinprick with the feeling of shame, say, at being confronted with one's mean-spiritedness. Both feelings are painful, and both have an intrinsic evaluative element. We cannot understand a feeling to be one of pain without seeing it as something bad or something felt as bad. But there is a difference between the ways in which the two feelings involve value (and, as well, between the kinds of value they are felt to involve). Pain presents itself as a *bad feeling*, whereas shame presents itself as a perception of (and response to) a disvalue that has nothing to do with the feeling that reveals it, namely a shameful (disvaluable) feature in oneself. Of course, since shame is painful, the experience of shame also presents us with an appearance of the badness of the feeling (whether or not it is warranted). Nevertheless, what is distinctive about shame is not that it is painful, but that it is a painful appreciation of a disvalue (demerit) that is entirely independent of any disvaluable feeling it might occasion. My shame's object is my shameful mean-spiritedness, demerit in me.

Similarly, pride is not, like the experience of a warm shower on a cold day, simply a pleasurable feeling, but a pleasurable appreciation (except when illusory) of either merit in oneself or reflected merit from someone to whom one is relevantly related. Thus, both pride and shame involve the appearance (and, when warranted, the appreciation) of values that are distinct from prudential value—merit and demerit, respectively.

Aristotle's terms for merit and demerit are "noble" and "base." He uses "noble" to describe forms of conduct and feelings that are worthy of us, that we should aspire to and attempt to emulate, that correspond to an *ideal* of conduct. And he uses "base" to describe what is beneath us, what we should look down upon and have contempt for, what falls short of the ideal, or perhaps, what corresponds to a "negative ideal."

Aristotle gets to his version of the Aristotelian Thesis via the function argument (1097b25–1098a18). The good of everything that has a characteristic function is functioning well. The characteristic function of human beings is activity of soul "implying a rational principle" (1098a13). Human good, then, must be "activity of soul in conformity with excellence" (1098a16). So far this gives us only that human well-being consists in

---

[23] For a general noncognitivist account of judgments about what "makes sense" or is rational, see Allan Gibbard, *Wise Choices, Apt Feelings* (Cambridge, MA: Harvard University Press, 1990). Compare also John McDowell, "Values and Secondary Qualities," in *Morality and Objectivity: A Tribute to J. L. Mackie*, ed. Ted Honderich (London: Routledge and Kegan Paul, 1985); and Justin D'Arms and Daniel Jacobson, "Expressivism, Morality, and the Emotions," *Ethics*, vol. 104 (1986), pp. 739–63. I also intend my normative claims in this essay about the relation between prudential value and the appreciation of merit and worth to be neutral with respect to contending metaethical theories of merit and worth.

excellent rational activity. What gets us to the conclusion that human well-being resides in activity that expresses a *conception* of excellence, specifically, an ideal of the noble, is the distinctive form that, according to Aristotle, human rational functioning takes. Aristotle contrasts merely goal-directed behavior (*poiesis*: producing or making) with the distinctively human activity (*praxis*) that, unlike *poiesis*, aims at an action for its own sake (1140b6–7). *Praxis* is activity engaged in as intrinsically valuable, as realizing an ideal of the noble (*kalon*). So human well-being must consist in excellent *praxis*, in noble actions chosen on account of their merit.

In addition to the function argument, Aristotle has various dialectical arguments that are addressed to those attracted to other views (1095b13–1096b11). A particularly persuasive one responds to the identification of *eudaimonia* with honor or esteem. Aristotle agrees that we want esteem (our own no less than others'), but he argues that this cannot be the root of the matter, since we value the esteem of those *we* esteem more than that of those we hold in low regard. What explains this, he claims, is that the esteem of the former assures us more of our *worthiness* of esteem, of our merit (1095b26–29). At bottom, then, we must wish to be virtuous and do what is noble for its own sake.

Aristotle is surely right about the centrality of ideals of merit and demerit in human life. It is obvious that human beings, "the blushing animal," are naturally subject to shame. And we don't need Thomas Hobbes, Francois La Rochefoucauld, or evangelical Christianity to persuade us of pride's role in the human psyche. We clearly care about the appearance of merit as well as about actually meriting esteem, as Aristotle's remark about honor shows. How else can we explain the enormous emotional resources we put into defending personal and public self-narratives in which we come off reasonably well.

As important as merit is to us, however, this does not yet explain the connection between noble activity and well-being that Aristotle has in mind. So far we just have that noble activity is essential to something we want to be true—that we have merit. It does not follow from this that noble *activity* has prudential value. It does not follow that a person gets intrinsic benefit from the activity *itself*. The benefit seems to come, rather, from the *fact* of merit or from knowledge or belief in that fact—as though the benefit of noble activity were that it made the narrative of one's life that of a noble character. As I understand the Aristotelian Thesis, however, the idea is not just that noble activity is essential to some intrinsically desired fact or state of affairs, but that noble activity is *itself* intrinsically valuable for the virtuous person.

IV. Appreciating Value and Worth

To work toward a more adequate understanding of the connection between virtuous activity and prudential value, let us consider a potential (but ultimately misguided) objection to Aristotle's claim that virtuous activity is chosen on account of its nobility. Aristotle tells us that to be virtuous, acts must be done as the virtuous person would do them, that is, out of motives that are distinctive of the specific virtue. To manifest the virtue of justice, just acts must be done justly, and to manifest temperance, temperate acts must be done temperately (1105a30). But Aristotle also says, as I have noted, that virtuous acts must be chosen as noble (1104b30–1105a1, 1105a31, 1117b8–10). What, then, is the relation between motives of these two different kinds? How can it be the case both that the virtuous person is moved by motives distinctive of the specific virtue she expresses and that she chooses the act on account of its nobility? For example, the courageous person is prepared to face fear and withstand danger when the values at stake warrant doing so. But the values that call for doing so cannot themselves be the nobility of withstanding danger, because it is only noble to withstand danger when the values at stake call for it. Or to take a non-Aristotelian example, good parenting is virtuous, but the distinctive motive of the good parent would seem to be a concern for one's children, not for the nobility of good parenting.

The proper response to this objection is that the motives in question need not be incompatible. To be moved by nobility of action in the right way, in the way a virtuous person is, is to be moved by an appreciation of the grounds that *make* the action noble. For example, the courageous person is moved by an appreciation of the values at stake that warrant facing fear and danger and that, therefore, make doing so noble. Facing the danger will not *be* noble unless it is called for by appropriate values (worth), so someone cannot be moved by a proper appreciation of an act's nobility unless he is moved also by an appreciation of the values that make the action noble.

There are two distinct points here. One concerns the content of motives expressed in virtuous activity, in particular, their relation to merit-making worth. The second concerns their "mode of awareness," specifically, their involving an *appreciation* of the relevant values.

The first point is a consequence of the relation between merit and worth, which I remarked upon above. Activity has merit when it is appropriately related to worth. In order for activity to be chosen as noble in the right way, then, it must be chosen for its relation to things of worth, since this is what makes it noble. The importance of children, for instance, calls for giving them good care; thus, doing so has merit. Parenting is virtuous, therefore, when it expresses an appreciation of the worth of children, the importance of their welfare, and, consequently, the merit of good parenting.

Note that, although on this view an action is meritorious on account of its relation to a form of value, namely worth, there is nothing essentially consequentialist about this idea. The act is still *intrinsically* choiceworthy since it has an intrinsically choiceworthy relation to worth. Neither does the fact that merit is derivative from worth entail that meritorious actions must maximize value. That would be so only if the relevant forms of worth were values to which the appropriate relation is promotion, rather than, say, respect, honoring, or some other attitude.[24] In fact, I think that this is not the case. I believe, for example, that meritorious parenting responds to the value of individual children. The good parent sees his child's welfare as mattering because he sees his *child* as mattering. It is the value of the child that is fundamental, not the value of the state of affairs of his child's faring well.[25] And this value is not one that can be promoted or produced. It is rather to be respected and cherished. That will, of course, involve promoting the child's welfare, but the fundamental reason for doing so will be that the child matters. Nonetheless, nothing in my general claims concerning the relation between prudential value and the appreciation of worth depends upon Kantian theses about worth.

The second point is that virtuous activity involves a distinctive mode of awareness of merit and worth, namely, *appreciation*, rather than just belief or knowledge. The latter are attitudes toward the proposition that something has merit or worth (or toward whatever is the proxy for that proposition in the correct noncognitivist account, if such an account is correct).[26] Appreciation, however, is an attitude toward the meritorious or worthy thing itself. It is impossible to be in the state of directly appreciating someone's merits, for example, without esteeming *her* and her traits, without seeing or feeling her (and their) merit, without its seeming to one as if she has merit. Similarly, it is impossible to directly appreciate something's worth without being in the state of deeming or holding *it* important, without seeing or feeling its importance, without its seeming to one as if it matters.[27] In this way, appreciation is a quasi-perceptual state. It involves experiences that are *as of* something's merit and worth, where this involves an experienced valuing relation to the particular thing.[28]

---

[24] On the relevance of this distinction to that between consequentialist and nonconsequentialist ethical theories, see Philip Pettit, "Consequentialism," in *A Companion to Ethics*, ed. Peter Singer (Oxford: Blackwell Publishers, 1991).

[25] For an elaboration and defense of this idea, see Anderson, *Value in Ethics and Economics*, pp. 19–30. See also Darwall, "Empathy, Sympathy, Care."

[26] For example, on Gibbard's norm-expressivism (in *Wise Choices, Apt Feelings*), the judgment that something is justified expresses the psychological state of acceptance of a norm warranting that thing. Suppose, as I have suggested, that the judgment that X has merit is understood as the judgment that esteem for X is justified. According to Gibbard's norm-expressivism, then, this judgment will express acceptance of a norm that warrants having esteem for X. The judgment that X has merit will thus express, not an attitude toward X, but an attitude toward an attitude toward X. Cruder noncognitivisms, such as emotivism, do hold that the judgment that something X has value expresses an attitude toward X, but they are problematic as accounts of value *judgment* for this very reason, since one can sincerely say or think that something has value even if one does not currently have a favorable attitude toward it, say, if one knows oneself to be depressed, in a perverse mood, or the like.

[27] Compare here David Velleman's view that love involves an appreciation of the worth of a person (Velleman, "Love as a Moral Emotion," *Ethics*, forthcoming).

[28] Here again, I intend to be taking no metaethical stands. I assume, for example, that noncognitivists can proffer some account of judgments about the appreciation of values. On my use of "as of," see note 32 below.

Return now to the criticism that if a person chooses to perform an act on account of the act's nobility, then he will not be moved as a virtuous person would. In effect, the objection assumes that Aristotle holds that the virtuous person is moved by a *de dicto* desire to act nobly, a desire that it be true that he does the noble thing, whatever that might be.[29] And the objection is that if that is so, then the person's motives will not have the appropriate relation to the specific things of worth with which the situation confronts him. We can begin to respond to this objection, I noted, if we say that a virtuous person will not simply act out of the conviction that a given act is noble, but, as well, out of convictions concerning the source of its merit in values (things of worth) to which the act responds. Thus, the good parent takes pains for his children in the belief that so acting is noble because it responds in the appropriate way to his children's worth.

If we go only so far, however, a version of the objection can be raised again at this stage. If I act simply in the belief that children have worth, mine included, without directly *appreciating* my children's worth, without appreciating this value *in them*, then the attitudes I express in parenting will be neither toward my parenting activity nor toward my children whose importance I take to warrant that activity. The attitudes will be toward the propositions that my children have worth and that, because they do, my parenting activity has merit. That this is not what Aristotle has in mind is shown by his distinction between virtue and continence (1145a15–1152a32).[30]

Unlike the merely continent, the virtuous person chooses noble acts "for *their* own sakes," in the sense that her favorable regard is directed to the acts themselves, not to propositions or states of affairs that include them (1105a30–32, emphasis added). She has an intrinsic regard that turns into enjoyment in the actual activity. She takes wholehearted pleasure in the activity itself. W. D. Ross's translation has Aristotle saying that the temperate person does not simply abstain from bodily pleasures, but "delights in this very fact" (1104b6). But clearly what Aristotle means is not that she delights in the (contemplated) fact of her temperance, but that she delights in temperate *activity*. She may also delight in contemplating the fact of her temperance, but that is not what makes her temperate. Terence Irwin's translation is better. "[I]f someone who abstains from bodily pleasures enjoys the abstinence it-

---

[29] Michael Smith makes a similar objection to externalism: that it must hold that what explains why the "good and strong-willed" person is motivated to act in accordance with his ethical judgments, even when these undergo radical change, is a *de dicto* desire to do what is right, whereas a morally good person would be moved, rather, by *de re* desires to do the very things he thinks morally good. See Smith, *The Moral Problem* (Oxford: Blackwell, 1994), pp. 71–76, 82–83.

[30] Aristotelian continence contrasts with *akrasia* or incontinence, acting against one's better judgment. The continent person does what she believes she should; for example, she chooses acts she believes to be noble. What she lacks, and what the virtuous person has, is wholehearted engagement with and enjoyment of noble activity.

self, then he is temperate."[31] Temperance is revealed in the temperate person's undivided engagement with and enjoyment of his temperate activity. His "activity is intensified by *its* proper pleasure" (1175a30, emphasis added).

There is a sense in which both the continent person and the virtuous person choose noble activities for their own sake, since both act in the conviction that their actions are intrinsically worth choosing. But there is another sense in which only the virtuous person chooses noble acts for *their* own sake, since only she acts out of a directly appreciative regard for the activity itself (and, if I am right, out of a regard for things of worth that make it meritorious). If we identify desires by that-clauses, then both the virtuous and the continent act out of the same desire: that they act nobly. A consequence of what we have just been saying, however, is that this identity observes an important difference in the *ways* that the continent and the virtuous respectively desire to do what is noble for its own sake.

This points to a more general distinction between ways in which someone may desire to do something for its own sake. Someone may think an activity intrinsically desirable and act out of a desire that she engage in it without having any favorable regard for the activity of a sort that would naturally become enjoyment were the activity to turn out as she envisages it. Having the belief, she may just want the narrative of her life to include the performance of that activity. If, contrary to fact, she could make it true that she had engaged in the activity without having actually to engage in it, she might be indifferent or even pleased. Consider the difference, for example, between an enthusiastic music-lover and someone who, lacking direct appreciation and enthusiasm for the activity, nonetheless engages in musical activity because she thinks it an intrinsically desirable thing to do. The first person takes pleasure in musical activity, whereas any pleasure taken by the second is in contemplating, self-reflectively, the fact that she engages in it.

Unlike merely continent actions, therefore, virtuous activity is actively enjoyed. The virtuous person favorably regards what he is doing, not just the fact that he is doing it. However, we must not lose sight of the fact that he is also acting on account of his activity's merit. So his enjoyment cannot simply be like the enjoyment one has in taking a warm shower on a cold day. It must be a pleasurable appreciation, not just of a quality of his own feeling, but of the value (merit) of his activity. It must involve an appearance that is as of his activity's merit, which appearance is itself properly related to what justifies or warrants his esteem.[32]

---

[31] Aristotle, *Nicomachean Ethics*, trans. Terence Irwin (Indianapolis, IN: Hackett Publishing Company, 1985), p. 37.

[32] Here and elsewhere I use the "as of" construction to stress the way the appearance seems to the person having it. Just as color experience is *as of* an intrinsic color feature, say, the redness of a book, so the experience of esteem involves an "appearance" that is as of an intrinsic "merit feature" of the object of esteem.

The lesson of our first point, however, is that it cannot involve only this. To choose an action on account of its nobility in the right way is to choose it out of a regard for its orientation to things of worth and, consequently, out of a regard for those very values. It follows that the proper enjoyment of virtuous activity involves an appreciation of these latter values also— appearances that are as of things of worth, which appearances are related appropriately to what justifies or warrants seeing things in that way.

There are two components, then, to a proper answer to the objection that virtuous activity involves motives characteristic of specific virtues rather than the desire to do what is noble. The first is that virtuous activity does, indeed, involve an appropriate relation to merit-making worth—not just to merit, considered abstractly. And the second is that this relation includes an intrinsically motivating appreciation of the ac- tivity's orientation to things that matter.

V. The Good of Merit- and Worth-Appreciating Activity

A friend once told me that she was unprepared for what a profoundly moving experience parenting would be for her. What she meant, I think, is that through parenting she was brought into a direct appreciation of deeply important values—the worth of her children, the importance of their being raised well, and, consequently, the value of the activity in which she was herself engaged. The activity itself included experiences and feelings that were *as of* her children's value and the value of parenting them well. Neither of us was in any doubt, moreover, about whether she meant also to be saying something about the contribution this activity was making to her own well-being, the value of her own life for her. She was saying that parenting had enriched her life, that she had found a depth of satisfaction in it for which she had not really been prepared.

I think I see a similar sense in the pianist David Golub's face. He may be having more fun than parenting can sometimes seem to involve, but any deeply worthwhile activity requires serious and painstaking atten- tion, and no doubt there are days when practicing a demanding piece seems anything but fun. What is common to both activities is the expe- rience of connecting with something of worth in a way that enables the direct appreciation of the value of one's activity.

Both activities give pleasure, but, as Aristotle says, pleasure is a sign of the activities' value, not its substance. What is pleasurable is, at least partly, the appreciation of merit and worth that these activities them- selves involve. And what makes these pleasures loom so large in our well-being is the sense that, through them, we are connecting with things that matter. The benefit comes through the appreciation of values—worth and merit—with which these activities connect us.

The same is true, I believe, with the more canonical Aristotelian virtues— courage, temperance, justice, and so on. What is so satisfying about meet- ing challenges with courage, for example? Is it the mere fact of overcoming

fear or lack of confidence? No doubt this is part of it, but surely it is
largely the sense of having dealt with these obstacles when and because
it *mattered*, when, that is, the values at stake called for doing so. We will
not count an act as one of bravery, or, at least, credit it as such, unless we
can see it as an appropriate response to things of worth.

That the primary source of prudential value is appreciation of valuable
activity, and not just belief in or knowledge of its merit or worth, can be
seen by considering how these respectively relate to self-esteem. It is
possible to believe that one deserves esteem, including one's own, but
nonetheless to lack self-esteem. Self-esteem is an attitude toward, and not
just a belief about, oneself. It is a way of regarding oneself that includes
a sense or feelings as of one's own value or a disposition to such feelings.[33] One can be racked by feelings of inadequacy and so lack self-
esteem even as one believes that one shouldn't.[34] Though one judges
there is no warrant for feeling this way, one may be unable to shake
feelings that are as of one's inadequate merit. It seems clear that a person
is substantially worse off by virtue of regarding herself in this way and
not just because of the undesirability of her feelings as feelings. Although
she believes she has merit, she is deprived of a stable appreciation of her
merit. From the standpoint from which she normally lives her life, it is as
if she has little or no merit, as if her activity does not connect in the right
way with what has real significance and worth.

How do we gain the appreciation of merit in which self-esteem consists? If merit consists in responding appropriately to worth, then we can
sense our merit only through sensing our responding appropriately to
worth. This is just what we gain in activities of merit, since they are
guided by an appreciation of worth. Of course, as Aristotle's remark
about honor reminds us, being honored by those we honor can support
self-esteem also. But it cannot do so simply by confirming the belief that
we have merit, since we can have that belief and lack self-esteem. It must
rather support a sense or appreciation of our merit, and it can do this only
if others have this sense also, which we can receive from them empathet-
ically, seeing ourselves through their eyes. For that to be true, however,
they must be able to sense or see merit in us by appreciating our virtuous
activity.

Subjective/objective. If this is right, then the good of virtuous activity
derives primarily from a perceptual-like relation between the person and
merit-making values that such activity usually involves. Both the subjective and objective elements are necessary. If what a person takes to have

[33] Just as "esteem" can refer to an attitude toward merit or one toward worth, so can
"self-esteem." Regarding self-esteem as an attitude and its relation toward feelings, I have
been helped by discussions with Peter Vranas.

[34] Robin Dillon points this out in her "Self-Respect: Moral, Emotional, Political," *Ethics*,
vol. 107 (1997), pp. 226–49. Dillon actually puts her points in terms of appraisal self-respect
(or as she calls it, following Stephen Hudson, "evaluative self-respect"). However, appraisal
self-respect is a species of self-esteem, namely, that concerned primarily with moral or
moral-like features of the person.

merit and worth does not have it in fact, then her life has less value (and, *therefore*, less prudential value) than she supposes. To check this, consider what kind of life you would want for someone you care about, for that person's own sake.[35] Will it be a matter of indifference to you whether what the person herself takes to ground her activities' merit really has worth or not? If you are convinced that what she is devoting herself to is worthless, would you want this for her for her sake as much as you would if the thing she were devoted to were something you thought had worth? It seems obvious to me that I would not. By the same token, however, it is not a matter of indifference whether a person whose activities actually have merit sees that they do so. The really significant benefits of virtuous activity require both subjective and objective elements. Related in the right way, these constitute an appreciation of the activity's merit and its relation to worth, that is, an appearance as of its merit and relation to worth, which appearance is itself appropriately related to actual merit and worth.

I need not claim, of course, that illusory satisfactions have no value for the person, nor that really meritorious, but unappreciated, activities are without value. My claim is simply that virtuous activity that includes an appreciation of its relation to worth has far greater (prudential) value for the person than either the subjective or the objective element, taken by itself.[36]

VI. VIRTUOUS ACTIVITY AND RELATIONSHIPS

Up to this point, I have been discussing individuals' virtuous activities more or less independently of their relations to others. I have been supposing, of course, that many virtuous activities, like parenting, derive merit from forms of relationship to others. But I have been abstracting from ways in which others are involved in virtually every form of valuable activity, ways in which shared valuable activities make possible distinctively valuable forms of relationship, and ways in which acknowledging the values that ground merit can lead one to acknowledge the value of persons.

The basic idea underlying many of these points is simple enough. Unlike welfare or well-being, merit and worth are personal-standpoint-neutral, rather than standpoint-relative, values. Something enhances welfare by being good *for someone*, but there is no such thing as merit or worth for someone, except in the sense of someone thinking something has merit or worth. There is only merit or worth period.

---

[35] Again, for a defense of the metaethical theory that being good for a person just is being something it would make sense for someone who cares about that person to want for her for her sake, see my "Self-Interest and Self-Concern."

[36] Derek Parfit makes a similar claim. See his *Reasons and Persons* (Oxford: Clarendon Press, 1984), pp. 501–2.

If worth or merit are normative for distinctive evaluative attitudes, consequently, they must be normative for *anyone's* attitudes, and, moreover, for attitudes and feelings we have or feel *as from anyone's perspective*. When we see something as worthy of admiration and emulation, we see it as having a feature, merit, that is there for anyone to appreciate who is capable of doing so. Similarly, if I see something, like fine music, to have worth, then I take it to be something anyone would be warranted in deeming important.

Compare this with the idea of welfare. On some influential accounts, prudential value is normative for desire from that person's *own* perspective. As I have said, I believe these accounts are mistaken. What is for a person's good, I believe, is what it would make sense to want, not from that person's perspective, but from the standpoint of someone (perhaps, the person himself) who cares about *him*. To judge that something will benefit someone, I think, is to make a claim that has normativity from that perspective, the standpoint of one who cares about him. But neither the concept of merit nor the concept of worth is standpoint-relative in either of these ways. Anything with merit or worth is worthy of one or another form of esteem, attitudes, or feelings we have as if from anyone's standpoint, regardless of who we are or whom we care about.

Merit and worth can thus be *common* values—they and their appreciation can be distinctively shared. Moreover, appreciating these values through shared valuable activity makes possible distinctive forms of valuable relationship, through which the good of valuable activity is both confirmed and ramified. This, in turn, creates new forms of shared valuable activity with others—forms that both add prudential value of their own and support that of the initial activities.

Merit ramifies both "up" and "out." It ramifies up, because when something has merit, then so do various second- and higher-order attitudes toward that thing. And it ramifies out, because when something has merit, then so do various attitudes of others toward it. The explanation for both phenomena derives from the very nature of merit, its consisting in an appropriate response to worth. For example, since individual persons have worth, and since various forms of love and respect are appropriate responses to their worth, these responses have merit. The appropriate response to merit is the esteem of admiration and the desire to emulate. Because these are appropriate responses to merit, they are also appropriate responses, at one remove, to worth. So they have merit also. Or alternatively, because merit is a form of worth, to which they respond appropriately, this gives them merit also. And this can ramify up again: since esteem for merit has merit, then esteem for esteem for merit has merit also; and so on.

Merit ramifies out, because if something has merit, then it calls for esteem from others no less than from the person who has it. Since merit consists in the appropriate response to worth, and esteem is the appropriate response to merit, then esteem is the appropriate response, at one remove, to worth. Thus, others' esteem of our merit has merit also. (Or, alternatively, this is so because merit is a form of worth to which others' esteem is the appropriate response.) And this can ramify out again: esteem for a person's esteem for another person's merit has merit also; and so on.

Merit's ramifying upward and outward creates a rich structure for the shared appreciation of valuable activity. And since, I have argued, the appreciation of her relation to worth is the major source of prudential value for a virtuous person, merit's ramifying up and out creates a rich set of possibilities for the appreciation of value to enhance well-being. When two people share esteem for merit, whatever its source, they are then in a position to appreciate this meritorious response in each other, and then, to appreciate the merit of their so doing, and so on. And when the merit they appreciate is in each other, these effects are accentuated. Moreover, since, as Joseph Brodsky put it, "a man is what he loves," in esteeming another's valuings one also appreciates and esteems that person as well.[37]

An unusual example will help illustrate these points. Oliver Sacks describes the remarkable case of two twins who had been variously diagnosed as autistic, psychotic, or severely retarded and institutionalized since the age of seven.[38] When Sacks first got to know the twins, they were twenty-six years old and considered to be relatively uninteresting *idiot savant* calculators, whose "trick" was that they were able instantly to calculate the day of the week of any date within the last, or the next, forty thousand years. It was thought they did this by mechanically applying an algorithm. The more Sacks got to know the twins, however, the clearer it became to him that they actually had a remarkable intuitive feel for mathematical structure and a rich shared imaginative life contemplating its beauty together:

> They were seated in a corner together, with a mysterious "secret" smile on their faces, a smile I had never seen before, enjoying the strange pleasure and peace they now seemed to have. I crept up quietly, so as not to disturb them. They seemed to be locked in a singular, purely numerical converse. John would say a number—a six-figure number. Michael would catch the number, nod, smile, and seem to savor it. Then he in turn would say another six-figure number, and it was John who received, and appreciated it richly. . . . *What were they doing? What on earth was going on?*[39]

Sacks finally conjectured that what was happening was that John and Michael were exchanging gifts of very large prime numbers. Somehow

---

[37] Joseph Brodsky, *On Grief and Reason: Essays* (New York: The Noonday Press, Farrar, Straus, and Giroux, 1995), p. 21.

[38] Oliver Sacks, "The Twins," *New York Review of Books*, vol. 32 (1985), pp. 16–20.

[39] *Ibid.*, p. 17.

each was able to see the primeness of a six-digit number and propose it as an object of shared contemplation. To test his hypothesis, Sacks returned to the ward with a book of primes. Finding the twins, "closeted in their numerical communion," he writes,

> I decided to join in, and ventured an eight-figure prime. They both turned toward me, then suddenly became still, with a look of intense concentration, and perhaps wonder on their faces. There was a long pause—the longest I had ever known them to make, it must have lasted a half-minute or more—and then suddenly, simultaneously, they both broke into smiles.[40]

This "great joy," Sacks remarks, was actually a "double joy." Sacks had introduced John and Michael to a new and remarkably large prime they had never before encountered, and he had made it evident to them that he had understood what they were up to, "admired it," and wanted to join in the activity himself. At this point, the twins made a place for Sacks, and the group continued on, now a prime-contemplating threesome, with Sacks sneaking looks at his book to confirm what John and Michael could see with mathematical intuition.

Sack's account recalls G. E. Moore's remark that "by far the most valuable things, which we know or can imagine" are "the pleasures of human intercourse and the enjoyment of beautiful objects."[41] Moore was speaking not of a person's good but of what he called "good absolutely."[42] However, his remark has something approaching the ring of truth when we read it as concerning well-being. What explains this, I think, is the interpretation of the Aristotelian Thesis I have been offering, namely, that the prudential value of virtuous activity consists largely in the appreciation of its connection to worth. Beauty is a form of worth, the appropriate responses to which include creation and appreciation. Both creating and appreciating beauty have merit, then; and these activities can enrich lives because they involve the pleasurable appreciation of this merit and worth. Similarly, the pleasures of human intercourse largely consist, I believe, in appreciating the merits and worth of other persons as well as the merit of relating to them in various ways.

Because merit ramifies up and out, its appreciation ramifies up and out also. This means that the prudential value of an individual instance is

---

[40] *Ibid.*, p. 18.

[41] G. E. Moore, *Principia Ethica*, with the preface to the second edition and other papers, edited with an introduction by Thomas Baldwin (Cambridge: Cambridge University Press, 1993), p. 237.

[42] Indeed, Moore argued that there is no coherent concept of a person's good. There is only the concept of the absolute goodness of something a person may possess or of his possessing it. Moore famously argued on these grounds that egoism is incoherent (*ibid.*, pp. 150–53).

likely to be substantially enhanced and supported by the prudential value of its branching offshoots. In this way, virtuous activity tends to create and partake of coherent structures of mutually supporting prudential value.

VII. CONCLUSION

Nothing I have said in support of the Aristotelian Thesis has presupposed any particular metaethics of well-being. Nonetheless, I believe that the theory that a person's good is what it would make sense for someone who cared about that person to want for her sake, and the arguments I have provided for the Aristotelian Thesis, are mutually supporting. When I ask myself what kind of life it makes sense to want for my children, it just seems obvious to me that it is a life in which they engage in activities whose merit and relation to worth they themselves appreciate. I would like it just fine if they came to have the same smile that I see on David Golub's face (or that Oliver Sacks saw on John's and Michael's faces).

The Aristotelian Thesis is plausible independently of any particular metaethics of a person's good. Because it is, it provides some support for the particular metaethics I have suggested, since that theory itself supports the Aristotelian Thesis. Of course, this support might not be very significant since it might be thought that something's being good for someone is what makes it make sense to want it for them for their sake, and not vice versa.[43]

In closing, I want to note how my arguments for the Aristotelian Thesis might be taken to suggest yet a further alternative metaethics of well-being. Perhaps it is true, not just that a person's life goes better to the extent that she appreciates her life's relation to worth, but that this is what prudential value *is*.[44] This is a metaethics of a person's good that those who find the idea philosophically puzzling, such as Moore, might find attractive.[45] The fundamental value concept is, as with Moore, that of a kind of intrinsic value that is independent of its relation to any conception of what is good *for* individuals. And the thought would be that being good for someone is identical with being an appreciation by that person of something intrinsically valuable (having worth).[46]

---

[43] I argue to the contrary in "Self-Interest and Self-Concern," and "Empathy, Sympathy, Care."

[44] Thus, we might take worth to include good experiences—pleasures including experiences that are appreciated as having worth *as experiences* and not as themselves appreciating further worth, such as beauty.

[45] "What, then, is meant by 'my own good'? In what sense can a thing be good *for me*? . . . When therefore, I talk of anything I get as 'my own good,' I must mean either that the thing I get is good, or that my possessing it is good" (Moore, *Principia Ethica*, p. 150). See also Thomas Hurka, "'Good' and 'Good For'," *Mind*, vol. 96 (1987), pp. 71–73.

[46] For example, the prudential value of pleasures (as such) would consist in their involving an appreciation of the value of certain experiences considered as such.

In the end, however, the case for the Aristotelian Thesis can be made independently of metaethics. No matter what metaethics of well-being we accept, I hope it now seems plausible that a good human life consists largely of activities that involve the appreciation of forms of value that are distinct from prudential value. Luckily, we do not need to worry that such a life is not also pleasurable. We have David Golub's smile to assure us that it is.

Philosophy, The University of Michigan

ANCIENT PERFECTIONISM AND ITS MODERN CRITICS*

By Georgios Anagnostopoulos

I. Introduction

The idea of flourishing has enjoyed a comeback in recent ethical theory, both from a historical and a systematic perspective. From a historical perspective, one finds a number of studies by scholars of ancient philosophy aiming to elucidate and defend the notion of flourishing; from a systematic perspective, the work of Thomas Hurka and Amartya Sen has contributed much toward the rehabilitation of the notion in contemporary ethical theory and discussion.[1]

Of course, to speak of a comeback is to assume that the notion enjoyed an earlier life, that it was a significant component of ethical theory in the past. It is well-known that this is indeed the case: several moral philosophers of the past have advocated flourishing in one form or another in their attempts to explain the good, happiness, or virtue. Most often these philosophers understand flourishing in terms of perfection, thus advocating perfectionist theories of the good, happiness, or virtue. At least Plato, Aristotle, Marx, and Nietzsche are among those who have put forth ethical theories that give a prominent place to flourishing and are perfectionist in character.

In Greek philosophy, perfectionism and flourishing go hand in hand, and both are most often connected to a view about human nature or essence. It is almost a given in Greek philosophy that there is a human nature or essence and, of course, that there is only one human essence. It is not surprising, then, to find that those who understand the human good in terms of flourishing or perfectionism come to the conclusion that the human good takes one form rather than many—it consists in the flourishing or perfection of those faculties or capacities that constitute human nature or essence. In addition, it is quite clear that this kind of framework implies an objective conception of goodness and of the good.

* I have benefited from comments on an earlier version of this essay from Stephen Darwall, Thomas Hill, Richard Kraut, Charles Larmore, and Douglas Rasmussen. I am most indebted for detailed comments and suggestions that have led to improvements of the final version to David Brink, Fred Miller, Mariana Anagnostopoulos, Andreas Anagnostopoulos, and the editors of this volume.

[1] Thomas Hurka, "The Well-Rounded Life," *Journal of Philosophy*, vol. 84 (1987), pp. 707–26; Hurka, *Perfectionism* (Oxford: Oxford University Press, 1993); Amartya Sen, *Collective Choice and Social Welfare* (San Francisco: Holden-Day, 1970); Sen, "Capability and Well-Being," in *The Quality of Life*, ed. Martha Nussbaum and Amartya Sen (Oxford: Clarendon Press, 1993), pp. 30–53.

The above features of perfectionism are by no means accepted by all. Almost all of them have been criticized or even rejected by many moral and political philosophers in recent times. The objectivism associated with perfectionist theories of the good was abandoned by the founders and most followers of utilitarianism, who argued for a form of hedonism as far as the good is concerned. Hedonism itself has been rejected by those objecting to the important similarity it bears to perfectionism—namely, its commitment to a single good or end (pleasure). Many theorists who reject both the objectivity and unity of the good or goodness tend to favor the desire-satisfaction conception of the good. According to them, the only intrinsic good is the satisfaction of desire. Such a conception is clearly subjective and, although it seems at some level to imply a single good or end (the satisfaction of desire), it is clear that it, unlike perfectionism, allows for a plurality of ends across different agents and even in the same agent. The things that agents, according to this view, aim at for the satisfaction of desire, and hence the kinds of lives they choose as their end, vary from individual to individual and even within the same individual. Recent liberal theorists have gone further, distancing themselves even from the kind of unity that can be attributed to the desire-satisfaction conception of the good by insisting that there are many different, conflicting, and often incommensurable *conceptions* of the good. Such a view may suggest that talk about the good is really empty, for it seems to imply that there can be no common or unified conception of the good. As a consequence, it might be best to speak only of the important implication of the liberal view about the ends of human life—namely, that there are different, conflicting, and often incommensurable ends. This implication is also shared by the desire-satisfaction conception. Lastly, much of the criticism of perfectionism has focused on its connection with human nature, essence, or teleology. Critics have sought to undermine perfectionism by attacking the very ideas or specific conceptions of human nature, essence, or teleology that are invariably given as its foundation. At times, even some who are sympathetic to the kind of shared purpose and unity of the good that theories of human flourishing and perfectionism espouse find the commitments these theories make to a metaphysical conception of human nature, function, or teleology problematic or unacceptable. Thus, Alasdair MacIntyre has recently attempted to ground the features of theories of human flourishing and of perfectionism that are abandoned by liberalism—for example, the unity of the good—in something other than essentialism or metaphysical teleology.[2]

It is quite difficult to adjudicate among these views about the good. Quite often the theories within which these views are embedded differ in their structure, some being teleological, others deontological, and still others fitting neither of these two types of theory. The structure of a theory is likely to have consequences. If John Rawls is right, such

---

[2] Alasdair MacIntyre, *After Virtue* (Notre Dame: University of Notre Dame Press, 1981).

differences in the structure of moral theories have quite important implications for the conceptions of the good that they endorse.[3] In addition, there are differences in what each moral theory presupposes. Whereas ancient philosophers and those advocating perfectionism begin with a conception of human nature, recent liberal thinkers begin with a specific political conception—for example, the liberal democratic society of the modern and contemporary world—and see their concerns as being exclusively political.[4] Thus, the questions that the various theorists address when they seek to specify the good may not be quite the same. In the one case, an account of the good is sought that is independent of any political framework or particular circumstances, while, in the other, the account sought must fit a preexisting or assumed social or political framework.

I shall begin by discussing two versions of perfectionism that seem not to start with or be based on a conception of human nature or teleology. One version (Plato's) is more important than the other (pre-philosophical perfectionism), since the former aspires to be a kind of comprehensive theory of value. Yet it might be useful to look at both of them; doing so may be of help in seeing what one can do with perfectionism without all the presuppositions about essence, nature, and teleology that so many find objectionable. It also may be instructive to see the limitations of these two different versions. Plato's perfectionism has some important implications for the political and educational theory he advocates in the *Republic*, some of which bear interesting similarities to some of the views of liberal theorists. Yet in the end neither of these perfectionisms that lack a metaphysical base will prove successful.

The rest of the essay will focus on Aristotle's discussion of the good that precedes his famous argument in support of perfectionism in Book I of his *Nicomachean Ethics*. This discussion is of considerable interest, for it can be interpreted as putting forth an account of the good that is nonperfectionist. Indeed, the account seems most similar to the view of the good advocated by desire-satisfaction theorists, which of course allows for different ends across different agents and a plurality of ends in the case of each agent. Yet even in this nonperfectionist account of the good, Aristotle argues in support of the life with a single final end and in support of the same end for all agents. Much of the discussion below attempts to identify the reasons for this difference between Aristotle and desire-satisfaction theorists by examining their corresponding presuppositions, especially with regard to the nature of rationality, the nature of the self, the nature and goals of the political association, and so on.

[3] John Rawls, "Social Unity and Primary Goods," in Amartya Sen and Bernard Williams, eds., *Utilitarianism and Beyond* (New York: Cambridge University Press, 1981); see also Rawls, *Political Liberalism* (New York: Columbia University Press, 1993), pp. 173–211.

[4] As Charles Larmore has aptly put it: "[B]y its very nature liberalism must be a philosophy of politics, and not a philosophy of man. . . ." Larmore, *Patterns of Moral Complexity* (Cambridge: Cambridge University Press, 1987), p. 25.

II. Pre-Philosophical Perfectionism in the Greek Tradition

The idea of perfection and the view that perfection is desirable and should be attained seem to have been a part of the Greek tradition before the philosophical theories that expound perfectionism of one kind or another were developed. Long before Plato and Aristotle, the good (*agathos*) man is thought to be someone who excels in some capacity or other, one who has some perfection. Most often the excellence or perfection is that of a physical attribute,[5] but not always. Thus, some of Homer's great men excel in strength, speed, endurance, fighting skills, or beauty, while others—admittedly, not many—excel in wisdom, cunning, or ability to rule over men. Excelling or surpassing others in such attributes is greatly valued and is considered a good; possession of some of these excellences is what makes an individual good. The importance that excellence and perfection have in the subsequent Greek culture is well-known. They constitute a defining feature of the Greek culture, where perfection of the human body and mind, their activities, and achievements are given a prominence that perhaps has no equal in any other culture.

This kind of pre-philosophical or pre-analytic "perfectionism" does not, of course, constitute a systematic theory of value in general or of ethics in particular. Yet it should not be dismissed as irrelevant. At least it may point to some important fact about human beings, something that even Rawls rather reluctantly is willing to admit when arguing against Aristotelian perfectionism—namely, that humans take enjoyment in the perfection of some capacities or attributes either in themselves or in others.[6] Such attitudes toward or beliefs about perfection constitute prima facie evidence of the value humans attach to perfection or of its being a good. Aristotle would not have dismissed such facts of human behavior or thought. For him the facts that all humans make happiness their end and that all humans desire health constitute important evidence for the goodness of these things. In any case, it is interesting to speculate in the present context about the role these pre-analytic attitudes toward perfection play in some rather cosmic views Plato and Aristotle hold about perfection and its effects. As is well-known, Plato insists that everything in the sensible world is striving to reach the supposed perfection of the world of the Platonic Forms, and Aristotle insists that everything is moved by a desire for the alleged perfection of the Aristotelian prime mover. Undoubtedly, there are deep philosophical foundations in Platonic and Aristotelian thought on which these views rest; yet the role the pre-analytic conceptions or attitudes about perfection in the Greek tradition

---

[5] According to Hurka, *Perfectionism*, pp. 37–39, perfectionism of physical attributes is one component of Aristotelian perfectionism. He claims that "Aristotelian perfectionism finds the highest physical good in great athletic feats."

[6] Rawls argues that perfecting certain capacities is rational and something that one's associates are likely to support as "promoting the common interest and also to take pleasure in . . . as displays of human excellence." See John Rawls, *A Theory of Justice* (Cambridge: Harvard University Press, 1971), p. 429.

might have played in the formation of these views of cosmic perfection-ism should not be dismissed.

As mentioned above, these pre-analytic views about perfection do not necessarily constitute a perfectionist theory of value. To begin with, in the pre-philosophical views just cited, perfection is viewed not necessarily as the final end or ultimate good, but rather as a means to attaining some other end that is clearly distinct from perfection. In Homer it is quite evident that the perfection of certain attributes is valued because it is thought to be a means to military victory, wealth, glory, immortality, or some similar final end. This is an instrumental or consequentialist per-fectionism that even an anti-perfectionist might find acceptable. A hedo-nist may very well wish, as indeed practical rationality dictates, to perfect those attributes or capacities that are instrumental to achieving the he-donist end, that is, greater pleasures. Even a theorist like Rawls, who holds a desire-satisfaction conception of the good and therefore admits different, conflicting, and incommensurable ends, can live with such "per-fectionism." Different ends or life plans will require the perfection of different attributes or capacities. If Hurka is correct, however, perfection-ism cannot have such extrinsic ends, since it recognizes no final ends other than perfection; even well-being, as ordinarily understood, cannot be an end of perfectionism.[7]

Yet given the importance attached to excellence and perfection in the Greek tradition, it might not be unreasonable to question the instrumen-talist interpretation of pre-philosophical perfectionism. A culture that prizes excellence or perfection to the degree the Greeks did surely must consider it worth having for its own sake, an ideal worth realizing independent of any consequences. Such an interpretation might not be out of place. In-deed, some have argued that even certain writings from Greek philo-sophical ethics are best understood as putting forth a theory of ideals.[8] Regardless of which interpretation of pre-philosophical perfectionism we may opt for, it is clear that neither is based on a conception of human nature or teleology. Neither interpretation appeals to the essence, func-tion, or end of humans in order to provide a foundation for the kind of perfectionism it advocates, or at least in order to identify a basis for determining which attributes are to be perfected.

Yet perfectionism without a foundation is likely to encounter problems of justification. Although both the instrumental and idealistic interpreta-tions of perfectionism might be able to provide some justification as to why some perfections are to be chosen over others, inevitably disagree-ments will arise about the final ends to which certain perfections are viewed as means or about the perfectionist ideals to be pursued. Where there are disagreements about ends, there will be differences about what

[7] Hurka, *Perfectionism*, p. 17.

[8] J. M. E. Moravcsik, "The Nature of Ethical Theorizing in the *Eudemian Ethics*," *Topoi*, vol. 5, no. 1 (March 1996).

is to be perfected. Soon after Homer we find the Greek poets Hesiod and Archilochus abandoning most of the ends of the Homeric individual and expressing strong disagreements about the excellences or perfections of Homeric culture. Perhaps what is most familiar to us are the disagreements about excellences and ends that are portrayed in Plato's dialogues; but Aristotle also seems quite aware of the deep and serious disagreements about ends and the excellences associated with them.

Someone like Rawls will likely respond that, outside of a set of perfections required by the basic structure of society, the instrumental justification mentioned above is the only kind of justification that could be expected, and therefore disagreements are inevitable. Beyond certain moral virtues, other perfections will vary from one person to the other, or even in the same person, as choices of ends vary or change. Differences in perfections cannot be avoided, given the variety of ends. And the same will be true if we choose to look at perfections as ideals; different agents will likely choose different attributes to perfect as their ideals or ends and will organize their lives accordingly. The only requirement is that ends do not violate the constraints of justice. Other theorists of liberal persuasion have gone further, denying that there can be any meaningful disagreements about ends or even that any discussion about ends is appropriate or makes sense (see below).

The response of some Greek philosophers to disputes or disagreements about the excellences or the good is strikingly different from that of the liberal theorists. Indeed, some arguments of the ancient thinkers in favor of perfectionism seem to be responses to disagreements or disputes about the excellences and the ends of human life. Obviously, the ancients think that (a) disagreements or disputes about ends should be eliminated, and that (b) disagreements or disputes about ends can be eliminated. Now (b) could be read in the way a liberal theorist might wish to read it—that is, as saying that there are no real disagreements about ends since the desire-satisfaction conception or any similar conception of the good does not allow any. Plato and Aristotle believe that there are genuine disagreements about ends and understand (b) as saying that they can be eliminated by reaching agreement in the strict sense. Indeed, they are not merely saying that agreement might be reached about a plurality of ends; they often argue that in an important sense there is only one ultimate end.

What lies behind Plato's and Aristotle's conviction that there is only one ultimate end, and therefore that disagreements about the good are both genuine and ultimately resolvable? Rawls has argued that their commitment to the unity of the good can be understood simply as a consequence of the teleological ethical theory they advocate, which gives priority to the good rather than to the right. Such an implication of the nature of their ethical theories, if it is one, would not necessarily lead them to perfectionism, for the condition of the unity of the good could be satisfied by any conception of the good that implied that there is one final end—for example, by hedonism. Others, however, have pointed to the role that functionalism—that is, the view that humans as well as many other kinds of things have a determinate and well-defined function—and the conception of human nature that it presupposes play in their perfectionist views, which in turn favor the unity of the good. Does Plato's perfectionism rest on a functionalism that is as much committed to certain metaphysical views about human nature and teleology as Aristotle's presumably is? And does Plato's perfectionism altogether exclude a plurality of ends?

III. Plato's Version of Perfectionism

Literally the whole of Book I of Plato's *Republic* is taken up by disputes or disagreements. Not only do Socrates and his interlocutors disagree about the nature of justice, they even disagree on whether justice is a virtue at all. In addition, they disagree on whether justice is advantageous, whose advantage it secures, whether it leads to the good life, and what the good life is.

At the very end of Book I, Plato responds to these pervasive disagreements and disputes by introducing the argument from function. He thus attempts to show that all the questions about the nature of the good life, of virtue in general, and of justice in particular can be answered by resorting to a perfectionism about virtue and the good that is based on a conception of function.[9]

This argument is interesting partly because it clearly antedates Aristotle's famous argument in the *Nicomachean Ethics* as well as his lesser-known argument in the *Eudemian Ethics* in support of perfectionism and human flourishing. Plato's argument has many similarities with Aristotle's arguments, but it also has important differences. The most significant difference is that the account of function Plato puts forth seems to avoid any explicit mention of a metaphysical nature or essence, or of teleology—features that figure prominently in Aristotle's functionalism and perfectionism and that have been considered by almost everyone as inseparable from both functionalism and perfectionism.

In his argument, Plato defines the function Φ of an F as that which only an F can do or that which an F can do better than any other thing (*Republic*, 352E). To illustrate the first condition for being the function of something, he gives as examples seeing in the case of the eye and hearing in the case of the ear. As an instance of his second alternative for being a function, Plato gives trimming in the case of the dirk, knife, and pruning knife; although all of them can do the job of trimming, the pruning knife does it best, and therefore trimming is the function of the pruning knife only and not of the others (353A). One way of understanding Plato's

---

[9] The functional account is not the only account of the good in the *Republic*. In Book VI, Plato presents a metaphysical account in terms of his theory of the Form of the Good. But it is the functional account that is of relevance to human flourishing and perfectionism.

account of function is as follows: Φ is the function of an F if and only if F is both a necessary and a sufficient condition for Φ-ing or F is a necessary and a sufficient condition for Φ-ing best. Plato then goes on to define the excellence of a functional thing as the condition(s) that is (are) necessary and sufficient for performing its function well, and the good of a functional thing as performing its function well. Once he has what he takes to be a general principle specifying the excellence and the good of a functional thing, Plato applies this principle to the case of the soul. He argues that the excellences of the soul are the necessary and sufficient conditions for living well, the latter being the function and good of the soul (353D–354C).

On the face of it, Plato's account of function is free of the metaphysical essentialism and teleology that are associated with Aristotle's conception of function. The definition of function Plato gives in terms of the two conditions stated above does not explicate function in terms of essence, nor does it appeal to any teleology. Plato does not explicitly state that the function of an F is identical to or in some way connected to the essence of F, or is the end of F, or is that for the sake of which F exists.[10] Thus, whatever objections one might have against metaphysical essentialism or teleology as they relate to function and to the corresponding perfectionism will not apply to Plato's view of function and the perfectionism based on it.

Plato's specification of the function of a (functional) thing X in terms of an activity that only X can do or can do best avoids an implication that is common to the essentialist and teleological accounts of function—namely, that the function, as well as the perfection or end, of each of the members of a species or a kind is identical to that of the other members. Hence, Plato's account of function has an important consequence for perfectionism: it leaves open the possibility that there is variation in the functions of the members of a species—since what only member x of species S can do (or what x can do best) may differ from what only member y of the same species can do (or what y can do best)—and therefore the account allows for different specific perfectionist ends or goods. In one sense, that is, stated at a certain level of abstraction and generality, the members of a kind all have one end—namely, the activity constituting the function or perfection of a functional thing; but specified more concretely, the particular functions, perfections, or ends could be different. Applied to the human species, the implication of Plato's perfectionism is that different individuals may very well have different functions and therefore different perfections.

This implication of Plato's account of function figures prominently in his conception of perfectionism and the role it plays in the political theory of the *Republic*. In his discussion in Book II of the origin of the political

---

[10] This was pointed out a few years ago by Richard Sorabji, "Function," *Philosophical Quarterly*, vol. 14, no. 57 (October 1964).

association and of the establishment of the most elementary city (the city of the "swine"), Plato argues that different individuals have different capacities and therefore are suited for different activities or tasks (369B–370C). The function of one individual, then, may very well be different from that of another, a consequence that plays a major role in Plato's argument in support of his claim that the political association is natural. Plato assumes that no individual is self-sufficient—that is, no one has all the capacities needed to perform the many tasks necessary for the good life—and that no individual is suited for performing more than one task well. Given these assumptions, Plato argues that each individual will be better off in restricting himself to the task he is suited for or can do best (his function) and, through exchange of the fruits of this type of division of labor, in securing the necessary means of life. Thus, some form of "political" association (the elementary city of the "swine") will naturally come into being.

Yet the implication for perfectionism in Plato's account of function can be best seen in his discussion of the excellences in his ideal city. In Book IV of the *Republic*, Plato argues that the ideal city will consist of three classes—the producers, guardians, and rulers—and each class will have distinct tasks or functions. The tasks or ends of these classes are different, according to him, as are some of their excellences or perfections. Of the four cardinal excellences Plato attributes to the city, wisdom is restricted to the rulers (428E) and courage to the guardians (429B–C). Only temperance and justice are, according to him, excellences of all three classes (432A, 434A). This supposed fact about the excellences of the city has its counterpart in the excellences of the soul, since, according to Plato, the number, nature, and excellences of the classes of the city are based on the number, nature, and excellences of the parts of the soul. According to him, there is almost a complete isomorphism between city and soul and their excellences.

Plato argues in Book IV that the soul has three distinct and irreducible parts or elements (appetitive, spirited, and rational), each suited for a certain task, activity, or function (437A–441C). He further argues that the magnitude or strength of each one of these parts differs among individuals, with some of them having one element as dominant and others a different one. The members of Plato's ideal city are divided into his three political classes on the basis of the strength of the elements of their souls, with those in whom the appetitive element is dominant constituting the largest class (the producers), those in whom the spirited element is dominant constituting the middle class (the guardians), and those in whom the rational element is dominant constituting the smallest class (the rulers).

As he does in the case of the excellences of the city, Plato argues that of the four cardinal excellences applicable to an individual two are excellences or perfections of distinct parts of the soul—wisdom of the rational element, and courage of the spirited element (442B–C)—and cannot be excellences or perfections of those in whose souls these elements either are not to be found at all or are of insufficient strength or magnitude. The remaining two excellences—temperance and justice—Plato attributes to all three parts of the soul, thus implying that they could be excellences or perfections of any individual. Yet in a sense these last two excellences are not really perfections of a part of the soul in the way the former two are. Temperance and justice do not relate to specific activities, functions, or flourishings of some one particular element of the soul in the way that wisdom relates to reason and courage relates to spirit. And the same is true in the case of the excellences of the city: Wisdom and courage are the excellences of specific tasks or functions constituting the perfections or flourishings of two classes (components) of the city or, ultimately, of two parts (components) of the souls of those belonging in these two classes. Temperance (the consent among classes or parts of the soul to have the rational class or part of the soul rule over all) is really a precondition for attaining the perfection or flourishing of any class (and city) or any part of the soul (and individual). And justice for Plato is nothing more or less than each class of the city or part of the soul performing its proper task or function and thus attaining the perfection or flourishing for which it is fit (433E, 434B, 443B, 443C).

Plato's account of function, then, and the perfectionism based on it, when coupled with his assumption that there is a wide variation among individuals with respect to their capacities or the strength of the three parts of the soul, allows for different activities, functions, or flourishings as well as differences in the excellences or perfections of individuals. Thus, it seems that there can be some version of perfectionism that allows for a plurality of ends, when these are identified at a certain level of specificity.[11] This version of perfectionism is the foundation of the strictly hierarchical political arrangement of Plato's ideal city as well as of his theory of justice, which aims to establish a structure within which the flourishing or perfection of each individual will be both possible and secured. It is also the foundation of the system of education Plato proposes for his ideal city, which is equally hierarchical and at the same time just, according to Plato's theory of justice, giving everyone an equal opportunity to rise to the level of perfection or flourishing that his/her capacities allow. Given the supposed variation in the strength of the parts of the soul or capacities among individuals, education cannot be the same for all individuals beyond a certain point, but must be suited to the different potentials of the members of the city.

It may seem from the foregoing discussion that Plato's perfectionism, by allowing a plurality of ends, is not very different from the position advocated by liberal theorists, at least with respect to the number of ends

---

[11] Clearly, much depends here on how the levels of specificity are to be determined; it might be a rather complicated matter. Martha Nussbaum argues (in "Aristotelian Social Democracy," in R. Bruce Douglass, Gerald M. Mara, and Henry S. Richardson, eds., *Liberalism and the Good* [New York: Routledge, 1990]) that even an Aristotelian version of perfectionism can allow for many flourishings.

it allows. Yet this is not the case. Not many have criticized or praised Plato for his liberalism, and for good reason. The overall argument in the *Republic* and the rest of Plato's ethical and political writings runs, on the whole, counter to the main tenets of the liberal tradition. For in the latter tradition it is almost axiomatic that the ends of individuals are set by their own desires, wants, or preferences. Desire or preference satisfaction is the primary determinant of the final end or ends of an individual. And surely there is very little discussion of desire or preference satisfaction in Plato's account of final ends or flourishings, at least in a straightforward sense.[12] Although he makes a gesture toward acknowledging the role desire plays in the motivation of the members of his first city (the city of the "swine"), it is clear that it is an individual's capacities that determine the activities he/she is to perform, which in turn determine his/her flourishing. The end (or ends) of a member of Plato's first city is (are) not determined by the individual's desires—at least not in terms of the desires the individual might be aware of, even though they might constitute a consistent whole or a rational plan. Rather, the end is determined objectively by the capacities an individual possesses, and therefore by the kind of flourishing an individual is capable of achieving.[13]

The same is of course true of the ends of the members of Plato's ideal city. Whatever plurality of ends is to be encountered in that city is not due to the variety of ends that satisfaction of desire or preference permits, but rather to the fact that different capacities are objectively correlated with different activities, functions, or flourishings. And it is clear that Plato's allowance for a variation of ends is, in contrast to the almost boundless possibilities of liberal theorists, quite limited. The variation of ends and of excellences is strongly constrained by the capacities of individuals, regardless of their desires or preferences.

Yet it remains to be seen whether the Platonic strategy of giving an account of function without any of the familiar Aristotelian metaphysical commitments can, in the end, succeed. It seems doubtful that function without any kind of presupposition connecting it to essence, nature, teleology, or something along similar lines, can do the work it is supposed to do for Plato. The account Plato gives seems inadequate for dealing even with the paradigmatic examples of functional things, for example, eyes and ears. Clearly, eyes are the only things that blink, and therefore blinking will have to be the function of an eye, according to Plato's first criterion of being a function of a thing—namely, that it is an activity only the thing can do. But Plato does not take the function of eyes to be

---

[12] Plato has often been interpreted as distinguishing between actual and "real" desires, the latter being those representing the agent's rational interests, which, of course, need not be the agent's actual desires. For a recent defense of the Platonic position, see Gary Watson, "Free Agency," in Watson, ed., *Free Will* (Oxford: Oxford University Press, 1982).

[13] Nussbaum (in "Aristotelian Social Democracy") argues that a thick but vague conception of the good along Aristotelian lines can be developed which is perfectionist in character and thus objective, but which allows for choice and a plurality of flourishings.

blinking and their excellence to be determined by reference to blinking. And Plato's second condition for identifying the function Φ of an F—that is, an F's Φ-ing better than anything else—does not resolve the difficulty. For if Alcibiades is better at stealing than anybody else, stealing would be his function. Indeed, if humans are the only animals that steal, it would seem that, on the first condition, stealing is everybody's function.[14]

To avoid such outcomes, Plato needs a more substantive conception of function, one that would connect the function Φ of an F with something like the nature of F—for example, one that would connect seeing with the nature of the eye, or hearing with the nature of the ear. A closer reading of the text of the *Republic* indicates that Plato himself probably had in mind such a conception of function, one that is more substantive than his definition of function may lead one to believe.[15] The organs (eye and ear) and components of an organism (body and soul) that are used as examples in Plato's discussion of function are treated in a way that tacitly connects the activities that presumably are their functions with their corresponding natures. The relations between eye and seeing, ear and hearing, and soul and living are clearly not accidental but essential ones for Plato and Aristotle. And it is the supposedly essential nature of a thing that determines its function, and not any peculiar or unique feature. Indeed, referring to functions as merely "peculiar" or "unique" activities, as translators often do in rendering the terms Plato and Aristotle use in singling out the function of something, does not tell the whole story. Peculiarity or uniqueness may in many cases be a necessary condition if an activity is to be the function of something, but it is not a sufficient condition. Both Plato and Aristotle consider the peculiarity or uniqueness an activity might have in relation to a thing only as one mark of being the function of the thing. In some instances, peculiarity or uniqueness is thought to reflect that special connection that distinguishes functions from mere activities. And Plato's use of certain terms in his discussion of function reflects this. The terms *idion* or *oikeion*, almost always rendered as "peculiar" or "proper," signify, as they do in Aristotle, something more than mere "peculiarity" or "uniqueness"; as most recent interpreters of

---

[14] Some of the problems concerning the relation of uniqueness to function are discussed in Hurka, *Perfectionism*, pp. 10–14.

[15] Plato seems to hint that at least some notion of teleology or design underlies the notion of function. According to him, the reason trimming is the function of the pruning knife and not of the other cutting tools he mentions is the fact that only the former has been fashioned for this purpose, while the other tools have not (353A). Yet understanding function in terms of design may have its limitations. Reference to design may be useful in understanding the function of artifacts of the kind Plato cites, but its role in explaining the functions of bodily organs or individuals is questionable. The design conception of function would be of some value for Plato's political objectives only if he were to presuppose that individuals are in some way *designed* or fashioned for some uses or functions. Plato does, of course, advocate in both the *Republic* and the *Statesman* something like fashioning citizens for certain purposes, but it seems quite clear that his use of function in determining the specific activities of individuals or classes in the *Republic* does not rely on a conception of function in terms of design, at least not of the type relevant to artifacts.

Plato and Aristotle argue, they make implicit reference to the nature or essence of the thing that is supposedly functional.[16]

Plato's strategy for resolving disputes about the excellences and the good seems to be both clear and reasonable. By proposing an explication of both these ethical elements in terms of a perfectionism which in turn rests on functionalism, he aims to provide an objective procedure for resolving disagreements about ethical matters. His perfectionism, if understood as resting on a functionalism that lacks any metaphysical, teleological, or other comparable foundation, has some implications that liberal theorists might find congenial—namely, its permitting different final ends for different agents. Yet Plato's functionalism so understood, and the corresponding perfectionism, seem insufficient even for Plato's purposes. They seem unable to resolve disagreements, even ones about the identity of the functions of things.

Yet Aristotle himself seems to have considered an account of the good that does not rest on the kind of metaphysical assumptions that his own perfectionism presupposes. This conception of the good seems to be nonperfectionist in character. As stated earlier, it rather resembles desire-satisfaction accounts of the good. Yet even when working with such a nonperfectionist conception of the good, Aristotle seems to favor a single end for a lifetime as well as unity of the good across different agents. Such positions seem, at least prima facie, puzzling when seen as part of a conception of the good that is similar to desire-satisfaction conceptions. I wish now to turn to a consideration of Aristotle's nonperfectionist argument and examine how these positions of his about the good fit together with some assumptions he makes about rationality, the self, and the nature and goals of the political association; in doing this, I hope also to locate more precisely the differences between his views and those of liberal theorists.

IV. Aristotle's Nonperfectionist Argument

Although Aristotle speaks of perfectionism in many of his extant writings, the argument from function in the later part of Book I of the *Nicomachean Ethics* has always been viewed as his clearest statement and defense of ethical perfectionism. But despite the extensive treatment Aristotle's argument has received, many aspects of it still remain unclear. This is especially true of the connection between the function argument

[16] See Sarah Broadie, *Ethics with Aristotle* (New York: Oxford University Press, 1991); Richard Kraut, "The Peculiar Function of Human Beings," *Canadian Journal of Philosophy*, vol. 9 (1979); Kraut, *Aristotle on the Human Good* (Princeton: Princeton University Press, 1989); and Jennifer Whiting, "Aristotle's Function Argument: A Defense," *Ancient Philosophy*, vol. 8, no. 1 (1988). The metaphysical presuppositions of Aristotle's claim that certain activities are unique or peculiar to certain functional things are altogether overlooked by Thomas Nagel's critical discussion of *eudaimonia* in his "Aristotle on *Eudaimonia*," in Amélie Rorty, ed., *Essays on Aristotle's Ethics* (Berkeley: University of California Press, 1980).

and Aristotle's earlier discussion in Book I (chapters 1 through 7) about the good, the end of human action, and happiness.

Most have read this early discussion as being a part of the perfectionist position Aristotle seems to be defending in the rest of the treatise, especially in Book I, chapter 7, and in Book X, chapter 6 and subsequent chapters. And there appear to be good reasons for interpreting the opening chapters of Book I as part of Aristotle's statement and defense of perfectionism. After all, there is no clear line dividing the early discussion from the function argument; on the contrary, the two segments of the text seem continuous. In addition, Aristotle's concern in the early discussion is with the end of human action and pursuit—a concern that is also a component of the function argument, since for Aristotle the function of a functional thing is its end.

To others, however, the function argument represents a break from the earlier discussion in the *Nicomachean Ethics* about the human good, the end of human action, and happiness. In their judgment, the perfectionist account of the good (and of the excellences) that the function argument puts forth is quite different from the conception of the good, end, and happiness that Aristotle is working with in the early chapters of Book I. In a recent essay, Gerasimos Santas has argued in some detail that the two accounts are not merely different, they are incompatible, since the first one is an account of the good as desire satisfaction, while the second is a perfectionist account.[17] According to Santas, Aristotle develops the desire-satisfaction conception of the good considerably, but in the end finds it inadequate. In order to meet the supposed inadequacies, Aristotle develops, in Santas's view, the functional/perfectionist conception. If this is indeed the case, examining the early discussion of the good might at least help us identify the problems Aristotle saw in the desire-satisfaction conception of the good and the ways in which the function argument can or cannot address these problems. It might be useful to see how far the desire-satisfaction argument can take Aristotle and at what point he needs to introduce considerations from function, and for what purpose. Can he, for instance, justify his claim that the best life has one final end, or is functionalism needed for even this conclusion?

Much of what Aristotle says in the early chapters of Book I of the *Nicomachean Ethics* could easily be interpreted as an account of the good in terms of desire satisfaction. And there are some good reasons for interpreting it in this way. First, it is clear that the language of desire and its ends dominates these early chapters, and there is little doubt that Aristotle's concern is primarily with the structure of desires and their ends and not with some objective property of goodness, either in terms of perfectionism or of some other similarly objective feature. In this discussion, Aristotle looks at the good as the end or object of desire or want

---

[17] Gerasimos Santas, "Desire and Perfection in Aristotle's Theory of the Good," *Apeiron*, vol. 22, no. 2 (1989).

(*epithymia, orexis*) or of pursuit (*diôxis*), this last term also presupposing an element of desire. Now this conception of end is clearly to be distinguished from that which we find in accounts of function, where functional things presumably have ends without necessarily having desires or pursuits—e.g., the end of an organ or a part of a living thing (e.g., the eye of an animal or the root of a plant) or an artifact. Ends are ascribed to functional things without desires or pursuits on the basis of some teleological framework that is often presupposed in accounts of function.

One might, however, object that Aristotle's allusion in this early discussion to a connection between desire and its ends on the one hand, and the good on the other, need not necessarily mean that he sees a link between desire and the good that is as strong as that implied by the desire-satisfaction conception of the good. Perhaps the link alluded to is far weaker and merely treated by Aristotle as evidence or as a starting point of the inquiry into the nature of the good.[18] Assuming that there is *some* kind of connection between desire and the good, a reasonable starting point in inquiring into the nature of the good might be an account of human desires and their ends. Admittedly, the relation between desire and the good in Aristotle's thought is quite difficult to understand. As John L. Austin once remarked, "the relation between 'being *agathon*' and 'being desired' is one of the most baffling puzzles in Aristotle's, or for that matter Plato's, ethical theory."[19] Yet while the connection between desire and the good may be unclear, the reason for connecting the two is quite transparent—namely, the need of a theory to provide a motivation for aiming at the good, which a desire-satisfaction account of the good squarely addresses and which, according to many, a perfectionist account does not. This problem is of concern to Aristotle and is treated by him in both his ethical and psychological works. In both types of treatises, he argues that the origin of action is desire of one form or another. Thus, Aristotle might have had a good reason for exploring an account of the good in terms of desire, and such a motive on Aristotle's part provides a second reason for interpreting the early chapters of the *Nicomachean Ethics* along the lines of a desire-satisfaction account of the good.

There is a third reason for treating Aristotle's early discussion as an exploration of a desire-satisfaction account of the good—namely, the kind of rationality that Aristotle seems to be working with in this part of his treatise. As Santas and other scholars have pointed out, Aristotle is concerned in this part of his ethical treatise with the rational structure of desires and of the orectic (appetitive) ends of an agent. As is the case with modern and contemporary desire-satisfaction theorists, Aristotle is attempting to distinguish the formal features of the good (those deriving from rationality or reason) from what is contributed by desire—the con-

---

[18] This objection was raised by Richard Kraut.
[19] John L. Austin, "*Agathon* and *Eudaimonia* in the *Ethics* of Aristotle," in his *Philosophical Papers* (Oxford: Oxford University Press, 1970), p. 31.

tent of the good.[20] He is considering some formal properties of desires and their structures—for example, consistency, transitivity, symmetry, and so on (see below)—and any implications they might have for the nature and number of the ends of human life.

Thus, Aristotle opens the discussion with the claim that "[e]very art and every inquiry, and similarly every action and pursuit, is thought to aim at some good; and for this reason the good has been declared to be that at which all things aim." On the basis of this statement, Aristotle has often been accused of at least two things: (a) making an unwarranted inference from the fact that every pursuit aims at some end to the conclusion that there is a single end at which all things aim, and therefore already reaching the conclusion that there is a single final end or a single good; and (b) committing himself to some kind of cosmic teleology with a single end or *telos*. As for (b), Aristotle does have some kind of cosmic teleology,[21] but it is not something that is stated or inferred from the opening sentence of the *Nicomachean Ethics*. Indeed, Aristotle does not seem to be stating anything categorically; on the contrary, as his language makes clear, he is saying that from the fact that every pursuit aims at some good, it would seem that the good is that at which all things aim. This does not, however, commit Aristotle to the view that there is such a single thing or a single end, the good, at which everything aims. And of course he does not commit himself to such a view.

In relation to (a), Aristotle immediately proceeds to state that there are many ends, which of course are not all the same. Some are means to other ends, while some are only ends; and where means and ends form a structure, certain formal properties are true of desires and their ends. The two most important formal properties for the present context are the transitivity and asymmetry of desire.[22] From these formal properties of desire as well as the assumption that not all desire is empty or vain, it follows that, if there is any desire, another formal requirement must be met—namely, there must be something that is pursued for its own sake or is pursued as an end in itself. Aristotle then gives a definition of what he

---

[20] This view of rationality is also shared by economists. Commenting on the economists' view, David Gauthier writes: "Rationality does not enter into what the individual considers to be a commodity or regards as a factor service. In this sense economic rationality is not concerned with the ends of action. . . . My greater good, or what has greater utility for me, is by definition what I prefer, and more of what is good is necessarily a greater good." See Gauthier, "Economic Rationality and Moral Constraints," *Midwest Studies in Philosophy*, vol. 3 (1978), p. 77.

[21] Of course, in the present context one thinks of Aristotle's unmoved mover; but in *Metaphysics* A, such cosmic teleology is suggested without any reference to any movers.

[22] The transitivity of desire is considered by many as an axiom of choice, stating that if some agent A desires x for the sake of y and y for the sake of z, then A desires x for the sake of z. The asymmetry of desire states that if an agent A desires x for the sake of y, then A does not desire y for the sake of x. Aristotle hints at both these formal properties of desire in the first chapter of Book I of the *Nicomachean Ethics* and presupposes them in his subsequent discussion about the good. For a discussion of some of these formal features of desire and preference and a defense of the transitivity of preference and choice, see R. C. Jeffrey, "Preference among Preferences," *Journal of Philosophy*, vol. 71 (1974), pp. 377-91.

calls "supreme" or "highest" good (*ariston agathon*) as that which is pursued for its own sake while all other things are pursued for the sake of it (*Nicomachean Ethics*, 1094a20).

At least two things need to be kept in mind about Aristotle's definition of a supreme or highest good. First, it can be easily understood within the framework of desires as stating that if there were something we desired for its own sake while we desired all other things for the sake of it, it would be the highest good. Aristotle need not be saying anything about an objective property of goodness which makes something a supreme or highest good or which explains why it is desired in the way it is desired. If Aristotle is working with a desire-satisfaction conception of the good, he cannot claim that the supreme good or end is so on account of its goodness.[23] And he does not. In addition, Aristotle's definition of a supreme good does not identify the good; it is not a specification of the content of the good, but only of some of its formal properties. Nothing Aristotle says about the supreme good or end is inconsistent with the desire-satisfaction conception of the good.

Second, the definition does not imply—and Aristotle does not say it does—that there is an end of human desire or pursuit which meets the conditions of the definition. As many commentators have pointed out, it is quite possible that human desires or pursuits form independent means-ends chains, with each chain aiming at some final end which is not pursued for the sake of anything else but without there necessarily being anything which is the final end of all chains. Indeed, it is possible for any individual to have a plurality of final ends at any particular time, as well as different final ends at different times. In addition, nothing Aristotle has said so far rules out the possibility that the independent chains and corresponding final ends of one individual are different from those of another individual.

Aristotle seems to be fully aware of the last possibility; there could be and there seem to be many ends (1094a8, 1097a23, 25). This is true even though there is verbal agreement that the end is one, namely, happiness (*eudaimonia*, 1095a20). For there is no agreement as to what happiness is—some identify it with (and therefore pursue as their final end) a life of wealth, some a life of pleasure, others a life of honor, still others a life of contemplation. Aristotle rejects most of these kinds of life as final ends by applying the test of finality or completeness or perfection (*teleiotes*, 1097a24).[24]

David Keyt interprets Aristotle's test as dividing ends into three classes: *subservient ends*, i.e., those pursued for the sake of other things (e.g., wealth, flutes, and, in general, instruments); *subordinate ends*, i.e., things

---

[23] For a discussion of the relation of desire to the good in different conceptions of goodness (e.g., subjective versus objective), see Amartya Sen, "Well-Being, Agency, and Freedom," *Journal of Philosophy*, vol. 82 (1985), pp. 192–200.

[24] The term *teleiotes*, as almost all translators point out, can mean a variety of things, including "perfection." If it means "perfection" in the present context, then Aristotle's finality test is not independent of perfectionism.

pursued for their own sake but also for the sake of some other things (e.g., honor, pleasure, intelligence, and every virtue, since these we choose for the sake of themselves as well as for the sake of happiness); and *ultimate ends*, i.e., things chosen only for the sake of themselves (e.g., happiness).[25]

Now the test of finality (or completeness or perfection) of ends must be understood within the desire-satisfaction conception of the good, and those who claim that Aristotle is entertaining such a conception of the good insist that it can be so understood. According to them, it concerns a formal feature of the good, something that has to do with the rationality of choice rather than with its content. When Aristotle distinguishes ends according to their finality, he speaks of what *we* desire as an end or means to an end, or of what are the ends of the various arts, e.g., medicine. But for the desire-satisfaction theorist, distinguishing among ends in terms of their finality must be relativized to an agent and his/her desires and their means-ends structures. Thus, one and the same thing might be an ultimate end for agent X, but a subordinate end for agent Y. Perhaps there is considerable overlap in the desires of agents and the means-ends structures such desires exhibit, and this justifies Aristotle in speaking of things *we* choose as means in contrast to other things *we* choose as ends, as well as of things *we* choose as both means and ends. Even though such an overlap may exist, however, it cannot rule out the possibility that what Callicles chooses as his final end (e.g., pleasure) is not what Socrates chooses as his. The overlap has its limits in deciding what is the best life for an agent, for this must be based on the desires of the agent and the life plan the agent chooses. The desire-satisfaction conception of the good cannot appeal to the life plans of others and to their means-ends structures, and certainly cannot appeal to some objective property that makes some things better or more final ends.

What kind of life, then, does the test of the finality of ends rule out? A life aiming only at subservient ends seems to be ruled out, since such ends are clearly pursued for the sake of other ends, either subordinate or ultimate.[26] What about a life that has at least one subordinate end, e.g., pleasure? Or a life with more than one subordinate end or more than one ultimate end? It is clear from what Aristotle says about the life of pleasure or honor that such lives are not the best a human being can achieve. According to Aristotle, even adding more subordinate ends to a life will not necessarily make it the best life. Even a life with a plurality of ultimate ends is not the best, for "[t]he supreme good seems to be something final. So, if there is one final end, this is what we are seeking, and if there are

---

[25] David Keyt, "Intellectualism in Aristotle," in John Anton and Anthony Preus, eds., *Essays in Ancient Greek Philosophy* (Albany, NY: State University of New York Press, 1983).

[26] Flutes seem to be a better example of a subservient end, one that Aristotle also finds paradigmatic of such ends. Some would say that it is even part of the meaning of the term "flute" that it is used for another final end, so that one cannot have the making of flutes as one's subordinate or final end. Wealth is clearly a much more complicated case, since so many—mistakenly, according to Aristotle—make it their subordinate or even final end.

more than one, the most final of these will be what we are seeking" (1097a28). This rules out the possibility that the best life for an individual can include a plurality of ultimate ends, and this and other statements in Aristotle's ethical and political treatises seem to rule out variation in the final ends of different individuals. He seems to leave no room for the possibility that the best lives of different agents might aim at different final ends.

It is most important to recognize that Aristotle reaches the conclusion that the best life has a single final end, which he takes to be identical for all, as soon as he distinguishes among the degrees of finality of ends and *before* he identifies happiness as the end that fits the requirement of highest finality, and certainly *before* he introduces the function argument. The conclusion about the single identical end should not then be supported by appealing to the supposed fact that people choose happiness as the most final end or by having recourse to the function argument. For if there are or if there *can* be more than one final end, the supposed finality of happiness and the nature of the human function may not be sufficient to explicate the content of all final ends.

Aristotle claims that there seems to be agreement that there is at least one final end—happiness:

> Now such a thing happiness, above all else, is held to be; for this we choose always for itself and never for the sake of something else, but honor, pleasure, intelligence, and every virtue we choose indeed for themselves. . . . [B]ut we choose them also for the sake of happiness, judging that by means of them we shall be happy. Happiness, on the other hand, no one chooses for the sake of these, nor, in general, for anything other than itself. (1097b)

And he adds: "Happiness, then, is something final and self-sufficient, and the end of action" (1097b20).

Aristotle is aware that the above characterization of happiness as a final end does not tell us what happiness or the best life is. It merely identifies a formal feature of happiness or of the good, but not its content. And this is very much the way a desire-satisfaction theorist would proceed in specifying the good—identifying its formal features and leaving its content open. Such a theorist, then, might say that Aristotle's claim that happiness is the most final end does not specify much, for happiness might consist of more than one final end (an inclusive conception of happiness), and different individuals may not have the same final ends. But such a possibility seems to be ruled out by Aristotle's claim that the good we are seeking is the final end or, if there are more than one, the most final. This seems to rule out a plurality of final ends. Aristotle appears to have concluded that the best life can have only one final end before attempting to specify the content of the good, end, or happiness in terms of the function argument.

Naturally, a number of questions arise in the present context. Why does Aristotle rule out the possibility that the best life can have more than one final end? And why is it not possible that the one final end he identifies (happiness) could be understood along the lines the desire-satisfaction theorist is urging—that is, in the inclusive sense? Or why cannot the best life have different final ends for different individuals? In addition, if Aristotle is working with the desire-satisfaction conception of the good, does this conception of the good alone imply his conclusion about a single identical end, or do additional considerations, unrelated to such a conception of the good, need to be introduced?

In the vast secondary literature on Aristotle's ethics, one can identify a number of suggestions by different commentators that can be seen as ways of reaching the single-end conclusion from within the desire-satisfaction conception of the good. There are, of course, even more suggestions as to why the conclusion cannot be reached from within such a conception of the good. The following are some suggestions of the first kind.

A. The implications of a supreme and most final end

As pointed out earlier, the definitions Aristotle gives of supreme and most final ends do not imply that there is either a supreme or a most final end. But Bernard Williams has argued that some other things are implied by Aristotle's definitions—namely, if there is a supreme end and a most final end, they are one and the same, and there cannot be more than one most final end.[27] Now Aristotle seems to think that happiness meets the conditions of being a most final end, and therefore, given the supposed implications of his definitions, he can say that there is at least one final end and that there can be no more.

The problem with this explanation is that, if Aristotle's definitions are strictly understood within the desire-satisfaction conception of the good, they would not justify the conclusion he wishes to draw. For these definitions would have to be applied to the structure of desires and ends of each agent, and each agent's supreme or most final end will be relative to his way of organizing his pursuits in terms of means and ends. It is difficult to see how we could arrive at an identical end for all, even though each person may have an end that he or she calls "happiness." Indeed, it is difficult to see how one could get to a single end for one agent; as Williams observes, one needs to relativize ends or goals not only with respect to an agent but also with respect to time.[28]

---

[27] Bernard Williams, "Aristotle on the Good: A Formal Sketch," *Philosophical Quarterly*, vol. 12, no. 49 (October 1962).

[28] *Ibid.*, p. 290.

B. Eliminating disagreements

Evidence from the Greek philosophical tradition clearly shows that disagreements about the end(s) of life are of great concern to Socrates, Plato, and Aristotle, and that all three philosophers show a strong preference for agreement on matters of conduct. Can Aristotle expect to eliminate disagreements about the good while still working within the desire-satisfaction conception of the good? Theorists who advocate such a conception of the good, and liberals in general, deny that this is possible. They claim that such disagreements or disputes are inevitable and ineliminable (Rawls, e.g., makes this claim), and some insist that there cannot even be any debate about final ends.[29]

Although there is no doubt that Aristotle, like his predecessors, has an interest in eliminating disagreements, it is not clear how this leads to an acceptable conclusion about the number of final ends. By itself, the desire to avoid disagreements about the end(s) of human life does not show anything about the nature or number of such end(s). In any case, similar disagreements are likely to exist about the nature of a single end. In addition, the move from a plurality of ends to a single one for the sake of eliminating disagreements may be too drastic. It surely raises the question of what it is rational to sacrifice for the sake of avoiding disagreements. Instead, it might be more reasonable to try to resolve disagreements by identifying that set of ends (possibly consisting of more than one end) acceptable to all or at least to most. Obviously, such an objective is less demanding, and it might be easier to attain than agreement about a single final end.

Disagreements about final ends might be bad (although liberals do not agree with this), but in order to move to some conclusion about the unity of the final end, one would need something more than a dislike of disagreements and a preference for agreement. One might try to show, and this will be more in tune with the desire-satisfaction conception of the good, that it is more rational to agree on final ends than to disagree, and thus to have a single end for a community or political association (see below). Or perhaps one might point to an objective procedure which is acceptable to all and which shows that indeed there is only one end; or one might point to something agreed upon by all that justifies agreement about ends. Now the function argument has often been viewed as providing a justification that fits the first of the two last alternatives—it is an objective procedure that leads to a conclusion about a single human end, assuming that the essence and function of a human being are what Aristotle says they are. As I pointed out earlier, however, Aristotle seems to have reached the conclusion about the unity of the good prior to the function argument.

---

[29] See John Rawls, *A Theory of Justice* (Cambridge: Harvard University Press, 1971), pp. 432–33; and Bruce Ackerman, "Neutralities," in *Liberalism and the Good* (*supra* note 11).

The very last alternative mentioned above might seem more promising for Aristotle. Aristotle might point to the fact that at some level there is agreement about the end of life. All or most seem to agree that happiness is the end. And this is something Aristotle introduces into the discussion before he concludes that the best life aims at a single final end. Now if all or even most humans subordinate their pursuits to happiness and to nothing else, and they do not subordinate happiness to anything, isn't that a reasonable ground for saying that there is only one final end?

Aristotle may very well have taken the above as a reasonable ground for concluding that there is one final end and that it is happiness. Yet the fact, if it is one, that happiness is most often or even always singled out as the final end does not show that there is only one final end. As I pointed out earlier, the inclusive interpretation of happiness still remains a possibility. More importantly, as Aristotle himself points out, different people mean quite different things by "happiness," and quite different ends are identified as happiness. Even the application of Aristotle's finality test cannot eliminate possible disagreements about ends as long as one remains within the desire-satisfaction conception of the good, despite the fact that at some level there is agreement about happiness being the end to which other things are subordinated. For it is possible for any of Aristotle's subordinate ends to be final ends for someone. Although pleasure can be desired for the sake of happiness, it need not be so; pleasure, as indeed Aristotle's own conception of a subordinate end implies, can be a final end. And one cannot argue from within the desire-satisfaction conception of the good or end alone that, since there is something to which pleasure could be subordinated, that thing is a preferable or more perfect end. To eliminate the possibility that subordinate ends have a claim to being final ends, one would need to interpret Aristotle's finality test as showing that some things are more perfect than others in some objective sense, and that our actual desires and the means-ends structures they exhibit are at times in agreement with the objective degrees of perfection of things. There is a possibility that Aristotle is thinking along these lines when he introduces the finality test, and, if finality were to be understood in this way, it might imply that there can be only one final end. But this way of looking at the matter makes little sense from the perspective of the desire-satisfaction conception of the good.

C. Aristotle's conception of a rational agent

Many Aristotelian scholars have argued that perhaps Aristotle's conclusion that there is only one final end makes good sense if one sees it in relation to his conception of a rational agent. Such an agent will be aiming to maximize consistency and minimize conflicts among his ends with a view to maximizing his good. This is best done if there is only one final end. More than one final end will inevitably result in situations of conflict and will most probably give rise to insoluble problems of choosing among equally competing final ends. Thus, the life plan with one final end is the most rational plan. Scholars point to Aristotle's own remarks in the *Eudemian Ethics* (1214b6) as evidence that he was indeed motivated by considerations of rationality:

> Having then in regard to this subject established that everybody able to live according to his own choice should set before him some object for noble living to aim at—either honor or else glory or wealth or culture—on which he will have his eyes fixed in all his conduct (since clearly it is a mark of much folly not to have one's life regulated with regard to some end) . . .

In addition, his remarks in the opening sections of the *Nicomachean Ethics* about the structure of human pursuits seem to confirm his concern with rationality.

Yet the kind of rationality Aristotle's interpreters seem to have in mind in the present context, the kind acceptable to desire-satisfaction theorists, raises several problems. On the one hand, it is not sufficient for deriving the kind of conclusion that Aristotle wants about final ends; on the other hand, desire-satisfaction theorists find the maximizing of rationality to the degree required to support even a rather weak conclusion about final ends to be inconsistent with the nature of the self. According to them, demanding the kind of rationality that Aristotle seems to demand from a life plan is too excessive and is stifling to the self.

What is needed to avoid conflicts among final ends? Rationality demands that an agent must have one final end at any one time, in view of which he chooses all he does. This, of course, leaves open the possibility of an agent's having different final ends at different times. This kind of rationality is consistent with multiple final ends throughout the life of an agent as well as different final ends across agents. But Aristotle wants something much stronger: a single final end throughout the life of an agent and an identical final end for all agents. The remarks quoted above from the *Eudemian Ethics* speak of a final end guiding an agent throughout a life, an end that is the ultimate end of a life, and leave no room for different ends among different agents.

Now there may be some advantages to having a single final end throughout a life, but it is not clear that this can be extracted from rationality alone or that it is wise to accept such a restriction on the number of final ends even if it could be extracted from rationality. What is clear, however, is the cost that the requirement of a rational plan of a whole life with a single end imposes: rationality that demands a single final end throughout the life of an agent eliminates the opportunity of revising one's life plan, at least with respect to the final end. Foreclosing the possibility of revising one's life plan with respect to its final end seems to be problematic for a variety of reasons. It seems to go against prudential considerations, since it overlooks the impact that changes in the desires and interests of an agent as she goes through life and as circumstances change are likely to have on her choice of ends. It eliminates the possibility of an agent—to use an example Aristotle might have appreciated—abandoning honor as his final end (political life) and devoting his life to contemplation (theoretical life).[30] Rawls goes even further and sees such a restriction on the final end not merely as lacking in prudence, given the uncertain course of human development and external circumstances, but also as violating the notion of a moral person. According to Rawls, to require a single identical end throughout the lifetime of an agent on the basis of rationality is to eliminate part of one of the two highest-order interests that, according to him, constitute the conception of a moral person—namely, the interest in exercising the capacity to revise one's own conception of the good.[31]

Yet Rawls has an even deeper objection to imposing such a restriction on final ends on account of rationality. He objects not only to the requirement of a single end for a lifetime (diachronic unity) but also to the requirement of a single end during any one period of an agent's life (synchronic unity). He finds such a demand of rationality on an agent's life—one that, at least, requires a single final end at each stage of an agent's life—too constraining on the self. According to Rawls, even this minimal demand of synchronic unity is at odds with the nature of the self; it disfigures the self, which, according to him, is heterogeneous.[32]

Rawls wishes to put limits on the demands of rationality as far as the number of final ends are concerned when these demands are inconsistent with the conception of the self. But if Aristotle has a different conception of the self, the disagreement between him and Rawls may not be as much about the limits of rationality as it is about the nature of the self. For Aristotle seems to be arguing in Book X, chapter 7 of the *Nicomachean Ethics* that the true or distinctive self of a human agent is not heterogeneous. According to him, it is homogeneous; it is constituted by that element in a human being which, "although small in bulk," is most powerful and unique to humans among animals and whose activity surpasses in worth every-

---

[30] See, in this connection, David Keyt, "The Meaning of *Bios* in Aristotle's *Ethics* and *Politics*," *Ancient Philosophy*, vol. 9 (1989).

[31] According to Rawls, "Social Unity and Primary Goods," pp. 164–65:

> [I]n formulating a conception of justice . . . we start by viewing each person as a moral person moved by two highest order interests, namely, the interests to realise the two powers of moral personality. These two powers are the capacity for a sense of justice . . . and the capacity to decide upon, to revise and rationally to pursue a conception of the good.

[32] See Rawls, *A Theory of Justice*, p. 554, where Rawls remarks:

> Human good is heterogeneous because the aims of the self are heterogeneous. Although to subordinate all our aims to one end does not strictly speaking violate the principles of rational choice (not the counting principles anyway), it still strikes us as irrational, or more likely as mad. The self is disfigured and put in the service of one of its ends for the sake of system.

thing else and constitutes the single final end and perfection of a human being (1177b27–35; see also 1177a13). Aristotle is not oblivious to the other elements of a human being—namely, those that are connected to the body and the remaining faculties of the soul. Yet he insists that the authoritative element is the one of "small bulk" and that all else is subordinate to it. To have as final ends things or activities that are not proper to this element that constitutes what it is to be a human being—that is, to subordinate the authoritative element to those that are by nature to be ruled, or to give equal weight to the ends of all elements—is, for a human being, to choose to be something other than one's self. And this, in Aristotle's view, would be to stifle or disfigure the self. It seems, then, that Rawls and Aristotle come out on opposite sides on the issue of how far rationality should constrain the number of final ends of an agent because the two have different views of the self. It is clear that Aristotle's conception is part of a view of human nature which is psychological/metaphysical in character; Rawls, on the other hand, insists that his conception has nothing to do with metaphysics—that it is political. How one would choose between these two conceptions of the self is clearly not a minor problem.

Yet even if we were to agree with Aristotle that rationality requires a single final end throughout the life of an individual, we would still not have shown that it also requires one identical final end across different agents. How could we get such an identity without appealing to factors other than rationality (e.g., human nature, teleology, nature of the self, perfection, and so on)? It would seem most natural to examine what rationality considerations alone imply with respect to the unity of the good when a number of individuals form an association to jointly pursue their final ends. Now Aristotle recognizes several distinct kinds of association (e.g., the household, the village, and the city or state or polis), but it is the political association or polis which is the most perfect or final, and which aims at the realization of the final ends of its members. The question, then, is whether rationality aspects of the political association—that is, aspects that do not involve substantive claims about human nature, teleology, the nature of the self, the content of desire, and so on—imply anything about the number of final ends in general or about the unity of the good in particular.

In his discussion of the end of the political association in the *Politics*, Aristotle unequivocally comes out in favor of the unity of the good. This is especially true in Books I, VII, and VIII, where he offers an explanation of the origin of and a justification of the existence of the state, as well as an account of the ideal constitutions. As he says at 1328a36:

> And the state is a certain association of similar persons, for the sake of the best life that is possible. And since the best thing is happiness, and this is some perfect activity or employment of virtue, and since it so happens that it is possible for some to partake of it, but for

others only to a small extent or not at all, it is clear that this is the cause for there arising different kinds and varieties of state and several forms of constitution. (See also 1252b30, 1282b15, 1295a25)

Such unity of the good implies a single system of education, according to Aristotle. As he puts it at 1337a23:

> Since the end for the whole state is one, it is manifest that education also must be one and the same for all and that the superintendence of this must be public, and not on private lines, in the way in which at present each man superintends the education of his own children, teaching them privately, and whatever special branch of knowledge he thinks fit.

Of course, it is such a single system of education that Aristotle describes and defends in the last two books of the *Politics*.[33] But these views of Aristotle about the unity of the good and of the educational system of the polis stem primarily from the kinds of substantive assumptions referred to earlier, especially functionalism, teleology, and perfectionism. If we were to accept such assumptions and what they presumably imply about the good, then the identity of the end for all members of the political association would follow. Aristotle himself points to such an implication in the *Nicomachean Ethics* (1094b) when he says that, if there were a supreme good (a single end for all human action), then this one end would be the end the state would aim to realize. It is clear, however, that these assumptions cannot be accepted in the present context, since to do so would be to beg the question. For the question is how to get from the assumption that rationality dictates a single end for the lifetime of each agent to the conclusion that the end is the same for all members of the political association, and how to get there by relying on rationality considerations alone.

As Aristotle's remarks quoted above indicate, however, there are different kinds and varieties of states and constitutions. In addition to the ideal or best states and constitutions, he recognizes lesser forms of both, the ones he designates as correct or deviant. In both correct and deviant states the identity of the end of the members of the state is not presupposed. Although Aristotle claims that in the correct state, as distinguished from the perfect state, the final end is virtuous activity (including virtuous military activity), the end of each member need not be identical. This is especially true in the case of the least perfect states, those whose constitutions are from the group Aristotle characterizes as the deviant. Mem-

---

[33] For a discussion of Aristotle's views on education and the end of the ideal state, see David Depew, "Politics, Music, and Contemplation in Aristotle's Ideal State," in David Keyt and Fred D. Miller, Jr., eds., *A Companion to Aristotle's "Politics"* (Oxford: Blackwell, 1991).

bers of states with deviant constitutions may retain goals such as wealth, freedom, or power. Now the correct constitution aims at the advantage of all members, but even this requirement need not imply identity of final ends for all members.[34]

If we assume, with Aristotle, the possibility of a plurality of final ends, are there considerations stemming from the political association that may lead to the unity of the good? In order to consider the possible implications of rationality for the final ends of the members of the polis, one would need to identify some of the basic features of Aristotle's ethical and political theories. For the question is, in part, whether a rationality that implies unity of the good is consistent with these basic features of Aristotle's ethical and political views. The following seem to be the most important features for the present purposes:

(i) The good is prior to the right (Aristotle's ethical and political theories are teleological).[35]
(ii) The state has an end or is telic.
(iii) Humans enter the political association for the sake of an end.
(iv) Politics presupposes the findings of ethics, especially those regarding the nature of the end(s) of individuals.

Two comments about (iii) are in order. First, the claim it makes is different from the one (ii) makes, since it is possible for the state to have an end that is not the same as that for the sake of which the members of the state enter or remain in it. But Aristotle argues that the end of the state is not different from that of its members. Second, at times Aristotle argues as if humans are moved by a kind of impulse in entering the state (*Politics*, 1253a30), but at other times he writes as if the members have in view specific ends they want to realize by entering or remaining in the political association. These ends, of course, need not all be in view prior to entering the political association (see below).

Although none of the foregoing claims constitutes a substantive view of the good or rests on some assumption about human nature or perfectionism, they nonetheless might have important consequences for the number of ends in a political association. Rawls has at times argued that by giving priority to the good over the right, Plato and Aristotle are committed to the view of the unity of the good, the view that there is one end that all

---

[34] See, in this connection, Fred D. Miller, Jr., *Nature, Justice, and Rights in Aristotle's "Politics"* (Oxford: Clarendon Press, 1995), ch. 5.

[35] Although most scholars agree on the teleological nature of Aristotle's ethical theory, those who take him to advocate a type of virtue ethics question the standard teleological reading of Aristotelian ethics. For a discussion of these issues, see Gerasimos Santas, "The Structure of Aristotle's Ethical Theory: Is It Teleological or a Virtue Ethics?" *Topoi*, vol. 15, no. 1 (March 1996).

rational agents will recognize.[36] It is not clear what follows from giving priority in one's ethical or political theory to the good or the right, but Rawls could be understood as follows. Assume (i) and (ii) and our earlier conclusion that rationality constraints favor a single end for a lifetime for each member of the political association. Usually (i) comes with a maximization principle—the goal of the state is to maximize the good. Aristotle hints at this in Book I, chapter 1 of the *Nicomachean Ethics*, when he says: "For even if the end is the same for a single man and for a state, that of the state seems at all events greater" (1094b10). Although Aristotle's remarks are somewhat ambiguous—they might mean that the state either aims at the greatest aggregate of good or at the good of the greatest number of members—the ambiguity does not affect the issue at hand.

Given the above assumptions, one might argue that it would be more rational for all members of a political association to aim at a single identical end. If a single identical end is adopted for all members, agreement on the final end will be attained, conflicts will be avoided, and maximization of the end of the state will be easier to achieve. The end of the state would be more likely to be realized and realized to the highest degree possible if all have an identical (and, *ex hypothesi*, single) end. Thus, rationality considerations might lead us to conclude that having a single end (unity of the good) is the best choice, if the goal of the state is to be optimally realized. Admittedly, this would not give us universal unity on the good, but even unity relative to a particular political association is not a small thing. Indeed, to liberal theorists it is far too much and is unacceptable.

Desire-satisfaction theorists and liberal theorists find little to agree with in the inferences Aristotle might draw about the unity of the good from such considerations of rationality. These theorists reject Aristotle's basic assumption about the state's being telic, its having a final end. According to Rawls, the state has no ends or goals whatsoever.[37] And without the telic view of the state, it is hard to see how the rationality of minimizing or eliminating conflicts among the ends of the state and achieving maximization of the good would lead us to the unity of the good. If the state does not aim at anything, why would it be rational to adopt one instead of many final ends?

Yet abandoning the telic view of the state, as liberal theorists insist on doing, does not necessarily settle everything. The state may have no ends, at least not any that are different from the ends of the individuals that are its constituents, but there still remain the end(s) of its members. As Fred Miller has argued, according to Aristotle, individuals form a political association in order to maximize their good, and Aristotle's talk of the priority of the city need not be interpreted as saying that there is an end that is prior to and above the ends of the individuals constituting the

---

[36] See note 3 above.
[37] Rawls, *Political Liberalism* (*supra* note 3), pp. 40–43.

city.[38] Aristotle argues repeatedly that the good of the state is not different from that of its individual members, and neither is happiness, which most people, according to Aristotle, take to be the end of both the state and its members (*Politics*, 1324a1, 1324a5). Aristotle also insists that individuals forming a polis "are also brought together by common interest, so far as each achieves a share of the good life. The good life then is the chief aim of society, both collectively for all its members and individually" (1278b20). The same is true in the case of the elementary associations, according to Aristotle: individuals come together in households or villages to satisfy their needs or realize their individual goals. They are motivated to form associations for mutual advantage, for the sake of mutually realizing their end(s). Yet the pursuit of mutual advantage does not require or imply identity of ends. According to Aristotle, the master and the slave enter into an association for mutual advantage, but obviously they do not have the same ends.

Setting aside, then, the telic view of the state, the question is whether rationality considerations alone might lead those who choose to form a community, society, or state to the view that it is best for them to aim at a single identical final end. Suppose, then, that Rawls is right in claiming that the state has no final end, and suppose for the moment that Aristotle is right in saying that rationality dictates that an agent has a single final end. Is it possible that coordination (i.e., rationality) considerations in a situation where each agent is trying to realize his or her single final end dictate that the best (rational) thing to do is for all to adopt the same final end—whatever the final end might turn out to be?

Perhaps one should not rule out the abstract possibility that some situation might arise in which coordination requirements may very well dictate the adoption of an identical end. But the prospect that some such demand is imposed by rationality in order for one to participate in social or political life seems most disquieting and problematic. If we merely assume that each agent has a single final end, thus leaving open the possibility for an initial diversity of final ends among agents, what end is to be adopted in view of coordination requirements and what connection would such an end have to desire satisfaction? A desire-satisfaction theorist would find nothing appealing in this. If such a theorist finds unacceptable the supposed constraint of rationality on the number of final ends for an individual—that is, a single end for any one stage of life, or a single end for a lifetime—it is not likely that he would accept the supposed requirement of one end for all. At least the first requirement allows that the single end be the end of the individual, while the second seems to take away even that.

What would Aristotle's response have been to such a requirement on the final ends of the members of the political association for the sake of

[38] Miller, *Nature, Justice, and Rights*, pp. 45–56.

rationality or coordination purposes? I think he would have resisted it. The fundamental principles of his political theory, as well as his assignment of priority to ethics over politics in the understanding of conduct, seem to be inconsistent with such a requirement on the final ends of members of the political association. Of course, Aristotle might have had different reasons for favoring the unity of the good—for example, reasons having to do with human nature—but that is clearly another matter.

The priority of ethics over politics implies that the good(s) of individuals can be specified prior to specifying the nature and structure of the political association. This, of course, does not necessarily imply that the good of the individual can be realized outside the political association, and Aristotle makes it abundantly clear where he stands on this. He insists that the final end of a human being, the good life, cannot be attained outside the political association. And this is precisely what motivates individuals to enter the political association—the interest in realizing an end or ends that they have prior to entering the association or that can be specified prior to specifying the nature of the association. Thus, Aristotle offers a specification of the good in his ethics—that is, he offers it prior to offering a political theory. The same is true of the excellences, including justice, which is both a moral and a political excellence. The account of justice in the *Nicomachean Ethics* is presupposed by the discussion of the same excellence in the *Politics*.

The fact that the account of the end(s) of the individual that Aristotle gives in his ethical theory is presupposed by his political theory is of considerable importance. For if there is diversity of ends among individuals, then the ends that are to be realized by the political association have already been or can be fixed without reference to the state. Whatever requirements rationality or coordination impose must be imposed with a view to realizing these ends, whatever they might be. It is difficult to see what would motivate individuals to enter the political association if they had to give up the ends that prompt them to enter such an association in the first place. And the question of motivation is of importance to Aristotle, something he clearly recognizes. Not only does he go to great lengths to identify the motives of female and male, master and slave, different households, and free individuals for entering into the various associations he identifies; he also insists that in thinking about the suitability of constitutions one must take into account what will move individuals to take part in a particular kind of state (*Politics*, 1289a).

The above, however, does not imply that individuals cannot alter or revise their end or ends. They might do so, and in a way that is consistent with Aristotle's political framework, even by the very process of participating in the political association and its educational institutions. For it is not necessary that individuals have their ends, at least not all of them, in clear view prior to entering the political association. Some of these ends may take shape when individuals are already a part of the association.

Aristotle probably has something like this in mind when he claims that the state comes into existence for the sake of life but exists for the sake of the good life. He could be understood as saying that before most individuals enter the state, they consciously desire only their own personal survival, but after they become part of the political association they learn that they have other ends, e.g., virtue. Thus, Aristotle may not disagree with Rawls about individuals revising their ends, but he would still resist the idea that they must forsake their actual natural ends for a political end or one dictated by the kind of rationality considerations that could be associated with the political association.

Yet one might argue that individuals would be willing to abandon their end(s) because being members of the political association is the most valuable thing to them, and therefore they would be willing to sacrifice everything for the sake of it. But if this were true, it would show that the final end of all is one and the same—namely, life within the political association—and that this is what ultimately motivates individuals to enter the political association. Now Aristotle does not discount the motivating role that the desire of an individual to be a part of the association plays in the formation or existence of the state. He clearly recognizes it when he claims that "man is by nature a political animal; and so even when men have no need of assistance from each other they nonetheless desire to live together" (1278b20; see also 1252b30). However, Aristotle's individuals are not primarily motivated by such a consideration in entering or remaining in the political association. Although he admits that sometimes individuals come together "for the sake of life merely, for doubtless there is an element of value contained even in the mere state of being alive" (1278b25; see also 1252b30), he insists that the political association is formed not for the sake of life or the life within the association, but for the sake of the highest good or the good life (1252a5, 1252b30, 1278b23, 1280a30).

The above considerations, I believe, also show that even Aristotle's telic conception of the state is, contrary to what Rawls says, inconsistent with the kind of rationality or coordination that would require citizens to alter their final ends in order to attain unity of the good. For if the end of the state is not something over and above the ends of the individuals—if it is not something competing with the ends of individuals—then admitting the telic nature of the state does not raise problems for Aristotle. The state is telic in the sense that it aims at the optimal realization of the highest end(s) of the citizens. And the better states, according to Aristotle, are those under whose constitutions "anybody whatsoever would be best off and would live in felicity" (1324a23). Such constitutions embody the principles of justice—that is, they aim at the good of all citizens in accordance with the principles of justice. Such a telic conception imposes certain restrictions on what considerations of rationality or coordination can be adopted. If the goal of the state, according to this conception, is to realize the end(s) of its members, and if the ends are determined prior to or without reference to the political association, then these are the ends to be realized and not some others that might be dictated by certain maximization or coordination principles. The goal of the state is to realize and not to change the end(s) of its members which have already been identified by ethics. If ethics specifies a single identical end for all, then of course the unity of the good or end at the political level will follow. But if ethics allows for a diversity of ends among individuals, the nature of Aristotle's telic conception of the state does not imply unity of the good and is not consistent with any rationality considerations (e.g., maximization) that might require such unity.

Now, were Aristotle to acknowledge different final ends across different agents in the state, he would need to reconsider his conception of education. As I pointed out earlier, the conception he outlines and defends in the last two books of the *Politics* is one that presupposes a single final end ("Since the end for the whole state is one, it is manifest that education must also be one . . ." [1337a23]). But if this presupposition is removed, the conclusion about the unity of education that Aristotle draws from it will also have to be reconsidered. Although Aristotle devotes Books VII and VIII of the *Politics* to an examination of education in the ideal state—that is, a state where the end of the citizens is the same—he says very little about the educational requirements of any other kind of state, and, as a consequence, there is little in the way of data with respect to his views on this issue. In Book IV, Aristotle points to the problem that those who enjoy too many goods to an excessive degree (e.g., strength, wealth, friends) pose for the political association; they are, according to him, "both unwilling to obey and ignorant of how to obey" (1295b15). He suggests that their problem stems from failures in education; they have not become habituated to be ruled, even in school.

In Book V, Aristotle returns to the question of education in the context of his discussion of possible means for securing the stability of less perfect constitutions or states, those in which citizens may very well have diverse ends. He writes:

> The greatest of all the means spoken of to secure the stability of constitutions is one that at present is slighted by all: it is a system of education suited to the constitutions. For there is no use in the most valuable laws, ratified by the unanimous judgment of the whole body of citizens, if these are not trained and educated in the constitution, democratically if the laws are democratic, oligarchically if the laws are oligarchic. (1310a12)

In the present context, Aristotle is concerned with the threat which the pursuit of certain ends (excessive wealth by the partisans of oligarchy, and excessive freedom by the partisans of democracy) poses for the stability of oligarchic or democratic rule. He urges that citizens be educated relative to the constitution—that is, in the things by which the oligarchs or the democrats will be able to run an oligarchy or a democracy, and not in what the extreme partisans of each type of constitution or state pursue. The types of ends that Aristotle sees as threatening oligarchy and democracy—wealth and freedom—are ends that, according to him, are built into the respective constitutional structures of these states. But the problem can be generalized; it is the problem of the relation between the ends pursued by the citizens and the stability of the state. Aristotle argues that the relation is a problematic one, even in the case where the ends pursued by the citizens are identical in kind to those the constitution protects. It would probably be even more problematic if the diversity of ends were greater than what Aristotle refers to in the remarks quoted above, if it included ends that might not be embedded in the constitution of a regime. His solution of the particular problems he raises with respect to oligarchy and democracy is to require a system of education that succeeds in habituating the citizens in the laws that each one of these constitutions approves. Aristotle's solution can be generalized and extended to cover cases of much greater diversity of ends than he imagines. It would require that the citizens, regardless of their particular ends, receive an education that habituates them in the laws of the state, so that the stability and preservation of the state and the constitution are safeguarded. At least this component of education, perhaps the minimum required for all citizens, would be identical for all. And, of course, there could be additional types of education that relate to the specific ends that different citizens or classes of citizens might have. Such a system of education may not be very different from what Plato elaborates in the *Republic*: it has elements that are shared by all citizens, but also components that serve the different ends of various political classes or members of the state.

V. Conclusion

One of the strongest objections to the idea of human flourishing, and to the perfectionism on which it rests, is that they both depend on a certain conception of human nature or make certain metaphysical assumptions about the function of human beings and their ends. The discussion above has shown that it is quite difficult to support the notions of human flourishing and perfectionism without relying on some conceptions of human nature or function that are strong enough to impose some limits on the number of final ends and to justify why certain kinds of life are indeed instances of human flourishing while others presumably are not. Thus, it was seen that ancient Greek pre-philosophical perfectionism faces considerable difficulties with respect to specifying the perfections that constitute human flourishing, if it is understood without any reference to a conception of human nature, function, teleology, etc. Plato's accounts of flourishing and perfectionism clearly depend on the notion of human function. But if function were to be understood, as Plato's text suggests, without any reference to some metaphysical or teleological views about humans, the Platonic project would encounter problems quite similar to those of pre-philosophical perfectionism. As pointed out earlier, it would not even be able to identify what the human function(s) is (are), and therefore would not be able to specify what kind of life constitutes human flourishing and explain or justify why it does so.

Aristotle's project in the early chapters of the *Nicomachean Ethics* poses a greater challenge. For while he appears to be working outside the perfectionist framework, he is unwilling to abandon one of the central features of theories of human flourishing and perfectionism—namely, the view that there is one final end and that it is the same for all. The discussion above has shown that if Aristotle is working with a desire-satisfaction conception of the good (and there is good reason to believe that he is), then the unity of the good he seems to advocate (a single identical end for all) cannot be assured. Such a unity of the good does not seem to follow from any rationality considerations alone that are consistent with some basic tenets of his ethical and political theories. A type of rationality, however, that he appears to find acceptable seems to imply that the best life for an individual is a life with a single final end. Although liberal theorists reject such a constraint on the number of ends on account of their commitment to the heterogeneity of the self, it was seen that Aristotle's conception of the self is not inconsistent with a view requiring a single final end for an individual.

Yet Aristotle's appeal to rationality and the nature of the self in support of the claim that the best life for an individual is one having a single final end is not likely to satisfy everyone. In particular, it is not likely to satisfy those who find theories of human flourishing and perfectionism objectionable on the ground that they rely on views about human nature, function, or teleology. For Aristotle's conception of the self is based on his views on human nature and whatever metaphysical claims these presuppose. Although these views have been criticized in recent years, some have found much in Aristotle's biology, psychology, and metaphysics that can be defended.[39] I cannot here defend Aristotle's views on the self or on human nature. All I wish to point out is that the disagreement between Aristotle and liberal theorists, all of whom might be working with the desire-satisfaction conception of the good, on the number of final ends for an individual comes down to a disagreement about the nature of the self. This last disagreement itself may be an implication of two different approaches to the self: one is clearly metaphysical/psychological/biological,

---

[39] See *ibid.* for the most recent discussion and assessment of Aristotle's views on biology and their presuppositions. For a more lengthy discussion and defense of Aristotle's biology and its metaphysical presuppositions and implications, see Montgomery Furth, *Substance, Form, and Psyche: An Aristotelian Metaphysics* (Cambridge: Cambridge University Press, 1988).

while the other is political. The first approach, whether or not it can succeed, is clearly the more foundational and has a wider scope.

Is there any possibility of defending Aristotle's conclusion about a single end for an individual, and possibly the unity of the good for all, without making any metaphysical commitments about human nature, function, or teleology? Alasdair MacIntyre, who is attracted to the kind of unity and shared purpose that views of human flourishing and perfectionism imply for human life, but finds the traditional metaphysical commitments such views make problematic, has sought to replace metaphysical commitments with social/political roles or goals. MacIntyre argues that both the good and the virtues can be determined by a kind of teleology that is not metaphysical or essentialist, and thus makes no reference to essentialist conceptions of human nature. According to him, the good of a person is determined by reference to the goals of the society of which the person is a member, and the excellences of a person are specified by reference to the social role he or she has within the social order. Thus, MacIntyre claims, one can avoid the traditional metaphysical commitments but retain teleology: "Although this [MacIntyre's own] account of the virtues is teleological, it does not require the identification of any teleology in nature, and hence it does not require identification of any teleology in metaphysical biology."[40]

MacIntyre's position, by eschewing the metaphysical and embracing the political/social, has one foot in the liberal tradition and, by permitting some vestiges of teleology, has the other foot within the boundaries of perfectionism or traditional theories of human flourishing. However, it is doubtful that such a position can meet the difficulties that similar attempts encounter. First, by advocating a teleology that relativizes ends to political goals, MacIntyre gives up on the possibility of identifying ends or excellences that are common to all. And if one is willing to relativize the good or excellences to political goals, why not relativize them to the goals of one's tribe, clan, group, or extended family? MacIntyre insists on the goals of the state or the polis as the goals relative to which the good and the excellences must be specified, but it is not clear that this cannot be done by choosing social/political units smaller than the state. Were one to admit this, there would be no obvious limits on what are to count as ends or excellences. Liberal theorists will probably welcome such a consequence, but one who, like MacIntyre, is critical of this aspect of liberalism, and wishes to speak of shared ends and excellences in a meaningful way, would not.

Second, and perhaps more importantly in relation to the ancient philosophical tradition, the kind of teleology MacIntyre proposes has an unpalatable consequence, one that even liberal theorists would reject.

---

[40] MacIntyre, *After Virtue*, p. 183. For a recent assessment of MacIntyre's views, see Miller, *Nature, Justice, and Rights*, esp. pp. 198, 336–46.

Whatever the undesirable aspects of Aristotle's essentialism might be, it has the feature of assigning an independence or "autonomy" to the individual. A member of the polis is, for Aristotle, an individual substance; a citizen is something that has an independent existence and nature—this is what being a substance implies. The final end(s) and excellence(s) of such a substance is (are) fixed by reference to its own essential form, which is not determined by any relation to anything else. But MacIntyre's teleology relativizes everything to the goals of the state, thus eliminating the independence Aristotle's teleology allots to the individual with respect to ends or excellences. MacIntyre's teleology treats the individual in the way Aristotle treats the functional parts of a substance or functional artifacts. The end of an eye or ear, according to Aristotle, is determined by reference to the goal (function) of the substance of which it is a part. And the end of an artifact, for example, a flute or an axe, is specified by something external to it, namely, the goals of those whose purposes such artifacts serve. Essentialism might have its problems, but giving up the kind of independence that is implied by the Aristotelian conceptions of substance and teleology, and thus subordinating the ends of individuals to something external to them, has consequences that many are likely to find unwelcome. In particular, given the priority that liberal theorists assign to autonomy, they are not likely to embrace the kind of consequence that MacIntyre's nonmetaphysical teleology seems to have.

Perhaps there are other ways that might lead us to Aristotle's conclusion that the best life for an individual has a single final end or even that the final end is the same for all, without having recourse to any metaphysical assumptions. It is possible, for example, that Aristotle's own account of finality of ends, from which he draws his conclusion about the number of ends for the best life of an individual (as well as the number of ends across agents), offers an alternative. His conception of finality is possibly much stronger than what the desire-satisfaction theory of the good would allow, and is perhaps strong enough to get him both the single end for an individual and the unity of end for all. It would be interesting to explore whether this stronger conception of finality requires only a more robust conception of rationality or ultimately rests on the same presuppositions as do Aristotle's views on human flourishing and perfectionism—namely, essentialism, functionalism, and teleology. But this is a topic for another project.

Philosophy, University of California, San Diego

ARISTOTLE'S ELUSIVE *SUMMUM BONUM*

By Sarah Broadie

I. The Main Question

The philosophy of Aristotle (384–322, B.C.E.) remains a beacon of our culture. But no part of Aristotle's work is more alive and compelling today than his contribution to ethics and political science—nor more relevant to the subject of the present volume. Political science, in his view, begins with ethics, and the primary task of ethics is to elucidate *human flourishing*. Aristotle brings to this topic a mind unsurpassed in the depth, keenness, and comprehensiveness of its probing.

"Which among humanly practicable goods is the *summum bonum* or highest good?" is his first and central question.[1] As we would expect, the answer he gives is rather abstract. Even so, he intends it to be informative and to provide guidance for action.[2] The present essay will focus on the account put forward in the *Nicomachean Ethics*, Book I, chapter 7, where Aristotle equates the *summum bonum* with "the soul's activity of excellence in a complete life."[3] This compact formula sets the agenda for Aristotelian ethics, which proceeds to explicate the *summum bonum* through detailed studies of (a) the *excellences* (or *virtues*)[4] and (b) the two most philosophically controversial components of *a complete life*, namely *friendship*[5] and *pleasure*.[6] Fully spelled out, the compact formula yields a conceptually rich, and substantial, ideal.

This essay will take the compact formula as given, and will not comment on the reasoning by which Aristotle arrives at it. Nor is it my present purpose to look closely at any portion of the content of his ideal. The main question addressed here is a formal one: What does it mean in the context of Aristotelian ethics to regard X as the *summum bonum*, whatever X may be? In discussing this question, we shall be led to consider the chief components of Aristotle's ideal to see how their interrelation constitutes a whole that fits the formal account of the *summum bonum*.

---

[1] Aristotle, *Nicomachean Ethics* (hereafter *NE*), Book I, ch. 4, 1095a15–16.
[2] *NE* I 3, 1095a5–6; II 2, 1103b26–28.
[3] *NE* I 7, 1098a12–20; cf. 10, 1101a14–16; Aristotle, *Eudemian Ethics* (hereafter *EE*), Book II, ch. 1, 1219a.
[4] *NE* II–VI.
[5] *NE* VIII–IX.
[6] *NE* VII 11–14; X 1–5.

II. Some Perspectives

The claim that X is the *summum bonum* seems to imply that X is the good which we should strive above all to realize. But is that what the claim means? And who are the "we" to whom the supposed implication applies?

To answer these questions we shall have to distinguish two levels of practical thinking. Before proceeding to the distinction, however, it is worth pausing over the obvious point that a practicable *summum bonum* cannot become an issue on any level except to rational beings with a multiplicity of needs and aspirations, and limited powers for satisfying them—practical beings, in short. The very phrase *"summum bonum"* implies different goods, ranking one beyond the rest. However, Aristotle remarks that everyone agrees in calling the highest good *"eudaimonia"*[7] (usually translated as "happiness," sometimes as "flourishing"), and he himself constantly uses this appellation. The word itself does not bring us much closer to understanding what the *summum bonum* is, since people have very different notions of *eudaimonia*.[8] But use of the latter, more colloquial, term gives Aristotle two advantages. It opens his topic to input from ordinary common sense (an important guide toward ethical wisdom, in Aristotle's view), whereas "the highest good" sounds a decidedly academic note. And the use of *"eudaimonia"* also brings the human ideal into relation with something more than human. For *eudaimonia* was a traditional attribute of the gods.[9] Aristotle can accept the attribution, though not because he accepts traditional portrayals of the gods. On the contrary, god, according to the Aristotelian philosopher's understanding, is a single unbroken, perfectly self-sufficient, eternal activity of reason.[10] There is no metaphysical margin here for any good except the activity itself. *"Eudaimonia,"* then, a term implying no comparison between other goods and the good which it names, is a suitable word for the divine attribute.

In Aristotle's eyes it is very significant that common sense recognizes the possibility of human *eudaimonia* too.[11] It surely is remarkable that the same word should be so naturally used both of the divine good, essential and unique in the divine life, and of a human good which is best among many and attainable only through the hazards of practicality.

We are already, with Aristotle, reflecting in a way that may seem out of place for the practical beings we are. From a "purely" practical point of view, as it might be called, our practical nature goes without saying.

---

[7] *NE* I 4, 1095a17–20.

[8] *NE* I 4, 1095a20–28.

[9] *NE* X 8, 1178b8–9.

[10] *NE* X 8, 1178b9–22; Aristotle, *Metaphysics*, Book XII, chs. 7 and 9.

[11] The well-being of nonrational animals is not *eudaimonia*; see *EE* I 7, 1217a20–29; *NE* I 9, 1099b32–1100a1; X 8, 1178b25–28.

When engaged in practical action we occupy the practical point of view, which like any perspective simply assumes its occupants as such. But Aristotle's ethics is built on a cosmic anthropology in which distinctively human existence is compared with other forms of life. We have just seen how the truism that the *summum bonum* is *eudaimonia* implies a comparison between human good and divine. The difference between human and divine invites, in turn, the comparison of humans with nonrational animals.[12] From the cosmic point of view it may even be cause for wonder that beings like ourselves exist at all to puzzle over how the capacity for godlike *eudaimonia* can occur interwoven with the needs of a vulnerable organism making its way in a physical environment. (Since the human organism makes its way only by learning, and we learn only from others of our kind, our way is essentially social,[13] which adds further dimensions of complexity to the multiple nature of the human good.) This cosmic-anthropological standpoint does not allow us to take our practical essence for granted.

Leaving wonder aside, however, there are also down-to-earth reasons why our practicality is not just a topic of speculation but for us an object of intense *practical* concern. The contrast just made between a practical perspective which takes itself wholly for granted, and the cosmological view which reflects upon the former, is compelling only if we ignore human nature and assume (legitimately, perhaps, for certain theoretical purposes) that as practical beings we are all committed to making good practical decisions, capable of discerning them, and geared to carrying them out. Were the assumptions true in practice, our practical decision-making could, of course, afford to overlook its own basis in the requisite organization of the soul. Practicality then might never have become a topic. (By the same token, when ethical theory confines itself to a universe of discourse where all agents are actively rational, the shift to an external perspective such as that of cosmic anthropology will seem gratuitous for ethics.) But since it is equally plain that the assumptions are false in practice and that we need them to be at least roughly true if only to satisfy our most obvious requirements, the cultivation of practical rationality becomes a pressing concern for the practical beings we are. The resulting reflection, along with experience, may even lead us to conclude that practical rationality, our paramount resource for obtaining the other things which we value, is best secured by means of the belief that in achieving it we achieve an *intrinsic* good, whether or not this belief is independently grounded or even meaningful. Inevitably, efforts to sustain and teach this conviction will sometimes be displaced by philosophical misgivings. How is it consistent with our *general* rationality to nurture our practical reason on a possibly irrational belief? In this way, a realistic practical point of

[12] See previous note; see also *NE* I 7, 1098a1–3.
[13] *NE* I 7, 1097b6–11; IX 9, 1169b18–19.

view naturally opens into a perspective every bit as external to practicality itself as the perspective of cosmic anthropology.

Whether we take good practice to be simply a resource for achieving
other goods or an end in itself, it poses a special kind of practical problem
because of the special way in which its reality is contingent and within
our power. It is not in our power as an external good is when close
enough for us to lay hands on it or when we have the legal right to use
it. "Possessing" good practical agency essentially depends on the would-be
possessor's commitment[14] to being a certain sort of person. Where others
are concerned, we can create conditions favoring such commitment, but
cannot inject the commitment itself. And since commitment is not an
external precondition but the core of good practical agency, the latter's
reality is contingent in a peculiar way. It is self-developing and self-
sustaining to the extent that commitment is present, and this fact, considered by itself, seems to place good agency in the class of things which
belong necessarily to their subjects given that they belong at all. To the
extent that commitment to it is lacking, good agency cannot install itself
any more than it can be installed from outside: which seems to place it in
the corresponding class of impossibilities. Since according to Aristotle we
begin neither as clear-cut haves nor as clear-cut have-nots in this respect,
but can develop in either direction,[15] the initial stages are critical, taking
us further and further away from alternative possibilities.[16] And since
individuals develop by absorbing the values of those around them, and
will pass them on in the same way, the self-propagating structure of good
and bad practice is found at the collective level too, in families and
communities.

There is plenty in these distinctively human facts to interest the cosmic
anthropologist, but in the *Nicomachean Ethics* Aristotle's interest is practical: he lays out the facts so as to educate moral educators in the fundamentals of their task. Perhaps as a moralist and educator Aristotle could
not afford to pause in puzzlement at the phenomena of human imper-
fection; but the anthropologist should surely wonder at some of them,
especially an anthropologist who, like Aristotle in his scientific studies,
operates under the assumption that "nature does nothing in vain."[17] For
instance, if we are essentially practical rational beings, how is it that
sometimes we fling ourselves into irrationality with such welcoming gusto
even in the teeth of its destructiveness? The Greek poets speak of Eros
and Ate sent by the gods, but experience knows that transports of lust or
rage do not always swoop upon us as if from outside. Often it is as if *we*
willfully release such forces, fueling them from within as though we find
ourselves in being consumed. Afterward we say: "I was not myself"; but

---

[14] Thus, Aristotle commonly uses "*spoudaios*" (literally: "serious") to mean "morally good."
[15] *NE* II 1, 1103a18–26.
[16] *NE* III 5, 1114a12–18.
[17] See, e.g., Aristotle, *Generation of Animals*, Book V, ch. 8, 788b21.

is it true? According to the Bible, "the imagination of man's heart is evil from his youth";[18] psychoanalysis has its own explanations; common sense talks of immaturity while acknowledging the need for an occasional vacation from responsibility. A suggestion which paves the way toward an Aristotelian response would be that what we seek when we kick over the traces of practical rationality is the taste of a fantasy *summum bonum*: a state of pure abandonment in the immunity of knowing that nothing else matters or even exists beyond some immediate enthralling object, whatever it may be.

We meet this human propensity with efforts to repress, contain, and sublimate. By themselves, though, such responses fail to come to terms with the fantasy *summum bonum*'s claim to *be* our *summum bonum*. The claim has power because it seems to ring true. Hence, various attempts have been made to take it seriously. In each case, the claim is acknowledged to represent an ideal of perfect fulfillment, and some form of approximation is recommended. One type of approach, emphasizing satisfaction rather than ecstasy, looks to raise the ratio of the individual's fulfilled to unfulfilled desires. This can be done either by keeping desires constant and finding surer ways of implementation, or by leaving the facts as they are and adjusting desires to whatever is at hand.

But an Aristotelian response would not follow either of these routes. Instead, it would begin by figuring out what sort of being one would have to be to live in perfect fulfillment. It would see that one would have to be independent of the mercy of circumstance. No needs could distract one, so one's only need (if so it can be called) would be for the fulfilling activity. One would not be beholden to a physical or social environment, but would constitute one's own company, one's own sustenance and instrumentation. One would be immortal, because one's activity could not fail unless the very love of life were to fail from within, which seems incompatible with perfect fulfillment. Fulfillment for such a being must consist in an activity suitable to its nature: an activity, therefore, that is endlessly interesting and perfectly self-contained. What has just been described is the life of a god, according to Aristotle's understanding.

Thus, if humans need sometimes to escape from practicality, not in order to fall asleep but because we crave positive engagement free from practical constraints, we have a model for the kind of activity in which it makes sense to seek liberation. The model is divine activity: free, self-sufficient, untouched by anything external. It hardly seems to matter for this argument whether we suppose this paradigm to be something real or only conceptual. Either way, Aristotle takes it seriously in practice when he fashions his famous defense of human theoretical reasoning ("contemplation"), arguing that we are at our most godlike in this purely intellectual activity, which shapes itself from within and seeks no satisfaction

---

[18] Genesis 8:21.

beyond itself.[19] Against those who caution mortals not to aspire beyond their mortal level, Aristotle encourages us to "act immortal" so far as our lives permit.[20] In this, he—and we, if we resonate to these intimations— have gone some way toward acknowledging the claim of what above was termed "the fantasy *summum bonum.*"

We are thereby led to recognize intellectual, or spiritual, or imaginative, activity for its own sake as *a* fundamental human good. A much more careful argument would be needed to support the position that such activity should be accorded the status of *highest* human good. In any case, this essay has yet to consider what a claim of this stronger form would mean. But the weaker conclusion is not necessarily less significant for anthropology and for education.

In the light of what has emerged so far, Aristotle's contribution to ethics can be seen as a double corrective for ethical theorizing that centers on what was earlier labeled the "purely practical" point of view. Such an approach takes for granted our reality as practical beings and our commitment to whatever is to count as practical success. It considers what principles a rational decider should use; how they should be applied; how they can be justified; whether they can be defended as objectively valid or binding on everyone; whether principles of morality take precedence over other kinds of principle, and if so, why they do. These, along with questions about the principles of justice, are still frequently assumed to be definitive of the field of philosophical ethics. Yet in Aristotle's ethical thinking these problems are not in the forefront. On the contrary, *his* two great problems reflect fundamental limitations of the purely practical perspective. The latter depends for its existence, just as studies which assume it depend for their practical relevance, on a not automatically guaranteed supply of good practical agents: hence the problem of moral education. Nor can the perspective, or studies which assume it, begin to confront, as a question for ethics, the problem of what we should do with ourselves when not called upon to be practical.

III. What Is It for X to Be the *Summum Bonum?*

A. A utilitarian answer

The theory of utilitarianism has shaped the course of debate among Western moral philosophers for more than two hundred years. So it is natural for us to understand the question "What is the human *summum bonum?*" in the way in which John Stuart Mill seems to understand it in the opening pages of his monograph *Utilitarianism.* Mill takes the question to expect an answer specifying *the good which we should strive above all*

---

[19] *NE* X 6–8; *Metaphysics* I 2; *Protrepticus* B 23–28 (Düring).
[20] *NE* X 7, 1177b31–34.

to realize, and he assumes that specifying this is the same as specifying *"the criterion of right and wrong,"* which he also calls "the foundation of morality." Thus, he writes:

> From the dawn of philosophy, the question concerning the *summum bonum*, or, what is the same thing, concerning the foundation of morality, has been accounted the main problem in speculative thought, has occupied the most gifted intellects, and divided them into sects and schools, carrying on a vigorous warfare against one another. And after more than two thousand years the same discussions continue. . . .[21]

This passage suggests a certain conception of what it is for X to figure as the *summum bonum*. It is for X to be one's ultimate objective, providing a universal rule for deciding what to do, namely: Strive to realize X.[22]

Is this conception Aristotelian? Before trying to answer, we should note that if (with Mill and Aristotle) one accepts that there is (in a practical sense) such a thing as the *summum bonum*, and further accepts the formal conception just outlined, one will be pulled (irresistibly, is another question) in the direction of the distinctively utilitarian substantial characterization of the *summum bonum* as general happiness or welfare, or the happiness/welfare "of the greatest number," however this is interpreted. Or rather, one will feel the pull if, like Aristotle and Mill, one has a good measure of respect for the ordinary moral consciousness; and one will not feel it if, flouting the latter, one believes that one's own happiness should be the one overriding goal, or that each individual's happiness should be the one goal for him or her. If there really is just one universal rule for me to follow in deciding what to do, and it is a rule referring to happiness or well-being (rather than to rationality as such, as with Kant), then unless I am an ethical egoist it will have to be a rule that refers to the happiness or well-being of a field of persons: my group, or all those whom my action might affect. For although this carries some paradoxical consequences for common sense, the package is less odious than the egoist alternative. Thus, the utilitarian *summum bonum* is a good which consists in a suitably extensive interpersonal multiplication of some other good such as well-being or happiness. But as we shall see, Aristotle does not think of the *summum bonum* as multiple in this way. In the light of the reasoning just given, this is evidence of his not sharing the formal conception of the *summum bonum* suggested by the above quotation from Mill's *Utilitarianism*.

[21] J. S. Mill, "Utilitarianism," in *Mill's Ethical Writings*, ed. J. B. Schneewind (New York: Macmillan, 1965), pp. 75–76.

[22] It is not clear whether Mill in fact takes this to be the formal meaning of *"summum bonum,"* or whether he even considers the question of the formal meaning.

Turning now directly to Aristotle, we must distinguish two levels of practical thinking: (1) that of the "statesman"[23] (*politikos*), whose chief task, in Aristotle's view, is to set and preserve values and principles, and shape accordingly the lives of those for whom he or she is responsible; and (2) that of the "individual" whose life is so shaped. It is a difference of roles, not persons. A statesman is an individual simultaneously, and in political constitutions where offices rotate, leaders revert to being mere individuals. For Aristotle, the paradigmatic statesman is, of course, the political leader, but the obligation to engage in the kind of thinking (*politikê*) that typifies the statesman is not confined to those who occupy or expect to occupy political office. The thinking in question may be described as "fundamental policymaking." It involves not only ethical reflection but planning in accordance with the values endorsed. Thus, the head of a family is or should be a "statesman" in relation to those under his or her responsibility, and every free adult should keep a statesmanly eye on his or her own life. The "individual," by contrast, is the person regarded as actually living out the detail of the life thus planned.

I turn now to the question whether Aristotle conceives of the *summum bonum* as *that which one should strive above all to realize*. If the question is posed with reference to the statesman, the answer turns out to be "No, but . . ." In other words, an affirmative answer would not be wholly misleading. Insofar as "Yes" implies or suggests that, according to Aristotle, the agent (on this level, the statesman) should make every decision with a view to realizing the *summum bonum*, "Yes" conveys the truth. But it also carries the false implication that the Aristotelian *summum bonum* owes its status as such to the way in which it figures in the good statesman's decision-making. If, on the other hand, the question is posed with reference to the individual, the answer is a definite "No." Not only is the affirmative false itself, but so is its implication that the individual ought to make every decision with a view to realizing the *summum bonum*.

So far, these are only summary conclusions. For clarification, let us turn first to Book I, chapter 2 of the *Nicomachean Ethics*, where Aristotle speaks of the *summum bonum* as the "goal (*telos*) of what we do, which we desire for its own sake, everything else being desired for the sake of it."[24] Within a few lines it becomes apparent that this is the goal of ideal statesmanship, the architectonic expertise which regulates the other goods in life in order to promote the *summum bonum*.[25] The philosopher's task is to explain the latter's nature so that statesmanship may aim at its target more effectively.[26] Just such a view of the philosopher's task would be taken "after more than two thousand years" by Jeremy Bentham, the founder of

---

[23] This word and its clumsy adjectives are high-flown and sexist, but less misleading than the alternative, "politician" and its cognates.

[24] *NE* I 2, 1094a18–19.

[25] *NE* I 2, 1094a26–b11; I 13, 1102a5–10.

[26] *NE* I 2, 1094a22–24.

utilitarianism, and by J. S. Mill.[27] But there is a crucial difference. Immediately after declaring the *summum bonum* to be the goal of statesmanship, Aristotle speaks of it as "the same, whether it is for a single individual or for a *polis* (city-state)." He then concedes that realizing it over a wide field (the wider, the better; it might even consist of many *poleis* or the whole Hellenic world) is "greater and more ideal," and "nobler and more god-like," although bringing it about for one person is not at all to be despised.[28] This tells us that the definitive goal of Aristotelian statesmanship is not a suitably extended interpersonal maximum of some given sort of good, but is itself a good of some sort which may be widely or narrowly realized. Statesmanship stands to its goal as the art of medicine stands to *its* goal, health. Medical knowledge does not dictate whom to heal or how many (except in the special case where patients reinfect one another unless all are treated); and the same is true of statesmanship. According to this system of concepts, the superiority of the *summum bonum* to all other goods is grounded on its nature (which has not yet been explained), not on its being the most extensive occurrence of a good which might also occur less extensively. Moreover, "Realize the *summum bonum*" is the rule governing the Aristotelian statesman's actions as such; but it is not *qua* statesman in Aristotle's sense that the practitioner undertakes to operate on a larger or smaller scale. Who and how many should constitute the field of operation depends on the practitioner's circumstances *as an individual*. (Thus, it is to the statesman or would-be statesman as *individual* that Aristotle addresses the comment that it is greater and more ideal, etc., to realize the *summum bonum* for many than for one.)

The fact that, in Aristotle's view, the *summum bonum* is the defining goal of statesmanship may lead one to think that, for Aristotle, this is what it is for X to be the *summum bonum*: it is for X to figure as the goal of the statesman as such. But the conclusion does not follow. Moreover, it denies Aristotle a reasonable explanation for why the statesman should seek to promote whatever it is that the *summum bonum* will turn out to be. Surely it is *because* X is the *summum bonum* that promoting X is the special responsibility of those with the power or expertise for managing the ordinary or well-known goods. But if so, to say that X is the *summum bonum* is to say something more than: "X is the goal that should govern the statesman's every action."

Let us now turn to what it is that the Aristotelian statesman tries to realize. Here we move to the other level of practical thinking, that of the "individual." For the statesman cannot directly produce the end of statecraft, because it consists in the happiness (*eudaimonia*) of those for whom he or she is responsible, and Aristotelian happiness, we are told, is "the

---

[27] Witness the title of Bentham's seminal *An Introduction to the Principles of Morals and Legislation* (1789). Mill, too, addressed policymakers and individuals, without distinction.
[28] *NE* I 2, 1094b7–10.

activity of excellence in a complete life."[29] "Excellence" here means that of a human being as such, considered not as a biological system but as rational and practical. Aristotle recognizes many excellences of *character* (also known as the "moral excellences"), as, for example, courage, good temper, highmindedness, justice; and he also recognizes two great excellences of *intellect*, namely, practical wisdom and theoretic cultivation. "Complete" implies a life of reasonable span, adequately blessed with health, material goods, the respect of others, friends, a satisfactory family, enjoyable pursuits, and perhaps other things that people generally regard as desirable. The statesman cannot directly produce an individual's happiness in the way in which a potter can produce a pot for someone, because several of the goods constituting Aristotelian happiness are or involve *activities* which (like the commitment spoken of earlier, in Section II) depend for their existence on the individual's participation. The statesman can do no more than create conditions for happiness.

Now we must ask: According to Aristotle, does the *summum bonum* enter into the life of the individual in the same way as it enters into the life of the statesman, that is, by being what the individual should essentially aim to bring about in as many lives as he or she happens to be responsible for in some measure? The answer depends on how Aristotle understands the individual's practical activity. Since this activity, issuing from practical excellence, is a major component of the complex good which is happiness and the *summum bonum*, our question collapses into the following: Insofar as happiness consists in the individual's practical activity of excellence, and insofar as the statesman's defining goal is to promote happiness, is it the statesman's defining task, according to Aristotle, to promote good *statesmanly* activity on the part of individuals? If so, then Aristotle must hold that the individual's practical activity of excellence is entirely structured by decisions governed by the one great principle of statecraft, interpreted as the philosophically enlightened statesman interprets it.

This is clearly not Aristotle's view, however. Promoting conditions for happiness, one's own and the happiness of those around one, is obviously an important concern for the person of practical excellence (who should also have a sound grasp of what in fact counts toward happiness in a given situation). But Aristotle does not present this as the person's one paramount goal.[30] Far from portraying the wise individual as acting always in accordance with a single rule, Aristotle warns his readers not to expect absolutely firm rules of practice.[31] (The person of practical excellence is always concerned to make good decisions, but "Make a good [or the right] decision" is not a rule that can help determine what a wise

---

[29] *NE* I 7, 1098a16–18.

[30] For a detailed interpretation, see Sarah Broadie, *Ethics with Aristotle* (New York: Oxford University Press, 1991), pp. 198–202.

[31] *NE* II 2, 1104a1–10.

decision would be.) Aristotle's discussions of the various excellences point in the same direction. The just person acts from considerations of fairness, which is determined by reference to desert and proportionality.[32] Promoting the conditions for happiness is not, as such, a mark of the just action. The courageous individual faces necessary danger in battle simply because it is his duty and anything else would be shameful.[33] (By contrast, statesmanship—in abeyance in the thick of the battle—should be able to justify the decision to go to war, by reference to the *summum bonum*.) There is no suggestion that the person of "tasteful wit" (*eutrapelia*, one of the Aristotelian virtues of character) enlivens conversation with pleasantries crafted with a view to promoting the conditions for happiness.[34] Again, in discussing practical wisdom Aristotle says that while practical wisdom perceives the means, excellence of character is what "makes the end right."[35] But excellence of character develops through upbringing and good conduct, not through philosophizing.[36] Statesmanship, by contrast, depends on philosophy to elucidate its goal.[37] If individual practical excellence is defined by aiming at happiness in the way in which good statesmanship is, then either the good statesman (presumably also an excellent individual) does not need Aristotle's ethical system to help "make the end right," or mere excellence of character is not, after all, sufficient for this function in the case of the individual. Either way, Aristotle's teaching is inconsistent.

B. An Aristotelian answer

The following results have just been reached: (a) if X is the *summum bonum*, then "Realize X" is the rule governing the Aristotelian statesman's every decision; but (b) this is not what it is for X to be the *summum bonum*; and (c) no such rule governs the good individual's every practical response. From this, a question arises. On the level of the statesman, we can see the relation of X to the other goods: it is the end to be achieved by managing them with a view to precisely that. But how does X stand in relation to the other goods in the life of the individual? And how does it enter into and (so to speak) affect that life if not by figuring as the end to be sought in all one's practical decision-making? To answer this is to answer our main question: (In the context of Aristotle's ethics) what is it for X to be the *summum bonum*? This is because the statesman seeks to craft the *summum bonum* not for himself, the statesman, as such, but for

---

[32] *NE* V 3–5.
[33] *NE* III 7, 1115b11–12; 8, 1116b2–3.
[34] *NE* IV 8.
[35] *NE* VI 13, 1145a4–6; cf. *NE* VI 12, 1144a6–9, 20–22, 31–36.
[36] *NE* II 4, 1105b9–18; X 9, 1179a36–b34.
[37] *NE* I 2, 1094a22–25.

the individual. The individual, in other words, is the locus of the Aristotelian *summum bonum*. Consequently, the relation of X to the other goods
in the life of the individual is the relation to them which constitutes X the
summum bonum.

According to Aristotle's understanding, for X to be the *summum bonum*
is for it to be "the principle and the cause of the [other] goods."[38] This is
not to be taken as implying that the *summum bonum*, whatever it is, causes
the existence of goods such as health and wealth and friendly connections, thereby doing duty for the ordinary causes of these things, such as
exercise, prudent management of resources, and willingness to cooperate.
The meaning, rather, is that the relation to the other goods which constitutes X *summum* is that of rendering them good and worth having, and
therefore worthy of past efforts to obtain and present concerns to preserve. (All this is on the level of the individual.) Now, although Aristotle
notes it as a point in favor of his own position that everyone speaks of
happiness as the highest good, *his* reason for accepting this identification
is somewhat esoteric. It is that once we understand happiness for what it
is—that is, once we understand it as activity of excellence in a complete
life—we see why happiness is the *summum bonum*. It is because activity of
excellence in relation to the various elements contributing to completeness of life is what makes those objects worth having.

Asked, "What is the highest good?" a person might answer: "Pleasure,"
or: "Love and friendship." It would be one kind of mistake to maintain
this seriously without qualification; some pleasures, some kinds of love
and friendship, are destructive, degrading, corrupting, etc. Faced with
plausible examples, the respondent might agree. In that case his or her
natural next move would be to modify the original claim to (for example):
"The highest good is *worthwhile* love and friendship." But a philosopher
would see this as embodying another mistake: the failure to grasp what
is at issue in claiming so-and-so to be the highest good. Perhaps the
respondent means: "It is what everyone should value most." It might
even be correct to say this of worthwhile love and friendship. But even if
so, worthwhile love and friendship cannot be the *summum bonum* according to the philosopher's understanding. If some forms of love and friendship are worthwhile, it is because of something about them over and
above the features that bring them under a general definition of love and
friendship. This something else is what makes good love and friendship
good; they do not make themselves so. Hence, the something else, not
they, performs the role of *summum bonum*. This argument can be generalized to show that the *summum bonum*, whatever it is, cannot be a good
form of something of which bad forms are also possible. Activity of

---

[38] *NE* I 12, 1102a2–4; cf. *NE* I 4, 1095a26–28 (reporting a position which Aristotle does not
reject although he rejects the Platonist interpretation of it; see *EE* I 8, especially 1218b7–14).

excellence in a complete life fills the bill (as does activity of excellence *tout court*). This cannot take bad forms; hence, it is superfluous to call any of its forms good.

The idea, then, is that activity of excellence in relation to the elements of a complete life, whether severally or together, is what makes those so-called advantages worth having. I say "so-called," because, although everyone wants them and acts and feels about them as if they are worth having and would contribute to happiness, outside the context of actual or assured activity of excellence, they are, at most, conditional promises of advantage. Activity of excellence, actual or assured, discharges the condition. It provides, as it were, a field—we could call it the "eudaimonic field"—in which those items take on the substantiality of goodness and count as ingredients of genuine happiness.[39]

But how does this come about? The point for which we now seek explanation is summed up in Aristotle's doctrine that "the good man [i.e., the person of excellence] is the measuring rod in matters of value."[40] This is by contrast with those of the opposite stamp. They, it turns out, are mistaken in valuing the things which everyone wants; or more precisely: they are mistaken in thinking those things worth having, when their own having them is meant. Certainly they think that if they pursue something as worth having (why else pursue it?), the thing is not going to lose its value once they have it. Otherwise they would not be better off then, as of course they think they will be. But will they? Go to the person of excellence. He or she contemplates the activities of one who does not merely fall short (the contemplator, too, may be less than perfect) but is facing in this or that wrong direction for developing excellence. In the eyes of the contemplator, the other's life is not desirable. The contemplator would not (even could not) live that way on any terms. Now suppose this contemplated agent is seen as achieving some of the usual desiderata, or as possessing them perhaps to an exceptional degree, or as operating through or about them to his or her pleasure or satisfaction. We ask the person of excellence: "Is that life now more desirable because of the feature which has just appeared?" If the latter wavers, we press: "Would *you* want that success or satisfaction on those terms—i.e., as part of a life like that?" The predictable negative answer implies that, according to the person of excellence, the contemplated life is not more desirable when it includes the usual desiderata than when it lacks them. Thus, according to the person of excellence, the one who lives that life is no better off with them than without them. For how could one *be better off* with X, yet *live no better* having X than not? So according to the person of excellence (who is a true measure), the usual desiderata are worthless insofar as they

---

[39] Cf. *EE* VIII 3, 1248b26ff.: "The good person is one for whom the natural goods are good." For a fuller development of the theme, see Plato, *Euthydemus*, 280b–282e.

[40] *NE* III 4, 1113a25–33.

relate to the contemplated agent as constituents, actual or possible, of *such an* agent's life.[41]

But does the negative judgment passed by the person of excellence somehow make it the case that the other life and the goods in it are worthless? Does the person of excellence rule this fact into being? One can see how Aristotle would reply to this, even though it is not easy for us to see how we could get back to the point—if we even wanted to—from which it would also be our considered reply as philosophers. Aristotle would say: "The person of excellence judges as he does because of what he sees about the other's life. He sees confusion of values: means being prized as if they were ends, ends precious in themselves exploited as means. He sees opportunities for good being missed through failure to understand the kind of good they are opportunities for—hence, in relation to this agent, they were never really opportunities. Since an opportunity for good is itself, as such, a category of good,[42] here we have an example of how the agent's personality cancels the value (so far as he himself is concerned) of a good which is present in his life. The person of excellence sees all this in the *activities* of the agent contemplated. He sees them as they are. *What* he sees is what leads him to form his judgment, and what he sees makes that judgment true. Thus, the so-called good things in the contemplated life are not worthless because the person of excellence thinks so. They are made worthless by the activity—its character and limitations—of the agent concerned. By contrast, an agent of opposite character makes worthwhile the goods in his life by acting about them in appropriate ways."

Obviously there can be no ground for congratulating a person on reaching some desired objective, or on a piece of good fortune, if he or she is in fact no better off. The same applies to self-congratulation or disappointment when one fares badly. If each is the final judge of his own worth, then the truth in these matters is as each sees it; getting what one wants is success and brings one closer to happiness. But if we can be blind to our human failings (the alternatives to blindness being: [1] we are free of such failings, and [2] we have them in full awareness of them and their nature as *failings*), then one who is blind in this way, yet cares about having the things which everyone finds desirable, lives in a dream. In reality, according to the present metaphysic of morals, there is for this agent no practical difference between failure and success in obtaining or keeping those things. I cannot lose an advantage the gaining of which would have brought no benefit to the person living *my* life. Disappoint-

---

[41] It is to be emphasized that this is intended as an analysis of what is implied by judging another to be of a character such that one would not be him no matter what advantages (as usually understood) might be attached. It is a further question whether such an undiluted attitude exists or should exist, even in the "good person."

[42] *NE* I 6, 1096a23–33.

ment and satisfaction at how things go for me presuppose my worth, actually or probably expressing itself in activity of excellence. For beings such as us, essentially practical, it is a chilling possibility that instead of its mattering how things turn out for us, we operate unknown to ourselves in a dark where success and failure are the same, ourselves rendering our efforts pointless at source. Nor, for such beings, could there be any more pressing necessity than that of ensuring the truth, more or less, of the practical assumption of our own worth which all our projects imply.

On this account, the *summum bonum*, so far as it consists in activity of excellence, is not primarily a good whose conditions we ought to act in order to secure. To the extent that it is true that we ought to act in order to secure it (different extents for individual and statesman), this truth follows from the more fundamental fact that the *summum bonum*, so far as it consists in activity of excellence, is the *sine qua non* of its mattering whether we secure anything else at all.

IV. Is the *Summum Bonum* No More Than Activity of Excellence?

In using the expression "the *summum bonum*, so far as it consists in activity of excellence," we seem on the brink of treating activity of excellence as identical with Aristotle's *summum bonum*. It is true that activity of excellence becomes happiness in the presence of the other elements (the ones making up a complete life), while they in turn, if sufficiently provided, become happiness in the presence of *it*. But these contributions to happiness are not symmetrical. Activity of excellence contributes by being already, from its own nature, unconditionally good. That is why it can make the otherwise valueless others good, rendering them constituents of a way of being which is properly called "happiness."

Activity of excellence, then, is a good not itself made good by happiness; it is prior to happiness and more fundamental. In view of this priority, as well as the fact that activity of excellence plays the principal role in the constitution of happiness (figuring as the metaphysical "agent" of good in relation to the "passive" other elements), one may be tempted to conclude that the *summum bonum* is activity of excellence *tout court*. This conclusion seems reinforced by the fact that Aristotle would certainly not want to say that goods which support activity of excellence even when there is no hope of its becoming happiness (through lack of some important component of the complete life) are therefore not worth having. Activity of excellence as such is good-making. Is *it*, then, rather than happiness, the *summum bonum*? Or is it identical with happiness? Neither alternative represents Aristotle's view. He not only repeatedly refers to the *summum bonum* as "happiness," but rejects any general identification of happiness with activity of excellence.[43] A happy individual, he says, is not "dislodged" from happiness except by major misfortune: but it can happen, and unless the person is killed or disabled, he or she continues in activities of excellence, making the best of harsh circumstances.[44]

Two points are relevant here. Firstly, Aristotle's ultimate paradigm of happiness is god. It might seem out of place to speak of the divine activity as "excellent," as if to exclude an alternative possibility. But, at any rate, since it is perfectly self-sufficient, happiness necessarily coincides with activity in this limiting case. Secondly, on the human level there is qualitative continuity between merely excellent activity, and happy activity, since the former, even at its most austere, depends on some measure of the other goods. One cannot exercise excellences such as temperance and justice except in relation to goods such as food and fellow-citizens.[45] And one must have the necessities of life to act at all. (Hence, there are, presumably, degrees of happiness. A person might lack one of the important elements of a complete life—for example, if he were blind—yet still count as happy rather than not.)[46] But the two points may pull in opposite directions if either is made a ground for identifying human happiness with human excellent activity *tout court*. The comparison with god could be drawn so as to suggest that humans are happiest when their excellent activity involves the minimum of other goods. (But what if one would welcome more of them? If so, one's dissatisfaction with the status quo would have to be interpreted as failure to recognize or fully appreciate one's happiness.) By contrast, the second point suggests the argument: mere excellent activity differs from conspicuous happiness only by degrees; so the former is happiness too. But since the degrees increase with the amount or number of other goods present (up to the point of superfluity), this argument indicates that our happiness is greater the less its structure approximates god's by minimal dependence on factors other than excellent activity.

The main difficulty of equating the *summum bonum* with activity of excellence *tout court* is that, on these terms, no one can reasonably want a good whose absence does not hamper his or her excellent activity, but whose presence would make it easier, say, or more enjoyable. For if the presence of the thing is superfluous so far as the subject's actual engagement in excellent activity is concerned, the thing is not part of his or her happiness, and should count as not worth having. Some philosophers

---

[43] This seems clear notwithstanding Richard Kraut's arguments to the contrary in his *Aristotle on the Human Good* (Princeton: Princeton University Press, 1989).

[44] *NE* I 10, 1100b22–1101a11.

[45] *NE* X 8, 1178a28–33.

[46] The example is from Gavin Lawrence, "Nonaggregatability, Inclusiveness, and the Theory of Focal Value: *Nicomachean Ethics* I.7. 1097b16–20," *Phronesis*, vol. 42, no. 1 (1997), pp. 32ff.

have defended the equation, even accepting the paradoxical conclusion just drawn, but Aristotle is not among them. Again, it would be strange to argue (if anyone has) that a person actively excellent but living in poverty should welcome improved circumstances not because prosperity contributes to one's happiness, but because it makes one more satisfied with the happiness one already exemplifies! If contentment is necessary for happiness, the argument falls short of showing that even the pauper's activity of excellence should count as happiness; and if it is not, the right-minded pauper has no business seeking to become less needy. But according to Aristotle, if in fact such a pauper wishes for, hopes for, tries for, welcomes improvement of his condition, these attitudes are entirely appropriate as attitudes of *this* person toward *this* person's situation and prospects, for (as before) in matters of value "the good man is the measure."

Obviously, difficult circumstances can make the activity of excellence harder for the subject. But that does not necessarily render it shorter or less frequent. Hardship stimulates greater activity of excellence in those who can rise to the challenge. Should they then embrace the hardship? One can hardly say "Yes," since this concession implies that one who looks back on an episode in which he rightly (as he believed then and still believes) refused under torture to betray his country's secrets, should, if he has proper values, treasure the event as an episode of *happiness* (and should wish happiness for those he loves?). Alternatively, it might be argued that the actively excellent person has reason to welcome better circumstances (as we normally call them) in that now he or she can be actively excellent in more contexts or bring more excellences into play. Certainly, this may be one's reason (and if so, surely a good one) for preferring to be free of hardship or privation. It is not the only good reason, however. Over and above that sort of reason for looking forward to having his sight again, the cataract patient looks forward to the pleasure of seeing well, of exercising the faculty of vision. This natural faculty is not an "excellence" in the sense relevant for Aristotle's ethics. The activity of vision is desirable per se as well as for facilitating other activities, including activities of excellence.[47] But it is not desirable per se because it is an activity of excellence itself. How do we know that it is desirable per se? We know from the fact that the good person, like everyone else, values it for what it is.

All practical activities aim to produce an ulterior result, but there is an important distinction which Aristotle might have said more to emphasize. In one sort of case, we aim to produce a result mainly as a basis for further activity of the same kind—for instance, farming, which is a way of life. In the other kind of case, the desired result will displace the circumstances which made the original activity necessary or possible—

---

[47] *NE* I 6, 1096b17–19; *Metaphysics* I 1, 980a20–28.

for instance, fighting a war for the sake of peace with security.[48] In times of peace, gentler excellences should come into play, upstaging those that show themselves most in times of crisis and austerity. No doubt peacetime offers more choices, but it would be difficult to make the case that the excellent activities of peace are necessarily more numerous or open to more individuals, or show greater or more various excellence, than their wartime counterparts. The rational desire for peace on the right terms is not grounded on the prospect of more, or more excellent, excellent activity, but on the distinct prospect of a happier way of life. The difference is made by such factors as freedom from fear, and from stress, privation, and hardship. Activity of excellence carried on under such conditions is more desirable than activity of excellence carried on in their absence—because of the character of the conditions themselves, not because they add to the sum of excellent activity. That they add to it is, as a general claim, much less obvious than that peace is preferable to war. It is preferable because of the independent natures of war and peace themselves. These independent natures do not, of course, make peace unconditionally more desirable than war. It still remains true that in the absence of suitable activities of excellence, peace will not have been worth fighting for.

Happiness, then, differs from activity of excellence. Each is an unconditional good that makes good the elements necessary for it. But happiness is unique in making good the objects necessary for activity of excellence *and other* objects universally desired.

V. In Conclusion

Finally, I want to offer two concluding reflections, one practical, one metaphysical.

1. It is a particularly important task of statesmanship, in changing times, to prepare individuals to switch into newly appropriate modes of excellent activity. The point about war and peace is good in itself, but Aristotle also brings it forward as an analogy for business and leisure.[49] Our natural desire for leisure will turn out to have been for something pointless to attain unless we are morally and intellectually equipped to employ it in suitable activities of excellence. Suitable activity, Aristotle argues, would be the kind of activity it makes most sense to ascribe to beings beyond the need of the special conditions that make leisure a human possibility. Aristotle recommends such activity precisely because it is godlike[50] (even more so, he thinks, than beneficent statesmanship on a grand scale). But the recommendation need not depend on theological

---

[48] *NE* X 7, 1177b4–12.

[49] See the previous note; see also Aristotle, *Politics*, Book VII, ch. 14, 1333a30–b11, and Book VIII, ch. 3, 1337b29–1338a13.

[50] *NE* X 7, 1177b19–34; 8, 1178b21–23.

assumptions or on Aristotle's conception of divinity. Leisure is a time for forgetting what had to be done to procure it, and for doing something quite different. In leisure, we act as if the infrastructure has nothing to do with us. It is not unreasonable, then, to choose leisure activities approximating those of absolutely free beings, whether or not such beings exist or are properly reckoned divine. In any case, worthwhile leisure activity is one way of instantiating the *summum bonum*. Engaged in it, we make the other goods worth having: both leisure itself, and the economic and social resources on which it depends.

2. It remains to respond to the metaphysical impulse that identifies the *summum bonum* with activity of excellence *tout court* on the ground that activity of excellence plays the leading part in the constitution of happiness. One response gives in to the impulse, respects Aristotle's equation of *summum bonum* with happiness, and consequently identifies happiness with activity of excellence. We have seen the difficulties of that. Another response would be to give in to the impulse, distinguish happiness and activity of excellence, and conclude *pace* Aristotle that happiness is not the Aristotelian *summum bonum*. But the impulse is not well founded. The unconditional good which is activity of excellence is prior to the good which is happiness. Because of this priority, activity of excellence *can* give worth to other things generally desired, and *would* give them worth *given that* they are available. But the prior good is not, because prior, the *summum bonum*, if the *summum bonum* is the good that *gives* worth to any of the usual desiderata, including those not necessary for unadorned activity of excellence. Activity of excellence needs more than its status as the prior (indeed, primary) good if it is actually to *make* the other things worth having and getting. The additional condition is that they, too, be at hand. If they are on the scene or in the wings, and if activity of excellence is present or assured, we either have or are set to have all the components of happiness together: the eudaimonic activity, and the items on which it can "act." This sounds like Aristotle's compact formula: "Activity of excellence in a complete life." But perhaps it would be better to think of the *summum bonum* not as happiness, the metaphysical product, but as activity of excellence in the act of *transforming itself into happiness* by taking advantage of available elements which can exist without it and without which it too can exist.

Philosophy, Princeton University

EUDAIMONISM, LOVE AND FRIENDSHIP, AND POLITICAL COMMUNITY*

By David O. Brink

I. Introduction

It is common to regard love, friendship, and other associational ties to others as an important part of a happy or flourishing life. This would be easy enough to understand if we focused on friendships based on pleasure, or associations, such as business partnerships, predicated on mutual advantage. For then we could understand in a straightforward way how these interpersonal relationships would be valuable for someone involved in such relationships just insofar as they caused her pleasure or causally promoted her own independent interests. But many who regard love, friendship, and other associational ties as an important part of a happy or flourishing life suppose that in many sorts of associations—especially intimate associations—the proper attitude among associates is concern for the other *for the other's own sake*, not just for the pleasure or benefits one can extract from one's associates. It is fairly clear how *having* friends of this sort is beneficial. What is less clear is how *being* a friend of this sort might contribute to one's own happiness or well-being. Even if we can explain this, it looks as if the contribution that friendship makes to one's happiness could not be the reason one has to care for friends, for that would seem to make one's concern for others instrumental, not a concern for the other for her own sake.

I would like to explore these issues about the role of love and friendship in a happy or flourishing life by examining and assessing themes in certain classical views of love and friendship, especially the views of Socrates, Plato, and Aristotle. In contrast with the comparatively minor role given to issues about love and friendship in many other traditions in the history of ethics and in contemporary moral philosophy, love and friendship play a prominent role in Greek ethical theory. Moreover, the Greeks, especially Socrates, Plato, and Aristotle, all recognize the contribution that love and friendship make to the lover's or friend's *eudaimonia*

* For helpful discussion of issues addressed in this essay, I would like to thank Georgios Anagnostopoulos, Julia Annas, Richard Arneson, Alan Code, Kathleen Cook, Stephen Darwall, Tim Hinton, Don Hubin, Thomas Hurka, Diane Jeske, Richard Kraut, Fred D. Miller, Jr., Allan Silverman, Steven Yalowitz, the other contributors to this volume, and its editors, as well as participants at the "Democracy and Self-Interest" conference at California State University at Fullerton in March 1998, and audiences at Ohio State University and Simon Fraser University. Work on this essay was supported by a President's Research Fellowship in the Humanities from the University of California.

or happiness, as they must if they are to respect the eudaimonist assumption that runs throughout (nearly all of) Greek ethics, according to which an agent's practical deliberations ought to be regulated by a correct conception of his own *eudaimonia*.

In exploring common themes in Greek views about love and friendship and their contribution to *eudaimonia*, I would like to focus on their ability to accommodate the common view that love and friendship involve concern for another for the other's own sake. As Gregory Vlastos rightly points out in his important essay "The Individual as Object of Love in Plato," accommodating intrinsic concern for another is an important test of adequacy for Greek conceptions of love and friendship.[1] This is a reasonable test for us to employ not just because intrinsic concern is part of modern conceptions of love and friendship but also because it is recognized in ancient conceptions as well. In discussing his own views about friendship in the *Nicomachean Ethics*, Aristotle makes concern for another for the other's own sake a defining feature of the best or most complete form of friendship:[2]

> Complete friendship is the friendship of good people similar in virtue. . . . Now those who wish goods to their friend for the friend's own sake are friends most of all; for they have this attitude because of the friend himself, not coincidentally. (1156b7–12)

Nor is this commitment to intrinsic concern for one's friends an idiosyncratic feature of Aristotle's own ethical theory. On this issue, as on many others, Aristotle sees himself as explaining and justifying common-sense commitments. In various places, he represents the common conception of friendship as involving concern for another for the other's own sake (1155b28–33, 1166a2–5). For instance, in the *Rhetoric* he defines friendliness in these terms:

> We may describe friendly feeling towards anyone as wishing for him what you believe to be good things, not for your own sake but for his, and being inclined, so far as you can, to bring these things about. (1380b35–1381a1; cf. 1361b35–37)[3]

[1] Gregory Vlastos, "The Individual as Object of Love in Plato," in his *Platonic Studies*, 2d ed. (Princeton: Princeton University Press, 1981).

[2] Though I treat the *Nicomachean Ethics* (*NE*) as my primary source for Aristotle's ethical views, I also rely on the *Eudemian Ethics* (*EE*) and the *Magna Moralia* (*MM*). In doing so, I assume that the *MM* is a useful source of information about Aristotle's ethical theory, even if Aristotle is not its author. Translations of passages from the *NE* are from *Nicomachean Ethics*, trans. Terence Irwin (Indianapolis: Hackett, 1985); translations of passages from other works by Aristotle are from the Revised Oxford Translation in *The Complete Works of Aristotle*, ed. Jonathan Barnes (Princeton: Princeton University Press, 1984).

[3] Whereas the previous passage from the *NE* requires only that A care about B for B's own sake, this passage from the *Rhetoric* requires that A care about B for B's own sake, *not* for A's sake. This contrast between intrinsic concern for another and self-concern is a familiar theme

These remarks suggest that the demand that an adequate account of love and friendship explain intrinsic concern for another is one that ancients, as well as moderns, have reason to take seriously.

One reason for focusing on this test of adequacy is that, as Vlastos argues, there are doubts about whether classical views of love and friendship can satisfy it. Though his focus is on Platonic conceptions of love and friendship, Vlastos discusses Socratic and Aristotelian conceptions as well. He credits Aristotle with explicitly recognizing the important truth that the best sort of friendship or love involves wishing another well for the other's own sake. Unfortunately, according to Vlastos, none of the classical views he considers can accommodate this truth. According to Vlastos, the Socratic view of love and friendship developed in Plato's *Lysis* cannot recognize concern for another for the other's own sake, because Socratic eudaimonism implies that the lover values the beloved only as an instrumental means to the lover's own happiness. The problem for the Platonic view of love represented in the *Phaedrus* and *Symposium*, Vlastos thinks, is different. The Platonic lover is concerned with making his beloved virtuous. This concern with the beloved's virtue, Vlastos thinks, is incompatible with caring about him for his own sake. Though Aristotle recognizes the requirement that the true lover love the beloved for his own sake, Aristotle's own account of love, Vlastos believes, is in essential respects Platonic; the lover's concern with the beloved's virtue, Vlastos thinks, prevents Aristotle from meeting his own demand that friends care about each other for the other's own sake.

Vlastos's discussion raises two main questions about the ability of classical views of love and friendship to accommodate intrinsic concern for another. One is the question of whether the lover's concern with the virtue of the beloved, emphasized by Plato and Aristotle, is compatible with concern for the beloved's own sake. The other question is whether eudaimonism is compatible with concern for others for their own sakes. Vlastos discusses this issue directly only in connection with Socrates, but the issue presumably arises for Plato and Aristotle insofar as they share Socrates' eudaimonism. My own view is that classical views of love and friendship—especially those of Plato and Aristotle—fare better than Vlastos supposes. Platonic and Aristotelian concern for the beloved's virtue is not only consistent with, but essential to, a concern for the beloved's own sake. Whereas Vlastos may be right about the difficulty Socrates faces in reconciling genuine friendship with his eudaimonism, Platonic and Aristotelian eudaimonism, by contrast, can recognize intrinsic concern for another.

---

in the *Rhetoric*'s reconstruction of common-sense thinking (cf. 1366a36–b6, 1367a4–6). It is not clear that the *Rhetoric*'s conception of selfless altruism can be reconciled with eudaimonism. However, it is significant that Vlastos typically understands the test of adequacy in terms of altruism, rather than selfless altruism, and that Aristotle rejects the popular contrast, articulated in the *Rhetoric*, between self-love and altruism (*NE* IX 8).

To defend Platonic and Aristotelian conceptions of love and friendship against this worry, however, is not to accept these conceptions without qualification. Platonic and Aristotelian conceptions of love and friendship do face difficulties, if not in their fundamentals, then in their application to issues about the appropriate form and scope of political association, especially in their application to Platonic and Aristotelian doubts about the nature and scope of democratic association. Associational bonds provide reason to value associates for their own sakes. Insofar as political activity is part of the good for rational animals, Platonic and Aristotelian conceptions of love and friendship arguably require fuller democratic commitments.

In arguing for these claims, I hope to explain the interest and appeal of Greek views about love and friendship, the contribution these relationships make to a good life, and the political significance of these relationships.[4] In order to pursue these issues as they arise in Socrates, Plato, and Aristotle, I must sometimes paint with rather broad strokes. Like Vlastos, I hope that pursuit of some common themes in classical views of love and friendship will compensate for the need to ignore or oversimplify certain interpretive issues.

II. Eudaimonism

Socratic, Platonic, and Aristotelian views of love and friendship all occur within a eudaimonist approach to ethics. Vlastos, in another context, describes eudaimonism this way:

> [T]he Eudaemonist Axiom . . . , once staked out by Socrates, becomes foundational for virtually all subsequent moralists of classical antiquity. This is that happiness is desired by all human beings as the ultimate end (*telos*) of all rational action.[5]

Socrates, Plato, and Aristotle are all eudaimonists; they think that an agent's practical reasoning should be regulated by a correct conception of

---

[4] My discussion of classical conceptions of love and friendship draws on parts of my discussion in "Self-Love and Altruism," *Social Philosophy and Policy*, vol. 14, no. 1 (1997), pp. 122–57; indeed, that article and this one have a common ancestry. There, I appeal to classical conceptions of love and friendship to help motivate a systematic conception of the rational authority of morality that attempts to reconcile other-regarding moral demands and self-interest by modeling interpersonal relations and concern on intrapersonal relations and concern. Here, I focus on the classical conceptions of love and friendship in their own right; I try to examine and assess their adequacy, in light of Vlastos's criticisms, in part by exploring their political implications.

[5] Gregory Vlastos, *Socrates: Ironist and Moral Philosopher* (Ithaca: Cornell University Press, 1991), p. 203. Cf. Terence Irwin, *Plato's Moral Theory* (Oxford: Clarendon Press, 1977), esp. pp. 51–54, 249–80; Irwin, "Aristippus against Happiness," *The Monist*, vol. 74 (1991), pp. 55–82; and Irwin, *Plato's Ethics* (New York: Oxford University Press, 1995), sections 36–37, 142.

his own happiness or *eudaimonia*. In Plato's early dialogues, Socrates is represented as a eudaimonist.[6] In the *Euthydemus*, Socrates assumes that we all aim at happiness (278e, 280b); the only issue is how to achieve it (279a, 282a). In the *Crito*, Socrates believes that his practical deliberations about whether to escape his death sentence should be guided only by whether that would be a just course of action (48c–d), because he thinks that a good life just is the life of justice (48b). In both the *Laches* and the *Charmides*, the investigations begin with the assumption that the virtues in question (courage and temperance) would improve and benefit young men if they were to acquire them. And at the end of the *Charmides*, Socrates assumes that if one has reason to be temperate it must be because temperance promotes the happiness of the person who has it (175d–176a). In later dialogues, Plato himself appears to accept eudaimonism. In response to doubts about justice in the *Republic*, he defends the claim that justice is a virtue, to be admired and practiced, by arguing that justice contributes constitutively to the *eudaimonia* of the agent who is just. And in the *Symposium*, Diotima takes the pursuit of one's own *eudaimonia* to be beyond the need for justification (205a). Aristotle, too, appears to be a eudaimonist. Though people have different conceptions of *eudaimonia*, he thinks we all treat *eudaimonia* as the final good (*NE* 1095a17–21). *Eudaimonia* is the only unconditionally complete good; all other things are choiceworthy for the sake of their contribution to *eudaimonia* (1097a27–b6). Aristotle makes clear in Book I of the *Nicomachean Ethics* that it is the agent's own *eudaimonia* that should regulate his practical reasoning. But this is also brought out later when Aristotle insists that one would rightly resist undergoing a substantial change, which one does not survive—for instance, one by which one was transformed into a god—even if this new being led a happier life (1159a6–12, 1166a1–23).

Eudaimonism implies that concern for one's friends or loved ones is justified just in case it contributes to the agent's own happiness. Whereas eudaimonism can explain instrumental concern for one's friends and loved ones, it is less clear how it can explain concern for them for their

---

[6] Plato's dialogues provide our most important evidence about the philosophical thought of Socrates. Though Socrates typically appears as the principal character in Plato's dialogues, the dialogues provide the basis for distinguishing between Socratic and Platonic thought. As is common, I divide Plato's dialogues into different periods or groups. I distinguish (1) early or Socratic dialogues, such as the *Apology, Crito, Euthyphro, Laches, Charmides, Euthydemus*, and *Lysis*; (2) transitional dialogues, such as the *Protagoras* and *Gorgias*; (3) middle Platonic dialogues, such as the *Meno, Phaedo, Republic, Symposium, Phaedrus, Parmenides*, and *Theaetetus*; and (4) later Platonic dialogues, such as the *Timaeus, Sophist, Statesman, Philebus*, and *Laws*. As is common, I treat Plato's early dialogues as a more or less accurate picture of Socrates' philosophical thought and the middle and late dialogues as representing mature Platonic thought. I regard the transitional dialogues as marking the emergence of Plato's own philosophical voice through reflection on the commitments in the Socratic dialogues. For other views of these matters, see Gregory Vlastos, "Socrates," *Proceedings of the British Academy*, vol. 74 (1988), pp. 89–111; Vlastos, *Socrates: Ironist and Moral Philosopher*, chs. 2–3, esp. pp. 45–47; and Irwin, *Plato's Ethics*, section 6.

own sakes. If friendship and love essentially involve such intrinsic concern, then it is not clear that the eudaimonist can defend genuine love and friendship. Though this is an issue that confronts all eudaimonists, it arises in an especially acute form for Socrates.

III. SOCRATIC FRIENDSHIP

Plato's *Lysis* is an early dialogue, representing Socratic thought, that is devoted to *philia*. Though *philia* can be and often is translated as "friendship," it includes intense and intimate relationships we would characterize as expressing love, such as parental love (207d).[7] As such, the *Lysis* is as much a discussion of love as of friendship. Socrates claims that love involves concern for the beloved's happiness (207d6–e5). But this concern for another is predicated on mutual benefit (214c). One who had a complete good would have no need of love or friendship; friendship can only exist between those who stand to gain from association with each other (215a–b). These claims fit nicely with Socrates' eudaimonism. For Socrates, however, such concern must be purely instrumental. Some things are chosen for the sake of something else, as when a patient chooses medicine for the sake of his health (219c1–2). But not all things can be chosen for the sake of something else; some things must be desired for their own sakes (219c1–d5). Only those things chosen or choiceworthy for their own sakes are good in themselves; those things valuable for the sake of something else, Socrates believes, are valuable only instrumentally:

> All such value as this [value in itself] is set not on those things that are procured for the sake of another thing, but on that for the sake of which all things are procured. . . . When we say we are friendly to things for the sake of a thing to which we are friendly, do we not clearly use a term with regard to them that belongs to another? And do we not appear to be in reality friendly only with that in which all these so-called friendships terminate? (219e8–220b1)[8]

Socrates believes that the lover values his beloved for the lover's own *eudaimonia*, as Socrates must if he is to reconcile friendship with his eudaimonism. It follows that a lover can love his beloved only instrumen-

---

[7] Hence, Vlastos writes: " 'Love' is the only English word that is robust and versatile enough to cover [*philia*]" ("The Individual as Object of Love," p. 4). Whereas Vlastos is surely right that *philia* includes intimate associations that we might more readily characterize as love than as friendship, it also includes less intimate associations that we might more readily characterize as friendship than as love. Hence, I am not sure that 'love' is versatile enough to do the job by itself.

[8] This translation from the *Lysis* is by J. Wright in *The Collected Dialogues of Plato*, ed. Edith Hamilton and Huntington Cairns (Princeton: Princeton University Press, 1961). Here Socrates is making perfectly general claims about the structure of a person's concerns; concern for persons—oneself or others—is a special case of concern for things.

tally, and this, as Vlastos observes, is incompatible with caring about one's beloved for his own sake.[9] If we assume that an adequate account of love and friendship must involve intrinsic concern for another, then the Socratic account appears defective.

IV. Platonic Love

Plato's own account of love (*eros*) is presented in the *Symposium* and the *Phaedrus*. In the *Symposium*, he describes an ascent of desire through various stages (210a–212a). This ascent moves from (1) love of a particular beautiful body, to (2) love of bodily beauty, as such, to (3) a love of all beautiful bodies, to (4) a love of spiritual beauty, that is, what is fine or beautiful in souls, to (5) a love of fine laws and institutions, to (6) a love of all kinds of knowledge, to (7) a love of what is fine, as such.

This last, best sort of love aims at what is good or fine (201a, 204d, 205d, 206b–e) and, in particular, at *propagating* what is good or fine (206c–208a, 212a). Plato believes that virtue is fine and that spiritual love aims at producing virtue. In middle dialogues, such as the *Republic*, he understands virtue as a psychic state in which one's appetites, emotions, and actions are regulated by practical deliberation about one's overall good. Virtue, so understood, is the controlling ingredient in a good or flourishing life. So when A loves B, Plato concludes, A will aim to make B virtuous (*Symposium* 209a, 212a).

Such love benefits the beloved, because one benefits by becoming virtuous precisely insofar as one is better off being regulated by a correct conception of one's overall good. But Plato also believes that the lover benefits from loving another (*Phaedrus* 245b), as Plato must if he is to reconcile interpersonal love with his eudaimonism. The key to seeing how Plato can reconcile interpersonal love with self-love is to appreciate the way in which he thinks that reproducing one's virtuous traits in another is the next best thing to immortality (*Symposium* 206c1–209e5; *Phaedrus* 276e–277a).[10]

According to Plato, my own persistence over time, despite both compositional and qualitative change, is a matter of reproducing my traits into the future:

> Now although we speak of an individual as being the same so long as he continues to exist in the same form, and therefore assume that a man is the same person in his dotage as in his infancy, yet, for all we call him the same, every bit of him is different, and every day he

---

[9] Vlastos, "The Individual as Object of Love," pp. 8–9.
[10] My account has benefited from those of Richard Kraut, "Egoism, Love, and Political Office in Plato," *Philosophical Review*, vol. 82 (1973), pp. 330–44; Irwin, *Plato's Moral Theory*, pp. 241–42, 267–73; Irwin, *Plato's Ethics*, ch. 18; and A. W. Price, *Love and Friendship in Plato and Aristotle* (Oxford: Clarendon Press, 1989), chs. 2–3.

is becoming a new man, while the old man is ceasing to exist, as you can see from his hair, his flesh, his bones, his blood, and all the rest of his body. And not only his body, for the same thing happens to his soul. And neither his manners, nor his disposition, nor his thoughts, nor his desires, nor his sufferings, nor his fears are the same throughout his life, for some of them grow, while others disappear. . . . In this way every mortal creature is perpetuated, not by always being the same in every way, as a divine being is, but by what goes away and gets old leaving behind and in its place some other new thing that is of the same sort as it was. (207d3–208b12)[11]

Though Plato mentions both physical and psychological persistence, it is clear that his real concern is with psychological persistence. For he regards the soul essentially as a capacity for deliberation, decision, and action (*Phaedrus* 245c–e), and he regards *eudaimonia* as consisting in the proper psychic ordering of the agent's soul. So my persistence requires my psychological reproduction into the future, and if this is to be good for me, I must reproduce my valuable traits into the future; if virtue is the dominant component of my *eudaimonia*, this requires me to reproduce my virtuous traits into the future. But interpersonal love involves the reproduction of my virtuous traits in another, who can live beyond me; this is why interpersonal love is correctly viewed as the next best thing to immortality. It also explains why spiritual intercourse and love are better than bodily love and intercourse; spiritual love begets greater and more valuable progeny (*Symposium* 209a1–e4). This explains why Plato would regard Socrates or Solon as more fecund and closer to immortality than the old woman who lived in the shoe (who had so many children she didn't know what to do).

On Plato's view, intrapersonal and interpersonal love are parallel; indeed, love of another appears to be just a special case of self-love. I extend myself into the future by reproducing my traits into the future. But I can also reproduce myself somewhat less systematically in others by sharing thought and discussion with them, in particular, thought and discussion about how best to live. In the intrapersonal case, I not only extend my interests; my self-reproduction is systematic enough to extend my life. Where my self-reproduction is, for various reasons, less systematic, I do not survive; but the very same sort of self-reproduction extends my interests.[12] On this view, the interests of those whom I love become part of my interests in just the sort of way that the interests of my future self are part of my overall interests.

---

[11] This translation from the *Symposium* is adapted from that of Michael Joyce in *The Collected Dialogues of Plato*, ed. Hamilton and Cairns (*supra* note 8).

[12] For a systematic development of these Platonic commitments about the difference between interpersonal and intrapersonal psychological reproduction, see my "Self-Love and Altruism," pp. 138–43.

V. ARISTOTELIAN FRIENDSHIP

Aristotle discusses friendship (*philia*) in Books VIII and IX of the *Nicomachean Ethics*. Like Plato, he believes that friendship is beneficial for both parties. Initially, he suggests that all forms of friendship involve reciprocal concern for the other's own sake (1155b28–33). He then identifies three different kinds of friendship: friendship for *advantage*, friendship for *pleasure*, and friendship for *virtue*, the last of which he regards as the best or most complete kind of friendship (VIII 3–8). Both advantage-friendship and pleasure-friendship, Aristotle claims, involve something *less* than concern for the other's own sake (1156a11–13). Advantage-friendship typically involves the concern one develops for other members of mutually beneficial cooperative schemes; such friends last as long as they share common and mutually advantageous goals. Pleasure-friendship involves strong and intense emotions among friends that reflect the pleasure each takes in the qualities and company of the other; these friendships involve a strong attachment and concern for the other, but these attachments are not stable insofar as they are based on transient emotional intensity. Both kinds of friendship are to be contrasted with virtue-friendship. This is friendship among people similarly virtuous in which each cares about the other for the other's own sake. Despite these and other differences between virtue-friendship, on the one hand, and pleasure-friendship and advantage-friendship, on the other hand, Aristotle insists that virtue-friendship supplies the "focal meaning" of friendship. In calling virtue-friendship the best or most complete kind of friendship, he signals that it is friendship to the fullest extent and that other associations are friendship by virtue of their approximation to it (1157a26–32).

Virtue-friendship cannot be widespread inasmuch as virtuous people are rare (1156b25) and this sort of friendship requires a degree of intensity that cannot be maintained on a large scale (1158a11–17, 1171a1–20). Complete friends share similar psychological states, such as aims and goals (1170b16–17) and live together, sharing thought and discussion (1157b8–19, 1159b25–33, 1166a1–12, 1171b30–1172a6). Virtue-friendship "reflects the comparative worth of the friends" (1158b28). The true friend aims at what is good (1162a5, b12, 1165b14–16) and fine (1168b28–1169a12). Because virtue is fine, the friend is concerned with his friend's virtue. This explains why Aristotle thinks that one cannot remain friends with someone who becomes irredeemably vicious (1165b14–21), that the vicious cannot even love themselves (1166b2–27), and that the person who values and aims to promote his own virtue is the true self-lover (1168a28–1169a12).

Virtue-friends care about each other for the other's own sake. If complete friendship is a virtue, then, as a eudaimonist, Aristotle must think that it contributes to the lover's, as well as the beloved's, *eudaimonia*.

Aristotle anticipates some of his claims about the justification of virtue-friendship (which begins at IX 4) in Book VIII, chapter 12, where he suggests that we should take parental friendship as our model of friendship. The parent is concerned with the child's welfare for the child's own sake. This concern is appropriate on eudaimonist grounds, because the parent can regard the child as "another-self" (1161b19, 28). The child can be regarded as another-self of the parent, because the child owes its existence and its physical and psychological nature in large measure to the parent; this both echoes and helps explain the common view that a parent's interests are *extended* by the life of the child.[13] Aristotle suggests that similar claims can be made about friendship between siblings. In virtue of living together, siblings causally interact in important ways and share many things in common and so can regard each other as other-selves (1161b30–35).

Despite important differences between familial friendship and virtue-friendship, Aristotle's account of familial friendship brings out clearly what is crucial to his justification of virtue-friendship. He explains the justification of virtue-friendship in terms of proper *self*-love (1166a1–2, 10, 1166a30–32, 1168b1–1169a12; *Eudemian Ethics* 1240a22–b13):[14]

> The excellent person is related to his friend in the same way as he is related to himself, since a friend is another self; and therefore, just as his own being is choiceworthy for him, the friend's being is choiceworthy for him in the same or a similar way. (*NE* 1170b6–9)

Aristotle believes that proper self-love requires a proper conception of the self and what is beneficial for the self:

> However, it is this [the virtuous person] more than any other sort of person who seems to be a self-lover. At any rate, he awards himself what is finest and best of all, and gratifies the most controlling part of himself, obeying it in everything. And just as a city and every other composite system seems to be above all its most controlling part, the same is true of a human being; hence someone loves himself most if he likes and gratifies this part. (1168b28–34; see also 1166a15–23)

---

[13] Insofar as this is true, Aristotle can provide further justification for his assumptions that there are posthumous benefits and harms and that the welfare of one's loved ones and the success of one's projects, after one is dead, are part of a complete good (*NE* 1100a10–31, 1101a23–30).

[14] My own account of these matters has benefited from those of Terence Irwin, *Aristotle's First Principles* (Oxford: Clarendon Press, 1988), esp. ch. 18; and Price, *Love and Friendship in Plato and Aristotle*, esp. chs. 4–7.

Here Aristotle identifies a person with the controlling part of his soul or his understanding. We know that he thinks a human is essentially a psycho-physical compound in which reason can regulate thought and action (1097b24–1098a16, 1102b13–1103a3). If so, it would be reasonable for him to think that the persistence of an individual consists in the continuous employment of his rational faculties to regulate his thought and action. Moreover, we know that the virtues of character involve the rational part of the soul regulating the nonrational part of the soul in such a way that the nonrational part of the soul harmonizes with the exercise of practical reason (1102b25–28), and we know that the correct exercise of practical reason—the proper realization of an individual's essence—is the controlling ingredient in his *eudaimonia* (1098b15–16, 1099b17–27, 1100b1–11, 1100b31–34). This would explain why Aristotle thinks that proper love for oneself involves a concern for one's practical reason and its virtuous exercise.

This account of proper intrapersonal love suggests a plausible interpretation of Aristotle's claims about the relation between interpersonal friendship and self-love that is reminiscent of Plato's analogy between intrapersonal and interpersonal reproduction in his account of philosophical *eros*. I preserve or extend myself by exercising my practical reason—forming beliefs and desires, deliberating about them, and acting as the result of deliberate choice. But the same sort of psychological interaction and interdependence can be found, presumably to a lesser extent, between two different persons. On Aristotle's view, friends share similar psychological states, such as aims and goals (1170b16–17), and they live together (1157b8–19, 1159b25–33, 1166a1–12, 1171b30–1172a6). Even if psychological similarity is necessary for friendship, it is clearly insufficient; it should be produced and sustained by living together and sharing thought and discussion (1157b5–12, 18–21, 1170b10–14).[15] This account of interpersonal psychological dependence among friends allows us to see how Aristotle thinks we can view a friend as another-self and, thus, how he can view the justification of friendship in terms of self-love. But then we

---

[15] We might wonder whether Aristotle should think similarity is necessary for friendship. Though he sometimes writes as if the relevant relations among friends must involve similar beliefs and values (1159b3–5, 1161b35, 1162a13, 1165b17, 1166a7, 1167a23–b10, 1170b16), it is not clear that this is or should be an essential feature of his position, at least insofar as he seeks to model interpersonal relations and concern on intrapersonal relations and concern. For within my own life, I exercise deliberative control and establish psychological connections with my future self when I intentionally modify beliefs, desires, or values, as well as when I maintain them unchanged. It may be that my successive selves will typically be fairly similar; perhaps wholesale and instantaneous psychological change is impossible or at least would involve a substantial change, which I would not survive. But intrapersonal psychological dependence is compatible with significant qualitative change. Our own persistence requires only continuous deliberative control, not fixity of character. If so, then it seems that, in the interpersonal case, Aristotle should allow for friends to be psychologically dissimilar provided the mental states and actions of each exert significant influence on those of the other. Indeed, much of the value of having friends depends upon their being no mere clones of me. See my "Self-Love and Altruism," pp. 144–45, 148–49.

can see how Aristotle can think that friendship involves concern for the friend's own sake and yet admits of eudaimonist justification. If B extends A's interests, then B's interests are a part of A's. This is true when A and B are the same person and when they are different people. My friend's good is a part of my own overall good in just the way that the well-being of my future self is part of my overall good.

This provides a eudaimonist account of why one should care about those with whom one is already friends. But it does not explain why one should cultivate friendships in the first place.[16] Indeed, if continued concern for friends is justified insofar as this contributes to the extended interests of the agent, this may look like a circuitous form of self-concern. Why not just spend my financial, emotional, and intellectual resources directly on myself, rather than cultivating relationships through which I can then benefit myself?

Aristotle argues that it is in my interest to exercise those capacities that are central to the sort of being I essentially am; because I am essentially a rational animal, the principal ingredient in my *eudaimonia* is the exercise of my deliberative capacities.[17] Interpersonal psychological interaction of the right sort promotes my *eudaimonia* by making possible the fuller realization of my deliberative capacities. The central premise of Aristotle's argument is that I am not self-sufficient at producing a complete deliberative good (1162a20–24, 1170a5–7; *EE* 1244b1–12; *Magna Moralia* 1212b24–1213b2; *Politics* 1253a25–27, 1261b10–15):

> For it is said that the blessedly happy and self-sufficient people have no need of friends. For they already have [all] the goods, and hence, being self-sufficient, need nothing added. But your friend, since he is another yourself, supplies what your own efforts cannot supply. (*NE* 1169b4–6)

Part of what Aristotle may have in mind is that cooperative interaction with others is mutually beneficial and that family, friends, and neighbors protect each other from misfortune by sharing their resources (1170a5). As important as these benefits are, however, they appear to give interpersonal interaction only instrumental value.

---

[16] These issues are distinguished in John Cooper, "Aristotle on Friendship," in *Essays on Aristotle's Ethics*, ed. A. Rorty (Los Angeles: University of California Press, 1980), pp. 318–19.

[17] It is common to contrast a *comprehensive* conception of *eudaimonia* that includes external goods and practical virtues or virtues of character, as well as intellectual virtues, with a *strict intellectualist* conception that identifies *eudaimonia* exclusively with contemplation. Whereas it appears that the formal criteria of *eudaimonia* (especially the completeness requirement and the function argument) introduced in *NE* Book I support a comprehensive conception and that *NE* II–IX conforms to this conception, *NE* X 7–8 appears to endorse strict intellectualism. My discussion of Aristotle's views about the justification of friendship and the political significance of his account of friendship fits most readily with the comprehensive conception, which I take to be Aristotle's considered conception (whether he holds it consistently or not).

Aristotle can and does have something more in mind. He focuses on the sharing of thought and discussion, especially about how best to live, as well as cooperative interaction. Sharing thought and discussion with another diversifies my experiences by providing me with additional perspectives on the world. By enlarging my perspective, it gives me a more objective picture of the world, its possibilities, and my place in it. Aristotle echoes Plato's claim in the *Phaedrus* that part of the value of intimates, with whom one shares thought and conversation, consists in their providing a "mirror" on the self (*Phaedrus* 255d5; *NE* 1169b34–35):

> Since then it is . . . a most difficult thing . . . to attain a knowledge of oneself . . . we are not able to see what we are from ourselves (and that we cannot do so is plain from the way in which we blame others without being aware that we do the same things ourselves; and this is the effect of favour or passion, and there are many of us who are blinded by these things so that we judge not aright); . . . when we wish to see our own face, we do so by looking into the mirror, in the same way when we wish to know ourselves we can obtain that knowledge by looking at our friend. For the friend is, as we assert, a second self. (*MM* 1213a13–24; cf. *EE* 1245a29–36)

Insofar as we regard the exercise of deliberative capacities as the chief ingredient in *eudaimonia*, we can see how self-understanding and self-criticism are both parts of *eudaimonia*. Interaction between those who are psychologically similar provides a kind of mirror on the self. Insofar as my friend is like me, I can appreciate my own qualities from a different perspective; this promotes my self-understanding. One need only think of the familiar way in which parents experience pride and sometimes chagrin when they see various habits and traits of their own manifested in their children. But there are limits to the value of mirrors; interaction with another just like me does not itself contribute to self-criticism. This is why there is deliberative value in interaction with diverse sorts of people many of whom are not mirror images of myself.[18] This suggests another way in which I am not deliberatively self-sufficient. Sharing thought and discussion with others, especially about how to live, improves my own practical deliberations; it enlarges my menu of options, by identifying new options, and helps me better assess the merits of these options, by forcing on my attention new considerations and arguments about the comparative merits of the options. Here Aristotle might appeal to Socratic claims about the deliberative value of open and vigorous discussion with diverse interlocutors. Moreover, cooperative interaction with others allows me to participate in larger, more complex projects and thus extend

---

[18] This is another reason Aristotle should not treat psychological similarity as a necessary condition of friendship (see *supra* note 15).

the scope of my deliberative control over my environment. In this way, I spread my interests more widely than I could acting on my own. Here too diversity can be helpful; cooperation is improved and extends each participant further when it draws on diverse talents and skills. In these ways, interpersonal psychological relations arguably make for fuller realization of my deliberative capacities. This may be part of what Aristotle has in mind in claiming that we are essentially political animals (*NE* 1097b9–12, *Politics* 1253a2) and that, as a result, the complete good for an individual can only be realized in a political community.[19]

VI. The "Cardinal Flaw" in Platonic and Aristotelian Love

As we have seen, Vlastos thinks that the Socratic view of love in the *Lysis* cannot recognize concern for another for the other's own sake, because the Socratic lover values his beloved as a means to advancing his own *eudaimonia*. On Vlastos's view, the egoism of the *Lysis* contrasts with the impersonal view of love represented in the *Phaedrus* and the *Symposium*, a view which emphasizes the lover's desire to propagate virtue. Despite these differences, Vlastos thinks that the Platonic account is no better able to explain the lover's concern for the beloved's own sake. On Vlastos's reading, the Platonic lover loves what is fine and virtuous in his beloved, not the beloved himself:

> We are to love the persons so far, and only insofar, as they are good and beautiful. Now since all too few human beings are masterworks of excellence, and not even the best of those we have the chance to love are wholly free of streaks of the ugly, the mean, the commonplace, the ridiculous, if our love of them is to be only for their virtue and beauty, the individual, in the uniqueness and integrity of his or her individuality, will never be the object of our love. This seems to me to be the cardinal flaw in Plato's theory.[20]

According to Vlastos, Aristotelian love is in essential respects Platonic, inasmuch as Aristotelian friendship, like Platonic love, aims at what is good and fine in the beloved:

---

[19] Is friendship, on this interpretation, a necessary part of *eudaimonia*? The answer may depend on the sort of modality at issue. Friendship is a part of *eudaimonia*, on this view, insofar as humans are not individually self-sufficient for a complete deliberative good. There may be conceivable circumstances (e.g., in which humans are omniscient) in which humans are individually self-sufficient for a complete deliberative good and in which an individual's deliberations cannot be improved by interaction and discussion with others. Friendship may not be part of *eudaimonia* in these circumstances. But these circumstances are remote from our own. Friendship is part of *eudaimonia* in circumstances, such as our own, of individual deliberative limitations.

[20] Vlastos, "The Individual as Object of Love," p. 31.

Aristotle's account of perfect *philia* does not repudiate—does not even notice—what I have called above "the cardinal flaw" in Platonic love. His intuition takes him as far as seeing that (a) *disinterested affection for the person* we love—the active desire to promote that person's good "for that person's sake, not ours"—must be built into love at its best, but not as far as sorting this out from (b) *appreciation of the excellences instantiated by that person....*[21]

Vlastos believes that, in explaining the lover's concern with what is fine and virtuous, Aristotle is unable to accommodate his own insight that true love requires concern for the beloved's own sake. This failure should manifest itself in Aristotle's account of self-love as well as in his account of interpersonal love. Whether the lover loves himself or another, he is to love what is fine or virtuous about him, and this, Vlastos thinks, is incompatible with loving him for his own sake.

VII. Impersonal Love

Vlastos's exact complaint is not entirely clear. Sometimes he seems concerned to insist that the object of proper love be a person, not his properties; at other times, he seems concerned to insist that proper love reflect concern for all aspects of a person's character, not just his best features. Part of his worry is that concern with another's virtuous traits is a kind of impersonal or generic concern, rather than a concern for the individual for his own sake. Valuing my friend as I would any virtuous person or someone capable of virtue may not seem to be valuing him for his own sake or to be attaching any significance to our historical relationship.

Something like this interpretation of Vlastos is reflected in Jennifer Whiting's discussion and defense of impersonal friendship in her provocative essay "Impersonal Friends."[22] But whereas Whiting thinks that Vlastos is right to attribute an impersonal conception of friendship to Aristotle, she thinks he is wrong to think this conception problematic. Because Whiting's discussion provides an extended account of the impersonal conception that troubles Vlastos, I shall discuss it in some detail.

On Whiting's view, Aristotle's account of virtue-friendship explains and justifies both *initial* and *subsequent* concern for one's friend by appeal to the virtuousness of his character. This account claims that one's choice of friends is to be justified on account of the quality of their characters. As such, this account of initial concern contrasts with a conception according to which initial concern is simply a brute fact that does not require

---

[21] *Ibid.*, p. 33n.
[22] Jennifer Whiting, "Impersonal Friends," *The Monist*, vol. 74 (1991), pp. 3–29.

justification.[23] This account of the justification of subsequent concern—which Whiting calls a generic conception—contrasts with what she calls an egocentric conception. Whereas the egocentric conception "takes the nature of one's reasons for concern to depend essentially on the nature of the *relationship* in which the potential object of concern stands to oneself,"[24] the generic conception claims that "the *substance* or *content* of another's character (as distinct from its *relationship* to one's own) is the ground of concern."[25] Whiting focuses on an egoist interpretation of the egocentric conception that justifies interpersonal love as a special case of self-love and objects to the "colonial" or imperial perspective that she thinks this requires the lover to adopt toward his beloved. In the wake of her criticisms of the egocentric conception, she defends a generic conception. It is this generic claim about the justification of subsequent concern that makes Whiting's conception of friendship impersonal; on this view, it is a virtuous character that grounds the virtuous person's reasons for concern about himself and his friends.

Vlastos objects to this conception of friendship, because he thinks it confuses loving a person for his own sake and loving him for his virtuous qualities. As I understand her view, Whiting's response is to distinguish between the *grounds* and *object* of concern.[26] She thinks that she can maintain the beloved as the object of concern while claiming that an impersonal concern with virtue is the ground of this concern. On her view, our grounds for caring about people are their properties, and it is appropriate to value good and bad traits differentially.[27]

We may be able to distinguish between the grounds and object of concern in the case of initial concern. One cannot be friends with everyone, and the quality of people's character may figure in the explanation and justification of decisions about whom to befriend. B's superior character may explain and even justify A's decision to befriend B rather than C. This seems compatible with A's coming to care about B for his own sake. But it is harder to distinguish between the grounds and object of concern in the case of subsequent concern. For if it is B's traits, rather than B's relationship to A, that ground A's concern for B, then it seems that A is essentially concerned with those traits and only incidentally concerned with B. The fundamental problem with the impersonal conception is that

---

[23] *Ibid.*, p. 7.

[24] *Ibid.*, p. 9.

[25] *Ibid.*, p. 11.

[26] I think that this distinction also underlies Cooper's attempt to reconcile Aristotle's claim that friendship, as such, involves concern for the other for the other's own sake and his insistence that pleasure-friendship and advantage-friendship involve concern for another only insofar as the other is pleasant or useful. Cooper's suggestion is that I can value another for his own sake, even if my reasons for doing so are the extrinsic benefits I get from him. See Cooper, "Aristotle on Friendship," pp. 312–13. I suspect, but will not argue here, that my doubts about Whiting's use of this distinction apply also to Cooper's reconciliation strategy.

[27] Whiting, "Impersonal Friends," pp. 12–13.

it attaches no intrinsic significance to the friendship relation itself.[28] The impersonal friend apparently has the same disinterested concern for her virtuous friend that she has reason to have for any virtuous person; the impersonal account does not explain why one should single out one's friends, from among the pool of virtuous people, for special concern. This objection to an impersonal conception of friendship is very much like the now familiar objection that impartial moral theories, such as utilitarianism and Kantianism, are unable to account for the significance of various kinds of special relationships, including those between intimates and friends.

Whiting is aware of this worry and defends the ability of the impersonal account to invest special relationships with normative significance:

> The virtuous person, having been properly brought up, finds herself in the world, with her particular virtues and in relationships with others and their particular virtues. She generally knows herself and those with whom she has spent more time more intimately, and is generally in a better position to cultivate and promote her generically valued ends in herself and her close associates than among those with whom she is less intimately acquainted. . . .[29]

Interestingly, this defense of the impersonal account of friendship appeals to the same considerations that the classical utilitarian invokes to explain special obligations. In *The Methods of Ethics*, Henry Sidgwick claims that common-sense morality is "inchoately and imperfectly Utilitarian" (*ME* 427).[30] He maintains that "the commonly received view of special claims and duties arising out of special relations, though *prima facie* opposed to the impartial universality of the Utilitarian principle, is really maintained by a well-considered application of that principle" (*ME* 439). He argues that the recognition of special obligations and a differentially greater concern for those to whom one stands in special relationships is in general optimal, because we derive more pleasure from interactions with associates, we often have better knowledge about how to benefit associates, and we are often better situated causally to confer benefits on associates (*ME* 431–39).

However, even if the demands of special concern and impartial concern often coincide, the coincidence is imperfect. I may derive more pleasure from interaction with my associates than from interaction with strangers, but those who are strangers to me have their own associates who derive

---

[28] For related criticisms of Whiting's impersonal conception of friendship, see Diane Jeske, "Friendship, Virtue, and Impartiality," *Philosophy and Phenomenological Research*, vol. 57 (1997), pp. 51–72.

[29] Whiting, "Impersonal Friends," pp. 21–22.

[30] Henry Sidgwick, *The Methods of Ethics* [*ME*], 7th ed. (London: Macmillan, 1907).

special pleasure from them. If so, it is not clear how an impartial concern with happiness explains why I would have any reason to privilege the claims of my associates. Moreover, often I am just as well positioned epistemically and causally to benefit strangers as to benefit my associates. When this is so, the classical utilitarian has no reason to regard an agent's investments in his friends as a more efficient use of his resources. There are comparable limitations in Whiting's impersonal defense of friendship. Suppose A and B are virtue-friends with each other but not as of yet with C. If A's reasons for caring about his friend B are exhausted by an impersonal concern with recognizing and promoting virtue, then his special concern for B must be limited. If C is more virtuous, or has greater potential for virtue, than B, then it is unclear why A should not abandon B for C or, at least in this case, prefer the stranger to his friend.

These accounts of special concern within an impartial or impersonal perspective appear unable to give a sufficiently robust account of special concern. We might entertain such views as revisionary challenges to the legitimacy of special concern but not, I think, as accounts or justifications of such concern. The problem is that they assign only *extrinsic* significance to special concern; special concern is valuable only insofar as it tends causally to promote happiness or virtue. By contrast, common sense attaches *intrinsic* significance to special relationships; the fact that A and B are friends gives A special reason to be concerned about B that he does not have to be concerned about C. Special concern may not always trump impartial demands to promote happiness or virtue; but the former cannot be reduced to the latter.[31]

We might put this point in terms of the distinction some have drawn between *agent-relative* and *agent-neutral* reasons.[32] The general form of agent-relative reasons makes essential reference to the agent who has them, whereas the general form of agent-neutral reasons does not. Reasons to promote the good or virtue, as such, are agent-neutral reasons, whereas reasons to promote the good of those to whom the agent stands in special relationships are agent-relative reasons. Friendship seems normatively significant, because it is a relationship that seems to transform the reasons the agent has independently of the friendship. If so, one's reasons to be concerned about one's friends are agent-relative and his-

[31] In a footnote, Whiting characterizes her justification of special concern as "pragmatic" and claims that it is not "purely instrumental" insofar as adopting this justification is a "minimal condition for the sort of agency we take to be intrinsically valuable" ("Impersonal Friends," p. 25, note 3). I am not sure how to understand these claims. Even if the impersonal account of special concern can recognize special concern that is psychologically noninstrumental, Whiting's account of its justification of special concern attaches only extrinsic significance to special relations.

[32] Cf. Thomas Nagel, *The View from Nowhere* (New York: Oxford University Press, 1986), pp. 152–53.

torical, whereas the impersonal conception of friendship represents them as agent-neutral.[33]

Whiting herself emphasizes the way an impersonal account of friendship grounds concern in the friend's virtuous character, rather than in the historical interaction between friends.[34] She fails to see how this prevents her from agreeing with common sense in assigning intrinsic significance to the friendship relation itself.[35] Unless our account of love and friendship attaches intrinsic significance to the historical relationship between friends, it seems unable to justify concern for the friend *qua* friend.

Unlike Whiting, then, I think that Vlastos is right to reject impersonal accounts of love and friendship on the merits.[36] However, unlike both Vlastos and Whiting, I do not think we need to attribute this impersonal conception to Plato or Aristotle. Both Platonic and Aristotelian accounts of love and friendship are agent-relative; they attach intrinsic significance to the historical interaction between lover and beloved. For Plato, as we have seen, the justification of the concern a lover has for his beloved depends upon the history of interaction between lover and beloved in which the lover reproduces his virtue in the beloved (*Symposium* 206c–209e). Aristotle, as we have seen, also insists that friendship essentially involves a condition of historical-causal interaction; friends must live together, sharing thought and discussion (*NE* 1157b8–19, 1159b25–33, 1166a1–12, 1170b10–15, 1171b30–1172a6). Moreover, Aristotle draws the agent-relative conclusion that the relationship in which one friend stands to another has independent normative significance that justifies differentially greater concern for friends than for others. He thinks that, all else being equal, it is better to help and worse to harm those with whom one

---

[33] Whiting claims that her account of friendship is in terms of *character-relative*, rather than agent-neutral, reasons, inasmuch as only the virtuous are party to virtue-friendship and, hence, have such impersonal reasons to care about their friends ("Impersonal Friends," p. 11). But even if these reasons apply only to the virtuous, they justify concern in proportion to the virtue or potential for virtue of the beneficiary and make no essential reference to the relationship in which the (virtuous) agent stands to the (virtuous) beneficiary. Moreover, insofar as Aristotle does or can claim that the relevant features of the best sort of friendship extend beyond virtue-friendship, it would be inadvisable to build character-relativity into his justification of friendship.

[34] Whiting, "Impersonal Friends," p. 4.

[35] *Ibid.*, p. 7.

[36] Though I agree with Vlastos that an impersonal account of love and friendship is defective, my diagnosis of the defect is somewhat different from his. My complaint that the impersonal account of friendship cannot justify concern for the friend *qua* friend does not, I think, entail that it cannot justify concern for the friend for the friend's own sake. As I shall argue (Section IX *infra*), the intrinsic value of a whole is compatible with, and indeed requires, the intrinsic value of its constituent parts. If so, an impersonal account of concern can justify intrinsic concern for another. If my friend is virtuous, or is capable of virtue, then an impersonal concern for all virtuous persons, or all those capable of virtue, justifies concern for her as a constituent part of this impersonal concern. If so, the complaint about the impersonal account of friendship is not that it cannot justify intrinsic concern for those who are friends but that it cannot justify intrinsic concern for them *as* friends.

has associational ties than it is to do these things to others (1160a1–6, 1169b12; *Politics* 1262a27–30).

Agent-relativity can come in different forms. In his important (and unjustly neglected) essay "Self and Others," C. D. Broad describes an agent-relative theory that he calls *self-referential altruism* and associates with common sense.[37] It is altruistic insofar as it recognizes nonderivative reasons to benefit others. But

> the altruism which common sense approves is always *limited in scope*. It holds that each of us has specially urgent obligations to benefit certain individuals and groups which stand in certain special relations to *himself*, e.g. his parents, his children, his fellow-countrymen, etc. And it holds that these special relationships are the ultimate and sufficient ground for these specially urgent claims on one's beneficence.[38]

On one interpretation, self-referential altruism is agent-neutral insofar as it recognizes nonderivative reasons to benefit others, but it is agent-relative insofar as the weight or strength of the agent's reasons is a function of the relationship in which she stands to potential beneficiaries. Self-referential altruism attaches intrinsic significance to the relationship in which the lover stands to the beloved.

Despite the intuitive appeal of self-referential altruism, Plato and Aristotle cannot, I think, be interpreted as self-referential altruists. Their eudaimonism commits them to a different kind of agent-relativity.[39]

---

[37] C. D. Broad, "Self and Others," in *Broad's Critical Essays in Moral Philosophy*, ed. D. Cheney (London: George Allen and Unwin, 1971), esp. pp. 279–80.

[38] *Ibid.*, p. 280. As I (would like to) understand him, Broad should say that the altruism that common sense approves is of *variable weight*, rather than of limited scope.

[39] Given the apparent incompatibility of impersonal and eudaimonic conceptions of love and friendship, it is somewhat surprising to find Whiting and Vlastos ascribing impersonal conceptions to Plato and Aristotle. Whiting recognizes the way in which the egocentric conception, which she rejects, appeals to eudaimonism ("Impersonal Friends," p. 9); she may see her case for ascribing a generic or impersonal conception of friendship to Aristotle as providing reasons for resisting the common interpretation of Aristotle as a eudaimonist. Vlastos, as we have seen, clearly interprets Plato and Aristotle, as well as Socrates, as eudaimonists, yet he apparently does not see this as an obstacle to ascribing to them an impersonal conception of love and friendship. Vlastos believes that Aristotle cannot consistently claim that the friend values another for the other's own sake and that the friend values his friend's virtue; he may think that adding eudaimonism just adds more inconsistency to the mix. However, Vlastos's attitude is complicated. In accusing Aristotle's conception of friendship of failing to distinguish (a) disinterested affection for the beloved—the desire to promote that person's good—from (b) appreciation of the excellences instantiated by that person, Vlastos comments that "(b), of course, need not be disinterested and *could be egoistic*" ("The Individual as Object of Love," p. 33n). Vlastos seems to be saying that there could be egoist as well as impersonal versions of (b): (1) A could value some of B's traits insofar as they are good, or (2) A could value some of B's traits insofar as they are beneficial to A. Presumably, Vlastos thinks that both (b1) and (b2) are incompatible with (a). Perhaps (b2) is more easily reconciled with eudaimonism than (b1). But, as I read Vlastos, (b2) is just a logical, not an interpretive, possibility; Aristotle's version of (b), according to

Eudaimonism, as I have noted, claims that an agent's practical reasoning should be regulated by a correct conception of his own happiness or *eudaimonia*. On this view, an agent has reason to do something just insofar as doing so contributes to his own *eudaimonia*. As such, eudaimonism, unlike self-referential altruism, implies that all reasons are agent-relative. Moreover, if the eudaimonist is to accord intrinsic significance to associational ties, he must claim that associational ties contribute in some essential way to the agent's *eudaimonia*. Plato and Aristotle can make this claim insofar as both claim that interpersonal love can be understood as a special case of proper self-love.

VIII. Loving Persons and Loving Virtue

Even if Platonic and Aristotelian conceptions of love and friendship, unlike impersonal conceptions, attach intrinsic significance to the shared history that friends have, it may still be unclear whether we can reconcile the lover's concern with what is good, fine, and virtuous with the requirement that he have intrinsic concern for his beloved.

Vlastos thinks that persons (as subjects) and their valuable or virtuous traits (as things predicated of subjects) are rival objects of love and friendship and that both Plato and Aristotle treat virtue, rather than the beloved, as the object of love. However, we ought to distinguish the *object* and *manner* of love and friendship. We do not need to read Plato and Aristotle as claiming that we should love virtue, rather than persons; rather, we can read them as claiming that we should love those persons, to whom we stand in the right relations of psychological interaction and interdependence, in a manner that prizes and promotes their virtue. Virtue explains *how* we should love, rather than *whom* we should love.

Interestingly, Whiting contrasts her own impersonal interpretation of Aristotle's claims about friendship's focus on virtue with remarks by the Christian theologian Paul Ramsey. Ramsey writes:

> How exactly do you love yourself? Answer this question and you will know how a Christian should love his neighbor. You naturally love yourself for your own sake. You wish your own good, and you do so even when you may have a certain distaste for the kind of person you are. Liking yourself . . . or not, has fundamentally nothing to do with [it]. . . . Unsubdued by bad qualities, not elicited by good ones, self-love does not wait on worth. In fact it is the other way around: *self-love makes you desire worth for yourself.*[40]

Vlastos, is (b1). If so, Vlastos must think that eudaimonism is inconsistent with an impersonal account of friendship.

[40] Paul Ramsey, *Basic Christian Ethics* (New York: Scribner and Sons, 1950), p. 100, quoted in Whiting, "Impersonal Friends," p. 16.

Not only does Whiting reject Ramsey's claim; she thinks Aristotle would as well. But Ramsey's claim seems quite plausible and suggests an attractive reading of Plato and Aristotle. He distinguishes implicitly, as I have explicitly, between the object and manner of love. Interpersonal love involves love of another, whereas intrapersonal love involves love of oneself. In both cases, love involves concern for the good of the beloved. Because Plato and Aristotle both believe that virtue, conceived of as a state in which one's emotions, appetites, and actions are regulated by practical deliberation about one's overall good, is the dominant component in an agent's *eudaimonia*, they believe that the appropriate expression of love for someone is a concern with the beloved's virtue. In caring about one's beloved, one cares about his virtue.

Thus, we can understand Aristotle's claim that interpersonal virtue-friendship reflects the comparative worth of friends as the claim that friends who care about each other for the other's own sake will prize and seek to promote the other's virtue. We can also explain why the true self-lover aims at his own virtue. In caring for himself, he cares for what he essentially is, and that involves concern for himself *qua* deliberative agent. But the good of an essentially deliberative agent involves the virtuous life, conceived of as a life expressing these deliberative capacities. So we can see why proper love for oneself involves a concern for one's practical reason and its proper exercise. Aristotle does say that one cannot love what is base (1165b15) and that the vicious cannot even love themselves (1166b2–27), and this may seem to conflict with Vlastos's and Ramsey's claim that we can, do, and should love imperfect beings. But Aristotle also says that we can and should maintain friendships despite corruption in our friend's character, provided only that the friend has not become *irredeemably* vicious (1165b13–18). This implies that we can and should love imperfect beings. Presumably, Aristotle's point is that we can love things that are bad things, but not *qua* bad things. Because to love things is to value them and wish them well (1155b2–28), love presupposes a capacity for value. But then love of another person requires a capacity for virtue. Vicious people can love themselves, but not *qua* vicious people; only the incurably vicious would be genuinely unable to love themselves. Loving persons and loving virtue, therefore, are not inconsistent. By distinguishing the object and manner of love, we can see how Ramsey is right to suppose that love of persons requires concern with their worth or virtues.

IX. EUDAIMONISM AND INTRINSIC CONCERN FOR ANOTHER

The foregoing claims explain how to reconcile love of persons and love of virtue within classical views of love and friendship. It does not yet explain how to reconcile love of virtue and eudaimonism. This is accomplished by Plato's and Aristotle's view that associational relationships extend the agent's interests. We are to love those persons with whom we are appropriately associated; loving them involves wishing them well, which for Plato and Aristotle involves a concern for their virtue. Concern for the virtue of one's associates benefits the agent, as well as his associates. This is because associational relationships extend the agent's interests. Both Plato and Aristotle see associates bound together by the same sort of deliberative glue that holds together a single life. What unifies a single life is that an agent's appetites, emotions, beliefs, deliberations, and actions at one point depend upon earlier ones; in particular, an agent preserves or extends himself by regulating his appetites, emotions, beliefs, choices, and actions in accordance with his deliberations. So too are associates bound together by deliberative interaction and interdependence; the experiences, beliefs, desires, ideals, choices, and actions of each associate depend to a significant extent on those of the other. This is why Plato thinks that interpersonal love is the next best thing to immortality (*Symposium* 206c1–209e5; *Phaedrus* 276e–277a) and why Aristotle thinks that a proper understanding of friendship undermines the popular contrast between self-love and altruism (*NE* IX 8).

But can this eudaimonist justification of interpersonal love and friendship justify concern for the other for the other's own sake? If the Platonic or Aristotelian lover cares about his beloved for the sake of the lover's own *eudaimonia*, mustn't such concern be at bottom instrumental? This was Vlastos's objection to the Socratic account of love and friendship. By Vlastos's own lights, Plato and Aristotle accept Socrates' eudaimonism; it is unclear why instrumental concern shouldn't infect their accounts of love and friendship as well. Whiting appears to be expressing a similar concern about the eudaimonist interpretation when she criticizes the colonial perspective that the egocentric interpretation imposes on interpersonal concern.[41]

As we saw, in the *Lysis* Socrates is committed to interpersonal concern that is purely instrumental:

(1) Insofar as x is desired for the sake of some other thing y, then x is only instrumentally valuable (219c–220b).
(2) If A and B are friends, A cares about B because of the contribution this makes to A's *eudaimonia*.
(3) Hence, friends care about each other only instrumentally.

If friends care about each other only instrumentally, they cannot care about each other for their own sakes. Vlastos is right, then, that Socrates'

---

[41] Related doubts about the eudaimonist justification of other-regarding concern are expressed in Section IV of Thomas Hurka's "The Three Faces of Flourishing," elsewhere in this volume.

eudaimonism renders his account of friendship inadequate.[42] But Platonic and Aristotelian eudaimonism do not require purely instrumental concern for the beloved. Whereas Socrates assumes that valuing something for the sake of another always reflects purely instrumental concern, Plato and Aristotle reject this assumption.

In the *Republic*, Glaucon and Adeimantus demand that Socrates show justice to be beneficial *in itself* and not simply for its normal causal consequences (357a–367e). Plato subsequently defends justice by arguing that justice secures the right ordering of the agent's soul and thus contributes to his *eudaimonia*. If we are to make sense of Plato's defense of justice as a response to the challenge that Glaucon and Adeimantus pose, we must interpret him as arguing that justice is valuable for its *intrinsic*, as well as its extrinsic, consequences. If justice contributes to the agent's happiness, because justice is a part of the agent's happiness, then Plato will have shown that justice is valuable "in and by itself" (367b4, e2–4). He regards justice as the controlling part of *eudaimonia*; he hopes to show that one is always better off being just than being unjust, no matter what the extrinsic consequences of justice and injustice turn out to be (360e–362c). But

---

[42] Vlastos is prominent among those who have rejected Irwin's suggestion that Socrates assigns virtue only an instrumental role in happiness. See Gregory Vlastos, "The Virtuous and the Happy," *Times Literary Supplement*, February 24, 1987 (and the subsequent exchanges between Irwin and Vlastos of letters to the editor), and Vlastos, *Socrates: Ironist and Moral Philosopher*, esp. pp. 6–10. Interestingly, Vlastos does not address an argument for Socratic instrumentalism that parallels this argument in the *Lysis*, which he does address. As Irwin notes, the argument of the *Lysis* might be applied to virtue itself (see Irwin, *Plato's Ethics*, sections 46–51):

(1) Insofar as x is desired for the sake of some other thing y, then x is only instrumentally valuable (219c–220b).
(2) Virtue is chosen for the sake of happiness.
(3) Hence, virtue is only instrumentally valuable.

But perhaps Socrates can avoid (3) while accepting (1) and (2) if he denies that virtue is distinct from happiness. Furthermore, it might well be claimed that he does deny this insofar as his strong claims about the necessity and sufficiency of virtue for happiness (*Apology* 28b, 29b–30b, 30d, 32b–c, 36c, 41d–e; *Crito* 48c–d, 49b) are best explained by the identity of virtue and happiness and insofar as he identifies justice and happiness (*Crito* 48b) and accepts the unity thesis that the various virtues all pick out one and the same state of an agent's soul (*Laches* 199e). On this reading, though virtue is chosen for the sake of happiness, it is not chosen for the sake of something *else*. Unlike Irwin, therefore, I think this gives us a way of avoiding *this* argument for attributing an instrumentalist attitude toward virtue to Socrates. My own view is that there is a tension between instrumentalist and noninstrumentalist attitudes toward virtue in Socrates. Whereas I agree with Vlastos, against Irwin, that it is hard to square instrumentalism with Socrates' view that virtue is necessary and sufficient for happiness and I believe that the *Lysis* argument does not commit Socrates to an instrumental attitude toward virtue, I do think that an instrumental attitude toward virtue fits with Socrates' craft analogy. Crafts have specific goals that can be specified prior to and independently of craft skills and methods, which these skills and methods are designed to secure causally (e.g., *Laches* 185b–e). But then it looks as if virtue ought to have some independent aim—happiness—and as if virtuous actions ought to be those that reliably secure this goal. If so, the craft analogy supports an instrumental attitude toward virtue. It is not, I think, until Book II of the *Republic* that Plato resolves this tension in Socratic thought in a noninstrumental direction.

the *comparative* claim that justice is always better than injustice does not entail that justice is sufficient for a complete good. In particular, the comparative claim allows Plato to recognize the value of external goods, independent of virtue (361e4–362a2). But then Plato's view seems to be that *eudaimonia* is a whole of which justice is a proper part. If so, justice is desirable for the sake of something *else*, namely, *eudaimonia*. But being desirable for the sake of *eudaimonia* does not imply that justice is only instrumentally valuable; it is valuable in itself for its constitutive contribution to happiness. If Plato can make this claim about justice, he can in principle make this claim about friendship and love. The lover can love his beloved for the contribution this makes to the lover's own *eudaimonia* and for the beloved's own sake if the good of the beloved is a constituent part of the lover's own *eudaimonia*.

On Aristotle's view, a good is complete if it is chosen for its own sake, and a good is unconditionally complete if all other things are chosen for its sake and it is not chosen for the sake of something else (1094a18–19, 1097a27–b6). He believes that *eudaimonia* is the only unconditionally complete good; all other goods are chosen for its sake. Some goods chosen for the sake of *eudaimonia*, such as money, though not choiceworthy in themselves, are choiceworthy as causal means to some ingredient of *eudaimonia*; these goods are incomplete, instrumental goods. But other goods — such as the virtues — that are chosen for the sake of *eudaimonia* are choiceworthy in themselves. They are chosen for the sake of *eudaimonia* in the sense that they are constituent parts of *eudaimonia*; they are valuable in their own right for their constitutive contribution to a valuable life. Such goods are complete or intrinsic goods, not mere instrumental goods, though they are not unconditionally complete goods. Here Aristotle is making explicit the sort of assumptions Plato must make about justice in *Republic* II–IV; in Aristotle's terms, Plato thinks justice is a complete good, but not an unconditionally complete good. If the lover treats the good of his beloved as a complete good that is also choiceworthy for the sake of his own *eudaimonia*, the lover is concerned for the other's own sake while valuing his beloved's well-being for the constitutive contribution this makes to his own *eudaimonia*.

Thus, both Plato and Aristotle have the analytic resources to provide a eudaimonist justification of interpersonal concern that is derivative but not instrumental. When I undertake a present sacrifice for a future benefit, I do so because the future interests are interests of mine. The on-balance rationality of the sacrifice depends upon its promoting my overall good. But because the good of my future self is a part of this good, concern for my overall good requires, as a constituent part, a concern for the good of my future self. In this way, concern for my future self for its own sake seems compatible with and, indeed, essential to self-love. If psychological relations can extend the agent's interests, then the good of others can be part of my overall good just as my own future good can be.

Though the on-balance rationality of concern for associates depends upon its promoting my overall good, concern for my overall good requires, as a constituent part, concern for the good of those with whom I am associated. Though the eudaimonic justification of interpersonal concern derives such concern from self-love, it can recognize concern for the other for another's own sake.[43]

So far, I have defended the resources of Plato's and Aristotle's conceptions of love and friendship to answer worries that they cannot accommodate intrinsic concern for the object of love and to do so within the constraints imposed by their eudaimonism. However, I do not mean to suggest that these conceptions of love and friendship are without problems; they face difficulties in their application to issues involving political association.

X. Concerns about Platonic Love and Authoritarian Rule

Though Platonic love involves intrinsic concern for the beloved, we may wonder whether Plato has an adequate conception of how this concern should be expressed. The paradigm of Platonic love is between a man and a boy. It is significant that Plato's paradigm is an asymmetrical relationship between unequals. More significant still is the comparatively passive role that the beloved plays in Platonic love. In the *Phaedrus*, Plato likens the relationship between lover and beloved to that between a sculptor and the statue or image that he fashions (252d5–253b1).[44] In this relationship, the lover apparently plays the active, creative role and the beloved the role of promising raw material. Presumably, Plato would insist on one disanalogy; a ball of clay, unlike the beloved, has no welfare with which to be concerned.[45] The lover will be concerned for the good and, hence, the virtue

---

[43] A somewhat different worry about whether my interpretation of Platonic and Aristotelian conceptions of love and friendship can accommodate intrinsic concern for another is this: Does interpersonal psychological interdependence justify associates (a) in being concerned about the other's overall good, though to a degree or strength that reflects the extent of their interdependence, or (b) in being concerned only about that part of the associate's good corresponding to the nature of their interdependence? Consider, for example, my reasons to be concerned about a casual acquaintance with whom I share a hobby. According to (a), our interaction gives me reasons to care about her overall good, though these reasons are weaker than my reasons to be concerned about the overall good of my family members or intimate friends; according to (b), I have reason to care only about those aspects of her welfare that are related to our shared hobby. Whereas (a) would recognize intrinsic concern for another, (b) might underwrite a version of Vlastos's worry that Plato and Aristotle can deliver concern for another's partial attributes but not for the other for the other's own sake. I believe, but cannot properly argue here, that the correct way to model interpersonal relations and concern on intrapersonal relations and concern vindicates (a), rather than (b). See my "Self-Love and Altruism," esp. Sections VII and XI.

[44] Irwin draws attention to this passage and expresses concern about the asymmetrical and passive aspects of Platonic love; see Irwin, *Plato's Moral Theory*, p. 269.

[45] Compare Aristotle's similar reasons for claiming that one cannot be friends with wine or other inanimate things (1155b28–31).

of the beloved, as the sculptor cannot be for his raw materials. But Plato still seems to suggest that the lover can and should express his concern for the beloved by molding him into a virtuous form. This suggests a passive role for the beloved in his own improvement. However, Plato has reason to reject this attitude toward the beloved. Concern for the beloved, he insists, involves concern for his virtue, because virtue is the controlling part of an agent's *eudaimonia*. Plato understands virtue as a condition in which an agent's appetites, emotions, and actions are regulated by practical deliberation about his overall good. However, the development of capacities for deliberative self-governance requires an educational process that exercises the student's deliberative capacities in part by providing him with various deliberative opportunities and responsibilities. A student cannot play a passive role in this sort of education. But this means that A cannot express concern for B in ways in which B plays an entirely passive role and which do not engage B's deliberative capacities. Unfortunately, it is not clear that Plato properly appreciates the way in which a concern for the beloved's own sake requires him to play an active and responsible role in the development and exercise of his capacity for virtue.[46]

Concerns about Platonic love are reflected, as Vlastos observes, in the political theory of the *Republic*.[47] Plato divides the ideal state into three classes. Artisans form the producing or economic class; auxiliaries are responsible for soldiering and policing; and guardians rule. Plato thinks that this division of labor should correspond to differences in people's psychological nature; this natural division of labor rests on the tripartite division of the soul (430e, 544d6–e3, 581b–c). The artisan class should be composed of those ruled by the appetitive part of their souls; the auxiliary class should be composed of those ruled by the spirited part of their souls; and the guardian class should be composed of those ruled by the rational part of their souls, namely, philosophers. In this natural division of labor, Plato thinks, everyone is performing his proper func-

---

[46] Plato is not always blind to the active and responsible role the student must play in his own moral education. I assume that Plato accepts the Socratic requirement that knowledge is necessary for virtue, even if he disagrees with Socrates about the sort of definitions required for knowledge. The mini-elenchus with the slave-boy in the *Meno* (82b–85d) shows how A and B might be unequal and yet how A might love and educate B without B assuming a purely passive role. Moreover, the educational system of the *Republic* clearly assigns students able to become guardians an active role in their own education (531e–541e). The active role that students must play in their own education is also reflected in Socrates' conception of his own role as philosophical midwife (*Theaetetus* 148e7–151d3).

[47] In "The Individual as Object of Love," Vlastos makes important connections between Platonic love and the political theory of the *Republic*. However, his misdiagnosis of the flaws in Platonic love infect his diagnosis of the flaws in authoritarian rule. Put briefly, we might say that just as the real flaw in Platonic love is not that the lover fails to have concern for the beloved's own sake but that he has an impoverished conception of the beloved's role in his own well-being, so too the real flaw in authoritarian rule is not that the guardians are not concerned with the well-being of auxiliaries and artisans but that the former have an impoverished conception of the role of deliberative opportunities and responsibilities in the latter's well-being.

tion. F is x's function just in case: (F1) it is best for x to F (407a, 420b, 421b–c); (F2) x can F better than x can do anything else (370a–b); (F3) x can F better than anyone/anything else can F (353a–b, 370a–b); and (F4) it is better for the state for x to F (420b–c, 421b). Indeed, Plato thinks that the state is just precisely when everyone performs his own function: the guardians rule over the artisans with the help of the auxiliaries; the auxiliaries carry out the edicts of the guardians; and the artisans agree to the rule by the guardians and auxiliaries (433a–434d). In particular, it is the function of the guardians or philosophers to rule because knowledge of moral and political matters is necessary for good ruling, knowledge of Forms is necessary for such knowledge, and only philosophers have knowledge of Forms (484b–d).

How should guardians rule? Their main imperative is to adopt institutions and enact laws that promote social justice by establishing and maintaining this natural division of labor (423d, 433a, 434c, 443c). Plato imagines that social justice will only be realized by authoritarian rule. Guardians need not be honest in their dealings with citizens; they have discretion to lie if this promotes social stability or happiness (389b–c, 459c). Guardians are allowed and expected to restrict various personal liberties of their citizens; they should censor literary and artistic works that do not adequately represent the virtuous life or promote unity (377b–389a, 399e, 401b), and they should install eugenics policies designed to produce the best possible offspring (456e, 459d–e, 460c, 536a). Moreover, because guardians alone have the knowledge necessary for good ruling, they should have exclusive political power. They should be politically unaccountable; the other two classes cannot hold political office and have no voting rights.

Plato thinks this political trust will not be abused. When properly educated, the philosophical nature is concerned with establishing and maintaining social justice, rather than material advantages for itself. Moreover, Plato introduces various institutional safeguards against the rulers' corruption. Most corruption is due to family ties and the temptations of wealth (491c). Therefore, rulers receive no pay and only necessary goods (that the artisans provide); they hold what property they are allowed in common; and they hold their spouses and children in common (416d–417b, 424a, 449c, 457d, 458d).

In assessing Plato's authoritarianism, it is important to remember that the political institutions of the *Republic* are for ideal theory, rather than nonideal theory. Unfortunately, Plato says very little about nonideal theory in the *Republic*. Although he does not regard the ideal state as impossible (499b–c, 502c), he thinks that real philosophers are rare (428e, 491a–b, 503b) and that popular prejudice will make it difficult to realize the ideal state (488a–489a, 502c, 516e–517a; cf. 592a–b). Though, at one point, he suggests that we try to approximate the ideal (437a–b), we should not suppose that he thinks we must accept authoritarian rule by nonphilosophers.[48] If so, we should assess Plato's authoritarianism in the circumstances he envisions, rather than be preoccupied with its liability to abuse in substantially nonideal circumstances.

It is a mistake to see the justification of Plato's authoritarian rule lying in appeal to some anti-individualist collectivist concern.[49] Plato's understanding of social justice in terms of a natural division of labor in which each performs his function implies that philosophical rule will be best for the state (F4), but it also implies that philosophical rule is best for each (F1). Because spouses and children are held in common, the guardians regard each other as family members (463c). But the harmony among the classes in the ideal state also ensures a degree of unity that allows all citizens to view one another as members of an extended family (414e–415a, 462a–463e). This explains why Plato thinks that the guardians will love their fellow citizens (412d) and will rule in the interest of the governed (342b–c, 345c–346c, 347d). But how can Plato claim that it is in the best interests of auxiliaries and artisans to be denied any share in their own governance? The guardians' love for auxiliaries and artisans is clearly a paternalistic love (463b, 463d). We know that Plato thinks that virtue, conceived of as a condition in which one's appetites, emotions, and actions are regulated by correct deliberation about one's overall good, is the controlling part of a person's *eudaimonia*. But he also believes that these deliberative capacities are distributed unequally.[50] He concludes that the next best thing to being ruled by one's own rational part is to be

---

[48] Plato's other political writings say more about nonideal theory. In the *Statesman*, Plato claims that the rule of law makes for imprecise justice (294b–295e); as a result, he thinks that constitutional government is a second-best option, behind case-by-case rule by some person or group that understands the art of good ruling (300c). Plato distinguishes among constitutions both by the number that rule (one, several, or many) and by whether the rule is wise and is in the interest and secures the consent of the governed (276d7–e6, 291d–292a, 293b6–8, 296d5–297b2, 301a–303b). Whereas monarchy is the best ideal constitution, democracy is the best nonideal constitution (302e6–8, 303a3–b8). However, even democratic government apparently excludes slaves and manual laborers from political participation (289d8–e3, 290a), regulates matters of marriage and procreation (310b–e), and imposes severe penalties for criticism of existing laws and institutions (299c, 300c). The *Laws* describes appropriate laws, institutions, and practices for nonideal theory (853b–c). In such circumstances, Plato thinks that the correct constitution should strike some kind of balance between monarchy and democracy (756e–757a). Although he is careful to insist that not every desirable social practice that the state might try to encourage should be mandated by law (772d–773e, 788a, 822d–823a, 885c8–d2), he nonetheless endorses a number of legal restrictions on marriage, procreation, association, expression, worship, and consumption (631d–632c, 656c, 662b, 721a–d, 746a, 780a, 783d–785a, 841d–e, 910b–d, 929e–930d, 950d).

[49] See Karl Popper, *The Open Society and Its Enemies*, 4th ed., vol. 1 (Princeton: Princeton University Press, 1963).

[50] It is somewhat puzzling that the assumption that deliberative capacities are distributed unequally—on which the justification of authoritarian rule rests—should be part of ideal theory. Wouldn't it be more ideal if everyone were a philosopher? Presumably, Plato could have no objection to democratic governance in a world of philosophers. Perhaps he thinks that the appropriate constitution for this possible world is not worth discussing in ideal theory, because he regards that world as too fanciful. Finding a world with a few philosophers, he might think, is improbable enough (*Republic* 428e, 491a–b, 503b).

ruled by the rational part of another (590c–d). In comparison with philosophers, nonphilosophers have weaker rational parts and less evaluative knowledge. It follows, according to Plato, that guardians express
their concern for the well-being of auxiliaries and artisans by aristocratic
management of the city's affairs.

The "cardinal flaw" in the political theory of the *Republic* is not that the
rulers are not regulated by a concern with the ruled, but rather that they
have a defective understanding of the interest of the governed. We think
that paternalistic rule is appropriate toward children, precisely because of
their underdeveloped deliberative powers. But even children need to
play an active part in their own development—being given suitable deliberative opportunities and responsibilities—if they are to be improved
by it. Moreover, even if deliberative capacities are not distributed equally,
artisans and auxiliaries are not children; they have deliberative capacities
too (518c). But then their good presumably involves the development and
exercise of these deliberative capacities. If, as Plato believes, political
institutions should be designed to promote the interests of each citizen
(F1), then political institutions should aim to develop the deliberative
capacities of all members of the community. But deliberative control of
this sort presumably involves participation in public deliberations, a significant sphere for self-control and private deliberation, and informed
and reflective assessment of alternatives in both public and private deliberation. If so, the interests of the governed arguably require democratic
political procedures, in which the democratic agenda is limited by certain
basic civic and personal liberties.

Plato's defense of authoritarian rule appeals to the comparative differences between philosophers and nonphilosophers. We might well challenge Plato's claims about the unequal distribution of rational capacities.
But even if we concede his assumptions, if only for the sake of argument,
comparative differences do not justify giving philosophers exclusive rule;
recognition of moral expertise does not require antidemocratic conclusions. In the *Protagoras*, Socrates expresses puzzlement that Athenians let
everyone speak and treat everyone as equally authoritative in the Assembly on moral and political matters, whereas they defer to expert testimony on technical matters (319b5–d8). However, after hearing expert
testimony on a technical matter, the Athenians still vote democratically,
though they allow expert testimony to shape their beliefs and preferences.
Socrates makes no objection to this practice; he does not suppose that the
votes on technical matters should be cast only by experts. If so, his belief
that Athenians ought to listen to experts on moral matters, if experts
could be had, is not inconsistent with a commitment to democratic institutions.[51] Citizens should be influenced by moral experts, and institutions

---

[51] Cf. Terence Irwin, "Socratic Inquiry and Politics," *Ethics*, vol. 96 (1986), p. 414. Insofar
as the *Protagoras* is a transitional or Socratic dialogue, it would be problematic to appeal to

ought to be designed so as to encourage this; but the resulting institutions could still be democratic ones, provided citizens, rather than the experts they listen to, are the ones to cast votes.

A democratic appeal to experts is not easy to articulate or achieve. On the one hand, if we merely let the experts speak but make the same decision we would have made had they not spoken, then we are not taking advantage of them and our decision making does not reflect a proper concern for getting it right about how life should be lived, even though our voting procedures are democratic. On the other hand, if we slavishly follow the advice of experts, the rest of us will not lead examined lives, even if we otherwise make the right decisions about how to live. Though a democratic community should seek and listen to expert views, democratic citizens should question expert testimony, attempt to understand the main grounds of expert recommendations, and follow expert recommendations just insofar as those recommendations can be reflectively affirmed. Democratic citizens might assume a kind of political responsibility, in relation to moral experts, not unlike the sort of responsibility assumed by young men and their parents in Plato's early dialogues when they consult Socrates and others in their decisions about the right sort of training and education for young men's souls. If so, it is arguable that the fullest political realization of Platonic love would attempt to make room for the contributions of moral experts *within* an account of democratic responsibility and governance.

XI. Concerns about Aristotelian Friendship and Political Community

Aristotle's political theory is intimately linked with his discussion of friendship.[52] General justice, which is complete virtue (in relation to another) (*NE* 1129b20–30), aims at the benefit of the community and the common good (1129b15–18). Aristotle's insistence on the connection among justice, the good of a community, and the common good suggests that his discussion of friendship should inform his discussion of political justice; friendship is the virtue appropriate to communities or associations in general and includes the perfection of justice (1155a22–28, 1159b25–1160a8), and justice obtains among members of associations united by friendship (*EE* 1242a19–b1).

---

its democratic commitments as evidence of democratic commitments in mature Platonic thought. But we can appeal to these claims in the *Protagoras* to identify a model, recognized by Plato, in which the operation of moral expertise takes place *within* a system of democratic governance.

[52] My account of Aristotle's political theory has benefited from those of Ernest Barker, *The Political Thought of Plato and Aristotle* (New York: Dover, 1959), chs. 5–11; Terence Irwin, *Aristotle's First Principles*, ch. 19; Irwin, "The Good of Political Activity," in *Aristoteles' Politik*, ed. G. Patzig (Göttingen: Vandenhoeck and Ruprecht, 1990); and Fred D. Miller, Jr., *Nature, Justice, and Rights in Aristotle's "Politics"* (Oxford: Clarendon Press, 1995).

At both the beginning and the end of the *Nicomachean Ethics*, Aristotle says that the highest or most complete good is studied by political science (1094a23–b12, 1181b13–25), and at the beginning of the *Politics*, he tells us that political association aims at the highest good (1252a3–7). Our discussion of Aristotle's claims about friendship puts us in a position to understand this claim about political association. In claiming that humans are political animals (*NE* 1097b9–12; *Politics* 1253a2), Aristotle is claiming that political association makes possible the more complete realization of the deliberative capacities of rational animals. Cooperative association with other members of my community contributes to the full realization of my deliberative powers by diversifying my experiences, by providing me with resources for self-criticism as well as self-understanding, by broadening my deliberative menu and improving my deliberations, and by allowing me to engage in more complex and varied activities. The deliberative value of this interaction is enhanced when others have diverse perspectives and talents. For political association to extend the interests of its members fully, the members of a polity must share in ruling; this provides the opportunity for widespread participation by people with diverse perspectives in a process of mutual discussion and articulation of ideals and priorities. Aristotle can then claim that the members of such a political association, like partners to the best sort of friendship, extend each other's interests. It is true that he believes that virtue-friendship cannot hold on the scale of a political community that is just (*NE* 1158a11–12, 1170b29–1171a20; *Politics* 1262b3–20) and that political communities are associations for mutual advantage and do not involve the best sort of friendship (*NE* 1160a11–15; *EE* 1242b22). Nonetheless, political communities that are just have, to a significant degree, the two features that are crucial to the justification of virtue-friendship and familial-friendship: there is commonality of aims and aspirations among members of the political association, and this commonality is produced by members of the association living together in the right way, in particular, by defining their aims and goals consensually (*NE* 1167a25–28, 1155a24–28). Insofar as this is true, members of such a political association can see the interests of other members implicated in their own interests. And members of such a community can aim at justice for its own sake, because justice, Aristotle believes, promotes the *common* good, which is presumably the good common to them insofar as they are members of an interdependent political community (1129b15–18).

This explanation of how the complete good for an individual can only be realized in a political community implies that political activity is part of the good of rational animals. Aristotle draws this conclusion explicitly when he contrasts parts and necessary conditions of wholes and argues that, whereas manual labor is a necessary condition of the happiness of the community, political activity is an organic part of happiness (*Politics* VII 8–9, esp. 1329a35–38; cf. *EE* 1214b11–27). This would seem to support some form of democratic government. But whereas Aristotle does think that some form of democracy is the best nonideal constitution, he is prepared to sacrifice democratic commitments in ideal circumstances and accepts significant restrictions on the scope of citizenship in nonideal circumstances.

An ideal form of government must concern itself with the common good (*Politics* 1279a18-22). Aristotle ranks three ideal constitutions in descending order of desirability: rule by monarchy (one), aristocracy (the few), and a constitutional polity (the many) (1279a32-b4, 1289a26-28). The nonideal states correspond to each of the ideal states but do not serve the common good: they are tyranny, oligarchy, and democracy (1279a20-21, 1289a28-31). Aristotle thinks monarchy is the best form of government in those (perhaps merely counterfactual) circumstances in which some one individual of unsurpassed virtue emerges (1254b31-1255a2, 1288a16-19, 1325b10-13, 1332b16-21).[53] However, unlike Plato in the *Republic*, Aristotle is not primarily interested in ideal theory. He believes that all existing states are nonideal (1260b35), and his chief concern is a special kind of nonideal theory:

> We have now to inquire what is the best constitution for most states, and the best life for most men, neither assuming a standard of excellence which is above ordinary persons, nor an education which is exceptionally favored by nature and circumstances, nor yet an ideal state which is an aspiration only, but having regard to the life in which the majority are able to share, and to the form of government which states in general can attain. (1295a25-32)

Because tyranny is clearly the worst nonideal constitution (1289a38-b3), much of Aristotle's discussion focuses on the merits of oligarchy, democracy, and mixed constitutions (1309b29-30), concluding that some form of democracy (or mixed constitution with democratic elements) is least bad (1289b4-10).

The oligarch thinks that happiness is founded on wealth, perhaps because this is an index of honor, and that the state should be viewed as a large firm whose main aim is the accumulation of wealth and the distribution of political responsibility and advantages according to one's property (1280a25-31). Political offices are subject to various property

---

[53] Although Aristotle allows that the best ideal constitution would assign rule to the ultra-virtuous—whether the ultra-virtuous are many or one (1288a34-36)—his considered claim seems to be that the best ideal constitution is a monarchy. But this invites the question why an ideal world would not be one in which everyone was ultra-virtuous and in which the constitution was, as a result, democratic. It may be that Aristotle's reason for not taking this possibility seriously within ideal theory is that it is just too fanciful; it is much more improbable that everyone would be virtuous than it is that one would be (cf. *Rhetoric* 1354a33-b1).

qualifications, with the more important offices having higher qualifications (1320b22–26); only the select few who possess these qualifications should participate in political rule (1298a34–b2).

By contrast, the democrat thinks that happiness consists in the gratification of one's appetites, and that happiness, as a result, requires that everyone be free to live as he wishes (1310a26–35, 1317a40–b16). For this reason, the democrat thinks that liberty is fundamental and that if there must be political rule of one over another, it is best that each take his turn in ruling and being ruled (1298a10–12, 1317a40–42, b14–16). The democrat thinks that each individual has rights to liberty and political participation, and believes that responsibilities and resources ought to be distributed equally (1318a5–10). There should be few, if any, property qualifications for citizenship; the rich and the poor alike should rule; political responsibilities should be frequently rotated and generally allocated by lot; and decisions should be made by majority rule (1291b30–38, 1317b17–1318b6).

Oligarchy and democracy are nonideal constitutions, because neither aims at the common good of its citizens; each rests on mistaken assumptions about happiness. Democrats want to be left free to indulge their appetites, whereas oligarchs aim at accumulating wealth; both must be concerned with amassing material goods. But whereas happiness does require some material goods, it is controlled by virtue, rather than material goods, and requires only modest amounts of the latter (1266b25–28, 1295a35–b1, 1323a15–1324a1).

Nonideal constitutions are also mistaken in their assumptions about the value of political activity. Each thinks that political rule is necessary to secure the appropriate distribution of wealth and liberty. But then political rule must be only instrumentally valuable. By contrast, as we have seen, Aristotle thinks political rule is intrinsically valuable. If political activity is an intrinsic good for rational animals, then all rational animals should have a share in ruling, and the proper constitution would be some form of democracy (1275b5–6, 1325b7–10). Citizenship involves having a share in judging and ruling (1275a22–33). If there are no qualifications for citizenship, then all will rule to satisfy their appetites, rather than to promote a common good. Oligarchy is right to demand qualifications for citizenship, Aristotle thinks, but wrong to conceive of the qualifications in terms of wealth or property. He believes that the right qualifications should exclude slaves and manual laborers from citizenship (1278a3–9); manual laborers ought to be drawn from the ranks of barbarians and natural inferiors (1329a24–26).

Good ruling presupposes leisure (1269a34–36, 1326b27–31), both because good rulers must be well educated, which requires leisure, and because, once educated, they must have leisure for proper deliberation. But to be self-sufficient and to sustain leisure, the state must contain manual laborers, including artisans, tradesmen, and farmers (1328b15–

1329a38). Aristotle thinks that manual labor is only instrumentally valuable (1329a35–36) and that it detracts from proper deliberation and pursuit of virtue (1329a37–38). So far, his claims do not settle whether people should be divided into citizens and laborers or whether all ought to partake in both (1328b25–30). Because he seems to think that manual labor destroys a person's capacity for virtue, he chooses the first option; some ought to labor so that others may have the leisure necessary for ruling. This would be inequitable if all had equal capacities for ruling and virtue, but Aristotle denies this. He thinks that some—such as slaves and, to a lesser extent, women—are naturally inferior (*Politics* II 4–7, 12–13). Such natural inferiors are well suited to be manual laborers who are excluded from citizenship.

These limitations in Aristotle's democratic commitments not only are troubling but also are difficult to square with his view about friendship, which justifies intrinsic concern among members of a political community. One limitation is that Aristotle recommends some form of democracy only in nonideal conditions. It is not clear, however, that Aristotle should think that monarchy is the best constitution even in those merely counterfactual conditions in which an ultra-virtuous figure emerges. Unlike Plato, who thinks that rule by the wise should be in the interest of the governed (*Republic* 463b5), Aristotle appears to think that the monarch would be entitled to view and treat his subjects as slaves (1254b34–37). Even if slaves had no share in reason (1260b13), this would not be true of all the monarch's subjects. Many have deliberative capacities, even if they are, by hypothesis, weaker than the monarch's. Aristotle unjustifiably assumes, as Plato did, that comparative inferiority justifies complete exclusion from citizenship.[54] If the ultra-virtuous man is to be concerned for others for their own sakes, then he must share political rule with them, because political activity is an intrinsic good for rational animals. As we saw in the earlier criticism of Plato, there are ways of recognizing comparative differences in rational agency within a system of democratic governance; these differences do not justify excluding some from citizenship.

Aristotle also limits the scope of citizenship in nonideal circumstances, excluding women, barbarians, slaves, and manual laborers. His discussion of friendship suggests reasons for a more inclusive conception of democratic citizenship. There already are significant forms of personal, social, and economic interaction and interdependence between Aristotle's citizens, on the one hand, and women, slaves, manual laborers, and resident aliens, on the other. The arguments for recognizing a common good based upon interpersonal self-extension require including them in the common good. Perhaps Aristotle thinks that they are part of a common

---

[54] Irwin usefully discusses Aristotle's reliance on this assumption in "The Good of Political Activity," section 11.

good but that concern for them for their own sakes does not involve giving them a share in ruling. Just as Plato justified aristocratic rule by appeal to the claim that the next best thing to being ruled by one's own reason is being ruled by the reason of another (*Republic* 590c–d), so too Aristotle thinks that natural inferiors are like the nonrational part of the soul—they can apprehend and follow the reason of another but they are incapable of the sort of deliberation required for proper management of their own affairs or those of the community (1254b20–24, 1260a12–22). Friendship toward the naturally inferior, Aristotle believes, does not require granting them citizenship.

This justification of limitations on the scope of democratic citizenship is problematic in several ways. For one thing, Aristotle excludes manual laborers from citizenship on the ground that manual labor is inimical to deliberation and virtue. But this seems to assume that manual labor can only be menial and of instrumental value. Dull and repetitive labor over which the worker has no control is menial and can only be instrumentally valuable to the extent that it furnishes life's necessities, but manual labor need not be menial in this way. As long as the farmer or artisan has responsibility for and control over production, distribution, and the organization of her labor process, manual labor can and will exercise important deliberative capacities. By Aristotelian criteria, meaningful manual labor ought to be an intrinsic good fully compatible with the life of virtue.

Aristotle excludes women and slaves from citizenship, because he believes that they are naturally inferior, able to follow the reason of another but incapable of the sort of deliberation necessary for ruling and human happiness. Sometimes, he seems to accept the noncomparative claim that some—especially slaves—are altogether lacking in deliberative capacities (1260a12). At other times, he appears to concede that all humans share in reason (1254b21–23, 1259b27–35) and to endorse only the comparative claim that women and slaves have weaker deliberative faculties than those to whom he would grant citizenship.

One obvious problem with these limitations on the scope of democratic citizenship is that there is no evidence for either the comparative or the noncomparative inferiority of women and slaves. Aristotle's observations about women and slaves might understandably lead him to suppose not simply that they had achieved less by way of individual and civic accomplishments than full-fledged citizens but also that they were, in one sense, capable of less. But this sort of incapacity is presumably the *product*, rather than the cause, of their being denied citizenship. Aristotle realizes that capacities must be cultivated and stimulated to develop properly. If I have not been given a proper education and training with suitable deliberative opportunities and responsibilities at various points in my development, I will not be prepared for proper deliberation about the management of my own affairs or those of the community. Thus, even if everyone had equal innate capacities, we should expect the unequal development of deliberative capacities in systems where education and deliberative opportunities and responsibilities are distributed unequally. But then the unequal capacities that discriminatory practices and institutions produce cannot be appealed to as justification for those practices and institutions. There appears, therefore, to be no good reason for Aristotle not to recognize the claims to citizenship that existing patterns of interaction justify.

Indeed, if there were evidence for significant inequalities in the distribution of deliberative faculties, we would be in precisely the situation that Aristotle imagines justifies monarchy or aristocracy. Like Aristotle's argument that monarchy is the best ideal state, his argument for restricting democratic citizenship in nonideal circumstances mistakenly assumes that comparative differences in the extent to which people possess qualifications for citizenship justify the complete exclusion from citizenship of those with weaker qualifications. At most, comparative differences in deliberative faculties should force us to make room for the operation of moral expertise *within* a system of democratic governance; they do not justify excluding some rational animals from citizenship.

Because political activity is an intrinsic good for rational animals, Aristotle's conception of friendship as justifying concern for one's friends for their own sakes requires him to extend political rule to all rational animals, and this requires him to drop his antidemocratic qualifications for citizenship. Existing patterns of association between Aristotle's citizens, on the one hand, and women, slaves, manual laborers, and resident aliens, on the other hand, provide a backward-looking justification for recognizing a more inclusive conception of the common good. The deliberative value of shared discussion with others, especially those with diverse perspectives and talents, provides a forward-looking justification for recognizing a more inclusive conception of the common good. Only by expanding the scope of citizenship can Aristotle hope to arrive at a political community that fully extends the interests of its members and achieves a complete and self-sufficient good (cf. 1281b4–15).

XII. Conclusion

Whereas Vlastos is probably right that Socrates' eudaimonism prevents him from recognizing that interpersonal love involves concern for another for the other's own sake, he is wrong to think that Plato's and Aristotle's conceptions of love and friendship are unable to recognize intrinsic concern for another. Vlastos is right that an impersonal concern with virtue is incompatible with genuine love and friendship. But if we distinguish between the object and manner of concern, we can see how Plato and Aristotle can reconcile the lover's concern with his beloved's virtue and his concern with his beloved. We can also reconcile intrinsic concern for the beloved with eudaimonism by seeing the way in which Plato and Aristotle both think that love and friendship extend the lover's interests.

Despite this defense of Plato's and Aristotle's conceptions of love and friendship, there are problems with the way they understand the nature and scope of interpersonal concern, which manifest themselves most clearly in their doubts about democratic association. As part of ideal theory, Plato's rulers express concern for the ruled in ways that do not engage the deliberative capacities of the ruled. Aristotle makes comparable claims, within both ideal and nonideal theory, about the scope of citizenship. Good government aims at a common good; but the best ideal government (monarchy) excludes all but one from a share in self-government, and the best nonideal government (democracy with significant restrictions on the scope of citizenship) excludes a great many rational animals from a share in self-government. The main features, if not the details, of my criticisms of these antidemocratic claims are probably not especially new. It is worth noting, however, that these criticisms are not based on some external or modern perspective, unavailable to Plato or Aristotle; their antidemocratic commitments are in tension with their own views about friendship and *eudaimonia*. For these antidemocratic political claims fail to appreciate the Platonic and Aristotelian insistence that associational bonds provide reason to value one's associates for their own sakes, which requires concern for them as rational animals. Because political activity is part of the good for rational animals, Platonic and Aristotelian conceptions of love and friendship require fuller democratic commitments. This would require significant changes in Plato's and Aristotle's political theories, but they are friendly amendments insofar as they are driven by deep features of Platonic and Aristotelian conceptions of love, friendship, and *eudaimonia*.

Philosophy, University of California, San Diego

NO FAMILIES, NO FREEDOM:
HUMAN FLOURISHING IN A FREE SOCIETY

By Jennifer Roback Morse

I. Introduction

This essay has one simple theme: the family does a very important job that no other institution can do. What is that job? Inside a family, helpless babies are transformed from being self-centered bundles of impulses, desires, and emotions to being adult people capable of social behavior of all kinds. Why is this job important? The family teaches the ability to trust, cooperate, and self-restrain. Neither the free market nor self-governing political institutions can survive unless the vast majority of the population possesses these skills. Why is the family uniquely situated to teach these skills and the values that go with them? People develop these qualities in their children as a side effect of loving them. What does this have to do with a free society? Contracts and free political institutions, the foundational structures of a free society, require these attributes that only families can inculcate. Without loving families, no society can long govern itself, for the family teaches the skills of individual self-governance.

There are, of course, many competing visions of what might loosely be called a free society. At the libertarian end of the spectrum are advocates of a "night-watchman state," a government that performs only the minimal functions of providing national defense, police protection, and a legal system to enforce contracts. A more conservative vision of a free society would allow the government a greater role for inculcating and enforcing moral norms. A New Deal liberal vision of a free society would include the provision of a social safety net, financed through taxes, to provide economic security. Finally, the most expansive view of the government's role would be that free political institutions allowing mass participation in the governing process are the only defining characteristics of a free society: the government may do anything selected through democratic political institutions, no matter how intrusive into the ordinary lives of citizens.

The argument of this essay applies to any and all of these visions of a free society, except possibly the last. Almost every society requires self-restraint on the part of the population. The skills taught by the family are critical to any society freer than a police state. I would make the point even more strongly. The freer the political and economic institutions of the society, the more necessary the skills of individual, personal self-governance. Conversely, without self-governing, self-restraining individuals, the scope of the organized governmental sector will necessarily grow.

Economic and political institutions can only remain free if they are self-regulating to a large extent. This is such an important aspect of free societies that economists and political theorists spend much of their effort trying to devise institutional structures that will allow ordinary people to conduct their activities with minimal government interference and still produce orderly social outcomes. All these institutional structures require individual citizens to possess certain personal characteristics.

One of the most famous self-regulating social systems is the decentralized market economy. Adam Smith's famous "invisible hand" insight shows that people pursuing their own self-interest can actually end up furthering the public interest, through no intention of their own. Since Smith's time, free-market economists have developed the invisible hand idea further, to show how far self-interested individuals might be left on their own in an unregulated marketplace. We economists have created a character, called *Homo economicus* or economic man. Economic man is a rational, calculating person who considers only his self-interest. This self-interested man calculates the costs and benefits of each potential action, and chooses the action that brings him the most happiness.

Libertarians as well as their critics and fellow-travelers have discussed the subject of self-interest and its proper role in human society.[1] Much of that discussion concerns "self-interest rightly understood," that is, how a reasonable person ought to understand his own self-interest. Behind that whole discussion is the realization that some persons cannot be safely turned loose to pursue their own self-interest. Members of street gangs, dishonest people, and people who have no scruples about using other people, cannot be trusted. Scholars who have turned their intellectual energy toward these problems have attempted to show that such behavior is not really in the interests of the people who engage in it and that society does have the right and the responsibility to limit certain classes of behavior, even if it is self-interested behavior and the person cannot be persuaded to abandon his own understanding of his interest.

My focus in this essay is quite different. I attempt to spell out some of the minimum necessary conditions for a person to develop a reasonable understanding of his own interest, and a reasonable understanding of his relationship to other members of the human race. After all, we are not born as fully rational adults, capable of grasping our true interests, able to make contracts and other agreements, able to defend our property rights and our other legitimate interests. We are born as helpless babies.

I will focus upon a libertarian argument for loving families because libertarians take a more expansive view of personal liberty than the ad-

---

[1] See, e.g., *Self-Interest*, ed. Ellen Frankel Paul, Fred D. Miller, Jr., and Jeffrey Paul (Cambridge: Cambridge University Press, 1997).

herents of most other political philosophies. If I can convince libertarians that their ideal political world makes demands upon individuals, then surely others who are more willing to accept constraints upon their own behavior would be inclined to agree. I show that the libertarian, minimal state requires loving families. Further, I argue that this requirement can only be sustained through self-enforcement by individuals. A government that attempted to enforce parental responsibility in any but the most obvious and observable areas would certainly be a nightmare to most people, but especially to libertarians.

I begin with a look at a child without a family, to show the relevance of family life to free markets and free political institutions.

II. The Child without a Family

Children who are abandoned by their families usually end up in one of two places: on the street or in an orphanage. The experience of children in orphanages reveals some things about the development of the human person during the formative years that we might otherwise overlook. The first thing to note is the widely observed "failure to thrive" syndrome that occurs in understaffed, minimal-care orphanages. Children who are deprived of human contact during infancy sometimes fail to gain weight or to develop.[2] All the bodily, material needs of the child are met in these orphanages. The child is kept warm and dry. The child is fed, perhaps by having a bottle propped into the crib. The child contracts no identifiable illness. Yet the child fails to thrive, and may even die. The widely accepted explanation is that the children die from lack of human contact.[3]

The second thing to observe about these children without families is that they often have difficulty forming attachments to other people. Even children who are later adopted by loving and competent families sometimes never fully attach to them or to anyone. The prevailing thinking is that children who do not develop attachments in the first eighteen months of life will have grave difficulty in forming attachments later. And if the parents of such children do not intervene by the time the child reaches twelve years of age, the prospects for successful future intervention are thought to be gravely diminished, to the point of hopelessness.[4]

---

[2] This syndrome is known as the Kaspar Hauser syndrome, or psychosocial dwarfism. See *Comprehensive Textbook of Psychiatry/VI*, vol. 2, 6th ed., ed. Harold I. Kaplan, M.D., and Benjamin J. Sadock, M.D. (Baltimore: Williams and Wilkins, 1995), ch. 40 and sections 43.3 and 47.3.

[3] See Robert Kareh, *Becoming Attached: First Relationships and How They Shape Our Capacity to Love* (New York: Oxford University Press, 1998), ch. 1, "Mother Love: Worst Case Scenarios," pp. 13–25, and the references cited therein.

[4] See *Comprehensive Textbook of Psychiatry/VI*, vol. 2, section 43.3, "Reactive Attachment Disorder of Infancy or Early Childhood." See also Foster Cline, *Understanding and Treating the Severely Disturbed Child* (Evergreen, CO: Evergreen Consultants, 1979), for an analysis of the most severely disturbed of attachment-disordered children. The classic works on the attachment process in the normal mother/child relationship are: John Bowlby, *Attachment and Loss, Volume 1: Attachment* (New York: Basic Books, 1969); and Mary Ainsworth, Mary

What do I mean by difficulty in forming attachments? What exactly is the problem? The classic case of attachment disorder is a child who does not care what anyone thinks of him or her. The disapproval of significant others is not a sufficient deterrent from bad behavior, because there is no other who is significant enough to matter to the child. Children with this disorder do whatever they think they can get away with, no matter the cost to other people. They do not monitor their own behavior, so authority figures must constantly be wary of them and watch them. They respond to physical punishments, and to suspension of privileges, but not to disapproval. They lie if they think it is advantageous to lie. They steal if they can get away with it. They may go through the motions of offering affection, but people who live with them sense a kind of phoniness. They show no regret at having hurt another person, or may offer perfunctory apologies. They may find it fun to torture animals.

As they grow into adolescence, these children may become sophisticated manipulators. Some authors refer to them as "trust bandits," because they are superficially charming, in their initial encounters with people. They can charm people for short periods of time, only to betray the people's trust by using them. They can con people for long enough to use them. In the meantime, their parents, and anyone else who has long-term dealings with them, grow increasingly frustrated, frightened, and angry over their child's dangerous behavior, which may include lying, stealing, violence, and fire-setting.[5]

As the parents try to seek help for their child, they may find that the child is able to "work the system." Such a child can often charm therapists, social workers, counselors, and, later, perhaps even judges and parole officers. This child is unwilling to consider others, or even to inconvenience himself for the sake of others.

Who is this child? Why, it is *Homo economicus*, rational, calculating, economic man—the person who considers only his own good, who is willing to do anything he deems it in his interest to do, who cares for no one. All of his actions are governed by self-interested calculation of costs and benefits. Punishments matter, loss of esteem does not. He does not self-monitor; so he can always find some opportunity to evade the rules. As to his promises, he breaks them if he deems it in his interest to do so.

This is the child who some social theorists might have imagined would have become "the noble savage," left alone by adults and not corrupted by them. This is the child in the state of nature, who takes care of himself, who has no society around him. This is the child who survived a life that truly was "nasty, brutish and short."

Plainly, this is a person who is not fit for social life. Most people would just call this person a sociopath, and not dignify this character by calling

---

Blehar, Everett Waters, and Sally Wall, *Patterns of Attachment: A Psychological Study of the Strange Situation* (New Jersey: Lawrence Erlbaum Associates, 1978).

[5] The terminology of "trust bandit" is due to Ken Magid and Carole McKelvey, *High Risk: Children without a Conscience* (New York: Bantam Books, 1987).

him *Homo economicus*. Certainly, this child who was actually left alone bears no resemblance to anyone's notion of a "noble savage."

An economist might object: "Self-interested behavior need not be selfish behavior in the pejorative sense. *Homo economicus* may very well consider the welfare of other people, if he cares about them and if their happiness matters to him." And that is exactly the point: the thing that keeps *Homo economicus* from becoming a sociopath is that he does care for someone other than himself.

Why did I shock you with this parable of *Homo economicus* as an attachment-disordered child? It is not because I believe that any economist, free-market or otherwise, believes that this is how children are or ought to be treated. It is not because libertarian political theorists abandon their children or encourage others to do so. It is because the desperate condition of this left-alone child shows us that we have been, all along, counting on something to hold society together, something more than the mutual interests of autonomous individuals. We have taken that something else for granted, and overlooked it, even though it has been under our noses all along. The missing element is none other than love.

III. What a Loving Family Does for a Child

How does love make the difference between the sociopath and the kind of person who could be trusted to pursue his own self-interest without causing too much trouble to other people? To see this, we must begin with the human person in infancy. As infants, we are helpless, needy, and immature.

The infant experiences his life in short bursts of neediness. He experiences a need which he cannot satisfy by himself. The child cries out for help. Help arrives. The help does more than satisfy the child's immediate need. The assistance of another person allows the child to learn to trust.

What happens when the child experiences an unmet need? Of course, he continues to be hungry or wet. The unmet need creates something in the child that cannot be fully characterized as an absence. He is sitting there hungry. She is sitting there wet. He has a bloody nose. She has diarrhea. They keep crying. Their cries grow louder and more frantic. No one comes.

What goes through the child's vulnerable little mind during this episode? He or she may get angry. She or he may despair. The child who despairs may very well become the "failure to thrive" child, who wastes away. The angry child, perhaps, has a better chance of survival. Neither type of child acquires any trust.

Many neglected children learn to stop crying for help. They have learned from experience that no one will show up. Crying is futile. They develop some other strategy for getting their needs met. But it is deeply pathological for an infant to be thrown on his own resources.

Sometimes, when caring adults eventually appear in such a child's life, they may misinterpret what they see. They may think, "What a good baby. She never cries." In spite of how convenient this silent child may initially appear to be, there is something seriously wrong with a child who never cries. When an adult finally realizes what is going on, there are few sights more pathetic than an obviously needy child who doesn't cry: a child with a huge mess of diarrhea, a child with a bloody nose, a child with a serious injury—just standing there, not crying—or trying to comfort himself, and resisting the assistance of other people.

With reasonable and supportive parenting, the baby learns to trust that he will be taken care of. As the adult world responds to the child's needs, the child learns that it is safe and beneficial to trust. Children of normal, loving parents learn that all the anxiety they work themselves up into is not really necessary. Mom and Dad are going to show up; they are going to do what is needed. Children eventually learn to relax into the care of the adults, who are in loving control of the situation.

In the process, the infant comes to know that there is more in life than the satisfaction of the bodily appetites. The infant learns from experience that human contact and love are the great goods that ensure his continued existence. As a by-product of caring for the most basic bodily needs, the parents call out the child's longing for human contact. The longing for human contact ultimately develops into a longing for the deeper attachment we ordinarily call love.

This is the job that loving families do. Why is it an important job?

IV. THE SOCIAL SIGNIFICANCE OF TRUST

The reader might wonder at this point: What is the significance of trust? It is a lovely thing, of course, if an infant learns to trust his parents. But what is the relevance of this for a free society?

Trust is the foundation of reciprocity. The ability and willingness to trust is intrinsic to our human nature, and to our survival. Indeed, trust is as deep a part of our human condition as is the self-centered impulse that economists spend so much of their time talking about. For the normal infant, the satisfaction of his needs in a personal way leads to the development of trust, and then to the capacity for reciprocity.

Even an infant can provide something of value and pleasure for the parents: the first smile. And in this exchange of smiles for satisfactions, the child begins to learn the value of reciprocity, of give-and-take, in human relationships. The child's continued existence depends not only on the presence of adults, but also on their willingness to give to and provide for the child. Being cute, making people laugh, and engaging other people, makes it easier for adults to provide help. As an economist would say, adults find it less costly to give to a cute infant than to an obnoxious one. This is the normal path of social development.

We can see these costs most clearly in two pathological cases of infant development. In the case of autistic or other unresponsive children, the child does not or cannot learn to engage other people. For reasons that are not understood, these children do not learn to be cute, do not learn to engage. Some of them resist being held, and will even arch their backs to escape their mother's embrace.[6] These children have only limited capacity to give benefits to those who care for them. Parenting these children is exhausting, in part because the child is giving nothing.

The second pathological case occurs when the child has no one to whom to give. Orphanage children, street children, and abused children may have little interaction with adults that is not exploitative or abusive. These unattached children often have difficulty developing the capacity for reciprocity in relationships. They may not develop relationships in any meaningful sense. These children become difficult to parent, because, like the unresponsive child, the unattached child is giving nothing.

V. THE PRISONERS' DILEMMA

Consider, as well, the prisoners' dilemma. Many social scientists and philosophers use this parable as a model for problematic cooperation. The prisoners' dilemma analyzes situations in which it is collectively beneficial for people to cooperate with each other, even while it is in their individual and private interest to be uncooperative.

The prisoners' dilemma takes its name from the following situation. Two people have jointly committed a crime and have both been arrested. The authorities do not have sufficient evidence to convict either prisoner. They offer the following deal to each prisoner separately.

If neither you nor your accomplice confesses, you will both go free, for we have insufficient evidence to convict you. If you confess, however, your accomplice will receive the full sentence, but we will give you a reduced sentence. If he confesses and you do not, you will receive the full sentence, while he gets the lighter sentence. When the prisoners pose the question, "What if we both confess?" the reply is, "You both get the full sentence allowed by law, for we will have all the evidence we could possibly need."

Both prisoners will confess as long as there are no possibilities for communicating with each other, or for offering each other bribes or side payments. This is a dilemma for the prisoners, because both would be better off if neither confessed. But since neither can be sure the other will cooperate with him, neither is willing to take the chance of being the only one to remain silent. They would be better off if they could cooperate

---

[6] See the title essay in Oliver Sacks, *An Anthropologist on Mars: Seven Paradoxical Tales* (New York: Alfred Knopf, 1995), pp. 244–96, for a sensitive treatment of the world of the high-functioning autistic person.

with each other. But the prison guards do everything possible to prevent cooperation, both by preventing communication and by the structure of the deal they offer the prisoners. Both prisoners confess and receive the heaviest sentence.

Many social interactions have a structure of payoffs similar to that described by the prisoners' dilemma. I would be better off if no one littered in the park. But I cannot stop others from littering. So why pay the cost of cleaning up after myself, if no one else has done so, or is likely to do so? I would be better off if no one ever made a frivolous liability lawsuit. But since I am already bearing the social cost of many such frivolous lawsuits, why shouldn't I "dial for dollars" with a liability suit of my own if a plausible occasion presents itself to me? I am better off living in a world in which everyone keeps his promises and contracts, than in a world without effective promise-keeping. But within the world of general promise-keeping, I am even better off if I renege on my own agreements when I can get away with it. Why should I shoulder the burden of keeping my contracts?

Theorists and experimentalists alike have shown that it is privately rational to play tit-for-tat in a prisoners' dilemma game, as long as the game has been started with a cooperative first move. In this context, tit-for-tat means that I will cooperate with you, if you cooperate with me. If you defect from our (implicit or explicit) agreement, I will retaliate by refusing to cooperate with you in the next round of interactions.

We can conceptualize the parent as the first mover in the child's life. The parent gives to the child in an unrequited way. Indeed, the child's very existence is a gift. The child receives the gift of life as well as many other gifts from the parent.

The child does not and, indeed, cannot reciprocate in kind. The child does learn to participate in reciprocity. The child learns give-and-take: the child learns to trade smiles with his parents. Sometime between the age of three months and six months, the child learns the cognitively trivial but socially complex task of playing peek-a-boo: looking, with anticipation, for another person; delighting in the moment of eye-contact. The only rewards for the game are laughter and looks. Ultimately, the child learns to take turns in a conversation. All these behaviors have elements of regard for others, elements of reciprocity, elements of mutual benefit and pleasure.

I have been focusing on the need for people to trust. I should also draw out the obvious fact that the ability to restrain oneself is an integral part of being trustworthy. Part of cooperating in the prisoners' dilemma is restraining oneself from taking advantage of opportunities for immediate gains. Both the willingness to trust and the ability to restrain oneself flow, in some sense, from the attachments of people to each other.

The child learns to suppress some of his immediate desires, for the sake of the comfort of others. He learns not to scream out for anything and everything he wants. He learns to wait his turn. He learns to share toys. These are all primitive forms of cooperative behavior. They all require self-restraint.

Child-development specialists have traced out the course of moral development along the following path. First, my parents will punish me if I do x. Next, my parents will not like it if I do x. Next, my parents might not find out, but if they did, they would not like it. Next, I won't like it if I do x. And finally, I am not the kind of person who even thinks about doing x.

The prohibition comes closer to the person with each of these steps. External costs and benefits become less relevant with each succeeding step. The child moves from calculating the costs of disobeying, and from calculating the probability of detection, to completely internalizing the prohibition. At this point, the prohibition has been incorporated into the child's set of preferences and his view of himself. And when the action becomes completely outside the choice set, costs and benefits become irrelevant. No calculation will take place, in any event.

For any of this progression of internalized prohibitions to take place, there must be a significant person in the child's life. This other person is significant precisely in the sense that the child cares what the person will do, and cares what the person will think. The disapprobation alone becomes enough of a cost to deter bad behavior.

The condition of the attachment-disordered child is instructive in this regard. Normal people care what other people think about them. Attachment-disordered people are dangerous precisely because they do not care what anyone thinks about them. No one can really control them. Only external sanctions have any impact on them, and they do not monitor their own behavior.

Social scientists have shown that people are more likely to be cooperative, the longer the time horizon of the interaction. In other words, people are more likely to play a stranger for a sucker, than they are to take advantage of a person they will have to deal with again later. Some of these social scientists make the following argument. Even if you feel nothing for the other person, you will be more likely to be cooperative and not press full advantage, if you know you will encounter that person again in future interactions. Even if you have no affection for or attachment to the other person, it will be in your rationally calculated self-interest not to exploit the other player, if you know you will have to deal with him again.

This argument is sometimes used to show how even people who have no psychological attachments to each other could be induced to cooperate, simply by following their rational self-interest. The argument is sometimes used to justify "minimal morals." Self-interest can be counted on to do the job that morals formerly had been asked to do.

But this argument assumes too much. The argument assumes that people have a long enough time horizon to take advantage of the future potential gains. The length of a person's time horizon cannot be taken as a parameter; it is a variable. In fact, a person's ability to look into the future, make a plan, and stick to it is an important variable in determining the person's success in life.

This is what I mean by "time horizon": Every genuine decision to act or not, has at least some component of hypothetical thinking and projecting into the future. "If I do this action, I will face the following consequence." People have to imagine the action, and its consequence, before they can really "choose" or "decide" what they are going to do. Most people can calculate the immediate consequences of their actions. But calculating the consequences of a long stream of actions and interactions is more difficult. It is difficult to accurately forecast the sequence of consequences. It may be even more difficult to restrain oneself in the face of immediate gain.

Social scientists ought not assume that every person has an equal capacity for accurate calculation of costs and benefits into the future. Nor is it safe to assume that every person has an equal capacity for postponing future benefits in the face of immediate costs. As a matter of fact, we do not know very much about how a person develops a longer time horizon.

We do know from both casual and systematic observation, that children have considerably shorter time horizons than do adults.[7] We do not know very much about how children move from the need for short-term gratification to an ability to delay gratification. A great deal of moral training focuses upon teaching a child to accept delayed gratification. With a bit of reflection, we can see that trust is a necessary element for teaching delayed gratification.

Most people do not instinctively or automatically learn to forgo future benefits when faced with immediate costs. We do not even learn it completely through trial and error, although many trials and errors may be involved. People usually need to have their experience explained to them. Little people especially need someone to tell them that they have a tummy ache because they ate too much candy. They are more likely to accept that information, and incorporate it into their thinking, if they trust the person who told them. The adults want the child to think to himself, "I am suffering now, because of something I did that seemed to be fun at the time. Perhaps I will remember to have less fun next time." The child is

[7] Margaret Brinig has done the most systematic work on the differences in time preferences among men, women, and children, as well as on the development of the length of time preferences. See Brinig, "Why Can't a Woman Be More Like a Man? Or, Do Gender Differences Affect Choice?" in *Neither Victim nor Enemy*, ed. Rita Simon (Lanham, MD: University Press of America, 1995); and Brinig, "Does Mediation Systematically Disadvantage Women?" *William and Mary Law Review*, vol. 2 (1995), p. 1.

much more likely to accept this message from someone he trusts as reliable and loving than from any person at random.

Trust, then, is a critical element in developing a longer time horizon. Trusting other people is one thing that an unattached person truly cannot do. Connectedness with others is related to the length of a person's time horizon, because connectedness to another person allows a child to trust in the first place. So trust is the mechanism through which a person with normal attachments to others first learns to delay gratification and lengthen his time horizon.

The attachment-disordered person has a lot of trouble participating in long-term interactions. The argument that repeated interactions by themselves induce cooperative behavior goes out the window with these people. For the attachment-disordered child, other people are truly interchangeable with each other. He cares as much about a stranger as he does about his mother. (Parents of attachment-disordered children often report that they believe their child would willingly go home with a stranger.) Therefore, if every person is truly interchangeable with any other, the attachment-disordered person is willing to find new trading partners for every interaction. He might literally "sell his mother down the river" if the price were right. A lost friendship means nothing to him. He can always find suckers. He can be a predator, in the economic arena and perhaps in other arenas.

From the social viewpoint, this is a dangerous character. From his own viewpoint, the attachment-disordered person is extremely limited in the kinds of transactions he can carry out. He can only engage in activities that do not require a particular person to interact with him for long periods of time. Unless he can truly restrain himself in the short run, using his rational calculating faculty, he will not be able to do anything very long-term. This seems to be characteristic of these people as they age. They keep conning people. Since all persons are interchangeable to them, they continue to find a steady supply of new suckers.

Losing the esteem of significant others is an important motivator for most people throughout their lives. Most people do not avoid crime because of anything the police or criminal justice system might do to them. There are many opportunities for committing crimes with low probabilities of ever getting caught. Yet people do not commit all the crimes they might get away with. Most people, most of the time, restrain themselves from committing crimes that might both be profitable to them and have low probabilities of apprehension. Why? I believe it is because they are afraid of what their parents would think.

It is only the attachment-disordered person who is literally running the cost-benefit analysis on every opportunity for theft, lying, and so forth. We can see from the behavior of such people that there are in fact many opportunities for antisocial behavior. Normal people do not even begin the calculations. The cost-benefit program is overridden by the thought

"What would your mother think?" or "What would your father say?" before the calculations even begin. In fact, that is what the mothers and fathers of the world want their children to do. "Don't even think about it." Why? Because if you think about it, you will find that some of the time, crime will pay. The parents' job is to short-circuit that entire line of thought.

The development of trust and self-restraint are responses to the give-and-take between parent and child. Reciprocity is necessary at the beginning of life. People learn about unrequited giving, because they are on the receiving end of it. They learn to allow other people to matter. They learn to be trustworthy and to trust. They learn to restrain themselves in the face of temptations. They learn to refrain from calculating the costs and benefits of activities that are likely to pose temptations. And from these lessons learned early in life, they become capable of participating in social life. They become capable of learning the further, complex tasks involved in a highly developed social order.

The capacity to participate in these profound and subtle relationships with intimates sets the stage for a capacity to engage in more limited trust relationships with strangers. It would not be reasonable to trust a stranger to the same extent that one trusts one's most intimate family members and friends. And at the same time, if one never has the opportunity or develops the capacity to trust one's most intimate family members, it is difficult to see how one would ever conclude that trusting more distant people could be beneficial.

A core of trust is created in children during infancy. Children come to believe that the world is a safe place, fit for their existence, and that they belong here, in some very deep sense. And this core belief can be transferred to people other than the parents. In fact, we have to teach children to be judicious in their trust of other people. The admonition not to talk to strangers would be unnecessary if children were not trusting. Just as we have to teach children to moderate their self-centeredness, even though we know some self-centeredness is necessary, we also must teach them to moderate their trust.

The fact that the core of trust within the family can be transferred outside the family has great social significance. For this is the foundation of larger social institutions based on trust. The child develops an ability to trust other people and institutions, in a moderate, mature way. That is, the child learns that some trust is necessary for his dealings in the world, and that, at the same time, some caution must be used in deciding whom to trust, for what purpose, and to what extent.

VI. Trust and Economic Institutions

Trade and exchange are the most basic economic activities. Trade and exchange are reciprocal behaviors. These most basic economic activities require some willingness to trust and some capacity for trustworthy behavior.

Experimental economists have observed that rats can be induced to do something akin to comparing costs and benefits. That is, experimental economists can show that rats will demand fewer food pellets when the cost of obtaining them is higher. In this very limited sense, rats are rational economic actors.[8]

But what the experimentalists cannot induce the rats to do, is to trade. That is, rats will not exchange food, or anything else, with each other. Demand is the economic action of an individual in isolation. Exchange is the economic interaction among individuals. Rats can be trained to "buy" commodities from a food dispenser, but rats do not trade among themselves. They appear to be incapable of reciprocal behavior.[9]

A commonplace transaction in a grocery store is, in a certain sense, comparable to the rats buying from a food dispenser. The person observes the commodity offered for sale and the posted price the seller asks for it. The consumer decides whether to buy or not. If he decides to buy, he parts with the required amount of money. The store dispenses the commodity to him. The transaction is completed.

But many more complex transactions are not at all comparable to the rat tapping for food pellets. Some transactions take place over longer periods of time. Such transactions often require people to deliver goods and make payments at staggered intervals. Other transactions are complex because the commodities are difficult to define precisely. Buyer and seller may have different conceptions of the good being traded. In both of these types of transactions, a certain amount of trust is necessary for the transaction to even begin. If the parties are both trustworthy and willing to trust, the transaction can be completed at far lower cost than if the transaction is clouded by mutual suspicion.

The banking system provides another example of the economic significance of trust. First and foremost, the banking system is based on trust: trust that your money will be there when you go to withdraw it, trust that your loan will not be called in ahead of schedule. Without trust of this kind, the banking system would collapse, no matter how it was regulated, and no matter how much deposit insurance was pumped into it.

The banking system of Europe was founded and for a long time dominated by wealthy families engaged in extensive trade and by religious

---

[8] John H. Kagel, Raymond Battalio, Howard Rachlin, and Leonard Green, "Demand Curves for Animal Consumers," *Quarterly Journal of Economics*, vol. 96 (1981), pp. 1–16; and Raymond Battalio, John H. Kagel, and Don N. McDonald, "Animals' Choices over Uncertain Outcomes: Some Initial Experimental Results," *American Economic Review*, vol. 75 (1985), pp. 597–613.

[9] For a discussion of why it might be that animals do not trade, see David Levy, *The Economic Ideas of Ordinary People* (London: Routledge, 1992), pp. 17-33.

orders.[10] One of the marvelous phenomena of economic development is the extension of those networks of trust, based on personal contact and/or highly developed reputations, into networks available even to strangers. The core of trust created among the religious orders and trading families spilled over into a vast financial system among strangers.

Can you imagine having a long-term contract, with thousands of dollars at stake over long periods of time, with someone who was calculating every short-term advantage? The law of contract cannot be enough to protect people from "efficient" breach of contract. The world could not do the amount and kind of business it does, if literally everybody played opportunistically on every occasion.

VII. Trust and Political Institutions

If trust and self-restraint are critical to free-market economic activity, these qualities are at least as important to constitutionally limited participatory democracy. To show why this is so, let me begin with a brief overview of the public-choice perspective on the policymaking process. The public-choice insight is that public policy is made through a self-interested process. Those who have the most at stake in the outcome of a regulatory decision, for example, have the greatest interest in getting themselves organized to influence the regulators. Typically, this means that producer organizations are favored over unorganized consumers. Well-defined, well-organized voting blocks are favored over more ill-defined groups. Many programs that superficially appear to be for the benefit of the poor, actually are controlled far more for the interests of certain middle-class constituents.

The modern democratic state offers many opportunities for the unscrupulous. The state is positioned to offer many favors in the form of tax breaks, favorable regulatory climates, and the like. Because of these potential favors, interested parties will be induced to try to manipulate the outcomes of these processes. Millions of dollars can be transferred by the stroke of a regulator's pen. Therefore, interested parties spend millions of

[10] See Randall Collins, *Weberian Sociological Theory* (Cambridge: Cambridge University Press, 1986), pp. 52-53. Collins uses the religious orders as examples of Max Weber's theories of the rise of capitalism. For an appreciation of just how far-ranging the activities of the military religious orders really were, see *The Atlas of the Crusades*, ed. Jonathan Riley-Smith (New York: Facts on File, 1991), especially the maps on pp. 53, 90-91, and 98, as well as the text on pp. 100 and 124. For the importance of the trading families and small corporations, see Rondo Cameron, *A Concise Economic History of the World: From Paleolithic Times to the Present*, 2d ed. (New York: Oxford University Press, 1993), pp. 66-68. See *Historical Atlas of the World* (Chicago: Rand-McNally, 1981), map 35, p. 71, for an appreciation of the extent of the banking activities of the Medici and Fugger families, as well as the league of Hanseatic towns.

dollars trying to influence the outcome. Public-choice economists refer to this phenomenon as "rent-seeking."[11]

There is a tremendous waste of resources in this process, as people spend valuable time either trying to live off the results of the political system of wealth transfer, or trying to protect themselves from predators who seek to do so. Most everyone realizes the destructiveness of this process. But once the process is in motion, no one can afford to step out of it. The temptation to engage in this kind of antisocial behavior is too strong for most people to resist. An old-fashioned Catholic might say that the modern state is a massive occasion of sin.[12]

This pessimistic view of government activity is widely associated with a particular public-choice brand of advocacy of limited government. But how is it related to our topic of trust? I believe that much of our modern state and its apparatus was established in good faith, by people who conscientiously believed that it would achieve its stated purposes. But they overlooked the fact that they were creating temptations. They were counting on people to be public-spirited, and to refrain from calculating the private benefits to themselves of taking full advantage of the system. Once people begin such calculations, lots of them are going to see that antisocial behavior really does pay.

Generally speaking, when we established many of our political institutions and instituted many of our public policies, we were counting on the core of trust and trustworthiness that is created in individuals by their family life. But these public institutions contain so many temptations for antisocial behavior that the habits of trust have become eroded. People who continue to behave decently are exploited by the unscrupulous. Game theory has a colorful name to describe people who cooperate when others defect: they are called "suckers." I believe that the state is parasitic on the core of trust created within the family. Perhaps the reason the state has not collapsed from the weight of its own corruption is that each generation continues to learn some of the core values of trust and trustworthiness upon which the continuation of mass political activity in fact depends.

The attachments between parents and children create a capacity to form lasting attachments with other people. Other, particular people become important enough to us that we are unwilling to take advantage of them. We are unwilling to sacrifice a long-term relationship with them for the sake of short-term advantage. Similarly, we exercise some forbear-

---

[11] See Anne Kreuger, "The Political Economy of the Rent-Seeking Society," *American Economic Review*, vol. 64 (1974), pp. 291–303. For a survey of recent work on rent-seeking, see Robert Tollison, "Rent-Seeking: A Survey," *Kyklos*, vol. 35 (1982), pp. 575–602.

[12] See, for instance, my "The Modern State as an Occasion of Sin: A Public Choice Interpretation of the Welfare State," *Notre Dame Journal of Law, Ethics, and Public Policy*, vol. 11 (1997), pp. 531–48.

ance, in *not* attempting to harness the power of the state for our personal ends on any occasion that might present itself.

It is not good enough to say, as libertarians and conservatives so often do, "We must make the state minimal. We must shrink and control the state so much that no one will be tempted to use it for his own benefit." I am inclined to agree with that statement, as far as it goes. The problem with that formulation is that it is unstable. A state with enough power to protect us from a military power like China or like the Soviet Union used to be, is a state that can do what it likes with us. Even the minimal state has power, enough to run a military establishment, a legal system, and a police force. All this power can be harnessed by private interests, if they are tenacious enough. Without some ethic of mutual forbearance among the citizens, the minimal state is highly unlikely to remain minimal.

This is why a discussion of trust and reciprocity belongs in a discussion about human flourishing within libertarian political theory. For the textbook description of *Homo economicus* appeared to be rational calculating man. Libertarian political theory relies upon the use of markets and other exchange relationships, to a far greater extent than most other political theories do. Constitutionally limited government relies to a great extent upon an ethic of mutual forbearance among the citizens.

In the background of rationally calculating economic man, economists and libertarians all along were assuming the presence of many particular capacities: for independent action, for definite preferences, for learning from one's experience, and for the use of language. These attributes are plainly necessary for economic life, and plainly beyond the capacity of the infant. While the infant is developing these capacities that prepare him for social life, he is also developing the capacity for trust and for reciprocity. The person who comes to the economic and political realms has already mastered these elementary skills, and has some ability to trust and be trustworthy.

Under normal developmental circumstances, persons learn these skills so automatically, so effortlessly, so painlessly, that we scarcely notice the process at all. I believe this is part of the reason why this aspect of the human person has been neglected by economists. Trust and reciprocity are so much a part of the human condition that we take them for granted. We notice them only in their absence.

VIII. The Short Version of the Problem

We could condense all these arguments and make the following simple statement from the economists' perspective. Contracts are the tools used by free people to arrange their economic affairs for mutual advantage. Constitutionally limited popular government is the heart of a free political society. But it is often not practical to make provisions for every possible contingency that might arise during the life of a contract. It is equally impractical to make explicit constitutional provision for every contingency that might arise during the life of a republic. In these economic situations, people become vulnerable to opportunistic and predatory behavior from their contracting partners. In the political arena, the citizens are vulnerable to constitutional interpretations that increase governmental power, all around the edges of explicit constitutional provision.

People can end up substantially dissipating the potential gains from trade by attempting to protect themselves both before and after the signing of a contract. Going into the contract, people who have reason to be suspicious must make ever more detailed provisions for ever more contingencies and for possibilities for noncompliance and shirking. During the life of the contract, if people find themselves in an unforeseen and vulnerable position, they must scramble around, trying to defend themselves or to cut their losses. Similarly, the benefits of a government of constitutionally limited power can be completely lost if a significant subset of the population tries to "push the envelope" of constitutionally permissible governmental power.

Because the potential losses from unscrupulous behavior can be so large, the system of contract law can operate at lower cost and greater benefit if it is supplemented by an ethical system of personal self-restraint. The political system of checks and balances needs to be supplemented by a personal system of checks and balances that operates in the interior of each person. The potential scope for the operation of this ethical code which places internal limitations upon behavior is simply enormous. It consists of all the social interactions in which implicit agreements are used, all the parts of contracts that cannot be completely specified, as well as all the aspects of life that rely upon civil behavior.

This is the importance of the job done by a loving family. The family calls out from the individual the capacity to have regard for other people. Libertarianism, in both the economic sphere and the political one, requires self-restraining, self-monitoring, self-governing adults. But we are not born as adults. In spite of what some romantics might think, actual babies are not noble savages. They are just cute savages, who have the potential to be civilized. They are totally self-centered, impulsive, and demanding. It is not a foregone conclusion that any particular child will be civilized.

IX. Is There a Close Substitute for the Family?

The family is the child's first link to the rest of the human race. The family quite literally socializes the child, in the sense of making the child capable of participating in the social order. Parents spend a lot of time wiping noses and tying shoes. These things might seem to be menial chores that any idiot could do. But as a by-product of doing these mundane things, the parents convey to the child that he matters to them. He comes to allow them to matter to him as well. The family is the natural and best institution for creating attachment and teaching cooperation.

Families can do this job well or poorly. We might ask, "Are there any substitutes for the family in doing this important task?" Let us be clear about what we are asking. If we are asking, "Is there a close substitute for a particular family that is negligent and abusive?" then, of course, the answer can sometimes be "yes." But the best substitute even for that family is another, more appropriate family. If we are asking, "Is there another institution that is more appropriate than the family?" then the answer is certainly "no."

I mean this in two senses. First, it may well be that there really is no family available to a particular child. Nevertheless, we must look to the family and what it provides under normal circumstances, to guide us in developing a reasonable alternative for that particular child. The family is still the benchmark for success or failure.

We have to use this benchmark with some discernment, however. For instance, the thinking behind the foster-care system probably was that placing children with families is better for them than keeping them in institutions. The reader might think that I would agree with this assessment that a family is better than an institution. However, institutions such as orphanages can sometimes provide something that a foster family cannot provide, namely, stability, continuity, and commitment. A foster family appears to be more like a real family, but the foster family lacks the very thing that is critical to attachment. The foster family cannot credibly say, "You are our child and no one will ever take you away. We will never get rid of you." The very premise of foster care is that it is temporary.

Second, the fact that some families fail should not lead us to conclude that the family as an institution is dispensable. The fact that some families are abusive does not imply that all children would be better off in state-sponsored daycare. The failures of some parents should not become an excuse for public distrust of all parents. Rather than jumping to the conclusion that no parents should be trusted or to the presumption that children are better off in daycare, we should see how the actual characteristics of well-functioning families can be supported or replicated in families that face greater challenges. In other words, strengthening the family, making it easier for it to do its legitimate and necessary jobs— these should be the first objects of government policy and social commentary. The family as an institution is far too important for us to throw up our hands when signs of strain appear.

There is no close substitute for the loving family in creating the "disposition to cooperate." Two possible substitute social institutions might come to mind. From the right-wing careerist corner, we might hear the claim that the market could solve this problem. We could hire someone to take care of our children. These hired substitute parents could be close enough substitutes for all practical purposes. From the left-wing statist corner, we might hear the claim that some government program could create the characteristics of cooperation. We could inculcate these dispositions in government schools and day-care centers. We could take the children from their parents at ever earlier ages, to assure that they were thoroughly trained and properly brought up for social life.

Before I address these points, I should remind the reader that my purpose is limited. I am not trying to show that there is never an appropriate situation in which to hire child-care help. Nor is my objective to offer a detailed critique of each and every government program that has been or could be devised for the care and development of children. My objective is to show that neither state programs nor hired child-care workers can be complete substitutes for parents in creating attachment and in teaching cooperation.

X. Is the Market a Substitute for the Family?

To deal with this possibility, let me summarize my activity as a stay-at-home mom on any given day. How are the basic jobs of instruction, limit-setting, direction, and guidance to be done with any particular child? One of my children has such a tender conscience that she bursts into tears at the realization of having done something wrong. The other requires a small two-by-four to even get the message that he has done wrong and needs to apologize. One child plays every injury for maximum drama: she demands a band-aid for microscopic boo-boos. The other child is so impervious to pain, and so resistant to accepting help, that if you hear a whimper out of him, it's best to just dial 911.

And the subtleties of settling quarrels! Who really started that fight? It looks for all the world as if big brother pushed and shoved, but little sister can be an irresistible provocateur. Who did what on this particular occasion?

They need help in their social interactions with each other and the other children in the neighborhood. They need more than a generalized instruction to share and be nice. Sometimes, they honestly have no clue how to do what they are supposed to do. They would like to persuade other children to play with them (on their own terms, of course), but they have no idea what to offer them, or how to speak to them. Sometimes, they are sorely tempted to do or say something they know they aren't supposed to, but they cannot quite see how to stop themselves, or how to manage the frustration inherent in controlling their impulses.

They might be able to formulate the thought, "I want that other kid's toy. I know my mom does not want me to punch him to get it," and then get stuck. They cannot see a course of action that gets them where they want to go, or, at least, to somewhere they can stand to be. The gap between what they want to do and what they are supposed to do is too broad for them to jump.

So, they need some coaching not only for their actions, but for their words and even their thoughts. Mom can intervene with suggestions such as, "Why don't you offer to trade?" or "Why don't you offer to play this game that will let you play with the toy together?" or, if all else fails, "Why don't you play with something else?" As the child gets a little older, helping him learn to manage his frustration is a more important objective than helping him find strategies to get his own way. "That toy belongs to him. He doesn't have to let you play with it." "You wouldn't like it if he took your toys." "Do you have enough toys? You need to be satisfied with what you have." Knowing when a particular child is ready for a new level of self-restraint, knowing what level of abstraction he can grasp, knowing how much frustration he can tolerate, and helping him move to a new level, all of these are part of the daily work of motherhood.

Now I ask you: Who am I going to pay to do all this? How am I going to give instructions of sufficient detail to a babysitter? The "market" cannot handle this problem completely. Of course, there is nothing wrong with hiring some help. But no one can completely delegate the innumerable tasks that go into raising any particular child. As a matter of fact, when people are particularly pleased with a nanny or babysitter, they often express this fact by saying, "She is just like one of the family." This statement means that this person has slid into the routine of the family, and has grasped its unstated rules, norms, and expectations. I have never heard someone praise a child-care worker by saying, "She is an employee," or, "She works for her paycheck." Usually, when parents say this kind of thing, they are at the end of their rope with someone who cannot draw any inferences or take any initiative.

The only plausible way to use the market still requires the family as a monitor. We hire people and use purchased goods in a variety of ways to help us raise our children. But the parents still have the primary responsibility for choosing which people, how much, and in what context. The parents still have the right and the responsibility for selecting the content of their "electronic babysitters," the TV, videos, and computer games. No one in his right mind would advocate turning children over to "the market" in some abstract way, and leaving the parents completely out of the decision-making loop. The family is still present in the process of selecting and monitoring any child-care services purchased on the market.

The problem with the market is that people sometimes use it too much or inappropriately. But no one in his right mind would conceptualize the problem of child care as fundamentally an economic problem which the impersonal market could solve. No one says, "Let parents turn their children over to the market, as infants. The parents need do nothing more. Let the system work itself out." Even parents who use the market most extensively recognize that they still have the primary responsibility for the upbringing of their child. The basic problem with the market as child-care provider is that people tend to rely upon it too much because it is convenient. People tend to let the priorities become garbled, as they do what is convenient for themselves rather than what is best for the child.

This is why I mention the market as a substitute for the family in this essay. Many Americans conceptualize personal liberty in a way that might be described as libertarian. This form of libertarianism means the right to perform any peaceful, noncoercive act. A typical statement of an individual's responsibility in this context is that the individual has a responsibility to refrain from the initiation of force, and from fraudulent activity. My argument is that this is an insufficient statement of the individual's responsibility even within a libertarian society, the society with the fewest external constraints upon people.

Parents have a positive responsibility to take care of their children. Completely delegating the care of children to hired help is not exactly an act of force or fraud. It is, however, an extremely negligent act. A libertarian society cannot long survive if large numbers of people choose to discharge their parental duties in this most perfunctory way. Individuals in a libertarian society need to have internalized this responsibility. Most people, even people who are in no way libertarians, would find it problematic to rely upon state enforcement of the parental obligation beyond the most minimal demands for material care.

XI. Is the Government a Substitute for the Family?

Most of the state's efforts currently are focused on helping infants whose parents are hopelessly incapable of parenting. The state itself uses the family as an institution, because its preferred solution is to place these infants into foster homes or, ultimately, adoptive homes.

So far, so good. There is a very good case to be made for the state to replace the most incompetent of families with better families. Even this modest effort, however, is fraught with difficulty, because child-welfare agencies are frequently unable to use everything they know about which children need to be removed and which parents really need to surrender their custodial rights completely. A caseworker may know perfectly well that a family has very minimal prospects of ever shaping up enough to provide an adequate home in which the children can attach to the parents and learn reasonable social skills. But all too often the social worker cannot prove her case in a court of law, which requires more than intuition, gut feelings, and tacit knowledge.

My point here is not to suggest reforms for the foster-care system. My point is simply this: If the agencies of the government have this much difficulty assisting families that are truly incompetent, why would we ever want to expand the governmental role in providing substitute services for the family? To create attachment, the infant's needs must be met in a personal enough way that the child feels that he matters to other people. To be a substitute for the family in this task, the state would have to remove the children from their parents as infants. But how would the employees of a government agency figure out the needs of each and every individual child charged to their care? It is far-fetched to even imagine such a thing. Replacing one family with another is probably as good a job as can be expected from an institution that is as fundamentally impersonal as the state. In the absence of gross neglect or abuse, the infant belongs with his parents.

The worst of the worst

Everything we know from experience about state-run programs, both from the U.S. and overseas, is that they are most likely to address nothing but the material needs of the child. The situation was the most stark in the orphanages run by the socialist governments of the former Soviet Bloc. The theory of those governments and the institutions they ran was that the person was nothing but his body. Solve the economic problem of providing for the material needs of the body, and the social problem is completely solved.

To show how bad non-family child care can get, let me relate something that took place at a conference I once attended. The conference was for the adoptive parents of children who had spent substantial time in former Eastern Bloc orphanages. In the course of the discussion, one mother remarked, "My son was fed like a hamster."

All of us in the audience that day knew exactly what she meant. Many of our children had been fed like hamsters too. The attendant at the orphanage takes the baby bottle, and wires it between the bars of the crib. The baby can eat whenever he wants, without anyone ever having to pick him up.

All of us were dealing with the long-term problems created for our children by being treated like hamsters. Our kids are shorter and smaller than average. They cannot control their bodies very well. They do repetitive, stereotypic behaviors, like repeatedly throwing an object into the air, rocking their heads, even banging their heads. Once they are placed in adoptive homes, most of them grow and gain weight very quickly. For most of the kids, the most severe of their stereotypic behaviors become more moderate and manageable. But you may be sure that if they had not been removed from the orphanage, they would still be unusually small. They would still be rocking and banging.

They have severe delays in developing speech, language, and social skills. They cannot draw inferences, especially in social situations. They have trouble attaching to other people, or caring about other people.

These difficulties seem to be persistent. Even after the child has spent substantial time with his new parents, he may still have these types of problems.

The reader might think that this case is much too extreme. Such a thing could never happen in America, or in any other Western country. We have the resources and the knowledge to do a better job creating attachments and teaching cooperation than the impoverished and corrupt Soviet Bloc.

Meeting the material needs of an infant is not enough. Yet meeting material needs is precisely the kind of thing that governmental programs and organizations are best equipped to do.[13] Feeding children can be observed and monitored. People can be held accountable for whether they have fed the children or not.

But government employees cannot be so easily held accountable for meeting the more subtle, nonmaterial needs of the child. Did you rock the baby? For how many hours? Did you hold the baby close to you, or did you stick him in an automatic rocker? Did you play peek-a-boo with those babies? How many of them? How many times? Did you look into the babies' eyes while you changed their diapers, or were you distracted by the cries of ten other children? Speaking of cries, how long did it take you to respond to each crying child? How many of them had to wait so long that they gave up on crying for help? We can see from the range and detail of the questions that it is hopeless to imagine that state-sponsored institutional care can ever provide what children need to become truly connected to the rest of the human race.

There is now some talk of reviving orphanages, from individuals who were raised in orphanages. The economist Richard McKenzie[14] is one of the most prominent of those who argue from the basis of their own experience in an orphanage. Their argument is that these institutions were not as bad as they are sometimes made out to be. Moreover, they argue that permanent placement in an orphanage is probably preferable to continual instability in a series of foster homes.

My response is that Richard McKenzie and the other advocates of this position were not raised in state-run orphanages. The orphanage Mc-Kenzie grew up in was sponsored by the Presbyterian Church. What

[13] Marvin Olasky makes substantially the same point with regard to state-sponsored poverty programs. For one of his more provocative statements of this point, see Olasky, "Persons, Not Pets," *Crisis*, vol. 13, no. 11 (December 1995), p. 6. He describes "bad" homeless shelters as ones in which the clients are, in effect, told, "Here's some food in your bowl, here's a place to sleep, that's a good boy."

[14] Richard McKenzie, *The Home: A Memoir of Growing Up in an Orphanage* (New York: Basic Books, 1996). Other prominent figures who have spoken publicly about how much they owe to orphanages include Tom Monaghan, Founder and CEO of Domino's Pizza, and Jude Dougherty, Chairman of the Philosophy Department at Catholic University of America. See Thomas S. Monaghan, "Why I Am Still a Catholic," *Crisis*, vol. 15, no. 8 (September 1997), pp. 22–26; and Patrick Fagan, "The Child Abuse Crisis: The Disintegration of Marriage, Family, and the American Community," Heritage Foundation Backgrounder No. 1115 (Washington, DC: Heritage Foundation, June 3, 1997).

prompted these people to start an orphanage for the care of other people's children? I think we can assuredly rule out some possible motivations. They did not do it to solve a great social problem. They no doubt knew that they were making a very modest contribution to solving a social problem. They did not do it because of the great salary and benefits they received as orphanage workers. They probably did not even do it because they had nothing better to do.

In all probability, the people of the Presbyterian Church ran that orphanage out of the love of God. They loved God. They thought it would please God to take care of these little children, so they did it. No doubt that is also what motivated them to do more than simply keep the little bodies alive. McKenzie's account makes it very clear that the workers in the orphanage gave the children instruction, guidance, and encouragement. Their religious commitment led them to extend themselves for the sake of the children of strangers. The children received from the orphanage the very things that families ordinarily provide: stability, attentiveness, moral direction, and love.

Can any modern Western state, self-consciously secular as they all are, replicate such motivation and commitment in its workers? I seriously doubt it. The state does not love anybody. Nor can we expect the state to hire professionals to love children.

It is true that families sometimes fail, and that the state may be required to intervene. But let's not kid ourselves. The best we can hope for is that these interventions will cobble together something that is not too harmful. The state cannot be a substitute for the family.

XII. CONCLUSION: LOVE IS NOT OPTIONAL

America has had some ambivalence about the meaning of freedom and liberty. Is liberty essentially a political condition of minimal government? Or is liberty a social condition that allows people unlimited freedom of action, subject to the prohibition on the use of force or fraud? Many Americans have replied that our national ethos includes both of these strands of thought.

In this essay, I have shown an area in which the freedom-of-action strand of American thought may very well be in conflict with the minimal-government strand. For the minimal state cannot exist without a substantial component of self-restraint and self-government within the citizenry. This internalized ethic cannot come into existence in the absence of loving families taking personal care of their own children. Scholars sometimes conceptualize the promise-keeping ethic, as though its primary impulse were rational and its primary foundation were utilitarian. We have had the luxury of describing it in that way because we have lived in a society in which most people had already imbibed these basic norms.

It seems, however, that promise-keeping for purely rational and utilitarian reasons cannot supply the foundation of contracts and ethical behavior that a free society really requires. For there are many occasions on which it is privately rational to break promises and contracts. When these temptations arise, something more powerful and more primal than rational calculation must overrule the urge to follow one's own self-interest, narrowly defined. The internal voice must say, "We don't do that kind of thing," before the calculation process ever gets started. That internal voice is the voice of the loving parent: the parent who proved himself trustworthy, long before we could even begin to demand proof or reasons for anything.

It is not sufficient to reduce family obligations to a species of contractual obligations, which may be renegotiated at will by consenting adults. The children who result from the union are not consenting adults, by definition. The needs of the children are not simply social constructs that can be redefined for the convenience of the adults. Some childhood needs are universal and non-negotiable.

Love is the key to fulfilling these obligations and inculcating these values. Love of the parents for the child keeps them engaged in the never-ending job of meeting the child's needs. Love of the parents for each other keeps them working as a team, so they are not overwhelmed by the task.

The child learns to trust his parents, not because he reasons from first principles that they have told him the truth, and that they are reliable sources of information. He trusts them because their loving actions have allowed him to feel safe. The loving actions take the place that a rational argument might take for an adult: they are utterly persuasive. From the parents' actions toward him, the child learns that making a generous first move is not the behavior of a sucker, but of the kind of fully human person that he would like to be. From his parents' love of each other, he learns that cooperation between people is not only possible, but quite wonderful.

Love is not optional in any free society. It is the foundation upon which the disposition to cooperate is based. It is the dynamic force that moves persons from being self-centered bundles of impulses to being the kind of persons who can be turned loose in a laissez-faire world. Love is a compelling argument.

Economics, Hoover Institution on War, Revolution, and Peace,
Stanford University

POLITICS, NEUTRALITY, AND THE GOOD*

By Richard Kraut

I. The Neutrality of the State

A large number of prominent philosophers have in recent years advocated the thesis that the modern nation-state should adopt a stance of neutrality toward questions about the nature of the human good. The government, according to this way of thinking, has two proper goals, neither of which require it to make assumptions about what the constituents of a flourishing life are. First, the state must protect people against the invasion of their rights and uphold those principles of justice without which there can be no stable and lasting social order. This goal is accomplished through a guarantee of basic civil liberties and the enforcement of a criminal code that prohibits murder, theft, fraud, and other widely recognized harms. Second, the state should promote the general welfare of the citizens by providing them with or helping them acquire the resources they need in order to lead lives of their own choosing. There are certain all-purpose means that people need in order to accomplish their goals—money, health, opportunities for employment—and it is legitimate for the state to pursue policies that enable citizens to acquire these goods. It may build roads, raise an army, regulate the economy, insure standards of safety, and supervise any other projects that give people the basic wherewithal they need to pursue their own ends.[1]

But what the state must not do, according to this way of thinking, is to take a stand on the question of what a good life is, or to try to exert its influence on citizens so that they find certain ways of life more desirable

* For criticism, I am grateful to the other contributors to this volume, and to its editors, as well as to Derrick Darby, John Deigh, David Hull, Thomas McCarthy, John McCumber, Martha Nussbaum, and Thomas Ryckman.

[1] The most influential advocate of this view is, of course, John Rawls, in both *A Theory of Justice* (Cambridge, MA: Harvard University Press, 1971), and *Political Liberalism* (New York: Columbia University Press, 1993). Despite significant changes in some of his views, I believe that the kind of neutralism I criticize here can be found in both works; see notes 7, 8, and 11 below. For other important defenses of neutralism, see Bruce Ackerman, *Social Justice in the Liberal State* (New Haven, CT: Yale University Press, 1980); Brian Barry, *Justice as Impartiality* (New York: Oxford University Press, 1995); Joshua Cohen, "Moral Pluralism and Political Consensus," in David Copp et al., *The Idea of Democracy* (Cambridge: Cambridge University Press, 1993); Ronald Dworkin, *A Matter of Principle* (Cambridge, MA: Harvard University Press, 1985); Charles Larmore, *Patterns of Moral Complexity* (Cambridge, MA: Harvard University Press, 1987); and Jeremy Waldron, *Liberal Rights* (Cambridge: Cambridge University Press, 1993). For a full and critical discussion, see George Sher, *Beyond Neutrality* (Cambridge: Cambridge University Press, 1997).

than others. The government must accept a certain division of labor regarding ends and means: it should leave individual citizens free to make up their minds about which ends they will pursue, because this is a matter about which the government has no special competence; but because of its great power to coordinate behavior, it must help the citizens acquire the means they are likely to need regardless of which ends they choose. So long as they do not harm others or interfere with their rights, citizens must be allowed to live as they see fit.

It is not difficult to understand why this thesis of neutrality has great appeal. Anyone who thinks that it is proper for the state to take a more active role faces an extremely difficult task. He must say precisely which ends the state should favor, and must give arguments for choosing those goals rather than others. Furthermore, he must confront the fact that in every large modern nation-state there are many conflicting views about what a good life is. If the state is to favor only one of these and discourage all others, what justification can be given to those whose way of life does not receive civic support? The history of moral philosophy shows us that no single conception of the good is uniquely rational and coherent: even if we confine ourselves to Western philosophy and religion, we see that rival conceptions of the good are held by Platonists, Aristotelians, Epicureans, Stoics, Skeptics, Jews, and Christians, among others. If the state favors one of these views and prohibits or discourages others, it must do so because there are arguments accessible to all rational beings that show the superiority of one single correct way of life over all others. Surely it is more plausible to suppose that the rational comparison of competing ways of life is difficult and inconclusive, and that therefore no single philosophy of life has so clear a superiority to all others that it alone should enjoy state support.

Furthermore, it is now widely agreed that it would be intolerable for a state to impose a detailed script on people's lives, dictating to them the kind of work they may do, the people they are to marry, or the kind of god they are to worship. Plato's *Republic* serves as a vivid example of how oppressive a regime would be, were it ruled by those who confidently claim to know what is good for others, and who allow no competing ideas to enter the minds of citizens. Such a regime could be imposed only through a system of indoctrination that suppresses freedom of thought and expression. It is far healthier for the state to allow divergent philosophies of life to compete with each other on their merits, and to allow new ideas about the art of living to be invented and explored. When each person is guaranteed a zone of freedom in which he may pursue his projects as he sees fit, so long as he does not interfere with others, human ingenuity and creativity are unleashed, and the political community achieves a rich diversity that is far more attractive than the oppressive uniformity and rigidity we find in the *Republic* or in any other alleged utopia modeled on a single conception of the good.

These ideas about diversity and freedom are now widely accepted, and I do not wish to challenge them. Nonetheless, I believe that the principle of neutrality ought to be rejected, because it in fact provides too weak a foundation for the kind of free and diverse society we would all like to live in. Neutrality only seems attractive because it is wrongly assumed that the only alternative to it is something like Plato's *Republic*—a rigid, uniform, intolerant, and authoritarian regime. I hope to show that this is not the case. A widely shared conception of human well-being provides a better support for the kind of political community we want to live in than does the principle of neutrality.[2]

II. PRINCIPLED VERSUS STRATEGIC NEUTRALITY

Before proceeding, more needs to be said about how the thesis of neutrality is to be interpreted. It holds that the actions of the state must not be based on assumptions about what is ultimately good or bad for human beings. But it is important to see that contemporary advocates[3] of this thesis regard it as a principled restriction on the role of the state rather than as a strategy for promoting well-being. It is easy to see how a strategic defense of neutrality would go: "Each individual," it might be said, "is in the best position to decide what kind of life is best for him. Such choices should be made in the light of information about one's talents, personality, preferences, and so on. These vary from one person to another, and no one is in a better position to acquire this information than the individual himself. Therefore, the state must not interfere with the citizen's decision about how he should lead his life."

Although there is some truth in this commonplace, it is nonetheless too hazardous a generalization to bear much weight. For it is also a commonplace that people often deceive themselves and are poor judges in their own case. There is no reason why a government official—a court-appointed social worker, for example—might not in certain circumstances make better plans for an individual than would that individual himself. So if we were to favor state neutrality solely as a strategy for the promotion of well-being, we would have to acknowledge that it works in some cases but not others. It is understandable, therefore, that contemporary advocates of neutrality should instead rest their case on the idea that as a matter of principle the state should not favor certain ultimate ends over others. Their idea is not that individual citizens will always or usually decide wisely on their own, but that the state has a duty to its citizens to

---

[2] I am hardly alone in rejecting the thesis of neutrality. Among those from whom I have learned a great deal are William A. Galston, *Liberal Purposes* (Cambridge: Cambridge University Press, 1991); Thomas Hurka, *Perfectionism* (New York: Oxford University Press, 1993); Stephen Macedo, *Liberal Virtues* (Oxford: Clarendon Press, 1991); Joseph Raz, *The Morality of Freedom* (Oxford: Clarendon Press, 1986); and Sher, *Beyond Neutrality*.

[3] That is, the authors mentioned in note 1.

let them freely choose their own ends and lead their own lives, even if in doing so they decide badly. Such advocates of neutrality would be willing to endorse this restriction on the state even if the result were a diminution in the well-being of citizens. Accordingly, the thesis of neutrality as I shall interpret it here, is that it is morally wrong for the state to enter into the question of whether its citizens are pursuing worthy or unworthy ends.

III. Freedom as a Good

There is another argument for state neutrality that must be distinguished from the one that I am concerned with here. Suppose it is said that the state should not interfere with the choices made by citizens because their freedom to choose is one of the greatest goods available to them. If the government narrows someone's options or brings pressure to bear by discouraging or discrediting certain alternatives, then that constraint robs the individual of something that is in itself quite valuable.[4]

It should be clear, however, that this argument, like the one that takes each to be the best judge in his own case, is not what lies behind the kind of neutrality I have in mind. The advocates of neutrality with whom I am concerned do not require the government to create a sizable zone of freedom because they propose a theory of the good according to which freedom is itself a constituent of human well-being. It is precisely the point of their defense of neutrality that a theory of the state should not rest on any single conception of what is intrinsically worthwhile. They do not require the state to leave a space for individual freedom because they hold that in fact freedom is good and therefore urge the state to adopt this view or impart it to citizens. On the contrary, their idea is that it is up to the individual citizen to decide whether freedom is one of the goods and how large a role it should play in his life. It would be out of place for a theory of the state or the state itself to make this determination on its citizens' behalf.

Another point should be noted: If someone were to defend the neutrality thesis by appealing to the good of freedom, he would have to explain why it is this good alone that the state should promote. Even if it is granted that it is good to have choices, and that more choices are better than fewer, it would be unreasonable to insist that choice is the only thing that is intrinsically valuable. If the defender of neutrality argues that neutrality promotes freedom and freedom is a good, we can ask why it may not sometimes happen that a person's use of his freedom deprives him of many other goods that are on balance more important than freedom. Appealing to freedom to support the thesis of neutrality not only misconstrues the meaning of the thesis, but also requires freedom to have a value that takes priority over all others. It is understandable that de-

---

[4] This is, of course, the argument proposed by John Stuart Mill. See *On Liberty*, ch. 3.

fenders of neutrality should not want to defend their thesis in this way. By saying that ultimate ends are none of the state's business, they relieve themselves of the burden of having to show why the goodness of freedom is greater than the value of all other goods combined.

IV. Assisted Suicide and the Value of Life

Thus far, I have merely been trying to explain how we should understand the thesis that the state is to abstain from judgments of intrinsic goodness and badness. We are construing that principle not as a strategy for promoting wise decisions but as a conception of the boundaries that civic officials are required to observe. Neutrality holds that the state's sphere of operation is constrained by certain moral limits. If it acts on a conception of the human good or restrains itself because it presupposes such a conception, it usurps a role that must be left to individual citizens.

I now want to show by means of a series of examples that this thesis is radically at odds with assumptions we reasonably make about civic life. My claim is that if citizens were to set aside their conceptions of human well-being, when they enact legislation or deliberate about constitutional matters, their common political life would become badly disfigured.

To begin with, let us consider an issue that has recently become the subject of widespread debate—the problem of assisted suicide—and ask what neutrality amounts to in this case. Suppose someone is ninety years old, gravely ill, in great pain, and so incapacitated that he must rely entirely on others to be fed and bathed. He wishes to die, but cannot do so without help. The question of assisted suicide is whether the legal system should allow this to happen. Presumably everyone will agree that requests to be killed cannot be treated lightly, and that there must be safeguards to insure that decisions are well informed and fully voluntary. Even if such precautions are workable, however, there still remains the question of whether in cases like these an exception should be made to the normal rule that no one should be complicit in another person's death. The question we are asking is not the fascinating but narrow legal issue of whether the due process clause of the U.S. Constitution's Fourteenth Amendment prohibits states from interfering with assisted suicide.[5] Our question is not about the interpretation of the law or about whether the issue of assisted suicide is best handled by the courts rather

[5] See Ronald Dworkin, Thomas Nagel, Robert Nozick, John Rawls, Thomas Scanlon, and Judith Jarvis Thomson, "Assisted Suicide: The Philosophers' Brief," New York Review of Books, vol. 44, no. 5 (March 27, 1997), pp. 41–47. The due process clause states that no state shall "deprive any person of life, liberty, or property, without due process of law." The legal question, then, is whether existing prohibitions of assisted suicide interfere with constitutionally protected liberty. On June 26, 1997, the U.S. Supreme Court unanimously decided that they do not. See Ronald Dworkin, "Assisted Suicide: What the Court Really Said," New York Review of Books, vol. 44, no. 14 (September 25, 1997), pp. 40–44.

than the legislature. We are instead asking a moral question: Should the state allow assisted suicide in such cases?

A defender of the thesis of neutrality holds that the state has no business addressing the issue of when a life is worth leading, and that it must leave this decision to the individual. Just as the state cannot take a stand on what is intrinsically good, so it cannot enter the issue of what is intrinsically bad. If an individual decides that his life is so bad that it is not worth leading, and requests assistance in dying, the state exceeds its proper role if it questions his decision. It can demand assurances that his decision is fully voluntary and rational, but if death is what he freely chooses, the government cannot substitute its judgment for his and prevent him from dying.

We must now point out that a remarkable move has been made. The neutralist argument for assisted suicide that I have just rehearsed contains no reference to the circumstances mentioned when I first explained the issue. I imagined someone who is old, gravely ill, in great pain, utterly dependent on others, and unable to carry out even the most basic activities of human life. But the defender of neutrality must say that these features of the case really distract attention from the real issue. The only point of referring to these circumstances is to give some plausibility to the idea that this person's life really is not worth living, that his decision to end his life is not only voluntary but also quite reasonable. But the neutralist must say that we badly miss the point if we favor assisted suicide for these reasons. From the perspective of neutralism, it is crucial to realize that assisted suicide is something to which each person has a right, regardless of whether officials of the state think his life is worth living or not. The neutralist holds that assisted suicide must be allowed not just in the case of those who are terminally ill and in great pain, but in all cases whatsoever (so long as the decision to commit suicide is fully voluntary). If someone decides that his life is not worth living because his lover has left him, or if he wants to get back at people whom he believes have been mistreating him, the state must allow him to receive assistance in committing suicide.[6] It is not up to a judge or a legislator to determine which grounds for suicide are adequate or inadequate.

The character of neutralism can be brought out more clearly if we bear in mind that at certain times all citizens who are eligible to vote become agents of the state, and in these circumstances the restrictions neutralism places on the state apply just as much to citizens as they do to members of the executive, legislative, or judicial branches of government. Imagine,

---

[6] To insure that the decision is fully voluntary, the state can require a considerable waiting period before allowing assisted suicide in these cases. But revenge and a sense of loss can be resilient and durable motives. Duly considered decisions can be based on extremely bad reasons. For a defense of an anti-paternalist policy toward suicide, see Joel Feinberg, *The Moral Limits of the Criminal Law*, vol. 3, *Harm to Self* (New York: Oxford University Press, 1986), pp. 344–74.

for example, that a referendum is being held about whether to make assisted suicide legal when a board of doctors has certified that someone willingly seeks to die because he is in great pain and incapable of basic human activities. The neutralist must hold that when citizens debate the merits or demerits of the proposed law, they are failing to live up to their responsibility as citizens if they argue in favor of it on the grounds that life is not worth living in these circumstances, or if they oppose it for the opposite reason. Since these citizens are making law, they are in effect agents of the state, and the state has no business taking a stand on what is intrinsically good or bad. For a public official to take into account questions of ultimate ends and the conditions in which life is worth living is already to overstep the bounds of legitimate state action; and since in a referendum all citizens are legislators, and therefore public officials, they too must leave aside their thoughts about well-lived lives, when they deliberate about assisted suicide. The principle of neutrality tells them that they are not to substitute their judgment about what is ultimately good or bad for the judgment of the person who requests to die. If citizens accept that principle, they must not invoke their conceptions of the good when they publicly discuss the merits of the proposed law.[7]

The extremity of this conclusion must be acknowledged. Most citizens would be outraged to be told that they exceed the bounds of good citizenship if they pay attention to the unbearable pain and degraded condition of the person who wants to die, and make these circumstances relevant to their wish to legalize assisted suicide. And surely there is much to be said in support of such outrage. The voter is being asked for his cooperation in bringing about the death of other human beings. In the referendum he is being asked whether he sanctions and supports future killings, and supporters of the principle of neutrality tell him that he may not legitimately inquire into the reasons for these deaths. Neutrality tells him that he must help bring about death merely because it is freely chosen by another. Surely a citizen may justly respond that he cannot decide whether or not to cooperate in the legalization of suicide unless he is given more information about the reasons people have for wanting to die.

---

[7] Rawls holds that "citizens and legislators may properly vote their more comprehensive views when constitutional essentials and basic justice are not at stake" (*Political Liberalism*, p. 235). By this he means that we are not to appeal to our fundamental religious and moral views, including our conception of human flourishing, when we collectively deliberate about "constitutional essentials and basic justice." It may be that the question of assisted suicide does not fit into this rubric, and that Rawls would therefore allow citizens voting in a referendum about this matter to justify their positions by appealing to a conception of human well-being. But it is not clear to me why it is legitimate to appeal to such a conception when one is considering lower-level legislation but not when higher-order principles are at stake. See also note 11 below. Note that Waldron expresses a more general ban: "It is not wrong for someone to favor a particular conception of the good life, but it is wrong for him in his capacity as legislator (and presumably as voter) to favor such a view" (*Liberal Rights*, p. 154).

What has forced the neutralist to adopt this extreme position? Recall an argument that was rehearsed earlier when we discussed the attractions of neutralism: we said that questions about what is ultimately worthwhile are matters about which reasonable people may differ, and it would be foolish to expect there to be a final and decisive resolution of these issues. But now that we have a concrete example before us, it should be apparent that the existence of reasonable disagreement and the unlikelihood of achieving unanimity provide no grounds for forbidding public officials from considering questions of intrinsic goodness and badness in their deliberations. Perhaps it is true that there will never be unanimity about the conditions under which life is worth living, but that is no reason for refraining from public debate about such matters when such issues are clearly pertinent, as they are in the case of assisted suicide. The fact that unanimity is unlikely does not mean that no minds will be changed. And even if no one's mind is changed, it is best for everyone to listen to all sides of an issue before enacting legislation. To decide the question of assisted suicide without even listening to debates about when a life is worth living would be to close one's mind to factors that are obviously relevant to the formation of a wise public policy.

V. Liberal Education

The next point to notice is that if the principle of neutrality were taken to heart and widely accepted, a number of the common practices and institutions of modern liberal democracies would become difficult to justify. Perhaps the best example of this is public support for nonvocational education. Public schools at all levels, from primary schools to state universities, use tax money to support classes in drama, music, literature, science, and history. Were we to accept the principle of neutrality, we could not justify these public expenditures by saying that the state should promote some of the constituents of a good life, and that the liberal arts are among those constituents.[8] Rather, we would have to say that such subjects as music, drama, science, and history give future citizens the means they need in order to achieve whatever goals they will have in the future. But an instrumentalist defense of a training in the liberal arts is unpersuasive. It is more honest and direct to acknowledge that although reading and writing skills provide students with means they are likely to need regardless of their ends, a large part of the traditional curriculum can be justified only if it is seen as an attempt to encourage students to develop new interests and goals. A large part of the cultural life of a

---

[8] Rawls writes: "[T]he government can no more act . . . to advance human excellence, or the values of perfection . . . than it can to advance Catholicism or Protestantism, or any other religion" (*Political Liberalism*, pp. 179–80). I believe that this approach makes it difficult to give the right kind of justification for a traditional liberal education.

nation will be inaccessible and of no interest to citizens who do not share the basic frame of reference that schools are designed to impart. This component of the curriculum does not provide all-purpose means that will be used regardless of the kind of life students later choose as adults; rather, it encourages the development of certain ends. A basic knowledge of history and science, for example, are part of the equipment a student will later need only if he makes certain choices rather than others about how to lead his life. These subjects might equip him to make better choices as a voter, but he may develop no interest in politics, and his job may require no knowledge of history and science. It might be replied that these subjects can encourage him to take more of an interest in politics and in the world of science, but that is not a reply the defender of neutrality can make, for neutrality requires the state to stay out of the business of shaping the ends of citizens.

The neutralist might therefore call for a radical change in the subjects taught in public schools; he might suggest that the curriculum be strictly vocational in nature. Such a move would bring out a point we have already noticed in our discussion of assisted suicide: neutralism is radically at odds with widely shared assumptions. Making public schools serve narrowly vocational purposes and nothing more is simply not on the agenda of any important political movement in any modern state.

The underlying assumption of a liberal education is that it is good to develop a love of such subjects as music, dance, theater, literature, science, and mathematics, and to participate to some degree in the institutions connected to these subjects. The state endorses this conception of a good life by approving and funding the curriculum of public schools. When these schools do not teach these subjects adequately, the wealthy respond by sending their children to private schools or by supplementing their public school education with private music lessons, dance classes, and the like. The poor can do no such thing; thus, in addition to the gap between rich and poor with respect to such all-purpose instruments as wealth, power, and status, there is a further disparity in the extent to which they can participate in the goods of culture and civilization, since these are accessible only to those who have been properly trained. Differences in wealth would not in themselves be so disturbing, if no one were so poor that he could not fully participate in the goods of culture and if everyone could guarantee that these goods will be as available to his children as they are to the rich. But advocates of state neutrality regarding ultimate ends are not able to express concern about this inequity. They hold that the state takes no view about what is good or bad in itself; it merely helps citizens acquire such all-purpose means as health, safety, and security. Since cultural goods are not all-purpose means, it is no business of the state to help all citizens to share in them. For the neutralist, the fact that the rich are better off than the poor in this respect should be of no greater concern to the state than the fact that the rich have more yachts than the poor.

VI. Basic Appetites

My discussion of liberal education may create the false impression that in my opinion the only goods or the best goods are those associated with high culture. For present purposes, however, there is no reason to make this assumption. Sexual pleasure, physical intimacy, the ability to make use of one's senses and to enjoy one's basic appetites—all of these are reasonably thought to be good in themselves. And this judgment of intrinsic value may in certain cases enter into political deliberations, thus providing another example of the inadequacy of neutralism. The neutralist presumably holds that the state can promote the health of the citizens, since health is an all-purpose means to any ends one may have. But suppose someone is sexually dysfunctional: is this a deficiency that state funds can legitimately be used to remedy, according to the neutralist? An individual may claim that in order to lead a full life he needs an expensive drug or operation that will restore his sexual capacities, but if the state is not allowed to accept any views about the constituents of a good life, it must treat this individual's demand for help as an expensive preference that has no more claim to state support than does the yearning of someone who thinks he cannot live well without owning a yacht. The enjoyment of sex and physical intimacy is not an all-purpose means to further ends; thus, for the neutralist there is no reason why the state should help those who have no capacity for it.

Such examples suggest that neutralism is simply too narrow a conception of the proper role of the state. All-purpose instruments are only some of the goods that the state ought to help provide to citizens. By forbidding the state to take a stand about what is intrinsically good or bad, neutralism prevents us from formulating a wise and humane approach to civic policy.

VII. Freedom and Religion

It might be thought that the sorts of examples I have been discussing are exceptional—that even if they create some difficulties, for the most part the principle of neutrality is the organizing idea behind many of the institutions of a modern liberal state and cannot be abandoned without upsetting our entire way of thinking about politics. This, however, is not the case, as I will now try to show. State support of liberal education is not an inexplicable exception to our normal civic practices. It is not the only or even the most important example of how the modern state operates with a substantive conception of what is intrinsically good and bad. The modern state is best viewed as an organization guided in part by the idea that citizens ought to be free to lead lives of their own choosing because such self-reliance and independence of mind is one of the most valuable ingredients of a flourishing life. Because it judges that self-actualization is intrinsically good, the state refrains from making constant and large intrusions in the lives of its citizens. It is not because it refrains from taking a stand about the good life that it leaves people free, but because it operates with a conception of the good that leaves individuals with a large zone of freedom in which to make their own choices.

The liberal state's attitude toward freedom may be usefully compared with the policy of parents who allow their children considerable freedom to make their own decisions, not because they suspend judgment about what is good for them but because they think that their children's lives would be worse if they lacked the ability and opportunity to make their own choices. The state allows citizens to choose the kind of work they do, the gods they worship, and the partners they marry because they would suffer great harm if their lives were so constricted that they lacked the capacity or opportunity to make these choices for themselves. For the most part, the choices they make for themselves are better than the choices that would be made on their behalf by others. If others were to make these choices for them, they would not develop the mental and moral powers whose exercise is one of the ingredients of a well-lived human life. The state is in the general business of promoting the common good, but since one of the goods is autonomy, there are limits to how intrusive the state can be in its efforts to help citizens.

My argument for looking at the modern liberal state in this way is that it provides a better way of organizing our thoughts about political issues than does the principle of neutrality. If we take the state to be in the business of promoting what is intrinsically good and opposing what is intrinsically bad, we can provide a single account of why it supports liberal education and also leaves citizens a large zone of freedom. We can also explain why in some cases it is reasonable to abridge people's freedom, and not allow them to pursue what they think is good. Autonomy is of great value, but it is not the only value, and in extreme circumstances other goods take priority over it. If someone wants to die but needs the cooperation of the political community in order to do so, the normal presumption in favor of allowing people to make their own choices can be rebutted if the political community makes the reasonable judgment that the individual's reasons for living vastly outweigh his reasons for dying.

The freedom of religion provides another way of clarifying the difference between taking the state to be neutral and viewing it as a partisan of the good. According to the neutralist, the state must take no stand about whether religion is a good or a bad thing. It should allow people to worship as they choose, but it must not in any way facilitate the practice of religion or give it any special encouragement or protection. By contrast, if the state can take a stand on what the ingredients of a well-lived life are, it would be appropriate for it to take special measures to insure that religious institutions or practices not be threatened or weakened. It can grant tax-exempt status to religious organizations, just as it does to educational institutions, because it recognizes that many people need religious practices and ties in order to lead their lives well. The state can therefore regard the destruction of temples or churches, or other attempts to interfere with the free exercise of religion, as an especially serious threat to the well-being of citizens. It can treat the burning of a church or the overturning of gravestones not as a destruction of property like any other, but as an outrage whose eradication deserves special resources because of the special role religion plays in the lives of so many citizens. When the state treats the free exercise of religion as a matter of great seriousness, it is not merely responding to the fact that people have intense feelings about religious matters. All sorts of preferences can be intensely felt, but this does not give them a special title to fulfillment. The only explanation of why the state devotes special attention to the protection of religious freedom is its recognition that religious institutions play a central role in the way the good is conceived by many citizens. In protecting and helping those institutions, the state is a partisan of a widely held conception of the good. It does not support one religious sect rather than another, but places all religions in a special category, because for many citizens these practices play an organizing role in their efforts to lead meaningful lives.

VIII. Democracy

There is one other institution of the modern liberal state that is best interpreted as a way of supporting a substantive conception of the good: democracy. The organizing idea of democracy is that power should not be the exclusive prerogative of elites, but must be divided equally among all citizens, who may appoint officials for various purposes, but whose collective decisions are the ultimate source of authority. This root idea is capable of being developed in many ways, and so there are many different kinds of democracy, some better and some worse than others. A phrase that has recently come into vogue—"deliberative democracy"[9]— emphasizes the notion that the best democratic forms are those in which citizens and officials do not merely form strategic alliances for purposes of gaining an advantage over less powerful groups, but also engage in

---

[9] For a detailed account, see Amy Gutmann and Dennis Thompson, *Democracy and Disagreement* (Cambridge, MA: Harvard University Press, 1996).

genuine deliberation with each other, offering objective reasons for proposals and entertaining the possibility that they have something to learn from public discussion. If we ask ourselves why this form of democracy has any claim to superiority over other varieties, one appealing answer is that institutions that encourage an open and honest discussion foster the development of certain traits of character that are in themselves good for people to have. In a way, this idea goes back to Plato, who proposed that democratic regimes and democratic people correspond to and mutually reinforce each other. We can adapt Plato's general idea by saying that the culture of a deliberative democracy encourages the development of a certain kind of person, and that such a political form can flourish only if people of a certain sort participate in it. There can be no genuine collective deliberation unless citizens are capable of rational and cooperative discussion. And one advantage of deliberative democracy is that it encourages the development of a certain kind of person, someone who is thoughtful, fair-minded, and public-spirited.

The point can be brought out more clearly if we remind ourselves that different kinds of democracy rely more or less heavily on the device of representation. It is widely assumed now that modern democracies cannot be governed by an assembly of all citizens, as were ancient democracies, because the number of citizens is simply too large by several orders of magnitude. But we should not complacently assume that large republics like India, the United States, and Germany have no alternative to the systems of representation they now employ. It is possible for all of them to make much fuller use of referenda and thus to approximate the system that exists in Switzerland.[10] If we ask whether such a move would be desirable, we can reply that one reason for moving toward a more direct democracy is that this would lead to a more public-spirited, well-informed, and thoughtful citizenry. If a larger role were assigned to the collective decision-making of all citizens, individuals would have a greater incentive to study and discuss issues than they do when they are confined to a more passive role. Perhaps the empirical claim that a system of regular referenda would have this beneficial effect is doubtful, but that does not matter for our current purposes. What we should acknowledge is that if a more direct democracy would have these effects, that would constitute one powerful reason in its favor. Note, however, that we can appreciate the force of this point only if we abandon the principle of neutrality and assess civic institutions by considering the contribution they make to intrinsically worthwhile ends. The principle of neutrality holds that the state must make no judgments about which ends are worthwhile and which are not. The government must not try to favor the

---

[10] For a brief overview, see "Full Democracy," in *The Economist*, vol. 341, no. 7997 (December 21, 1996).

development of a certain kind of person on the grounds that it is good to have certain character traits. Accordingly, the neutralist cannot agree that the choice between different kinds of democracies should be based in part on the ways in which they foster good lives. Once again, a factor that seems entirely appropriate to consider in our political deliberations is ruled out of court by neutralism merely because it ventures into the forbidden realm of intrinsic good and evil.[11]

IX. DIGNITY AND HUMILIATION

We should recall at this point that defenders of neutrality do not claim that the state should be neutral about all questions of norms and values. On the contrary, they insist that the state must uphold principles of justice and the basic rules of morality that forbid people to harm each other. But they draw a distinction between these moral principles and other questions of value about which they say the state should take no stand. Justice is to be upheld, but this can be done in the absence of any conception of the *summum bonum*. Justice is a matter of setting limits on how we treat each other and distributing such all-purpose instruments as wealth, power, and rights. To pursue justice or rectify injustice does not require or presuppose having a view about what is intrinsically good or bad.

This view certainly seems to be correct in some cases. We can insist that theft is wrong, for example, without claiming that the stolen objects are in themselves worth having. It is far from clear, however, that this applies in all or even many cases of justice and injustice. Consider, for example, an act in which one person publicly humiliates and cruelly degrades another — for example, by assaulting him, insulting him, spitting on him, and the like. This is the sort of behavior that must of course be condemned by any just and humane code of law. But why so? The amount of physical harm done or even threatened may be slight. Something terrible is being done to a person in this case, but we would not come close to capturing it by saying that the victim is being deprived of something he needs as a means to whatever goals he may have. He is not being deprived of a physical capacity or of money. Rather, the injury consists in the very fact that his dignity as a human being, the honor he is due as a member of the human community, his claim to equality of respect, is being denied. He is being treated as someone who belongs to a lower order; his membership in that subhuman realm is being affirmed; and this by itself deprives him of a

---

[11] Recall at this point Rawls's idea that in public debate "constitutional essentials" ought to be defended without appealing to "perfectionist values" or "comprehensive views" about the value of human life. See *Political Liberalism*, pp. 179–80 and 235; see also notes 7 and 8 above. If this means that one cannot seek to make the basic political institutions of society more democratic by appealing to a conception of human flourishing, then Rawls is placing too great a limitation on discussions of human flourishing in public life.

good that is his due.[12] In describing the case in this way, we are presupposing that one of the things that makes a human life go well is the recognition received by the person who lives it that he is fully human, and the social forms in which that recognition is expressed. This social recognition is needed not merely as a means to further ends, but also because it is in itself a good thing to have. A person who is treated with respect by his community is already better off than someone who is not, apart from any other differences there are between them. And public officials can play an important role in determining whether citizens receive this recognition from each other. States can officially encourage acts of cruelty and degradation, and they can passively stand by while these acts take place. Public officials can insure that citizens receive each other's respect only if they design institutions that promote this goal and take severe measures against those who seek to dominate others. The importance of this form of justice cannot be recognized unless the state upholds a substantive conception of the good.[13]

X. OBJECTIONS AND REPLIES

I will close by considering two objections to the position I have defended. The first is that allowing the state to operate with a partisan conception of the good opens the door to oppression. Suppose, for example, that the majority of citizens hold that the good consists in fellowship with God, and legislation reflecting this point of view is adopted. Nothing I have said explains why it would be wrong for the state to be so sectarian.

My reply is that we must distinguish between the thesis that the state should promote the good and the thesis that whatever the state thinks is good really is such. If the good is not fellowship with God, then civic officials are not justified in making the contrary assumption the basis of their legislation. On the other hand, if the good does consist in having the proper relationship to God, then surely there is *something* to be said in favor of a state that is guided by this conception.

[12] It might be said, against this, that to be humiliated is to be wronged but is not in itself to be deprived of a good or made to suffer a harm. This objection is highly implausible, however. Honor is widely recognized as an intrinsic good. Accordingly, its opposites—various forms and degrees of *dis*honor (being subjected to shame, humiliation, embarrassment)—are plausibly regarded as evils. It would be impossible to understand what is objectionable about humiliating someone (when it is objectionable), if such treatment attaches nothing bad to its victim. If various forms of mistreatment are regarded as injustices but not as intrinsically bad for the victim, the topic of good and evil can be too easily dismissed as peripheral. For a helpful analysis of various forms of dishonor, see William Ian Miller, *Humiliation* (Ithaca, NY: Cornell University Press, 1993).

[13] If being unemployable is a source of shame, then my argument would provide a further reason, besides economic reasons, for job training. The question is not psychological (how does it feel to be unemployable?) but sociological (are the unemployable treated as a caste?).

In many modern societies, however, there is a great deal to be said against such a state—even if the religious conception of the good is correct. Any attempt made in a country like the United States to propose a religious conception of the good as the guiding principle of the government would be a political disaster; to abandon stable and workable traditions of religious impartiality would cause so much distrust and turmoil that one cannot imagine how any real good would result. One does not need to invoke the principle of neutrality in order to explain why one should be opposed to any such change. One only needs good political sense.

In other societies, however, where religion has traditionally been a component of political life and a broad consensus exists about the need for these practices, no moral objection can be made to civic endorsement of sacred rites. The ancient Greek city-states were polities of this sort, and there may be other examples in our own time. Members of such communities can reasonably defend the integration of religion and politics by claiming that it is the role of the state to promote the good of citizens, and that participation in common religious practices is beneficial for all. It would be a mistake to think that the only way to resist applying this model of religious-political integration to the United States is by affirming the principle of neutrality. A more sensible form of resistance is to accept that principle but to insist upon the sociological and historical differences between this country and those that are far more uniform. There is nothing wrong with the state acting for the good of citizens, but in contemporary America far more harm than good would result if the government played a major role in guiding the spiritual lives of citizens.[14]

A second objection should now be considered. It might be said that allowing the state to take a stand on what is intrinsically good is a recipe for disaster because there simply is no rational way to support a conception of human well-being. The multiplicity of competing conceptions of the good is evidence that in this area reason has great difficulty finding its way. To substantiate this charge, a critic might list the various things that I have taken to be good in this essay: autonomy, pleasure, the liberal arts and sciences, honor, respect, and the like. Why settle on this particular list of goods? Why not some other? Unless there is some systematic and defensible theory of goodness—and I have offered none—it is best to require the state to base its reasoning on something more accessible to the human mind.

---

[14] There is a large literature on politics and religion in pluralistic societies that I cannot adequately discuss here. See, for example, Kent Greenawalt, *Religious Convictions and Political Choice* (New York: Oxford University Press, 1988); Michael Perry, *Love and Power* (New York: Oxford University Press, 1991); and Philip Quinn, "Political Liberalisms and Their Exclusion of the Religious," in *Proceedings and Addresses of the American Philosophical Association*, vol. 69, no. 2 (1995), pp. 35–36.

But such pessimism about our ability to find some degree of under-standing and consensus about the good is unjustified. That pleasure and at least some of the other items I have assumed to be good really are so is as uncontroversial and reasonable an assumption as can be made in moral philosophy. There is nothing mysterious or suspect about the thesis that certain goals are worth pursuing for their own sake, apart from or in addition to the instrumental value they have. In ordinary life, we cannot dispense with making judgments of this sort, since we often reasonably decide to devote far more effort to certain projects than their instrumental value would justify. Moral and political philosophy are continuous with the sort of thinking we do in our everyday lives, and there is no reason for philosophers to prune away our ordinary moral categories, unless some argument is given to undermine them.[15]

It is therefore sensible to ask whether our political institutions are doing as good a job as can reasonably be expected to help citizens lead good lives. It is equally sensible to ask whether our communities would be-come less humane and enriching, if public funds were not used to foster an autonomous, thoughtful, and enlightened citizenry, or to guarantee an equal measure of dignity for all, or to promote the widespread accessi-bility of the sciences and the arts. If these are worthy goals that citizens generally accept, and the state already plays an important role in helping us achieve them, there is no good reason to insist that it reduce its role and confine itself to the provision of purely instrumental goods. The fact that the history of philosophy reveals deep disagreement about the *sum-mum bonum*, that Stoics have disagreed with Epicureans, and Christians with Jews, should not blind us to the workable consensus we have achieved about more concrete goals, and to the possibility that we might arrive at further agreement through rational discussion.

XI. Conclusion

What we should avoid in political philosophy is the adoption of a conception of the good that cannot serve as the common goal of all citizens because it is too narrow and sectarian. In a pluralistic society like the United States, where religious impartiality has been a long tradition, civic endorsement of one particular religious conception of the good would be deeply disruptive of stable and workable institutions. Neutralism seizes upon this fact and infers a broader conclusion, namely, that no conception of the good—whether religious or secular—should guide the state in its

---

[15] Here I am responding to Brian Barry, who cites the clash between rival religious conceptions of the good to support a form of skepticism, which in turn is used to justify a principle of neutrality (*Justice as Impartiality*, pp. 168–73). I think he overlooks the point that there is considerable agreement about at least certain intrinsic goods.

HUMAN FLOURISHING AND UNIVERSAL JUSTICE*

By Thomas W. Pogge

I. Introduction

The question of what constitutes human flourishing elicits an extraordinary variety of responses,[1] which suggests that there are not merely differences of opinion at work, but also different understandings of the question itself. So it may help to introduce some clarity into the question before starting work on one answer to it.

That human persons are flourishing means that their lives are good, or worthwhile, in the broadest sense. Thus, the concept of human flourishing, as I understand it, marks the most comprehensive, "all-in" assessment of the quality of human lives. This concept is broader than many other concepts that mark more specific such assessments—including those of pleasure, well-being, welfare, affluence, and virtue, as well as those denoting various excellences and accomplishments. Understanding the

* Many thanks to Marko Ahtisaari, Christian Barry, Ellen Frankel Paul, Peter Koller, Angelika Krebs, Jonathan Neufeld, Brian Orend, and the members of the Columbia University Seminar for Social and Political Thought, for many very helpful critical comments and suggestions.

[1] One can get a sense of this variety by recalling the more influential discussions of human flourishing just within analytic philosophy of the past twenty years. Among these are the discussions in the following books: Julia Annas, *The Morality of Happiness* (Oxford: Oxford University Press, 1993); Jon Elster, *Sour Grapes* (Cambridge: Cambridge University Press, 1983); Harry Frankfurt, *The Importance of What We Care About* (Cambridge: Cambridge University Press, 1988); William Galston, *Justice and the Human Good* (Chicago: University of Chicago Press, 1980); Allan Gibbard, *Wise Choices, Apt Feelings* (Cambridge, MA: Harvard University Press, 1990); James Griffin, *Well-Being* (Oxford: Clarendon Press, 1986); Alasdair MacIntyre, *After Virtue* (Notre Dame: Notre Dame University Press, 1981); Thomas Nagel, *Mortal Questions* (Cambridge: Cambridge University Press, 1979); Robert Nozick, *The Examined Life* (New York: Simon and Schuster, 1989); Martha Nussbaum, *The Fragility of Goodness* (Cambridge: Cambridge University Press, 1986); Nussbaum, *The Therapy of Desire* (Princeton: Princeton University Press, 1994); Derek Parfit, *Reasons and Persons* (Oxford: Oxford University Press, 1984); Joseph Raz, *The Morality of Freedom* (Oxford: Clarendon Press, 1986); Raz, *Ethics in the Public Domain* (Oxford: Clarendon Press, 1994); Richard Rorty, *Contingency, Irony, and Solidarity* (Cambridge: Cambridge University Press, 1989); Thomas Scanlon, *What We Owe to Each Other* (Cambridge, MA: Harvard University Press, forthcoming 1999); Michael Slote, *Goods and Virtues* (Oxford: Oxford University Press, 1983); Slote, *From Morality to Virtue* (Oxford: Oxford University Press, 1992); Charles Taylor, *Sources of the Self* (Cambridge, MA: Harvard University Press, 1989); Ernst Tugendhat, *Vorlesungen über Ethik* (Frankfurt: Suhrkamp, 1993); Bernard Williams, *Moral Luck* (Cambridge: Cambridge University Press, 1981); Williams, *Ethics and the Limits of Philosophy* (Cambridge, MA: Harvard University Press, 1985); Williams, *Shame and Necessity* (Berkeley: University of California Press, 1993); Williams, *Making Sense of Humanity* (Cambridge: Cambridge University Press, 1995); and Richard Wollheim, *The Thread of Life* (Cambridge, MA: Harvard University Press, 1984).

conceptual relations in this way, one need not deny the substantive claim that the most comprehensive assessment of human lives is exhausted by one of the more specific assessments—that pleasure, say, is all there is to human flourishing. For this claim, that human flourishing is nothing more than pleasure (or virtue, or affluence, or any of the others), does not entail that the *concept* of human flourishing is no broader than the *concept* of pleasure. This latter conclusion would follow only if the contrary claim, that human flourishing is more than just pleasure, were self-contradictory, which, on my understanding of the concepts, it clearly is not.

Let me try to give some more structure to the concept of flourishing. A straightforward distinction, which goes back at least to Plato, is the distinction between *components* of flourishing, which are good for their own sake, and *means* to flourishing, which are good for the sake of their effects.[2] Something (e.g., happiness, wisdom) is a component of flourishing just in case it is constitutive of flourishing, part of what flourishing does or can consist in. Something (e.g., affluence, education) is a means to flourishing just in case it tends to enhance the components of flourishing on balance. These two categories of what one might broadly call *contributors* to flourishing are not mutually exclusive: a component of flourishing may also be a means to other components.[3] It is evident that the first of these categories has a certain priority: we cannot determine whether something is a means to flourishing until we have a sense of what flourishing consists in.

Even if we ask more precisely, "What constitutes human flourishing, a comprehensively good or worthwhile life for human persons?" the diversity of responses is still overwhelming. One obvious reason for this is that we have diverse substantive conceptions, which differ in what they single out as components of human flourishing and in how they weight and relate these components. As a first step toward clarifying these differences, one might distinguish between *personal* value, a life being good for the person living it, and *ethical* value, a life being worthy or (in the broadest sense) ethically good. There are surely features of human lives (e.g., friendship, knowledge, art, or love) that contribute to both its personal and its ethical value. But—though the ancients resisted this insight—it is manifest that the two measures weight even these features differently and also diverge strongly in regard to other features. Pains from chronic gout, for instance, detract from the personal value but not from the ethical value of a life[4]—while, conversely, menial and solitary labors for good causes tend to contribute to a life's ethical value but not to its personal

---

[2] See Plato, *The Republic*, trans. G. M. A. Grube (Indianapolis: Hackett, 1974), 357a–358d.

[3] In fact, Plato's argument seeks to show that being just is good in both ways (*Republic*, 357c–358a)—that it is a component in its own right (*Republic*, Books 2–7, esp. 444d–e) and a means to other components, such as well-being, pleasure, and esteem (*Republic*, Books 8–10, esp. 587e–588a, 612d–614b).

[4] Kant offers this example in his *Critique of Practical Reason*; see Immanuel Kant, *Kants gesammelte Schriften*, vol. 5, ed. Königlich Preußische Akademie der Wissenschaften (Berlin: Georg Reimer, 1913), p. 60.

value. Given such divergences, substantive conceptions of human flourishing will differ in how they relate the overall quality of a human life to its personal and ethical value.

The two more-specific notions are themselves complex. Thus, personal value is related to a person's *experiences*: it is related to their being, for instance, enjoyable, intense, interesting, rich, and/or diverse. But personal value would also seem to be related to a person's *success* in the world. These two ideas easily come apart: persons may not know about some of their successes and failures; and, even when they do, their inner lives may be dulled by successes and much enriched by failures.

The notion of ethical value also suggests two main ideas. It is associated with the idea of good *character*, of a person having admirable aims and ambitions, virtuous maxims and dispositions, noble feelings and emotions. But it is also associated with ethical *achievement*, with the ethical significance of the person's conduct.[5] These two ideas, as well, come apart easily: how one's character manifests itself in the world is significantly affected by one's social starting position and talents, as well as by circumstances and luck. And worthy achievements may well result from base motives.

Distinguishing these four dimensions—experience, success, character, and achievement—may give some structure to the concept of human flourishing. Within this structure, one can then ask further whether these dimensions are jointly exhaustive, how and how much each of them contributes to human flourishing, and what more-specific components of flourishing should be distinguished within each of them (different ways in which experiences may be good and undertakings successful, different character traits and kinds of achievement). The complexities indicated by these questions are one major reason for the diversity of views about what constitutes human flourishing.

Another important reason is the multiplicity of perspectives on human flourishing, which make this notion appear to us in various ways. It makes a difference whether one poses the question of flourishing *from within*, in regard to one's own life, or *from without*, in reference to the lives of others. And it matters also whether the question is posed *prospectively*, with practical intent and in search of normative guidance for how to use one's power to shape one's own life and the lives of others, or *retrospectively*, in the spirit of mere evaluation.

The relevance of these distinctions can be appreciated by noting that the choice of perspective has a substantial bearing on (at least our perception of) the relative importance of the dimensions of human flourishing distinguished above. It seems appealing, for example, to give more weight to ethical (relative to personal) value when one reflects prospec-

---

[5] Achievement, in turn, might be understood in different time frames, i.e., more narrowly, in terms of the ethical quality of a person's *deeds*, and/or, more broadly, in terms of the ethical significance of her life's historical *impact* on the world.

tively on one's own life than when one reflects prospectively on the life of one's child: we are more likely to approve of someone who sees a large part of her child's future flourishing in this child's happiness than of someone who sees an equally large part of her own future flourishing in her own happiness.[6] Similarly, it seems appealing to give more weight to experience and character (relative to success and achievement) when we think about another's life prospectively (with practical intent) than when we assess it retrospectively. We may conclude in the end that these are perspectival distortions that should be explained away en route to a unified conception of human flourishing. But in order to reach any such adequate conception, we must first notice that human flourishing appears differently to us depending on the perspective we take.

The perspective in which we encounter the question of what constitutes human flourishing also makes an important difference in another way. When one thinks prospectively (with practical intent) about the life of another person, a certain deference seems to be called for. It is widely agreed, nowadays, that the autonomy of adult persons ought to be respected and that the measure of a person's flourishing—the specification of its various dimensions, their relative weights, and their integration into *one* measure of the comprehensively good life—is then, to some extent, to be posited by this person herself. This is not just the trivial thought that, if one wants to make another person happy, one must give her what she enjoys and not what one would enjoy oneself. For this thought still assumes an underlying common currency—happiness or joy—in terms of which the personal value of *any* life can be assessed. To respect the autonomy of another means, however, to accept *her* measure of human flourishing. If she cares about knowledge rather than happiness, for example, then one should give her a good book for her birthday. This is likely to make her happy—both because the book will enhance her knowledge and also because one has chosen one's gift with care. Nevertheless, if one truly respects her autonomy, then one will give her the book not for the sake of her expected joy but for the sake of enriching her knowledge. One is respecting another's autonomy insofar as one takes her flourishing to consist in whatever *she* takes it to consist in.

---

[6] We see an extreme instance of this phenomenon in act-utilitarian doctrine according to which the personal value of a human life is measured by the quantity of happiness it contains while its ethical value is measured by its impact on the general happiness. When a utilitarian reflects on the value of a human life from within, its ethical value will predominate: what matters is that one's life should have the greatest possible positive impact on the general happiness. To what extent one should seek one's own happiness is an empirical-instrumental question: one should seek one's own happiness whenever this is the best way of promoting the general happiness—and otherwise one ought to promote the general happiness, even at the expense of one's own. When a utilitarian reflects on the value of a human life from without, its personal value will predominate: what matters is that others be as happy as possible. To what extent one should also want them to be promoters of happiness is an empirical-instrumental question: one should promote the ethical value of human lives whenever this is the best way of promoting the personal value of human lives—and otherwise one ought to promote personal value, even at the expense of ethical value.

This is certainly not tantamount to the introduction of autonomous living as a universal currency (on a par with how the classical utilitarians conceived of happiness). To respect another as autonomous does not mean seeing him as someone whom one should try to goad toward free and deep reflections about his own life. It does not even mean accepting him as someone who has managed, through free and deep reflections, to develop his own measure of the value of his life. To the contrary, I respect someone's autonomy only insofar as I accept *his* measure of his flourishing—without demanding that he must have come to this measure on a certain reflective path that I approve of. This notion of autonomy is connected, then, not to self-legislation, to the *giving* of directives to oneself, but, more simply and more literally, to *having* one's own directives: a purpose of one's own.

II. SOCIAL JUSTICE

The idea of human flourishing is central not only to our personal and ethical reflections about our own lives and the lives of those around us, but also to our political discourse about our social institutions and policies. Here it is, in particular, our idea of justice that affords yet another perspective on the question of what constitutes human flourishing. In its ordinary meaning, the word "justice" is associated with the morally appropriate and, in particular, evenhanded treatment of persons and groups. Its currently most prominent use is in the moral assessment of social institutions, understood not as organized collective agents (such as the United States government or the World Bank), but rather as a social system's practices or "rules of the game," which govern interactions among individual and collective agents as well as their access to material resources. Such institutions define and regulate property, the division of labor, sexual and kinship relations, as well as political and economic competition, for example; and they also govern how collective projects are adopted and executed, how conflicts are settled, and how social institutions themselves are created, revised, interpreted, and enforced. The totality of the more fundamental and pervasive institutions of a social system has been called its basic structure (the term used by John Rawls) or institutional scheme.[7] Prominent within our political discourse, then, is the goal of formulating and justifying a criterion of justice, which assesses the degree to which the institutions of a social system are treating the persons and groups they affect in a morally appropriate and, in particular, evenhanded way.[8] Such a criterion of justice presupposes a measure of human flourishing, and one specially designed for the task of evaluating

---

[7] "Social order" and "regime" are also used.

[8] The moral assessment of social institutions may thus involve more than a criterion of justice, as one may also want to consider, for example, how institutions affect other species of animals or how well they accord with God's will. My definition places such issues outside the discourse about justice, which can therefore contribute only one essential component of the moral assessment of social institutions.

how social institutions treat the persons they affect. This task differs significantly from other tasks for which a measure of human flourishing is likewise needed, and its execution may therefore require a distinct conception of human flourishing.

When we think of how social institutions treat persons, we generally have in mind the persons living under those institutions, the persons to whom those institutions apply. But this focus on present participants may be too narrow in two respects. First, social institutions may have a significant impact on present nonparticipants. The political and economic institutions of the United States, for example—through their impact on foreign investment, trade flows, world market prices, interest rates, and the distribution of military power—greatly affect the lives of many persons who are neither citizens nor residents of this country. We should allow, then, that the justice of an institutional scheme may in part depend on its treatment of outsiders. Second, social institutions may also affect the flourishing of past and future persons—through their impact on pollution, resource depletion, and the development of religions, ways of life, and the arts, for example.

Here it may be objected that social institutions cannot possibly affect the flourishing of past persons in any way. Already Aristotle has shown, however, that this thought is at least disputable.[9] To dispute it, one might argue as follows: It is relevant to a person's flourishing whether her confidence in her successes and ethical achievements is mistaken. This is so when her confidence concerns the present (e.g., if the love she ascribes to her husband or the knowledge she ascribes to herself are not real) and also when it concerns the future (e.g., if she wrongly believes that her invention will lead to great future benefits). But it seems arbitrary to hold that the—to her, in any case, unknown—true impact of her life is relevant to her flourishing only up to the time of her death. A person's flourishing may therefore depend in part on the long-term success and ethical achievement of her life. It may thus be in a person's interest that her last will be followed, that her creative productions remain available, or that her projects be continued by others. And social institutions can then arguably be unjust by avoidably causing the nonrealization of such interests.[10]

In thinking about the justice of social institutions, we should not, then—as is so often done—ignore, or exclude in advance, the interests of past and future persons or those of present nonparticipants. Recognizing these interests does not preclude us from acknowledging the special status of present participants, who generally are more significantly affected by

[9] See Aristotle, *Nicomachean Ethics*, trans. Terence Irwin (Indianapolis: Hackett, 1985), Book 1, ch. 10, 1100a10–31.

[10] For further discussion of this topic, see Lukas Meyer, "More Than They Have a Right To: Future People and Our Future-Oriented Projects," in *Contingent Future Persons: On the Ethics of Deciding Who Will Live, or Not, in the Future*, ed. Nick Fotion and Jan C. Heller (Dordrecht: Kluwer, 1997), pp. 137–56.

social institutions and also, through their role in continuing and upholding them, tend to bear a greater moral responsibility for their shape.

It makes no sense to try to assess the justice of social institutions one by one. Doing so, we would detect various supposed injustices that turn out to be illusory when examined in a broader context: compulsory male military service, for instance, is not unjust so long as men are not disadvantaged overall in comparison to women. Doing so, we would also be likely to overlook comparisons and reforms that involve discrepancies in regard to several institutions: even if each of our social institutions is perfectly just so long as all the others are held constant, it may still be possible to render them more just by redesigning several of them together.[11]

Assessing the social institutions of each country together as one scheme is, in the modern world, only a partial solution to this difficulty. For both the formation and the effects of such national basic structures are heavily influenced by foreign and supranational institutions. This is especially evident in the case of politically and economically weaker countries, where the feasibility and effectiveness of national institutions (meant to secure, perhaps, the rule of law, or access to adequate nutrition for all) depend on the structure of international institutions and also on the structure of the national institutions of more powerful states. We need, then, a holistic understanding of how the living conditions of persons are shaped through the interplay of various institutional structures, which influence one another and intermingle in their effects.

These interdependencies are of great significance—and are nonetheless frequently overlooked not only by moral philosophers, but also by social scientists, politicians, and the educated public. We tend to assess a country's institutions, and also the policies of its government, by reference to how they treat its citizens, thereby overlooking their often quite considerable effects upon foreigners. Similarly, we tend to overlook the effects of global institutions, which may greatly affect national basic structures and their effects upon individuals. These institutional interconnections—an important aspect of so-called "globalization"—suggest that we need for the contemporary world a single *universal* criterion of justice that would allow us to assess together all social institutions of diverse scope whose interplay shapes the living conditions of individual persons.

Both moral and pragmatic reasons demand that we should try to formulate this criterion of justice, which is to be applied universally (that is, to all institutions worldwide), so that it can gain universal acceptance. This desideratum suggests that respect of autonomy should be extended beyond persons to include societies and cultures as well. While a shared

---

[11] This point is analogous to one that arises when we seek to optimize some process of production. Even if it is true that each part of the process is designed in the best possible way given the way the other parts are designed, it may still be possible greatly to improve the entire process: by redesigning all the parts together or, more importantly, by altering the process's very structure (including its division into parts).

criterion of justice will of course impose important constraints, it should also be compatible with a significant diversity of (national) institutions and ways of life. Here, again, the wider, more literal sense of "autonomy" (*having* one's own way of life) is appropriate, rather than the narrower one (*choosing* one's own way of life). What matters is that a society's institutions and way of life be endorsed by those to whom they apply— they need not be endorsed reflectively. The shared criterion of justice we seek should not, then, hold that cultures have an autonomy worthy of respect only insofar as they sustain supra-cultural reflection, discourse, and choice in matters of human flourishing.[12] In fact, it must not make this demand, if it is to be widely acceptable worldwide and thus immune to the complaint that it manifests an attempt to impose Western enlightenment values upon other cultures.

III. Paternalism

Respect of autonomy was first mentioned above in the context of relating to an adult whose ideas about flourishing differ from our own: rather than promote his good as we see it, we should often promote his good as he defines it for himself (while sometimes perhaps also engaging him in a discussion of this subject). It is tempting to advocate a like deference in the domain of justice, defining each person's flourishing as whatever this person takes it to be. Such a nonpaternalistic strategy fails, however, in this domain, for at least two separate reasons.

First, since there is not one set of social institutions that best meets the values and aspirations of all persons affected, and since persons always differ in how they define flourishing for themselves, we must, in deciding between two institutional alternatives, compare the relative gains and losses in flourishing of different persons or groups. Such comparisons evidently presuppose a common measure. If we are not to go beyond how the relevant persons themselves define a good life for themselves, then this common measure can only be the *degree* to which particular social institutions meet the disparate values and aspirations of the persons affected by them. Such a measure can indeed be constructed for simple cases where persons have divergent preference rankings over outcomes.[13]

---

[12] The goal of free intercultural agreement on a universal criterion of justice does, however, involve the hope that most cultures can sustain reflection and discussion about matters of *justice* that transcend the confines of their own traditions and are sensitive to the outlooks prevalent in other cultures. Sections IV and VI below indicate how cultures might fulfill this hope even without fulfilling the demand I reject in the text.

[13] Here a person's most favored outcome is assigned the value 1, and her least favored outcome is assigned the value 0. The value of any other outcome Q is then that $n (0 \leq n \leq 1)$ which makes the following true: The person is indifferent between Q with certainty, on the one hand, and a lottery pursuant to which her most-favored outcome occurs with probability n and her least-favored outcome with probability $(1 - n)$, on the other hand.

But the conceptions persons have of their own flourishing are not simple preference orderings over states of the world. They involve deeper issues, which block any straightforward conversion of preferences and facts into a numerical value on a one-dimensional flourishing scale. One such deep issue concerns the question of whether what matters is the fulfillment or the satisfaction of aspirations and desires,[14] where *fulfillment* is the actual realization of a person's desire in the world, while *satisfaction* is her belief that her desire is so realized.[15] Here one might respond that a nonpaternalistic strategy should defer to each person's own desires regarding fulfillment versus satisfaction—that is, we should go by where she herself would place the outcomes *fulfilled but not satisfied* (she is loved but believes that she is not) and *satisfied but not fulfilled* (she believes falsely that she is loved) between *fulfilled and satisfied* (she correctly believes that she is loved) and *neither fulfilled nor satisfied* (she correctly believes that she is not loved). But this amendment runs into awesome complications: Is there, for each desire of every person, a fact of the matter regarding the relative weight this person would attach to the fulfillment versus the satisfaction of that desire? How can such relative weights be ascertained in an objective way? And how feasible is a social-justice calculus whose operation requires that such fulfillment-versus-satisfaction weights be ascertained for every desire of every person?

Another deep issue concerns how we should deal with a person's desires about desires—for instance, with her desires concerning her own desires. A person may desire active enjoyment over passive contemplation, yet regret this desire—and then again wish that she did not have this regret. Such tensions across levels are commonplace when persons seek to define a good life for themselves. And it is not clear how, when there are such tensions, the degree to which a particular institutional scheme meets a person's values and aspirations is to be measured. Should we go with her first-order desires,[16] with the first-order desires she would prefer to have, with the first-order desires the person she desires to be would prefer to have, or what?

---

[14] This issue of fulfillment versus satisfaction confronts any account of human flourishing and thus is quite independent of my focus on such accounts within the context of developing a globally shareable criterion of justice for the moral assessment of institutional schemes.

[15] Thus, your aspiration to be loved is *fulfilled* insofar as you truly are loved, and *satisfied* insofar as you live in the happy consciousness of being loved. Obviously, an aspiration may be fulfilled without being satisfied and also may be satisfied without being fulfilled: you may be loved while believing that you are not; or you may believe falsely that you are loved. The fulfillment of an aspiration may be a matter of degree insofar as its realization in the world may be more or less complete. The satisfaction of such an aspiration may then be a matter of degree twice over, for it also depends on the degrees of confidence with which a person ascribes particular degrees of fulfillment to the aspiration in question.

[16] A person's first-order desires are those desires that are not about her own desires. Many of our desires fall into this category. But many do not, as when I desire to shed, to strengthen or to weaken, to indulge or to frustrate, to attend to or to neglect one of my present desires, for example, or when I desire to acquire a new one.

A second reason for the failure of the nonpaternalistic strategy is that social institutions shape not merely the environment and the options of the persons living under them—but also their values and aspirations, which cannot then provide an impartial standpoint from which alternative institutional schemes could be compared. We can have no determinate idea of how human persons define a good life for themselves apart from information about the social conditions under which they grew up. In response to this difficulty, one might propose that social institutions ought to meet the values and aspirations of existing persons and/or the values and aspirations that persons raised under those same institutions would develop.[17] But these proposals by themselves cannot deliver an adequate criterion of justice. Otherwise highly oppressive institutions would be rendered just by the fact that the oppressed are raised so as to accept their abysmal status, and dictatorships would be rendered just by the fact that those living under them are brainwashed into adoring the leaders.

The failure of the nonpaternalistic strategy to deliver a determinate criterion of justice should not be surprising. It reflects our predicament. We will unavoidably bequeath a social world to those who come after us—a social world into which they will be born without choice and one that will ineluctably shape their values and their sense of justice, in terms of which they will then assess the social world we left them with. Facing up to this daunting responsibility requires that we develop, within a normative conception of the justice of social institutions, a substantive conception of human flourishing.

Designing social institutions with such a conception in mind inevitably involves a dose of paternalism, which can, however, be made more palatable by honoring the following four desiderata: (1) The sought universal criterion of justice ought to work with a thin conception of human flourishing, which might be formulated largely in terms of (unspecific) means to, rather than components of, human flourishing. Though disagreements about what human flourishing consists in may prove ineradicable, it may well be possible to bypass them by agreeing that nutrition, clothing, shelter, and certain basic freedoms, as well as social interaction, education, and participation, are important means to it—means which just social institutions must secure for all. Such a thin conception would express some respect for the autonomy of diverse cultures, favoring social institutions acceptable to persons from different (religious, social, ethnic, etc.) backgrounds representing a wide range of diverse more-specific conceptions of human flourishing. (2) The sought universal criterion ought to be modest. Rather than define justice as the highest attainable point on

---

[17] The latter demand is that social institutions should engender fitting pairs of values and options—should work so that persons have the options they value and value the options they have.

an open-ended scale, it should define justice as a solid threshold compatible with an international diversity of institutional schemes that are merely required to treat the persons affected by them in a minimally decent way. (3) The requirements of the universal criterion should not be understood as exhaustive. They should, for instance, leave the various societies free to impose their own more demanding criteria of justice upon their own national institutions and even to judge foreign or global institutions by the lights of such more ambitious criteria.[18] (4) The supplementary considerations introduced by such more ambitious criteria of justice must not, however, undermine the universality of the modest criterion and therefore must not be allowed to outweigh the latter in situations of conflict or competition (e.g., over scarce resources). The requirements of the universal criterion ought therefore to be understood as preeminent within any more ambitious national criterion.

Taking all four desiderata together, the envisioned universal criterion should be able to function as a *core* in a dual sense—as the core in which a plurality of more specific conceptions of human flourishing and of more ambitious criteria of justice can overlap (thinness and modesty); and as the core of each of these criteria, containing all and only its most important elements (preeminence without exhaustiveness).[19] The task is then to formulate a criterion of basic justice that is morally plausible and internationally widely acceptable as the universal core of all criteria of justice.

IV. JUSTICE IN FIRST APPROXIMATION

On the basis of the reflections introduced thus far, our task has taken on the following form: We are seeking a widely acceptable core criterion of basic justice that assesses social institutions on the basis of how they treat persons. Such a criterion presupposes interpersonal comparability,[20] but it should also respect the autonomy of the various persons and cultures involved. This suggests formulating the sought-after criterion in terms of certain basic goods, broadly and abstractly conceived—in particular: in terms of the extent to which the persons affected by an institutional scheme have the goods they need to develop and realize a conception of a personally and ethically worthwhile life. In the last few decades many

[18] There must be tight limits, however, on how one society may sanction another when it judges the institutions of the latter to accord with the universal criterion but not with the former's own more ambitious criterion of justice. Agreement on a universal criterion would lose much of its point, if fulfillment of this criterion did not shield national regimes against coercive reform efforts from the outside.

[19] I do not here mean to rule out the possibility that some societies or other groups may think of the universal criterion as exhausting what justice requires. This criterion—though it should not be understood as exhaustive—should not be understood as nonexhaustive either. Both of these understandings would needlessly undermine its widespread acceptance and hence the plausibility of its claim to universality.

[20] See Section III above, second paragraph.

theorists have indeed developed criteria of justice along these lines. Those
following this general approach must answer three questions in order to
specify an operational criterion of justice.

Question 1. How should these basic goods be defined? Here one might
work with something like Rawls's social primary goods or Ronald Dworkin's resources, adding perhaps freedom from pain as a further component, as Thomas Scanlon suggests.[21] An important alternative to this
answer is Amartya Sen's account of capabilities.[22] Insofar as the quest
is for a modest criterion of basic justice, one that marks only a solid
threshold, the demand for basic goods should be severely limited in
four respects: (a) Only really essential goods, ones that are truly needed
for developing or realizing a conception of a worthwhile life, should be
placed on the list of basic goods. (b) The demand for the basic goods
listed should be limited both quantitatively and qualitatively to what I
will call a *minimally adequate* share. Food and freedom of association
are necessary for a worthwhile life, but we need these only in limited
amounts and can get by entirely without delicacies and without meetings at certain times or places. (c) Persons truly need *access to* certain
basic goods, rather than these goods themselves. It is no intolerable
flaw in a social order that some persons living under it choose to fast
for long periods, to participate in boxing matches, to live as hermits
cut off from human interaction, or even to obtain help in committing
suicide—provided they could gain the basic goods they are renouncing
without thereby incurring a serious lack in other basic goods. (d) Basic
goods should also be limited probabilistically. Social institutions cannot
be so designed that everyone affected by them has absolutely secure
access to all goods that he needs. U.S. society, for example, cannot be
so structured that your physical integrity is guaranteed 100 percent. It
cannot be completely ruled out that some punks or even police officers
will attack you without provocation. Even when this can, or does, happen, we should nevertheless say that you have secure access to the
basic good of "physical integrity," so long as the probability of such an
attack does not exceed certain limits. What sounds paradoxical is nev-

[21] Paradigmatic for this answer is Rawls's broad list, which includes various basic liberties as well as income and wealth, powers and prerogatives of office, and social bases of
self-respect. See John Rawls, *A Theory of Justice* (Cambridge, MA: Harvard University Press,
1971), esp. section 15; and Rawls, "Social Unity and Primary Goods," in *Utilitarianism and
Beyond,* ed. Amartya K. Sen and Bernard Williams (Cambridge: Cambridge University Press,
1982), pp. 159–86. Cf. Ronald Dworkin, "What Is Equality? Part II: Equality of Resources,"
Philosophy and Public Affairs, vol. 10, no. 4 (Fall 1981), pp. 283–345; and Thomas M. Scanlon,
"Preference and Urgency," *Journal of Philosophy,* vol. 72, no. 19 (November 1975), pp. 655–69.

[22] Capabilities are defined in terms of what a person can do or be. In contrast to the
Rawlsian answer, this way of conceiving basic goods makes their measurement sensitive to
differences in persons' specific needs and endowments. Thus, Sen has us focus, for example,
not on a person's income as such, but on her income relative to her specific nutritional (and
other) needs. See Amartya K. Sen, *Commodities and Capabilities* (Amsterdam: North-Holland,
1985), and also the anthology *The Quality of Life,* ed. Martha Nussbaum and Amartya K. Sen
(Oxford: Oxford University Press, 1993), esp. the helpful essay on Sen by Gerald A. Cohen,
pp. 9–29.

ertheless plausible: it is possible that your physical integrity, but not that of your black colleague, is sufficiently well protected in the U.S. even if you are in fact assaulted while she is not.

When social institutions work so that each person affected by them has reasonably secure access to minimally adequate shares of all basic goods, then these institutions are—according to our core criterion of basic justice—fully just. But a criterion of justice should also facilitate comparisons of institutional schemes that are not fully just. We therefore need answers to two further questions that have to do with aggregation.

Question 2. How should the chosen basic goods be integrated into *one* measure of a person's standard of living? How should relevant shortfalls—for example, in nutrition, freedom of movement, and liberty of conscience—be weighted vis-à-vis one another so that it can be ascertained, for any affected person or group, how far it falls below the minimum standard of living required by our core criterion of basic justice? Here one might ascribe a standard of living 1 to all affected persons who reach the threshold in regard to all basic goods and then ascribe lower numbers (greater than or equal to 0, but less than 1) to all those who fall below the threshold with regard to one or more basic goods.[23] My use of the new expression "standard of living" is not merely meant to flag that we are dealing here with a thin core notion of human flourishing which, to be appropriate to the global plane (and in contrast to the thicker notions that particular countries or groups might employ), is severely limited in the four ways—(a) through (d)—described above. It is especially also meant to flag the further point that the construction of a standard of living, and of a criterion of justice more generally, is a pragmatic task: the constructed standard should be a good proxy for the appropriately thin core notion of human flourishing, of course, but it should also, when used within a public criterion of justice, promote human flourishing so conceived through its compelling unity, clarity, simplicity, easy applicability, etc. It is such pragmatic reasons that justify constructing the international standard of living as a numerical measure with a threshold. And one can therefore support this standard even if one does not believe that human flourishing itself is either discontinuous (so that gains and losses above some threshold are much less significant than gains and losses below it) or quantifiable.

Question 3. How should the measurements of the standard of living of the various affected persons (or groups) be integrated into *one* overall measure for the justice of social institutions? Here one might work with the arithmetic or geometric mean, for example, or else choose sum-ranking, maximin, or some indicator of inequality as an interpersonal

---

[23] One might need to rethink this formulation if it can plausibly be maintained that even persons falling below the threshold in regard to one or more basic goods should be assigned standard of living 1 so long as they sufficiently exceed the threshold with regard to other basic goods.

aggregation function.[24] One might also want to give differential weights to persons depending on whether they are insiders or outsiders, and on whether they lived in the past, are living in the present, or will live in the future.

V. Essential Refinements

Before thinking further about these questions, we must take account of a further complication which has been neglected in recent writings about justice. In assessing the justice of social institutions, it is relevant *how* such institutions affect the flourishing of individuals. Let me introduce the point through a quick example. Imagine a hypothetical scenario in which every year some 10,000 U.S. residents (or twenty-seven per day) are killed by the police. U.S. residents would then, on average, face an approximately one-quarter percent probability of dying through police violence.[25] If this were really the case, we would surely want to dispute that the physical integrity of U.S. residents is here reasonably secure. We would want to say that the social institutions of the United States are unjust in this regard and ought to be reformed with the aim of reducing the number of police killings. This might be done through better police training, for instance, or through more effective and more severe punishments of police officers who engage in unjustified violence.

Persons are actually killed in motor vehicle accidents in the U.S. at a rate that is over four times higher than the imaginary rate in the preceding story: over 43,000 deaths annually in 1995, 1996, and 1997, or about 119 per day.[26] At this rate, the average U.S. resident has a better than 1 percent chance of dying in a motor vehicle accident.[27] In this case, too, institutional reforms might bring relief. One might allow only cars with a built-in maximum speed of fifty miles per hour, for example, or might greatly increase the punishments for drunk driving (which plays a role in some 40 percent of the fatalities in question).[28]

---

[24] The arithmetic mean is the sum of the measurements for the various affected persons divided by the number of persons, N. The geometric mean is the Nth root of the product of those measurements. Sum-ranking simply uses the sum of all measurements. Maximin takes the lowest measurements to be representative. Inequality is measured in many different ways—one straightforward indicator is the ratio of the arithmetic mean of the bottom 20 percent of affected persons to the arithmetic mean of the top 20 percent.

[25] Their risk each year would be only about 0.0036 percent (10,000/275,000,000) on average, but they would face this risk over their full lifespan (approximately seventy-five years, on average).

[26] The National Safety Council gives a figure of 43,360 deaths for 1995, and 43,300 for 1996, and offers a preliminary estimate of 43,090 for 1997.

[27] The risk each year is only about 0.01574 percent (43,300/275,000,000), but, again, the risk increases over a lifetime to about 1.18 percent over seventy-five years.

[28] According to the National Safety Council, the latest figures for alcohol-related road traffic fatalities are 16,589 out of 42,524 (39.01 percent) in 1994; 17,274 out of 43,360 (39.84 percent) in 1995; and 17,126 out of 43,300 (39.55 percent) in 1996.

The juxtaposition of these two cases makes it evident that we assign very different moral weights to different institutional influences on our risk of premature death. We view a significant and avoidable risk of premature death through police violence as a much greater injury to the justice of a society than an otherwise equal risk (or even a considerably greater risk) of premature death through traffic accidents—and we do this even on the assumption that all other things (such as citizens' acceptance of these risks, and the possibility and social cost of reducing them) are equal in the two cases.

If we did not think in this way, if we assigned equal moral weight to such different kinds of institutionally reducible risks of premature death, then we would have strong reason to support the death penalty for the most dangerous drunk drivers. An institutional "reform" that caused some one hundred of the worst offenders to be executed in the U.S. each year—more than doubling the annual number of executions for all current capital offenses—would presumably have a very considerable deterrent effect, thus resulting in a significant reduction in the incidence of drunk driving. If it could reduce the total number of alcohol-related traffic fatalities by merely 5 percent (about 860 deaths annually), then some 760 fewer persons would die prematurely each year, and all U.S. residents would face a statistically lower risk of premature death.[29]

If we want to avoid embracing this proposal as an easy and obvious step toward a more just society, then we need to make moral distinctions. We must not assess social institutions from the perspective of rational prospective participants, as modern hypothetical-contract theories (starting with Rawls) have been doing. For such prospective participants would prudently favor the imagined execution regime over the status quo, so long as it really does entail an overall reduction in citizens' risk of premature death. This is so, because they are conceived as ranking feasible institutional arrangements solely in terms of the quality of life they could expect under each, and thus are conceived as not caring *how* one institutional scheme produces a higher expected quality of life than another.

The dubious implications of consequentialist and hypothetical-contract theories are due to the fact that they assess social institutions *solely* on the basis of the quality of life they afford to their prospective participants. To

---

[29] This argument is presented more fully in Thomas Pogge, "Three Problems with Contractarian-Consequentialist Ways of Assessing Social Institutions," *Social Philosophy and Policy*, vol. 12, no. 2 (Summer 1995), Section VC, pp. 260–64. As I mention there, a full calculation would have to subtract, from the number of traffic deaths avoided (860 annually in the example in the text), not only those who will die prematurely by execution (100), but also people who may be killed by drunk drivers desperately trying to evade capture. And the reform could have further (positive or negative) effects on the number of premature deaths as well. Sections VA and VB of the same essay discuss how similar reasoning may support other morally dubious reforms in the criminal-law domain, such as increased use of strict-liability statutes, rougher methods in the apprehension and treatment of suspects, and lower standards of evidence.

avoid such implications, we must distinguish different ways in which social institutions affect the lives of individuals and then incorporate this distinction into our criteria of justice, including the universal core criterion sketched in the preceding section. This core criterion must not define basic-good shortfalls simply as institutionally avoidable shortfalls from reasonably secure access to minimally adequate shares of basic goods, but must also take into account how social institutions relate to such shortfalls.

Let me illustrate this thought by distinguishing, in a preliminary way, six basic ways in which social institutions may relate to human flourishing. Because of my specific focus here, I will formulate this sixfold distinction in terms of institutionally avoidable basic-good shortfalls—without assuming, however, that the universal core criterion we seek ought to be sensitive to shortfalls of all six kinds (classes 5 and 6, in particular, may well fall outside the core). For illustration, I will use six different scenarios in which, due to the arrangement of social institutions, a certain group of innocent persons is avoidably deprived of some vital nutrients V (the vitamins contained in fresh fruit, perhaps, which play a major role in the maintenance of good health). The six kinds of institutionally avoidable shortfalls are arranged in order of their moral significance, according to my intuitive, pre-reflective judgment: First-class shortfalls are officially mandated, paradigmatically by the law (legal restrictions on the sale/purchase of foodstuffs containing V to/by certain persons). Second-class shortfalls arise from legally authorized conduct of private agents (sellers of foodstuffs containing V lawfully refuse to sell to certain persons). Third-class shortfalls are foreseeably engendered through the uncoordinated conduct of agents under rules that do not specifically require these shortfalls (certain persons, suffering severe poverty within an ill-conceived economic order, cannot afford to buy foodstuffs containing V). Fourth-class shortfalls arise from private conduct that is legally prohibited but generally tolerated (sellers of foodstuffs containing V illegally refuse to sell to certain persons, but enforcement is lax and penalties are mild). Fifth-class shortfalls arise from natural factors whose effects social institutions avoidably leave unmitigated (certain persons are unable to metabolize V due to a treatable genetic defect, but they are not receiving the treatment that would correct their handicap). Sixth-class shortfalls, finally, arise from self-caused factors whose effects social institutions avoidably leave unmitigated (certain persons are unable to metabolize V due to a treatable self-caused disease—brought on, perhaps, by maintaining a long-term smoking habit in full knowledge of the medical dangers associated therewith—and are not receiving the treatment that would correct their ailment).

This differentiation of six ways in which social institutions may be related to human flourishing is preliminary in that it fails to isolate the morally significant factors that account for the descending moral significance of the shortfalls in question. Since trying to do this here would lead us too far afield, let me just venture the hypothesis that what matters is not merely the *causal* role of social institutions, how they figure in a complete causal explanation of the shortfall in question, but also (what one might call) the implicit *attitude* of social institutions toward the shortfall in question.[30] To illustrate: A high incidence of domestic violence (a shortfall in women's reasonably secure access to physical integrity) may show a society's legal order to be unjust, if it could be substantially reduced through more vigorous enforcement of, and more severe punishments under, existing laws. But the same abuse of the same women would indicate an even greater injustice, if it were not illegal at all—if spouses were legally free to beat each other or, worse, if men were legally authorized to beat the women in their households.

My preliminary classification is surely still too simple. In some cases, one will have to take account of other, perhaps underlying causes; and one may also need to recognize interdependencies among causal influences and fluid transitions between the six classes.[31] It is to be hoped that the formulation of a universal core criterion of basic justice, which is to be internationally acceptable, will be able to bypass most of these complications by focusing narrowly on the morally most important institutionally avoidable basic-good shortfalls. In any case, I will bypass these complications here, merely emphasizing once more the decisive point missed by the usual theories of justice: To be morally plausible, a criterion of justice must take account of the particular relation between social institutions and human flourishing. In the special case of a core criterion of basic justice, this relation may affect whether some institutionally avoidable basic-good shortfall counts as a basic-good deficit (a core injustice)[32] at all and, if so, how morally significant this deficit is (how great a core injustice it indicates).[33]

We have now seen, at least in outline, that a morally plausible criterion of justice must consider institutionally avoidable basic-good shortfalls not merely in regard to their magnitude and frequency, but also in regard to how social institutions are related to them. The identification of this new

[30] This implicit attitude of social institutions is independent of the attitudes or intentions of the persons shaping and upholding these institutions: only the former makes a difference to how just the institutions are—the latter only make a difference to how blameworthy persons are for their role in imposing them.

[31] The case of smoking, for instance, may exemplify a fluid transition between classes 2 and 6 insofar as private agents (cigarette companies) are legally permitted to try to render persons addicted to nicotine.

[32] A core injustice is one identified by the core criterion, and thus an injustice recognized as such by all the more demanding conceptions of justice overlapping in this core criterion. I have explored this notion from a somewhat different angle in my essay "A Global Resources Dividend," in *Ethics of Consumption: The Good Life, Justice, and Global Stewardship*, ed. David A. Crocker and Toby Linden (Lanham, MD: Rowman and Littlefield, 1998), pp. 501–36.

[33] To illustrate: Whether it is unjust for social institutions not to entitle indigent persons to treatment for a certain lung disease—and, if so, how unjust this is—may well depend on whether this disease is contracted through legally authorized pollution by others or self-caused through smoking in full awareness of its risks.

weighting dimension suggests that we need to ask whether there might be additional weighting dimensions that the usual theories of justice have overlooked. I believe there are two such additional dimensions, which I can only mention here. One further weighting dimension concerns the social costs that would arise from the institutional avoidance of a morally significant basic-good shortfall. Whether and how urgently justice demands reforms toward reducing the traffic-related risk of premature death may depend on the cost of such reforms. In order to save 2,000 pedestrians annually, would we merely have to lower the speed limit within residential areas from thirty to twenty-five miles per hour or would we have to invest billions into constructing tunnels and overpasses? To avoid 20,000 cases of child abuse annually, would we merely need to modify the training of school teachers or would we have to spy on millions of private homes with video equipment? Such questions are surely relevant to deciding whether given basic-good shortfalls are unjust at all and, if so, how much they detract from the overall justice of the relevant social institutions.

A second additional weighting dimension concerns the distribution of basic-good shortfalls. Many of the usual theories of justice are, of course, distribution-sensitive through their aggregation function (using, e.g., maximin, the geometric mean, or some measure of inequality in this role). But these theories also tend to accept what economists call the anonymity condition. On the face of it, this condition looks harmless enough: it requires merely that permutations of persons over social positions should make no difference to judgments of justice. Thus, the injustice of certain basic-good deficits is exactly the same regardless of who is suffering these shortfalls. This requirement seems to express the very essence of justice: surely, one wants to say, our moral assessment of an institutionally avoidable hardship ought not to be affected by whether this hardship is suffered by me or by you, by someone like us or unlike us, by someone we like, dislike, or do not even know—every person matters equally. But the anonymity condition becomes problematic in reference to certain groups. It may indeed not matter whether a particular hardship is suffered by a man or a woman, by a white or a black, by a Mormon or a Jew—but what if women or blacks or Jews are greatly overrepresented among those suffering the hardship? Is this still to be considered morally irrelevant, as the anonymity condition requires?[34] It would seem that a morally plausible criterion would have to take account of some such correlations. Whether such correlations are unjust and, if so, how unjust they are, may well depend on how large a role social factors play in their genesis and on

[34] To be sure, the anonymity condition permits a criterion of justice to be sensitive to whether two different kinds of hardship are correlated (e.g., to count it as a greater injustice if the groups of those excluded from higher education and of those excluded from political participation overlap than if they are disjoint). But being black, female, or Jewish are not, as such, hardships. Sex, color, and religion are precisely the kinds of factors that the anonymity condition was meant to screen out.

how salient such correlations are. For illustration, consider severe and avoidable poverty suffered by a certain fraction of a population. The injustice indicated by this poverty would not be much affected by the fact that some nonsalient group (e.g., those with blood-type B) is, due to statistically inferior natural endowments, overrepresented among the very poor. The injustice might be seen as greater if women (a salient group) were overrepresented due to statistically inferior natural endowments. And it would be seen as greater still if women were overrepresented among the very poor due to sexist cultural practices under which they do most of the housework and have fewer educational opportunities.[35]

In this section, I have, at least in broad outlines, displayed the general structure of a morally plausible criterion of justice—and, in particular, the various parameters in regard to which alternative specifications of such a criterion would differ from one another. This structure is unfortunately rather complicated. The criteria of justice currently available tend to be simpler. Rawls's perspective of the original position ignores the first and third new dimensions entirely and the second for the most part, because the parties who are choosing principles of justice are conceived as interested solely in the quality of life of prospective citizens, irrespective of the institutional mechanisms that may condition such quality of life.[36] As I could here show only generally and in outline, the simpler theories of justice advocated by Rawls and others imply various demands that are either morally dubious or unable to cope with the actual complexities of contemporary social systems.[37]

VI. HUMAN RIGHTS

What terminology might be most suitable for expressing a complex and internationally acceptable core criterion of basic justice? I believe that the concept of human rights is most likely to be equal to this task, at least if we are prepared to understand this concept in a special institutional way.[38] Surprisingly, this special understanding of human rights, which I

---

[35] The injustice would be even greater, if women were legally required to do most of the housework, or legally barred from many educational opportunities—but this is a matter of the first typically overlooked weighting dimension (class 1 versus class 3) extensively discussed at the beginning of this section.

[36] Something similar can be said of the much vaguer approach advocated by Jürgen Habermas through his Principle U. See, in particular, Habermas, *Moralbewußtsein und kommunikatives Handeln* (Frankfurt: Suhrkamp, 1983), pp. 75f.; and Habermas, *Erläuterungen zur Diskursethik* (Frankfurt: Suhrkamp, 1991), pp. 130–76.

[37] For more detail, see my "Three Problems" (*supra* note 29), and Thomas Pogge, "Gleiche Freiheit für alle?" in *John Rawls: Eine Theorie der Gerechtigkeit*, ed. Otfried Höffe (Berlin: Akademie Verlag, 1998), pp. 149–68.

[38] I speak of *institutional* understandings of human rights in contrast to *interactional* ones, according to which human rights are constraints on the treatment of human beings by other human agents and are thus independent of the existence of social institutions.

will now proceed to explicate, fits quite well with how human rights are understood in the 1948 *Universal Declaration of Human Rights*.[39]

According to one common institutional understanding, a human right to X is a kind of meta-right: a moral right to an effective legal right to X. So understood, human rights require their own implementation: the governments and citizens of every state ought to ensure that all human rights are incorporated into their state's fundamental legal texts and are observed and enforced within their state through effective judicial institutions.[40]

This understanding leads to demands that are, in my view, both too strong and too weak. They are too strong, because a society may be so situated and organized that its members enjoy secure access to X, even without a legal right thereto. Having corresponding legal rights in addition is good, to be sure, but not so important that this additional demand would need to be incorporated into the concept of a human right. A human right to adequate nutrition, say, should count as fulfilled when one has secure access to adequate nutrition, even when such access is not legally guaranteed. A human right would require its own legal instantiation only if it is empirically true—as it may be for some civil and political rights—that secure access to its object presupposes the inclusion of a corresponding legal right in the law or constitution.

The demands entailed by this conventional understanding are also too weak, because legal and even constitutional rights, however conscientiously enforced, often do not suffice to ensure secure access. Here I am not merely thinking of the many showcase constitutions around the world that detail a comprehensive list of strong protections but are widely ignored in governmental practice. It is likely that the proponents of the conventional institutional understanding would not rest content with such "rights" either. I am mainly thinking of cases where, though legal rights are effectively enforced, poor and uneducated persons are nevertheless incapable of insisting on their rights, because they do not know

---

[39] This declaration was adopted and proclaimed by the General Assembly of the United Nations on December 10, 1948, as resolution 217 A (III). For the full text, see *Twenty-Four Human Rights Documents* (New York: Columbia University Center for the Study of Human Rights, 1992), pp. 6–9.

[40] Thus, for example, Habermas writes: "The concept of human rights is not of moral origin, but ... *by nature* juridical." Human rights "belong, through their structure, to a scheme of positive and coercive law which supports justiciable individual right claims. Hence it belongs to the meaning of human rights that they demand for themselves the status of constitutional rights." Jürgen Habermas, "Kants Idee des Ewigen Friedens—aus dem historischen Abstand von 200 Jahren," *Kritische Justiz*, vol. 28, no. 3 (1995), pp. 293–319. The quotes are from p. 310 and p. 312; italics are in the original; the translation is mine. Though Robert Alexy explicitly refers to human rights as moral rights, he holds an otherwise similar position which equates the institutionalization of human rights with their transformation into positive law; see Alexy, "Die Institutionalisierung der Menschenrechte im demokratischen Verfassungsstaat," in *Die Philosophie der Menschenrechte*, ed. S. Gosepath and G. Lohmann (Frankfurt: Suhrkamp, 1998), pp. 244–64.

what their legal rights are or because they lack either the knowledge or the economic independence necessary to have these rights enforced through the proper legal channels. Even if there exists in India a legal path that would allow domestic servants to defend themselves against abuse by their employers, their human right to freedom from inhuman and degrading treatment (*Universal Declaration*, article 5) remains nevertheless unfulfilled for most of them.

Contrary to the understandings of human rights currently prevalent in the literature, I thus propose to explain this concept as follows: A human right is a moral claim *on* social institutions and therefore a moral claim *against* all those who participate in the coercive upholding of such institutions. The postulate of a human right to X is tantamount to the demand that social institutions are to be (re)designed in such a way that all persons affected by them have secure access to X.[41] Through this explication, one can clear away from the start the common suspicion that human rights promote individualism or even egoism, a mentality of everyone-for-himself, which threatens communal values.[42] According to my understanding, the point of human rights is not to educate persons to conceive of themselves as the holders of individual rights on whose enforcement, even against the majority or common good, they are entitled to insist at any time. The point of human rights lies rather in the insight that social institutions, which human beings impose upon one another with open or at least latent violence, must minimally be such that all persons affected by them have secure prospects for obtaining the means that are necessary to lead a life in dignity. Human rights are not legal rights, on which one can insist in a court of law, but morally binding elementary needs that ought to be fulfilled under any social institutions we design or uphold.

Two things must be said to soften this point. First, it is clear that legal rights can be, and often are, an effective means for fulfilling human rights. Such legal rights need not, however, have the same content as the human rights they help fulfill. Depending on the context, the best way of fulfilling a human right to minimally adequate nutrition may not be legal rights to foodstuffs when needed, but rather some other legal mechanisms—such as legal rights to child-care or retraining subsidies, to unemployment benefits, to a start-up loan or a piece of land, or laws against usury or against hoarding of, or speculation in, basic staples. Secondly, it is at least theoretically possible to include certain legal rights in the object of a human

[41] This proposal is elaborated in more detail in my "How Should Human Rights Be Conceived?" *Jahrbuch für Recht und Ethik*, vol. 3 (1995), pp. 103–20.

[42] Such criticism to the effect that human rights lead persons to view themselves as Westerners—as atomized, autonomous, secular, and self-interested individuals ready to insist on their rights no matter what the cost may be to others or the society at large—has been voiced, for instance, by Singapore's semi-retired ruler Lee Kuan Yew.

right. An example would be a human right to constitutionally protected freedom of religion. I am worried, however, that such demands might excessively dilute the conception of human rights we are seeking. A society whose citizens know that their enjoyment of religious liberty is secure—perhaps because religious tolerance is an unquestioned way of life in that society—does not deserve the charge that it fails to fulfill human rights merely because there is no legal statute that explicitly guarantees freedom of religion.

The concept of human rights is especially well suited to take account of the necessary differentiations that need to be made in regard to how social institutions relate to basic-good shortfalls. Such differentiations are already being made in regard to some constitutional rights. The German constitution, for instance, postulates: "Everyone shall have the right to life and to inviolability of his person."[43] According to the developed judicial understanding of this right, it is not the case that every avoidable death constitutes a violation of this right to life—let alone an exactly equally weighty violation. Death during a violent police interrogation would certainly count as a weighty violation of the basic right in question. Death due to unofficial violence condoned by state officials would count as a less weighty violation. And a death that could have been prevented by expensive medical treatment that the patient was unable (and the state unwilling) to pay for would not count as a violation of the right to life at all. The concept of human rights I am proposing involves similar differentiations—though with the difference that human rights are not addressed to a government and its agents, but to the institutional structure of a society (or other comprehensive social system). Human rights are not supposed to regulate what government officials must do or refrain from doing, but are to govern how all of us together ought to design the basic rules of our common life. This suggests the probabilistic *ex ante* perspective which I have already sketched above: a valid complaint against our social institutions can be presented by all those whose physical integrity is not sufficiently secure, not by all those who happened to fall prey to an assault. This is why it makes more sense, in the institutional context relevant here, to speak not of the violation of human rights, but of their fulfillment or nonfulfillment. A human right to life and physical integrity is fulfilled for certain persons if and only if their security against certain threats does not fall below certain thresholds. These thresholds will vary for different human rights and even for different sources of threats to one human right; and they will also be related to the social cost of reducing the various threats and to the distribution of these threats over various salient segments of the population.

---

[43] Grundgesetz, Article 2.2, in Press and Information Office of the Federal Government, *The Basic Law of the Federal Republic of Germany* (Wiesbaden: Wiesbadener Graphische Betriebe GmbH, 1979), p. 14.

These differentiations have to be incorporated into the specification of human rights.

VII. Specification of Human Rights and Responsibility for Their Fulfillment

The proposed path toward the formulation of an internationally acceptable core criterion of basic justice is now open to view. We start out from the personal and ethical value of human life—not in order to ascertain wherein this value lies, but in order to determine the social context and means that persons normally need, according to some broad range of plausible conceptions of what human flourishing consists in, to lead a minimally worthwhile life. This goal expresses respect for human autonomy, especially insofar as the criterion we seek is to be based on very weak assumptions about the components of ethical value. The main assumption here is merely existential: it is a historically and geographically universal fact that almost all human persons feel a deep need for an ethical worldview by reference to which they can judge whether their own life, and also the lives of others they may care about, is good—not merely for themselves, personally, but also, in a larger sense, ethically.

Beyond this, one can perhaps make one further general statement: In today's highly interdependent and communicatively closely interconnected world there exists in every culture an insuppressible plurality of ethical worldviews and of opinions about the objectivity and universality of such worldviews as well as about the relative importance of ethical (as against personal) quality of life. Even a modest criterion of basic justice should therefore demand that social institutions be designed so that the persons affected by them can develop, deepen, and realize an ethical worldview of their own. The essential presuppositions for this capacity can be presented under two headings. The first of these is liberty of conscience: the freedom to develop and to live in accordance with one's own ethical worldview so long as this is possible without excessive costs for others. This freedom must include various other liberties, such as freedom of access to informational media (such as books and broadcasts) and the freedom to associate with persons holding similar or different ethical views. The second heading is political participation: the freedom to take part in structuring and directing any comprehensive social systems to which one belongs. This includes the freedom publicly to express ethical criticisms of political institutions and decisions as well as the freedom to participate on equal terms in the competition for political positions and in the struggle over political decisions.

Other, more elementary basic goods are important for both the ethical and the personal value of human life. Among these are physical integrity, subsistence supplies (of food and drink, clothing and shelter), and freedom of movement and action, as well as health care, education, and economic participation. All of these basic goods should be recognized as the objects of human rights—but only up to certain quantitative, qualitative, and probabilistic limits: what human beings truly need is secure access to a minimally adequate share of any of these goods.

It is well known that many human beings today do not have secure access to a minimally adequate share of these goods, that the fulfillment of human rights has been only very partially achieved. This poses the question of how responsibility for the underfulfillment of human rights can be ascribed to particular social institutions—and thereby also to particular persons, namely, those who have participated in designing and upholding those institutions. This question involves special difficulties in this era of global interdependence when social institutions influence one another and their effects intermingle. It is convenient, and therefore common, to ignore these interdependencies in the way of what I have elsewhere referred to as *explanatory nationalism*.[44] This notion is well illustrated by how economists and the financial media tend to analyze Third World poverty: as a set of national phenomena explainable mainly by bad domestic policies and institutions that stifle (or fail to stimulate) national economic growth and engender national economic injustice. It is difficult to design policies and institutions that promote both growth and economic justice (and the pundits differ on how this should best be done), but some countries have succeeded rather well, and so could the others, if only they had better economic institutions and pursued better economic policies. If the governments of presently poor countries had done better in these regards, there would now be much less poverty in the world; and, if such governments were to do better from now on, severe poverty would gradually disappear.

This dominant view is quite true on the whole, but it is also totally one-sided. For it holds fixed, and thereby entirely ignores, the economic and geopolitical context in which the national economies and governments of the poorer countries are placed. The modern state, after all, is itself an institution: the land surface of our planet is divided into a number of clearly demarcated and non-overlapping national territories. Human beings are matched up with these territories, so that (at least for the most part) each person belongs to exactly one territory. Any person or group effectively controlling a preponderant share of the means of coercion within such a territory is recognized as the legitimate government of both the territory and the persons belonging to it. It is entitled to rule "its" people through laws, orders, and officials, to adjudicate conflicts among them, and also to exercise ultimate control over all resources within the territory ("eminent domain"). It is also entitled to act on behalf of these

---

[44] Thomas W. Pogge, "The Bounds of Nationalism," in *Rethinking Nationalism* (*Canadian Journal of Philosophy*, Supplementary Volume 22), ed. Jocelyne Couture et al. (Calgary: University of Calgary Press, 1998), pp. 463–504.

persons against the rest of the world: to bind them vis-à-vis outsiders through treaties and contracts, to regulate their relations with outsiders, to declare war in their name, to represent them through diplomats and emissaries, and to control outsiders' access to the country's territory. In this second role, a government is considered continuous with its predecessors and successors: bound by the undertakings of the former, and capable of binding the latter through its own undertakings.

This global context (of which I could here only sketch a few central features) is of crucial importance for explaining the incidence of unfulfilled human rights and the persistence and severity of global poverty. Explanations by reference solely to national factors and international differences leave important questions open. They leave open why national factors (institutions, officials, policies, culture, climate, natural environment, level of technical and economic development) have *these* effects rather than others. It is quite possible that, in a different global environment, the same national factors, or the same international differences, would have quite a different impact on human flourishing.[45] Such explanations also leave open why national factors are the way they are in the first place. Global factors significantly influence national policies and institutions, especially in the poorer and weaker countries. It is quite possible that, in a different global environment, national factors that tend to generate poverty, or tend to undermine the fulfillment of human rights more generally, would occur much less frequently or not at all.[46] These

[45] An analogous point plays a major role in debates about the significance of genetic vis-à-vis environmental factors: factors that are quite unimportant for explaining the observed *variation* of a trait (e.g., height, IQ) in some population may be very important for explaining this trait's *overall level* (frequency) in the same population. Suppose that, in some province, the observed variation in female adult height (54 to 60 inches) is almost entirely due to hereditary factors. It is still quite possible that the height differentials among these women are minor compared to how much taller they all would be (67 to 74 inches) if it had not been the case that, when they were growing up, food was scarce and boys were preferred over girls in its distribution. Or suppose that we can predict quite accurately, on the basis of genetic information, who will get cancer and who will not. This would not show that the overall incidence of cancer is determined by the human gene pool. For it is still quite possible that, in a healthy environment, cancer would hardly occur at all.

[46] This point is frequently overlooked—by Rawls, for instance, when he attributes the human-rights problems in the typical developing country exclusively to local factors: "[T]he problem is commonly the nature of the public political culture and the religious and philosophical traditions that underlie its institutions. The great social evils in poorer societies are likely to be oppressive government and corrupt elites." John Rawls, "The Law of Peoples," in *On Human Rights*, ed. Stephen Shute and Susan Hurley (New York: Basic Books, 1993), p. 77. This superficial explanation is not so much false as incomplete. As soon as one asks (as Rawls does not), *why* so many less developed countries (LDCs) have oppressive governments and corrupt elites, one will unavoidably hit upon global factors—such as the ones discussed in my two examples: Local elites can afford to be oppressive and corrupt, because, with foreign loans and military aid, they can stay in power even without popular support. And they are so often oppressive and corrupt, because it is, in light of the prevailing extreme international inequalities, far more lucrative for them to cater to the interests of foreign governments and firms rather than to those of their impoverished compatriots. Examples abound: There are plenty of LDC governments that came to power and/or stay in power only thanks to foreign support. And there are plenty of LDC politicians and bureaucrats

considerations suggest that the worldwide underfulfillment of human rights cannot be explained by reference to national factors alone.

The thoughts expressed in the last paragraph are not especially subtle, and economists are well aware of them in other contexts. When they think about how to structure world trade (Bretton Woods, the Uruguay Round, and the World Trade Organization), they do try to anticipate how alternative global trading regimes would affect international trade flows and worldwide economic growth. Only in their attempts to explain global poverty is our global economic order strangely neglected. The tunnel vision of economists rubs off on the rest of us. We regret that so many countries have bad institutions and governments, but we do not ask further why this may be so. In particular, we do not ask how we ourselves might be involved in this sad phenomenon.

If we did pay attention to this question, we would soon come across global factors that play an important role in the reproduction of human misery and whose reform would greatly advance the fulfillment of human rights. Elsewhere, I have tried to analyze some such factors, which codetermine what sorts of persons gain power and influence in the poorer countries, what options these persons face, and how the pursuit of any of these options affects national poverty and the fulfillment of human rights.[47] What I want to add here is only this: If global factors figure in the explanation of Third World misery, then this misery may also be our concern. This could be so, provided we accept that all persons involved in upholding social institutions have a shared moral responsibility to ensure that these institutions satisfy at least the universal core criterion of basic justice, which is to ensure that the human rights of all persons affected by these social institutions are fulfilled. If a particular underfulfillment of human rights—hunger in Brazil, say—comes about through the interplay of global and national factors and could be remedied through global as well as through national institutional reforms, then the responsibility for this underfulfillment lies with both institutional schemes, and therefore also with both groups of persons: with all those who participate in the imposition of either the global or the Brazilian basic structure without

---

who, induced or even bribed by foreigners, work against the interests of their people: *for* the development of a tourist-friendly sex industry (whose forced exploitation of children and women they tolerate and profit from), *for* the importation of unneeded, obsolete, or overpriced products at public expense, *for* the permission to import hazardous products, wastes, or productive facilities, *against* laws protecting employees or the environment, etc. It is perfectly unrealistic to believe that the corruption and oppression in the LDCs, which Rawls rightly deplores, can be abolished without a significant reduction in international inequality.

[47] See Pogge, "A Global Resources Dividend" (*supra* note 32), and Thomas W. Pogge, "Menschenrechte als moralische Ansprüche an globale Institutionen," in *Current Issues in Political Philosophy: Justice in Society and World Order*, ed. P. Koller and K. Puhl (Vienna: Hölder-Pichler-Tempsky, 1997), pp. 147–64.

making compensating contributions to their reform. Acceptance of this view would entail, then, that the citizens of the developed countries bear some responsibility for the world hunger problem.[48]

For each of us this responsibility means that we should either refrain from participating in unjust social institutions—hardly a realistic option—or else compensate for such participation by working simultaneously for the reform of these institutions or for the protection of their victims. The word "compensate" is meant to indicate that how much someone should be willing to contribute toward reforming unjust institutions and toward mitigating the harms they cause will depend on how much he is contributing to, and how much he is benefiting from, their maintenance. Obviously, these matters deserve a far more elaborate treatment than I can give them here.

Explanatory nationalism sends a message that has become deeply entrenched in common sense. It makes us look at poverty and oppression as problems whose root causes and possible solutions are internal to the foreign countries in which they occur. To be sure, we deplore the misery abroad and recognize a positive moral reason to help out with aid and advice. When poverty is due to natural causes, we demand that "there should be certain provisions for mutual assistance between peoples in times of famine and drought and, were it feasible, as it should be, provisions for ensuring that in all reasonably developed liberal societies people's basic needs are met."[49] Insofar as "the great social evils in poorer societies are likely to be oppressive government and corrupt elites,"[50] we may be able to help by exerting some pressure on the rulers—perhaps through loans, trade, or diplomacy. But, since we see no causal link between global factors and the incidence of oppression, corruption, and poverty, we will not even ask whether those who shape global institutions and, more generally, the global context in which the poorer countries are placed have a negative moral responsibility for global poverty. Some quick reflections may show the importance of such causal links. A large portion of the huge quantities of natural resources we consume is imported, much of it from repressive, undemocratic countries. We deplore this lack of democracy and wonder what we might do to help. As good explanatory nationalists, however, we see no connection between the international transaction and the domestic tyranny. The former involves us, but is a fair exchange at market prices; the latter is unjust, but

---

[48] Acceptance of such a responsibility would not reduce the responsibility of corrupt Third World elites in any way. It is quite wrong to think that the sum of responsibility is fixed by the harm done, as is shown by reflection on the fact that those who commit murder together may each bear full responsibility for the crime, rather than a fraction inversely proportional to the number of perpetrators.

[49] Rawls, "The Law of Peoples," p. 56.

[50] Ibid., p. 77.

involves us only marginally as potential helpers. This separation again makes it very hard to ask the right questions: e.g., What entitles a small global elite—the affluent citizens of the rich countries and the holders of political and economic power in the resource-rich developing countries—to enforce a global property regime under which they can claim the world's natural resources for themselves and can distribute these among themselves on mutually agreeable terms?

VIII. Conclusion

This essay is about what measure of, or proxy for, human flourishing is needed for purposes of assessing the justice of social institutions and what role this measure should play within such assessments. We saw in the course of the discussion that measures of human flourishing differ in stringency and specificity (among other things). An internationally acceptable core criterion of basic justice requires a measure of low stringency and specificity. In this role a conception of human rights is far more suitable than all the theoretical constructs currently discussed by academics—or so I have argued. Such a conception is, on the one hand, substantial enough to support a severe and constructive critique of the status quo. And it also respects, on the other hand, the autonomy of the diverse cultures of this world—provided we are prepared to understand human rights not as demands for legal rights, but as moral claims on social institutions. A conception of human rights demands, then, simply that all social institutions are to be designed so that all human beings have secure access to the objects of their human rights. Precisely this demand seems to me to be expressed in article 28 of the *Universal Declaration of Human Rights*, which says: "Everyone is entitled to a social and international order in which the rights and freedoms set forth in this Declaration can be fully realized."

Acceptance of such a universal core criterion of basic justice does not preclude particular societies from subjecting their national institutions to a richer criterion of justice that involves a more stringent and more specific measure of human flourishing. Such a national measure might, for example, ascribe to citizens additional basic needs, such as: to have certain legal (constitutional) rights; not to be too severely disadvantaged through social inequalities; to be adequately compensated for natural handicaps and bad luck; or to receive a subsidy for the discharge of important religious duties.[51] But such additional basic needs would everywhere be understood as secondary to the universal human needs

---

[51] Such measures would still function in the context of assessing social institutions and would thus presumably be probabilistic (*ex ante*) and focused on publicly ascertainable *access* to a quantitatively and qualitatively *adequate* share of certain goods. In these regards they would differ from measures of human flourishing that we employ in small-scale contexts, where we may be concerned to enrich the life of a friend, for example, or our own.

recognized by the globally shared conception of human rights: the pre-eminent requirement on all social institutions is that they afford each human being reasonably secure access to minimally adequate shares of basic freedoms and participation, as well as minimally adequate shares of food, drink, clothing, shelter, education, and health care. Achieving the formulation, global acceptance, and realization of this requirement is the preeminent moral task of our age.

Philosophy, Columbia University

INDEX

Abelard, Peter, 72
Ackrill, J. L., 1, 4, 9 n. 20
Actualization, 24, 33, 34, 36, 37
Adaptation, 36
Agency: and activity, 29–30; moral, 21, 179 n. 9; practical, 236; rational, 286
Agent-neutrality, 7–9, 16, 22–25, 29, 41, 52, 269–71
Agent-relativity, 148 n. 14, 177 n. 7, 269–72; and egoism, 10; and human flourishing, 6–10, 21–23, 25–26, 29, 52
Agents, 337, 348; and deliberation, 273–74; and ends, 198–99, 202, 218–21, 224–25; moral, 160; rational, 7, 34, 148, 157, 175 n. 66, 218–20, 224–25, 235; of the state, 320–21, 332; and valuation, 138; and well-being, 124–26
Agent sovereignty, 116–17
Alexy, Robert, 352 n. 40
Altruism, 113, 160, 254 n. 3, 271–72, 274
Annas, Julia, 58 n. 23, 60 n. 25, 67, 68 n. 38, 69
Anscombe, G. E. M., 44, 54, 59, 145 n. 2
Appetites, 324. *See also* Desires; Preferences
Aquinas, 5 n. 14, 12 n. 27, 22 n. 51
Archilochus, 202
"Aristotelian Thesis," 176–77, 179–82, 194–96
Aristotle, 28 n. 63, 190, 271, 338; and *eudaimonia*, 5, 10, 11 n. 23, 46, 176–77, 234–35, 241, 256, 263, 272–77, 289; and friendship, 253–56, 260–66, 270, 272–74, 282–83, 286, 288–89; and function, 204, 208–11, 215, 217, 232; and the good, 10, 41, 101–2, 176, 181–85, 202, 209–18, 221–28, 230–31; and happiness, 143, 145–46, 149, 215–16, 218, 225, 250–51, 283; and human nature, 12–13, 37, 221, 230; and perfectionism, 199–200, 203, 209–10, 230, 232; and political association, 221–29, 232, 265, 282–89; and rationality, 219–28, 262; and self-direction, 11–12, 37; and the *summum bonum*, 233–51 passim; and teleology, 35, 212, 232; and virtue, 16, 177, 185, 187–89, 260–62, 272–74
Association, 225, 282, 288; personal, 252, 257, 264, 272, 274; political, 205, 209, 221–28, 255, 277, 283, 289. *See also* Community; Relationships; State
Atlas Shrugged (Rand), 76–77, 91 n. 22

Austin, John L., 211
Authoritarianism, 278 n. 47, 279–81, 317
Authority, 326
Autonomy, 165, 232, 325, 336–37, 339–40, 342, 343, 355, 360; and rationality, 29 n. 65, 157

Banking, 302
Barry, Brian, 331 n. 15
Beneficence, duty of, 163–67, 169, 172–73
Benevolence, 56, 57, 163
Berlin, Isaiah, 40
Biology, 230–31
Brazil, 358
Brinig, Margaret, 299 n. 7
Broad, C. D., 271
Brodsky, Joseph, 193
Butler, Joseph, 47

Categorical Imperative, 152, 155, 169 n. 59, 171 n. 61
Causation: final, 34, 38; formal, 35, 38
Censorship, 279
Character, 10, 41–42, 65, 85, 158–59, 160 nn. 46 and 48, 242–43, 246, 262, 266–67, 273, 327–28, 335–36
Charmides (Plato), 256
Children, 281, 290, 292–301, 304, 306–14
Choice, 76, 167, 173; and agency, 29–30; and beneficence, 164–65, 169, 174; freedom of, 318, 321, 324–25; and the good life, 97–98, 101–2; and human nature, 171; and information, 317; and nobility, 189; theory of, 212 n. 22, 214, 220 n. 32
Christianity, 272
Citizens, 228–29, 232, 279–82, 285, 290–91, 305–6, 315–32 passim, 339, 352, 360
Citizenship, 284–89, 321
Civil liberties, 315
Civil order, 27
Coercion, 156, 164
Commitment, 236
Community, 282, 328–31; political, 265, 283, 286–88, 316, 325, 332. *See also* Association; State
Competition, 161, 337, 355
Compossibility, moral, 13, 27, 42
Compulsion, 30
Consent, 164, 166, 174

363

Consequentialism, 2, 5 n. 14, 16 n. 38, 83–92, 93 n. 26, 94, 151 n. 22, 155
Constitution, German, 354
Constitution, U.S., 319
Constitutions, 222–23, 226–29, 280 n. 48, 284–86, 352
Contemplation, 237–38, 245. *See also* Reason, theoretical
Continence, 187–88
Contracts, 290, 297, 303, 305–6, 314
Conventionalism, 21, 25
Cooper, John, 10 n. 22, 102, 145 n. 2, 263 n. 16, 267 n. 26
Cooperation, 263–65, 283, 290, 296–98, 300, 307, 314, 321, 325, 327
Coordination, 225–28, 316
Courage, 189–90, 205–6, 243
Crito (Plato), 256
Culture, 323–24, 327, 339–40, 342, 343, 355, 357 n. 46, 360
Cummiskey, David, 151 n. 22

Delbrück, Max, 35–36
Deliberation, 83–84, 86, 88–89, 155, 263–65, 280–81, 283; and democracy, 326–28; and happiness, 146, 151, 159; moral, 16, 161–63; and neutrality, 319, 321, 324; and political activity, 285–88; practical, 107–8, 253, 256, 258, 262, 264, 273, 278; and rationality, 104–6, 109
Democracy, 255, 280 nn. 48 and 50, 281–89, 290, 303, 322, 326–28, 359; and stability, 228–29
Den Uyl, Douglas J., 12 n. 29, 20, 25 n. 57, 28, 33 n. 78
Deontology, 2, 19 n. 46, 93 n. 26
Depew, David, 222 n. 33
Desires (Passions), 28–30, 41–42; and ends, 207, 211–19; formation of, 128–30, 134, 137; fulfillment of, 114, 123–28, 131–35, 139–40, 341; and the good, 28–29, 198–99, 202, 209–18, 230, 232, 237; and human flourishing, 3, 47–48; informed, 126–34, 178 n. 8, 181 n. 19; and love, 258, 274; and nobility, 187–89; nonprudential, 125–26; and rationality, 207, 211, 225; and reason, 171. *See also* Appetites; Preferences
Dialogue between a Philosopher, a Jew, and a Christian (Abelard), 72
Dignity, 179 n. 9, 328, 331, 353
Dillon, Robin, 190 n. 34
Diversity, 316–17
Driving: regulation of, 346–47, 350
Due process, 319
Duties, 317, 360; and the categorical imperative, 152 n. 24; and happiness, 143, 144 n. 1, 153, 158–60, 162–68; and human flourishing, 171; imperfect, 158, 164–65,
169, 173; other-regarding, 45, 46, 52–53, 57, 64, 65–67; parental, 310. *See also* Obligations
Dworkin, Ronald, 135–36, 139, 344

Economics, 301–3, 305–6, 309, 356, 358
Education, 206, 278, 282; moral, 238; and neutrality, 322–24, 326; and the state, 222, 228–29
Egoism, 57, 79, 194 n. 42, 239, 267, 271 n. 39, 353; and agent-relativity, 10; and consequentialism, 84–85; flourishing-based, 73, 76, 81, 82, 89, 93–94; and hedonism, 83, 84–85, 87; and human flourishing, 45–46, 66–70; objections to, 74–76, 80–82, 90–93; and rationality, 51–53, 182; and virtue, 54, 56, 59, 64, 66–70
Eminent domain, 356
Emotions, 41, 260, 274
End (*Telos*), 3, 9, 12 n. 28, 32–40 passim, 180, 212, 255; final, 4, 9, 143, 181, 199, 201, 207, 209–10, 212–30, 232; inclusive, 4; ultimate, 83. *See also* Function
Ends, 147 n. 10, 149, 165, 167, 169–74; and desire, 211–19; kingdom of, 163; and neutrality, 315–21, 323–24, 327; and persons, 154–55; plurality of, 198–99, 202–7, 213–19, 223, 225–32; and rationality, 214, 217–28, 230
Equality, 155
Essentialism, 32, 48–49, 51, 197–99, 201, 204, 208–9, 231–32, 262–63, 265
Ethics, 7–8, 14–15, 19, 21, 72–73, 95, 143–44, 238; neo-Aristotelian, 13, 16; and politics, 223, 226, 228, 233; virtue, 54, 59–60, 160, 223 n. 35. *See also* Morality
Eudaimonia, 2, 5, 10, 11, 46, 53 n. 13, 144, 145 n. 2, 146 n. 3, 176–77, 184, 234–35, 241, 252–53, 256, 259–65, 272–78, 280, 289
Eudaimonism, 251, 253–61, 263, 271–77, 288–89
Eudemian Ethics (Aristotle), 101–2, 203, 219
Eugenics, 279
Euthydemus (Plato), 256
Euthyphro, 3 n. 5
Excellence, 120, 200–202, 209, 226, 231–33, 266, 271 n. 39, 322 n. 8; and activity, 176–77, 183–84, 242, 244–51; and function, 204–8
Experience, quality of, 121–23, 126
"Experience machine," 121–23
Externalism, 187 n. 29

Fairness, 243
Family, 308–10; and freedom, 290, 292; and love, 290–92, 294–95, 306–7, 313–14; and trust, 301, 304

Flourishing, concept of, 44, 144–45, 176–77
Flourishing, human, vii, 70–71, 141–42, 233, 258, 333–37, 357; as agent-relative, 6–10, 19, 21–23, 25–26, 29; and egoism, 45–46, 66–70, 73, 76, 81, 82, 89, 93–94; and *eudaimonia*, 2; and freedom, 305; and happiness, 143–46, 167–75, 197, 336; and human good, 176–77, 180; and human nature, 1, 14, 29–41, 43, 44–45, 46–53, 71; as inclusive, 3–5; as individualized, 5–6, 15–16, 25–26, 42–43; and justice, 26–28, 337–51, 355, 360; and Kant, 167–75; and life plans, 97, 100, 102; as objective, 3, 6 n. 16, 8–9, 24, 207; and perfectionism, 1, 12, 197–98, 203, 206, 229–32; and practical wisdom, 15–21, 42; and prudential value, 113; and rationality, 29–30; and relationships, 252; as self-directed, 10–12, 28–30, 33, 37; and self-interest, 72–73, 89, 92–95; as social, 12–13, 26–27; and the state, 315, 321 n. 7, 325, 328 n. 11; and value, 178; and virtue, 44–45, 53–66, 71; and worth, 179. *See also* Eudaimonia; Good life; Happiness
Forms, Platonic, 115, 200, 203 n. 9, 279
Fountainhead, The (Rand), 78–79
Fourteenth Amendment, 319
Freedom, 30, 168, 172, 175, 229, 316–21, 344–45, 353, 355, 361; external, 155–57; and the family, 290, 292; moral, 165–66; of religion, 324–26, 354; and society, 290–91, 295, 305–6, 310, 313–14. *See also* Liberty
Free market, 290–92, 303, 305, 308–9
Free will, 12 n. 27
Freud, Sigmund, 161 n. 51
Friendship, 12, 33 n. 79, 121, 123; character, 91 n. 22; and eudaimonism, 252–63, 265, 271 n. 39, 272–77, 288–89; impersonal, 266–72; and justice, 282; and political association, 283, 286–89. *See also* Relationships
From Morality to Virtue (Slote), 159
Function (*Ergon*), 32 n. 72, 278–79; and the good, 37–39; human, vii, 3, 11 n. 23, 32, 37, 46–47, 183–84, 198, 201, 203–12, 215, 217, 229–30, 232; and virtue, 180. *See also* End

Gauthier, David, 212 n. 20
Genericism, 33–34
Germany, 327
Gibbard, Allan, 133–34, 186 n. 26
Glendon, Mary Ann, 353 n. 42
God, 329
Good, 7, 12 n. 30, 36–37, 192, 194–96, 212, 245–51, 257–61, 265, 281, 328; common, 177 n. 6, 282–89 passim, 325; concep-

tions of, 316, 319, 321, 323–24, 326, 329–31; conflicts of, 113; and desire, 28–29, 198–99, 202, 209–18, 230, 232, 237; divine, 234–35, 237, 248, 250–51; and egoism, 75, 80–82, 90–92; and *eudaimonia*, 256, 263, 276; final, 145; and freedom, 318–20; and friendship, 269; and function, 37–39, 203–4, 210; and happiness, 144–45, 148, 150–51, 160 n. 46, 161 n. 50; highest, 213, 222, 233–34, 238, 244; human, 2–3, 4 n. 13, 9, 14, 22–24, 33, 37, 44–48, 53, 56, 70–71, 96–99, 103, 106, 111–12, 113, 117, 120, 176–77, 180–83, 197–203, 210, 220 n. 32, 221–28, 234–38, 315; and human flourishing, 333–34, 340; and ideal-advisor theory, 127–30, 133–36; intrinsic, 91 n. 23, 198, 235, 320–22, 324–26, 329 n. 12, 332; and knowledge, 10, 19; and love, 265–66, 273, 277; nonmoral, 181 n. 19; objective theory of, 47, 70, 98, 104, 114–17, 118–21, 124, 126, 132–42; and perfectionism, 119–20, 136; and rationality, 51–52, 103–4, 105, 109–11; and the right, 223–24; subjective theory of, 47–48, 114–19, 135–36, 140–41; ultimate, 72; and utilitarianism, 198, 238–39, 241; and value, 334, 355; and vice, 62; and virtue, 53–71 passim. *See also* Goods; *Summum bonum*; Value
Good life, 100–103, 105–6, 111–13, 120, 122, 134, 137, 139 n. 29, 176, 179, 203, 225–28, 255–56, 315–16, 322, 324, 336, 340–42. *See also* Flourishing, human
Goods, 233–34, 243–44, 251, 318; cultural, 323–24; external, 276; first-order, 52; generic, 4, 5–6, 17, 19, 41; and happiness, 248, 285; and human flourishing, 10, 14–15, 17, 19–21, 42; instrumental, 113–14, 331; intrinsic, 114, 118–20, 127, 276; and justice, 343–45, 348–56, 360 n. 51; objective, 3, 47; primary, 4 n. 10; second-order, 51–52, 57; and self-interest, 79; and the state, 315
Good will, 144 n. 1, 146 n. 4, 148, 161, 168, 171, 178
Government, 284, 289, 290–91, 308, 310–12, 316, 318, 320, 330, 352, 356–59; goals of, 315; and justice, 155–58, 168; limited, 304–6, 313
Greek culture, ancient, 200–202
Griffin, James, 124 n. 13, 126 n. 14, 134, 135–36, 139

Habermas, Jürgen, 351 n. 36, 352 n. 40
"Habits of thought," 85–89
Habituation, 65–66, 228–29
Hampshire, Stuart, 15 n. 36

Happiness, vii, 53 n. 13, 72, 73, 83, 96, 103, 112, 115, 213, 221, 243, 247–51, 279, 287; ancient views on, 143–46, 149; and *eudaimonia*, 2, 176 n. 4, 234, 241–42, 256, 272; as final end, 215–18; and the good, 210, 244; and human flourishing, 143–46, 167–75, 197, 336; and justice, 275–76; Kant on, 143–44, 146–75; and pleasure, 117, 121, 146, 218; and politics, 283, 285; and preferences, 161; and relationships, 252, 254, 269; and self-interest, 291, 294; and utilitarianism, 7, 239; and value, 160–67; and virtue, 146, 149, 159–60, 161 n. 50, 175. *See also Eudaimonia; Flourishing, human*
Harm, 325, 328, 329 n. 12, 359
Hedonism, 114, 115, 118, 121, 197, 201; and egoism, 83, 84–85, 87
Hesiod, 202
Holtman, Sarah, 156 n. 35
Homer, 200–202 passim
Homo economicus, 291, 293–94, 305
Honor, 329 n. 12
Hubin, Donald C., 133 n. 24
Human nature, vii, 1, 117–18, 143, 148, 157 n. 39, 161, 170–71, 175, 295; and essentialism, 48–49; and human flourishing, 1, 14, 29–41, 44–45, 46–53, 71; and perfectionism, 120, 180, 197–99, 203, 229–31; as practical, 234–36, 238, 247; and rationality, 49–53; as teleological, 32–37
Humiliation, 328, 329 n. 12
Hurka, Thomas, 120, 197, 200 n. 5, 201
Hursthouse, Rosalind, 56, 58
Hypothetical-contract theory, 347
Hypothetical imperative, 169–70, 174

Impartiality, 7, 104, 108, 268–69; religious, 330, 331
Impersonalism, 7–8, 16, 288; and love, 266–72
Inclinations: natural, 163, 166–67. *See also* Preferences
Incontinence (*Akrasia*), 187 n. 30. *See also* Weakness of will
Independence, 325
India, 327, 353
Individual, 232, 240–44, 317, 320
Individualism, 15–16, 353
Ineluctabilism, 33, 37
Inequality, 345, 346 n. 24, 357–58 n. 46, 360
Information, 128–31, 134, 317, 321
Institutions: civic, 324, 326–27, 329; political, 279, 281–82, 288, 290–91, 303–4, 331; religious, 326; social, 307, 337–56, 358–61
Integrity, 89
Intellectualism, 263 n. 17
Intention, 34

Interests, 77, 79, 81–82, 87, 89–90, 109–10, 163, 181, 219–20, 259, 263, 265, 274, 276, 283, 338; and preferences, 104–5; rational, 207 n. 12; and values, 92
Internalism, 70, 127–28
Intuitionism, 150
"Invisible-hand" explanations, 291
Irwin, Terence, 51 n. 9, 187–88, 275 n. 42, 277 n. 44, 286 n. 54

Johnson, Samuel, 97–98
Judgment, 325; conventional, 118; ethical, 187 nn. 29 and 30; expert, 117–18, 123, 129; and the good, 116; and happiness, 169; moral, 161; and neutrality, 320–21, 324, 327, 332; value, 41, 186 n. 26
Justice, 26–28, 151 n. 22, 202–3, 206, 220 n. 31, 226, 256, 321 n. 7, 334 n. 3, 356; as aim of government, 155–58; and *eudaimonia*, 275–76; political, 282; principles of, 152–53, 155–56, 227, 315, 328; social, 279–80, 337–39; universal, 339–40, 342–51 passim, 355, 358, 360
Justification, 267, 269 n. 31

Kant, Immanuel, 143–75 passim, 178, 334 n. 4
Kantianism, 16, 268
Kaspar Hauser syndrome, 292 n. 2
Kenny, Anthony, 22
Keyt, David, 213–14
Khawaja, Irfan, 4 n. 9
Knowledge, 23, 49–50, 279; and the good, 10, 19, 33 n. 79, 40; and virtue, 278 n. 46
Kraut, Richard, 139 n. 29, 211 n. 18
Kripke, Saul, 48

Labor: division of, 278–80, 316; manual, 283, 285–88
Laches (Plato), 256
Larmore, Charles, 199 n. 4
Law, 229, 321, 348, 352–53; obedience to, 153, 156; universal, 154–55
Lawrence, Gavin, 248 n. 46
Laws, The (Plato), 280 n. 48
Legislators, 321
Leisure, 250–51, 285–86
Lennox, James G., 34, 36
Lewis, C. I., 149
Liberalism, 198–99, 202, 206–7, 209, 217, 224, 230–32; New Deal, 290; and paternalism, 136
Libertarianism, 290–92, 305–6, 310
Liberty, 117, 136, 156–57, 279, 281, 285, 291, 310, 313, 319 n. 5, 354–55. *See also* Freedom

Life, 105–6, 110–12; and action, 90; and choice, 76–77; examined, 100–101; and happiness, 96–99, 103; and meaning, 111–12; quality of, 133, 135–36, 139–40, 333, 335, 347, 351, 355; of reason, 99; as shared, 91; ways of, 92–93, 118, 316, 340; worth of, 320–22

Life plans, 118, 201, 214, 219; ancient Greek views on, 100–102; and human flourishing, 97, 100, 102; objections to, 96–100, 105–12; and rationality, 96, 102 n. 13, 103, 105–6, 109–10; Rawls on, 102–5

Lomasky, Loren, 29 n. 65

Love, 91 n. 22, 161, 186 n. 27; and democracy, 282; and eudaimonism, 252–62, 265, 271 n. 39, 272–77, 288–89; and families, 290–92, 294–95, 306–7, 313–14; impersonal, 266–72

Luck, 98

Lying, 152, 154

Lysis (Plato), 254, 257, 265, 274, 275 n. 42

MacDonald, Scott, 4 n. 13, 12 n. 30

MacIntyre, Alasdair, 33, 198, 231–32

Marx, Karl, 197

McKenzie, Richard, 312–13

Meaning, and life, 111–12

Meno (Plato), 278 n. 46

Merit: ethical, 94; and value, 178–80, 182–94 passim; and worth, 178–81, 185–87, 189–94

Metanorms, 27

Metaphysics of Morals, The (Kant), 155

Methods of Ethics, The (Sidgwick), 268

Mill, John Stuart, 7, 114, 117–18, 121, 122–23, 157–58, 238–39, 318 n. 4

Miller, Fred D., Jr., 224–25

Monarchy, 280 n. 48, 284, 286

Moore, G. E., 148 n. 13, 149, 150, 194, 195

Moral development, 298

Moral excellence, 11, 16, 26

Morality, vii, 19, 76, 113, 143, 144 n. 1, 148 n. 14, 159, 170 n. 60, 174, 239; commonsense, 268; and rationality, 255 n. 4. *See also* Ethics

Moral self-indulgence, 67–69

Moral theory, vii, 199. *See also* Ethics

Moral worth, 158–59, 162

Motivation: and desire, 207, 211; moral, 33, 158–59; and political association, 226–27; and virtue, 65–70, 185, 187, 189

Mutual advantage, 225, 252, 260, 283, 305

Myth of Er, 101

Nagel, Thomas, 209 n. 16

Nationalism, explanatory, 356–57, 359

Nation-state, 315–16. *See also* State

Naturalism, 47, 150

Naturalistic fallacy, 32–33

Needs, 294–95, 344 n. 22, 353, 360

Neo-Aristotelianism, 2, 8–9, 11, 13, 18 n. 44, 21, 32–33, 38, 42–43; objections to, 21–30; and underdetermination, 15–16

Neutrality, 315–32

Newman, John Henry Cardinal, 60 n. 25

Nicomachean Ethics (Aristotle), 46, 199, 203, 209–12, 219–20, 222, 224, 226, 230, 233, 236, 240, 253, 256, 260, 283

Nietzsche, Friedrich, 160, 197

Noble (*Kalon*), 177–79, 183–85, 187–89

"Noble savage," 293–94, 306

Noncognitivism, 186

Norms, 151–52, 328; moral, 290

Norton, David L., 43

Nozick, Robert, 121

Nussbaum, Martha, 206 n. 11, 207 n. 13

Objectivism, 77

Objectivity, 115–16, 143, 146, 190–91; and ends, 207, 217–18; and the good, 23–24, 197–98, 207 n. 13, 209, 213–14; of human flourishing, 3, 6 n. 16, 8–9, 24

Obligations, 2, 5 n. 14, 16 n. 38, 268, 271; parental, 310, 314. *See also* Duties

Olasky, Marvin, 312 n. 13

Oligarchy, 228–29, 284–85

On Liberty (J. S. Mill), 117–18

Orphanages, 292, 307, 312–13

Pain, 130–32, 183

Parenting, 185–87, 189

Parfit, Derek, 67, 74–75, 115, 139 n. 29, 191 n. 36

Paternalism, 117, 136, 280–81, 340–42

Peace, 250

Perfectionism, 37, 42, 119–20, 136, 159, 180, 322 n. 8; and Aristotle, 209–32; and human flourishing, 1, 12, 197–98, 203, 206, 229–32; and human nature, 120, 180, 197–99, 203, 229–31; and Plato, 197, 199–209, 229–30; pre-philosophical, 200–203, 229–30

Perry, R. B., 149

Phaedrus (Plato), 254, 258, 264–65, 277

Philosophy, 96, 99, 111, 243; ancient Greek, 197; history of, 316, 331; moral, 331; political, 156–57

Philosophy of Loyalty, The (Royce), 102–3

Plato, 284, 286–87, 327, 334; and authoritarianism, 279–82, 316–17; as a eudaimonist, 255–56, 271–72; and justice, 275–76; and love, 254, 258–59, 270, 272–78, 282, 288–89; and perfectionism, 197, 199–209, 229–30

Pleasure, 83, 122, 130, 331, 334; and happiness, 117, 121, 146, 218; and pain, 130–

31, 132 n. 23; proper, 187–88; and
relationships, 252, 260, 268–69; and
value, 117–18, 120, 122–23, 130–31, 139
n. 29, 141, 176, 183, 189, 195 n. 46, 196;
and vice, 62–63, 64 n. 31; and virtue,
63–64
Pluralism, 6, 13, 14, 21, 40, 42, 108, 331
Polis, 28 n. 63
Political activity, 283, 285–89
Political participation, 281, 283, 285, 355
Political science, 233, 283
Political theory, 278–79, 281–82
Politics, 13, 223, 226, 323, 324, 330
Politics (Aristotle), 221–22, 226, 228, 283
Poor, the, 323–24
Potentiality, 24, 33–37 passim
Poverty, 356–59
Power, political, 279, 305–6, 358, 360
Preferences, 108, 212 nn. 20 and 22, 298,
299 n. 7, 324, 326, 340–41; and ends,
207; and happiness, 161; and interests,
104–5; and life plans, 106; and pleasure,
117, 122–23, 131. *See also* Desires
Pride, 183
Principles, 238; moral, 151, 153, 155, 157,
175 n. 66, 328. *See also* Rules
Prisoners' dilemma, 296–301
Prohibitions, 298
Projects, 111, 164–66, 174, 331
Promise-keeping, 166, 297, 313–14
Property, 284–85
Protagoras (Plato), 281, 282 n. 51
Proust, Marcel, 96
Prudence, 105, 108–9, 111–12, 113, 166,
169–70, 172, 174, 220. *See also* Value,
prudential
Public-choice analysis, 303–4
Public officials, 321–22, 329
Public policy, 303–4, 322
Public-spiritedness, 327
Putnam, Hilary, 48

Railton, Peter, 82–87, 127, 128
Ramsey, Paul, 272–73
Rand, Ayn, 76–82, 91 n. 23, 92–93, 160
Rasmussen, Douglas B., 12 n. 29
Rasselas (S. Johnson), 97–98
Rationalism: ethical, 14–15, 21, 41
Rationality, 57, 84, 89, 93 n. 26, 108, 212 n.
20, 239, 276–77, 283; and autonomy, 29
n. 65, 157; and choice, 320; and cooperation, 297; and deliberation, 104–6, 109,
327; and desire, 207, 211; and egoism,
182; and ends, 181, 214, 217–18, 230;
and function, 183–84; and the good,
103–4, 105, 109–11, 149, 316, 330; and
happiness, 144 n. 1, 148 n. 14, 166 n. 56,
167; and human flourishing, 29, 39,

41–42, 170–74; and human nature, 49–
52; and justice, 347; and life plans, 96,
102 n. 13, 103, 105–6, 109–10; and morality, 255 n. 4; and perfectionism, 200
n. 6, 201; practical, 49–52, 157 n. 40,
201, 235, 237; and ruling, 280–81, 285–
89; and self-interest, 291, 298, 314; and
the soul, 205–6, 262; theoretical, 49–51;
and tradition, 31; and values, 92; and
virtue, 50, 51 n. 9. *See also* Reason
Rawls, John, 157, 225, 315 n. 1, 321 n. 7,
357–58 n. 46; and the good, 198–99, 201,
217, 223–24; and justice, 155–56, 351; on
life plans, 100, 102–6, 109, 110; and
perfectionism, 200–202, 322 n. 8, 328 n.
11; and primary goods, 4 n. 10, 344;
and rationality, 220–21
Realism, 32, 116–17
Reason, 11–12, 20, 84 n. 20, 99, 102, 286–87;
and the categorical imperative, 152 n.
24; and desire, 29–30, 41–42, 171; and
eudaimonia, 234; and motivation, 33;
practical, 5 n. 14, 12, 15, 17, 24–25, 29,
30, 39, 107–8, 146, 154, 156, 157 n. 39,
170 n. 60, 171, 174, 182, 235, 255, 262,
272; and self-direction, 28, 37; theoretical, 15, 19, 107–8, 171 n. 61, 237. *See also*
Rationality
Reasons, 327; for action, 45–46, 53–56, 59,
64, 65–67, 69–71, 74, 80–82; agent-
neutral, 269–71; agent-relative, 269–72
Reciprocity, 295–97, 301–2, 305
Reflection, 84
Reflective equilibrium, 131
Regulation, government, 315
Relationships, 26–27, 252, 268, 274, 295–96;
loving, 140–41; and virtue, 191–94
Relativism, ethical, 40
Relativity, and subjectivity, 117–18
Religion, 316, 330, 331; and freedom,
324–26
"Rent-seeking," 304
Republic (Plato), 101, 199, 203–5, 207–8, 229,
256, 275–76, 278–81, 284, 316–17
Respect, 168–69, 173, 178–79 n. 9, 329,
336–37, 339–40, 342, 343, 355, 360; for
self, 190 n. 34
Responsibility, 237, 278, 281–85, 287–88,
310; and character, 30; of citizens, 321;
moral, 37, 161 n. 50, 162, 170, 173, 339,
356, 358–59; parental, 292
Rhetoric (Aristotle), 253, 254 n. 3
Rich, the, 323–24
Right, the, 223–24
Rights, 157, 161–62, 164, 315–16, 320;
human, 351–58, 360–61
Risk, 347
Ross, W. D., 60, 149, 150, 153, 187
Royce, Josiah, 102–3

Rules, 242–43, 337, 354; moral, 151–54, 328; utilitarian, 239. *See also* Principles

Sacks, Oliver, 193–94
Sacrifice, 79–80, 87, 92, 113, 125, 276
Santas, Gerasimos, 210, 223 n. 35
Scanlon, Thomas, 116, 344
Self, 12 n. 29, 219–21, 230, 261, 264, 276
Self-conception, 103
Self-directedness, 10–12, 20, 28–30, 33, 37, 97
Self-esteem, 190
Self-government, 289, 290–91, 306
Self-interest, vii, 152 n. 24, 255 n. 4, 291, 293–94, 298, 303, 314; and ethics, 72, 90; and flourishing, 81–82, 89, 92–95; Rand on, 78–80; and virtue, 72–73, 77, 80, 93–94; and well-being, 81
Selfishness, 77, 294
Self-love, 163, 254 n. 3, 258–59, 261–62, 266–67, 272–74, 276–77
Self-perfection, 12, 20, 43, 180 n. 14
Self-reliance, 325
Self-restraint, 290–91, 297–301, 303, 306, 313
Self-sufficiency, 205, 248, 263–64, 265 n. 19, 285, 288
Self-understanding, 264, 283
Sen, Amartya, 197, 344
Shame, 183–84, 329 n. 12
Sidgwick, Henry, 7, 268
Singer, M. G., 166
Slaves, 285–88
Slote, Michael, 64 n. 31, 74, 105, 159–60, 162–63
Smith, Michael, 187 n. 29
Sober, Elliott, 36 n. 86
Sociality, 12–13, 26–28, 235
Social order, 315
Society, 294; and freedom, 290–91, 295, 305–6, 310, 313–14
Socrates, 3 n. 5, 100–101, 203, 255–58, 274–75, 278 n. 46, 281–82
Sorabji, Richard, 204 n. 10
Soul, the, 204–6, 235, 259, 262, 275, 278, 287
Spontaneity, 110
Stability, 279; political, 228–29
Standard of living, 345
State, 221–29, 231–32, 278–79, 284, 310–13, 356; minimal, 290, 305; modern, 303–4; and neutrality, 315–20, 323–32; and rights, 352. *See also* Association, political; Community, political
Statesman, 240–43
Statesman (Plato), 208 n. 15, 280 n. 48
Stoicism, 140
Subjectivism, 6, 21, 25, 114–16, 190–91; and flourishing, 145; and the good, 198; and

happiness, 143, 146–47; and relativity, 117–18
Suicide, assisted, 319–22
Sullivan, Louis, 78–79
Summum bonum, 6, 159, 233–38, 240–48, 251, 328, 331; and utilitarianism, 238–39
Sumner, L. W., 40 n. 102, 115 n. 2, 119, 123 n. 12, 128, 139 n. 29
Supererogation, 55, 64
Supervenience, 149
Switzerland, 327
Symposium (Plato), 254, 256, 258, 265

Taylor, Charles, 178 n. 8
Teleology, 30, 171, 180, 223, 231–32; and human nature, 32–37; metaphysical, 198–99, 201–5, 208 n. 15, 211–12
Temperance, 187–88, 206, 256
Territory, 356–57
Theory of Justice, A (Rawls), 100, 102 n. 13
Third World, 356, 358, 359 n. 48
Tiberius, Valerie, 161 n. 49
Time horizons, 299–300
Tolerance, 354
Trade (exchange), 301–2, 358
Tradition, 31
Trust, 290, 293–95, 297–305, 314
Truth, 31 n. 70
Tyranny, 284, 359

Unanimity, 322
United States, 327, 330, 331–32, 338, 344–47
Universal Declaration of Human Rights, 352, 360
Universality, 23–24
Universalizability, 22–24
Unmoved mover, 200, 212 n. 21
Utilitarianism, 7, 16, 67–68, 150–52, 162–63, 198, 238–39, 241, 268–69, 336 n. 6, 337
Utilitarianism (J. S. Mill), 117–18, 121–22, 238–39
Utility, 136–37, 212 n. 20

Value, 87, 99, 246, 328; and activity, 177, 184–95; agent-neutral, 7–8; agent-relative, 9, 148 n. 14; and endorsement, 135–38; ethical, 334–36, 355; and friendship, 257, 263, 266, 274–76; and happiness, 160–67; instrumental, 9, 263, 274–76; and interests, 81, 90; intrinsic, 149, 150 n. 20, 151, 168, 177, 179, 195, 270 n. 36, 275, 285, 318, 324; and life, 76–77, 81; and love, 265, 273–76; and merit, 178–80, 182–94 passim; moral, 158; and perfectionism, 199–200; personal, 334–36, 355; and pleasure, 117–18, 120, 122–

23, 130–31, 176; prudential, 113–17,
    119–20, 122, 125, 129, 132–33, 135, 139–
    41, 181, 183 n. 23, 184–86, 190–96; and
    sacrifice, 79; ultimate, 6, 9, 77. *See also*
    Values
Values, 40, 77, 92, 240, 328, 340, 353. *See
    also* Value
Veatch, Henry B., 12 n. 28, 24, 39 n. 101
Velleman, J. David, 128 n. 20, 186 n. 27
Vice, 44, 62–63, 64 n. 31, 67, 68, 93, 143,
    260, 273; and rationality, 50–51
Virtue, vii, 16, 256, 275 n. 42, 279, 284 n.
    53, 285–87; and activity, 188–95, 222;
    and egoism, 66–70; and friendship,
    260–62, 266–70, 272–73, 283; and happi-
    ness, 146, 149, 159–60, 161 n. 50, 175;
    and human flourishing, 44–46, 53–66,
    71, 173, 197; and the human good, 176,
    179 n. 10; and human nature, 48–49;
    and love, 254, 258–59, 265–67, 270,
    272–73, 278; moral, 41–42, 149; and
    nobility, 184–85, 187–89; and perfection-
    ism, 203; and rationality, 50–52; and
    self-interest, 72–73, 77, 80, 93–94; and
    value, 77, 80, 94. *See also* Virtues
Virtues, 84, 93–94, 189–90, 231, 233, 262,
    263 n. 17; and choice, 76; conflicts be-
    tween, 58; and human flourishing, 4,
    5–6, 10, 14, 17, 19–21, 41; moral, 44,
    143, 202; and Objectivism, 77; other-
    regarding, 58, 65, 67; and rationality,
    50, 51 n. 9; self-regarding, 57–58; unity
    of, 55. *See also* Virtue

Vitalism, 33
Vlastos, Gregory, 253–55, 265–66, 267, 271
    n. 39, 272–75 passim, 278 n. 47, 288
Voluntariness, 320
Voting, 320–21

Waldron, Jeremy, 321 n. 7
Weakness of will, 137, 140. *See also* Inconti-
    nence
Wealth, 229, 284–85, 323
Welfare, 115, 117, 120, 125, 127, 181–82,
    186, 191–92, 239, 261 n. 13; general, 315.
    See also Well-being
Welfare, Happiness, and Ethics (Sumner), 139
    n. 29
Well-being, 13, 44 n. 2, 66 n. 34, 73, 81,
    87–88, 91, 93, 113–17, 120, 123, 133,
    141–42, 145, 181–84, 189, 192–96, 201,
    239, 252, 263, 278 n. 47, 281, 317–18, 321
    n. 7, 326, 330; and desire formation,
    128–30, 134, 137; and desire fulfillment,
    123–28, 131, 135, 139–40. *See also* Wel-
    fare
Whiting, Jennifer, 11 n. 23, 226–74 passim
Wilkes, Kathleen V., 29–30, 39 n. 100
Williams, Bernard, 100–101, 107–9, 216
Wisdom, 112, 205–6; practical, 11, 15–21,
    25, 28, 41–43, 242, 243
Worth, 182, 244–47, 251, 272–73; and merit,
    178–81, 185–87, 189–94; moral, 178; of
    persons, 162; and value, 178–80, 185,
    189–95, 334